Portrait of William Hine (1687–1730) by Sir Godfrey Kneller

The Three Choirs Festival: A History

The Three Choirs Festival: A History

New and Revised Edition

Anthony Boden and Paul Hedley

THE BOYDELL PRESS

First published 2017
The Boydell Press, Woodbridge

ISBN 978 1 78327 209 9

The Boydell Press is an imprint of Boydell & Brewer Ltd
PO Box 9, Woodbridge, Suffolk IP12 3DF, UK
and of Boydell & Brewer Inc.
668 Mt Hope Avenue, Rochester, NY 14620–2731, USA
website: www.boydellandbrewer.com

A catalogue record for this book is available from the British Library

The publisher has no responsibility for the continued existence
or accuracy of URLs for external or third-party internet websites
referred to in this book, and does not guarantee that any content
on such websites is, or will remain, accurate or appropriate

This publication is printed on acid-free paper

Designed and typeset in Adobe Caslon Pro by
David Roberts, Pershore, Worcestershire

Printed and bound in Great Britain by
TJ International Ltd, Padstow, Cornwall

Contents

List of Illustrations

Frontispiece: Portrait of William Hine (1687–1730) by Sir Godfrey Kneller (© Bridgeman Images).

Plates Group 3 – The Twenty-First Century
(between pp. 300 and 301)

The Frontispiece portrait of William Hine (1687–1730) by Sir Godfrey Kneller is published by courtesy of Bridgeman Images. Unless otherwise stated, other eighteenth- and nineteenth-century illustrations in this book are taken from the Extra-Illustrated ('Grangerized') edition of the 1895 *Annals of the Three Choirs*, compiled by A. M. Broadley and presented to the City of Gloucester by Alderman Edwin Lea in 1917. Formerly housed in the City of Gloucester Library, the collection has now been transferred to the Gloucestershire Archives, where it is catalogued under Refs. DY3/15019 to 15030GS.

Preface

THIS book is a revised, updated and expanded edition of *Three Choirs: A History of the Festival*, researched and written between 1989 and 1991, and published by Alan Sutton in 1992. Now, a quarter of a century later, further research has enabled me to revise and amplify the early chapters; to throw additional light upon the origins of the Festival; to rewrite Chapter 22; and to add Chapter 23, covering the period from 1992 to 1999, years during which I was personally involved as Festival Secretary/Administrator at Gloucester. However, rather than attempting to write about the twenty-first-century Festivals myself, I turned to Dr Paul Hedley for assistance in the preparation of this new edition. Paul, who took on the job of central management in 2008, has written an account of the Festival during the years from 2000, thereby completing this history of Three Choirs up to its tercentenary year, which was celebrated in 2015.

The complete list of works performed in the cathedrals and other principal venues at the Festival, formerly collated by the late Christian Wilson, were published in the 1992 edition of this book. Henceforth, in order to give readers access to the latest version of the *Annals*, it is intended that detailed listings will be updated periodically and hosted on the Three Choirs Festival website.

Between 1989 and 1990, I had set out to contact as many people with Three Choirs connections as possible, and they and numerous others assisted me in a variety of ways. My very first telephone call was to Harold Watkins Shaw (who preferred to be known as Watkins Shaw). His excellent book *The Three Choirs Festival*, published in 1954, set the bar high for any writer contemplating following in his footsteps, and I confess to having been rather nervous about approaching him, and concerned that he might have viewed me as an interloper in his sphere of expertise. However, my fears proved to be groundless: he invited me to visit his Worcestershire home, where he and Mrs Shaw welcomed me most warmly and where he was only too pleased to talk openly during a long, informative and helpful discussion.

Sir David Willcocks, Wulstan Atkins, Herbert Sumsion, Melville Cook and Meredith Davies are among the several others who were particularly helpful in sharing their experiences of the Festival. In his letter, for instance, Meredith Davies revealed some of the issues that had concerned him after his arrival at Hereford in 1950, and we were able to talk about these when we met. His main preoccupation had been with the standard of performance which prevailed in the early post-war period:

> The Cathedral choirs were not very good – at least to young men recently associated with Oxford & Cambridge – and the chorus tackled an enormous weight of music, with (at times) some necessarily perfunctory and superficial preparation. There was pervading enthusiasm, but not much refinement!

... The previous week [to the 1952 Hereford Festival] was spent in London, with orchestra and soloists; I think the orchestra rehearsed in the cathedral only on the Monday – 'Black Monday' it was called, with good reason. The more serious members of the London Symphony Orchestra – who admittedly enjoyed the week immensely – thought it very unrealistic. One had, too, to appreciate that the upstart nascent festivals at Edinburgh & Aldeburgh were setting standards and winning musical prestige which could leave Three Choirs looking like a very old-fashioned junketing – as, indeed, some critics were beginning to suggest.

Meredith Davies's comments echoed a critique by William Mann, published in *The Times* following the 1967 Hereford Festival (see Chapter 19), and confirmed my impression that, throughout its long history, the Festival had undoubtedly seen low points when either unacceptable standards or unimaginative programming had marred its reputation. Certainly, by 1967 radical reform of the appalling 'Black Monday' rehearsal system was long overdue; happily, 'old-fashioned junketing' would eventually come to an end, vital innovation in programming was soon to be addressed, and the Festival concluded the twentieth century in good heart and voice. As Roderic Dunnett so aptly put it in November 1992, in his *Church Times* review of the first edition of this book:

> William Mann was not alone in sniffing at artistic 'senile decay'. Yet the list of commissions, or revivals, seems far from staid: John McCabe's *Notturni ed Alba*; Leighton, Bennett and Mathias; Szymanowski's Polish *Stabat Mater*; or Penderecki conducting his own *Te Deum*; the Italians, Dallapiccola and Petrassi. Not all, it seems, was Stanford and Ebenezer Prout.

Even so, towards the end of the twentieth century the necessity for a major structural shift in the management of the Festival began to be contemplated. In order to secure the long-term future of Three Choirs, the need to bring together the administration at each of the three cities under a unified, professional leadership – seen by some members of the executive as obvious, but as anathema by others – presented a bone of contention which would only be resolved in the wake of unforeseen events. A refreshing change was in the air; a change that would be implemented within the first few years of the new millennium.

A. N. B.

May 2016

Acknowledgements

FIRST EDITION, 1992

SINCE starting out in 1989 to research and write this history, the list of those to whom I have turned for information, advice and help has steadily and inevitably increased. From the outset my closest companion and colleague was Christian Wilson, who not only took upon himself the task of updating the *Annals* of the Three Choirs, but also willingly volunteered to type out my manuscript.

It has been my good fortune to meet many people whose memories of the Festival over long years have helped to enliven these pages. I am particularly indebted to Basil Butcher, Maurice Hunt and Reginald Woolford, who were kind enough to lend me their valuable collections of Three Choirs photographs, press cuttings and memorabilia, and then to allow me to keep them by my side for many months as most useful sources of reference.

I have been helped greatly by the reminiscences of past organists of Gloucester, Hereford and Worcester: Melville Cook, Meredith Davies, Douglas Guest, Donald Hunt, Richard Lloyd, Roy Massey, Christopher Robinson, John Sanders, Herbert Sumsion and Sir David Willcocks. I also acknowledge with gratitude the help of many kinds which I received from Jean Armstrong, Wulstan Atkins, John Aukett, Rodney Bennett, Ray Boddington, Vernon Butcher, Tony Clark, Hugo Cole, Pat David, Jeremy Dibble, W. A. DuBuisson, Alice Dyson, Sir Keith Falkner, Diana Feilden, Tom Fenton, Joy Finzi, Derek Foxton, Brian Frith, Patience Gobey, Mike Grundy, John Harris, Jenny Houston, Laurence Hudson, Brendan Kerney, Jerrold Northrop Moore, Christopher Palmer, Rosemary Passmore-Rowe, Arthur Pritchard, Peter Roberts, Watkins Shaw, Edith Sterry, Alice Sumsion, R. S. Thompson, Ursula Vaughan Williams, Canon David Welander, Sam Driver White, Howard Williams, Francis Witts and Percy Young.

I am most grateful to Robin Stayt, himself a former Festival Secretary at Gloucester, who, having offered to assist in researching the first edition of this work, accepted the specific but unenviable task of seeking out the precise origins of Three Choirs. His enquiries over many months and in many places included the study of numerous manuscripts, family correspondence and other documents, and interviews with several historians of the eighteenth century. Although unsuccessful in adding substantially to the store of Three Choirs knowledge, his efforts have been of enormous value in eliminating from further consideration those areas of research which he proved to be without profit, thus saving me many hours of fruitless labour.

My researches would not have been possible without the cooperation and assistance of a number of professional librarians and archivists. For their unfailing courtesy and consideration I owe sincere thanks to Sue Hubbard, Jill Voyce, Barbara Griffiths, Graham Baker, and the staffs of the City Libraries and

Records Offices/Archives in Gloucester, Hereford and Worcester; the National Sound Archive; Christopher Bornet and his colleagues at the Library of the Royal College of Music; Ian Ledsham at the Music Library of Birmingham University; Godfrey Waller of the Manuscript Department, Cambridge University Library; Robert Tucker at the Barbican Music Library; and Meg Kimmins, Joan Williams and Ron Stratton at the Cathedral Libraries of Gloucester, Hereford and Worcester respectively.

I am grateful to the Oxford University Press for permission to quote from *Walford Davies* by H. C. Colles; *R. V. W.: A Biography of Ralph Vaughan Williams* by Ursula Vaughan Williams; and *Elgar on Record* by Jerrold Northrop Moore; and to Gollancz Ltd for permission to quote from *Elgar as I Knew Him* by W. H. Reed.

My thanks are due to Gareth Rees-Roberts for copies of his photographs of the 1991 Hereford Festival, and to the late Jack Farley for his care and photographic skill in copying, often from very poor originals, many of the illustrations in this book.

Finally, I must thank my wife, Anne, for her constant support and forbearance throughout the past two years.

A. N. B.

1992

REVISED EDITION, 2017

WE are grateful to past and present Three Choirs Festival Artistic Directors Geraint Bowen, David Briggs, Adrian Lucas, Peter Nardone, Andrew Nethsingha and Adrian Partington for sharing their memories of the Festival.

Many of those who contributed their recollections, gave help and advice in the preparation of the first edition of this book, and were acknowledged in 1992, have sadly passed away. However, we have been helped in the preparation of this new edition in many ways and by many people, and acknowledge with great thanks the ready assistance that we have received from William Armiger, Roger Dubois, Roderic Dunnett, John Gilden, John Harris, Donald Hunt, Dominic Jewel, Roger Jones, Graham J. Lloyd, Roy Massey, Alexis Paterson, John Quinn, Clare Stevens, Lindsay Wallace, Lucy Watson and Stephen J. Williams.

We are indebted to Jeremy Wilding and the Three Choirs Festival Society for providing financial support towards this project, and we are especially grateful to Michael James for the many hours that he has willingly spent in the preparation of an up-to-date, computer-compatible version of the revised text of this book.

A. N. B. & P. H.

2016

Abbreviations

Annals Rev. Daniel Lysons *et al.*, *History of the Origin and Progress of the Meeting of the Three Choirs of Gloucester, Worcester and Hereford and the Charity connected with it* (Gloucester, 1812; rev. edns 1864 and 1895)

ARCO Associate of the Royal College of Organists

CBSO City of Birmingham Symphony Orchestra

CUP Cambridge University Press

FRCO Fellow of the Royal College of Organists

LPO London Philharmonic Orchestra

LSO London Symphony Orchestra

MT *The Musical Times*

MW *The Musical World*

OUP Oxford University Press

RLPO Royal Liverpool Philharmonic Orchestra

RPO Royal Philharmonic Orchestra

(G) Gloucester ⎫

(H) Hereford ⎬ following a year to denote the venue of a Festival

(W) Worcester ⎭

Cathedral Organists

THERE follows a list of the organists of Gloucester, Hereford and Worcester from the time of the earliest Music Meetings to date.

Gloucester	Hereford	Worcester
		1688 Richard Cherington
	1707 Henry Hall junior	
1712/13 William Hine (deputy from 1707, but effectively in charge)	1714 Edward Thompson	
	1720 Henry Swarbrick	
		1724 John Hoddinott
1730 Barnabas Gunn		
		1731 William Hayes
		1734 John Merifield
1740 Martin Smith		
		1747 Elias Isaac
	1754 Richard Clack	
	1779 William Perry	
1782 William Mutlow		
	1789 Miles Coyle	
		1793 Thomas Pitt
	1805 Charles Dare	
		1806 Jeremiah Clarke
		1807 William Kenge
		1813 Charles Clarke
	1818 Aaron Hayter	
	1820 John Clarke-Whitfeld	
1832 John Amott	1832 Samuel Sebastian Wesley	
	1835 John Hunt	
	1843 George Townshend Smith	
		1844 William Done

Gloucester	Hereford	Worcester
1865 Samuel Sebastian Wesley		
1876 Charles Harford Lloyd		
	1877 Langdon Colbourne	
1882 Charles Lee Williams		
	1889 George Robertson Sinclair	
		1895 Hugh Blair
1897 Herbert Brewer		1897 Ivor Atkins
	1918 Percy Hull	
1928 Herbert Sumsion		
	1950 Meredith Davies	1950 David Willcocks
	1956 Melville Cook	
		1957 Douglas Guest
		1963 Christopher Robinson
	1966 Richard Hey Lloyd	
1967 John Sanders		
	1974 Roy Massey	
		1975 Donald Hunt
1994 David Briggs		
		1996 Adrian Lucas
	2001 Geraint Bowen	
2002 Andrew Nethsingha		
2007 Adrian Partington		
		2012 Peter Nardone

It was … a fortuitous and friendly proposal, between a few Lovers of harmony, and brethren of the correspondent Choirs, to commence an anniversary visit, to be kept in turn: Which voluntary instance of friendship and fraternity, was quickly strengthened by social compact: And afterwards, being blessed and sanctioned by a Charity-collection, with the word of exhortation added to confirm the whole, it arrived to the figure and estimation, as ye see this day.

Thomas Bisse, Chancellor of Hereford (1729)

A remarkable, unique institution lying at the heart of British life – the Three Choirs Festival.

Radio Times (27 July 2015)

I

Origins

THE most frequently asked question about Three Choirs history is a simple one: 'when exactly did the Festival begin?' Finding an answer, however, has from the outset proved to be far from simple. The engraver and publisher Valentine Green, writing in 1796, stated that the first Meeting of the Three Choirs took place at Worcester in August 1722, whereas we now know that the inception of the Music Meetings (as they were termed until 1836, when the designation 'Festival' was adopted) must pre-date that by some years.[1] Even as long ago as 1812, the Rev. Daniel Lysons, the earliest chronicler of the Festival to write a detailed history, was forced to admit that 'It is in vain that I have endeavoured ... to trace anything like the time of their first establishment.'[2]

Two lengthy suspensions of Three Choirs, both of them caused by war, added to the confusion. The Festival was discontinued for six years during World War I: from 1914 to 1919. In 1920, Sir Ivor Atkins, Organist of Worcester Cathedral, was charged with restarting Three Choirs on the return to peace; he gave official recognition to the year 1715 'by reckoning the first Festival after the suspension ... as the two hundredth'.[3] This was generally accepted, such that Dennis Stoll, writing in 1938, in his book *Music Festivals of Europe*, felt able to state with confidence that 'The three choirs met for the first time in 1715.'[4] But neither Atkins nor Stoll based his claim upon firm documentary proof. The outbreak of World War II, in 1939, silenced debate on the matter for seven more years: the Festival was again suspended throughout the duration of hostilities.

As late as 1966, in an historical note for a Worcester Festival programme book, the music critic A. T. Shaw pronounced that 'any attempt to fix the date of the [first] meeting is predestined to failure'.[5] But even so, the search for a start-date has continued. Dr Percy M. Young (1912–2004) – musicologist, writer, conductor, authority on Elgar, frequent lecturer at Three Choirs Festivals, and a distinguished scholar of English music of the eighteenth and nineteenth centuries – contributed a valuable essay, 'The First Hundred Years', to a booklet

---

[1] Valentine Green, *The History and Antiquities of the City and Suburbs of Worcester* (Worcester, 1796), p. 76.

[2] *Annals* 1812, p. 159.

[3] Watkins Shaw, *The Three Choirs Festival: The Official History of the Meetings of Gloucester, Hereford and Worcester, c. 1713–1953* (Baylis for Three Choirs Festival, 1954), p. 5.

[4] Dennis Gray Stoll, *Music Festivals of Europe* (John Miles, 1938), p. 20.

[5] Worcester Festival programme book, 1966, p. 14. Copy held in the Three Choirs Festival Office, Gloucester.

published in 1977 in association with the celebrations at Gloucester marking 250 years of the Festival. In it, Dr Young summarised the personalities and qualities of early eighteenth-century musicians of Gloucester, Hereford and Worcester:

> [Three Choirs], as it is now generally recognised, was created principally by musicians, and those who were most active at the beginning were the cathedral organists. At the beginning of the eighteenth century the organist of an English provincial cathedral was not thought to be a person of importance either socially or musically. Those who held the office were either local men who had worked their way up from an apprenticeship or those whose talents were not considered likely to guarantee advancement in London.
>
> At Gloucester and Worcester the eighteenth century was played in by two drunks. Jeffries, organist at Gloucester for almost thirty years, was so renowned for intemperance that on that account only he is memorialised in the History of the straight-laced Hawkins. Cherington of Worcester, who kept his place for thirty-six years and superintended the music for the Treaty of Utrecht Thanksgiving … was a combative individual, once compelled by his Dean to do penance in the cathedral for fighting with a lay clerk. Such robust behaviour, it may be said, also distinguished various worthy members of the German Bach family at the same time. At Hereford, on the other hand, some acknowledged distinction was brought to the cathedral by the Halls, father and son, who played the organ between 1688 and 1713 … Those who took up the Music Meeting according to Bisse's intention were William Hine (1687–1730), at Gloucester; John Hoddinott (1688–1731), a former chorister, at Worcester; and Edmund Thompson (d. *c.* 1721) and Henry Swarbrick (d. 1754), possibly a relative of the German-born organ-builder who improved the Worcester organ in 1752, at Hereford.[6]

In seeking the origins of Three Choirs and its first author, or authors, it is therefore necessary to examine the competing claims of each organist, to seek evidence to show that one or more of them possessed above-average qualities, and to review any relevant contemporary publications.

The earliest printed evidence for the origins of the triennial Music Meeting appears in a 1719 edition of the *Worcester Postman*, where a notice advertises arrangements for 'the yearly Musical Assembly', thus indicating that an annual event must already have been established before 1719. Since 1920 the numbering of the Festivals has, in line with Sir Ivor Atkins's statement, been counted from 1715. Hence, the tercentenary of the founding of the Three Choirs was celebrated at the Hereford Festival of 2015, by which time the number of Festivals actually presented had reached 288.[7]

---

[6] Percy M. Young, 'The First Hundred Years', in Barry Still (ed.), *Two Hundred and Fifty Years of the Three Choirs Festival* (Three Choirs Festival Association, 1977), p. 13.

[7] The Three Choirs Festival could not meet during the six years of World War I or the seven years of World War II. So 2015 minus 1715 = 300 years (plus 1, to count the year 1715 itself), minus 13 (6 + 7) = the 288th by 2015.

The earliest record that the Rev. Daniel Lysons had been able to trace was contained in an announcement in the *Gloucester Journal* of Monday 12 August 1723, showing that by that year a subscription scheme was already firmly in place:

> All Gentlemen who are subscribers to the Annual Meeting of the Three Choirs at Gloucester, Hereford and Worcester are desired to take Notice, That the Day and Place of Meeting this year is at Hereford, Tuesday, Sept. 3rd., in order to a performance of Musick the two Days following, pursuant to their subscription. Tickets to be had at Mr John Hunt's, Bookseller, and at Mr Ford's at the Redstreak Tree, in Hereford.

In 1723 the *Gloucester Journal* was only in its second year of publication, and no references to a Music Meeting at Worcester appear in the 1722 editions. However, the *Worcester Postman* had then already been in existence for more than a decade, and the edition dated 14–21 August 1719 contains the following notice, first traced by Sir Ivor Atkins:

> The Members of the yearly Musical Assembly of these Parts are desired to take Notice, That, by their Subscription in September last at Gloucester, they are obliged (not withstanding a false and groundless Report to the contrary) to meet at Worcester, on Monday the last day of this instant August; in order to publick performance, on Tuesday and Wednesday following.[8]

In an easily overlooked footnote added to his 1864 Continuation of the *Annals*, and replicated in the 1895 edition, John Amott, Organist at Gloucester, revealed that he 'had in his possession an old family account book, in which subscriptions to the Music Meetings from 1718 to 1728 were recorded'.[9] No records have been found for Meetings held before the subscription scheme was introduced, which explains why there is uncertainty about the first few years. Clearly, an annual event had already been established by 1718, and it is improbable that a regular subscription series would have been initiated immediately following a single informal gathering. Surely, a minimum of three experimental Meetings, one in each city, would have been trialled before a subscription series could have been instituted, or even contemplated with confidence, and this thought may have been in Sir Ivor Atkins's mind when he determined that 1715 was the most likely year in which Three Choirs was inaugurated.

Unlike the cathedrals of Gloucester and Worcester, there was no monastic tradition at Hereford. Having a secular (i.e. non-monastic) body of clergy, it underwent no constitutional change at the Dissolution of the Monasteries under Henry VIII. In the early Middle Ages the clergy of the cathedral included the dean and twenty-seven canons, along with a number of chantry priests, or vicars choral (cantarists), who were required to sing or recite mass at the many altars in the cathedral. Richard II incorporated the vicars choral as a college in 1395, by which time their number had increased to twenty-seven, one of whom was

[8] Watkins Shaw, *The Three Choirs Festival* (Three Choirs Festival Worcester, 1954), p. 1.

[9] *Annals* 1895, p. 14, n. 1. The subscription to the Music Meeting was 10s. 6d. (52½p) in 1718, and in the following year had risen to 6s. 0d. per quarter.

elected custos. The buildings of the College of Vicars Choral at Hereford were begun in 1475. The Laudian statutes of 1637 provided for only twelve vicars choral, together with five lay members.

The vicars choral served Hereford over many centuries. As clergy specially chosen for their musical gifts they had no parallel in Gloucester or Worcester. Until the mid-nineteenth century the vicars choral provided all the alto, tenor and bass parts in the cathedral choir. The college was dissolved in 1937.

During the Civil War the cathedral was closed and, in spite of the vicars choral sending a petition to the Committee for Sequestration, the college was disbanded; it did not reopen until 1660, when, as the Rev. W. Cooke reported:

> The Buildings and Premises of the College had necessarily fallen into sad decay and dilapidation during the late Rebellion; and the Expences of reparation were a heavy tax upon the General Funds; to [Humphrey] Fisher [a vicar choral] was committed the superintendence of restoring the Common Hall and the Library.[10]

The College Hall and Library were finished by 1 September 1676, and soon, perhaps immediately, the hall became the focus for a college music club – a venue for the performance and enjoyment of secular music, which was, of course, banned from cathedrals. And it is certain that the vicars choral knew how to enjoy themselves, as did Henry Hall, successor in 1688 to the first post-Restoration Organist at Hereford, John Badham.

Hall (*c.* 1656–1707) had been a fellow chorister with Purcell in the Chapel Royal before successive appointments as Organist at Exeter and, in 1688, at Hereford. Dually gifted as both poet and composer, he wrote 'a verse tribute "To the Memory of my Dear Friend Mr Henry Purcell" published in 1698 at the beginning of Part One of *Orpheus Britannicus*, Henry Playford's great collection of Purcell's songs'.[11]

> No convincing evidence has been found to suggest that Hall felt isolated in Hereford, regretting its remoteness from London. On the contrary, he lived happily with his wife and two children, William and Henry, enjoying the musical life of the cathedral and the city. He took a full part in the social life of the college and wrote secular music for the evening concerts of the vicars which were popular and held regularly in the college hall after it had been refurbished following the decay of the buildings during the interregnum.
>
> Both of Henry Hall's sons were musicians. William was a violinist, who from 1692 until his death in 1700 was a musician in ordinary to the king, and the younger Henry lived to succeed his father as organist of the cathedral.[12]

---

[10] W. Cooke, 'Biographical Memoirs of the Customs and Vicars' (1851), 2 vols in 1 (MS), held in Hereford Cathedral Library and Archives.

[11] See Paul Iles, 'Music and Liturgy since 1600', in Gerald Aylmer and John Tiller (eds), *Hereford Cathedral: A History* (Hambledon Press, 2000), pp. 405–7.

[12] Ibid.

Hall senior composed a great deal of music especially for the Hereford choir. Also, confirmed Cooke, 'exclusive of musical talent, Mr Hall had a great turn for poetry; and making allowances for the depraved taste and ribaldry, in those days still prevalent, there is considerable point and humour in his verses'.[13] The following catch by Henry Hall, written on King William's return from Flanders, proves Cooke's point that Hall was an ardent Jacobite.

> Rejoice ye fools, your Idol's come again,
> To pick your pockets, and to slay your Men.
> Give him yr. Millions – & his Dutch yr. lands,
> Don't *ring* ye *Bels*, you fools, but *wring* yr. Hands.

Of Mr Hall's secular music, little now remains; some of his catches may be found in Lames collection, a few are still in MS at Hereford; but since among his Poems several songs are inserted, it is presumed that in his two-fold capacity of Poet and Musician, he had no difficulty of giving proof of this combination of talent, by carolling those ditties in the *Black Lion Club Room* where frequent carousals are spoken of among his jovial & political associates; compeers of those nightly revelries, which most likely diverted his thoughts from the greater duties of his professions, for which Education & Genius had so abundantly qualified him.[14]

The Black Lion still stands in Hereford, and the Hereford vicars choral seem to have enjoyed such opportunities for conviviality; undoubtedly many of the Gloucester and Worcester lay clerks would have felt likewise. The Chapter Act books give examples enough of admonishments meted out to lay clerks who dared to take their musical talents to town – witness the following entry made at Worcester on 25 September 1684:

> Whereas scandall has been given by Roger Fosbrooke the Elder a Lay Clerk of this Church, by his associating himself with the Town-Musick, it is hereby decreed, that he shall Determine and give his Answer before the first of March next, whether he will relinquish the Town-Musick, or resign his Lay Clerk's place. And if he shall presume after that time to play in any public house, or at any public meeting, or to associate himself with the Town-Musick any more, that then he be immediately, *ipso facto*, suspended from his sayd Lay Clerk's place and from the benefitt and profitts thereof for a period of one whole year from the time of such offence committed. And to prevent all further scandall that may arise upon the matter, It is hereby decreed and enacted that for the future every Lay Clerk before his admission shall with one sufficient Surety give Bond to the Dean and Chapter in the Summe of One Hundred pounds, That he the said Lay Clerk to be admitted, nor his wife, nor any other from him shall keep any Tavern, Ale house or Victualling House; and that he will not accept or

---

[13] Cooke, 'Biographical Memoirs of the Customs and Vicars'.
[14] Ibid.

perform any service in any publick Musick, nor at any time play in any public house whatsoever.[15]

Given that 100 pounds in 1684 represented ten years' pay to a lay clerk, presumably the intention of this admonishment was not only to terrify Roger Fosbrooke into compliance, but also *pour encourager les autres*. What this and other Chapter Acts like it show is that the pull of secular music for sheer pleasure was understandably strong – but where was it to be heard? Throughout the Commonwealth period, even in London, there had been no specially designed concert halls, no true opera, no ballet, few theatres, and no music festivals. In general, those seeking to enjoy popular music would gravitate to inns and taverns.

However, by the time of Henry Hall senior's death in 1707, at the age of fifty-one, a change was already well under way. Rising middle-class affluence, albeit at the price of a widening gap between 'haves' and 'have-nots', increased the demand for popular entertainment of all kinds, and the exploitation of printing, which began in the middle of the seventeenth century and accelerated in the 1690s, was fundamental in bringing a scattered population to entertainment, and *vice versa*.

Effective publicity, the availability of printed music, and the social and cultural aspirations of a rising middle class created ideal conditions for the steady expansion of provincial entertainment in the eighteenth century. The vicars choral at Hereford had been among the privileged few in having a splendid hall and music club, enabling them to hear and to make music from such an early date; it would not be long, however, before the people of Gloucester and Worcester, including the cathedral organists and lay clerks, were to demand secular entertainment of their own. Music composed for anything other than services was not permitted in cathedrals; it was therefore inevitable that the secular element of the earliest Music Meetings would have been held in music clubs, with Hereford leading the way.

Henry Hall senior was succeeded at Hereford by his son, Henry Hall junior, who 'possessed much of his father's talent for music and poetry but, unhappily, also the like Bacchanalian propensities'.[16] His counterpart at Gloucester, though older, was a kindred spirit – Stephen Jeffries, whose single long-lasting contribution to the music at Gloucester was the composition of a tune for the cathedral chimes:

> This was the first tune to include Great Peter, and the necessary adjustments to the medieval chime machine were made by Abraham Rudhall, the well-known Gloucester Bellfounder. He was paid £5 for this in 1698 ... I tracked down a printed sheet of *c.* 1700, in the library of the University of Texas. This gives a three-part choral arrangement by Stephen Jeffries of his tune, set to words by Maurice Wheeler, then Master of the College School. These are entitled *A Meditation upon Death*.[17]

[15] Chapter Act Book 1684. Worcester Cathedral Library and Archive.

[16] Cooke, 'Biographical Memoirs of the Customs and Vicars'.

[17] Jonathan MacKechnie-Jarvis, *Friends of Gloucester Cathedral Newsletter* 73 (Autumn 2015), p. 17.

Born at Salisbury, where he was a chorister and later Assistant Organist in the cathedral, Jeffries was appointed Organist at Gloucester Cathedral in 1682 when only twenty years old. Soon after his arrival he was admonished by the Dean and Chapter 'for manifold neglect and unreasonable absence from the Church without leave desired or obtained', in spite of being given £2 by them shortly before 'for his encouragement'. In 1688, Jeffries was again admonished for playing on the organ 'a common Ballad' which caused female members of the congregation to dance.

> This was reputed to have been in the presence of between 1,500 and 2,000 people. On being warned, Jefferies' [*sic*] reply seems to have been to repeat the performance, and yet he kept his position long enough that he suffered another warning in 1699 for being frequently absent, especially on Sunday mornings, and also for not educating the choristers in the grounds of music.
>
> Jefferies was an eccentric who, according to Hawkins in his *History of Music*, was addicted to staying out late in taverns … Hawkins also refers to the occasion when a singer from away, with a good voice, was asked to sing a solo anthem in the Cathedral, and for this purpose stood by the elbow of the organist in the organ loft [in the Quire]. Stephen Jefferies, finding him trip in the performance, instead of helping him and setting him right, promptly rose from his seat and leaning over the gallery, called aloud to the choir and to the whole congregation, 'He can't sing it!'[18]

Surprisingly, Jeffries continued to hang on as Organist at Gloucester until his death in 1712, aged fifty-four, but he had effectively been replaced some five years earlier by William Hine, a man of a very different stamp. The Gloucester Treasurer's Accounts for 13 October 1707 record the payment of £6 5s. od. to 'Mr Hynde [*sic*] the new organist', yet the drunken Jeffries continued to be listed as organist, while Hine bore the burden as his deputy. In 1709/10 Hine received £27 10s. od. for his year's salary, with an additional gratuity of 2 guineas, and continued to receive part-payment until Jeffries's death. The Dean and Chapter most certainly did not wish to lose the talented and reliable Hine, and by voluntarily increasing his salary by £20 they ultimately ensured that his services were secured.

Henry Hall junior, the sharp-witted poet, musician and *bon viveur*, and William Hine were almost exact contemporaries; both were aged twenty or twenty-one in 1707, when they were appointed to Hereford and Gloucester respectively. There is good evidence to show that these two young men were collaborating from at least as early as 1709, the year in which they jointly composed a Morning Service, 'Hall and Hine in E flat': the *Te Deum* is by Hall; the *Jubilate* by Hine. Though highly regarded in the eighteenth century, this joint venture has long been considered rather dull, and cannot be said to have ignited an instantaneous launch of the Music Meetings. However, it does indicate that the Service was composed to be sung by the combined Hereford and Gloucester cathedral choirs. The Gloucester Treasurer's Accounts show that

---

[18] Brian Frith, *The Organs amd Organists of Gloucester Cathedral* (Gloucester Cathedral, 1972), p. 56, quoting Sir John Hawkins (1719–1789), *A General History of the Science and Practice of Music*, 5 vols (1776; repr. Novello, 1853 and 1875).

on an unspecified date in 1709, Hall, 'the organist fromward Hereford', was paid two pounds;[19] a large sum which may well represent a payment for Hereford's participation in a combined service – undoubtedly 'Hall and Hine in E flat' – and it is possible that the ultimate aim of these two young musicians was to bring their new joint composition and both of their choirs to Worcester in 1710. Such a gesture of *hommage* to the senior cathedral could only have reinforced ancient ties and established a dialogue between the organists and singing men of the three cities. If Hall *was* accompanied by his Hereford choirmen on the visit to Gloucester in 1709, and if both choirs were indeed in Worcester in 1710, they would have been free to enjoy convivial entertainment together following Morning Service for, by 1711, Gloucester and Worcester had caught up with Hereford and could boast music clubs of their own.

However, these experiments, important as they were in signifying the first eighteenth-century flutterings into life of collaboration between cathedral organists in the Three Choirs counties, do not constitute a full-scale, two-day Music Meeting featuring both sacred and secular music. Such a development would be achieved within a very few years, but it would not be organised exclusively by the Church. Instead, it was the result of cooperation – of lay Stewards working *with* the Church. The organisational demands were considerable: the Meetings required effective direction (both musical and administrative), financial support, the sale of tickets, and the use of one or more secular venues. Nonetheless, from these small, unrecorded beginnings the idea suggested in 'a fortuitous and friendly proposal' gained strength, was encouraged by music-lovers, and within less than a decade had grown into a flourishing series of Music Meetings.[20]

The Worcester Organist during Hall and Hine's time, Richard Cherington, was older than either of his *confrères* and, as we have seen, was a man of brittle temper; in 1697 he had been ordered to do penance for quarrelling and fighting with one of the lay clerks.[21] While he seems not to have been involved in the 1709 gathering at Gloucester, it is quite possible that the Worcester singing men *were* there, even if Cherington was not. Little is known about him, and it seems unlikely that he possessed either the necessary dedication or motivation to be the sole instigator of the Music Meetings. Equally, as organist of the senior of the three cathedrals, it is inconceivable that he was not involved in the formulation of any ambitious strategy devised by Hall and Hine.

---

[19] Treasurer's Accounts. Gloucestershire Archives (D 936A 1/5).

[20] The quotation is from a sermon preached by Thomas Bisse, Chancellor of Hereford, at the meeting of the Three Choirs in 1729; see *Annals* 1812, p. 127. Copies of Bisse's semons are held in Hereford City Library.

[21] John E. West, *Cathedral Organists Past and Present* (Novello, 1899), p. 90. Updated by Watkins Shaw, *The Succession of Organists of the Chapel Royal and the Cathedrals of England and Wales from c. 1538* (OUP, 1991).

H ENRY Hall junior died in 1714, too early to take part in establishing the
earliest of the triennial Music Meetings. The gatherings pre-dating any
charitable purpose are known to have been held during the tenures of Hine
and Cherington, so it is to Hine that we now turn in an effort to assess his
contribution in establishing the Three Choirs Meetings.

Unusually among cathedral organists, Hine was not a local man and had
not worked his way up from an apprenticeship. But by the time he arrived in
Gloucester, Hine, like Henry Hall senior, had already made his mark in London:

> [Hine] was born at Brightwell, Oxfordshire, in the year 1687 [two years
> after the births of both Bach and Handel], who having a fine Voice, and
> talents for Music obtained a Choristership at St Mary Magdalene College,
> Oxford, where, having been taught by Mr Hyte, Organist and Master of
> the Choristers there, he soon distinguished himself, and in time became
> an accomplished Singer; he was made Choice of by John Weldon, then
> Organist of New College, to sing and act in his *Judgement of Paris*, which
> obtained the Prize, after the death of Henry Purcell, (whose Pupil he had
> been) upon the presentation of it in Town [London]. While he remained
> in Oxford, he also learnt the Harpsichord of Mr Hyte, and became his
> Assistant.[22]

At Magdalen, Hine progressed rapidly from chorister to lay clerk, and by
1701 had gained success in the world of secular music, singing in opera on the
London stage. A notice, dated 18 March 1700, was placed in the *London Gazette*
by a group of English nobles who, envious of the popularity of Italian opera in
London, had offered a 'Musick Prize' for the best all-sung English opera setting
of Congreve's libretto *The Judgement of Paris*.[23] The sponsors, headed by Lord
Halifax, offered four prizes: the first of 100 guineas; the second, 50 guineas; the
third, 30 guineas; and the fourth, 20 guineas. Four composers entered: John
Weldon, John Eccles, Daniel Purcell and Gottfried Finger. Their entries were
performed during the spring of 1701, then staged together in a grand final at the
Dorset Garden Theatre on 3 June 1703. Weldon was the winner and Hine was
engaged to sing the title-role, thereby becoming sufficiently known and admired
in both high society and the London musical world to warrant the painting of
his portrait by Sir Godfrey Kneller (see Frontispiece).

Kneller (originally Gottfried Kniller; 1646–1723) was an eminent German-
born painter who had settled in England; hailed as the leading British portraitist,
he was created a baronet in 1715. Both Kneller and Lord Halifax were members
of the famous Kit-Kat Club, a group of thirty-nine noblemen and gentlemen,
formed about 1700, whose interests lay in the spheres of politics and the arts. All
were pledged to uphold the Protestant succession; all were strong supporters of
the Royal House of Hanover; and all were painted by Kneller.

Unfortunately, the 'Musick Prize' competition did little to advance the
progress of opera in English. Italian opera gained the ascendancy, and both John
Eccles and Daniel Purcell chose not to write any more music for the theatre.

---

[22] Samuel Arnold, *Cathedral Music*, 4 vols (London, 1790).

[23] All-sung opera, as opposed to the more usual English form of semi-opera in
which music and spoken drama were mixed.

It is probable that Hine, his reputation growing, travelled widely, including from Oxford to Gloucester early in the 1700s, perhaps to sing and/or to play the organ in the cathedral, thereby getting to know Stephen Jeffries and other local worthies, including Abraham Rudhall, and finding an affinity with the building, the city, and its people – but not yet realising that within so provincial a setting his future lay.

Then, in Oxford in 1705, having allowed passion to overrule discretion, he found himself dismissed summarily from Magdalen College, charged with fornication. One door closed firmly but, for so talented a young man, another opened wide. He was 'placed under Jeremiah Clarke, Organist of St Paul's [and Joint Organist of the Chapel Royal, with William Croft], from whom the Pupil imbibed the Master's excellence and became distinguished for his elegant manner in playing on the Organ'.[24] Not only would Hine have studied and absorbed the musical style of his master, which he emulated, but in the capital, the heart of music-making in Britain, he was also privileged to meet and to hear the finest singers and instrumental musicians. At St Paul's he would also have encountered the functioning of a unique charity, instituted there in 1655 and granted a royal charter in 1678: the Corporation of the Sons of the Clergy, a body that was later to provide the model and the *raison d'être* for the Music Meetings of the Three Choirs of Gloucester, Hereford and Worcester.[25]

Jeremiah Clarke, who had been a pupil of John Blow at the Chapel Royal, was at St Paul's from 1695 and at the Chapel Royal from 1704. He is mainly remembered today for his *Prince of Denmark's March* (widely known as the 'Trumpet Voluntary'), which was for a long time incorrectly attributed to Purcell. In 1707, at age thirty-four, Clarke was consumed by a violent and unrequited love for a lady of high social standing, and descended into a deep, suicidal melancholy. 'Before shooting himself, he considered hanging and drowning as options but, to decide his fate, he tossed a coin; however the coin landed in the mud on its side.'[26] Instead of consoling him, this prompted his choosing the third method of death, and he performed the deed in the cathedral churchyard on 1 December 1707.

In the meantime, William Hine had left London, escaping to the quietness of Shropshire, where he took the post of Organist at Ludlow Parish Church. The choice of location was not a random one: the Ludlow organist that he was to replace was Henry Hall junior, who, following the death of his father, was appointed Organist of Hereford Cathedral on 5 June 1707. The coming together of these two young musicians of similar tastes and abilities proved to be a seminal event in the history of Three Choirs, their like-mindedness probably stimulating exciting thoughts about the potential for music-making in the west.

Ludlow is situated only some 25 miles due north of the city of Hereford, and Hine will have wasted no time in visiting the city, almost certainly with Hall, and acquainting himself with the music and organisation of both its cathedral and its music club. Remaining at Ludlow for a short while, Hine then moved on to

[24] Arnold, *Cathedral Music*.

[25] E. H. Pearce, Preface to *The Sons of the Clergy, 1655–1904* (John Murray, 1904), pp. ix–x.

[26] Solomon Piggott, *Remarkable Modes of Suicide* (J. Robins & Co, 1824), p. 175.

Gloucester Cathedral to join Stephen Jeffries as his deputy – but undoubtedly aware that he would soon be required to take the reins.

From London, where he had been a small fish in a big pond, Hine now found himself to be a relatively big fish in a rather small pond. He settled into his new surroundings, his mind probably filling with ideas and ambitions, and his reputation steadily rising. Although he was certainly in favour with the Dean and Chapter, ahead lay the challenge of persuading them that sacred and secular music *could* somehow be linked to mutual advantage.

Singled out for praise in the *Annals*, William Hine was described by Lysons as 'a musician of considerable eminence', and he was soon taking steps to climb Gloucester's social ladder. On 21 September 1710:

> He married Alicia, daughter of Mr Ruddell [Abraham Rudhall], the famous Gloucester Bell-founder, by whom he had one Daughter, who lived to be married. His amiable, polite manners, gained him the respect of all who knew him. He sang elegantly in a feigned voice [falsetto, i.e. countertenor] and was esteemed an excellent Teacher of singing &c. Among his pupils was Dr William Hayes, Music Professor at Oxford, who when a Boy, was much admired for his singing, and thro' the Recommendation of his friend and Patroness Mrs Viney who had taught him to play his first Tune on the Harpsichord he was articled for a term of years to Mr Hine, to be regularly bred in Music ... Mr Hine's Talents shone conspicuously even in a place not prone at that time to encourage Music. His compositions chiefly consisting of Church Music were written for the use of Gloucester Cathedral.[27]

By 1712 Hine was fully in charge of the music at Gloucester, where he and Alicia would have moved into the organist's house within the Palace Garden, by the Infirmary arches (demolished in the 1860s). During his tenure:

> he brought a new professionalism to the musical life and choral tradition of the Cathedral and established new standards of excellence. The rough-and-ready amateurish approach of the seventeenth century was no longer acceptable. In particular the Annual Music Meeting provoked a certain amount of rivalry between the three cathedral choirs, and challenged their organists and choirs to increasingly high standards.[28]

Three years later at Gloucester, in 1715, the first tentative, two-day, Annual Music Meeting of the Three Choirs is believed to have taken place. Nor does it seem unreasonable to suppose that similar, experimental Meetings might have been held at Worcester and Hereford in 1716 and 1717 respectively. By the time of the second Meeting at Gloucester, in 1718, the year of the first Three Choirs subscription society concert, Hine had successfully persuaded the Dean and Chapter there that the organ should be removed from beneath the south crossing arch to a central position over the west entrance of the Quire. A major structural

---

[27] Arnold, *Cathedral Music*. Another of Hine's pupils was Richard Church, later Organist of New College, Oxford.

[28] David Welander, *The History, Art and Architecture of Gloucester Cathedral* (Alan Sutton, 1991).

operation, organised by Hine himself, this brought his instrument to the most prominent position in Gloucester Cathedral; it was 'a bold and imaginative move which evoked considerable controversy at the time, and indeed has since'.[29] While certainly bold and imaginative, it was also costly and ambitious:

> According to the Rev. T. D. Fosbrooke, the Gloucester historian writing in 1819, the organ was moved … in 1718. At that date Abbot Wigmore's pulpitum was pulled down and the 'square stone pulpit' … was destroyed, its place being taken by the Organ. The Gloucester Corporation Minutes of 1717 approve a present of £50 to the Dean, as a contribution to his 'work of large expence by Beautifying and Enlarging the Choir' for the better accommodation of the Corporation and Citizens – and specifically for moving the organ.[30]

The move could hardly have failed to spur Hine's creativity, furthering his aspiration to excel as an organ recitalist and composer. His skill is clearly in evidence in works such as a sparkling little organ piece written for the flute stop, and in his Voluntary in F major we hear the work of a composer able to move easily between varied and contrasting moods, between exuberance and melancholy. The pianist Graham J. Lloyd, who knows this Voluntary in the edition prepared by Gwilym Beechey (see Chapter 3), suggests in a letter to me that:

> Whilst in no way a challenge to the keyboard works of his more brilliant contemporaries J. S. Bach and G. F. Handel, William Hines's Voluntary in F major is nevertheless an attractive addition to English liturgical organ music. Using well-established Baroque techniques, it makes much use of 2 and 3 part textures; a heavy reliance on sequences (where phrases are repeated 2 or 3 times at a different pitch) and elaborate ornamentation, in some cases in every bar.
>
> In its eight distinct sections, contrast is achieved by alternating slow and fast sections. In terms of tonality the home key of F major is maintained with occasional moves to D minor and, in one case, F minor; the latter key also providing some of the work's more serious moments.
>
> Interestingly, Hine indulges in more elaborate counterpoint as the piece progresses, saving his best ideas for the final section. The only change of time signature, from 4/4 to 3/4, also occurs here and it is these factors allied to the introduction of triplets in the right hand that create more excitement and give the music added propulsion as it draws to its close.

Hine knew his worth as a first-rate musician, but his plans for Gloucester clearly did not end there. 'At that time in respect of the organists of the three cities the tenant of the Gloucester loft appeared as *primus inter pares*'.[31]

---

[29] Ibid.

[30] Ibid.

[31] Young, 'The First Hundred Years'.

BEFORE 1715 the Music Meetings at the three cities are likely to have evolved only gradually, starting with occasional visits to 'sister' cathedrals by singing men and organists in the seventeenth century, then possibly progressing to occasional but unrecorded ties involving secular as well as sacred music-making early in the eighteenth century. A formal subscription society was established by 1718, and finally, in 1724, a union was forged between the Music Meetings and a charitable purpose (see Chapter 2).

This steady strengthening of cooperation could only have been boosted in 1713, when the signing of the Treaty of Utrecht ended the War of the Spanish Succession and ushered in three decades of relative stability and peace in Europe. The constant danger posed by the old French monarchy was at an end, and the maritime, commercial and financial supremacy of Great Britain was assured. The Treaty was marked by widespread rejoicing in Britain, which in Worcester included a major celebration with a fireworks display in the city, and in the cathedral a large-scale Service that was also an important musical event, presumably superintended by Richard Cherington, and noted with justifiable pride in the *Worcester Postman*:

> **Worcester, July 10.** Tuesday last, being the day appointed for a general Thanksgiving. The same was observed here with general Solemnity and Regularity in the following manner. The Bells began to ring as soon as day appeared, and about 10 in the Forenoon ... our Mayor, was met at the Town Hall by the Aldermen and other Members of the Chamber, and the several Companies of this City met at their Halls, and meeting together near the Cross, proceeded in great Order with their Streamers, and Musick before them to the Cathedral, where was performed Mr Purcell's great *Te Deum*, with the Symphonies and instrumental parts, on Violins and Hautboys, and afterwards a Sermon suitable for the Occasion was preached by Mr Phillips.

Three days earlier, a far less ambitious service was given at Gloucester Cathedral. The Treasurer's Accounts there show that on 7 July '£1 13s. 4d. was paid for a 'Thanksgiving for ye Peace to ye Preacher, Choir and Ringers'. Nonetheless, having seen the positive impact of the grand Worcester occasion, the clergy and organists of all three cities may have been persuaded that, should they cooperate in a regular musical celebration, the potential for musical, devotional and financial advantages could be substantial. By this time, too, the lay clerks and members of the music clubs in all three cities had presumably agreed to implement the 'fortuitous and friendly proposal ... to commence an anniversary visit, to be kept in turn'.[32]

However, there are two factors which make it unlikely that any sort of joint celebration would have been either attempted or appropriate in 1714, the year following the celebrations attached to the Treaty of Utrecht. First, Queen Anne, the last Stuart monarch of Great Britain, died on 1 August 1714, ushering in the reign of our first Hanoverian king, George I; second, Henry Hall junior died on 21 January 1714, aged only twenty-seven; he was buried in the vicars choral cloister, near his father. Hall's place was taken by Edward Thompson, who

[32] *Annals* 1812, p. 127.

moved to Salisbury in 1718, leaving a gap at Hereford until the appointment of Henry Swarbrick on 10 November 1720. Nothing is known of an organist between 1718 and 1720, but perhaps William Hine acted as caretaker: the organ had been repaired in 1707, Hine was familiar with it, and Swarbrick arrived in Hereford too late to have been able to participate in the known three-yearly cycle of pre-charitable Music Meetings: 1718 Gloucester, 1719 Worcester and 1720 Hereford.

No Music Meetings appear to have been held in 1713 or 1714; Sir Ivor Atkins concluded that the first pre-charitable assembly of Three Choirs took place in 1715; John Amott's family account book shows that a subscription scheme was introduced in 1718 – but the year 1715 fits with the known three-yearly cycle, placing the inaugural Music Meeting at Gloucester, with William Hine as its guiding spirit, artistic director, organist, harpsichord virtuoso and singer.

2

A Fortuitous and Friendly Proposal

THE musical club which met in the hall belonging to the vicars choral at Hereford was, as Lysons pointed out, 'an establishment of little expense: the performances were all *gratis*, except that of Mr Woodcock, their leader, whose nightly pay was five shillings. The members were regaled with ale, cyder and tobacco.'[1]

The Woodcocks were a musical family. Hawkins, speaking of Robert Woodcock, famous as a flute-player and composer for that instrument, adds:

> He had a brother named Thomas, who kept a coffee-house at Hereford, an excellent performer on the violin, and played the solos of Corelli with exquisite neatness and elegance. In that country his merits were not known, for his employment was playing country-dances, and his recreation angling. He died about the year 1750.[2]

At some time before mid-century, the Hereford musical club meetings had fallen into abeyance. They were revived in 1749 by William Felton, a vicar choral from 1741 to 1769, who transferred the concerts from the College Hall to the coffee house in St John Street, then owned by Frank Woodcock, which possessed the only room in the city large enough for the purpose. This new arrangement seems to have been quite profitable to Woodcock. The articles of the society, drawn up by Felton, show that Woodcock was to be paid 7s. for his performance (presumably on the violin) and 15s.: 'for the use of his Room, Fires, Forms & Candles for the two Sconces & Desks and Harpsichord'. In addition, Frank Woodcock's son, Francisco, was also to receive 2s. 6d. as a performer, and the Treasurer of the society was one John Woodcock. In the face of a potential monopoly it was perhaps prudent of Felton to ensure that the articles allowed that: 'It shall be in the power of the Performers (who are not paid) to remove this meeting to any other place they shall think proper.' Among the performers who *were* paid, apart from Woodcock and son, appear the Hereford Cathedral Organist, Henry Swarbrick, who played the harpsichord and was also responsible for ensuring that it was tuned, and a Mr Dyer, both of whom received 7s. 6d., and one Jemmy George, who was paid 10s. 6d. The Treasurer was also required 'to provide an Hautboy [oboe] to perform Each Night as cheap

---

[1] *Annals* 1812, p. 161.

[2] Sir John Hawkins, *A General History of the Science and Practice of Music. A New Edition with the Author's Posthumous Notes*, vol. 2 (Novello, Ewer & Co., 1776), p. 826.

a Rate as he can'; in 1749, a player named Clarke was paid £1 6s. to come from Worcester.[3]

The Hereford musical club had its equivalents in Gloucester and Worcester, and Lysons tells us that 'at Gloucester the meetings of the club were held in a large room within the walls of the Deanery', an arrangement that continued until 1763.[4] But an advertisement in the *Gloucester Journal* of Monday 17 September 1722 shows that from early in the eighteenth century music was also performed in the College Library.

Looking to Worcester, we find an advertisement in the *Worcester Postman* of 17–26 August 1720:

> This is to give Notice to all Gentlemen, Ladies and others that are lovers of music that on Friday 26th August at the Green Room in the Tower will be a concert for the benefit of Claudius Phillips, whereat he will perform several Pieces by himself. N. B. Tickets may be had at Mr Corfields at the Cross in the City of Worcester, at 2s and 6p each, beginning at 6 in the evening.

The joining together once per year, in each of the three cities in rotation, of the members of the musical clubs had, at first, no purpose beyond providing a pleasurable opportunity for listening to or sharing in the performance of music in a social gathering. The Meetings were, from the beginning, of two days' duration: extended Matins, accompanied by an orchestra, was held in the cathedral each morning, followed by performances in various secular buildings each evening.

Then, in 1716, Dr Philip Bisse, Bishop of Hereford, appointed his brother, Thomas, to the chancellorship of that diocese. Dr Thomas Bisse was a Gloucestershire man, born in 1675 at Oldbury-on-the-Hill, where his father was rector. He graduated at Oxford and held an appointment at the Rolls Chapel in London before joining his brother in Hereford. Thomas was an eloquent preacher with a genuine concern for the wretched state of so many of his clerical brethren and their families.

On 6 December 1716, Thomas Bisse preached a sermon at St Paul's Cathedral before the Corporation of the Sons of the Clergy. From the outset, the purpose of the Corporation was charitable. Even though over more than three centuries it has been best known to the public for an annual festival of music held in St Paul's, the Corporation's historian, Nicholas Cox, has pointed out that until relatively recently this was not part of the Corporation at all.[5] This is the reverse of the original purpose of Three Choirs, which began as a Music Meeting with social rather than charitable ends.

In addressing the Sons of the Clergy, Thomas Bisse was following in the footsteps of his brother, Philip, who had preached for the Corporation in 1708 and was its president from 1717 to 1721, thus retaining an association with that

---

[3] Minute Book and Accounts of the Hereford Musical Society, 1749–57. Hereford Cathedral Library and Archives (MR.4.D.xii).

[4] *Annals* 1812, p. 162.

[5] Nicholas Cox, *Bridging the Gap: A History of the Corporation of the Sons of the Clergy over Three Hundred Years, 1655–1978* (OUP, 1978).

body after his appointment as bishop, first to St David's in 1710, and then to Hereford in 1713. This was a significant period for the evolution of Three Choirs. As we have seen, Henry Hall junior, in the final months of his short life, had by 1709 forged valuable links with William Hine, introducing his Gloucester colleague to the Hereford Music Club as an exemplar for secular music venues. And in the ambitious Thanksgiving Service for the Treaty of Utrecht in 1713, Richard Cherington had raised the sacred music of Worcester Cathedral to a new level.

Unsurprisingly, Thomas Bisse, wishing to emulate the fundraising success of the Sons of the Clergy, soon pressed forward the idea that the annual Music Meetings of the Three Choirs should embrace a similar charitable purpose. He demonstrated thereby the unequivocal favour of the Church for a gathering centred on music, conceived both as a perfect expression of praise and as a universal source of pure pleasure.

Thomas Bisse's first sermon at Three Choirs was published in 1720:

> A Rationale on Cathedral Worship or Choir Service. A sermon preached in the Cathedral Church of Hereford, at the Anniversary Meeting of the Choirs of Worcester Gloucester and Hereford, Sept. 7, 1720. By Tho. Bisse, D. D., and Chancelor of the said Church. Printed for W. and J. Innys at the Prince's Arms at the West End of St Paul's. 1720.[6]

But in 1724 at the Gloucester Meeting his sermon promoted the cause of the charity, details of which were contained in a handbill circulated on the previous day:

> These are to give notice, that tomorrow, viz. – Thursday, the 10th instant, (September) there will be a collection made after morning service, at the Cathedral-door, for placing out, or assisting the education and maintenance of the orphans of the poorer clergy belonging to the dioceses of Gloucester, Worcester, and Hereford, or members of the three respective choirs; to be disposed of by six stewards, members of the Society, a clergyman, and a gentleman respectively belonging to the said dioceses.[7]

In the following two years, first at Worcester and then at Hereford, Bisse persisted in his purpose. His 1726 sermon at Hereford was based upon a text from Ecclesiastes 2.8: 'I gat me men-singers and women-singers, and the delights of the sons of men, as musical instruments, and that of all sorts.' And in a note to the sermon, he says: 'having first proposed this Charity with success at Gloucester, in 1724, and recommended it at Worcester in 1725, I thought myself obliged to promote it in this way, in the church and diocese to which I belong.'

---

[6] See footnote by E. F. Rimbault, *Annals* 1864 and 1895, p. 3.

[7] Copies of the sermons of Thomas Bisse are held in Hereford City Library.

THANKS to its many benefactors, the charity initiated by Thomas Bisse prospered. Among its earliest supporters, two philanthropists deserve particular mention: Colonel Maynard Colchester of Westbury, and his neighbour Catharine Boevey at Flaxley, both of whom were also prime movers in inaugurating the Society for the Promotion of Christian Knowledge.[8]

Maynard Colchester succeeded to the manor and estates at Westbury-on-Severn in 1696. His near neighbour at Flaxley Abbey, the rakish William Boevey, a wealthy merchant of Dutch descent, died in 1704 leaving a widow. Well-educated, cultivated and still young, 'Catharine Boevey regularly spent winters in London and summers at Flaxley entertaining notable personalities, including bishops and the writers Steele and Addison, who were said to have portrayed her in *The Tatler* as the perverse widow wooed in vain by Sir Roger de Coverley.'[9]

There was an ancient link between Westbury and the College of Vicars Choral at Hereford, forged in 1384 when some of the vicars attempted to obtain the revenue of the church at Westbury. This led to a dispute about their right to hold property, which was settled in 1395 when Richard II incorporated the vicars choral as a college. In addition to enjoying the revenues of the church, the college also controlled the lease of the rectory at Westbury. Details of seventeenth- and eighteenth-century leaseholders are recorded in the Accounts Book of the college, which is lodged in the Hereford Cathedral Library, and includes an entry showing that from 1675 to 1682 the lease was granted to Sir Thomas Brydges, later Lord Chandos.

Catharine Boevey died on 21 January 1726, aged fifty-seven, and was much mourned throughout Gloucestershire. At the Gloucester Music Meeting in 1728, the Rev. Peter Senhouse preached a sermon on 'The Use of Musick'. It was printed later in the year, with a dedication to 'Mrs Pope', sometime companion to Mrs Boevey, and an acknowledgement 'how much is owing' in respect to the Meeting of the Three Choirs, 'to the wisdom and goodness of your late excellent friend, and our kind and memorable patroness, Mrs Boevey, who laid the foundation of the good work, and during her life liberally contributed to the support of it'.[10]

As the charity founded by Bisse was barely a year old when Catharine Boevey died, it appears clear that she had given substantial support to the pre-charitable Music Meetings since their inception. And, of course, only after she was widowed, aged twenty-two (thirteen years after Peter Senhouse was admitted as a vicar choral at Hereford), would she have enjoyed any financial independence.

The charity was soon proving its effectiveness. In the first year, 1724, the collection amounted to £13 10s. 0d. divided equally between the three dioceses for disbursement by the six Stewards.[11] The Minute Book (opened in 1612) of

---

[8] See Joan Johnson, *The Gloucestershire Gentry* (Alan Sutton, 1989), p. 190.

[9] Ibid., pp. 196 and 197.

[10] *Annals* 1895, p. 3n.

[11] The Stewards of the charity should not be confused with the Stewards of the Music Meeting, of whom there was only one in the earliest years. For a short history of the Three Choirs Charity, see Brian Frith, 'The Festival Charity', in Barry Still (ed.), *Two Hundred and Fifty Years of the Three Choirs Festival* (Three Choirs Festival Association, 1977), pp. 25–6.

the Haberdashers Company in Hereford shows that, on 5 November 1725, one Posthumous Whitney, son of Hester Whitney, widow of the vicar of Clifford, was bound apprentice to a local 'Barber Chyrurgeon and Perukemaker (by the Charity having been paid out of the Contribution of the three Choirs of Hereford, Worster, & Gloster for ye assistance of Clergymens Widdows & Orphans).' It is also heartening to find in the same venerable Minute Book that by 1758 Posthumous Whitney had risen to the exalted position of Master of the Haberdashers Company![12]

By 1778 the collections at the Music Meetings were proving inadequate for the relief of the clergy widows and orphans in Worcestershire, and so at the Worcester Meeting in that year a subscription scheme was initiated whereby the beneficed clergy and some of the opulent laity donated an annual sum not exceeding 1 guinea each. The subscription in the first year amounted to £200. Similar schemes began at Gloucester in 1786 and at Hereford in 1791, building upon the strength of Bisse's initial proposal.

In 1729, at Hereford, Thomas Bisse preached once more for the charity and was able to say with some pride:

> In one thing our Society hath a perfect resemblance to that greater [The Corporation of the Sons of the Clergy], that it sprang, too, from a very small and accidental origin. It was in like manner a fortuitous and friendly proposal between a few lovers of harmony and brethren of the correspondent choirs, to commence an anniversary visit, to be kept in turn; which voluntary instance of friendship and fraternity was quickly strengthened by social compact; and afterwards, being blessed and sanctioned by a charity collection, with the word of exhortation added to confirm the whole, it is arrived to the figure and estimation as ye see this day ... Though the members of that communion we have entered into, being voluntary, may go off as their wills vary or as their affairs require, yet, by the accession of others, the Society may subsist unto many years, yea, generations, tending to the furtherance of God's glory, in the exaltation of His holy worship, to the improvement of our choirs, the credit of our foundations; to the benefit of our cities, the comfort of the fatherless; to the delight of mankind, of ourselves, and all that come nigh us. Upon these grounds it commenced, and upon these let our brotherly love continue.[13]

B UT the *first* seeds of Three Choirs pre-date any charitable purpose. It is possible to look back much further – and to begin with a misty legend.

In his monograph *1890–1990: The Centenary of the Birth of a Friendship: Edward Elgar and Ivor Atkins and their Influence on the Three Choirs Festival,* Sir Ivor Atkins's son (and Elgar's godson), E. Wulstan Atkins, recollected his boyhood years in the Worcester Cathedral Choir, 1913–19. He remembered hearing from 'the oldest lay clerk, James Smith, then nearing eighty, about a

---

[12] Minute Book of the Haberdashers Company in Hereford. Hereford City Library (338.6).

[13] *Annals* 1812, pp. 127–30.

"legend" which was handed down from one generation of lay clerks to the next, relating to the start at Worcester of the Three Choirs Meetings':

> I was fascinated, and told my father, who said that he knew all about the romantic legend, but without confirmation it could not be treated seriously … Some years later I found that Elgar … knew all about it, having, he thought, been told it by his father when he was about 12. I asked him to tell me the version he had heard. It was almost word for word what I had been told about it in about 1918, and what my father had heard in 1897 when he first became organist at Worcester. All three versions stated definitely that it was Worcester who had started the Meetings in 1662, by the lay clerks inviting their colleagues in Hereford and Gloucester to join them in celebrating the recent full restoration at Worcester of daily sung services with organ. Neither Elgar nor my father, being good historians, would accept the legend without written proof; it sounding to them too much like an old monk's tale. They admitted, however, that there were points of great interest to them in the story, particularly the date for the start of the Meetings at Worcester in 1662. Both knew that this would be the first year after the 1660 Restoration [of the monarchy] in which the lay clerks could have invited their colleagues, but in itself this did not prove anything.[14]

Why should the Worcester lay clerks have invited their colleagues from two other cathedrals to join them in 1662? What ecclesiastical connections can we find to link the three cathedrals *before* 1662? The Rev. Stephen J. D. Williams provides answers to these questions:

> The number of English dioceses with which we are familiar in the twenty-first century (above forty) was not always so. From 1066 to 1540, when there were a mere fifteen dioceses, growing to twenty-seven, Worcester Diocese always looked after the county of Gloucestershire east and south of the Severn river (including Bristol), whilst Hereford Diocese embodied Gloucestershire west and north of the Severn.
>
> Even at the Reformation, after a brand new Diocese of Gloucester was formed around the former Abbey of St Peter, with John Wakeman, last Abbot of Tewkesbury, as its first bishop, Gloucester still relied on the other two for financial support and had so many impoverished parishes that its independence waxed and waned: at some time merely again an Archdeaconry of Worcester (1552–1554), then for ideological reasons on its own once more; for some time with, and sometimes without Bristol, but always, as an abbey church which remembered how for the last half a millennium its constituency had looked to two other older establishments as 'mother church'. And personal links continued, in that Godfrey Goldsborough (Bishop of Gloucester 1598–1604) was a former prebendary

---

[14] E. Wulstan Atkins, *1890–1990: The Centenary of the Birth of a Friendship: Edward Elgar and Ivor Atkins and their Influence on the Three Choirs Festival* (Trinity Press, 1990), pp. 1–2.

of Worcester; and Henry Parry, at first Bishop of Gloucester 1607–1610, was translated to Worcester, continuing there till 1616.

When, 9 October 1646, the English episcopacy was abolished by Parliament, remaining so throughout the Commonwealth and Protectorate periods, those who saw value in some formality, and viewed a Prayer Book as a protection of traditional values, were thrown even closer together in the way that any embattled minority can be. In the seeming chaos of the English Civil Wars, churchmen who travelled with the king, and then later with his son, grew used to working closely with each other and reliant on one another and were thus very ready, at the Restoration, to continue to co-operate when necessary.

The great project, where such co-operation was of the essence, was to reinstate Prayer Book worship at the earliest opportunity, as soon as the Interregnum was ended.[15]

And what musical links can we find to connect the three cathedrals? Let us begin with Worcester and Gloucester, and a celebrated family of musicians. Thomas Tomkins (1572–1656) was born and bred at St David's in Pembrokeshire, where his father, Thomas the elder, a clergyman with a number of family connections in Worcestershire, served until 1586. By 1594, Tomkins senior was installed as a minor canon at Gloucester Cathedral; he was elected precentor by 1605 and was, from 1596 until his death in 1627, also the vicar of St Mary de Lode in the city.[16]

Thomas Tomkins the younger, a master composer and former pupil of William Byrd, was appointed Organist at Worcester in 1596 and made a gentleman and later Organist of the Chapel Royal. When, in 1616, William Laud, afterwards Archbishop of Canterbury, became Dean of Gloucester with a mandate from James I to set right much that was amiss, it was to Tomkins at Worcester that he turned for advice about the organ. Thomas Dallam, who had built a new organ at Worcester in 1613, inspected the Gloucester instrument and found it 'very mean and very far decayed'.[17] On Dallam's advice, Laud decided to follow the example of Worcester Cathedral and appeal locally for funds for a new organ. On 12 March 1616, Laud wrote to 'the right worshipful our verry worthy and lovinge Friendes the Gentrey and others of the Countie and Citty of Gloucester' for financial assistance, but there is no record of the response made to his appeal.[18] Perhaps in a Puritan city, where Laud's liturgical changes were thought to smack of popery, money was deliberately withheld. The old organ was patched, nothing more was done, and by 1637 it was considered beyond repair. Sackbuts and cornets were introduced to accompany the choir.

Then, in 1640, John Okeover (Oker) – who had been appointed Organist and vicar choral at Wells in 1619/20, appointed Master of the Choristers there in 1625,

[15] Rev. Stephen J. D. Williams, author of a forthcoming monograph on the events surrounding the legendary Meeting of 1662.

[16] See Anthony Boden, *Thomas Tomkins: The Last Elizabethan* (Ashgate, 2005).

[17] Boden, *Thomas Tomkins*, pp. 103–4.

[18] Very Revd Henry Gee, *Gloucester Cathedral: Its Organs and Organists* (Chiswick Press, 1921), pp. 7–8.

and granted the BMus degree at Oxford in 1633 – was appointed Organist and Master of the Choristers at Gloucester. Okeover, whose liturgical settings were in the repertoire of all three cathedrals, finding himself organist without a useable organ, turned for guidance, like Laud before him, to Worcester. He sought the advice of Thomas Tomkins, who no doubt advised the Gloucester Chapter to negotiate with Thomas Dallam's son, Robert. The accounts show that 6s. was given to 'a messenger to Worcester two severall tymes to Mr Thomkins about the agreemt with Dallam for the new organ'.[19]

Choral services continued for at least two years after the new organ was set up. But in 1642 the dark clouds of Civil War finally broke. Worcester remained loyal to Charles I; Puritan Gloucester supported Parliament; and even John Okeover became a soldier, taking up arms in Cromwell's cause. In September 1642 the Parliamentary army under the Earl of Essex effected 'the profanation of the Cathedral' [in Worcester], wrote Sir William Drysdale, 'destroying the organ, breaking in pieces divers beautiful windows wherein the foundation of the church was lively historified with painted glass, and barbarously defacing fair monuments of the dead'.[20]

Tomkins will have succeeded in having his organ repaired after these atrocities, but in 1646 Worcester was besieged. Parliamentary reformers again fell upon the cathedral. 'The organs being two fair pair, all bishops' beards, noses, fingers, and arms and all, if they had any white sleeves, were broken.'[21] Thomas Tomkins was deprived of his living, his life's work seemingly in ruins about him. He went to live with his son, Nathaniel, at the village of Martin Hussingtree near Worcester. He died there, a disappointed man, in 1656.

Cirencester fell to Royalist troops in 1643. Prince Rupert then rode on to Gloucester to demand its surrender. Gloucester refused. In August, Charles I surrounded the city with 30,000 men. A Parliamentary force arrived on 5 September, relieved the siege within two days, and the Earl of Essex entered Gloucester in triumph.

Tradition has it that Gloucester Cathedral was spared excessive damage, but an ordinance abolishing all choral services in England and Wales, and directing the demolition of all organs in cathedrals and other churches, was passed by Parliament in 1644. Deans and Chapters were dispersed, and for sixteen years the choirs fell idle.

Following the Restoration of Charles II in 1660, all confiscated church lands and buildings were given back. Surviving members of chapters, lay clerks and others returned, and a massive programme of repairs was set under way. But it would be a long time before all was back to normal. Wulstan Atkins summarised the situation at Worcester:

---

[19] Worcester Cathedral Treasurer's Accounts. Worcester Cathedral Library and Archive.

[20] See Vernon Butcher, *The Organ and Music of Worcester Cathedral* (Worcester Cathedral, 1981), p. 9.

[21] Ibid., quoting Carte's letter (Worcester Cathedral Library and Archive 1.15): 'The organs being two fair pair' (a single organ was described as 'a pair', just as today we refer to 'a pair of trousers').

1660, Cathedral partly ruinous, no choir, no organ, no Master of the Choristers and no music. Morning Prayer was said for the first time on August 31st, 1660. The new Dean, Dr Oliver, President of Magdalen College, was installed on September 13th, and strenuous efforts were made to 'settle the church in order', including re-establishing the choral services, since it was understood that Charles II would visit Worcester on 3rd September, 1661, the anniversary of the Battle of Worcester. (The visit did not take place.) Only four of the Minor Canons who had served the Cathedral in 1646 and six of the former lay clerks were still alive. The full complement of ten lay clerks was reached in April, 1661, but it was not until May, 1662 that the Minor Canons were up to the ten required by the statutes. The choristers had been formally admitted by November, 1660, but they would require many months' training before they could take their part in the choir.

In June 1661, the chapter appointed Giles Tomkins, a nephew of the former organist Thomas Tomkins, as organist and Master of the Choristers … In July, 1661, an organ loft was constructed and George Dallam built an organ, probably from the remains of his father's 1613 organ and of other smaller organs taken down in 1646.[22]

Giles Tomkins visited the Dean and Chapter of Gloucester in the latter part of 1661, thus re-establishing musical links between the two cathedrals. He would have found a city, unlike Worcester, under the deep suspicion of Charles II. If Worcester had been the 'Faithful City', the last to hold out in defence of the Crown, the king 'had not forgotten Gloucester's earlier sympathies, and took steps to make sure that the city would not oppose him again':

By the Corporation Act of 1661, the town councillors, aldermen, and officers all had to take an oath of allegiance, and to forswear the Puritan's Solemn League and Covenant … The Council was also purged of all its anti-Royalist members: 10 aldermen, 25 councillors (more than half) and John Dorney, the town clerk, were all removed.[23]

It comes as no surprise to learn that at the bishop's Visitation of Gloucester Cathedral in February 1663, John Okeover had failed to return to his post:

there was lately an Organist in the said Church who is lately gone away, And that at present there is no organist there, & we further say that ever since his Majesty's most happy restoration the teaching of the Choristers or singinge boys, hath been committed by the Deane & Chapter to Richard Elliott, one of the Lay Clerks of the said Church for the said time, being two whole yeares, & we know not where it may be continued on him longer, & for his paynes and care, we leave it to your Lordshipps Consideration.[24]

[22] Atkins, *Birth of a Friendship*, pp. 2–3.

[23] Caroline Heighway, *Gloucester: A History and Guide* (Alan Sutton, 1985), p. 127.

[24] 'Episcopal Visitations of the Dean and Chapter of Gloucester, 1542–1751'. Gloucester Cathedral Archives and Library.

The Commonwealth period was a hard one for Okeover:

> On 28 March 1651 the Trustees for the Maintenance of Ministers recorded that "John Oker Organist and M[aste]r of the Choristers of the late Cathedrall Church of Gloucester hath discovered unto the said Trustees the tithes of Corne and Hay ... and all other tithes of the Impropriate Rectory of Upton St. Leonards in the County of Gloucester to bee in Lease and that the rent reserved thereupon being £4. 3s. 6d. a yeare hath bin in arrears for severall yeares before the 6th. of January 1649 and the said Trustees have received from Thomas Pury, M.P't that the said Mr Oker is very well affected to the Parliament having bin in Armes for them and that hee is in a necesstuos [sic] Condicion It is therefore ordered that hee shall have 1 yeares rent ...".[25]

Nothing further is known of Okeover's military activities, but no doubt he played some part in the defence of Gloucester during the siege in 1643. He lived out his time as long as possible as a former servant of the cathedral, but at the Restoration he seems to have left Gloucester and returned to Wells, where he died, probably about 1662. He wrote a number of pavanes and fantasias, now in the British Library, and other works in the Bodleian Library, and the Cathedral Library at Gloucester contains three books of his *Fancies of three parts*.[26]

In the absence of an organist, the task of answering the bishop's questions fell to two of the singing men: Robert Muddin and the aforementioned Richard Elliott, whose son was a chorister. From them we learn that there were seven singing men and eight choristers at Gloucester in February 1663. Wulstan Atkins again:

> To replace the destroyed music books the [Worcester] accounts show that in 1661 the Chapter purchased a set of Barnard's 1641 '[The first Book of] Selected Church Music', and later other music was obtained from King's College, Cambridge. The accounts for 1662 have a number of entries of payments for copying music. Complete sets of music for the choir were not available until 1662. The Chapter's troubles regarding the organist were not over, however, since the accounts show Giles Tomkins absented himself before December, 1661. Richard Browne, one of the Minor Canons, was elected in March and admitted as organist on 26th April, 1662. The Cathedral was, therefore, without an organist for about six months, though probably Richard Browne carried out the duties.
>
> From all these facts it is clear that the Chapter, who would naturally have wanted the music for the services to be of the highest standard, and the lay clerks themselves, would not have been in a position to invite their colleagues from Hereford and Gloucester to visit them before September, 1662.

---

[25] Quoted by F. S. Hockaday in his Abstracts for Upton St Leonards: Lambeth Palace Library MS 978, p. 221. Hockaday's Abstracts are held in the Gloucestershire Archives.

[26] Brian Frith, *The Organs and Organists of Gloucester Cathedral* (Gloucester Cathedral, 1972), pp. 51–2.

At first sight all this would appear to confirm the 'legend', but unfortunately, despite the detailed entries already referred to, no trace can be found of later entries making any reference to the three Cathedral choirs meeting at Worcester in 1662. It is true that the legend claims it was the Worcester lay clerks who issued the invitation and possibly therefore there was no expense to the Chapter, but nevertheless one would have expected some entry in the official archives, if only to record the date and that official approval had been granted.[27]

Nonetheless, we have evidence of strong musical links between Gloucester and Worcester over half a century, first through Thomas Tomkins and then, after the Restoration, through his nephew Giles Tomkins. It is also reasonable to assume that Gloucester would be anxious to demonstrate loyalty to Charles II by sending a delegation and taking part in Restoration celebrations in the 'Faithful City'. But these were hectic and uncertain times for the Worcester Chapter. It would have taken considerable time for the effects and awful legacy of the recent 'distracted times' to be replaced by tranquil normality and, in any case, perhaps the chapter did not entirely approve of a joint celebration, including a loosening of formality in a convivial social get-together, organised by the lay clerks of the three cathedrals.

As one might expect, although the Treasurer's Accounts reflect an immense amount of cathedral repair work in progress, the ledger is far less neatly maintained than it was to be in the settled days to come. Also, unless the visit of the Gloucester and Hereford lay clerks involved expense to the Chapter, no entry *would* appear in the Worcester accounts. Again, the Gloucester Cathedral accounts yield a complete blank – but not so for the following year. Here, at last, in an entry dated 24 August 1663, is strong evidence of a joint celebration:

> Given to the Worcester Choirmen and Organist with the consent of Dr Washbourne ... £1 0. 0.[28]

Then, on 6 November 1663, the Worcester Treasurer's Accounts show that 5s. was 'Paid for ringing when Mr Deane came from Gloucester'.[29]

Clearly, the Worcester lay clerks and Richard Browne were in Gloucester at about the time of the anniversary of the legendary Worcester 'Music Meeting'. The Dean of Worcester, Dr Thomas Warmestry, also travelled to Gloucester – and his return to Worcester was welcomed by a peal of bells – a modest gesture when compared with the pomp that had accompanied his arrival in Worcester as dean on 27 October 1661, an event celebrating the resumption of spiritual and temporal normality following two decades of war and privation. On that occasion Dr Warmestry had been escorted into Worcester by:

> about 100 Horse ... the clergy band stood ready to receive him in the City. The 40 king's Scholars at the College Gate. He alighted at his house the Deanery, put on his robes. And the prebends and quire met him in the

---

[27] Atkins, *Birth of a Friendship*, p. 3.

[28] Gloucestershire Archives (D 936A 1/2). Thomas Washbourne was a prebendary.

[29] Treasurer's Accounts. Worcester Cathedral Library and Archive (A.26).

Cloisters, sung *Te Deum*. Then came into the Quire ... The Sub-Dean Mr Giles Thornborough, installed him.[30]

Six months later, on 23 April 1662, the first anniversary of 'The King's Coronation Day [was] solemnly kept by the Dean and Chapter in the Cathedral.'[31] This, of all days in 1662, would surely have been the one upon which Worcester, the senior cathedral of the three, would have invited the singing men of Gloucester and Hereford to join their own lay clerks in putting on as impressive a celebration as possible. Equally, one might expect such an invitation would have been penned by the Worcester Dean and Chapter. However, 'there is an amusing [1661] letter extant written by Bishop Skinner of Worcester to Archbishop Sheldon, telling of the difficulty Dean Warmestry was having in the erection of a great organ in the cathedral, "the dean being utterly ignorant of music"'.[32] This might explain why the legend claims the invitation to have been extended by the Worcester lay clerks themselves. The result was certainly majestic:

> Clergy band attended. 6 Trumpets; after prayers and sermon, which was not ended until half an hour past one, the Dean feasted; gave a largesse to the soldiers and trumpets. At night bonfires in College, trumpets sounding, 2 drums beating, and some guns. Before evening prayer the Dean, Dr. Britten, petty canons, and quire went from the Church door, trumpets first sounding. Then *Te Deum* was sung round about the sanctuary in church yard, and so round to College gate into the Church.[33]

So, although the legendary Meeting of 1662 cannot be proved, evidence for visits from Worcester to Gloucester lends support to the strong possibility that there had indeed been an initial celebration in Worcester in 1662. Such a legend is unlikely to have persisted over three centuries unless *some* sort of Meeting had taken place. However, not even fragmentary evidence exists to indicate that Hereford was involved in these first Meetings.

An undated entry in the Worcester Treasurer's Accounts for the year 1670 records:

> Given by order to Mr Elliott of Gloucester Choire ... £2 0. 0.[34]

Elliott was paid £10 per year for his duties as a lay clerk at Gloucester. It is highly unlikely that he would have received £2 at Worcester entirely for himself, and it is reasonable to assume that this sum represented a payment to him as senior lay clerk on behalf of all the Gloucester choirmen. This entry is followed by another:

> A messenger to Gloster by Mr Tompkins order for a Singing man ... 0 3. 0

---

[30] *Diary of Henry Townshend*, ed. J. W. Willis Bund (Worcester Historical Society, 1915), p. 81.

[31] J. W. Willis Bund (ed.), *Diary of Henry Townshend of Elmley Lovett, 1640–1663*, vol. 1 (Worcestershire Historical Society, 1920), pp. 66–7.

[32] Bertram Green, *Bishops and Deans of Worcester*, rev. edn (Worcester Cathedral, 1979), p. 48.

[33] Ibid., p. 88.

[34] Treasurer's Accounts. Worcester Cathedral Library and Archive (A.26).

Had one of the Gloucester men failed to arrive in Worcester? Certainly, two of Richard Elliott's contemporaries, Richard Broadgate and John Payntor, had been sacked in 1666, 'admonished to depart this church for often absences & contempt of the Dean and Chapter',[35] and their successors may well have been no more reliable. But the reference to 'Mr Tompkins' shows that the influence of that family was still strong. This was Nathaniel Tomkins, a strong Royalist, High Churchman, amateur musician, canon of Worcester Cathedral from 1629, and the son with whom the great Thomas Tomkins had lived for the last ten years of his life.

Throughout the years 1662 to the end of the century there is only one other ledger entry which might be significant. It appears in the Gloucester Treasurer's Accounts and is dated 21 November 1665:

Paid to a Hereford Singing Man by Mr Deane's order ... o 5. o[36]

Was this a visit to Gloucester by a single singing man? He could have been in company with other Hereford choirmen; we can never know. What is clear is that no regular payments were made by Chapter after 1663. This does not, of course, mean that Meetings did not take place. If arrangements for visits were made between lay clerks no Chapter expenditure would have been incurred and, therefore, no ledger entries made. Equally, although Chapter approval would have been required, no decision as such would have been entered in Chapter Act books. From the few documentary fragments that *do* exist it is reasonable to conclude that *some* meetings between two, and possibly all three, of the cathedrals' choirmen took place in the latter part of the seventeenth century, but no regular sequence can be deduced.

[35] Chapter Act Book (1 February 1666), Gloucester Cathedral Archives and Library.
[36] Gloucestershire Archives (D 936A 1/3).

3
A Numerous Appearance of Gentry

Iᴺ his later years, William Hine seems to have become disillusioned with his provincial lot at Gloucester. The *Gloucester Journal* of 19 September 1722 has a reference to 'A Consort of Vocal and Instrumental Musick' given in his benefit, and this included 'several songs in English and Italian with their Symphonies, perform'd by Mr Priest's ꜰᴀᴍᴏᴜꜱ ʙᴏʏ from Bristol',[1] but after that, nothing. And by 1730 his life was, in any case, drawing to a premature close. He died on 28 August in that year, aged forty-three, just days before the start of a Gloucester Meeting of the Three Choirs.

Life in eighteenth-century England may not have been quite so nasty and brutish as in former times, but it was very often short. Hine was buried in the cloisters of Gloucester Cathedral, where a small tablet to his memory, erected a few paces to the left of the Chapter House door, bears the following inscription:

M. S. Gulielmi Hine,
hujusce Ecclesiae Cathedralis
Organistae et Choristarum Magistri.
Qui morum candore et eximia in
arte cœlesti peritia omnium amorem
et admirationem, venerandi autem
Decani et Capituli gratium (voluntario
Stipendii incremento testatum) meritissimo
affectus est. Morte præmatura ereptus
Obiit Aug. 28vo, Anno Christi 1730, ætatis 43.

Sacred to the Memory of William Hine,
Organist and Master of the Choristers of this Cathedral Church,
whose upright character and outstanding mastery of the heavenly art
most deservedly won the admiration and love of all,
as well as the favour of the Reverend Dean and Chapter,
shown by their decision voluntarily to increase his salary.
Snatched away by premature death he died August 28th
in the year of Christ 1730, aged 43.

A further couplet was added to the inscription, recording the death of Alicia Hine, also at the age of forty-three, on 28 June 1735.

Hine's compositions, chiefly consisting of music for Gloucester Cathedral, remained unpublished in his lifetime but, after his death, Alicia had published

---

[1] Brian Frith, *The Organs and Organists of Gloucester Cathedral* (Gloucester Cathedral, 1972), pp. 56–7.

by subscription *Harmonia Sacra Glocestriensis, or Select Anthems for 1, 2, and 3 Voices, &c.* The volume contains the anthems *Save me, O God, for thy name's sake*, *Rejoice in the Lord O ye righteous*, and *I will magnify Thee O God my King*, the *Jubilate* (with Hall's *Te Deum*), and a Voluntary for organ.[2] The exceptionally long subscription list for the publication (231 subscribers for 309 copies) included some celebrated musicians well known to Handel: Bernard Gates, Thomas Chilcot of Bath, and, best-known and most importantly, Maurice Greene, described as 'Dr Green, Organist of his Majestys Chappel Royal, and of the Cathedral of St Paul's'.

Alicia had showed her heartfelt gratitude by inserting the following note in the collection:

> To all lovers of Divine Harmony; and in particular to those who by their Generous Subscription have Encourag'd the Publication of the following compositions. This Book Is with the utmost Gratitude Most humbly Dedicated by Their Most Oblig'd, Most Obedient, And most Devoted Servant, A. H.

William Hayes marked Hine's passing by the composition of a communion and Evening Service in continuation of 'Hall and Hine in E flat', the correct title of the whole being 'Hall, Hine and Hayes'.

D ETAILS of music performed at Meetings of the Three Choirs in the first half of the eighteenth century are tantalising but sketchy, even though local newspapers, published primarily to serve the interests of the nobility and gentry, regularly carried notices advertising the dates and places of the Music Meetings. After the event, a gushing paragraph could be expected, of which the following from the *Gloucester Journal* of Tuesday 17 September 1728 is typical:

> **Worcester, Sept. 12.**   On the 4th and 5th Instant was held here the Anniversary Meeting of the Three Choirs, Worcester, Gloucester and Hereford, when there was a numerous Appearance of Gentry of the first Rank. A very good sermon was preach'd upon the Occasion by the Revd. Mr. Brooks of Hanly; and the Musical Performances were executed to great and general Satisfaction. The Charity Collection for placing out the Children of the poorer Clergy, &c., amounted to £40 the Mayor with the principal Gentlemen holding the Basons at the Cathedral-Doors.

Should a lord and his lady honour the Meetings by their presence this would be reported grandly, but many decades were to pass before the provincial press thought it any part of its duty to publish so much as one line of musical criticism in its very brief record, in spite of the fact that the Music Meeting quickly came to be regarded as an event of prime professional as well as social interest.

When, in 1721, the *Worcester Postman* revealed which two pieces were to be performed in Gloucester Cathedral at the Music Meeting that year, we find mention of two *Te Deum*s, one by Purcell and the other by William

---

[2] See Gwilym Beechey (ed.), *Ten Eighteenth-Century Voluntaries* (A. R. Editions, 1969).

Croft.[3] The Hereford Meeting of 1726 was reported in the *Worcester Weekly Journal:*

> **Hereford, Sept. 10.** At the Anniversary Meeting of the Three Choirs here there was an handsome appearance of Gentry; and the Performance both Vocal and Instrumental perform'd with great Approbation, and a Sermon upon the occasion preach'd by Dr Bisse, which the Society and Gentry have desir'd him to print; and the Charity Collection for the placing out the children of the poorer Clergy amounted to nearly £50, notwithstanding the Detention of much Company by the Report of the Small-Pox being frequent in the City.

A footnote to the *Gloucester Journal* notice advertising the Meeting starting in Hereford on Tuesday 2 September 1729 shows that a day of rehearsal had by then been found to be necessary: 'N. B. The Performers have obliged themselves by a separate Article to meet on Monday.'[4] In 1731 the *Gloucester Journal* makes its first mention of specific musical items at the Meetings – and Purcell is still supreme:

> **Worcester, Sept. 9.** [1731]. Yesterday being the first day of the Annual Meeting of the Three Choirs, a suitable Sermon was preached by the Rev. Mr Phillips, Sacrist of our Cathedral, before a grand and numerous Auditory. The same evening was perform'd a Concert of Vocal and Instrumental Musick at the Town Hall which was very much crowded, several Persons of Quality being present. And this Morning Dr Purcel's [*sic*] Great *Te Deum* was sung to Musick at our Cathedral, at the Doors whereof was collected upwards of £45 for charitable Uses.[5]

But no mention is made of the name of the conductor at this concert: William Hayes. Having completed his apprenticeship to Hine two years previously, Hayes had applied successfully for the post of Organist at Worcester Cathedral in 1731.

Meanwhile, a musician of towering genius, dubbed 'the man-mountain' by Hayes, had arrived on British shores. In 1711, George Frederick Handel had accepted an invitation to write a new opera in the Italian style for London. The result was *Rinaldo*; Handel returned to England in 1712, went on to write four more operas by 1715, received a life pension from Queen Anne, and wrote for her both a Birthday Ode and the *Te Deum* on the Treaty of Utrecht. Handel never returned to his post as *Kappelmeister* at the court of the Elector of Hanover, who, following the death of Queen Anne in 1714, ascended to the throne of Great Britain as King George I.

WILLIAM Hayes (1706–1777), composer, conductor, organist and singer, was born in Gloucester, the son of a family of cordwainers (i.e. shoemakers), and was baptised at St John's Church in the city on 27 January 1706. His family is thought to have had close associations with that of his tutor, William Hine, and it would have been surprising if the death of Hine in 1730 had not left Hayes

[3] Gloucestershire Archives (D 936A 1/5).
[4] *Gloucester Journal*, 19 August 1729.
[5] *Gloucester Journal*, 14 September 1731.

deeply saddened. However, it appears that he was also left smarting with envy and resentment because he had not been selected to replace his revered master as Organist of Gloucester Cathedral. The Dean and Chapter had, instead, chosen Barnabas Gunn, whose reputation as a talented improviser had been made at St Philip's, Birmingham.

Hayes, although ultimately destined to become a celebrated conductor and singer, had not yet achieved his high reputation. Unkindly, he began to pursue a long-standing grudge against Gunn. The depth of Hayes's animosity was still evident when, two decades later, he issued a bitingly satirical pamphlet purporting to have been written by Gunn, entitled *The Art of Composing Music by a Method entirely New*. In it, Hayes poked fun at Gunn, amusingly suggesting that he 'composed music by means of an imaginary device called a *Spruzzarino*, which squirted ink randomly onto ruled music paper', a method 'suited to the meanest capacity, whereby all difficulties are removed, and a person who has made never so little progress before, may, with some small application, be enabled to excel'.[6]

Hayes's own compositions include chamber cantatas and ceremonial odes of high quality, and his collections of catches, glees and canons proved to be very popular. An ardent Handelian, Hayes became the most active conductor of Handel's choral works outside London, often performing a dual role as both conductor *and* singer. However, as Percy Young pointed out, 'conductor is the wrong word':

> Cathedral organists were not so well placed in the musical hierarchy that the distinguished, and sometimes vainglorious, singers and instrumentalists who came down from London felt obliged to pay overmuch attention to them … Oratorio performances were for long co-ordinated more through luck than judgement, with the keyboard player and the leading violinist each endeavouring to correct the miscalculations of the other.[7]

Hayes was responsible for introducing many of Handel's works to the provinces, including to Three Choirs, and his influence on the Music Meetings was profound. From 1731 to 1734 he was Organist at Worcester Cathedral, and in 1733 he visited Oxford to be present when Handel famously directed a series of his own works there, including the première of his new oratorio, *Athalia*, at the Sheldonian Theatre.

In 1734, Hayes moved permanently from Worcester to Oxford, embarking upon a distinguished academic career at Magdalen College while continuing to direct major choral works in a number of provincial centres. In Oxford he initiated the building of the Holywell Music Room, and in 1741 he was appointed Professor of Music at the university. In 1754 he acted as both Deputy Steward and Director of the Music Meeting in Gloucester, returning there in 1757 to both conduct and sing in, *inter alia*, the first performance at Three

[6] See Simon Heighes, *The Lives and Work of William and Philip Hayes* (Routledge, 1996), pp. 5–6.

[7] Percy Young, 'The First Hundred Years', in Barry Still (ed.), *Two Hundred and Fifty Years of the Three Choirs Festival* (Three Choirs Festival Association, 1977), p. 13.

Choirs of Handel's *Messiah* (see Chapter 4). He performed there again in 1760 and 1763.

Following Hayes's death in 1777, his son, Philip Hayes, followed in his father's footsteps at Oxford. And it was Philip Hayes who presented Sir Godfrey Kneller's portrait of William Hine (see Frontispiece) to the Music School at Oxford. In a final, generous tribute to Hine, Philip Hayes wrote of him that he had 'possessed a happy genius':

> Hine was an excellent organ player, as I have frequently heard my Father and others who knew him say, but being fix'd in a place not very prone to encourage musical abilities, found himself neglected, which made him the less solicitous about improving those talents nature had given him, & thereby became a lost man to the Musical World, who otherwise would have done the greatest honour to it. He was much respected and esteem'd a Genteel worthy man.[8]

The achievements of William Hayes far exceeded those of his master. Sadly for Hine, his former glory long since eclipsed, he was destined to remain largely forgotten for three centuries.[9]

O UR first certain knowledge of a performance of music by Handel at the Meetings appears in the *Gloucester Journal* of Tuesday 17 August 1736. A notice states that 'Mr Purcell's *Te Deum* will be performed on the Wednesday Morning, and Mr Handel's on the Thursday Morning.' Thereafter, new works by Handel were gradually introduced by William Boyce, composer to the Chapel Royal, who took over as conductor of the Three Choirs Meetings in 1737 and went on to become Master of the King's Music in 1755. Two advertisements for 1739(G) announce a performance of *Alexander's Feast* – 'an Ode written by Mr Dryden, and set to Musick by Mr Handel, with Trumpets, French Horns and Kettle-Drums' – and in a later edition of the paper the following is added: 'The two Evening Performances of Musick will be at the Booth-Hall, on one of which will be performed *Alexander's Feast*.'[10] Obviously, a larger venue for the secular concerts had become essential.

Lysons was unable to obtain very much information about the principal performers before the year 1755, other than that the leader of the band was Thomas Woodcock of Hereford, famous for playing Vivaldi's Violin Concerto No. 5. Woodcock was paid up to 1½ guineas for his performances at the Meetings.

From 1733(G) onwards, Lysons believed 'the most eminent performers were engaged from the metropolis'.[11] A *Gloucester Journal* advertisement for that year notified that 'No Hands will be paid, but those that are apply'd to by the Steward, or his Assistants', and that 'We hear that the Steward of the Musick Meeting

[8] Samuel Arnold, *Cathedral Music*, 4 vols (London, 1790).

[9] See also *William Hine (1687–1730): Four Pieces for Organ*, an excellent YouTube short documentary online film produced by Andreas Osiander (9 May 2014); online at https://www.youtube.com/watch?v=cDGXfgC75wo [accessed 9 January 2017].

[10] *Gloucester Journal*, 7 August 1739 and 4 September 1739.

[11] *Annals* 1812, p. 163.

has engaged 2 French Horns, a Trumpet, and other Hands from London, a great many Persons of Distinction being expected here.'[12] The subsequent 'review' reported that:

> there was the greatest appearance of Gentlemen and Ladies of Distinction, and the best Performance that ever was known upon that Occasion; the Steward having collected out of London ... the best Performers, both Vocal and Instrumental, consisting of French Horns, Trumpets, Hautboys, German Flute, and a fine Treble Harp, &c. The famous Mr Powell of Oxford did us the Honour of singing in our Church on both days.[13]

Walter Powell had been a member of the choirs of Christ Church and other colleges, and was the principal male oratorio singer at Oxford during Handel's celebrated visit there in July 1733. Powell, apparently a countertenor, had made such an impression on this occasion that he was immediately appointed one of the Gentlemen of the Chapel Royal. Following his death in 1744, an extravagant obituary appeared in the *Gentleman's Magazine*:

> Is Powell dead? Then all the earth
> Prepare to meet its fate:
> To sing the everlasting birth,
> The Choir of Heaven's complete.

It seems likely that the additional expense and effort on the part of the Steward of the Three Choirs Music Meeting in 1733 would have been directed towards the performance of some more than usually ambitious work, almost certainly by Handel.

In 1738, though not at a Music Meeting, Handel's *Esther*, composed as a Masque, *Haman and Mordecai* and revised in 1732 as his first English oratorio, was performed at the Town Hall, Worcester, on 11 September for the benefit of John Merifield, the organist.[14]

Merifield's contemporary at Gloucester from 1730 to 1740 was, as we have seen, Barnabas Gunn, a man of unusual versatility. Besides his musical responsibilities in Gloucester, he supplemented his organist's salary of £35 *per annum* by entering into partnership with a dealer in timber from London: they sold oak and deal at premises in Lower Westgate Street.[15] In 1736, Gunn published two cantatas and six songs, settings of verses by Congreve, Prior and others, which, as Percy Young pointed out, 'like some of his Harpsichord Lessons published by Robert Raikes in Gloucester [from whom Alice Elgar was descended] and his Violin and Cello Solos later published by J. Johnson of Birmingham, may well have provided evening entertainment at Meeting time'.[16] Gunn collected the remarkable number of 464 subscribers for this volume:

[12] *Gloucester Journal*, 14 August 1733.

[13] *Gloucester Journal*, 11 September 1733.

[14] *Gloucester Journal*, 12 September 1738.

[15] *Gloucester Journal*, 12 October 1736 and 8 August 1738.

[16] Young, 'The First Hundred Years', p. 11.

Among the names it was that of Mr Handel which shone the brightest. Why it may be asked, did Handel show such favour (as in 1745 he did in respect of Chilcot's Shakespeare songs)? There is, it is felt, a possibility of *quid pro quo.*[17]

As Frith points out:

Whilst in Gloucester Gunn organised a number of concerts, some of them held in a room at the old Tolsey, at the Cross. For these concerts he called on the best singers from the choirs of Hereford and Worcester, as well as 'the Gentlemen of the Musick-Clubb' in Gloucester.[18]

Gunn returned to Birmingham in 1749 where, enterprising as ever, he combined his duties as Organist with those of postmaster for the town, and also put on many concerts and theatrical performances in local theatres.

The single Steward of the Music Meeting was always a musical man: a member of one of the music clubs, and generally either a clergyman or a lay clerk belonging to one of the choirs. The Steward of the Meeting engaged and defrayed the expenses of the band, and was responsible for losses. Hardly an enviable task – by mid-century lavish productions at the secular concerts were proving expensive!

At Gloucester in 1745 a dramatic pastoral entitled *Love's Revenge, or Florimel and Myrtillo,* by Maurice Greene, and Handel's *Acis and Galatea* were performed at the Booth Hall. On 3 September the *Gloucester Journal* reported:

London, Aug. 29. This Day Dr Greene, Master of his Majesty's Band of Musick, with several gentlemen belonging to the Chapel Royal, Westminster Abbey and St Paul's set out for Gloucester, where they are to meet the Gentlemen belonging to the Choirs of Worcester, Hereford and Gloucester, in order to perform, at the last mentioned place, on Wednesday and Thursday next, a Grand Concert of Musick, both Vocal and Instrumental, for the Benefit of poor Clergymen's Widows and their Children.

Samson, composed by Handel in 1743, reached Three Choirs in 1748(G): 'the musical Performance was greatly applauded, particularly the celebrated Oratorio of Samson. And the Assembly, each night, at The Bell, was so crowded, that there was scarce Room for the Gentlemen and Ladies to Dance.'[19]

The Music Meetings and their attendant attractions – 'ordinaries', balls and horse races – provided a focal point in the social calendar of nobility, gentry, better-off clergy, and any family the head of which could lay claim to the title 'gentleman'. Timed to follow the annual harvest, the Meetings provided an interlude of civic hospitality in late August or September, before the more serious business of winter hunting began.

In addition to the 'ordinaries' – lunches for patrons of the Music Meeting held in local hostelries – it became traditional by mid-century for the Steward

[17] Ibid., pp. 11–13.
[18] Frith, *Organs and Organists of Gloucester,* pp. 58–9.
[19] *Gloucester Journal,* 20 September 1748.

to invite the performers to dine with him on the first day of the Meeting. This, in addition to all the other expenses, threatened the future of the Meetings for lack of volunteers to take up the heavy financial burden of Steward. In 1784 a contributor to the *Gloucester Journal*, writing under the pseudonym 'Philo-Harmonicus', suggested a solution:

> Having for many years, attended your Annual Meetings, and being a sincere Well-Wisher to the Continuance of them, it gives me no small concern to hear it frequently said they are likely to drop … [that] the Musical Performances were becoming so expensive as, sometimes, not be sustain'd by the Profits of the two Concerts, and that this made the Members of the Musical Societies diffident as to taking upon them the Office of STEWARD, and even to decline it.
>
> That all due encouragement may be given to Lay Members belonging to either of the Choirs … that the Organist of each Choir, and the Steward of each Musical Society, do nominate and appoint a moderate Number of Vocal and Instrumental performers, to attend the Rehearsals and Performances at every Meeting as well as the two others as that they belong to; and that their Expences be allow'd them, either by the Steward of the Annual Meeting, or by the private Society, as shall be deemed most practicable. As this would be an Incitement to the younger Practitioner to study more in order to be distinguished, as would it, perhaps be a means of unclosing the Lips, and untying the Hands of some who are already qualified to be useful.
>
> … let the Steward disburse no more at Dinner, on the first Day of the Meeting, than will be barely sufficient to entertain such as are actual Performers; I mean such who are not only Performers in their own Choirs or Concerts, but intend to assist in the Performances on the two succeeding Days … unless it can be prov'd that Dining together on that Day is of any particular Use or Emolument to the Society, it were far better abolished. This would, effectually, lessen the Expences, but the Trouble and Fatigue, of the Steward also.

At the heart of Philo-Harmonicus's letter was a suggestion of sound economic sense:

> That each Subscriber instead of being entitled to Tickets Gratis, do pay, at the time of Subscribing, into the Hands of the Steward for the year ensuing, the Sum of Ten Shillings and Sixpence: In consideration of which he shall be entitled to a Ticket each Night, and his Ordinary paid each day by the Steward. But if he does not appear, that then the said Ten shillings and Sixpence shall be deem'd forfeit to the Society as usual.[20]

All of these ideas were endorsed the next week in a letter to the paper by a former Steward. The inclusion of 'Forfeits' in future statements of Music Meeting accounts suggests that they were taken up.

At the same time the balls, free to patrons of the Music Meeting, had

---

[20] *Gloucester Journal*, 30 August 1748. 'Ordinary' – eighteenth-century usage: living expenses, i.e. for meals or, perhaps, dinner.

become overcrowded by gatecrashers: a problem solved in Gloucester in 1757 by transferring the balls to the Booth Hall, where they followed immediately after the concerts. In 1752 the following advertisement appeared in the *Worcestershire Journal*:

> **City of Worcester, Sept 14.** As it has been the desire of several ladies of distinction, that some method might be thought of to remove the many inconveniences which arise from the great number of people who crowd the ballroom at the Music Meetings, on account of their being admitted *gratis*, the Mayor (in order to carry on the balls with more decency and regularity) has taken the management of them into his own hands, and gives this public notice, that every lady, as well as gentleman, shall pay half-a-crown each night for their admittance, as is usual at the other meetings; and the money collected shall be disposed of in a proper manner. And, that the Stewards of the Meeting may not suffer by the necessary alteration, notice is hereby given, that no person shall have the liberty of coming to the balls without providing tickets (which will be given at the hall-door in exchange for concert tickets) for the satisfaction of the conductor of the ball, that they have favoured the concert with their company.

All this sounds entirely reasonable and businesslike – but it led to a major row at the next Worcester Meeting, in 1755. In that year it had been decided that the number of Stewards should be increased to two, no doubt to ease the financial burden on any one individual. The Dean of Worcester, Dr Waugh, and the Honourable Edwin Sandys agreed to take on the task. Noting that the balls of 1752 had produced a profit of £178 3s. for the City Corporation – money, as they saw it, lost to the charity – they applied to the mayor for the use of the Guildhall (Town Hall) for the balls. Permission was refused. The distinguished but angry Stewards determined to hold the balls in the College Hall instead of the Guildhall, but not until they had inserted a lengthy notice, highly critical of the Mayor and Corporation, in the newspapers:

> It is thought proper to state to the public the following facts, merely lest the Charity … should suffer by misrepresentation … That the taking separate pay for the balls, by persons who bear no part of the expenses of the musical performances, might not only hurt the collection, but reduce the number of concert-tickets so much, as not to raise a sufficient sum to pay the performers; by such means the Meeting itself would be ruined.
>
> That application was made to the Mayor by the Stewards, in the most respectful manner, for the use of the hall and ball-rooms over it, which, considering the benefits arising to the city by this Meeting, and the charitable purpose for which they are asked, it was natural for them to expect it would be granted; but some, it seems, of those in power in the city thought otherwise: *the request was not granted – the ball-room was refused*; and Mr Mayor transmitted to the Stewards a printed account how the money arising from the balls in 1752 had been applied: by which it appeared that not one shilling of it was given in charity.[21]

---

[21] See *Annals* 1812, pp. 174 and 181.

The mayor, Benjamin Pearkes, was clearly furious, and responded with a document entitled 'The Corporation of the City of Worcester vindicated from a most injurious reflection', in which he said that the proceeds from the balls had never previously been applied in favour of the charity, and

> That several former Stewards of the Concert, and also the *Balls*, whose minds have been actuated by the *Principles of Humanity*, have, in some Degree, applied the Surplus arising therefrom, to *charitable* Uses; but then have always discover'd the most passionate Regard for that valuable old Maxim – CHARITY *begins* at Home.[22]

The 'overplus' from the 1752 balls had, it seems, been spent on painting, gilding and lacquerwork, both inside and outside the Guildhall. The Worcester Corporation hit back at the Stewards in 1755 by advertising rival balls and selling tickets at 2s. 6d. each from the two local coffee houses. But peace returned in 1758 when, once again, 'balls every evening, *gratis*' were advertised.

From primitive beginnings, horse racing grew rapidly in the first half of the eighteenth century and, as with the Music Meeting, newspapers played a vital role in its development. By 1722, 112 cities and towns in England were holding race meetings, and at large county towns the races were organised to coincide with their assizes.[23]

Worcester has one of the oldest racecourses in England. Horse racing has taken place on Pitchcroft for more than 280 years, and it may well have formed part of the city life from much earlier times.[24] A notice in the *Worcester Journal* for 20 June 1718 advertises that:

> On Friday the 27th June there will be run for in Pitchcroft, Worcester, a Saddle and Bridle £3 value by any Horse, Mare or Gelding carrying ten stones … the winning Horse to be sold for seven pounds … There will be at the same time, a pair of Silver Buckles run for by Men round Pitchcroft, Gratis: and a handsome Hat to be run for by young Women, the length of Pitchcroft. Also a very good Silver laced Hat to be won at Backsword, that Hat being 14s value. Those that are willing to enter their horse must enter the 26th of the instant, at the Crown in Broad Street, Worcester.

Racing at Hereford is first mentioned in the *Racing Calendar* as on 17 August 1731, and at Gloucester on 24 September 1734, but it was not until shortly after mid-century that the Race Meetings and the Music Meetings were deliberately timed to coincide. At Worcester in 1737 the Music Meeting was 'deferr'd a Week longer than the usual time, on Account of several Principal Performers

---

[22] See Watkins Shaw, *The Three Choirs Festival: The Official History of the Meetings of Gloucester, Hereford and Worcester, c. 1713–1953* (Baylis for Three Choirs Festival, 1954), p. 26.

[23] Andrea Theodore Cook, *A History of the English Turf*, vol. 1 (H. Virtue, 1901), pp. 160 and 199.

[24] See E. J. Witt, 'Racing at Worcester' (1981). Worcester City Library (WG 798.4/255227).

being engag'd at Oxford Races',[25] and at Gloucester in 1748 the date of the
Meeting was altered because it clashed with the Burford Races.[26] A sure way
to ensure maximum attendance, and to avoid divided loyalties, was to bring the
Race Meetings and Music Meetings together. In Gloucester, for instance, the
races were advertised for Tuesday and Friday in the Music Meeting week. On
Tuesday night there was always a ball at the Bell Inn, called the Stewards' Ball,
'at which the Lay-steward of the Meeting, who was also a Steward of the races,
presided'.[27]

Although racing continues at Worcester and Hereford, it was already in
decline at Gloucester by 1793, when the link with the Music Meeting was
severed. Thirty years earlier, the Rev. Robert Gegg, a Gloucester man, had been
unimpressed:

> **Sep 6th 1763.** A great deal of company in Town; the Meeting of the 3
> Choirs of Gloucester, Worcester and Hereford, being held here this Week.
> An Horse-race in Maisemore Meadow this Afternoon, but (unfortunately
> for the Fools of Fashion) poor Sport.[28]

J. C. Whyte, writing in the following century, described the Gloucester course:
'The races take place in a meadow, on the banks of the Severn, the course being
an oblong of about a mile and a half, with a straight run-in of 400 yards.'[29]

So great a gathering of eighteenth-century wealth in one place drew to the
Music Meetings an unofficial 'fringe' of attractions, as well as a fair number of
the light-fingered gentry who continued to stretch police patience and resources
well into the reign of Queen Victoria. Sideshows such as the following, noticed
in 1748, would have been commonplace: 'We hear that Mr Bridges designs
being here at the Music-Meeting on the 13th of next Month, to exhibit, to the
Gentlemen, Ladies, &c., his Curious MACHINE, called the MICROCOSM.'[30] Not
least of the attractions would have been the presence, in the Three Choirs cities,
of groups of strolling players.

One of the earliest provincial theatres was built in Bath in 1705. Its company
spread its nets wide, and strolling players from Bath soon included Devon and
Wiltshire, as well as Gloucester, Hereford and Worcester, in their itinerary. On 15
July 1729, a Hereford Music Meeting year, the *Gloucester Journal* announced:

> The Bath Company of Comedians are building a large commodious Booth
> in the White Lyon Yard, near the Market-Place, to entertain the Public at
> the Approaching Assizes, Races and the Triennial Meeting of the Three
> Choirs: they have with them Mr Hippisley, and other Actors from both of
> the Theatres in London; their Cloaths and Scenes far exceed any yet seen
> here. They will open on 28th Instant with the Beggars Opera, or Provok'd
> Husband.

[25] *Gloucester Journal*, 9 August 1737.
[26] *Gloucester Journal*, 19 July 1748.
[27] *Annals* 1812, p. 182.
[28] Diary of Rev. R. Gegg (1763). Gloucestershire Archives.
[29] J. C. Whyte, *History of the British Turf*, vol. 2 (Colburn, 1840), pp. 242–3.
[30] *Gloucester Journal*, 23 August 1748.

The company in its summer progress was evidently strengthened by recruits from London.[31] Some few years later Joseph Yarrow, a York comedian and playwright, recounted in verse 'An Epilogue, made by a Gentleman of Hereford, occasioned by meeting a Company of Strolers [*sic*] on the Road':

> From Hereford the Jovial Crew departed,
> Kings walk'd on Foot, the Princesses were Carted:
> In pure Compassion to the Maiden Queen
> That wanted but a Month of Lying-In
> Thus on a Heap lay pil'd; there the Brandy Bottle,
> Here the Child.
> Great Montezuma hir'd an humble Hack,
> And he that grasp'd the World bestrid a Pack:
> Great Orronoco from his Privy Purse,
> Cou'd not afford Imoinda poor a Horse:
> Young Amon, staying late behind the rest,
> Was in great danger too of being prest.
> But Faith it would have made the Greatest laugh,
> To see the Truncheon knuckle to the Staff.
> Thus, on the Road, no more but common Men,
> Once got to Ludlow, then all Kings again.[32]

---

[31] See Sybil Rosenfeld, *Strolling Players and Drama in the Provinces* (CUP, 1939), p. 176.

[32] *A Choice Collection of Poetry* (1738), quoted by Rosenfeld, *Strolling Players and Drama*, p. 19.

4

'The Musick of My Admiration Handel'

FOLLOWING the first known Three Choirs performance in 1736(G) of one of his *Te Deum*s, the music of Handel rapidly rose into a position of absolute command at the Music Meetings. *Alexander's Feast* was repeated, and *L'Allegro, Il Penseroso* introduced at Gloucester in 1751. In the following year the *Worcester Journal* gave a detailed programme for the 1752(W) Meeting:

> On Wednesday will be perform'd, at the Cathedral, in the Morning, Purcel's [*sic*] Te Deum and Jubilate, an Anthem by Dr. Boyce, and Mr. Handel's celebrated Coronation Anthem; and at the Town-Hall in the Evening, a concert of Vocal and Instrumental Musick. On Thursday will be perform'd, at the Cathedral, in the Morning, Mr. Handel's Te Deum and Jubilate, A New Anthem by Dr. Boyce, and the same Coronation Anthem; and at the Town Hall, in the Evening, the Oratorio of Samson.
>
> J. Arnold, Steward[1]

The *Te Deum* and *Jubilate* of Purcell would be that in D, which he wrote for St Cecilia's Day 1694, the year before his death. Handel wrote a set of four anthems for the coronation of George II in 1727, but the 'celebrated' one is most likely to have been either of the two most popular: 'The King shall rejoice' or 'Zadok the Priest'. Handel's *Te Deum* and *Jubilate* could have been either that written in 1713 for the Treaty of Utrecht or, more likely, that written in 1743 for the victory of Dettingen which, according to Lysons, was introduced to the Music Meetings at Gloucester in 1748. But, as Watkins Shaw has pointed out:

> one notices that whereas in 1752, for example, we hear of a *Te Deum* by Handel, in 1755 and 1756 the announcement speaks of the 'New *Te Deum*' by Handel. (Those dates, however, refer to Worcester and Hereford Meetings.) After 1755 there is no doubt that the 'Dettingen' setting was in regular use.[2]

The anthem by Boyce would have been either *Lord, thou has been our refuge* or *Blessed is he that considereth the poor*. But it was the performance of *Samson* which incurred the greatest expense.

Mr Arnold was feeling the pinch, and one month after the initial notice of the Meeting appeared in the newspapers, it was followed by another:

---

[1] *Worcester Journal*, 23 July 1752.

[2] Watkins Shaw, *The Three Choirs Festival: The Official History of the Meetings of Gloucester, Hereford and Worcester, c. 1713–1953* (Baylis for Three Choirs Festival, 1954), pp. 8 and 9.

The additional Expence in preparing for the ORATORIO of SAMSON, and the larger Demands of the London Performers and Others, make it absolutely necessary to raise the Price of the CONCERT TICKETS from Half-a-Crown to Three Shillings. And that it may not be imagined that the Steward proposes any Advantage to himself, he assures the Publick, that if there be any Overplus, it shall be faithfully applied towards continuing the Charitable Meetings of the THREE CHOIRS which cannot be supported, unless the Stewards are to be indemnified.[3]

Arnold was careful to ensure that his full accounts were published in the *Worcester Journal*, thus proving that far from gaining any 'advantage to himself', the *overplus* remaining after meeting all expenses amounted to the princely sum of 1s. 5½d! Furthermore, the accounts show that he had made a loss of £10 16s. 8d. on the Meeting held as far back as 1744 and that these arrears had only been recouped after the 1752(w) Meeting. Income from tickets and books of words for the two nights amounted to £234 12s. 0d. against expenditure relating to the musical performance of £149 14s. 6d., including:

Performers	£120
Transcribing the Oratorio of Samson, Paper and Binding	£22 18s. 6d.
Mending a Tenor Fiddle	10s. 0d.
Purchas'd a Pair of Kettle Drums	£6 6s. 0d.

Further expenditure was incurred on 'Stewards' Dinner, Wine, Ale, etc. used at the several Rehearsals and the Performance', printing costs, an assortment of items including mayor's officers, candles, sconces and snuffers, and even a bill for 15s. for mending the Guildhall windows.

At Hereford in 1750 a proposal had been made by friends and supporters of the music club to rebuild and enlarge the College Hall. The necessary amount was raised through voluntary contributions and the hall opened in time for the evening concerts at the 1753(H) Music Meetings. As a result of this initiative, Hereford now extended the Meeting to three evenings, an example not followed by Gloucester and Worcester until 1757 and 1758 respectively. Thereafter, either two or three evening concerts were given at each Meeting until 1770, after which three became the regular number.

The first evening in 1753(H) was devoted to a Miscellaneous Concert, the precedent for what was to become a long-lived Three Choirs tradition; the second concert was given over to Handel's oratorio *Samson*; and the third to a dramatic piece called *The Shepherds Lottery*, written by Moses Mendez and set to music by William Boyce. As at Worcester in the previous year, the high costs involved in presenting *Samson* necessitated an increase in the price of tickets to 3s.[4]

William Hayes acted as Deputy Steward at Gloucester in 1754. In addition to *L'Allegro, Il Penseroso*, Handel's *Judas Maccabeus* was given twice: on Thursday evening and, in aid of 'the laudable Undertaking of erecting a County-hospital', a repeat performance on Friday morning at which a sum of just over £50 was collected.

[3] *Worcester Journal*, 27 August 1752.
[4] *Worcester Journal*, 27 December 1753.

From the year 1755 we have a regular account of the performers. The notice for the Worcester Meeting of that year states:

> The Oratorio of Sampson [*sic*] by Mr Handel, and Dr Boyce's Solomon, with several other Pieces of Musick, will … be perform'd in the Great Hall in the College at Worcester, the Corporation of Worcester having refused the Stewards the Use of the Ball-room in the Town-hall, which they requested that all the Profits arising from the Meeting might be applied to the Charity for which it was instituted.
>
> Care has been taken to engage the best Masters that can be procured. The Vocal Parts (beside the Gentlemen of the Three Choirs) will be perform'd by Mr Beard, Mr Wass, Mr Denham, Mr Baildon, Miss Turner, and others; the Instrumental Parts by Mr Brown, Mr Millar, Mr Adcock, Mr Messing &c. The Musick to be conducted by Dr Boyce.[5]

The first name among the singers is that of John Beard, the leading tenor of his day and the man who established the popularity of that type of voice in England – he took the principal part in numerous pieces, and was the original tenor in Handel's *Esther*. Beard was one of the singers in the Duke of Chandos's Chapel at Cannons. In 1739 he caused a great scandal by marrying Lady Henrietta Herbert, only daughter of James, Earl of Waldegrave, and widow of Lord Edward Herbert, second son of the Earl of Powis – a thing unheard of. In *The Wealth of Nations*, published in 1776, Adam Smith summed up a contemporary view of opera-singers and other entertainers:

> There are some very agreeable and beautiful talents of which the possession commands a certain sort of admiration; but of which the exercise for the sake of gain is considered, whether from reason or prejudice, as a sort of public prostitution. The pecuniary recompense, therefore, of those who exercise them in this manner must be sufficient, not only to pay for the time, labour, and expense of acquiring the talents, but for the discredit which attends the employment of them as the means of subsistence. The exorbitant rewards of players, opera-singers, opera-dancers, etc. are founded upon those two principles; the rarity and beauty of the talents, and the discredit of employing them in this manner.[6]

Aristocratic reaction to Beard's marriage to Lady Herbert provides a clear insight into contemporary social attitudes. Lady Mary Wortley Montague, in one of her letters to Lady Pomfret, wrote:

> Lady Herbert furnished the tea-tables here with fresh tattle for the last fortnight. I was one of the first informed of her adventure by Lady Gage, who was told that morning by a priest that she had desired him to marry her the next day to Beard, who sings in the farces at Drury Lane. He refused her that good office, and immediately told Lady Gage, who (having been unfortunate in her friends) was frightened at this affair, and asked my advice. I told her honestly that since the lady was capable of such amours I did not

---

[5] *Gloucester Journal*, 8 July 1755.

[6] Adam Smith, *Wealth of Nations* (Penguin, 1986), p. 209.

doubt, if this was broke off, she would bestow her person and fortune on some hackney-coachman or chairman, and that I really saw no method of saving her from ruin, and her family from dishonour, but by poisoning her, and offered to be at the expense of the arsenic, and even to administer it with my own hands, if she would invite her to drink tea that evening.

Her relations have certainly no reason to be amazed at her constitution, but are violently surprised at the mixture of devotion that forces her to have recourse to the church in her necessities, which has not been the road taken by the matrons of her family.[7]

Lady Herbert's 'friends' were disappointed. Beard was a man of liberal attainments, pleasing manners, good principles and respectable conduct. He and his wife enjoyed much happiness together. After her death Beard married a daughter of the theatre manager John Rich, and eventually became one of the proprietors of the Covent Garden Theatre. He sang at Three Choirs in 1755(w), 1758(w), 1760(G) and 1761 (w). He died in 1791.[8]

Among the instrumentalists named in 1755(w) was Abraham Brown, Leader of the band before the arrival of Felici Giardini in 1770. Brown succeeded Festing as Leader of the king's band and most of the public concerts. He is said to have had 'a clear, sprightly and loud tone, with a strong hand, but was deficient in expression'.[9] The other performers mentioned were Miller and Adcock, both celebrated bassoonists, and Messing, an eminent French horn player.

At Hereford in 1756 the great attraction at the Music Meeting was the first Three Choirs appearance of the Italian soprano Giulia Frasi, who came to England in 1743:

> young and interesting in person, with a sweet and clear voice: though she never ranked as first woman at the Italian opera, yet, by learning English, she became of much importance at our oratorios, theatres and public concerts, when singers of a higher class, without qualification, could be of no use. She pronounced our language in singing with a more distinct articulation than native performers; and her style being plain and simple, with a well-toned voice and a good shake, she delighted the ignorant and never displeased the learned. She became, in consequence, an established favourite with the public, and sang at the Meetings of the Three Choirs nine successive years. Frasi, after many years' residence in this country, where she made from £1,100 to £1,800 *per annum*, was obliged to retire to Calais, in order to avoid being arrested for debts, the consequence of her want of economy; and after subsisting for some time on small pensions from her friends in England, which gradually diminished, died almost literally for want of bread.[10]

Accepting the truth of notices which appeared in the papers that 'the City is very healthy, and quite free from the Smallpox', the crowds descended upon

---

[7] See *MW* 1860, p. 584.

[8] *Annals* 1895, p. 31n.

[9] *Annals* 1812, p. 183.

[10] Ibid., pp. 184–5.

Hereford in 1756, three noblemen and twelve members of Parliament among them, and £182 was collected at the doors for the charity.[11] However, this figure was greatly exceeded in 1757(G), when Handel's *Messiah* was given at Three Choirs for the first time:

> by a numerous Band of Vocal and Instrumental Performers from London, Salisbury, Bath, Oxford, and other places; particularly Signora Frasi, Mr Beard, Mr Wass, and Mr Hayes; Three Trumpets, a pair of Kettle-drums, Four Hautboys, Four Bassoons, Two Double-basses, Violins, Violoncellos, and Chorus Singers in Proportion. The Musick to be conducted by Dr Hayes.[12]

Messiah immediately became an indisputable favourite at Three Choirs, performed complete or in part at all but two Music Meetings until 1963(w). In 1757 the large sum of £300 was collected at the doors, but in addition there was an unprecedented 'overplus' of £60 added to the charity. A full statement of accounts was published in the *Gloucester Journal*:[13]

Received from Oratorio Tickets,	
1st Night [*Judas Maccabeus*]	162. 00. 0
2nd Night [*Acis and Galatea*]	136. 00. 0
3rd Night [*Messiah*]	207. 00. 0
Forfeits	024. 19. 0
From the Sale of Oratorio Book, Printing and Dispersing Expences cleared	000. 05. 0
Received	530. 04. 0
Disbursed to Singers and Instrumental Performers	267. 04. 6
To Doctor Hayes for Singing, and conducting the Musick	22. 01. 0
For collating, writing and adjusting Parts	005. 05. 0
For Advertisements and Carriage of Parcels, paid by Dr Hayes	006. 09. 0
To Frasi	052. 10. 0
Frasi's and Beard's Expences	046. 05. 9
Ball-Musick	022. 01. 0
To R. Raikes for Advertisements and Tickets	007. 02. 0
Wax Candles	021. 10. 6
Stewards' Dinner	012. 06. 6
To Officers and Porters	007. 08. 9
Disbursed	470. 04. 0

Received	530. 04. 0
Disbursed	470. 04. 0
Balance to be added to the Charity	60. 0. 0

George Talbot
Norborne Berkeley

---

[11] *Gloucester Journal*, 14 and 21 September 1756.

[12] *Gloucester Journal*, 12 July 1757.

[13] *Gloucester Journal*, 1 November 1757.

So Giulia Frasi was rewarded with a fee which amounted to more than double that paid to William Hayes in his dual role as both conductor and singer. According to measuringworth.com, £1 in Handel's time was worth about £140 today (2016).

At Worcester in 1758 the band was led by Thomas Pinto, a prodigious violinist of whom Dr Burney wrote that, 'With a powerful hand and a marvellous quick eye, he was so careless a player, that he performed the most difficult music better the first time he saw it, than ever after.'[14]

In 1759(H) the Rev. Benjamin Mence joined Frasi and Wass as a principal singer. Recording the death in 1796 of this remarkable clergyman, the *Gentleman's Magazine* described him as one 'in whom the classical world has lost a scientific genius, and whose vocal powers as an English singer remain unrivalled'. In addition, 1759 was the second year in which the famous oboist Thomas Vincent, a pupil of Sammartini, played at Three Choirs. In that same year we also find the name of Storace, a double-bass player and father of the composer Stephen Storace, a friend of Mozart, and that of the soprano Ann Selina (Nancy) Storace.

Of greater significance than the names of the performers in 1759 was the venue for *Messiah*, transferred from the evening concerts to the cathedral – previously the exclusive preserve of services and anthems. Why should this change have happened? Certainly, the Hereford College Hall would have been too small for the scale of *Messiah* performances given in the public halls at Gloucester and Worcester, even though it was adequate for a 'Grand Concert of Vocal and Instrumental Musick' on the Thursday evening in 1759.[15] But why could *Messiah* not have been performed in the Hereford Guildhall?

The answer is to be found in a document still preserved in the City of Hereford Archive, recording an agreement between the Mayor, Aldermen and Citizens of Hereford of the first part and the Bishop of Hereford of the other part, that:

> The Guildhall of the City of Hereford being ruinous and necessary to be rebuilt and it having been proposed that by the voluntary Contributions of the Gentlemen and Clergy within the County and Diocese of Hereford added to the fund raised by the Corporation of the said City, a Guildhall should be built upon a more extensive plan, and in a more Convenient Situation than the present, so as to have a Room proper for the reception of the Company at the Meetings of the Choirs of Hereford, Gloucester and Worcester as well as for the General Convenience and use of the said City *Be it known* that for the satisfaction of all parties who are or may be concerned in so Generous an Undertaking *We* the Mayor Aldermen and Citizens of the said City *Do* Grant and agree to and with the Lord Bishop of Hereford and his Successors that the said Room when built as aforesaid shall at all times be free for the use of the said Meeting whenever requested by the Stewards thereof *Given* under our Common Seal the

---

[14] *Annals* 1812, p. 188.

[15] *Gloucester Journal*, 14 August 1759.

Twentieth day of July in the Year of Our Lord One Thousand seven hundred and fifty nine.[16]

Three weeks after this agreement was reached, notices were placed in the papers advertising that *Messiah* would be performed in the cathedral, the only building in Hereford of sufficient size which was not 'ruinous'. Surely, the deal struck with the bishop for free use in perpetuity of the new Guildhall for the Music Meeting, with its implied advantage in terms of income to the charity, was of paramount significance in the granting of reciprocal approval for the use of the cathedral for oratorio performances. There was also another compelling reason why, in September 1759, the Stewards of the Music Meeting at Hereford would not have wished to be seen as the poor relations of Gloucester or Worcester in their *Messiah* performance: Handel had died in the previous April.

In the decade from 1754 the Gloucester Meetings were conducted by William Hayes; those at Worcester were conducted by a prince among composers of the English Baroque, William Boyce, until his appointment as Organist of the Chapel Royal in 1758.[17] The first of the cathedral organists to be recorded as conductor on his home ground is thus Richard Clack, Organist at Hereford from 1754 to 1779, who was in charge of the 1759 Meeting. Perhaps he too used his limited influence to gain access to the cathedral for *Messiah*. Worcester followed Hereford's example in 1761, but Gloucester barred the cathedral to *Messiah* until 1769.

The 1760 Meeting at Gloucester was devoted to the memory of Handel. Hayes conducted *Esther* on Wednesday evening, followed on the second night by '*The Passions*, an Ode written by Mr. Collins and set to music after the Manner of an Oratorio by Dr. Hayes, to which will be added an ODE to the Memory of Mr Handel; with a Variety of Instrumental Pieces between the several Parts.'[18]

Elias Isaac (1734–1793), the Worcester Organist, took over as conductor of the Worcester Music Meetings from 1761, and of the Gloucester ones from 1769. He also conducted at Hereford in 1777, two years before the death of Richard Clack. The principal tenor at Three Choirs was, for many years, Charles Norris, Organist at St John's College and Christ Church, Oxford. As a boy, Norris was a chorister at Salisbury Cathedral, and it was as a treble that he first appeared at Worcester in 1761. Norris was greatly admired, particularly for the deep feeling and expression with which he sang in *Messiah* and in Purcell's 'From Rosy Bowers'. He died in 1790 at little more than forty-five years of age, a victim of alcoholism. As Rimbault put it:

> from an early disappointment in love, [he] unhappily gave way to excesses falsely glossed over as *convivial*, to which he fell a premature victim. At Westminster Abbey, in 1790, he could not hold the book from which he sang, and excited emotions of pity in place of the rapture that was wont

---

[16] Herefordshire Archive (AE 75).

[17] Boyce conducted at Worcester in 1755 (see *Gloucester Journal* notice, 8 July 1755), though Lysons claims he was there earlier, from 1737. Deafness forced him to give up much of his work during his later years. He died in 1779.

[18] *Gloucester Journal*, 29 July 1760.

to follow his performance. He died at Himley Hall, the seat of Viscount Dudley and Ward, Sept 5th, 1790.[19]

Norris sang at Three Choirs for the last time in 1788(w).

In 1765, Giulia Frasi was replaced by Charlotte Brent, a pupil of Thomas Arne, in whose opera *Eliza* she made her first appearance in 1755. She was the original Mandane in Arne's opera *Artaxerxes*, and in 1766 became the second wife of the violinist Thomas Pinto. Charlotte Brent spent the latter part of her life at 6 Vauxhall Walk, London, where in 1802 she died in poverty.

In 1769, at Gloucester, John Crosdill, the best English cellist of his time, made his first Three Choirs appearance, as did Johann Christian Fischer, the celebrated oboist. Fischer appeared regularly at Three Choirs for more than twenty years. In 1780 he married the daughter of the painter Thomas Gainsborough, but the match was an unhappy one. Fischer toured the Continent between 1786 and 1790, playing before a less-than-admiring Mozart in Vienna in 1787. He died in London in 1800.

Among the portraits of musicians painted by Gainsborough are studies of both his son-in-law Fischer, and of Elizabeth Linley, the daughter of Thomas Linley, a singing-master, composer and organist of Bath Abbey who with his son, also Thomas, wrote the music for Sheridan's play *The Duenna*. Elizabeth Linley first sang in her father's concerts in Bath, and made her London and Three Choirs debuts in 1770(w). Considered to be the most accomplished singer that this country had produced, she enjoyed huge popularity wherever she appeared. But in 1773, between the time of her engagement for Three Choirs and the Meeting at Worcester, she eloped with Sheridan, having already married him in secret. It was feared that she would not fulfil her engagement, but Sheridan not only allowed his wife to appear but also presented £100 to the charity – the sum which was to have been Elizabeth Linley's fee.

In 1770(w) also, Felici Giardini became the Leader of the band – a position he filled for seven years – and the Italian castrato soprano Giusto Ferdinando Tenducci returned to Worcester, where he had first appeared in 1767.

Tenducci came to England in 1758, toured Scotland and Ireland with Arne, but later returned to Italy to escape his debts. Rimbault describes how Tenducci was engaged to sing at Worcester in 1767 for 50 guineas:

> When the money was paid to him, with true operatical dignity he refused to give a receipt for it, alleging 'that he should be sent for to sing at all the *horse-races* and cock-fighting in the kingdom; and that he would rather *give* his performance.' The stewards, the Right Hon. W. Dowdeswell, Chancellor of the Exchequer, and the Rev. Sir Richard Wrothesley, Bart., Dean of Worcester, being informed of his objection and the terms in which it was made, conveyed a hint to him that 'they should be thankful to him for the fifty guineas.' The hint was not lost upon him; he condescended to give a receipt for the sum for his own use.[20]

Tenducci, who married three times, died in Genoa in 1790.

[19] *Annals* 1895, p. 39n.

[20] Ibid., p. 47n.

Mary Linley, the younger sister of Elizabeth, sang at the Meetings from 1771 to 1773, and in 1775 and 1776. From 1774 her more famous sister's place was taken by Cecilia Davies, an Englishwoman who had won a great reputation in Italy, where she was called 'L'Inglesina'. In July 1832 Rimbault visited Cecilia Davies at her home in London. She was then ninety-two years of age. He was 'surprised to find that she retained all her faculties, was very communicative, and recollected the former events of her life perfectly, which she related with great distinctness and vivacity. She died a few years after, in the extreme of old age, disease and poverty.'[21] It seems this is a recurring theme.

At Gloucester in 1775, Handel's *Israel in Egypt* was performed at Three Choirs for the first time. Between the first and second parts of the oratorio a 'Miscellaneous Act' was given, consisting of songs performed by Mary Linley and the Italian castrato soprano Venanzio Rauzzini, and instrumental pieces by Giardini, Fischer and Crosdill.

Rauzzini sang at three Meetings, 1775 to 1777, after which he regularly appeared as a member of the audience until his death in 1810. He had made his operatic debut in Rome in 1765, and two years later entered the service of the court of the Elector of Bavaria in Munich. In 1772 he created the leading role in Mozart's *Lucio Silla* in Milan, and Mozart wrote the *Exsultate Jubilate* for him. In 1774 he settled in England, appearing both as singer and composer, and his opera *Piramo e Tisbe*, performed as an oratorio, was given in full at Hereford in 1777. From 1778 he lived in Bath, where he gained a high reputation as a singing teacher, numbering among his pupils Gertrud Mara, John Braham, and Nancy Storace and Michael Kelly, both of whom sang in the first performance of Mozart's *La nozze di Figaro*. Nancy Storace appeared as a 'juvenile performer' at the 1777(H) Meeting: she was not quite twelve years old!

In addition to the three cathedral choirs, other choral singers from 'London, Salisbury, Bath, Oxford and other places' had been mentioned in the notice for the first *Messiah* performance in 1757(G), and such augmentation became the norm at Three Choirs. By 1772 it was acknowledged that the choirs at the Meetings lacked balance due to a shortage of trebles. Then, in 1772(G), 'were engaged this year, for the first time, to assist the trebles in the choruses, Miss Radcliffe and others, of the celebrated female chorus singers, as they were called, from the North of England'.[22] The *Gloucester Journal* reported that their 'exact and spirited accompanyment added greatly to the grandeur of the several choruses'.[23] The 'Concert of Ancient Music', an annual royal and aristocratic affair during nearly three-quarters of a century from 1776, used also 'to import mill-girl sopranos from Lancashire and Yorkshire, and maintain them in London throughout the concert season'.[24] The northern ladies were engaged regularly for Three Choirs throughout the last quarter of the eighteenth century.

[21] Ibid., p. 51n.

[22] *Annals* 1812, p. 203.

[23] *Gloucester Journal*, 14 September 1772.

[24] Percy A. Scholes, *The Mirror of Music, 1844–1944: A Century of Musical Life in Britain as Reflected in the Pages of the 'Musical Times'*, vol. 1 (Novello, 1947), p. 49.

Among the singers from the North who appeared at Gloucester in 1772 was one Miss Harrop. Six years later this lady returned to Gloucester as a soloist, able to command a fee of 100 guineas. She had married Joah Bates, a Yorkshireman – 'one of the Commissioners of the Victualling Office, a scientific amateur in music'[25] – who had taken her from her music-master, Sacchini, and completed her musical education himself. According to Burney, the result was that Mrs Bates's

> seraphic voice and disposition for music were so highly cultivated by him as to render her one of the most enchanting singers ever heard; and that her performance of Handel's pathetic songs, in particular, had made it impossible to be pleased with her successor in them [Madame Mara] at the concerts of Ancient Music.[26]

Joah Bates (1741–1799) was the conductor of the Concert of Ancient Music in London from its inception in 1776. He conducted at the Handel Commemoration of 1784 at Westminster Abbey when, strangely, he employed Madame Mara and not his wife.

Samuel Harrison was one of the treble soloists with the Concerts of Ancient Music. His voice remained unbroken until the age of eighteen, when it failed at once in a single day – the day of his engagement at the 1778(G) Music Meeting. Harrison went on to become a much sought-after tenor.

In 1778, Lamotte led the band, and 'the matchless Cervetto', as Burney styled the famous cellist, appeared as an instrumentalist for the first time. Two years later, at Hereford, William Cramer took over as Leader, beginning a long association of the Cramer family with Three Choirs. He was a brilliant violinist, a member of the Elector's orchestra at Mannheim from 1752 to 1772, after which he settled in London. He was nominated chamber musician to the king and appointed Leader at the Ancient Concerts.

Following the transfer of *Messiah* to the cathedrals at Hereford in 1759, Worcester in 1761 and Gloucester in 1769, three morning events – *Messiah* and two church services – became a regular pattern at Three Choirs until 1784. In that year the (inaccurately calculated) centenary of Handel's birth was, as we have seen, celebrated at Westminster Abbey under the direction of Joah Bates. Similar celebrations were held elsewhere in the country, including at Gloucester, where, on the second morning in the cathedral:

> on which till this time the church services had been repeated, and to which admission was gratuitous, there were substituted the music which had been performed in Westminster Abbey on the first day of Handel's commemoration; and the admittance to this performance was fixed at 5s. 6d., the same as the other concerts.[27]

The 'Westminster Abbey Selection' now became the regular item for the second morning at each Meeting (except in 1787(G), when *Israel in Egypt* was performed). After 1791 it became a 'Grand Selection of Sacred Music by Handel'.

[25] *Annals* 1812, p. 210.

[26] *Annals* 1895, p. 55n.

[27] *Annals* 1812, p. 218.

The famous Madame Mara made her Three Choirs debut in 1784(G), fresh from her huge success at Westminster Abbey, of which Burney said:

> She had the power of conveying the softest and most artificial inflexions of her sweet and brilliant tone to the remotest corner of that immense building, whilst she articulated every syllable with such neatness, precision and purity, that it was rendered as audible and intelligible as it could possibly have been in a small theatre by mere declamation.[28]

Gertrud Mara (née Schmeling) was born at Cassel in 1749 and was taken on tour by her father as a child-prodigy violinist. While visiting England her talent as a singer was discovered and she had lessons from Domenico Paradisi. She sang under Hiller in Leipzig in 1769, and in 1771 married the cellist Mara and entered the service of Frederick the Great in Berlin. When, in 1780, she tried to leave Prussia she was imprisoned for her attempt – a fate which also befell Voltaire when he had tried to leave Frederick's court! When, at last, she was able to get away, she appeared with great success in Vienna, Paris and London.

Among the singers who made their first Three Choirs appearance at Gloucester in 1784 were, in addition to Mara, Miss Cantelo, a young singer who later married Samuel Harrison, and James Bartleman, the leading bass of his generation, but appearing in 1784, as Harrison had done before him, as a treble.

On Easter Monday 1786 the whole of the west end of Hereford Cathedral collapsed, taking with it several bays of arches in the nave. Quite obviously, there was no possibility of using the building for the morning performances at the Music Meetings in the following September. The two gentlemen who had been nominated as Stewards, fearing a large financial loss, withdrew from office and others could not easily be found to take their places. At last, James Walwyn Esq. and the Rev. Canon Morgan agreed to accept nomination. The Meeting took place as usual; the morning performances, the 'Westminster Abbey Selection' and *Messiah* were transferred to St Peter's Church. On the first and third evenings there were Miscellaneous Concerts; and on the intermediate evening 'a Concert of Ancient Music' on the plan of those held in London. What might the audience have heard at these Miscellaneous Concerts?

Only one printed programme of an eighteenth-century Three Choirs Miscellaneous Concert is known to survive. It is to be found in the Painswick House Collection held in the Gloucestershire Archives and refers to the year 1790 when, among other artists, the young son of the Gloucester Organist, William Mutlow, appeared as a treble in a melodramatic ballad, 'The Ghost of Edwin', written by one Colin Roope Esq.

A Selection of Songs
for the
Performances at the Booth Hall
on Thursday Evening
September 9, 1790
Gloucester: Printed by R. Raikes

[28] Ibid., pp. 218–19.

Act I

Overture, 'Ariadne'	
Song, Madame Mara Gia trionfar	(Anfossi)
Concerto Oboe, Mr. Parke	
Song, Miss Parke Dove sei	(Handel)
Concerto, Corelli	
Song, Madame Mara 'Softly sweet'	
Recit, 'Search round the world' – Solomon	
Chorus, 'May no rash intruder' – Solomon	

Act II

Grand Concerto, Handel	
Glee, 'Sigh no more Ladies' – Stevens	
Song, Master Mutlow 'Pale was the Moon'	
The Ghost of Edwin (new)	(Hayes)
Quartetto, Pleyell	
Song, Miss Parke 'The prince unable'	(Handel)
Concertante, Wilton	
Song, Madame Mara 'Dunque corri'	(Giordanielli)
Chorus, 'The many rend the skies'	

In June 1788, George III suffered a particularly bad series of 'bilious attacks' (he was suffering from porphyria), and his physician, Sir George Baker, advised him to visit Cheltenham for a course of treatment, taking the spa waters there. The king arrived in Cheltenham on Saturday 12 July, accompanied by Queen Charlotte, the Princess Royal, the Princesses Augusta and Elizabeth, Lord Courtoun (comptroller of the Royal Household), Lady Weymouth (in charge of the ladies-in-waiting) and other members of a large party, including Fanny Burney.

While in Cheltenham, the king learned that the triennial Music Meeting was to be celebrated at Worcester on 27, 28 and 29 August. He signified his intention of being present at the Meeting, provided that it could be brought forward to the 6, 7 and 8 of that month – and the alteration was accordingly made. Two days before the Meeting, the king wrote to his daughter, Princess Sophia, opening his letter with the following paragraph:

My Dearest Sophia,

The account of this Day of Mary is so charming that it has quite put me into Spirits and prepared me for going tomorrow after Dinner to Worcester where I shall remain till Friday Evening that I may attend the three Mornings at the Cathedral the Musick of my Admiration Handel.[29]

The royal party arrived in Worcester on the evening of Tuesday 5 August as planned, and took up residence at the bishop's palace. The next day at 5 a.m. the king walked out to view incognito many parts of the city before returning for

[29] Letter from King George III to Princess Sophia (4 August 1788). Gloucestershire Archives.

various levees, followed by Divine Service in the cathedral. This included the overture to *Esther*, the Dettingen *Te Deum*, *Grand Jubilate*, an anthem and two coronation anthems. The following morning the 'Westminster Abbey Selection' was performed; and on the third morning an audience of almost 3,000 attended *Messiah*.

Up until 1834 all cathedral performances at Three Choirs were given in the quire, but for the royal visit of 1788 the nave of Worcester Cathedral was handsomely fitted up for the occasion. A gallery for the royal family was erected under the Great West Window: 'It was spread with a rich Worcester carpet, lined and faced with crimson silk, and shaded with a lofty canopy of the same material and surmounted with a crown.'[30] On the right hand of it was a seat for the bishops of the three dioceses, and on the left another for the Dean and Chapter of Worcester. Behind these seats were others for the Stewards of the Meeting and for the royal suite. 'The orchestra was at the opposite end of the nave. Below the Royal Gallery were rows of seats raised one above another for the Nobility and persons of Distinction. There was also a small Gallery on each side of the Nave for the Corporation and their families. The area was filled with seats for the audience in general.'[31]

At seven o'clock on the Friday evening the royal family went to the College Hall to hear a Miscellaneous Concert. An elegant box had been prepared in the centre of the gallery for their reception.

> The King was dressed in a Blue and Gold uniform. The Queen and Princesses in royal purple gowns with silver tissue petticoats. The Queen's head dress was a cap decorated with purple ribbands and studded with beads of polished steel as brilliant as the finest diamond ... The Princesses wore their hair ornamented very gracefully with gauze and flowers; their slippers adorned with polished steel rosettes, lately invented by Bailey of Gloucester.[32]

Fanny Burney attended the concert and recorded in her diary:

> I was much more pleased than in the morning [*Messiah*], but was obliged to come away at the end of the first act, as it was already ten o'clock ...
>
> The box for the Royals was prepared upstairs and made very handsome; but there was no sort of resting-place considered for the attendants who were forced to stand perpendicular the whole time. Miss Hawkins, Betsy and myself had places behind the Royal Box. The King, Queen, and Princesses had very handsome large chairs; their poor standing attendants were Lady Harcourt, Lord Oxford, Mr Fairly, and the two Colonels to fill up, for in form and order the Equeries are never admitted to the Royal Box, but in the country this etiquette is cast aside ... Poor Lady Harcourt was so weakened by her influenza that she was ready to drop, and after the first

[30] *Gentleman's Magazine* 57, pt. 2, no. 3, p. 756.

[31] Rev. James Nankivell, *The Royal Visit to the Three Choirs Meeting in 1788* (Trinity Press, 1950), p. 13.

[32] *European Magazine* 14 (1788), pp. 150–1.

act was forced to entreat permission to resign her place to Lady Pembroke, who was in the gallery; and, being another Lady of the Bed Chamber, was equally proper for it.[33]

The principal singers at the royal Music Meeting were Gertrud Mara and Mrs Ambrose (née Mahon); Charles Norris, singing for the last time at Three Choirs; Hindle and Wilson, countertenors; and the basses Sale and Griffiths. The instrumental performers, according to Lysons, were: 'Mr Cramer, leader, Fischer, Mara [the cellist husband of Gertrud Mara], Mahon, Ashley, with the double drums &c., &c., aided by the powerful support of His Majesty's private band. The music was conducted by Mr Isaac.'[34]

In 1789(H) the principal soprano was the celebrated Elizabeth Billington, daughter of Carl Weichsal, a German oboist who had settled in London. She was a pupil of J. C. Bach, appearing first in public as a child pianist in 1774. She married the double-bass player James Billington in 1783. 'When I first heard her in 1783,' wrote Lord Mount Edgcumbe,

> she was very young and pretty, had a delightful fresh voice of very high compass, and sang with great neatness several songs composed for Allegranti, whom she closely imitated … yet something was wanting; for she possessed not the feeling to give touching expression, even when she sang with the utmost delicacy and skill.[35]

But Haydn, in his diary of 1791, spoke of Mrs Billington as a singer of genius. Like Cecilia Davies before her, Elizabeth Billington gained the rare distinction of acceptance as a first female singer in Italian theatres, and she was a great favourite at Three Choirs for many years. Although advertised to appear at Worcester in 1791, Mrs Billington did not appear and her place was taken by Gertrud Mara. John Marsh, an amateur composer of note, writer about music and diarist, was present at the first evening performance:

> After seven I hurried to the performance of Acis and Galatea at the college-hall, fearing I should lose the overture, but found they had not begun, though much after the time announced for the beginning, being waiting for Madame Mara, who was to sing the first song, and who, when she thought proper to make her appearance, did not choose to sit in the orchestra with the other singers, but with the company in the room, whence she never went to the orchestra without being waited upon, to be handed up by Mr. Wigley, the member for Worcester. As she notwithstanding this behaviour met with great applause after every song she sang, Miss Poole, the next singer, to shew her satisfaction, also joined in the applause by wrapping [sic] with her fan; which (it seemed) much displeased Mara, who observed that it was as much as to say she sang

[33] *Diary and Letters of Madame d'Arblay* [Fanny Burney], *edited by her Niece*, vol. 4: *1788–9* (Henry Colburn, 1843), pp. 228–31.

[34] *Annals* 1812, pp. 227–8.

[35] *Annals* 1895, p. 70n.

almost as well as Miss Poole did herself, and that she had a great mind to box her ears for her impertinence.[36]

As the eighteenth century drew towards its end Europe was in turmoil. The American Revolution had ended in 1783, dealing a crushing blow to the policies of George III and forcing him to make concessions to public opinion in England. The French Revolution began in 1789, and Louis XVI was guillotined in January 1793. Napoleon rose to power – and Britain was at war with France.

Against this background, the following statement appeared in the *Hereford Journal* of 26 July 1798:

> **Hereford.** The Dean and Chapter having no expectation, in the present exigencies of the country and in the absence of many of the principal inhabitants of the diocese, that any gentleman will undertake the large and increasing expenses of conducting a Music Meeting, submit to the consideration of the Nobility, Gentry and Clergy, the propriety of raising a subscription to answer the charitable purposes of it.

The idea was a failure and the subscription unproductive.

Fortunately, the Duke of Norfolk had gathered together a large number of singers and instrumentalists at his Holme Lacy country house, all of whom offered their services free at two performances in aid of the charity on 5 and 6 September. When this plan was published in the *Hereford Journal* it prompted a meeting of the gentry of the county at which it was resolved that, in preference to accepting this benevolent offer, the Meeting of the Three Choirs should go ahead as usual on 26, 27 and 28 September, and that the number of Stewards should, from then on, be increased to two or more lay and two or more clerical. In fact, six Stewards accepted office in 1798, one of them being Canon Morgan, who had stood forward in a similar way in 1786.

John Marsh paid three more visits to Three Choirs, in 1808(G), 1819(H) and 1821(W). His description of the first of these will serve to take us into the Music Meetings of the nineteenth century, and into the congenial company of William Mutlow, Organist of Gloucester from 1782 until 1832; Marsh travelled into Gloucestershire from Monmouth:

> I made a famous breakfast; and about eleven we set out for Ross, eleven miles, to which we had a very pleasant ride, great part of the way by the river, Wye, the scenery about which was delightful. Here we went, to see the fine view from the church-yard; after which, we got our dinner at the inn, and about three set off again for Gloucester, which we did not reach till near seven o'clock, when we took possession of a small lodging in St. Mary's churchyard, taken for us at a great price, three guineas and a half for cooking, for the music meeting week by Mr. Mutlow, the organist.
>
> On Tuesday, the sixth, we got in to the rehearsal at the cathedral, and were much pleased, the principal vocal performers being Mrs Billington, Mr and Mrs Vaughan, Mess. Harrison, Goss and Bartleman, and the principal instrumental Mess. Cramer, leader, Lindley, Griesbach, Mahon,

---

[36] Diaries of John Marsh, 16 vols (MS), Cambridge University Library, Add. MS 7757.

Holmes, Boyce etc. With all these, except the females and Harrison, and near twenty others I dined this day at Mr Mutlow's, who gave us a fine turbot, turtle soup, venison, and plenty of game, which was sent him by the Stewards of the meeting. On the next morning we went immediately after breakfast to the cathedral to get good places; and at eleven the service began with the overture of Esther, performed by the band, and afterwards were introduced the Dettingen Te Deum, one of Dr Boyce's charity-anthems, and the coronation anthem; beside which the full band and chorus joined in the Gloria-patri of the psalms, which had a very striking effect. After the prayers there was an appropriate sermon, and a collection at going out for the widows and orphans of the clergy of the three dioceses; for which one of the plates being held by the bishop, Dr Huntingford, he was so good as to recognise me, as we passed. At a quarter before six we went to the room and were much entertained with the oratorio of Alexander's Feast, finely performed. On the next morning we went to a grand selection at the cathedral, of which the first and third parts were mostly from Handel, and the second consisted of the first act of Haydn's Creation. In the evening, the room being much crowded, we did not enjoy the concert so much as on the evening before, neither did it go off so well, as in consequence of the heat of the room the performers were much oppressed, and found it expedient to shorten the concert by leaving out a concertante of Mozart's for six obligato instruments and the concluding full piece. We here took our leave of the music at Gloucester, as instead of going to the Messiah the next morning at the cathedral, which we had so often heard, we devoted this our last morning at Gloucester to going to see the new jail there, built on Mr Howard's plan with a penitentiary, and proper distinction between the debtors and felons, and Mr Weaver's pin-manufactory.[37]

[37] Ibid.

5

The Gentlemen and the Players

FOLLOWING the rescue of the Festival by the Duke of Norfolk in 1798, the number of Stewards rose to six, three clerical and three lay, in each city. Even so, rising costs and falling receipts placed an increasingly formidable burden upon these gentlemen. After 1817(G), when receipts exceeded expenditure and the Stewards were able to invest a surplus in consols, the Festival made a loss every year until 1853(G). In 1836 it was rumoured that at a meeting of the Worcester Stewards 'some good round sums were offered by certain of them to be released from their impending responsibility'.[1] This is hardly surprising: deficits in the previous decade had exceeded £750 *per annum*, reaching a peak of £1,365 1s. 0d. in 1832(G).

Between 1836 and 1838 three meetings took place at the Episcopal Palace in Worcester of a committee appointed 'to consider the best means of ensuring a more enlarged and efficient support of the Triennial Musical Festival in Worcester'.[2] The result was the setting up in Worcester of a guarantee fund amounting to £746 in which thirty-two gentlemen and members of the clergy, including the Bishops of Worcester and Rochester and three members of Parliament, agreed to subscribe the whole, or such proportions as necessary, of amounts from £5 to £20 each towards the Worcester Music Meetings. This sum, together with £50 from each of the, by then, eight Stewards was used to defray expenses, the payment from each subscriber being made in proportion to the amount of their subscriptions.

In 1844 a guarantee fund was opened in Gloucester too, but there the preferred method of raising an extra subsidy was to increase the number of Stewards. In 1847 James Henry Brown took over as secretary of the Gloucester Festival. Not only was he a first-class administrator but he also had a gift for attracting men of means and influence to the ranks of the Stewards; in 1853 there were twenty-three, in 1862 fifty-four, and by 1868 there were no fewer than 106.

If anything, the difficulty was greater at Hereford than at either of the other cities. Although the Hereford Stewards made every effort to keep Festival expenses down, they could do nothing to increase the number of seats in the smallest of the three cathedrals. In consequence, financial losses at Hereford were often greater than at Worcester or Gloucester. In 1858 their plight was so severe that the secretary of the Hereford Festival Committee wrote to his counterpart in Gloucester to ask if there was any possibility of changing the Festival of that year from Hereford to Gloucester and delaying Hereford's turn until 1859. The Gloucester Committee refused to accept this proposal but suggested instead that

[1] *MW* 1842, p. 305.
[2] *Annals* 1895, p. 135.

Hereford too should increase the number of Stewards serving the Festival.[3] By the end of the century at both Gloucester and Worcester the Stewards numbered around 200, and at Hereford 300.

While to have a large number of generous Stewards was financially advantageous, the arrangement created its own problems. The possession of a noble title, wealth, civic status or a seat in Parliament is not necessarily a guarantee of musical sensitivity. On the other hand, a Steward pledging large sums of personal money might expect to have his opinions heard in the process of Festival decision-making. Inevitably, committees grew larger, subcommittees were formed to debate even minor matters, meetings grew in number and duration, stress on the secretary and conductor increased, and the resulting decisions were sometimes patently wrong.

The Rev. F. E. Witts (1783–1854), vicar of Wick Rissington in Gloucestershire, left in his diary a delightful pen-picture of the activities of a Festival Steward in the early nineteenth century. On 13 September 1826 Witts wrote:

> The town was all alive with company, some crowding towards the college, some arriving at the inns and lodgings, all in gay attire and nothing could be more lovely than the weather. A large posse of constables under the able generalship of a Bow Street Officer was posted at the Cathedral door, and their services were likely to be needed for the admission this morning was free. Each Steward's share of tickets for the galleries was 25, and the lay and clerical galleries held about 60 persons and were each day almost exclusively occupied by the first ladies in point of rank and connection, who attended the meeting, a most beautiful sight and the present style of female dress tended to justify the appelations affixed: a *parterre* – a bed of roses.
>
> My own ladies were each day accommodated in the first row of the clerical gallery, and from the extent of my acquaintance I was each morning soon drained of my tickets, and had I twice as many could have disposed of them to various applicants. By 11 o'clock the inner choir of the Cathedral was fearfully crowded … an occasional scream or groan indicated distress or fainting, some were carried out, some struggled into the outer choir, the most persevering stood their ground …
>
> The concert at the Shire Hall was very fully attended, nearly a thousand persons were present and the pressure at the upper end of the room was great. Lady Lyttleton and the Misses Witts were there and as soon as I had provided for their accommodation by a fresh bench between those already occupied and the orchestra,[4] the well-known and obtrusive Alderman Matthew Wood of London, coveting similar accommodation addressed himself to me.[5] I explained it had been the constant rule with the Stewards

[3] Gloucester Festival Minute Book, 1858. Gloucester Cathedral Archives and Library.

[4] The word 'orchestra' referred to the platform upon which the musicians (i.e. the 'band') performed.

[5] Sir Matthew Wood, MP, Lord Mayor of London. Two silver cups, presented to him in 1820 and 1821 for the part he played in championing the cause of Queen

to reserve accommodation for their own parties, and with very few forms kept back and the Lord Lieutenant not yet arrived he would have to find accommodation in the seats already placed. In reply the Alderman (who since the death of the sister of his namesake the eccentric and wealthy Jemmy Wood, Banker of Gloucester, has been a summer resident here where the old lady left him a good house in consideration of his championship of the late Queen Caroline, and where he hopes to worm himself into the good graces of Banker Jemmy) dilated on the ill-usage of the public by the Stewards: then exit in rage.

When the conversation reached the ears of Bowles[6] the following day when we were summing up the receipts at the Cathedral door, the poet extemporised:

> What money our music produces;
> For surely a meeting is good
> Where are Beauforts and Sherbornes and Ducies
> And Lansdownes and Alderman Wood.[7]

In the following year, 1827, royal patronage was extended to the Music Meetings by King George IV, a privilege continued to the present day.

Though generally courteous in helping the public to their seats at Festival performances, the Stewards could often be guilty of a pompous arrogance, especially to the gentlemen of the press:

So long as the Gloucester Festival has the good fortune to retain the services of such a secretary as Mr. J. H. Brown there is no fear of any paucity of stewards; but with all respect to these public spirited gentlemen I would venture to suggest that the administrative [*sic*] should be in fewer hands. We all know the proverb about 'Too many cooks', and this week it has been most painfully exemplified. Personally speaking I am making no complaint – on the contrary, so far as I am concerned individually, I have received the greatest possible courtesy and politeness from every steward with whom I have been brought in contact; but it has not been the case with all my London *confrères*, one of whom was told on Friday, upon requesting a seat, that 'no one had asked him to come there, and if he did come it was either for his own pleasure or profit.' ... On Thursday, while Mr. Reeves was touching the heart of everyone by his exquisite singing of 'Total Eclipse', one of the stewards (the most exalted functionary of Gloucester), was moving about, whispering in the ear of one or other of his colleagues, to the annoyance of everyone in his

---

Caroline, are now in the possession of the City of Gloucester. Caroline, Princess of Brunswick, married the Prince of Wales in 1795. Described by the historian Dr J. H. Plumb as 'eccentric .... coarse-fibred ... flamboyant, dirty and highly-sexed', Queen Caroline was tried by the House of Lords on charges of adultery and scandalous behaviour when the Prince ascended the throne as King George IV in 1820. Quotation from J. H. Plumb, *The First Four Georges* (Batsford, 1956), p. 170.

[6] The Rev. W. L. Bowles, another Steward.

[7] Rev. F. E. Witts, *The Diary of a Cotswold Parson*, ed. D. Verey (Alan Sutton, 1978).

neighbourhood, who wished to listen to the greatest treat of the whole Festival.[8]

A few years earlier there had been similar complaints:

Of the grand dress ball at the Shire Hall last night, I am not in a condition to send you a report. On entering the Hall, I presented my ticket, as usual, and entered the room, when a gentleman tapped me on the shoulder, and requested to know if I belonged to the London press. I told him I had that honour; whereupon he expressed a desire that I should follow him to the orchestra, whither he had received orders to show gentlemen of the press who might think proper to attend the ball. I was too indignant to remonstrate – 'surprise held me mute' – so I left, convinced that the stewards of the Hereford Festival were not by any means courteous to strangers, and this was my last impression of the Meeting of the Three Choirs in 1855.[9]

In his autobiography published in 1908, Joseph Bennett describes the ordeal of a young and inexperienced reporter attending the Festival for the first time:

In 1865, for some months before the Gloucester Festival took place, I had acted as a reporter of concerts, and such like, for the *Sunday Times* ... The paper was of no weight in the councils of music, and I was absolutely unknown – a mere waif, or stray, that had drifted by accident into the area of the art, and, like all such things, liable to be swept up and cast into the fire. But I felt none the less ambitious on that account, and as the Festival drew near, my mind was made up to attend it. So, one day, I presented myself before Mr Seale, the proprietor of my first journal, and enlarged upon the fitness with which the *Sunday Times* might place itself among other important papers in the Festival jury-box. My eloquence, though very sincere, proved of none effect. Seale remarked that the *Sunday Times* was a London weekly, and that musical doings in Gloucester did not concern it. He graciously added, however, that as I seemed to wish it, he would accept a report of the Festival, provided it cost him nothing. Let me confess that, for the moment, I was staggered by the proferred conditions. But only for a moment. My resolve to go held fast, though I had to support a wife and family upon means which left nothing to spare. I 'pinched' to do it – pinched myself, that is; going to Gloucester by the cheapest way, and securing a bedroom in one of a row of cottages some distance from the centre of the city. My food I could get as opportunity offered, but, of course, I was outside the zone of hospitality in my character as a friendless stranger. That, however, troubled me not at all, so long as I had a shilling in my pocket.

The next morning saw me bowing before the majesty of the Festival secretary, and pleading for a ticket of admission to the performances. The official's name was Brown; his ordinary role, if I rightly remember, was that of drawing-master at an important school hard by, and he lived in a

[8] *MW* 1868, p. 652.
[9] *MW* 1855, p. 562.

quaint old house on the eastern side of the cathedral yard. Said Mr Brown, as I approached him in his secretarial office, 'Well, sir, what can I have the pleasure of doing for you?' That was promising, and I could see, further, that I had to deal with a kindly little man. 'I represent the *Sunday Times*, Mr Brown, and shall be obliged by a ticket of admission for the week.' A cloud of doubt settled on the secretary's face. Opening a drawer, he took out a note-book and examined a particular page. Then he spoke again: 'I don't find the name of the *Sunday Times* in the list of papers to which admission has been granted.' 'No, sir,' I replied, 'but I have lately been appointed its critic, and I want to change all that and much else.' 'That's right', said Brown; then, after a pause for consideration, he filled up, and handed to me a ticket for any vacant seat in the north aisle. That second-class place I took to be a compromise between good nature and official strictness, but anyhow it served my purpose very well; and, as none of the critics knew me, and I was equally ignorant of them, there was no occasion for false shame …

Here let me say that Festival authorities forty years ago were not always remarkable for politeness or suavity when dealing with members of the press. I quite agree that allowance should be made for them in this regard, because it sometimes happened that members of the press were as lacking in the graces of behaviour as themselves; standing too much upon an unduly heightened sense of their own importance, and so on. Since the time of which I speak, a great change for the better has taken place, but still there is room for improvement, and much further good might be done by abolishing the journalist's free pass, which, I have always thought, degrades him in the common eye. I could say much on this question, but I touch it now only in passing.

Forty years ago the Festivals at Gloucester, Worcester, Hereford and Norwich (all these being cathedral cities) ended with a ball, the sole survivor of various 'side shows,' which clung more or less tenaciously to the main attraction …

The ball of the Three Choirs I never cared to witness, and I came too late on the scene to refuse the Gloucester 'Ordinary' – not a Bishop but a sort of public dinner – together with Gloucester Races, both functions being left-handed appendages of the Festival. Lastly, the ball vanished also. The air of the seventies was not good for it, but that its demise was lamented by the county Misses I can well believe.

Do you ask how the free press-tickets affected the amenities between festival officials and festival reporters? The answer is that fifty years ago, and for a good while later, journalists who attended festivals in the provinces, and received free tickets, were not looked upon as gentlemen, albeit, when referred to as a body, they were sometimes styled 'gentlemen of the press', that form being employed as a sort of compliment if toasts were about. They may have been famous critics in London, but, generally speaking, the provincial mind recognised no difference between them and the newspaper men whose ordinary vocation it was to attend coroner's inquests, and make notes of police court proceedings. This was not all. Your festival official, in the long-past time to which I refer, appreciated in a wonderful manner his four days' brief authority, and exerted himself to the extent of unblushing impudence; without deliberate purpose, in many cases, I firmly believe, but simply because he thought it the proper course to take with a journalist. I remember how, on one occasion, I walked to a certain cathedral, rather carefully 'made up' for the part of a gentleman, and was received by a local magnate, acting as steward, with pleasant smiles and a friendly mien. I showed him my ticket, which was prominently marked 'Press', and, alas! the smiles vanished, and the bearing became stiff and hard as, waving his hand, he cried 'Pass up.' I did not blame the poor man, because there was the question whether he knew any better, and likewise was there the fact, avowed on the ticket, that I had entered as a mere dead-head.[10]

For the great majority of nineteenth-century Stewards, Three Choirs was a highlight of the social calendar, presenting an opportunity to meet, and to be seen with, a larger number of the nobility and gentry than at most other occasions in the three shires. For the ladies there was always the task of assisting as plate-holders in the collections for the Festival charity. This simple duty could be quite an ordeal for an aristocratic young lady unused to public exposure in Victorian England. In her memoirs, written a century ago, the Margravine of Anspach recalled her experience at a Gloucester Festival. This lady was the youngest daughter of Augustus, fourth Earl of Berkeley. Her first husband was Lord Craven, and her second the Margrave of Anspach. But the extract has to do with her maiden days, when she was the 'toast' of Gloucestershire:

> In the summer after the grand *fête* at Berkeley, there was a music-meeting at Gloucester, to which I went with Lady Berkeley [her stepmother]. An unexpected summons came to me to request that I would leave the pew where I was, and hold one of the plates for the money collected for the poor, at one of the doors of the Cathedral. This requisition was made by desire of the Bishop of Gloucester, and to this door all the gentlemen of the three counties rushed to get a sight at the young novelty. As I naturally must have felt abashed at such a situation, where I was so very conspicuous, the consequence was that I averted my face when I curtsied for the guineas that were given, and they all fell sliding from the plate, to the entire dismay of the two beadles who attended. So great was my confusion at this unlucky circumstance that, on my return to the Bishop's palace, where I was staying, I was obliged to retire to my bedroom, where I remained to cry and sob at my misfortune. It was only Lord Berkeley [her brother] who could rouse me, by telling me peremptorily that I must go to the ball, where I was again mortified because he scolded me for refusing to dance with an odious Baronet, whom he liked and I hated because he had ventured to tell me that he was in love with me; and as there were others who talked love to me I disliked them all.[11]

[10] Joseph Bennett, *Forty Years of Music, 1865–1905* (Methuen, 1908), pp. 295ff.
[11] Quoted in *MT*, 1 October 1897, pp. 668–9.

Given the Victorian perception of women as guardians of the home, consigned to a subordinate, domestic role, it is not surprising that the notion of ladies becoming Stewards at the Festival was not even discussed until the latter part of the century. The Gloucester secretary suggested in 1889 that the Executive Committee might invite ladies to be Stewards. The proposal was considered but rejected several times in the remaining years of the century, and nothing more was done until 1907, when it was agreed to confer with the Hereford and Worcester Stewards. A resolution was then made that invitations should be sent to 'Ladies who are Householders, and whose husbands, brothers or sons, would have been eligible to become stewards'.[12] Even so, no lady actually became a Steward until after World War I, by which time an irreversible change in the social order was, in any case, under way.

Throughout the nineteenth century, although the main burdens of the musical direction and administration of a Festival fell to the conductor and the secretary respectively, there was no question of them being treated by the gentlemen of the Executive Committee as their equals. Rather, their status appears to have been that of highly respected senior servants. A glimpse into the Committee Room will prove the point.

After Secretary Brown's death, his place in Gloucester was taken by a young man called F. W. Waller. Brown's honorarium had been £50 per Festival; but on Waller's appointment in 1874 the Stewards immediately halved this sum. The new secretary soon found himself in difficulties and, before the 1877 Festival, took the courage to write formally to his chairman:

I must ask your consideration of one point ... before the year gets too far advanced in case you desire to make any change in consequence of what I have to put before you.

When I first accepted the duties of the office, it was fully represented to me by the Stewards that the payment was very small & quite out of proportion to the work & I took it for the year 1874 on that understanding ...

Though I was influenced by the very small remuneration, still I hoped to clear my expenses for as I am dependent on my own exertions I cannot afford to be a loser by the Festival, but such was the case on the last occasion from the following cause.

The duties of the Secretaryship absorbed so much of my attention especially just before & at the time of the Festival that it became absolutely necessary for me to employ an additional clerk in my office to do work, all of which I should have easily accomplished myself under ordinary circumstances.

The payment for this assistance amounted to over £40, thus it will be seen, as I received £25 from the Festival, that in addition to the time & labour expended upon the work, I was out of pocket £15 besides incurring many incidental expenses quite inseparable from the Secretaryship.

[12] Gloucester Festival Minute Book, 1907. Gloucester Cathedral Archives and Library.

Under the circumstances, I hope I shall not be considered unreasonable in asking the Stewards to increase the payment sufficiently to recoup me for any outlay to which I may be put in the coming year so as to ensure my not being out of pocket by the undertaking.[13]

The Stewards were gracious enough to see Waller's point of view and to award him the same honorarium as his predecessor. They were less gracious in 1880 when the Gloucester Cathedral lay clerks refused to accept the terms offered to them, i.e. £6 for singing at all the oratorios, the special service on Friday evening and the usual services, except the three evening services for which 15s. would be paid by the Dean and Chapter. Two lay clerks, Thomas and Hargrave, attended a meeting of the Music Committee to explain their views. They had, they said, received from Dr Wesley in 1874:

For Oratorios	£5 0s. 0d.
For Special Service	£1. 1s. 0d.
For three Evening Services	5s. 0d.
Total	£6 16s. 0d.

They now required £7 7s. 0d., being 11s. extra, and if the Stewards would give them that amount they would give their assistance at the Friday evening service. The Stewards pointed out that the evening service would be paid for by the Dean and Chapter; the lay clerks would not be moved: 'They said that the £7 7s. 0d. was the sum which they must have and that they considered that [they] had been unfairly treated in the matter of the Festival Charity.'[14] (The widows and orphans of lay clerks had originally benefited from the charity but this was discontinued when the services of the lay clerks ceased to be gratuitous.)

The special service on Friday evening, introduced at Gloucester in 1874 in place of the traditional ball, had not been universally welcomed:

The Ball is as dead as a dodo, and the 'light fantastic toe' now reposes, with the foot to which it belongs, on cathedral hassocks … As regards the musical service, I am bound to write severe things. The members of the Three Choirs, clad in surplices, made a great show on the lower benches of the orchestra; but their singing was almost beneath criticism, lacking, as it did, the very elements of such merit as alone could satisfy reasonable expectations.[15]

Perhaps remembering this slovenly performance, the Committee refused to discuss the lay clerks' grievance; Thomas and Hargrave left the room. When they had gone it was agreed that no increase on the £6 would be allowed but that the Friday evening service would be optional – a clear sign of their belief that the service could hardly suffer!

[13] Gloucester Festival Minute Book, 1877. Gloucester Cathedral Archives and Library.

[14] Gloucester Festival Minute Book, 1880. Gloucester Cathedral Archives and Library.

[15] *MW* 1874, p. 621.

The attitude of polite nineteenth-century society towards musicians was much the same as the attitude towards tradespeople. Performers were considered as purveyors of music just as grocers were purveyors of food and wine. Music could be enjoyed as food and wine could be enjoyed; but the musician and the grocer would not be invited to tea.

By 1811 Three Choirs had already begun to assume much of the aspect which it would have for the rest of the century. It had progressed from a small gathering of amateurs and cathedral choristers to become a major national festival engaging celebrated singers, solo instrumentalists and orchestral players, and augmenting the choral forces of Gloucester, Hereford and Worcester with choral societies and choirs from other cities.

In the early part of the century, the size of the orchestra varied year by year. In 1812(w) there were twenty-two violins, eight violas, four cellos and four double basses; two flutes, two oboes, two clarinets, two bassoons, two trumpets, two horns, drums and a 'double trombone', which is the standard 'Mozart' orchestra, plus a bass trombone.[16] In 1831(H) we read that 'the instrumental band, with Mr F. Cramer as principal first violin, was small but select'.[17]

Following the transfer of the oratorio performances from the quire to the nave (1834(H)) an expanded orchestra could be accommodated, comprising more or less the same players who performed at other major festivals and drawn 'from the Concert of Ancient Music, Philharmonic, Italian Opera and other establishments from London'. In 1839(w) the band, judiciously selected, consisted of the following performers:

Violins: F. Cramer, Loder, Blagrove, C. Reeve, Wagstaffe, Griesbach, Guynemer, Kearns, Loder, jun., N. Mori, Patey, Piggott, Watkins, Anderson, Mackintosh, W. Cramer, J. Marshall, Hope, Perry, D'Egville, J. D'Egville, Martin, Newson, Newsham, Holmes.

Violas: Moralt, Daniels, Nicks, S. Calkin, Abbott, Glanville, Davis, Marshall.

Violoncellos: Lindley, Crouch, W. Lindley, C. Lindley, Hatton, Piggott.

Double Basses: Dragonetti, Anfossi, Howell, G. Smart, Flower, Griffiths.

Flutes: Ribas, Hill.

Oboes: Cooke, Keating.

Clarinets: Willman, Williams.

Bassoons: Baumann, Tully.

Horns: Platt, Rae, Kielbach, C. Tully.

Trumpets: Harper, Irwin, Harper, jun.

Trombones: Smithies, Smithies, jun., Albrecht.

Drums: Chipp.

Organ: Mr Amott.

Pianoforte: Mr. Hunt.[18]

[16] See Shaw, *Three Choirs Festival*, p. 40.
[17] *Annals* 1895, p. 119.
[18] *MW* 1839, p. 307.

Among these players were some of the finest instrumentalists of the first half of the century. F. Cramer, Loder and Blagrove all belonged to famous musical families and each performed the duties of Leader at different concerts.

François Cramer (1772–1848) first played at a Music Meeting in 1788, the year of George III's visit, succeeded his father as Leader in 1800, and continued to appear at Three Choirs until he retired in his seventy-sixth year. In 1830, on his way to the Worcester Festival with his wife and daughter, Cramer narrowly escaped serious injury or worse. The coach on which they were travelling from London was heavily laden with baggage which was much too high on the top; more was put on at Cheltenham and Tewkesbury. The Cramers and one other person were inside the coach but there were eleven passengers and the coachman outside. They had reached Severn Stoke, seven miles from Worcester, by ten o'clock on the night of Saturday 11 September. Coming down a steep hill the coachman failed to lock the wheel and lost control of the horses. The coach careered down the hill and 'after going for a few minutes at a rapid pace, came to a curve on the road, when, from the immense weight of passengers and luggage at the top, the coach swung, and was thrown to the earth with a tremendous crash'.[19] Few of the passengers escaped injury, and two of them were killed: Joseph Hughes, a maltster from Sidbury, and Frederick Bennett, the Organist of Christ Church and New College, Oxford.

Robert Lindley (1777–1855), a Yorkshireman, was the principal cellist at the Italian Opera House in London, where he played at the same desk as the great double-bass player Domenico Dragonetti (1763–1846). For half a century the two were seen playing together not only at the opera but also at the Ancient Concerts, the Philharmonic, and all the provincial festivals; and Dragonetti's dog, Carlo, was often to be seen sitting beside them.

> Next came that 'Concertante duett' of Corelli's by Lindley and Dragonetti. This was a treat to which all lovers of harmony had been for some time looking forward, and the whole audience and orchestra were on tiptoe in anxious expectation. The veterans, on coming in front, were greeted with loud cheers by all parties, and then, after a 'majestic silence', the strain began. Words would fail us if we endeavoured to express our admiration of this wonderful performance; the tone, expression, and taste displayed by Lindley in the slow movement, and his execution in the allegro were 'beyond compare'. As to Dragonetti, it will ever remain a wonder with us, how he could move his fingers with such astonishing rapidity on his unwieldy Behemoth of an instrument. The performance of this work of Corelli's was in the musical sphere one of those 'angel visits' which are few and far between. It was finished amid thunders of applause.[20]

Lindley and Dragonetti were remembered in the autobiography of the baritone Henry Phillips:

> Giants they were in talent, such as had never existed before, and possibly may not again. The tone of Lindley's violoncello it is far beyond the

---

[19] *Worcester Herald*, 15 September 1830.

[20] *Worcester Herald*, 14 September 1839.

power of words to convey, it was so pure, so mellow, so harmonious. He was so perfectly skilled in all he had to do, that you might as well have tried to confuse an automaton as turn him from his path. One of his great achievements was accompanying Mr. Braham in Arne's celebrated cantata 'Alexis.' Many a listener must have left the concert-room fevered with wonder at the marvellous execution of the two artists. Another quality Lindley possessed, which I have never found in any other violoncellist, viz. that when accompanying a recitative, he gave the full chord, and frequently the note on which the singers were to commence. Some one or two tried to imitate his mode, but all failed. When accompanying a song, his last symphony would be most elaborate; he would play wonderful harmonies, and running roulades that one thought could not possibly terminate in the proper key. I well remember, at a musical festival, his accompanying Mr. Braham in that beautiful air, 'Oh, Liberty, thou choicest Treasure.' At the morning performance in the cathedral, when he came to the concluding symphony, he played, to the astonishment of the whole orchestra, in harmonics, 'Over the hills and far away'. This, I presume, was his idea of Oh, Liberty! The bishop and nobility present were delighted, and a repetition was immediately demanded. Lindley laughed to such a distressing degree, and took so much snuff, in both of which offices Dragonetti joined, that he said he couldn't play it again, and he wouldn't, and he didn't.

Then Dragonetti! In him what a strange being I shall have to describe: he was a kind-hearted man, abounding with eccentricities; by nature a lover of the fine arts; and on his instrument, the double bass, *perfection*. The power and tones he produced from his unwieldy instrument were wonderful, and to this he added great and rapid execution. The ends of his fingers had become, by practice, broad, covered with corns, and almost without form. Take him out of his profession, he was a mere child, given to the greatest frivolities. He led a single life, and occupied one lodging for years; which lodging, consisted of a bed-room, sitting-room, and a vacant apartment, which contained his collection of paintings, engravings, and dolls. Dolls – do not start, reader! A strange weakness for a man of genius to indulge in, but so it was; white dolls, brown dolls, dark dolls, and black, large, small, middling, and diminutive, formed an important feature in his establishment. The large black doll he would call his wife, and she used to travel with him sometimes to the festivals. He and Lindley generally journeyed together inside the coach, and when changing horses in some little village, he would take this black doll and dance it at the window, to the infinite astonishment and amusement of the bystanders. Such was one of the strange eccentricities of this really great man. So powerful was the tone he could produce from his instrument, that I have frequently heard him pull a whole orchestra back with one accent if they wavered in the least.

One of his and Lindley's great performances was a duet of Corelli's for violoncello and contra-basso, a surprising performance, and one which never failed to elicit an encore. The copy, in Dragonetti's handwriting, was played from, for nearly fifty years; it eventually fell into my possession, having been presented to me by Vincent Novello after Dragonetti's death.[21]

Thomas Harper (1787–1853) was a Worcester man with a national reputation as the leading performer on the slide trumpet in the country. When in his prime his playing was said to need 'no praise of any critic – it speaks indeed "trumpet tongued"'.[22] After his death he was succeeded as principal trumpet by his son. Another father-and-son partnership in the Festival band was that of the Smithies, senior and junior – the most accomplished trombonists of their time.

Before the invention of the bass tuba the lowest brass notes were provided by the ophicleide, a player being hired as required.[23] Liberties were sometimes taken with the orchestration of works in order to include the impressive ophicleide sound. An example of this was Edward Taylor's adaptation of Mozart's Requiem, the *Redemption*: 'In the score which Mozart has made perfectly symmetrical, an ophicleide had been intruded, and an oboe substituted for one of the *corni di bassetti*. These liberties … are highly reprehensible.'[24] The most respected ophicleidist of the nineteenth century was a Mr Ponder; having been engaged for the 1841 Festival, he arrived in Gloucester by coach from London, immediately burst into a fit of violent coughing, and died within minutes. The demise of the ophicleide itself followed only a very few years later. During the nineteenth century the technology of the valve brought to all brass instruments an advantage previously available only to trombone players: every note in the range of each instrument could now be played.

Before 1840 there were comparatively few amateurs in Britain with an extensive knowledge of music. By mid-century a steady increase in the number of brass bands and choral societies had begun. Collective music-making was thereby extended for the first time from the upper to the 'respectable' members of the lower classes – and smiled upon by society as a virtuous and moral activity.

Increased access to music and music-making was boosted by the introduction of modern methods in the production of instruments and sheet music. In 1850, for example, the possession of a piano was a rare luxury; by 1871 it was estimated that there were 400,000 pianos and a million pianists in Britain. By the end of the century the availability of the three-year hire purchase system had brought less expensive pianos within the budgets of many thousands more. At the same time, sheet music was becoming increasingly affordable. The cost of a vocal score of *Messiah* in 1837 was a guinea; in 1887 it was 1s.

An equally important factor in the increasing practicality of establishing choral societies was the introduction of classes for choral singing. John Hullah (1812–1884) was a Worcester man who went to Paris in 1839–40 to study

---

[21] Henry Phillips, *Musical and Personal Recollections during Half a Century* (Skeet, 1864).

[22] *MW* 1836, p. 56.

[23] The ophicleide was made from a metal, wide-bored, conical tube, 8–9 feet long, with a U-bend about halfway. It was played with a cup-shaped mouthpiece, had holes covered with keys in the side, and had a compass of about three octaves.

[24] *MW* 1846, p. 431.

G. L. Wilhelm's method of teaching singing in classes. On his return he started similar classes in England, and in 1841 began to teach schoolmasters at Exeter Hall in the Strand, London, demonstrating successfully that everyone might learn to sing – a completely new notion at the time. Hullah's was the first attempt in England to spread a general knowledge of music, but his system ultimately gave way to Curwen's tonic sol-fa.

Exeter Hall was home to the Sacred Harmonic Society from 1834 to 1880. In the early years of the Society's life there were so few amateur performers available in London that singers were brought from Yorkshire and Lancashire to strengthen the chorus, and were found employment in the capital. By 1842 professional members of the Sacred Harmonic Society were beginning to resent the influx of amateurs, and the *Musical World* took up their cause when singers from Exeter Hall were engaged to perform at the Worcester Festival:

> **Worcester Festival.**   We promised to afford the Exeter Hall amateurs the advantage of as much notoriety as we could procure for them – the strictures we have from time to time felt it our duty to publish, on the unfairness of unprofessional persons supplanting artists in their legitimate engagements, have had the double effect of considerably reducing their numbers, and inducing every possible means of disguise, change of name, and incognito – we, however, have the pleasure to gratify the following gentlemen, to whom this public announcement will, doubtless, prove more satisfactory than the several fees of six pounds each, suborned by them from the pockets of the regular chorus singers, for filling, but certainly not supplying their places: – Mr. H. Withers, pastry cook, Blackfriar's Road – Mr. T. Carmichael, coal clerk – Mr. A. Carmichael, coal clerk – Mr. W. Pocock, stock broker – Mr. J. Taylor, plumber, Clement's Lane – Mr. W. Cowell, tailor and draper – Mr. Robert Bowley, boot maker to the Duke of Cambridge, Charing Cross – Mr. J. Windsor, oil and colourman – Mr. Benjamin Ward, retired painter and glazier – Mr. H. Paine, coach trimmer – Mr. H. Muggeridge, custom house clerk. We shall hope to extend this list in our next.[25]

By 1830 the band and chorus at Exeter Hall had increased to 700 and the Society had built up a high reputation for the performance of complete oratorios, especially those by Handel and Mendelssohn.

The tradition of importing additional singers had, as we have seen, been established at Three Choirs long before the foundation of the Sacred Harmonic Society in 1832. By 1850 the advertisements for the Gloucester Festival could boast proudly and in heavy type that the 'Instrumental Band and Chorus' comprised 'nearly three hundred performers, selected with care from the Orchestra of the Philharmonic, and from the Choral Societies and Choirs of Exeter Hall, Bristol, Norwich, Windsor, Worcester, Hereford, etc.'[26] During the second half of the century the visiting choral singers came from many

---

[25] *MW* 1842, p. 310.

[26] The quotation is from posters of the time. See also Barbara Young, *In Our Dreaming and Singing* (Logaston Press, 2000), for a detailed study of the evolution of the Festival Chorus.

other towns and cities, including Leeds, Bradford, Liverpool, Huddersfield, Cheltenham and Birmingham.

The Crystal Palace, built in Hyde Park to house the Great Exhibition of 1851, became a venue for Sacred Harmonic Society performances of Handel's oratorios in 1857 and 1858. In the following year, 1859, the centenary of Handel's death was marked by a festival at the Crystal Palace. At each performance the choir exceeded 2,700 and the orchestra 450. So popular were these large-scale productions that the Handel Festivals became a triennial event. An era of monster oratorio performances had arrived; so much so that by the 1880s, the peak of the Handel Festivals' popular appeal, the chorus numbered 4,000 and the orchestra 500.

Three Choirs performances of *Messiah* never reached the excesses of scale which so delighted Victorian audiences at the Crystal Palace; lack of space in the cathedrals would, in any case, have limited the numbers of choir and orchestra to a smaller army. Nonetheless, the same version of the oratorio, reinforced by Mozart's 'additional accompaniments', was demanded by provincial festival audiences. Handel was distorted for mass effect. As Winton Dean has pointed out, 'the Victorians worshipped Handel; they did not know him'.[27]

Visiting choral singers continued to swell the ranks of the Three Choirs until the closing years of the nineteenth century. Many of these, along with professional orchestral players from London, travelled the circuit of major music festivals each year – a system which in 1872 brought them very close to disaster when the passenger train in which they were travelling from Worcester to the Norwich Festival collided with a luggage train. By good fortune, the only casualties were musical instruments, destroyed in the crash; the performers, including leading soloists, escaped with nothing worse than bruises and shock.

Until 1864 the custom at Three Choirs was for the organist of the host cathedral to act as Festival conductor, for one of the visiting organists to play the piano, and for the other to play the organ. For at least the first thirty years of the century the word 'conductor' had a very different meaning from that understood today. In purely orchestral works the direction of the orchestra was the responsibility of the principal violinist, while another musician 'at the pianoforte', with a full score before him, played or made gestures as necessary. In choral works the role of the 'conductor' was that of beating time and indicating entries with a roll of paper – and a sketch of William Mutlow, drawn by Maria Malibran in 1829, shows him doing just that (see Plate 23).

The change to modern conducting practice began in 1820 when Louis Spohr visited England to take part in a season of Philharmonic concerts. While rehearsing a manuscript symphony of his own, billed in the programme to be 'Conducted by the Composer', Spohr, instead of taking his place 'at the pianoforte', carried a music desk to the front of the orchestra, drew a baton from his pocket and began to direct the players in the manner already gaining popularity in Germany. When Mendelssohn conducted in London in 1829 he too used a baton. The old method gradually gave way to the new.

But the new method was a severe trial for provincial organists whose training came from their predecessors, who lacked any experience of directing

[27] Winton Dean, *Handel's Dramatic Oratorios and Masques* (OUP, 1959).

professional players and singers, and who were required to don an uncomfortable mantle for only one week in every three years. Add to these difficulties the severe lack of rehearsal time available to the conductor, who was unable to drill his resident and visiting forces together until the day before the Festival, and it would be surprising if the invariable outcome had been a polished performance. Only the perennial repetition of *Messiah* and, later, *Elijah* engendered confidence through familiarity. 'Novelties' could present a worrying challenge.

While the gentlemen of the local press were more often than not enthusiastic about Three Choirs performances, it was inevitable that London critics, accustomed to the panache of professional conductors such as Joseph Surman and Sir Michael Costa, should make unfavourable comparisons and question the contribution of Three Choirs to the cause of art. What *is* surprising is how frequently, in spite of daunting obstacles, the cathedral organists of the nineteenth century *did* succeed in drawing their disparate forces together to achieve highly creditable results.

The tenure of William Mutlow at Gloucester spanned half a century and the reigns of George III, George IV and William IV. Throughout these many years he was much loved as a kindly, good-tempered and eccentric character with a zest for living and a pointed disregard for the use of the King's English. Something of the waggish Mutlow can be gauged from the following anecdote recorded by the Gloucester historian and attorney George Worrall Counsell (1758–1843), referring to an incident which took place in 1824:

Gloucester Pedestrianisms

On Saturday evening last a most extraordinary feat of pedestrianism was exhibited at the Mitre in this City by two very singular personages. Mr Mutlow, the fat Organist of our Cathedral, 64 years of age, five feet in height and four feet in circumference, challenged an old gentleman of this City of the name of Rogers who is in his 70th year, who has been for a long time past a martyr to the gout, subject to flatulence and bending under the weight of age and infirmities, (and who) agreed to run for a wager ten times round the landlord's garden, a distance of 500 yards.

The Organist ... had unfortunately that day partaken of a most splendid dinner and an extra quantity of wine to which he super-added two pints of Goodwin's ale. His friends were therefore apprehensive of his falling down with his load during the race, in which case he would most likely have burst asunder, notwithstanding which he appeared quite in glee, being screwed up to Concert pitch and, jumping up like the jack of a harpsichord, went off at (speed) ... but the old gentleman, his antagonist, being perfectly sober, shook off the gout and appeared to gain strength at every round, whilst the Organist's bellows were soon out of wind and, being a bar behind, he lost his time, began to shake, was out of tune and, looking like a flat between two naturals and his pipes being nearly choked, came to a finale, and his opponent then after a few eructations took the lead, went forwards *con spirito* and, although he suffered so much from an accumulation of wind as the Organist did for want of it, he finally won the bet.[28]

---

[28] Document now deposited in the Gloucestershire Archives.

A behind-the-scenes view on the Festival of 1826 is given in a letter from Mutlow to 'Mr. Hedgley, 20 Castle Street, Pimlico, London.' (Hedgley was a well-known music copyist and librarian.) It was published in the *Musical Times* of October 1901:

Dear Sir,

Respecting Mr. Bond, I am sorry to say I cannot comply with his terms. I have Dragonetti, Philpots, and Chattaway. If Mr. Bond will come for Twelve Guineas, I shall be glad to see him, if not I shall see for one on less terms. Harper is engaged. I have his answer saying he will come – 25 guineas. I will thank you to see him. I cannot take three of the Lindleys and Marshall of Warwick. Respecting the London chorus singers, my terms are eight guineas each, and if either of the following should object to the terms, you must engage others in their room – Taylor, Lewis, Tett, Hennies, Birt, Doane, Buggins, and Fisher. Say nothing to Doane on the subject.

Have you the vocal principals and chorus parts of the new words of the Creation? I want but 4 *st*, 4 *2d*, 3 [?] violas, 4 violoncs. Of anything you may send with the flutes, oboes, etc., will you send two cantos and two tenors of 'He sent a thick darkness'?

I wish you would spend a week with me before the Meeting – you would relieve my mind very much.

I am, yours truly,
W. MUTLOW
Gloucester, August 20, 1826

Mutlow's last Music Meeting was that of 1829. After his death on 1 January 1832, in his seventy-second year, Counsell wrote of him, 'it may with truth be asserted, that few men died more sincerely regretted'.[29]

The stability afforded to Gloucester by Mutlow was not enjoyed by Hereford until 1835. Charles Dare made no significant contribution to the Festival, was dismissed his post due to 'bibulous tendencies',[30] and died in 1820. His successor, Aaron Hayter (appointed in 1818), also disgraced himself, and was dismissed after only two years in post, during which he was the conductor at the Music Meeting of 1819. After serving as Organist of the Collegiate Church of Brecon for fifteen years, he emigrated to the United States. There he became organist of the most important churches in New York and Boston, and was much esteemed.

John Clarke-Whitfeld was already fifty years old when he relieved Hayter at Hereford in 1820. Born in Gloucester on 13 December 1770, John Clarke assumed the additional surname of Whitfeld in 1814 on the death of his maternal uncle, H. F. Whitfeld, in anticipation of receiving an inheritance. Unfortunately his only gain was a name; the inheritance never materialised.

---

[29] *Gloucester Journal*, 7 January 1832.

[30] Mr. Gretton, 'Memories Hark Back', reproduced in Watkins Shaw, *The Organists and Organs of Hereford Cathedral* (Hereford Cathedral, 1988).

Clarke-Whitfeld was a composer as well as an organist. He presented two of his own oratorios at the Hereford Music Meetings: *The Crucifixion* in 1822 and *The Resurrection* in 1825. Although neither work was successful, Clarke-Whitfeld had set the precedent which would form a pattern later in the century of cathedral organists composing sacred works specifically for Three Choirs performance.

Soon after his arrival at Hereford, Clarke-Whitfeld had been dogged by ill health. He tendered his resignation in April 1823 but withdrew it in June. In 1832 the Chapter were reluctantly obliged to relieve him of his responsibilities as a result of an attack of paralysis, and he died, aged sixty-five, on 22 February 1836.

In October 1832 the ailing Clarke-Whitfeld was replaced by a young man of a very different stamp. Samuel Sebastian Wesley (1810–1876), twenty-two years old when he came to Hereford, had already held various organist posts in London during the previous six years as well as gaining valuable experience of secular music-making in the capital. The illegitimate son of the composer Samuel Wesley (1766–1837), Samuel Sebastian's grandfather was the hymn-writer Charles Wesley (1707–1788), and his great-uncle was the religious reformer and founder of Methodism, John Wesley (1703–1791). Samuel Sebastian soon set his sights on reform too: reform of the abysmal state into which cathedral music had slumped in the nineteenth century.

Wesley remained at Hereford for only three years (1832–5). After London he found provincial life lonely and unrewarding. His income was insufficient for his needs, forcing him to take on significant teaching commitments. He was already a superlative organist whose ambition was to devote his life to composition, and at Hereford he completed his famous anthem *The Wilderness*. But an organist at that time depended upon the Church for his livelihood – the same Church whose low musical standards he was bravely prepared to attack; turbulence lay ahead.

At the 'away' Music Meetings of 1833(w) and 1835(G), Wesley took his place at the pianoforte. But in 1834 the Meeting at Hereford was under his direction. The programme included three pieces by the conductor: a *Sanctus*, a sacred song entitled *Abraham's Offering*, and a manuscript overture. Also in 1834 a major Three Choirs innovation, aiming to make the Meeting more attractive, was announced in the programme:

> in furtherance of this view, as well as in compliance with scruples to which [the Stewards] willingly defer, they have concurred with the Dean and Chapter in a determination to transfer the scene of the musical performances from the choir to the nave of the Cathedral, where the more ample accommodation for the auditory, the impressive character of the architecture, and the improved sphere for the undulation of harmonious sounds, will combine to augment that unspeakable fascination which is the never-failing effect of the grand compositions selected for the occasion.[31]

Surely it must have been Wesley, with his sure ear for the diagnosis of ills in the performance of cathedral music, who suggested to the Stewards how 'the undulation of harmonious sounds' should best be heard.

[31] *Annals* 1895, p. 123.

Wesley resigned his post at Hereford in September 1835, and his next contribution to Three Choirs followed after an interval of full thirty years: years spent in turn at Exeter Cathedral, Leeds Parish Church and Winchester Cathedral; years too in which his finest music was composed; but years in which he was frequently dispirited in searching for increased discipline and excellence in the choral services of the Church of England by the lack of understanding shown by a seemingly indifferent clergy. In 1865 Wesley was appointed Organist and Master of the Choristers of Gloucester Cathedral, where he remained until his death.

Following Wesley's resignation, the Hereford Chapter appointed John Hunt to take his place. He too was a young man – only twenty-eight years old when he took up his post on 1 October 1835. Hunt had been brought up as a chorister and articled pupil at Salisbury, moving to Lichfield, where he was a vicar choral, in 1827. At his first Music Meeting at Hereford, Hunt impressed not only as a conductor but also as a singer:

> Mr. Hunt, the organist of the cathedral and conductor of the festival, possesses a sweet counter-tenor voice; and which appears to be a real chest voice – not often the quality of an alto. It is unfortunately not always audible; but when heard, the effect is very agreeable. Moreover the style is chaste and correct. We heard him to the best advantage in the leading solo to the last chorus of the *Dettingen*, 'Lord in thee have I trusted'.[32]

Considerable difficulty had been experienced in obtaining Stewards for the 1837(H) Meeting. 'On 26th June an advertisement appeared in the Hereford newspapers stating that the Stewards of the preceding Hereford Meeting had made every effort to obtain successors, but had only procured the names of three gentlemen who were willing to act.'[33] The 1834 Meeting had made a loss of £933 8s. 0d. as a result of Wesley's decision to include only a selection from *Messiah* instead of the complete work. Within four weeks sufficient Stewards had been found, but meanwhile Hunt had persuaded the soloists to appear for reduced fees. The Stewards were so grateful that they presented him 'with some articles of plate, as an acknowledgement of his zeal and exertions on behalf of the Meeting'.[34]

During Hunt's time as Organist, the fabric of Hereford Cathedral once more gave cause for concern. In 1841, at the request of Bishop Musgrave, a survey was carried out. The piers of the central tower were found to be in a dangerous state, and the eastern gable of the Lady Chapel was about to collapse. Restoration and repair, superintended by Dean Merewether (S. S. Wesley's brother-in-law) and his successor Dean Dawes, continued for over twenty years, but John Hunt did not live to see the outcome. He died, aged thirty-five, on 17 November 1842 after having fallen over a dinner wagon laden with plates and glasses, which had been left in a dark part of the cloisters after an audit dinner. Three days later his

---

adopted nephew, a chorister, died from the shock of his uncle's death and was buried in the same grave.[35]

At Worcester the early years of the nineteenth century were marked by three fairly rapid changes in the incumbent of the organ loft. Thomas Pitt resigned in 1806 and was relieved by Jeremiah Clarke (not to be confused with the more famous composer of the same name who committed suicide in 1707). Clarke had been a chorister at Worcester, was a noted violinist, and first played at Three Choirs in 1800(W) as principal second violin, a position which he filled at other national festivals also. Following his death in 1807, Clarke was replaced by William Kenge. Clarke conducted only one Music Meeting, 1806, and Kenge two, 1809 and 1812. Long-term stability was then achieved by the appointment of Charles Clarke in 1813.

Clarke was born in Worcester in December 1795 and was a chorister at the cathedral. He was appointed Organist of Durham Cathedral when still only sixteen years old but resigned that post in 1813 in order to return to Worcester to take over from Kenge, and there he remained until his death on 28 April 1844.

A royal visit made to the Worcester Music Meeting of 1830 by the Duchess of Kent and her twelve-year-old daughter, Princess Victoria, must surely have been a highlight of Charles Clarke's career. George IV had died in June 1830, and was succeeded by the 'sailor king', William IV, who, alone among George IV's six brothers, enjoyed a measure of popularity with the public. Victoria's father, the Duke of Kent, was a soldier – hated by the army for his love of severe punishments, and hated by George IV for his hypocrisy and intrigues. Her mother was a princess of Leiningen.

Excitement mounted during the week preceding the Music Meeting, as first one and then another royal or noble guest arrived to take up their quarters in Malvern:

> There has been a great influx of rank and fashion at Malvern during the week. The Duchess de Berri and suite arrived there yesterday; after visiting St. Ann's Well, the Church, and Library, her Royal Highness partook of refreshments at the Foley Arms, and continued her route to this city. Her Royal Highness arrived last evening at the Hop Pole Inn, where she slept, and proceeded, at an early hour, this morning, to Birmingham. The Marchioness of Bute and family are amongst the recent arrivals; the Marquess is shortly expected, and likewise Sir Robt. Peel, on a visit to his brother, Colonel Peel, who has been for some time past residing at this delightful spot.
>
>   Directions have been received at the Foley Arms for apartments to be prepared for the reception of Prince Leopold, whose arrival is daily looked for. It is expected that her Royal Highness the Duchess of Kent will prolong her stay until the month of October, Earl Beauchamp will display

---

[35] See Shaw, *Three Choirs Festival*, p. 23; and John E. West, *Cathedral Organists Past and Present* (Novello, 1899), p. 43, updated as Watkins Shaw, *The Succession of Organists of the Chapel Royal and the Cathedrals of England and Wales from c. 1538* (OUP, 1991).

his accustomed hospitality by entertaining the Princess Esterhazy and a host of fashionables during the ensuing week, at his seat at Madresfield.[36]

On Tuesday 14 September the royal visitors arrived in Worcester:

> The Mayor and Corporation on receiving an intimation of the intended visit, eagerly embraced the opportunity of evincing that loyalty and attachment to the Royal Family, for which this city has at all times been so eminently conspicuous; and preparations were accordingly ordered, on an extensive scale, for the suitable reception of the illustrious visitors at the Town Hall.[37]

Their efforts and expense were quite wasted. On arrival in the city the Duchess of Kent announced that she wished to avoid a public reception, and the Body Corporate was asked to attend an audience at the deanery instead. But the people of Worcester saw their future queen as she drove by in an open landau:

> During their progress through different parts of the city they proceeded at a slow pace, with the laudable view of gratifying the eager desire of the assembled populace to approach the carriage – a condescension which was duly appreciated; indeed, the courteous demeanour of their Royal Highnesses won the affections of all classes. The Princess ... possesses a most intelligent and interesting countenance, and displays at this early age intellectual powers of no ordinary kind. The incessant care with which these powers are cultivated, and the maternal solicitude with which the best feelings of the heart are fostered, are clearly perceptible, and open a bright prospect for the future. A feeling of deep interest is naturally excited for the welfare of this Princess who will, in all human probability, one day rule over the destinies of this country.[38]

After more than a century under the first four Georges there must have been many fingers crossed for 'a bright prospect'!

The arrangements in the cathedral and chapter house were elaborate and carefully planned:

> As the Duchess of Kent and the Princess Victoria would necessarily be the principal objects of attraction, the seats prepared for them are so situated and so much elevated, that their Royal Highnesses are visible from almost every part of the Church: they occupy that space which is between Prince Arthur's Chapel, and the doorway into the south aisle of the choir; the whole compartment is covered with scarlet cloth; two antique chairs are provided for the Duchess and her interesting daughter; the cushions were those used by the revered George III, and his Consort; they have been recently found. The royal arms are in the centre, richly emblazoned in gold. The approach to the seats is from the garden of the Deanery; a staircase

---

[36] *Worcester Herald*, 10 September 1830.

[37] Ibid.

[38] Ibid.

is erected up to a window in the Dean's Chapel; this window being taken out, forms an entrance to a raised platform which leads directly to the seats, so that their Royal Highnesses and suite have an opportunity of passing into the choir without interruption. The Chancel Gallery extends from the back of the altar to the east window, and is capable of accommodating 800 persons; it is a beautiful piece of carpentry; when filled with company, the effect is singularly fine; two other galleries extend over portions of the north and south aisles. In the Chapter Room (which is appropriated to the entertainment of the Nobility and Gentry invited by the Bishop of Rochester and Lady Sarah Murray) the arrangements are equally good. Round this fine apartment tables are laid with convenient intervals, and round the column in the centre there is a table for the Duchess and the Princess and those distinguished individuals who may accompany them. Their Royal Highnesses and suite enter the Chapter Room from the Deanery, one of the windows of which is taken out, and a covered way made to one of the Chapter Room windows, whence a staircase descends into the apartment.

TUESDAY, SEPT. 14 – At an early hour this morning, persons began to assemble about the Cathedral, and before the hour of opening the doors (half past nine), a considerable crowd was waiting for admission; by half past ten there was scarcely a place vacant, though the accommodation was so ample. Their Royal Highnesses the Duchess of Kent and the Princess Victoria arrived with their suite at twenty minutes before eleven at the Deanery, where they were received by the Bishop of Rochester and Lady Sarah Murray; they soon after passed into the Cathedral. Our venerable Diocesan conducted the Duchess of Kent, and the Bishop of Rochester led the interesting Princess Victoria. Both their Lordships wore their robes. A long train of Nobility occupied seats near the Royal Highnesses, towards whom every eye was directed. At this moment the Church presented an appearance equally striking and beautiful; the magnificent chancel gallery was filled in every part.[39]

During the Opening Service, while the choir was singing 'When thou had'st overcome the sharpness of death', the cathedral grew dim; a thunderstorm blackened the sky outside, 'and the rolling peals mingling their awful sounds with the music, added to the solemnity of the general effect'.[40]

In contrast, a short distance away at Worcester County Gaol the same thunderstorm underlined the despair of William Haydon, George Bromfield and Richard Ray, awaiting transportation for seven years; and of Joseph Fletcher, James Rastall, John Reynolds and William Workman, sentenced to transportation for life. All seven men were removed to a ship at Chatham the next day.

[39] *Worcester Herald*, 15 September 1830.
[40] Ibid.

A FTER William Mutlow's death in 1832 his place at Gloucester was taken by John Amott, a pupil of Mutlow, who, from 1820, had been Organist of the Abbey Church, Shrewsbury. Amott seems not to have been a very distinguished musician: one of his old choristers told Sir Herbert Brewer that his ability as an organist was:

> of an elementary character. The pedals were rarely used, and when he did play on them he would allow the choristers, as a special favour, to go to the organ loft to see how it was done. As a rule a board was placed over the pedals on which his feet rested.[41]

To Amott and his contemporaries fell the task of adapting to the new method of conducting with a baton at the Festivals. Even after a quarter of a century of experience, the Gloucester Organist still clearly lacked an adequate technique. In a review of the 1856 Gloucester Festival, the music critic of the *City Press* put his finger on the causes for less than satisfactory performances at Three Choirs:

> The execution of the works at these festivals has not kept pace altogether with musical advancement in other places. It is true that the *Messiah* and *Elijah* were better performed than on previous occasions, but on the whole, with the materials of principals, chorus, and band, engaged for the four morning performances in the Cathedral and the three evening concerts in the Shire-hall, greater precision, more delicacy, and a finer *ensemble* ought to have been secured. Where the deficiency lies is patent to everybody. So long as the conductor's baton at these festivals remains in the hands of the inexperienced local organist, so long must there be mishaps, mistakes, and contrarieties. It is not reasonable to expect that, once in three years, a provincial professor, however respectable his talents may be, can bring together a mixed body of choralists and instrumentalists, and a cosmopolitan phalanx of leading singers, and with one rehearsal insure a steady and finished interpretation of most intricate oratorios, and of selections from the music of operatic masters and concert composers of every school ... How is it, that when the orchestra, with Sainton and Blagrove as leaders, and conductors too, thought proper to run away from the 'traditional' beat, the overtures and symphonies went so briskly, as in the *Zauberflöte*, *Anacreaon* and *Der Freischütz*, and in Haydn's sparkling No. 8 Symphony? But when the *baton* of the conductor and the bow of the *chef-d'attaque* came into collision, as in the accompaniments to many of the vocal pieces, what a 'confusion worse confounded' ensued! As instances, let Mendelssohn's *Lorely* finale, and Beethoven's 'Crown ye the altars,' from the *Ruins of Athens*, be cited. What a 'gachis' were the accompaniments to 'Casta Diva,' sung by Viardot, and 'Il segreto,' sung by Alboni. What must foreign amateurs have thought of these exhibitions at a great English musical festival – a time-honoured institution fast approaching to an existence of a century and a half?

In 1856 the Stewards paid Amott £130 for his services, plus 20 guineas travelling expenses, £5 for the special instruction of choristers, and six free tickets

---

[41] Herbert Brewer, *Memories of Choirs and Cloisters* (Bodley Head, 1931).

for each performance. At the next Gloucester Festival, in 1859, his terms were unchanged except that the allowance of free tickets was reduced to two – 'For Mr and Mrs Amott only'![42] Amott's standing with the critics was unchanged too. Describing how the position of the organ in the Gloucester Shire Hall prevented members of the audience sitting at its side from getting a good view of the conductor, the critic of the *Musical World* added: 'Not that the latter fact need be such a matter of regret, as far as the gentleman who wields the baton at Gloucester is concerned.'[43]

In fairness to Amott it must be said that what he lacked as a musical director he more than made up for in his aims for the development of the Festival. At his first Music Meeting in 1832 he reintroduced 'the full band of trombones' which had been a feature of the Handel commemoration of 1784. The expansion of choral and orchestral forces at Gloucester from 1835 must have resulted from Amott's initiative. And above all, we owe a debt of gratitude to him for continuing the *Annals* of the Three Choirs, from the point at which Lysons had left them in 1811, to the year before his death, 1864.

Happily, at Amott's last Festival as conductor (1862(G)) providence granted him a real success. Even though three of the oratorios were performed without any rehearsal at all, the critics of the national and musical press were united in their praise for his direction of *Elijah*. Amott was able to reproduce proudly and in full in the *Annals* a glowing report which appeared in *The Times*, and he must have been delighted with what he read in the *Musical World*:

> We can with … justice make the *amende* to Mr. Amott, for the really admirable manner in which he directed his forces in *Elijah* … Not only were the respective times correctly taken throughout, Mr. Amott merely adopting the medium course, and neither following the example (of which we have such frequent instance in London) of accelerating the speed, with the mistaken notion of increased brilliancy, nor of dragging the time, as has been generally the case with the conductors of the festivals of the [three] choirs. Taken altogether, it is hardly too much to say that this was one of the most unexceptionable performances of *Elijah* ever heard.[44]

Amott was the last to live in the Gloucester Organist's house within the Palace Garden by the Infirmary arches (demolished in the 1860s), and the first to occupy what has since 1861 been designated the Organist's residence in Miller's Green. He died there on 3 February 1865.

Twelve days later a General Meeting of the Stewards was called at which the secretary read out a letter from W. P. Price Esq., who was unable to attend. In it he suggested 'the present time would be a favourable opportunity to apply to the Dean and Chapter for permission, in future, to employ a London Conductor, instead of the Organist, for the time being, of the Cathedral'.[45] Faced with such

---

[42] Gloucester Festival Minute Book, 1856 and 1859. Gloucester Cathedral Archives and Library.

[43] *MW* 1859, p. 612.

[44] *MW* 1862, p. 582.

[45] Gloucester Festival Minute Book, 1865. Gloucester Cathedral Archives and Library.

an important decision, the Dean and Chapter determined to seek the advice of England's most eminent cathedral organist, Samuel Sebastian Wesley. To their astonishment and pleasure Wesley offered to take the Gloucester post himself and, even though they must surely have known that the long-suffering Winchester Chapter had asked him to resign as a result of neglect of duty, his offer was gratefully accepted.

Wesley was fifty-five years old when he arrived in Gloucester and, although only middle-aged, had suffered from ill health for many years; he was lame, having broken a leg badly while crossing a stile in 1847, and was embittered by his long and discouraging experience of cathedral life.

In spite of concern about the safety of the Great West Window, Wesley persuaded the Stewards that the orchestra should be relocated at the west end of the cathedral for his first Festival – a layout which had been introduced successfully at Hereford in the previous year. This necessitated the hire of an organ from Henry Willis. The arrangements proved far more expensive than anticipated and, although receipts were larger than any since 1853, at a General Meeting of the Stewards on 11 October 1865 it was resolved that:

> The conductor should be kept in due subordination to the Stewards. This important point was only secured after a series of struggles which threatened more than once to impede the Festival and the Stewards should be careful now not to give the staff out of their own hands. It was thought by more than one that too much was left to the discretion of the Conductor at the last Festival, e.g. in the engagement of the principals, the alteration of the position of the orchestra, involving the expense of hiring a special organ, etc. etc., and thus contravening the principle of scrupulously avoiding all unnecessary outlay.[46]

To be fair to Wesley, in the engagement of the principals he had *tried* to economise. The finest British tenor of the day, John Sims Reeves, had asked for a fee of £315, would not accept less, and so was not engaged. Another Festival favourite, the contralto Charlotte Sainton-Dolby, was also dropped, as was her husband, the violinist Prosper Sainton, who often led the evening concerts. Unfortunately, this was precisely the wrong area in which to try to save money. The substitute tenor, Herr Gunz, was a German who had never before sung in English and who proved totally inadequate for the position of a principal. Two young ladies engaged to replace Sainton-Dolby, the Misses Wilkinson and Elton, were unequal to the task. The *Queen* magazine, acknowledging that the Festival had been a commercial success, summed up its artistic achievement:

> With respect to the receipts, it is expected that the stewards will be relieved from any liability, although the 'penny wise and pound foolish' system of making the engagements will tell more heavily than was anticipated, by the getting rid of Sims Reeves, M. Sainton and Madame Sainton-Dolby. The financial success is cited by the superficial and interested as an approval on the part of the public of the musical arrangements. A greater fallacy cannot exist. If the argument of receipts be worth anything, it would be to assert

[46] Ibid.

that let the engagements be ever so bad, the execution ever so indifferent, success must attend these meetings from extraneous causes, such as the splendid sermon preached by the Rev. Canon Kennaway, the glorious weather of the week, and the determination of the county not to submit to the clerical intolerance. As regards public opinion of the week's musical doings, how is it to be gathered? If you read the local organs here, there never was such a conductor as Dr. Wesley, nor such perfect performances. If you look at the reports supplied by 'manifold' copy by one single reporter to the *Morning Post*, *Daily News*, *Advertiser*, and *Star*, although not quite up to the provincial puffery, success sanctifies the musical *mistake*. Indeed, the *Times*, cautious as it is with respect to Dr. Wesley's conducting and his programme, thinks it may fairly point to the result to whitewash him. The *Morning Herald* and *Morning Advertiser*, and some of our weekly contemporaries, are more outspoken; they state, without equivocation or qualification, that the programmes, the performances, and the conductor, were altogether a complete mistake; in other words, that the festival was artistically a failure. Now, any impartial person, whose opinion is entitled to the smallest consideration as a critic, whether professor or amateur, will endorse the statement as perfectly accurate, that the selections were never worse conducted, that the order of their execution displayed a total want of judgment as to light and shade, and that the engagements of the chief artists were not judicious or up to the mark.

All was not quite so black as painted by the *Queen*. In his programming of the evening concerts Wesley had initiated an important change of emphasis from popular and often trivial miscellanies towards the performance of more serious and complete major works. The real problem was less with the selection of works than with their execution – especially when Wesley took up the baton.

In 1865 the pianist Arabella Goddard was engaged to play in Beethoven's *Fantasia*, op. 80 (the 'Choral Fantasy'), at the first evening concert, and Mendelssohn's Concerto in G minor at the second. Reviewing both concerts, the critic of the *Morning Herald* reported on the Beethoven that:

> the chorus was too numerous for the band, and worse than that, did not know their parts. The conductor [Wesley] whose affection for his score is so great that he can never take his eyes off the copy, was not the general who by a glance of his eye could call together dispersed troops. It was an awful *gachis* … How disheartening for a pianiste to perform the obbligato of the fantasia under such circumstances may be conceived.

On the following evening 'the conductor resigned his baton, and permitted Mr. Henry Blagrove [the Leader] to conduct with his violin bow'.[47] Joseph Bennett was present:

> The music went on well enough in such accustomed hands as those of the pianist and the 'leader', the Doctor's beat being little regarded – a circumstance which did not appear to trouble him. Gradually Wesley's face lightened and beamed. The music having hold of him, presently took entire

---

[47] *Morning Herald*, 1 September 1865.

possession. He swayed from side to side; he put down the baton, treated himself to a pinch of snuff with an air of exquisite enjoyment, and then sat motionless, listening. Meanwhile Blagrove conducted with his violin-bow.[48]

By the end of Wesley's first Festival the Gloucester Stewards were probably beginning to lament the passing of even the unremarkable Amott. At least he, unlike his successor, had not been encumbered by temperamental genius, and his ability as a conductor was hardly any worse. Brewer tells us that:

> Wesley was essentially an organist and composer and not a choir trainer or conductor. In fact, towards the end of his time the training of the choristers was left in the hands of one of the lay clerks. When a full rehearsal of the choir took place the men made no attempt to sing out but just whispered their parts.[49]

In 1866, even though acknowledged as the finest organist and the greatest composer of church music in the country, Wesley was not invited to compose anything for the Worcester Festival. On the eve of the Festival he withdrew, suggesting to the Committee that his place at the organ should be taken by Hamilton Clarke of Queen's College, Oxford:

> Mr. Townshend Smith, of Hereford, was again at the organ, the Festival Committee having declined the substitute proposed by Dr. S. S. Wesley, of Gloucester, whose absence is being accounted for in all sorts of ways, not one of which, however, approximates to the truth. We have reason to believe that the learned Doctor is busily engaged in bringing through the press his long-expected great Psalmody book – *The European Psalmist* – which at present engrosses his exclusive attention ... From another point of view the absence of so eminent a professor is, perhaps, less significant. Not a single composition of his was put down in the programme; nor was he asked to play an organ voluntary ... Whether Dr. Wesley felt piqued, it is impossible for us to know.[50]

To add insult to injury, the Organist of St Paul's Cathedral, John Goss, *was* invited to compose an anthem for the 1866 Festival. It would be difficult to defend Wesley's action, but honour was restored at Hereford in 1867. The first performance in the cathedral included Wesley's anthem *Ascribe unto the Lord*, conducted by the composer.

As Festival conductor Wesley was characteristically eccentric. During Beethoven's Mass in C in 1868(G):

> an unfortunate breakdown at the commencement of the Kyrie, owing to the uncertainty of the tempo adopted, created an uneasy feeling that more disasters were in store and, by the time Miss Edith Wynne came in with her solo, hopeless confusion reigned supreme, so that the movement came to a sudden collapse, and was recommenced.[51]

[48] Bennett, *Forty Years of Music*, p. 35.
[49] Brewer, *Memories*.
[50] *MW* 1866, p. 599.
[51] *Annals* 1895, p. 239.

The *Musical World* decided that the week's performances included 'points of excellence which not even Dr. Wesley could spoil'.[52] Once again, Joseph Bennett had been in the audience:

> On the Saturday of the Festival week at Gloucester (1868), all the music being ended, and all who helped to make it at rest from their labours, myself and a friend ventured upon a visit to the conductor-organist, and found him at home in the old house which was once the residence of Robert Raikes. After some desultory chat, the Doctor was begged to go into the cathedral and play to us anything he pleased. It was a bold request, for the poor man must have been suffering more or less from fatigue. He protested that he could not play if he would, and that he would not if he could; but the chance of hearing him was too good to be lost, and we pressed him hard. In the end, and perhaps thinking that assent was the quickest way to get rid of us, he agreed to go into the cathedral, sent for the blowers, flung off his slippers, put on a pair of thin boots, and led the way, keys in hand. 'Mind,' he said, 'you are not to come up into the gallery with me. You are to go and sit on the steps leading to the altar rails, and wait there until I have finished.' We took up our positions forthwith, but as he turned to the foot of the gallery stairs, the Doctor cried out: 'Mind, I can't play; haven't touched the organ for months, and the instrument is in a very bad state.' With this damper upon our expectations, Wesley began his display. There was a great deal of noise with the stops – ungainly things, as long as a man's forearm – and the Doctor started upon one of Bach's fugues. He made a bad beginning, stopped and shouted to us: 'I told you I couldn't play!' 'Never mind, Doctor, go on.' Another attempt ended much as did the first, after which we called out: 'Extemporise, Doctor.' We could hear him grumbling, but in a minute or two he began, and soon got into the mood. His performance was lengthy, but quite magnificent. My companion had heard Mendelssohn extemporise, and even he, with such a comparison to make, expressed his astonishment at the Doctor's wonderful resources. The organ became silent after a fugal climax, and we waited for more. We waited long, so long that we feared something had happened. What had happened was this: The Doctor had crept behind the front of the gallery, stooping so that he was not visible below; then silently descended the stairs, and, giving word to the blowers, left the cathedral. We called again and again, and there was no reply. We returned to the organist's house, and found our runaway once more in his slippers, and chuckling over the little joke he had played upon us. But for the sake of that extemporaneous performance, we would have put up with twenty jokes.[53]

The arrival of Wesley at Gloucester in 1865 broke up a triad of Three Choirs conductors who had worked together for over a decade: John Amott, George Townshend Smith and William Done.

---

[52] *MW* 1868, p. 645.

[53] Bennett, *Forty Years of Music.*

Townshend Smith was born at Windsor on 14 November 1813, the son of Edward Smith, a lay clerk of St George's Chapel, Windsor, where he became a chorister under Highmore Skeats. Afterwards he studied under Samuel Wesley senior. Before he was chosen as Organist of Hereford on 5 January 1843, Townshend Smith was Organist of the Old Parish Church, Eastbourne, and of St Margaret's, King's Lynn.

Of the three contemporaries, Townshend Smith seems to have been the most energetic and able in the cause of Three Choirs. Of his first Festival, in 1843, the *Musical World* was pleased to report that:

> As a *whole*, we never witnessed a meeting go off more successfully, and praise, well deserved, sits brightly upon the conductor, Mr. Townshend Smith, who in this, his first essay as conductor of the Triennial Festival in this city, has earned the applause of every well-wisher to the meeting, as well as the true lover of sterling music.[54]

Townshend Smith not only conducted at Three Choirs but also acted as Festival secretary – a prodigious double burden. On several occasions during his thirty-four years in office the Hereford Festival was in danger of winding up due to lack of financial support. The zealous exertions of Townshend Smith were always able to save the day. Unlike Amott, who never enjoyed personal popularity, owing perhaps to a stiff reserve of manner, Townshend Smith was held in great affection.[55] His was a genial and kindly presence in Hereford, a man of antiquarian interests and greatly admired as a musician. Joseph Bennett said of him:

> Smith had strength. The orchestra would follow him without any sense of risk; he knew what he wanted, and, generally, how to get it – a state of things highly valued because singularly rare … I can give an instance of his energy and alertness. After conducting a long morning performance it was not his custom to sink into an easy chair, crying, like the despairing lover in 'Solomon's Song': 'Stay me with flagons, comfort me with pomegranates.' Rather would he make up his returns of attendance and collections, then himself starting out to leave copies at the hotels where musical critics were lodging. We always looked for Townshend Smith within an hour of his laying down the baton; and he, with his zeal and devotion to duty, never failed us.[56]

After Smith's death there was a genuine sense of loss which, as the *Musical Times* put it, 'evidenced the high estimation in which he was held, even by those whose attachment to him could in no degree be influenced by local position'.[57] Samuel Sebastian Wesley died on 19 April 1876, and George Townshend Smith on 3 August 1877.

[54] *MW* 1843, p. 310.
[55] See Amott's obituary notice in *The Times*, 4 September 1865.
[56] Bennett, *Forty Years of Music*.
[57] *MT* 1877, p. 427.

FOR fifty-one years from 1844 William Done was the Organist at Worcester, where he was born on 4 October 1815, a few months after the Battle of Waterloo. He was a chorister in the cathedral and a pupil-assistant to Charles Clarke, whom he eventually succeeded. Done never sought a post away from the city of his birth and, although he made great improvements in the cathedral services at Worcester, was an unremarkable but reliable Three Choirs conductor, considering himself to be primarily a teacher of music. He lived quietly in the Organist's house in College Green, where the attic was fitted up as an aviary for his many canaries. Describing the quiet, plodding Done, Joseph Bennett said that he was a 'good, amiable man – as feebly built as a suburban villa'.[58]

Although Done received his share of mixed reviews for his efforts with the baton, the *Musical Times* balanced the record in a report of the 1881 Worcester Festival:

> Looking back upon the artistic results of the week, we cannot but feel that very much of the success of the Festival was owing to the exertions of the local Conductor, Mr. Done. It is too much the custom to underrate the services rendered at these meetings by the Cathedral organist simply because some experienced Conductor might be brought from London who, it is said, would exercise more control over the executants. But, apart from the ungracious act of placing a stranger in a Cathedral where the musical arrangements are always presided over by one well known to the residents, is it fair to ignore the hard work which has devolved upon the organist for many months before the performance? We happen to know, for example, that Mr. Done had for a very long period toiled hard with different sections of the choir, and even journeyed to Leeds, in order to insure an adequate rendering of Cherubini's Mass; and we emphatically say that the choral singing in this work would have done honour to any Conductor. The general performances under his direction, too, were very far above the average.[59]

François Cramer's long reign as Leader of the Festival orchestra ended in 1844, four years before his death at the age of seventy-six. His place was taken by John Loder at William Done's first Festival as conductor, in 1845(w). Loder (1788–1846) had relieved Cramer at the evening concerts for many years but predeceased the older man by two years.

The Leader at the Festivals of 1846(H) and 1847(G) was Thomas Cooke (1782–1848), the Irish tenor, violinist and composer who at the age of seven had performed a violin concerto in public 'with an effect and precision rarely equalled by so young a performer'.[60] Cooke was an amazingly versatile musician: for twenty years he had not only sung at the Drury Lane Theatre, but also led the orchestra, played nine different instruments, managed the house and composed musical stage pieces for it.

---

[58] Bennett, *Forty Years of Music.*

[59] *MT* 1881, p. 512.

[60] *Annals* 1895, p. 134n.

No British musician of the nineteenth century was more versatile than John Liptrot Hatton (1809–1886). Born in Liverpool, Hatton was a violinist, pianist, organist, singer and composer. At the Hereford Festival in 1846, he appeared as both singer and pianist. At the first of the Miscellaneous Concerts in the Shire Hall he played the piano part in Beethoven's early Quintet in E flat for piano, clarinet, oboe, horn and bassoon. In the second part of the concert Charlotte Dolby, accompanied by Hatton, sang two songs – 'The Chapel' and 'The Shepherd's Winter Song' – both announced as the compositions of P. B. Czapek (*czapek* being the Hungarian for 'hat on'!). Hatton himself sang a chansonette, 'Le Savoyard', acknowledged as his own composition: 'a piece of drollery which was vociferously encored, and the words of which consisted in a mixture of the French and Italian languages common to the Italian frontier'.[61] In addition, Miss Birch accompanied herself in Hatton's cavatina, 'The Syren's Invitation'.

The music critic of *The Times*, J. W. Davison, took Hatton to task concerning his 'Czapek' songs:

> These songs are the compositions of Mr J. L. Hatton, an English artist of distinguished talent, who should know better how to regard his art and respect the public, than to adopt an uncouth hyperborean signature 'Czapek.' They are exceedingly clever and musician-like, and will win favour on the score of their own merits, without the subterfuge of pseudonymous parentage.[62]

But the same critic was much kinder to Hatton when, in the third evening concert, he played the solo part in what was then a rare performance of Mozart's Piano Concerto No. 22 in D minor, κ466:

> These works of the immortal master who has enriched the repertory of the piano to a greater extent than any other composer, except the universal Beethoven, are too much neglected by our performers, and Mr. J. L. Hatton deserves credit for endeavouring to bring them to notice.

After Thomas Cooke's death, Henry Blagrove (1811–1872) took over as Leader; he too had been a prodigy, appearing before the public from the age of five. His brother, Richard Manning Blagrove (1826–1895), became the leading British viola player, and was appointed Professor of this instrument at the Royal Academy of Music. He was also an accomplished and celebrated concertina player, formed a Concertina Quartet, published the *Concertina Journal* (from 1853), and composed fantasias, etc. for concertina and piano. Richard Blagrove remained the leading viola at Three Choirs until 1890(w), and also played the concertina occasionally at evening concerts. Two of his sons, Arthur and Stanley, were also musicians, playing cello and violin respectively in the orchestra at the 1893(w) Festival.

During Henry Blagrove's long reign as Leader – 1845 to 1870 – the evening concerts were often led by Prosper Sainton (1813–1890). Sainton was born in Toulouse, where, in 1840, he became a professor at the Conservatoire. In 1844 he visited London and played under Mendelssohn, returning in the following year to settle in England as a member of the Beethoven Quartet Society, an orchestral

---

[61] *Annals* 1895, p. 155.

[62] Reproduced in *MT* 1909, p. 644.

leader and a teacher. In 1860 he married the contralto Charlotte Dolby, and in 1871 succeeded Blagrove as sole Leader of the Festival orchestra at Three Choirs.

At the third evening concert of the 1866(w) Festival, Sainton and Blagrove were joined by J. T. Carrodus and Henry Holmes in a performance of Ludwig Maurer's *Symphonie concertante* for four violins. This proved so popular that it was repeated at the Festivals of 1867(H) and 1868(G). Although once famous, by the 1860s the Maurer work was already considered showy and trivial. Nonetheless, the brilliant playing of the four violinists was such 'that all idea of its triviality was lost in the admirable ensemble of its execution'.[63]

In 1869(w) Carrodus returned to thrill the Three Choirs audience with a performance of the first movement of the Beethoven Violin Concerto, into which he introduced a cadenza by Molique: 'For purity of tone, finished correctness of mechanism, delicacy of expression, and thorough comprehension of the composer's intentions, Mr. Carrodus stands second to no living English violinist.'[64]

John Tiplady Carrodus (1836–1895) was the head of yet another family of musicians. He was a Yorkshireman who appeared before the Keighley public at the age of nine, and before the London public four years later. His foreign-sounding surname is thought to be a corruption of the Scottish 'Carruthers'. He had been a pupil of Bernhard Molique and became the Leader of the orchestra of the Philharmonic Society. In 1882 Carrodus took over from Sainton as the Leader of the Three Choirs Festival orchestra, and in 1894, at Hereford, his family possibly set a record: in the orchestra were J. T. Carrodus and his five sons.

Without doubt, the family name to emerge as the most famous from among the members of the Festival orchestra through the late-Victorian years was that of Elgar. William Elgar and his brother Henry played second violin and viola respectively in the orchestra for many years. And at Worcester in 1878, William was joined among the second violins by his son, Edward.

[63] *MW* 1866, p. 601.
[64] *MW* 1869, p. 641.

6

Avoiding Shipwreck

IN its long history, Three Choirs has not always sailed in untroubled waters. In the nineteenth century it sometimes appeared that the Festival was steering an uncertain course between the opposing fleets of High and Low Church, and in danger of foundering upon the rocks thrown up by those who sought to banish it from the cathedrals altogether.

It is difficult for us to imagine that a music festival should generate controversy and rancour; but Three Choirs is as inseparable from the cathedrals of Gloucester, Hereford and Worcester as religion was from nineteenth-century England. It was religion, the Christian religion, which permeated every aspect of life: political, educational, social, artistic and scientific. Some discord was inevitable.

One of King George IV's subjects whose opposition to the Festival was expressed almost as strongly as his protest against the way in which the country was being governed, was the Radical reformer William Cobbett. For a decade after the rout of Napoleon at Waterloo, depression and political reaction gripped England. Poverty and distress were widespread. Between 1822 and 1826 Cobbett made a number of journeys through the southern counties, on horseback, to see for himself the condition of the people and the changes in the countryside. His arrival at Gloucester in 1826, recorded in his diary account, *Rural Rides*, coincided with Three Choirs.

> From Stroud I came up to PITCHCOMB, leaving PAINSWICK on my right. From the lofty hill at PITCHCOMB I looked down into that flat and almost circular vale, of which the city of GLOUCESTER is in the centre. To the left I saw the SEVERN, become a sort of arm of the sea; and before me I saw the hills that divide this county from Herefordshire and Worcestershire. The hill is a mile down. When down, you are among dairy-farms and orchards all the way to Gloucester, and, this year, the orchards, particularly those of *pears*, are greatly productive. I intended to sleep at Gloucester, as I had, when there, already come twenty-five miles, and, as the fourteen which remained for me to go, in order to reach BOLLITREE, in Herefordshire, would make about nine more than either I or my horse had a taste for. But, when I came to Gloucester, I found, that I should run a risk of having no bed if I did not bow very low and pay very high; for, what should there be here, but one of those scandalous and beastly fruits of the system, called a 'MUSIC MEETING'! Those who founded the CATHEDRALS never dreamed, I dare say, that they would have been put to such uses as this! They are upon these occasions, made use of as *Opera-Houses*; and, I am told, that the money, which is collected, goes, in some shape or another, to the *Clergy of*

the Church, or their widows, or children, or something. These assemblages of player-folks, half-rogues and half-fools, *began with the small paper money*[1] and with it they will go. They are amongst the profligate pranks which idleness plays when fed by the sweat of a starving people. From this scene of prostitution and of pocket-picking I moved off with all convenient speed, but not before the ostler made me pay 9*d.* for merely letting my horse *stand* for about ten minutes, and not before he had *begun* to abuse me for declining, though in a very polite manner, to *make him a present* in addition to the 9*d.* How he ended I do not know; for I soon set the noise of the shoes of my horse to answer him. I got to this village, about eight miles from Gloucester, by five o'clock; it is now half past seven, and I am going to bed with an intention of getting to BOLLITREE (six miles only) early enough in the morning to *catch my sons in bed if they play the sluggard.*

He was obviously in a foul temper! Fortunately his sons *were* up when he arrived the following morning and the beauty of the Herefordshire countryside soon calmed him down.

The year 1832 was a time of crisis. The previous September a Reform Bill to abolish rotten boroughs, widen the franchises and introduce representation in Parliament for the new industrial towns was defeated in the House of Lords by forty-one votes (twenty-one of which came from the bench of bishops); revolution seemed imminent. Serious rioting took place in London and elsewhere; in Bristol the mob rampaged for two days. Finally, in May 1832 William IV threatened to create sufficient new peers to push the Bill through the House of Lords. The Reform Act of 1832 was passed and the crisis was averted; but, by then, many had no courage to travel to Gloucester for the Music Meeting.

In addition to the political turmoil in the country, cholera broke out in 1832 and spread widely, reaching Gloucester in June: 'its ravages, though not so great as in many other places, did not finally cease until about the period of the [Music] Meeting.'[2] Cancellation was expected, but, in spite of public nervousness, the Meeting ultimately went ahead on 11 September. Then another blow fell: two of the principal singers engaged – Maria Caradori and Henriette-Clementine Meric – failed to turn up. The Festival was so poorly attended in that year that a huge shortfall in income had to be made up by the hapless Stewards. Only the generous donation of £100 from Lord Redesdale prevented the Festival charity from suffering.

All these problems beset the new Organist at Gloucester Cathedral, John Amott, on taking up his duties as conductor of the Music Meeting for the first time in 1832. In the preface to his continuation of the *Annals* from 1812 to 1864,

---

[1] The Stamp Act, requiring a government stamp to be fixed to newspapers, advertisements and various legal documents, was introduced in 1765. In 1802 Cobbett started the *Weekly Register*, a Radical newspaper, but in 1810 was fined £1,000 and sent to gaol for two years for having criticised flogging in the army. In 1816 he reduced the price of the paper from 1*s.* to 2*d.* so that it escaped the stamp duty.

[2] *Annals* 1895, p. 120.

Amott wrote that 'the meetings of the Three Choirs have, upon several occasions, narrowly escaped shipwreck'. In 1832 the Festival was sailing towards very choppy waters indeed.

In his review of the 1836 Festival at Worcester, the critic of the *Musical World* commented on the audience's behaviour at the first concert in the College Hall:

> So far as the audience were concerned, it was of little consequence how the band performed ... for the indifference manifested by the auditory was most uncomplimentary both to their own understandings – to say nothing of good education – and to the efforts of the performers ... The English people have no doubt made considerable advance of late years in musical taste and knowledge; but the good folks of Worcester are leagues in the rear of the general improvement. They are mere Goths, for instance, compared with their Birmingham neighbours.

The same critic, reporting from Hereford in 1837, wrote:

> The effect of the orchestra appeared to be almost poverty-stricken after having emerged from the great volumes of sound that had been ringing in our ears at Birmingham ... The Birmingham performances have damped the zeal of many amateurs in this neighbourhood: added to which Hereford in itself is not of sufficient importance to uphold a festival on a grand scale.

The Birmingham Festival had originated in 1768 with performances in aid of the funds of the General Hospital; by 1800 it had become a triennial event. The rapid growth of the city, fuelled by industrial expansion, caused a doubling of the population during the nineteenth century, to reach 437,000 at the census of 1881. The Birmingham Town Hall was opened in 1834: a symbol of civic pride which, quite naturally, became the grand new venue for the Birmingham Festival.

England was steadily passing from a rural to an urban society. By 1851, for the first time, more than half of the population lived in towns and cities; thirty years later the figure had risen to 70 percent. Industrialists and businessmen were founding a new aristocracy. A desire to give expression to that status, along with the presence of an increasing number of choral singers and sometimes, as at Birmingham, a new town hall, ensured the industrial towns and cities of the Midlands and northern England enjoyed both the will and the resources to develop existing festivals and to establish new ones. Not one important city wished to be outdone by another for very long.

Although Three Choirs had provided the example for others, such as Birmingham, Liverpool, Leeds and Norwich to follow, the three cathedral cities now found themselves in competition with their large industrial neighbour – a neighbour who could afford not only to engage the same soloists at the same enormous expense, but could also provide a larger venue and larger orchestra under the batons of celebrity conductors for both secular concerts and oratorio performances. The managers of the Birmingham Festival did not have to consider the problem of ecclesiastical censorship, either.

At the Worcester Festival of 1836 the third morning began with a performance of Mozart's Requiem, adapted by Edward Taylor under the title of *Redemption* for performance in English:

Not only was the title of *Requiem* altered by Mr. Taylor, but additional music was introduced, some of which was not by Mozart. This, together with the substitution of English words for the original Latin to which the music had been expressly composed, justly excited the opposition of the critics, so that the strange mixture has since been very properly rejected.[3]

In addition to this massacre of Mozart's Requiem, anti-Catholic feeling was manifest in a number of late alterations to the printed programme. On the third morning Miss Hawes sang Cherubini's *O salutaris*: English words were substituted, objection being taken to the Catholic ones. The next day, in a Miscellaneous Selection, Clara Novello had been announced to sing Cherubini's *Ave Maria* and Hummel's *Alma Virgo*, but an objection had been raised against the words of these pieces too. Handel's 'Holy, holy' and Haydn's 'With verdure clad' were substituted. But why this censure in 1836, when, only three years earlier at Worcester, Maria Malibran had delighted her audience with Cherubini's *O salutaris* sung in the original Latin, and when Mozart's Requiem had been performed in full in 1834 at Hereford?

The Worcester Stewards were so grateful to Clara Novello in 1836 for agreeing without fuss to substitute non-contentious works at short notice, that they presented her, by the hands of Lady Harriet Clive, with an ornament costing 50 guineas: 'If our Church are afraid of Popish words biting them, why', asked the *Musical World* angrily, 'do they not quash the whole of our Liturgy?'

In the century before the 1830s, evangelicalism – 'the call to seriousness' – had established itself in a dominant position in British Protestantism. Then, in the 1830s and 1840s, evangelicalism was challenged, under the impetus of the Oxford Movement, by a reawakening of the Catholic spirit within the Anglican communion. Evangelicals, resisting a revival of the Catholic tradition, took up the fight with zealous energy for the next forty years; only at the end of the nineteenth century was it possible for compromise to still this bitter struggle.

Against such a background the choice of items for performance at the Music Meetings became a matter requiring great delicacy. When, for instance, a selection from Beethoven's Mass in C was performed in 1847(G), it was called 'Service in C' – 'to suit Protestant tastes!'[4] (The name stuck for some time afterwards, too.) When the same work was performed in 1850(G), a large proportion of the audience walked out, 'marking painfully the schism in the High and Low Church'.[5]

The first Festival appearance of Beethoven's *Mount of Olives* (*Christus am Olberg*), in 1842(w), was in an English adaptation and with a changed title: *Engedi*, or *David in the Wilderness*, because the original libretto includes a conversation between Our Lord and an angel, which was considered 'unthinkable except to an audience of sceptics or freethinkers'.[6] The result was that 'Beethoven's intentions were outraged from the beginning to end, and, in spite of the perfection of the

[3] Ibid., p. 129, n. 1.

[4] Ibid., p. 156.

[5] *Illustrated London News*, 14 September 1850.

[6] *Worcester Journal*, 8 September 1842.

performance, the effect was nearly lost from the absurd inapplicability of the words to the music'.[7]

In 1871(G), S. S. Wesley conducted the *St Matthew Passion*. It was the first complete performance of an oratorio by Bach ever to be heard at Three Choirs, and even this was censored. 'Mr. Bayly and Mr. Gambier Parry consulted with the conductor as to certain parts of the Passion Music which the Stewards desire to be omitted, especially that of Our Lord's Words on the Cross.'[8]

Having become accustomed to navigating carefully around the shoals and breakers of censorship, in 1838 the Festival sailed into the cannon fire of a powerful opposition which threatened to scupper it completely.

At Hereford in 1834, possibly in response to the competition of the Birmingham Festival and regular financial losses, the twenty-four-year-old S. S. Wesley had obtained approval for the nave of the cathedral to be used for the first time for oratorio performances. A similar arrangement was adopted by Gloucester in the following year and by Worcester in 1842. The Festival was now expanding to meet increased audience expectations: by 1838, the year following Queen Victoria's accession, the orchestra and chorus at Gloucester had grown from 200 to 300, and the Meeting was designated a 'Festival' in the programme for the first time. Huge and expensive efforts were made to present a perfect setting for the performances:

> The preparations in the cathedral, for the accommodation of the audience, presented a splendid *coup d'oeil* from the orchestra. At the bottom of the nave, embracing the whole extent between the pillars, ran a long sloping gallery, reaching from the bottom of the large window to about ten feet from the ground. This gallery was fitted up with rows of benches having backs, each bench containing numbered seats; by which means places might be secured by a timely application, and by ballot, in any part of the gallery. The whole of the nave, from the front of the gallery to that of the orchestra, contained rows of benches without backs. Here twelve shillings and sixpence purchased a seat; those in the gallery cost a guinea. On the side of the nave next to the choir, rose a splendid orchestra, affording easy accommodation for three hundred performers. It was on a level with the gallery, and rose as high as the foot of the organ, which formed the background of the picture. The seats were decorated with scarlet cloth, which, with the scarlet and gold ornamental work on the fronts of the gallery and orchestra, formed a rich and bold contrast with the quiet tint of the noble nave and its massive columns. The aisles were fitted up with plain seats for the accommodation of persons of humbler pretensions than the occupants of either the gallery or the nave. The arrangements at the Shire-hall Evening Concerts were made upon a scale as liberal as those of the cathedral, and with equal attention to the comforts of the audience.[9]

---

[7] *MW* 1842, p. 308.

[8] Gloucester Festival Minute Book, 1871. Gloucester Cathedral Archives and Library.

[9] *MW* 1838, p. 37.

If William Cobbett's complaints of a dozen years earlier had failed to blow the Festival ship off course, his line of attack was now followed up by a highly influential clergyman whose salvo opened up a breach which had still not been fully repaired by the end of the century.

A sermon given by the Rev. Francis Close, a staunchly evangelical clergyman, at St Mary's, Cheltenham, on the Sunday before the 1838 Festival was reported in the *Cheltenham Journal*:

> There are other amusements, less obviously inconsistent with 'the love of the Father', in which the great majority of pious persons think it wrong to participate. They are aware that the specious garment of a charitable object is cast over them; that the hallowed sanction of religious services is in measure imparted to them, by introductory prayers, and even the preaching of a sermon:– but when they view the Music Meeting as a whole, – when they investigate more narrowly its details and its accompaniments, they are forced to the conclusion that it is 'not of the Father, but of the world'.

Strong condemnation of the Festival followed. 'May the eyes of many', said Close, 'be opened to see "the end of these things".'

A meeting of the Stewards was called in the ensuing week, at which Baron Segrave made the following speech which was reported in the *Gloucestershire Chronicle*:

> I have attended these meetings now for thirty-six years, and have been absent from none, with one single exception. I have afforded them, during that time, the best support in my humble power to give, and have been under the impression that in so doing, I was pursuing a praiseworthy and charitable line of conduct. I, therefore, admit that I should not feel satisfied with myself if I omitted to notice a very severe attack that has been made on this institution from a neighbouring pulpit. I should have hoped that the countenance given to this charity and these meetings, by the stewardships of Bishop Ryder, Bishop Bethell and the present Diocesean, would have been sufficient to have protected us from the charge of irreligion; but that charge has nevertheless been deliberately and gravely made. If it had been made by an obscure or ignorant individual, it might have been suffered to pass by unnoticed. But Mr. Close is neither the one nor the other. He is a clergyman of undoubted talent and acquirement, and of considerable influence in the large and populous town of Cheltenham. He is not a contemptible adversary. I have therefore thought this a proper occasion to call the attention of the friends of the charity to this question, but I am of opinion that it would be not only a very unfit opportunity to discuss it, but more, that we are not the tribunal by which it ought to be settled. But as a member of the Church of England, I most respectfully submit that, those clergymen who are friendly to this institution should refute the charge brought against it, and fairly tell us whether we are upholding a system of folly and sin, or whether we are supporting, by laudable means, a charity, the ends of which are beneficial.

The effect of this appeal was quite the opposite to that desired by the Rev. Francis Close. Fearing for the future of the charity, the clergy rallied around the Festival. Pointing out that they had, in the past, failed to give the charity the support which it deserved, either by their presence or their contributions, the Dean of Hereford, the Very Rev. John Merewether, wrote to every clergyman in the diocese requesting their attendance in gowns on the first day of the Festival:

> You are probably aware of the difficulties which have attended the continuance of the Festival for another occasion. What would the poor recipients of its funds do if they were deprived of its support, which is actually, in some cases, almost all they have to depend upon? Might they not cast an upbraiding look on those who have not lent their aid and countenance in promoting its valuable object? That object is peculiarly one which the Parochial Clergy are interested in promoting, and when the Bishops of each diocese, the Archdeacons, the Cathedral Clergy, all concur in giving it their sanction, can we justify our unconcern without impropriety? ... The whole may be regarded, and ought to be conducted, as an occasion of innocent enjoyment, sanctified by its dedication at the outset, and endeavouring to obtain a result of the most benevolent and charitable kind.

The Stewards breathed a sigh of relief: a considerable number of clergy appeared in gowns at the Opening Service of the 1840(H) Festival; and for the next thirty-four years, although frequently beset by financial difficulties, the Festival enjoyed a period of relative calm, punctuated by the periodical pricking of clerical conscience. Had there been no charitable purpose behind the Festivals, it is certain that they would not have survived the mid-nineteenth century. As it was, the income from the charity was essential to the maintenance of the widows and orphans of the poor clergy of the dioceses. In the absence of any other source of support, the clergy felt obliged to continue their sanction of the Festival. In October 1852 the Bishop of Gloucester and Bristol wrote:

> I feel it my duty to continue to extend to this charitable scheme all the support and encouragement in my power; unless any other plan for securing similar benefits to the families of our poorer brethren could be suggested, which should be equally efficient and less exposed to objections ... I can only say that my determination remains unaltered, and that no substitute for the Music Meetings has been proposed.[10]

Any alternative proposal would have necessitated the raising of £1,000 in each diocese every three years. Not surprisingly, none could find support.

And the Rev. Francis Close? He became the Dean of Carlisle on the recommendation of Lord Shaftesbury to Palmerston and, after his death, the Cheltenham school which bears his name was dedicated to the memory of Dean Close.

---

[10] *Annals* 1895, p. 171.

IN 1863 Lord Palmerston, acting on the advice of Lord Shaftesbury, appointed Charles John Ellicott as Bishop of the United See of Bristol and Gloucester.[11] (It seems he was chosen partly because he had opposed answering *Essays and Reviews*, the work of six distinguished Broad Churchmen.)[12] Dr Ellicott was not a lover of music. On first encountering Three Choirs in 1865(G) he selected Festival week to cross 'from Lauterbrunnen over the Tschingel glacier to Kandersteg'. The Dean of Gloucester, Henry Law, who was appointed in 1862, also absented himself, as did two of the cathedral canons. So marked a disapproval of the Festival prompted a lively exchange of correspondence in the columns of the musical, national and local press. One 'Button of Birmingham' wrote to the *Birmingham Daily Post* and the *Musical World*:

> Musical Festivals are not always so harmonious as they seem to be. While band and chorus pour forth a swelling flood of sweet sounds in cathedral or hall, there may be a dreadful squabble going on in the Committee Room. It is in cathedral towns, I believe, that these little difficulties happen with the greatest frequency; and here another element of discordance comes in, by the necessary interference of the clergy. Either the Bishop won't preach, or the Dean has doubts about the lawfulness of oratorio music, or an eccentric canon goes off with a highly Protestant bang – and then what is called a 'scandal' arises, and the Festival which ought to be the perfection of harmony, becomes an occasion of strife and a source of bitterness. Something of this kind, it seems, but lately happened at Gloucester.[13]

The correspondent of *The Times*, reporting on the Festival, had noted that:

> Although the Dean is absent, the Deanery is occupied by Lord Ellenborough, who exercises the accustomed and expected hospitality; and although Bishop Ellicott – also absent – objected to preach on behalf of the widows and orphans, he has found a most admirable substitute in the Rev. C. E. Kennaway, Canon of Gloucester and Vicar of Chipping Camden, whose sermon of this day, built upon the text 'For *all* are thy servants' (Psalm 119, v. 91) is the talk of every one. Never was good cause more eloquently supported from the pulpit. Mr. Kennaway not only pleaded for the charity, but for the Festival; and not merely for the Festival in the abstract, but for the performances of sacred music in the Church.[14]

Three Choirs survived the Festival of 1865, but Dr Ellicott's lack of interest in music could never be reversed, not even by his wife, who was a keen amateur musician, an able contralto, and founder-member of the Handel Society (f. 1882) and of the Gloucestershire Philharmonic Society. In spite of the bishop's absence at Festival time, she restored the tradition of throwing open the Palace with generous hospitality. On 3 September 1886 she wrote to A. M. Broadley:

[11] The Sees of Gloucester and Bristol were joined in 1836, and divided in 1897, with effect from 1 January 1898.

[12] See David Welander, *The History, Art and Architecture of Gloucester Cathedral* (Alan Sutton, 1991).

[13] *MW* 1865, pp. 594–5.

[14] *The Times*, 6 September 1865.

I am sorry to say the Bishop will not be at home for the Festival … I shall be most happy to see you after the oratorio on Tuesday afternoon. I am 'at home' all through the week so pray look in whenever you like. Besides Lady Westbury and Miss Simpson my guests are as follows: Lord and Lady Norton and Miss Adderley, Mr. and Mrs. Power, Mr. and Mrs. Travers, Revd. H. R. Haweis, Mr. Frederic Cowen, Mr. Lionel Monckton, Professor Thomas Wingham, Mr. Alfred Barnett, Mr. Henry Lazarus, Mr. William Wing and Mr. W. de Manby Sergison. So you see music is well represented – all these seven gentlemen being artists – with the exception perhaps of Mr. Monckton who wishes to be considered an amateur for fear of spoiling his career as a Barrister – but he writes charmingly.[15]

Perhaps you are not aware that I have an artist in my own daughter. She is bringing out an Overture (her second Orchestral work) at the Tuesday Evening Concert and to judge from its reception by the band at the rehearsal on Wednesday morning I think it is likely to produce a sensation. She calls it 'dramatic' because one of its leading features are *recits* for celli – I hope you will be able to go and hear the work on Tuesday evening.

My daughter was a student at the R.A.M. and is in all respects a member of the musical profession and *not an amateur*.

You may be amused by my emphatic underlining but she is always annoyed at being spoken of as a 'talented amateur'.[16]

The *Dramatic Overture* by Rosalind Ellicott (1857–1924) was indeed well received, and was praised by the *Musical Times* as a work of exceptional merit. Her other compositions for Three Choirs, all performed at Gloucester, include a song entitled 'To the Immortals', sung by Hilda Wilson in 1882; *Elysium* for soprano, chorus and orchestra in 1889; *Fantasie* in A minor for piano and orchestra in 1895 (Sybil Palliser was the soloist); and in 1898 a choral ballad for men's voices, *Henry of Navarre*, setting verses by Macauley.

Like her mother, Rosalind Ellicott was a good singer – a soprano who often sang at charitable concerts in Gloucestershire. Sir Herbert Brewer recalled an occasion when the unmusical bishop arrived home one winter afternoon to find his wife and daughter entertaining some friends:

They were singing a duet. The fire was black and cheerless; the Bishop took up the poker and began to stir it vigorously. Mrs. Ellicott stopped singing and, in a reproachful voice exclaimed, 'My dear, my dear!' The Bishop, holding up his hand in a becalming manner, replied, 'Don't stop, my love, don't stop! You don't disturb me in the least!'[17]

When Dr Ellicott died in 1905, his had been the longest episcopate in the history of the diocese of Gloucester – forty-two years.

[15] Lionel Monckton (1861–1924), composer of *The Quaker Girl*, etc.
[16] Letter from Constantia Ellicott to A. M. Broadley (3 September 1886). Held in the Broadley Collection in Gloucester City Library.
[17] Herbert Brewer, *Memories of Choirs and Cloisters* (Bodley Head, 1931), p. 86.

Also in 1865, during Ellicott's boycott of his first Three Choirs, rumour was spreading that powerful outside influence would soon compel Worcester to give up *its* triennial Festival. *The Times*, reporting on the extraordinary success of the Gloucester Festival, suggested that the large turnout of inhabitants and supporters represented a protest against 'clerical interference', adding that the people had 'little mercy on their Bishop, less on their Dean, and least of all on Lord Dudley, who is generally supposed to be harbouring unfriendly intentions towards the Worcester Festival of 1866'.[18] The Dean of Gloucester, in granting the use of the cathedral, had yielded, against his own conviction, to the force of public opinion. At Worcester, opposition to the Festival was led by one of the richest noblemen in the land: the great Worcestershire magnate Earl Dudley. Writing to *Berrow's Worcester Journal* on 4 October 1865, Dudley had said:

> When a better religious feeling banished the festival from the choir – from the Holy of Holies – where it had degenerated from a service by the united choirs, to a performance of works on sacred subjects by English and foreign artists – of indifferent reputation, greedy of pay then as now, and the latter barely able to pronounce the language they were paid to sing in – when this took place, the nave, the neglected, dusty, broken-floored, never-used nave – a mere ante-chapel to the choir, was suggested as a convenient place, and has been so used ever since. Is this any reason that it should go on? Warmed, lighted, fitted for service, used for it, ordinarily and specially restored to Divine use – performed in it, save service alone? Ask the candid, even of those who attended the Gloucester Festival in a spirit of opposition, if the Cathedral was not desecrated? and if it was, as I know it was, you will not be a party to ours being so used and misused.

The argument rumbled on for the next few years but the Festival continued.

The year 1873 marked the beginning of the so-called Great Depression in Victorian Britain; the year in which, following decades of industrial omnipotence and boom, British manufacturers were faced for the first time by competition from abroad. The following year brought depression to the Three Choirs Festival.

In April 1874, Worcester Cathedral was reopened following extensive restoration. The Gloucester Festival in September of that year ended with a service in the cathedral instead of the usual ball; the sermon was given by the Rev. Dr Barry, a canon of Worcester Cathedral. In it, he implicitly confirmed a rumour which had been circulating for some weeks: that the Dean and Chapter of Worcester would not permit the Festival of 1875 to take place in its traditional form. At the end of the sermon Dr S. S. Wesley made his comment in music: he played the Dead March from *Saul*.

The reasons put forward by the Dean and Chapter of Worcester for withholding permission for the use of the cathedral for the Festival were twofold. First, the cathedral having been completely restored, and the nave as well as the choir being devoted to public worship, they no longer felt at liberty to transfer the charge and control of it to other hands. However, their real motive was revealed in the second reason alleged – that the Dean and Chapter 'are of the opinion that musical performances which are unconnected with any religious

---

[18] *The Times*, 8 September 1865.

service, and to which admission is given only by purchased tickets, should no longer take place in the Cathedral'.

In fact, Lord Dudley had offered a sum of £10,000 towards the restoration of Worcester Cathedral on condition that the Music Meetings should no longer be held there. In the face of strong public opposition to such a condition Lord Dudley retracted his first offer and subscribed £5,000 on condition that Lord Hampton would raise the rest. The result was a subscription not of £5,000, but of £11,000.

In Lord Hampton's view, this large sum was subscribed and bestowed upon the cathedral on an understanding that the Festival would not be discontinued. The newly appointed Dean of Worcester, Dr Grantham M. Yorke, remained unmoved. The Stewards of Gloucester and Hereford were dismayed, as were the citizens of Worcester, not a few of whom would suffer financial loss if the Festival were cancelled. Protests poured into Worcester Cathedral.

The issue was taken up in the national as well as the local press and the musical journals:

It seems, on the face of it, a great pity that a beautiful Musical Festival, which a custom of a century and a half has rendered little less than an institution in the West, should be so summarily put an end to, and the reasons ought to be very strong on which the Dean and Chapter rely. It is easy to see that the feeling which has dictated the refusal is connected with the novel sentiments of ecclesiastical propriety which have gained so much ground of late years among the clergy, and the moment for thus enforcing a strict ecclesiastical standard has, at least, been very unfortunately chosen. It would have been more graceful if the new Dean had exerted his influence to permit the holding of the first Festival which occurs since his appointment, and he could have interfered afterwards with much greater effect.[19]

An 'indignation' meeting was held in Worcester, presided over by the mayor and attended by deputations from Gloucester and Hereford. In a series of resolutions, which were forwarded to the Dean and Chapter, the meeting regretted that the friendly relations which had 'so long subsisted between the Dean and Chapter and the City of Worcester should be imperilled'. Lord Hampton insisted that the Chapter were morally bound by the understanding which he contended was arrived at in 1870, when the public raised £11,000 for the completion of the cathedral – that the Festivals should be continued. It was this latter point upon which the response of the dean concentrated:

[The Dean and Chapter] desire to call special attention to the second resolution, in which they observe, with much surprise and regret, that the Stewards have thought it fit publicly to accuse them by implication, of taking advantage of the absence of a 'literal obligation' to depart from an 'honourable understanding', and have thus encouraged those ignorant of the circumstances to represent the Dean and Chapter as 'having obtained money under false pretences'.

[19] *The Times*, and reported in *MW*, 31 October 1874, p. 715.

The dean maintained that in seeking subscriptions towards the restoration of the cathedral 'every condition was withdrawn, and that every question of opinion, whether with respect to Musical Festivals or otherwise, was left entirely open and unprejudiced'. In support of his argument he quoted the text of a letter from the Lord Bishop of Worcester dated 3 October 1874:

> I always understood that, when contributions were solicited on the last occasion for the restoration of the Cathedral, it had been agreed on all sides that the question of the continuance of the Musical Festivals was to be considered open, the Dean and Chapter being left free to decide it one way or the other, as they might think fit, without reference to the opinions of the persons contributing. My own contribution certainly was given on this understanding.
>
> I am yours, very truly
> sgnd: H. Worcester

What Dean Yorke failed to say was that he had quoted only an extract from a much longer letter. The rest of the bishop's text was as follows:

> Lord Hampton and other contributors might, perhaps, fairly encourage the hope that the Dean and Chapter, being relieved from the pressure of Lord Dudley's offer and the apparent difficulty of completing the restoration without accepting the conditions, would eventually decide in favour of continuing the Festivals, but I do not think that they have any ground for saying that the Dean and Chapter are under any obligation to continue the Festivals because the liberal contributions of some who wished them to be continued relieved them from the embarrassment of returning an answer to Lord Dudley's offer.
>
> My own opinions about the Festivals have been always the same. I enjoy the oratorios in the Cathedral very much myself, and I think that they are edifying and profitable to the great mass of people who attend them. I do not see any objection to such use of the Cathedral, nor to the admission of hearers by paid tickets. But I admit a very great evil in the erection and removal of the huge platform hitherto thought necessary, and I hope that if the Dean and Chapter will allow the use of the Cathedral for oratorios they will insist upon some other arrangement. My feeling on this subject is so strong that, if the oratorios cannot be performed satisfactorily without turning the cathedral into a carpenter's shop for many days before and after the Festival, I would rather that they were discontinued.[20]

Interestingly, the problem of noise in constructing and removing the complicated wooden platforms had been a source of irritation to the Dean and Chapter at Gloucester as well as at Worcester. The Dean of Gloucester had asked the Stewards there if screws, instead of nails, could be used in the construction so as to reduce the noise to a minimum. The problem was solved by asking the contractor, Mr Clutterbuck, to prefabricate all the parts required to make the staging and then to assemble the timbers in the cathedral using iron bolts.

[20] *MW* 1874, p. 755.

The *Musical World* was forthright in its condemnation of proceedings at Worcester:

> The Dean and Chapter of Worcester Cathedral have, at last, taken a decisive step and positively refused the use of the Cathedral for the next Festival of the Three Choirs. Their decision can only take by surprise those who are ignorant of the capacity of clergymen for doing the wrong thing. With some bright exceptions, clergymen only in name, the 'parsons' have gone on blundering from the beginning, spoiling every good work to which they have put their hands, and only succeeding when the object has been to do mischief. So, now, the clerical trustees of Worcester, for the sake of a principle waived by scores of men as good or better than themselves, fly in the face of public opinion, and shut the doors of a national building against their neighbours and the public. Be it so. The new Dean will have his reward from those among whom he has just gone as a stranger, and the Chapter must look forward to a day of reckoning. The temper of these times is not in favour of clerical assumptions, and Church dignitaries should remember that what the nation gave it can also take away. In possession of handsome incomes (for doing little) and comfortable residences, they, no doubt, think themselves 'lords over God's heritage', whose power nothing can touch. But every such act as the one under notice lengthens an already formidable indictment against a rotten ecclesiastical corporation, which will ere long tumble about the ears of those who wax fat and kick beneath its shadow. When that event happens, the nation, and not a sect, will possess the national buildings, and all danger of their refusal for an innocent and laudable purpose will have passed.[21]

A final conference between the Worcester Stewards and the Dean and Chapter took place just before Christmas 1874. The Stewards described it as 'a useless ceremony'; at the request of the Mayor of Worcester they sent a petition to the queen in Council, together with one to the same effect from the citizens of Worcester, protesting that:

> Application has been made to the present Dean and Chapter of Worcester for the Cathedral as heretofore for the festival of the year 1875, but the Dean and Chapter have declined to grant the use thereof, and have proposed to substitute for a festival, such as those which have so long and so satisfactorily been held in the Cathedral, religious services and sermons, which some sections of your Majesty's subjects would be unable to attend … Your petitioners, therefore, humbly pray that your Most Gracious Majesty, as the head of the Church of this realm, will be pleased to use your influence with the Dean and Chapter of Worcester to induce them to permit the holding of the triennial festivals in the Cathedral Church of this city, under such arrangements as will best promote the object in view.[22]

[21] *MW* 1874, p. 705.
[22] *MW* 1875, p. 4.

One last skirmish took place before the end of 1874: an exchange of carefully controlled civilities between the Bishops of Worcester and Gloucester:[23]

Hartlebury
Kidderminster
Dec. 9th. 1874

My dear Bishop of Gloucester,

At a general meeting of subscribers to the Society for the relief of Clergymen's Widows and Orphans in the Archdeaconry of Worcester, held this day, the secretary informed them that the usual remittances had not been received from the Stewards of the Musical Festival held this year at Gloucester. As the meeting was further informed that the remittance was withheld under your sanction and advice, I was requested by the members present to write to your Lordship on the subject in the hope that further consideration may induce the Stewards to follow the course which has been usual on such occasions. ... In the advertisement of the Festival of 1874, it was announced to the public that the money collected would be devoted to the benefit of the Widows and Orphans of the Clergy of the three Dioceses. It is to be presumed that money was given on this occasion for such purposes, and it is contended that money so given cannot properly be diverted from the object for which contributions were solicited. Again, the members of the Worcester Choir were invited to take part in the performances, and did actually take part, on the understanding that the Festival was for the benefit of the three dioceses in common; and it is contended that if the share due to the Worcester Diocese be now withheld, such withholding is as much a breach of faith as if the understanding had been a contract executed under hand and seal between the Stewards of the Festival on the one hand and the members of the Worcester Choir on the other. Our Society entertains no doubt that if the question was submitted to a Court of Equity, the Court would direct the Stewards of the Gloucester Festival to pay the Worcester Charity its third as usual.

The reasons which I have stated appear to be sound and good, even on the supposition that no Musical Festival may be held in Worcester next year. But I may mention that the question of the continuance of the Festivals at Worcester is not yet settled, arrangements having been recently made for a conference between the Stewards of the Proposed Festival of 1875 and the Dean and Chapter of Worcester, with the view of determining the conditions under which the Festival may be held satisfactory to both parties.

I am, my dear Bishop,
Yours very faithfully,
(sgnd.) H. Worcester

[23] Gloucester Festival Minute Book, 1874. Gloucester Cathedral Archives and Library.

Reply from the Bishop of Gloucester and Bristol:

> I thank you for your kind letter. Having heard from our local Treasurer
> (a) that it appears by documentary evidence that the cycle of Festivals
> commenced with Gloucester and (b) that an assurance (now in my
> judgement equitably necessary) had not been received that the sum usually
> sent from Worcester would be forthcoming next year for our widows and
> orphans, I approved of our Treasurer waiting till such assurance should be
> received. Feeling, however, that the advertisement to which you refer may
> carry with it technical liability, I wrote to our Treasurer suggesting that he
> should invite our Stewards to a meeting, place before them your letter, take
> their decision thereon and report to me. I will then have the pleasure of
> writing to you again.
>
> December 11th. 1874

The Gloucester Stewards met and, with considerable reluctance, authorised the
treasurer to pay over forthwith to the treasurer of the Worcester charity the
one-third of the collection of the 1874 Festival.

The 'reformed' Festival of 1875 went ahead in an atmosphere of civic gloom
and anger. No solo performers or orchestra were engaged, no platform was
erected in the cathedral, no tickets were sold, and no secular concerts were held.
Only about sixty people turned up for the Opening Service on 28 September. The
music performed during the three days of the 'Festival' – quickly dubbed the
'Mock Festival' by the unhappy townsfolk of Worcester – was less than exciting:
no oratorios, not even *Messiah*, were heard. Three choral services were held on the
second day (at 8.30, 11.00 and 3.30) and the Festival was brought to a close on the
third day with services at 11.30 and 3.30. The music consisted almost entirely of
settings of the canticles, with anthems by Ouseley, Wesley, Mendelssohn, Spohr,
Handel, Attwood and others.

> Thus ended the Worcester Festival of 1875. Amongst other signs of
> disapprobation it was noticed that the cabmen had crepe bows tied to their
> whips, and one or two black flags were displayed in the streets.[24]

Years later, Sir Edward Elgar described the prevailing gloom to Sir Ivor Atkins:
how the only redeeming feature had been S. S. Wesley's wonderful organ playing
of Bach's 'Wedge' and 'Giant' Fugues at the end of evening services; and how, to
Elgar's delight, it had rained incessantly during the Mock Festival, though the
weather had been fine up till then, and brilliant sunshine returned the day it was
over.[25]

The atmosphere of mourning prompted the following epitaph, which
appeared in the *Birmingham Town Crier*:

IN MEMORY OF THE
WORCESTER MUSIC FESTIVAL
Died September, 1875
Though of humble origin

[24] *Annals* 1895, p. 265.
[25] E. Wulstan Atkins, *The Elgar–Atkins Friendship* (David & Charles, 1985), p. 474.

And for years having only
A very
Modest existence
It tried to attain
Great importance,
And to
Achieve many great and good works,
When in the height of its
Influence and prosperity,
And after ministering to the
Wants of hundreds,
And elevating the
Minds of thousands,
It was unfortunately discovered that it was
Unfit to live.
It was fired at by a
Noisy Canon,
Attacked by a
Military Dean,
And denounced by a
Religious nobleman.
Persecuted by prigs, Puritans and parsons,
Choked by a highly Christian Chapter,
It faintly and feebly
Breathed its last
Before the eyes
And in the presence of its
Chief assailants and assassins.
Weep, Worcester, weep,
Thy lyric glory's gone
No more, alas, to be
Till Dean and Chapter
All translated are
Into the silent see.

The Festival went ahead as usual in Hereford in 1876 and Gloucester in 1877, and by 1878 the Dean and Chapter of Worcester had thought fit to capitulate. The Worcester Festival was reborn. At the Opening Service the sermon was preached by the bishop himself, and the scruples of the clerical authorities were effectively satisfied by the introduction of prayers before the performance of sacred works in the cathedral.

Since 1875 the only interruptions in the otherwise unbroken annual Three Choirs tradition have been those caused by the two world wars, but an element of opposition to the Festival continued until well into the twentieth century.

7
Prima voce

FOR the first three-quarters of the nineteenth century, Britain was the unchallenged supplier of the world's goods, skills and services. Although one-third of the people lived in a residuum of wretched poverty, the nation as a whole attracted unprecedented wealth, as a result of which the finest foreign singers were drawn to London opera houses and concert halls to perform alongside the best British artists.

At a time when the radio and the gramophone were less than dreams, a public hungry for music was prepared to pay high prices for opera and concert tickets, and national and international celebrity singers could demand huge fees for their appearances. At the end of the London season each year, these stars would tour the country, singing at regional music festivals such as Leeds, Liverpool, Norwich, Birmingham and Three Choirs.

To enable provincial concert-goers to see and to hear as many of their renowned favourites as possible, it was customary for the solo parts of a work performed at Three Choirs to be divided between a first and second singer of the same voice, the former receiving a higher fee than the latter. Not surprisingly, this division sometimes led to rivalry and to contractual problems.

In addition to singing in performances of sacred works in the cathedrals, the same stars would take part in the evening Miscellaneous Concerts in secular venues. To modern tastes these concerts would seem to have been over-long and indigestible mixtures of operatic arias, ballads, humorous songs and instrumental and orchestral pieces. However, they gave people living in rural communities the occasional opportunity to experience a cross-section of the entertainment enjoyed regularly by their compatriots in London. To them it seemed not the least bit incongruous that, as at Gloucester in 1847, Marietta Alboni should share the bill with, among others, John Parry – a comic singer and 'shaker of sides' – and that following Alboni's performances of operatic arias and duets with the great bass Joseph Staudigl, Parry was 'received uproariously, was in uproarious humour, and was uproariously encored in both his ingenious pasticcios'.[1]

In the early years of the nineteenth century Three Choirs soloists included a few whose reputations had been made in the eighteenth century. Gertrud Mara sang for the last time at a Music Meeting in 1801(H), and Elizabeth Billington in 1809(W). James Bartleman carried on until 1817(G):

> It is melancholy to record that many of the latter years of Bartleman's life were passed in almost unremitting pain. His ardent mind long struggled

---

[1] *MW* 1847, p. 616.

against disease, and he was often delighting crowded audiences with his performance, while the dew of bodily agony stood upon his brow.[2]

Bartleman was so ill by 1819 that he was unable to attend his own benefit concert. He died on 15 April 1821 at the age of fifty-one and is buried in Westminster Abbey. Dr Rimbault records that 'after his decease, his large and valuable library of ancient music was sold by auction, and the respectable auctioneer ran away with the proceeds, which thus became lost to his two sisters who survived him'.[3]

Throughout the nineteenth century Three Choirs was notable for the engagement, year after year, of a galaxy of star singers which, to a later age, would have been the equivalent of regular appearances by Caruso, Melba and Chaliapin. The Italian soprano Angelica Catalani (1780–1849) was among the foreign celebrities whose first appearances at the Music Meetings were made in the early years of the century. She sang at Gloucester in 1811 and at Worcester in 1812. Catalani came to England in 1806 and, with performances at Covent Garden and elsewhere, had in less than six months earned almost £10,000. Her fee to sing in Gloucester was the highest ever before paid by Three Choirs: 450 guineas! However, she was famous not only for her magnificent voice but also for her generosity: while in Gloucestershire she visited the county prison and donated a large sum to the prison charity. She then proposed and took part in a concert held in the Cheltenham Assembly Rooms, which was so successful that there was money to spare for the county infirmary too. Furthermore, she donated 50 guineas of her Three Choirs fee to the Festival charity.

Maria Malibran (1808–1836) sang at three Music Meetings in the last few years of her short, brilliant and tragic life: 1828(G), 1830(W) and 1833(W). Taught by her Spanish father, Manuel García, and by Hérold in Paris, she made her London debut in 1825 as Rosina in *The Barber of Seville* before she was seventeen. At the end of that season she went to America with her father, where, one day after her eighteenth birthday, she married Malibran, an elderly Frenchman. 'The marriage proved to be a ghastly failure. Whatever may have been M. Malibran's musical attainments, his only known composition was a composition with his creditors. The bankruptcy of the elderly bridegroom took place within a year of the nuptial ceremony, and Maria left him.'[4] In 1830 she found love with the Belgian violinist Charles de Beriot, whom she married in 1836 and with whom she appeared at the Music Meeting of 1833(W).

The glorious voice of Malibran was contralto in quality, with a compass of three octaves. She was a woman of remarkable personality and amazingly varied accomplishments:

> She was an intrepid horsewoman, a capital dancer, an inimitable caricaturist,[5] a humorous concocter of charades and riddles, and – though some 'superior' persons may regard this as a weakness in her character – she could make a very good pun. Yet, upon the slightest indication, she

---

[2] *Annals* 1895, p. 63n.

[3] Ibid.

[4] *MT* 1901, p. 585.

[5] See Plate 23 for an illustration showing Malibran's caricature of William Mutlow.

would … discuss with discriminate enthusiasm the genius of Dante or Shakespeare, Raphael or Michaelangelo. She was an excellent pianist, and composed many very creditable songs … in short, her versatility was quite phenomenal.[6]

Reporting on the Music Meeting of 1829(G), the *Gloucester Journal* records that a great crowd attended the morning service, at which 'many females were carried out in a fainting state'. The prayers were read by the Rev. W. W. Mutlow, a son of the cathedral organist and a minor canon of the cathedral. Of Malibran's achievements at the Music Meeting we learn from the paper that:

> To remarkable powers of voice, she unites singular clearness of articulation; and her style of singing is strongly characterised by that depth of feeling which constitutes the very soul of the music. There is something in her demeanour, too, which is very pleasing; and we were delighted to observe that both she and Mrs. Knyvett invariably took a prominent part in the responses of the day – a point not always attended to by the principal singers on such occasions as the present … The whole company was enraptured by Madame Malibran's execution of the Bishop air, 'Should he upbraid', and a general encore was the natural consequence. Madame Malibran still further charmed the company by the ready and obliging manner in which she complied with the request of one of the Stewards to favour them with another song, when she instantly took her seat at the piano, and with a degree of archness and good humour peculiarly her own, gave the lively and playful air 'Rampataplan', which was loudly commended.[7]

Following her triumph in Gloucester, Malibran was invited to sing at Worcester in the following year, 1830, the year in which Princess Victoria and her mother, the Duchess of Kent, attended the Music Meeting.

In the spring of 1836 Malibran, by then pregnant, fell from her horse. In spite of the seriousness of her condition, she insisted upon travelling from Paris to Manchester in the following September in order to fulfil an engagement at that city's music festival. Though weak and ill she sang on both the morning and evening of Tuesday 13 September and again on the following day. At the Wednesday evening concert she took part in a duet with Maria Caradori Allan – 'Vanne se alberghi in petto' from Mercadante's *Andronica*. It was received with immense enthusiasm, and she even repeated the performance; but at its end, while the concert room was still ringing with applause, she was fainting in the arms of her friends. Nine days later – 23 September 1836 – at the Mosley Arms Hotel, Manchester, Maria Malibran passed away at the age of twenty-eight.

The life of Malibran's brother, Manuel García (1805–1906) was as full of years as Maria's was deprived of them. He was an eminent singing teacher and the inventor of the laryngoscope, who retired at the age of ninety-five and lived for five more years.

---

[6] *MT* 1901, p. 586.

[7] *Gloucester Journal*, 26 September 1829. The 'Rampataplan' was Malibran's own composition – her 'Rataplan'.

Malibran's sister, the mezzo-soprano and composer Pauline Viardot-García, sang at the Music Meetings in 1841(G), 1854(W) and 1858(H). She too was a woman of formidable talents who married a much older man: the French writer Louis Viardot was twenty-one years her senior. In 1843 she met the novelist Turgenev in Paris and formed an intimate relationship with him. When both men died in 1883, Pauline withdrew from society and lived as a semi-recluse until her death in 1910 at the age of eighty-nine.

It was Maria Malibran who sang the role of Leonora in the first performance in English of Beethoven's opera *Fidelio*, at Covent Garden in 1835. Eleven years earlier the soprano parts in Beethoven's *Missa solemnis* and Symphony No. 9 (*Choral*) had been sung at their first performances by Henriette Sontag in the presence of the composer, who was by then profoundly deaf. In 1823 Weber had chosen her to sing the title part in *Euryanthe*. After her marriage to the Count de Rossi in 1828 she retired, but, following the revolutions in Europe of 1848, she returned to the stage. Her reappearance in London after twenty years caused a sensation, and in 1850 she sang at the Gloucester Festival:

> the anxiety to hear Madame Sontag was so great that all other considerations were overlooked. Her first song, Donizetti's cavatina, 'Se crudele il cor', is by no means a remarkable composition, but the original and perfectly executed cadenza which Madame Sontag introduced at the end of the largo, and the exquisite fancy with which she embellished the cabaletta, raised the greatest enthusiasm. In Arne's 'Soldier tired', Madame Sontag obtained a unanimous encore: ... Madame Sontag has made an indelible impression on the Gloucesterians, who never gave a stronger proof of their good taste than by the unbounded applause they bestowed upon the efforts of this gifted and accomplished artist.[8]

In 1852 Henriette Sontag went to America. While in Mexico City she contracted cholera and died there on 17 June 1854.

A contemporary of Sontag and Malibran, the Scottish soprano Mary Ann Paton (1802–1854) appeared at the Festivals in 1825(W), 1828(H), 1829(G) and 1830(W). She had made her first stage appearance in 1822 and married Lord William Pitt Lennox in 1824, but they separated later and she married Joseph Wood, tenor, of the Covent Garden Theatre, ultimately settling in Manchester and then Leeds as a teacher of singing. Mary Paton was the first Reiza in Weber's *Oberon*; and it was with an aria by Weber, 'Softly sighs' from *Der Freischütz*, that she thrilled the Gloucester audience in 1829. She died at Radcliffe Hall, Yorkshire on 23 July 1864.

The Worcester Festival of 1842 brought to prominence a young contralto who was to remain a Three Choirs favourite for a quarter of a century. Charles Clarke, the cathedral organist, was too ill to conduct and the Stewards engaged Joseph Surman of the Exeter Hall in London to take his place. The Stewards had by this time already engaged the principal soloists, among whom was the contralto Maria Hawes, whose first Three Choirs appearance had been at Hereford in 1834. Surman wrote to Miss Hawes, sending her the programme, in response to which she replied in a letter:

[8] *MW* 1850, p. 593.

containing sundry protestations against the (as Miss H. terms it) unwarrantable distribution of various solos and duets, which she has been accustomed to sing, among sundry other vocalists – also containing certain *commands*, that such and such a song should be placed in such and such a place – that such a duet should be reversed – that so and so should not sing this or that – and that she (Miss Hawes) insisted upon doing this or that, or the other.[9]

Surman suggested various compromise solutions to Miss Hawes but she wrote back immediately to him, and later to the Festival Committee, insisting upon having her own way or declining her engagement. The Committee despatched a Mr Rogers to London forthwith to obtain a replacement for Miss Hawes, and he engaged the twenty-one-year-old Charlotte Dolby, who had recently made her debut there following her studies at the Royal Academy of Music.

Miss Dolby rushed to Worcester without knowing anything of the music which she would have to perform and without the advantage of a single rehearsal. Her appearance was a triumph.

Miss Hawes was never again asked to sing at Worcester, and only once more in a Three Choirs Festival: at Gloucester in 1844. However, Charlotte Dolby (who became Madame Sainton-Dolby on marrying the French violinist Prosper Sainton, Leader of the Festival orchestra from 1871 to 1882) achieved fame and distinction. In 1845 she was invited by Mendelssohn to sing with Jenny Lind at Leipzig; and on 26 August 1846 she sang in the first performance of *Elijah* under the direction of the composer at the Birmingham Festival, along with Maria Caradori-Allan, Charles Lockey and Joseph Staudigl.

Three Choirs had a vintage year in 1847. Not only did the four soloists who had performed in the Birmingham première of *Elijah* repeat the work in Gloucester, but also the famous contralto Marietta Alboni (1822–1894) was engaged to sing in the second and third Miscellaneous Concerts. Alboni, a pupil of Rossini, had made her debut at La Scala, Milan, in 1843. In London she shared star billing with Jenny Lind at Her Majesty's Theatre.

Alboni, the gorgeous Alboni, with her portly frame and winning smile, came forward and sang 'Una voce poco fa' after her own peculiar fashion, and at once produced an impression which has had no parallel in the musical annals of Gloucester … She was rapturously encored, and repeated the allegro with increased brilliancy. There was scarcely a note of Rossini's text, but the thing had a charm of its own that was quite irresistible … Alboni is the whole theme of Gloucester *causerie*: you cannot pass up and down the streets without hearing an earnest discussion of her merits in almost every corner, nor can you approach a house where there is a piano, without hearing some young lady endeavouring to emulate [her] fervour and *intensity*.[10]

Alboni was not only celebrated for her beautiful voice but also for her bodily size. Madame Girardin was once asked by someone who knew nothing of opera:

[9] *MW* 1842, p. 308.
[10] *MW* 1847, p. 629.

'What is Alboni then?' Madame Girardin replied: 'What is she? Why, she is an elephant who has swallowed a nightingale!'[11]

Another, more slender, nightingale became the most sought-after of all sopranos. Jenny Lind (1820–1887), 'The Swedish Nightingale', studied with García in Paris and came to settle in England in 1847. Within a very short time she established a huge reputation.

In December 1847, the Bishop of Worcester wrote inviting her to appear at the Worcester Festival of 1848. To this she replied that she would have great pleasure in being able to aid so excellent a charity. The only condition Jenny Lind made was that a sufficient interval should be allowed to elapse between the end of the London opera season and the Festival, so as to allow her to recover from the fatigue of her opera engagements.

William Done was despatched to London to make the necessary arrangements, and had an interview with Jenny Lind, who referred him to Mr Lumley, the Director of Her Majesty's Theatre, to ascertain when the opera season would close. However, Done was obliged to return to Worcester with nothing settled.

The Festival secretary, the Rev. Robert Sargeant, wrote to Jenny Lind reminding her of her letter to the bishop and advising that the start of the Festival had been deferred to 5 September for her convenience. He received a letter from Mr Lumley expressing regret that Mlle Lind's previous engagements would not permit her appearance at Worcester. Sargeant went to see Lumley but was unable to change his mind; a little later he received a letter from Lumley containing a cheque for £50 from Jenny Lind, as a donation from her towards the Festival charity.

In the second week of August 1848 advertisements appeared in the newspapers announcing that Jenny Lind had accepted engagements to sing at Birmingham and Cheltenham during the same week that the Worcester Festival was to be held. The indignation of the Worcester Stewards was extreme. Sargeant wrote to Jenny Lind pointing out that her appearance at the two towns 'must inevitably be productive of the most serious injury that the festival can sustain'.[12] It is not known if he received any reply. However, for Lumley the seasons of 1847 and 1848, thanks to Jenny Lind, were a huge success. It was rumoured that in 1847 alone he pocketed £22,000 clear of all expenses.

In 1852, Jenny Lind married the composer and conductor Otto Goldschmidt and toured widely with him. For the 1856 Festival the Gloucester Stewards authorised John Amott to negotiate with her for a sum not exceeding £500 (in that year Alboni received £275 and Viardot £180), but he was not successful. He tried again for 1859 but 'she declined to enter into any engagement to sing at the Festival'.[13] Finally, in 1862 the Festival chairman, Sir George Jackson, High Sheriff of Gloucester, was asked to approach Jenny Lind. This time her reason for refusal became plain: in her letter declining yet again to sing at the Festival

[11] *MW* 1855, p. 544.

[12] *MW* 1848, pp. 567–8.

[13] Gloucester Festival Minute Book, 1859. Gloucester Cathedral Archives and Library.

1 Hereford Cathedral

2 Thomas Bisse

3 William Hayes,
by John Cornish, c. 1749

4 John Beard

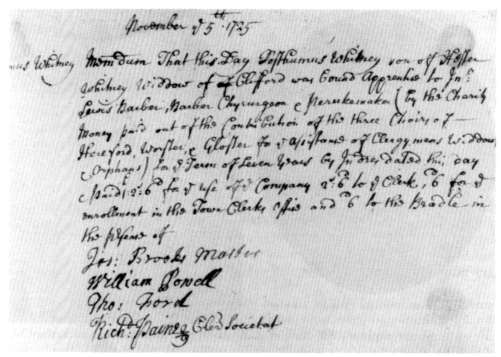

5 Entry dated 5 November 1724, in the Minute Book of the Hereford Haberdashers Company, recording the apprenticeship of Posthumous Whitney to a local 'Barber, Chyrurgeon and Perukemaker' with funds provided by the Three Choirs charity

6 Eighteenth-century catch singers

7 Giusto Ferdinando Tenducci

8 Giulia Frasi

9 *Johann Christian Fischer*, by
Thomas Gainsborough

10 *Mrs Richard Brinsley Sheridan*,
née Elizabeth Linley,
by Thomas Gainsborough

11 Hereford Cathedral, 18 April 1786

12 Gertrud Elisabeth Mara

13 John Braham

14 James Bartleman

15 Worcester Cathedral at the beginning of the nineteenth century, by J. Powell

16 Angelica Catalani

17 Elizabeth Billington

18 Nancy Storace

19 Robert Lindley and Domenico Dragonetti

20 François Cramer

21 Maria Malibran

22 Charles de Beriot

23 Caricature of William Mutlow drawn by Maria Malibran at Gloucester in 1829

24 William Mutlow

25 Giovanni Mario

26 Antonio Tamburini

27 Luigi Lablache

28 Giulia Grisi

29 Henriette Sontag

30 Clara Novello

31 John Sims Reeves

32 Joseph Staudigl

33 Mary Ann Paton

34 Therese Tietjens

35 Jenny Lind

36 Henry Phillips

37 Marietta Alboni   38 Samuel Sebastian Wesley   39 George Townshend Smith

40 Hereford, 1852

MUSIC

GLOUCESTER MUSICAL FESTIVAL

(From our own Correspondent.)

GLOUCESTER, WEDNESDAY

GLOUCESTER CATHEDRAL.—THE SUPPOSED PILGRIM'S DOOR.

THE GRAND MUSICAL FESTIVAL IN GLOUCESTER CATHEDRAL.

41 Gloucester, 1850

42 William Done

43 Worcester, 1863 (probably the last photograph taken before the fine screen surmounted by the organ was removed)

44 Worcester, 1890: William Done (wearing top hat), Hugh Blair (wearing mortar board) and choristers

45 Worcester, 1866

46 Gloucester, 1841

48 Iron bridge over the River Wye at Hereford, from a drawing by J. Clayton

47 A railway poster from 1883

49 Gloucester, 1865: the nave of the cathedral looking west

50 Hereford, 1897

51 Gloucester, 1853: the Secular Concert in the Shire Hall. The three soloists are Mme Castellan, Miss Dolby and Theodore Formes.

52 Bishop Ellicott: a caricature by 'Spy'

53 Lord Dudley: a caricature by 'Spy' (1875)

54 Rosalind Ellicott

55 The Very Revd Francis Close

56 Langdon Colborne

57 Sir Hubert Parry in 1892

58 Sir Frederic Cowen

59 Sir Arthur Sullivan

60 Hereford, 1891. *Standing:* G. R. Sinclair; *seated, left to right:* J. T. Carrodus, W. H. Eayres, R. M. Blagrove, and C. Ould

61 G. R. Sinclair and Dan

62 *Left to right:* Ivor Atkins, George Robertson Sinclair and Herbert Brewer, *c.*1899

she added that in any engagement she might make, she would require Mr Otto Goldschmidt to be the conductor.[14]

At last, in 1867, Jenny Lind-Goldschmidt agreed to sing in her husband's oratorio *Ruth* at the Hereford Festival in a performance conducted by him. While there she also sang in *Elijah* and *Messiah*. In these two long-established masterpieces she scored a fair success:

> Those who know the intense absorption of Madame Goldschmidt in her work, and the wonderful combinations of earnestness and intelligence she brings to its performance will not require to be told what an effect she made in the impassioned music of her part [in *Elijah*]. Years have produced their inevitable effect upon the voice which once cast a spell over every listener, but the instinct of the artist remains strong as ever, and asserted, this morning, all its old power.[15]

The reviewer continued: 'The rendering of the sublimest of airs, "I know that my Redeemer liveth" by Madame Goldschmidt ... was a marvel of artistic skill and profound expression.'[16]

The 'instinct of the artist' was insufficient to make a success of *Ruth*, a work described by the *Musical World* as 'an unsymmetrical corpse'. *The Times* noted that not one of the many choruses was gone through from end to end without impediment, and the *Hereford Journal* reported that 'Madame Lind-Goldschmidt's exertions in the part of Ruth were almost painful to witness; her once fine voice is gone.'

Giulia Grisi (1811–1869) was an Italian prima donna with an international reputation. She sang in the Festivals of 1838(G) and 1855(H), and was considered by many to be the finest dramatic soprano of her generation. She was typical of the many singers of both sexes who rose to fame on the stages of the world's opera houses and who, although not specialists in oratorio singing, were in huge public demand to sing at the regional festivals. To opponents of the Music Meetings the very fact that these stars were theatrical performers was anathema: a cathedral was a House of God, not an opera house. At the same time, within the musical establishment there was a rising tide of opposition to the policy of engaging foreign stars at huge expense in preference to British singers for so absolutely British an institution as the Three Choirs Festival.

Pre-eminent among the English women singers of the mid-nineteenth century was the soprano Clara Novello (1818–1908), daughter of Vincent Novello, the composer and founder of the famous music-publishing firm. Clara Novello made her debut at the Worcester Music Meeting of 1833 and sang regularly at Three Choirs for almost three decades. During her career she earned the praise of both Mendelssohn and Schumann, and her reviews read like a litany of praise. For her final performance in 1860, again at Worcester, the *Musical World* reported:

[14] Gloucester Festival Minute Book, 1862. Gloucester Cathedral Archives and Library.

[15] *MW* 1867, p. 576.

[16] Ibid., p. 592.

To say that she sang to perfection would be faint praise … It made everyone feel a regret that we are so soon to lose such a voice from among us, and that future festivals must look long and far before they again find any one conveying the sensations produced by those clear ringing bell-like notes.[17]

It was seventeen years before the festivals found such a voice again. The first principal soprano from 1861 to 1876 was the Hungarian Thérèse Tietjens (1831–1877), who settled in England in 1858 and first sang at Three Choirs in the evening concerts in 1859(G). Although engaged to sing at Gloucester in 1877, Tietjens fell ill in the June of that year. The Stewards, fearing that she might be unable to sing at the Festival, authorised Charles Harford Lloyd to negotiate for a possible stand-in. He considered Madame Helen Lemmens-Sherrington, who had not sung at Three Choirs for five years, but found that she was already booked to appear in a series of concerts during the Festival week. To obtain her services would have involved buying up those concerts at a cost of £130, in addition to paying her fee of 150 guineas for singing with Tietjens, or 200 guineas if she took on all the work alone. The Stewards considered this to be out of the question.[18]

On 12 July the manager of Her Majesty's Theatre in London, Col. J.H. Mapleson, who was Tietjens's agent, wrote to Lloyd saying that she was very much better and that her medical attendant had authorised him to announce that she would be fit to perform before the close of the opera season. Even so, Lloyd continued to plan for the possibility of her not being able to appear. He had, in any case, determined to engage a soprano of the finest quality for this, his first Three Choirs Festival. He contacted Frederick Gye, the agent of Mlle Emma Albani, a Canadian singer who had settled in England in 1872 after making a successful debut at Covent Garden.[19] Gye wrote to Lloyd saying that as Three Choirs had agreed to pay Tietjens 350 guineas, he presumed that there would be no objection to paying 'such an Artiste as Mdlle Albani considerably more'. He asked for 450 guineas: far more than the cost of engaging Helen Lemmens-Sherrington *and* buying out her previously booked concerts.

On 11 August 1877, just three weeks before the start of the Festival, Mapleson wrote to Lloyd:

I am very sorry to say that Mdlle Tietjens is not making the progress we had all wished. Her medical attendant Dr Spencer Wells up to last Saturday gave me a full assurance that her services were to be relied upon. During the last three or four days she has become much weaker and feels she will be unable to undertake the engagement.[20]

---

[17] *MW* 1860, p. 587.

[18] Gloucester Festival Minute Book, 1877. Gloucester Cathedral Archives and Library.

[19] Albani's real name was Marie Louise Cecile Lajeunesse. She later married Gye, after which she was known as Madame Albani-Gye.

[20] Gloucester Festival Minute Book, 1877. Gloucester Cathedral Archives and Library.

Lloyd persuaded the Stewards to engage Emma Albani, in spite of the cost. We are told 'She threw her whole soul into *Elijah*', and so began her thirty-four-year association with Three Choirs.[21] Thérèse Tietjens died on 3 October 1877.

Madame (afterwards Dame Emma) Albani became the 'Queen of Song' of this and all the English musical festivals of the day. The impression she made was still vivid many years later. In reminiscences communicated to Watkins Shaw in 1952, Sir Ivor Atkins recalled the magnificent effect of her singing of the aria 'Hear ye, Israel' at the beginning of Part II of *Elijah*, particularly her soaring phrases at 'I, thy God', an effect enhanced by her practice of requiring the earlier soprano music of the oratorio to be sung by a soloist of lesser calibre. Atkins recalled, too, how she would not come on the platform until Part II was about to begin, when she entered with her copy of the music tied in ribbon, and held up the proceedings while she knelt for a moment in prayer. He mentioned also her ostentatious reluctance – and refusal – to rehearse, even to use her singing voice; and her elaborate progress in carriage and pair, even if it were only the eighty yards from where she stayed (at what later became the Worcester deanery, and is now the King's School office) to the south cloister gate of Worcester Cathedral. But as Dr Shaw has pointed out, 'before her active career was over, a style came to be required which demanded more personal effacement, a greater degree of artistic and intellectual subtlety', and H. C. Colles notes that her instinct was right when in 1902 she was reluctant to sing in Walford Davies's *The Temple*.[22]

Janet Patey, née Whytock (1842–1894), a Scottish contralto, appeared regularly at Three Choirs from 1866(w), the year following that of her first concert tour, and the year of her marriage to John Patey, the English baritone. There was great disappointment when in 1877(w) Madame Patey was not invited to sing at the Festival. Both she and Charles Santley were dropped 'from motives of economy'.[23] Although Santley was back in the following year, Patey never returned.

Of the second rank of female principal singers in the latter half of the nineteenth century, mention must be made of the soprano Anna Williams and the contralto Hilda Wilson; both were Festival favourites for many years, Williams appearing regularly from 1878(H) and Wilson from 1880(G) until 1904(G). In fact, Hilda Wilson (1860–1915) was a local girl, the daughter of James Wilson, a 'professor of music' and bandmaster who also seems to have kept 'The Running Horse' at 38 Barton Street, Gloucester. Her younger sister Agnes was a soprano, and her brother, H. Lane Wilson, a well-known songwriter, accompanist and bass singer who appeared as a soloist at Three Choirs in 1898(G) and 1902(w).[24] Hilda Wilson's musical training had been generously paid for by Gloucester ladies.[25]

---

[21] *The Times*, 4 September 1877.

[22] H. C. Colles, *Walford Davies* (OUP, 1942), p. 73.

[23] *Annals* 1895, p. 289.

[24] I was indebted to the late Mr Brian Frith for this information.

[25] See Watkins Shaw, *The Three Choirs Festival: The Official History of the Meetings of Gloucester, Hereford and Worcester, c. 1713–1953* (Baylis for Three Choirs Festival, 1954), p. 79.

Among the famous foreign male opera singers to appear at Three Choirs in the first sixty years of the nineteenth century were the tenors Giovanni Rubini and Giovanni Mario, the baritones Antonio Tamburini and Giovanni Belletti, and the great bass Luigi Lablache.

Lablache (1794–1858) was born in Italy of French and Irish parents, made his debut in Naples in 1812 and quickly became world famous. In 1827 he was a torch-bearer at the funeral of Beethoven and in 1830 made his first appearance in London, returning to England every year except 1833 until the closure of Her Majesty's Theatre in 1852. He sang at Three Choirs for the first time in 1835(G) and in the following year was appointed singing-master to Queen Victoria. He returned to the Festival in 1838(G), 1840(H) and 1848(W). In 1850 the *Musical World* heaped praise upon Lablache:

> Lablache's voice is an organ of extraordinary power. It is impossible by description to give any notion of its volume of sound. He is an ophicleide among singers. One may have some idea of the power of tone, when it may be asserted, that, with the entire opera band and chorus playing and *singing forte*, his voice may be as distinctly and separately heard above them all as a trumpet among violins.[26]

The German bass Theodor Formes sang at Three Choirs each year from 1850 to 1854 and again in 1857. His voice was described as colossal and impressive but, in common with other stars of the day, he sometimes saw no purpose in attending rehearsals of works he had sung many times. On one occasion (1851(W)), he failed to turn up for an evening concert, sending word that he was indisposed. Rumour had it that 'Formes was off to sing somewhere else that night' and when 'towards the end of the evening the Stewards came up in solemn file and announced that Herr Formes was got better [*sic*] and would certainly sing the morrow morning in the *Messiah* … there was a good deal of laughing, and it was pronounced to be a case of a very sudden cure.'[27] The only countertenor of distinction to be heard at Three Choirs in the nineteenth century was William Knyvett (1777–1856), a member of a famous family of English musicians, who was appointed a Gentleman of the Chapel Royal in 1797. Knyvett was a conductor and composer as well as a singer; he first performed at a Music Meeting in 1799(G), when he was described as 'a most chaste counter-tenor singer' and 'one of the very few English singers remarkable for correctness in the musical enunciation of the words of the English language'.[28] Knyvett's wife, Deborah, was also a singer and they performed together for many years, making their last Three Choirs appearance in 1838(G).

One other, albeit reluctant, countertenor made his brief mark in the period. At the Opening Service of the Worcester Festival in 1854, Charlotte Dolby became suddenly unwell. At a moment's notice the alto parts were taken 'and most creditably executed' by Mr Jones, the Organist at Tewkesbury.[29]

---

[26] *MW* 1850, p. 617.

[27] *Worcester Herald*, 30 August 1851.

[28] *Annals* 1895, p. 79.

[29] *MW* 1854, p. 610.

John Braham (1777–1856), whose real name was Abraham, was a Jew of German extraction: a small man (he was 5′3″ tall) with a huge, trumpet-like tenor voice. His singing career began as a treble at the Covent Garden Theatre in 1787; in 1794 he made his debut as a tenor at Rauzzini's concerts in Bath. He appeared in London and at the Gloucester Festival in 1796. The composer Stephen Storace was so impressed by Braham's singing that he began writing *Mahmoud* for him, but died in 1796, at the age of thirty-three, before completing the score. Shortly afterwards Braham left for the Continent with Storace's sister Nancy, the first Susanna in Mozart's *Le nozze di Figaro* (1786), who had been a pupil of Rauzzini and who had become Braham's mistress. He returned to England in 1801 following huge acclaim in France and Italy, and in the next twenty-five years is said to have earned an average of £14,000 *per annum*.

Braham reappeared at Three Choirs in 1809(w) and sang at the Music Meetings until 1838(G). He was greatly admired as an opera singer, but less so in oratorio and popular ballads, which he tended to 'Italianise'. At Gloucester in 1817:

> The performance of *Messiah* was considerably marred by Mr Braham, who sang 'Comfort ye, my people' in a manner so ill-fitting the subject, and with such redundancy of false ornament, as to draw upon himself the censure of the critics of that period, who were naturally disposed to indulgence, especially towards one whose popularity was then at its zenith.[30]

When Braham was nearly sixty years old, the critic of the *Musical World* was kinder to him in reviewing the Worcester Festival of 1836:

> After nearly forty years of acquaintance with Mr. Braham's public life, it was delightful to hear him pour out with such youthful vigour the 'Sound the Alarm!' It is good to listen to him, if it be only to cheat oneself into the belief that both we and he are the same as when we used to think that there never had been such a voice and such fine singing since the creation of our first parents.[31]

Braham frequently sang with Maria Malibran and with the baritone Henry Phillips. In his autobiography, *Musical and Personal Recollections during Half a Century* (1864), Phillips describes Braham as 'a rare mimic, and at times very witty':

> He would often refer to one of [Angelica] Catalini's weaknesses, viz: boasting of the various articles of jewellery she possessed. Certainly they were very costly, and she would walk round our room saying, – You see dis brooch? de Emperor of Austria gave me dis. You see dese earrings? de Emperor of Russia gave me dese. You see dis ring? de Emperor Napoleon gave me dis', and so on. Mr. Braham, in imitation of this, would say, pointing to his umbrella, – 'You see dis? de Emperor of China gave me dis.' Then, pointing to his teeth, 'de King of Tuscany gave me dese.'

[30] *Annals* 1895, p. 101.
[31] *MW* 1836, p. 56.

Phillips tells another story about Braham, which refers to a Three Choirs performance in which Maria Malibran, Braham and Phillips took part under the baton of William Mutlow. In his book *Cathedral Organists* (1899), John West suggests that this anecdote should be taken *cum grano salis*. Even so, it is a good tale:

> Mr. Braham was a man generally of most reserved manners, which gave the impression of pride, yet no one entered more into jest than he did, whether practical or otherwise. One of a laughable character occurred at a celebrated triennial festival, in connection with the conductor, who was organist of the cathedral. He chanced to be a gentleman of eccentric habits and appearance, very short and fat, an epicure of no ordinary stamp, the length of whose arm was as near as possible the measure of his baton. Though an especial favourite with Madame Malibran, she delighted to play him all sorts of tricks, at which he never took offence. On one occasion of a morning performance, of selected sacred music, Madame Malibran and Braham had to sing a duett, John Loder being leader of the orchestra; the three consulted together as to what trick they could play the conductor, and one having been agreed upon, the morning performance arrived, all went very well, the band and singers going on smoothly in one time while the conductor beat another – that was of little consequence in those days. At length came the duett by Malibran and Braham, which had a long symphony preceding it; the conductor, with more than ordinary energy in honor of so grand an occasion, waved his baton in the air, till down it came as a signal for the first chord, but not a semblance of sound issued from the orchestra. 'Hallo!' shouted the conductor, with a raised head, in amazement, 'can't you all see? Now, then, we'll try again.' He did, and the result was the same. 'Why, what the devil's the matter? – are you all mad?' cried the little fat man, the huge drops falling from his forehead, which, as he drew his handkerchief to remove, the symphony began, to his great astonishment, and almost defied his beating a bar correctly till it had nearly finished, the singers nearly fainting with suppressed laughter at the success of the trick they had so ingeniously planned.
>
> When this little conductor gave a lesson on the pianoforte, it was always in a room next to the kitchen: in the middle of the lesson he would say, 'There, go on; I can hear ye, I'm only going to baste the air' (hare), so he walked into the kitchen, did what he proposed, came back, and finished the lesson. The Queen's English was a matter sadly disregarded by this gentleman: luckily, not being at court, he escaped the condemnation it must otherwise have brought upon him; when going out he would call to the servant, 'Hann, where's my 'at?' He was, however, a kind, good-tempered soul, took all that happened in the best part, and when the festival had terminated said, 'Some very droll things have occurred this week; but never mind, come and dine with me, and we'll enjoy the haunch of venison and drink success to the next festival in some of the finest port wine in England.'

The most prominent British tenors for the remainder of the nineteenth century were Charles Lockey, John Sims Reeves and Edward Lloyd.

Charles Lockey (1820–1901) first sang at a Music Meeting in 1846(H), the year in which he came to prominence by taking the tenor part in the first performance of Mendelssohn's *Elijah* in Birmingham. He repeated this success in Gloucester in 1847, for which he received £42, and continued to sing at the Festivals until 1856(G), by which time his career had been rather eclipsed by that of Sims Reeves.

John Sims Reeves (1818–1900) was the king of tenors in this country for over thirty years from his first London appearance in 1847. He sang regularly at Three Choirs from 1848(W) until 1877(G) and was equally popular and successful in the performance of operatic arias and oratorios. He also endeared himself to the British public as a singer of ballads such as 'Tom Bowling', 'The Death of Nelson', 'The Bay of Biscay' and 'My Pretty Jane'.

Sims Reeves would never agree to sing unless he was in good voice, and once stated that he had lost £80,000 during his long career through his conscientiousness. He always preferred to disappoint an audience than to turn up and sing to them 'with a throat', and Three Choirs audiences were often disappointed. As early as 1849(H) he failed to turn up for *Messiah* and Charles Lockey was obliged to substitute without notice. His absences from concerts became so notorious that *The Orchestra* magazine suggested that promoters resort to a new form of advertisement:

> ON THIS OCCASION THE AUDIENCE WILL
> POSITIVELY HAVE A * CHANCE OF HEARING
> MR. SIMS REEVES
>
> * Here insert 'good', 'fair', 'small', or
> 'poor' as the case may be

So used did the Three Choirs Stewards become to Sims Reeves's absences that they were not prepared to be sympathetic when, genuinely ill, he left the platform halfway through the Wednesday evening concert in the Shire Hall at the Gloucester Festival of 1859; a shocking and faintly comic scene ensued, and was reported the next day in *The Times*:

> No less than four speeches were adventured in the course of about one hour last night – three short, and little to the purpose; one not very long, but *much* to the purpose. Of the short speeches one was delivered by Mr. T. Gambier Parry,[32] a 'steward', and two were furnished by the Mayor of Gloucester: the not very long speech flowed gently from the lips of Madame Clara Novello. The origin of all these improvised orations may be briefly stated. The indisposition of Mr. Sims Reeves has been alluded to. It was observed on all sides during the performance of *The May Queen*, and no one ought to have felt surprise, however he may have experienced disappointment, at the omission of a ballad allotted to this gentleman in the second part of the concert. When, however, Madame Novello

[32] Father of Sir Hubert Parry.

had sung 'Prendi per me' out of its place, and on her retiring there were no signs of Mr. Reeves, the audience began to be restive, and would not be pacified until one of the stewards (Mr T. G. Parry) came forward and addressed them. He said (as clearly as we can remember), 'Ladies and Gentlemen, – It seems to be the principal duty of the stewards to make apologies for Mr. Sims Reeves. The stewards have done all in their power, but as Mr Sims Reeves has quietly walked off, the stewards cannot fetch him back, and I hope they will not be blamed. He has found a good friend in Madame Novello, who has kindly consented to sing a song in his stead.' This address was received with mingled applause and hisses. It did not, however, satisfy Mr Reeves's substitute, who, protesting that it conveyed an erroneous statement of the facts, declared that she would not sing until it had been corrected. The Mayor of Gloucester (on the refusal of his colleague to set matters right) then volunteered a further explanation, which amounted to this: –

'Ladies and Gentlemen, – I have the pleasure to inform you that Madame Novello will give another song in place of Mr. Sims Reeves.' Cries of 'Not enough' – 'We know that already' – greeted the ears of his worship as he left the platform, having delivered himself of this weighty piece of information. Being apprised of the inadequate manner in which he had accomplished his self-imposed task, the Mayor returned to the charge, and addressed his turbulent co-citizens afresh: – 'Ladies and Gentlemen,' he said, 'I am to state that Mr. Sims Reeves, being ill, was compelled to leave.' This speech, a worthy pendant of the other, was answered by shouts of laughter, and it seemed unlikely now that the disturbance would be quelled at all. After a long interval, during the progress of which the Shire hall threatened to be turned into a bear-garden, Madame Clara Novello made her appearance on the platform, to fulfil as was generally surmised, the task she had undertaken as deputy. Shouts, cheers, and plaudits greeted her from every part of the room, and when these subsided, she opened her lips – but not to sing. Instead of 'Bonnie Prince Charlie' it was 'Ladies and Gentlemen.' Calmly, unaffectedly, yet firmly, Madame Novello, like a musical Portia, admonished her hearers. She spoke to the following purport: – 'Before he went away, very ill, Mr Reeves explained to the conductor his total inability to sing his ballad in the second part; but, with a desire that the audience might not be losers through his indisposition, which was not his fault, he applied to me to introduce something in its place, and even sent for a copy of the ballad I am now going to have the honour of singing to you, with much less ability than he would have shown.

'Mr. Amott, with whom alone the artists engaged at the festival can communicate on business, was consulted, and gave his approval; and, not satisfied even with this, Mr. Reeves spoke with one of the stewards, who also consented to the change. Had this been stated, no fault could possibly have been laid at his charge. I thus take the liberty to address you, Ladies and Gentlemen, because I will not allow a brother artist to be unjustly accused, as Mr. Reeves was – of course unintentionally – in the explanation given this evening, or to be blamed when he is entirely innocent, and especially when he had taken all the precautions in his power to compensate for any disappointment.' The tones of this nightingale had more persuasive eloquence in them than the voices of the steward and the Mayor. The fair apologist (who speaks, by the way, quite as musically as she sings) was completely overwhelmed with the demonstrations of complete satisfaction that her quiet speech had elicited, and the peace of her 'brother artist' was made with the public. We do not remember a more graceful act on the part of one artist to another – an act implying a strong sense of right, no little moral courage, and the total absence of a certain feeling of jealous rivalry from which even the most distinguished members of the profession are not invariably exempt.

The next day, Sims Reeves was confined to bed, but was able to sing in *Messiah* on the Friday. The reason for his illness was made clear in the press: one night in the week before the Festival, he had been staying in a London hotel which had caught fire. He had joined in the efforts to extinguish the blaze which threatened to destroy the whole building. Then, with his family, he had been obliged to spend the night camping on the wet grass of a nearby park and had caught a cold.

The Gloucester Stewards made a public apology for their blunder and Sims Reeves donated 25 guineas to the Festival charity to compensate for the disappointment, pointing out that he would have given more, but that he had in any case charged 50 guineas less than his usual terms.[33] He was known for his generosity: following *Messiah* in Hereford in 1867, the collection plate was found to contain a cheque for £100 from Sims Reeves.

Although he must have earned vast sums, Sims Reeves was never a saver and ended his days in poverty. In 1896 he was reduced to appearing at music halls, and in April 1900 he was given a Civil List pension of £100; six months later he was dead.

Edward Lloyd (1845–1927) had been a choirboy at Westminster Abbey until 1860 and one of the Gentlemen of the Chapel Royal from 1869. His first important public appearance was at the Gloucester Festival of 1871, when S. S. Wesley chose him to sing the part of the Evangelist in the first Three Choirs performance of Bach's *St Matthew Passion*. His beautiful singing brought him the approval of the critics, a fee of 30 guineas, and a foothold on the ladder to fame. Lloyd retired from public life after the Hereford Festival of 1900.

THE leading British singers to perform the bass solos at Three Choirs in the nineteenth century were Henry Phillips, W. H. Weiss and Sir Charles Santley.

Phillips (1801–1876) was born in Bristol, appeared on the stage when still only a boy, sang in the chorus at the Drury Lane Theatre in London and gradually worked his way up to become the leading British baritone of his generation. He appeared not only on the opera stage and concert platform but also in table entertainments. After performances at Three Choirs, where he sang between 1826

---

[33] Gloucester Festival Minute Book, 1859. Gloucester Cathedral Archives and Library.

and 1852, he would sometimes take to the boards in local theatres, singing parts such as that of Tom Tug in Dibdin's *The Waterman*.

Willoughby Hunter Weiss (1820–1867) was considered to be second only to Joseph Staudigl (1807–1861) as an interpreter of the name-part in *Elijah*. He first sang at Three Choirs in 1844(G), when an eighteen-year-old soprano from Gloucester, Georgina Ansell Barrett (1826–1880), was making her debut. Weiss and Barrett became man and wife, frequently sharing the concert platform until her last Festival appearance in 1864(H).

In 1859 Weiss came into collision with the Gloucester Stewards as a result of a bungle by John Amott, who had engaged Giovanni Belletti to share the bass parts with Weiss. In accepting his engagement, Weiss wrote to Amott on 28 June making the condition that there should be a fair arrangement of the music between Belletti and himself. On 9 July he wrote again saying: 'I hope I shall have the Elijah.' Unfortunately, Belletti had insisted that he would only appear 'on the understanding that he would not be called upon to learn music or English words with which he was not already perfectly acquainted'.[34] As Belletti *was* acquainted with *Elijah*, Amott gave the part of the prophet to him. The fat was in the fire; the Festival Committee received a spiky letter from Weiss:

> the terms on which I accepted the Engagement at your Festival, have not been complied with, and any person conversant with musical matters will, I feel convinced, agree that I have not been fairly dealt with – and that in justice to my own professional reputation I cannot do otherwise than refuse to go into the Engagement with the music allotted to me, which certainly is not that of first principal Bass, for which I expressly stipulated.

Gloucester had to manage without Weiss in 1859, but he sang at the next five Festivals; his final appearance, in which he was again magnificent as Elijah, was at Hereford in 1867, the year of his death at the age of forty-seven. Weiss is still remembered as a writer of lyrics and composer of ballads, the best-known of which is *The Village Blacksmith*.

A Gloucestershire man who built a successful international career, the baritone Robert Watkin-Mills was born in Painswick on 5 March 1856, studied in London and Milan, and made his first public appearance at a Crystal Palace concert in 1884. He was back in Gloucester for the Festival of 1886 and appeared frequently as a Three Choirs principal soloist until 1906(H). Watkin-Mills finally settled in Toronto, where he died in 1930.

The greatest British baritone of the latter half of the nineteenth century was Sir Charles Santley (1834–1922). Trained by Gaetano Nava in Milan and by Manuel García in London, his career spanned the five decades from 1857. Enormously successful as an opera singer, Santley sang the role of Valentine in the first performance (in Italian) of Gounod's *Faust* in England at Her Majesty's Theatre on 11 June 1863. Following this success, Santley was engaged for Three Choirs and became the principal bass soloist at all the major festivals until the beginning of the twentieth century. In January 1864 he again sang Valentine at Her Majesty's Theatre, in an English version of *Faust* prepared by Henry Chorley. Gounod composed a new aria especially for Santley, 'Even bravest heart may

[34] Ibid.

swell', and this was destined to become one of the most popular numbers in the opera. However, after 1877 he was heard only in concerts and oratorios – and at the start of the new century in a medium which would make his voice immortal: the gramophone.

THERE can be no doubt that throughout the nineteenth century, audiences had been attracted to Three Choirs chiefly by the appearance at the Festival of star artists. The double-cast system, coupled to the enormous fees of soloists, had regularly plunged the Festival into deficit, generously underwritten by the hard-pressed and sometimes reluctant Stewards. The cost of engaging principal singers in three typical years is of interest: 1865(G) – £1,058; 1866(w) – £1,220; 1867(H) – £1,208. Under pressure from the Stewards, the Festival conductors made periodic attempts to economise: at Gloucester in 1871, S. S. Wesley engaged neither Sims Reeves nor Santley – to the disappointment of public and critics alike. Even so, the fees of the principal singers during the three days of the Festival amounted to £915, the equivalent purchasing power of which would be some £76,000 in real terms today (2016).

As the nineteenth century drew to a close, so too did the provincial clamour for international star singers. 'Taste and education in music were developing with such rapid strides, that Festival Committees had to realise that the chief attraction was the music itself.'[35] The gramophone played an important part in developing taste and education in music. The demand for miscellaneous concerts of operatic arias, ballads, humorous songs and instrumental pieces, already fading out of fashion by mid-century, declined further as the public were enabled to listen to their favourite artists on records at home. The opera star who also sang in *Messiah* and *Elijah* gave way to the specialist oratorio singer – the path chosen by Charles Santley in 1877. And in the year in which Santley was knighted, 1907, the first sod of earth on the site of the future Gramophone Company factory at Hayes, Middlesex, was cut by a famous tenor whose career had begun at the Three Choirs Festival of 1871: Edward Lloyd.[36]

---

[35] Herbert Brewer, *Memories of Choirs and Cloisters* (Bodley Head, 1931), p. 91.

[36] The Gramophone Company was responsible for the His Master's Voice gramophone records; later it became part of EMI Records Ltd.

8

Favourites and Flops

THROUGHOUT the eighteenth century the music of Handel had dominated Three Choirs and, supreme among all his works, *Messiah* remained safely anchored to the Festivals for the whole of the nineteenth and much of the twentieth centuries. It was a brave S. S. Wesley who, in his first Festival as conductor at Hereford (1834), dared to present only a selection from *Messiah* instead of the whole work – an experiment which he was not allowed to repeat. However, the Handelian domination did slowly subside as successive Festival conductors, by patient persistence, gradually stimulated the appetites of their provincial audiences to accept a more varied oratorio diet. The turning point came in 1800(w).

Joseph Haydn (1732–1809) had attended the Handel Festival at Westminster Abbey in 1791. The experience had an enormous effect upon him. After one performance of *Messiah* he said of Handel: 'He is the master of us all', and, as a result of this festival, began to consider the possibility of composing an oratorio of his own. Haydn completed *The Creation* in 1798. The work occupied him for two whole years, of which time he said, 'Never before was I so devout as when I composed *The Creation*. I knelt down each day to pray to God to give me strength for my work.' When urged to bring it to a conclusion, he calmly replied, 'I spend much time over it, because I intend it to last a long time.'

The Creation was published in 1800, performed in London in March, and heard for only the third time in England at the Worcester Music Meeting of that year. The individuality of Haydn's genius was not at first fully understood by Three Choirs audiences nurtured on the style of Handel, but selections from *The Creation* became ever more popular as the century progressed.

There was less of individuality or genius in the oratorio *Palestine* by Dr William Crotch (1775–1847), and yet the work was in great demand for a short time. Extracts from it were given in 1827(w) and 1833(w). Following a complete performance in 1839(w), the *Musical World* even went so far as to describe it as 'the best specimen of oratorio writing in this country'.[1] When it was repeated in 1840(H) the same journal acknowledged that *Palestine* contained much that was plagiarised Handel, and adjusted its earlier assessment: 'it is the oddest mixture of great talent and servile, drivelling imitation that can be conceived.'[2] Following Crotch's death in 1847, a poorly attended performance of the work was given in a final salute at the Worcester Festival of 1848. As far as Three Choirs was concerned, the oratorio died with its composer.

[1] *MW* 1839, p. 326.
[2] *MW* 1840, p. 203.

Even more rapid obscurity awaited Neukomm's *Mount Sinai* (extracts 1832(G)) and Schneider's *The Deluge* (extracts 1833(W)), neither of which survived to a second Three Choirs performance. The same fate befell two oratorios by Dr John Clarke-Whitfeld, the Hereford Organist, and presented under his own direction: *The Crucifixion* (1822(H)) and *The Resurrection* (1825(H)). The ever-outspoken critic of the *Musical World* was cruel enough to describe a piece by Clarke-Whitfeld as 'grave though sapless twaddle', and it is inconceivable that modern listeners will ever be given the opportunity to judge for themselves.[3]

At the Music Meeting of 1832(G), John Amott introduced not only the ill-fated *Mount Sinai* but also Mozart's Requiem and extracts from the best-known oratorio of Louis Spohr (1784–1859), *The Last Judgement*. Other choral works by Spohr were taken up by Three Choirs: *The Fall of Babylon* (1846(H)), *Calvary* (1849(H)) and *The Christian's Prayer* (1855(H)), each of which received a handful of performances in succeeding years but failed to achieve the sensational success of *The Last Judgement*, which was demanded time and again until 1901.

Now almost completely forgotten and ignored, in its day *The Last Judgement* was considered to be 'the mighty conception of a master-mind'.[4] Composed by Spohr in 1825, it was first performed in England at the Norwich Festival of 1830 when, as in a full performance at the Worcester Festival of 1836, the bass solos were sung by Edward Taylor, who was also responsible for preparing the English adaptation of the original German libretto (*Die letzten Dinge*). It was Taylor who adapted Mozart's Requiem under the title of *Redemption* for the controversial performance in English at Worcester in 1836.

Sir Herbert Brewer recalled an incident at one of the Three Choirs Festivals when a Steward gently informed a lady that she was occupying the wrong seat. With indignation she replied: 'I sat in this seat for *The Creation* and I intend to remain here for *The Last Judgement*!'[5]

In the first half of the century Beethoven's *Mount of Olives* (1842(W)) and Mass in C (1847(G)) were introduced to Three Choirs, both with altered titles – *Engedi* and Service in C – and 'Protestantised'. But the coming man was Felix Mendelssohn (1809–1847); his oratorio *St Paul* (1837(H)) and the sinfonia cantata *Hymn of Praise* (1841(G)) became immediate Festival favourites. His next choral work proved to be the most popular of all – a masterpiece which marched in step with *Messiah* at all but two of the Festivals between 1847 and 1929, was programmed many times thereafter, and remains a firm favourite to the present day. In the spring of 1846, Mendelssohn wrote to Jenny Lind about his new oratorio: 'I am jumping about my room for joy! If it only turns out half as good as I fancy it is how pleased I shall be!'

Mendelssohn's *Elijah* was given a triumphant first performance at the Birmingham Festival on 26 August 1846 under the direction of the composer. Its repetition at the Gloucester Festival of 1847 was sufficient incentive to bring the correspondent of the *Musical World* hastening back from his first-ever assignment

---

[3] Ibid., commenting on the spirit scene from Charles Whitfeld's *The Lay of the Last Minstrel*.

[4] *Gloucester Journal*, September 1835.

[5] Herbert Brewer, *Memories of Choirs and Cloisters* (Bodley Head, 1931).

in 'the ancient, celebrated, and never-enough-to-be-extolled city of Paris' – a city which within the year was plunged once more into revolution.

> The journey from Paris to Gloucester involves a distance of between three and four hundred miles. I left Paris on Sunday morning, and (after sleeping on Sunday night at Boulogne) arrived here on Tuesday morning, in the middle of the night – to employ an Irishism – by the mail train from London. You will say that I am a great amateur of festivals to travel such a long way for the sake of assisting at one, and to leave such a city of delights as Paris for an out-of-the-way corner of the world like this very ancient and venerable city of Gloucester – and in such strong stormy weather especially. But 'business before pleasure' is an axiom from which I have so often swerved, that the novelty of sticking to it, for once in a way, amuses me. And I have not been ill repaid for my trouble, since I have listened once more to *Elijah*, the greatest masterpiece of modern music – and exceedingly well rendered, by the way … The sensation produced by *Elijah* justified all that the Gloucester amateurs had anticipated. Its success, both in an artistic and pecuniary point of view, was triumphant. There was but one opinion about it. Worcester, next year, and Hereford, the year after (unless Mr Done and Mr Smith, the organists of either cathedral, be not the men for whom I take them) will imitate the example of Gloucester, and make the *Elijah* the prominent attraction of the Festival.[6]

Elijah marked the culmination of Mendelssohn's career: he died on 4 November 1847 at the age of thirty-eight, leaving unfinished a third oratorio which could well have been something beyond *Elijah*, just as *Elijah* had been something beyond *St Paul*. This was *Christus*, the fragments of which were performed in 1853(G) and 1870(H).

Contemporary music found eager audiences in Victorian Britain, and the first name among popular contemporary composers was that of Mendelssohn. For more than a generation after his death it was the genius of Mendelssohn which dominated the musical taste of this country, during which time any new oratorio fell inevitably under the shadow of *Elijah*. The *Stabat Mater* of Rossini (1792–1862) was given eight Three Choirs performances between 1849(H) and the end of the century, but his *Petite Messe solenelle*, given in 1869(w) and 1874(G), found less favour. Sir Michael Costa's *Eli* (1856(G) and 1857(w)) and *Naaman* (1866(w)) made no lasting impression.

The most prominent British composer of the early Victorian period, also well known as pianist and conductor, was Sir William Sterndale Bennett (1816–1875). A friend of Mendelssohn and Schumann, his music was strongly influenced by the former. Sterndale Bennett's popular cantata, *The May Queen*, received three performances at the Festival in secular evening concerts (1859(G), 1860(w) and 1878(w)) but his only oratorio, *The Woman of Samaria*, was not given until 1888(H). After long neglect, his music is now enjoying a limited revival, but England owes an especially important debt to Sterndale Bennett for his promotion here of the proper appreciation of Bach and other great foreign composers. He founded

[6] *MW* 1847, pp. 614–29.

the Bach Society in 1849 and gave the first performance in England of Bach's *St Matthew Passion* in 1854.

Pieces by Bach had occasionally been included in Three Choirs Miscellaneous Concerts much earlier: in 1836(w) the chorale from the *St Matthew Passion* was encored – not by cheering and stamping but by a gesture from the bishop's finger! By the initiative of S. S. Wesley a complete performance of the *St Matthew Passion* was introduced to the Festivals for the first time in 1871(G). Sadly, the performance was under-rehearsed, badly conducted and at one point broke down completely. The cathedral was barely half-filled for a programme which began at 11.30 a.m. and did not finish until nearly 5.00 p.m. It included not only the Bach and the first (and last) Three Choirs performance of *Gideon* by William Cusins, but also a selection from Spohr's *Calvary* 'performed to a weary and vanishing audience'.[7]

In spite of all, the wonder of the *Passion* shone through, and William Done was successful in recommending it to the Worcester Committee for the following year. Five more years passed before the newly appointed Charles Harford Lloyd included the *St Matthew Passion* in the Gloucester Festival programme of 1877. Two years later at Hereford, Langdon Colborne introduced the *Christmas Oratorio*, which was repeated in 1894(H) by George Robertson Sinclair and, in 1896(w), by Hugh Blair. And it was Hugh Blair who, standing in for William Done, gave the first-ever performance at Three Choirs of Bach's *Mass in B minor* in 1893(w). The work had been given in Leeds in 1886 and 1892, and the Leeds Choir of 100 voices formed half the chorus at Worcester.

The bounds set by the first Three Choirs performances of the *St Matthew Passion* and *Mass in B minor* mark a span of more than two decades, during which innovation slowly gained pace. In 1880 the *Musical Times* was able to say of the Gloucester Festival:

> Mr C. H. Lloyd having felt his power at the Festival three years ago, when but recently appointed organist at the Cathedral, was evidently ambitious on the next occasion to present us with a work of acknowledged high interest, but one not generally known; and in choosing Beethoven's Mass in D (*Missa Solemnis*) we think he made a wise selection. The rage for novelty should not blind us to the fact of the existence of several excellent works which not only the general public, but many musicians, are entirely unacquainted with, and we therefore, in addition to Beethoven's Mass, cordially welcome Leonardo Leo's *Dixit Dominus* and Palestrina's *Stabat Mater*, not only for their intrinsic merits, but as proof that the programmes of the Three Choirs Festivals are not, as many persons tell us, always composed of works which everybody knows!'[8]

The veteran William Done sought to match Lloyd's success when planning the Worcester Festival of the following year. The Mass in D minor by Luigi Cherubini (1760–1842) had been brought to the notice of the English public at a Bach Society concert under the direction of Otto Goldschmidt in 1881. Done wasted little time in deciding to bring the Cherubini work to Worcester:

[7] *Annals* 1895, p. 250.
[8] *MT* 1880, p. 498.

Mr Done deserves every credit for affording us the opportunity of hearing the effect of this sublime composition in its true home – a Cathedral. Comparable only in power and grandeur to Beethoven's Mass in D, which was one of the great attractions at the last Gloucester Festival. Pedantic amateurs, who are sometimes apt to cast a slur upon these 'country meetings', may now perhaps begin to think that if they wish to hear the greatest sacred works rendered amidst the greatest sacred architectural surroundings, they must journey to one of the Three Choirs Festivals.[9]

Thirty years after the death of Mendelssohn, a major choral work by a living foreign composer was once again introduced to Three Choirs. *Ein deutsches Requiem* (*A German Requiem*) by Johannes Brahms (1833–1897) received its first public performance in England in 1873, and was repeated brilliantly by Lloyd at his Gloucester Festival debut in 1877, with Sophie Lowe and Charles Santley in the principal solo parts. *The Times* described the work as a 'colossus' which had been 'rendered with the greatest fluency and precision'.

The oratorios of Charles Gounod (1818–1893) enjoyed some popularity at Three Choirs, particularly *The Redemption*, which in its day was universally acknowledged as a masterpiece; it was introduced by Charles Lee Williams in 1883(G), and repeated in 1884(W), 1885(H), 1887(W), 1892(G) and 1897(H). Williams also brought Gounod's *Mors et Vita* and *Messe solenelle* to Gloucester (in 1886 and 1889) but neither work struck root, and today all memory of *The Redemption* has withered away.

Worcester celebrated in grand style at the 1884 Festival to mark the 800th anniversary of the founding of the cathedral. The full Festival orchestra and chorus took part in the Opening Service on Sunday 6 September; Monday was taken up by rehearsals, and on the Tuesday morning Gounod's *The Redemption* was accorded the position usually occupied by *Elijah*, which was deferred until the Wednesday evening. William Done repeated his success of 1881 with Cherubini's Mass in D minor in the first part of the Wednesday morning concert. But the chief interest of the Festival centred on the next day, when the largest audience of the week assembled in the cathedral to hear the second performance in England of the *Stabat Mater* by Antonín Dvořák (1841–1904), conducted by the composer and with Albani, Patey, Lloyd and Santley in glorious voice.

The *Musical Times* awarded Dvořák's oratorio the accolade 'one of the greatest compositions of modern times' and recorded how the silent audience had been visibly moved by the performance.

At the secular concert in the Shire Hall in the evening, the audience was released from all restraint when Dvořák appeared again – to conduct his Symphony in D major.[10]

On his entry into the orchestra, the applause was so overwhelming that it was many minutes before he was allowed to give the signal for commencing; a similar demonstration followed the end of each movement, and at the end of the work he received such an ovation as we trust will

[9] *MT* 1881, p. 511.

[10] Originally published as his first symphony, the D major op. 60 was, in fact, Dvořák's sixth.

convince him that English people are ever ready to recognise and give welcome to, the highest representative men in art, whatever may be the country of their birth.[11]

It is unlikely that Dvořák spotted this hint of misplaced chauvinism. In any event, he returned to England five times in the next two years and in 1891 was asked by the Birmingham Festival Committee to compose a setting of John Henry Newman's poem *The Dream of Gerontius*. Instead, he gave them his colourful and dramatic *Requiem Mass*, a work which was repeated at the Hereford Festival of 1894 under the direction of George Robertson Sinclair. Birmingham had to wait until 1900 for its Newman setting: it came from a composer born no further away than Broadheath in Worcestershire, and destined to become the first name in English music.

Meanwhile, the nation was content to lionise the prodigious son of a military bandmaster and 'probably the most widely popular English composer who has ever lived'.[12]

By the time he was twenty-five, Arthur Sullivan (1842–1900) was well known as a song-writer, the composer of a fine symphony (*Irish*), and had achieved considerable success with a suite of incidental music to *The Tempest*. Collaboration with W. S. Gilbert was two years in the future and a knighthood twelve more, but already he was the respected member of a circle which included Alfred Tennyson, John Millais, George Grove, Henry Chorley, and Jenny Lind and her husband, Otto Goldschmidt. Sullivan's overture *In Memoriam* had been performed at the Norwich Festival of 1866 under the direction of Sir Julius Benedict, and now he was ready to strengthen his links with the major festivals – the *sine qua non* at that time for a British composer wishing to present large-scale choral works to the public.

Sullivan completed his oratorio *The Prodigal Son* in only three weeks. The biblical texts, which he selected personally, were arranged by George Grove; and the first performance, under the composer's baton, was given at the Worcester Festival of 1869. Otto Goldschmidt, still smarting from the failure of his *Ruth* in 1867, wrote a cautionary note to Sullivan:

> In the case of Hereford two years ago, the chorus – numbering about 160 – came from Hereford, Worcester, Gloucester, Bristol, Bradford [and] London. They had not met together until the general rehearsal [for both choir and orchestra] in the Cathedral on the Monday. Your choruses may be so well written and easy that this single hasty rehearsal is sufficient. As a rule I should say it was not. Certainly it did not prove so in my case. I had again asked for one joint rehearsal, but the answer was that it was impossible … Experience, however, has shown me that though the chorus may not be able to meet collectively before the Monday noon, they *can* meet after, viz. in the evening of that day … You will know how to profit by this friendly hint.[13]

[11] *MT* 1884, p. 584.

[12] Ernest Walker, *A History of Music in England*, 2nd edn (OUP, 1924).

[13] Arthur Jacobs, *Arthur Sullivan: A Victorian Musician* (OUP, 1984).

Perhaps the hint was heeded – the *Musical World* review of *The Prodigal Son* tells us that 'our most rising English composer conducted his own work as he had already done at the *rehearsals*'. In any event, the work was hailed as a triumph of originality; 'the principal parts were sung to perfection by Mdlle. Tietjens, Madame Trebelli-Bettini, Messrs. Sims Reeves and Santley, the band and chorus went marvellously well, and altogether a more perfect first performance could hardly have been possible.'[14] Sullivan had passed the critical Rubicon.

The Prodigal Son was repeated at Hereford in 1870 and again, under Sullivan's baton, at Gloucester in 1889, when his overture *In Memoriam* was substituted for the National Anthem at the beginning of the programme in memory of Thomas Gambier Parry, who had died the previous year.

By 1889, with his reputation firmly built not upon oratorios but upon the outstanding success of the Savoy operas, Sullivan was at the height of his fame. *The Prodigal Son* had already fallen into neglect and it had been a decade since he had conducted the only Three Choirs performance of his oratorio *The Light of the World*, a work described by Ernest Walker as having 'hardly any vitality, even to be vulgar'.[15] However, he achieved huge popular acclaim for his secular cantata *The Golden Legend*, composed for the Leeds Festival of 1886 and repeated under his own direction at the Worcester Festival of 1887, when the chorus was composed entirely of the Leeds contingent of the Festival Choir. Sullivan returned to conduct *The Golden Legend* at Hereford in 1888 – and did so with no rehearsal at all; his diary entry for 11 September 1888 reads: 'Left Paddington 12 … arrived Hereford 5.31 … Eight o'clock, conducted performance of *Golden Legend* in Shirehall – crammed house. Very good performance – only band *rough*, a lot of fossils amongst them.'[16] *The Golden Legend* was performed at Three Choirs for the last time in 1898(G), when the conductor was Herbert Brewer.

Posterity has decreed that Sullivan will be remembered above all for his light operas, but there were many other British composers of the late Victorian period whose contributions to oratorio- and cantata-writing lie forgotten and whose names are barely remembered at all. The following list covers the years from 1869 to 1895; works performed at secular concerts are distinguished by (s).

1869	Sullivan	The Prodigal Son (repeated 1870 and 1889)
1870	Barnby	Rebekah
1871	Cusins	Gideon
1873	Ouseley	Hagar
1876	Barnett	The Raising of Lazarus
1878	Armes	Hezekiah
1879	Sullivan	The Light of the World
1880	Holmes	Christmas Day
	Parry	Prometheus Unbound

[14] *MW* 1869, p. 641.

[15] Walker, *A History*.

[16] Jacobs, *Arthur Sullivan*.

1881	Caldicott	Widow of Nain
	Mackenzie	The Bride (s)
	Barnett	The Building of the Ship (s)
1882	Garrett	The Shunammite
	A. M. Smith	Ode to the Passions (s)
1883	Stainer	St Mary Magdalene (repeated 1891)
	Arnold	Sennacherib
	Lloyd	Allen-a-Dale (s)
	Parry	The Glories of our Blood and State (s)
1884	Lloyd	Hero and Leander (s)
1885	J. Smith	St Kevin (s)
	Lloyd	The Song of Balder (s)
1886	Rockstro	The Good Shepherd
	Lloyd	Andromeda (s)
	Cowen	Sleeping Beauty (s)
1887	Cowen	Ruth
	Sullivan	The Golden Legend (s) (repeated 1888, 1889 and 1898)
	Stanford	The Revenge (s)
1888	Bennett	The Woman of Samaria
	Colborne	Samuel
	Cowen	Song of Thanksgiving
	Parry	Blest Pair of Sirens
1889	Parry	Judith
	Lee Williams	Last Night at Bethany (repeated 1890)
	Mackenzie	The Dream of Jubal (s)
	Ellicott	Elysium (s)
1890	Bridge	The Repentance of Nineveh
	Parry	Ode to St Cecilia (s)
1891	Edwards	Praise to the Holiest
	Lloyd	Song of Judgement
	Parry	De Profundis
	Stanford	Battle of the Baltic (s)
	Sullivan	Te Deum
1892	Bridge	The Lord's Prayer
	Lee Williams	Gethsemane
	Parry	Job (repeated 1893 and 1894)
1894	Bridge	The Cradle of Christ
	Mackenzie	Bethlehem
	Lloyd	Ballad of Sir Ogie and Lady Elsie (s)
1895	Parry	King Saul
	Cowen	The Transfiguration
	Lee Williams	Dedication

Of all the works listed, only Parry's *Blest Pair of Sirens* is heard with any regularity today

In the main, the volume of compositions resulted from the demand each year to include one or more 'novelties' in the Three Choirs programmes – and after 1880 that demand was fuelled by a clearly increasing rivalry between the three cathedral cities to attract the first names in contemporary music to compose substantial pieces specifically for the Festivals. One example will suffice: Sir Frederick Cowen (1852–1935), a West Indian by birth, was celebrated as both composer and conductor and was knighted in 1911. His Symphony No. 3 (*Scandinavian*), composed in 1880, had been hailed by *The Times* as 'the most important English symphony for years'; his operas, orchestral pieces and many songs are filled with delightful melodies of the lighter kind. The announcement that Cowen had been commissioned to write an oratorio for the 1887 Worcester Festival excited widespread interest and a great demand for tickets. In view of Goldschmidt's experience in 1867 it is perhaps surprising that Cowen, with Joseph Bennett as librettist, chose *Ruth* as the subject and title of his oratorio. Over 2,600 people packed into Worcester Cathedral to hear it, prompting the *Musical Times* to comment:

> *Ruth*, therefore, appeared in the light of a good investment on the part of the committee, and the fact may have an important influence on future policy. At the same time, we must bear in mind that composers with the special popularity of Mr. Cowen cannot be 'turned on' at any time, nor can musician and subject be always so admirably suited to each other as in the present case.[17]

Unfortunately, the libretto of *Ruth* caused eyebrows to rise, and Joseph Bennett explained why:

> The public [applied] to an innocent Bible story the rigid conventionality of the suburban mind. As it stands in the Sacred Book, the tale of Ruth and Boaz is as chaste as anything from the pen of Jane Austen, but knowing the tendency of nice people towards ideas which are the reverse, I made slight changes to humour their nicety. But they took their old stand – that is to say, they would have an Eastern tale only after it had been brought as far as possible into conformity with the notions of their 'straitest sect.' I really could not prevent Ruth from paying a nocturnal visit to Boaz. Had I done so I should now be recording my own shame, and inditing apologies to the Bible.
>
> *Ruth* was produced at a Festival of the Three Choirs, and I greatly fear that Dr Cowen's extremely beautiful dance-music in the festival scene was grievous to the 'unco guid.' I wonder why they have not called a meeting, and passed a vote of censure upon King David for dancing before the Lord in Gilgal.[18]

Cowen was not writing in his most comfortable *métier*, he regarded himself primarily as a symphonist. His best works have not survived the eclipse of

---

[17] *MT* 1887, p. 601.

[18] Joseph Bennett, *Forty Years of Music, 1865–1905* (Methuen, 1908), pp. 385–6.

Victorian musical taste and, unlike Sullivan, he found no collaborator of the genius of W. S. Gilbert to whose words he could wed his melodic gift.

Not all the 'novelties' presented at Three Choirs were even so well received as those by Sullivan and Cowen; there was much which was banal. Commenting on the 'musical platitudes' in Rockstro's *The Good Shepherd* the reviewer of *The Musical Times* asked why the composer was 'permitted to arrest our attention when greater men are waiting for a hearing?'[19] But at least new British works were being heard in increasing numbers. It *was* possible for a newly appointed cathedral organist like Charles Lee Williams to make his debut as a Festival composer in 1889 before an immense audience with his cantata *Last Night in Bethany*, to have it performed by the leading soloists and finest choral singers of the day, and to have the satisfaction of knowing that the piece was booked for performance in several places as an immediate result of its Three Choirs success. This was in startling contrast to the lack of adventure in Festival programmes at the beginning of the century; and even if much of this music did little more than give devotional sentiment to words culled from a multitude of biblical texts, a chance was given for much rarer gold to shine through.

As a direct result of that more adventurous spirit the 'greater men' eventually found an audience and modern English music was born. Even so, the first precious glimmerings were not discovered in a packed cathedral, but in the far less auspicious surroundings of a secular concert in the Gloucester Shire Hall.

---

[19] *MT* 1886, p. 592. The composer in question is William Rockstro (1823–1895, originally Rackstraw).

9

Sacred and Profane

> If we seek for a definite birthday for modern English music, September 7,
> 1880, when *Prometheus* saw the light at Gloucester and met with a mixed
> reception, has undoubtedly the best claim.[1]

WITH his cantata *Prometheus Unbound*, a setting of scenes from Shelley's
epic poem, Hubert Parry (1848–1918) strode into the midst of all that was
conventional and 'safe' in English choral music and unwittingly became, in the
words of Herbert Howells, 'a near revolutionary'.[2] Every conceivable obstacle
stood in the way of his success.

In spite of his championship of Three Choirs as a Steward over many years,
Parry's father, Thomas Gambier Parry, squire at Highnam Court near Gloucester,
would not tolerate music as a profession for his children and forbade his eldest
son, Clinton, to pursue it. Following his education at Eton and Oxford, Hubert
was obliged against his will to take up a career in insurance and to limit his
musical activities to those of an amateur. His first offering to Three Choirs was
an *Intermezzo religioso* (1868(G)) which, in the judgement of the *Pall Mall Gazette*
of 12 September 1868, 'in no way belied its amateur origin'. In 1877, following
seven years at Lloyds Register of Shipping – which ended in financial disaster –
he was at last able to take up music as his chosen profession. Meanwhile, in
1873, he had begun regular lessons with the concert pianist Edward Dannreuther,
who introduced Parry to the music of Wagner and provided him with
free tickets to visit Bayreuth for the first performance of *The Ring* there in
1876.

Parry returned from Bayreuth aglow with inspiration; but many of the
English critics were scathing about the 'so-called Prophet of the Future,
Richard Wagner'.[3] Except for Dannreuther, Parry's friends pilloried him for
turning towards 'the music of the future' in his own composition. By this time
he had also further alienated himself from his father and contemporary society
by renouncing Christian doctrine. Even so, uncomfortable isolation was no
deterrent from his boldness in choosing a poem by Shelley as the inspiration for
his first major choral work. Alas, the performance was under-rehearsed and quite
beyond the bass soloist, a Mr Francis, who sang the title role:

> The chorus of 250 voices, selected from Worcester, Hereford, London,
> Huddersfield, Oxford, Bristol, and other towns, as well as with the

---

[1] Ernest Walker, *A History of Music in England* (OUP, 1924).

[2] Herbert Howells, Crees Lecture delivered at the Royal College of Music on 7
October 1968.

[3] *MT* 1880, p. 499.

Gloucester choir, was, together with the already practised band, kept at rehearsal yesterday [Monday, the day before the concert] from ten in the morning till five in the afternoon, and again from half-past seven in the evening until past midnight. As a matter of course the 'three choirs' assembled for cathedral service this morning [Tuesday]; but independent of this duty, there was a return to the previous night's work of rehearsal solely on account of Mr. Hubert Parry's work.[4]

In low spirits following the late-night rehearsal and unaware that the chorus, on the initiative of the Huddersfield contingent, would volunteer to rehearse again the next day, Parry wrote in his diary for Monday 6 September 1880: 'Rehearsal of *Prometheus* in the evening which was literally agonising. Not time to do much more than go through it. Everything at sixes and sevens and chorus literally bewildered. Everybody tired with rehearsing other things all day, and general misery all round.'[5] On top of this, Parry was depressed about his difficulty in finding a publisher for the work.

The secular concert in which *Prometheus Unbound* was performed began with Beethoven's overture to *Fidelio*, followed by four arias by Mozart, Gluck and Gounod before Parry's piece was heard. After the interval, an over-long evening continued with a Mozart symphony, several arias, and Gounod's Jupiter Festival March from *Polyeucte* for orchestra and choir.

> A generous welcome was accorded to Mr. Parry on his taking the conductor's place. Any pleasure which his work may have afforded was not demonstrated with enthusiasm. That the second part of the concert was a very late affair needs hardly to be said … the most extremely adverse judgements do not deny the composer a strength which he may apply at will, and which, if applied with less inveterate determination to out-Wagner Wagner, would no doubt be capable of greater, if not of more elaborately artificial, work than this most ambitious essay.[6]

Players, singers and audience were all weary; the parts were peppered with mistakes and difficult to read in the dim gaslight; but thanks to the Huddersfield Chorus and the magnificent singing of Edward Lloyd, the performance held together and, at the end, Parry was called forward and loudly applauded. The critics took up positions which ranged from the generously defensive to the pointedly hostile. But nearly forty years later Sir Henry Hadow remembered the significance of 7 September 1880; 'No-one seems to have had any idea that, on that evening in the Shirehall, English music had, after many years, come again into its own and that it had come with a master-piece in its hands.'[7]

Parry's biographer, Professor Jeremy Dibble, has reassessed that significance:

[4] *MW* 1880, p. 515.

[5] Jeremy Dibble, 'Parry: Some Fresh Thoughts', Gloucester Festival programme book, 1989, p. 24. Copy held in the Three Choirs Festival Office, Gloucester.

[6] *MW* 1880, p. 576.

[7] W. H. Hadow, 'Sir Hubert Parry', *Proceedings of the Musical Association* 45 (1918–19), pp. 135–47.

There can be little doubt that *Prometheus Unbound* excited many scholars and critics (including Bernard Shaw) because, in embracing, at least in part, Wagnerian techniques of declamation and leitmotif, Parry's cantata automatically set itself apart from other contemporary English works in the same idiom. The association, however, of the revolutionary vision and intellect of the atheist Shelley and Parry's apparent literary audacity has tended to overemphasise the work's true musical quality. In fact, along with the extraordinary juxtaposition of Wagner and Brahms, one is also aware of some areas that are entirely indebted to the traditionally conservative Handelian and Mendelssohnian conditioning of his early musical training. The work suffers from stylistic inconsistency and suggests more readily someone with an admirable technical proficiency, but with as yet insufficient conviction. Moreover, with its obvious eclecticism, *Prometheus* bears all the symptoms of immaturity, experiment, and the uncertainty of a composer who had not yet found himself.'[8]

Whatever the musical quality of *Prometheus Unbound*, it is certain that so powerful an expression of humanitarian ideology would not have been granted admission to a cathedral. If Gloucester *can* lay claim to the birth of modern English music, no matter how immature the work, then the essential condition of the delivery of that birth, and the single advantage available to Parry, was the existence of the Three Choirs secular concerts.

The hugely popular secular evening concerts were given splendid new venues in the nineteenth century when shire halls were built in each of the Three Choirs cities. The one at Gloucester, designed in the Greek Revival style by Robert Smirke, architect of the British Museum, was constructed between 1814 and 1816. The secular concerts were transferred there from the old Booth Hall in 1817 when, on the second evening of the Music Meeting, upwards of 1,400 tickets were sold. The exterior of the building, with its four heavy, unfluted Ionic columns, is most impressive. Unfortunately, the interior of the Grand Hall, approached via a staircase rising from the vestibule, was not ideal for concerts: the acoustic was dry, and the organ occupied too large a space in the centre of the platform to allow a satisfactory arrangement of the chorus and orchestra. (In 1910 Sir Hubert Parry donated £1,500 towards the cost of improving the hall, his wishes being that the platform should be reconstructed, side seats removed, and a gallery erected facing the platform. This was done, and at Herbert Brewer's suggestion the organ was moved, rebuilt and bracketed on the wall.)[9]

Robert Smirke was again engaged to design the Shire Hall in Hereford, which was built, immediately following completion of the Gloucester Shire Hall, between 1817 and 1819. This time Smirke gave the façade a noble portico of eight pillars in Doric style, imitating the temple of Theseus at Athens. The Three Choirs secular concerts moved to the Shire Hall from the Hereford Music Room in 1819 but, as at Gloucester, the new hall was not ideal as a concert venue. Various improvement schemes were put forward during the nineteenth century:

---

[8] Dibble, 'Parry: Some Fresh Thoughts'.

[9] Gloucester Festival Minute Book, 1910. Gloucester Cathedral Archives and Library.

the question of alterations arose as early as 1846, strenuously advocated by George Townshend Smith. By 1854 a definite scheme was drawn up, which then lapsed owing to lack of funds but was revived and successfully carried out in 1862, in good time for the Hereford Festival of 1864.

> Since the Festival of 1861 important changes and modifications have been made in the large room in the Shire Hall. The space formerly given to the orchestra is now absorbed by the auditorium; while a new orchestra, occupying a recess under an arched roof, exactly opposite the portico, or great entrance, and fitted up alike with taste and simplicity, is an object as grateful as the former one was ungrateful to the eye. Besides this, the old raised benches are discarded, which not only enlarges the accommodation but imparts freedom and boldness to the general appearance of the area. The acoustic properties of the building are wonderfully improved by the alterations, and the Hereford people may now lay claim to the possession of a room for their festival and evening concerts, balls and other such entertainments far superior to the Shire Hall at Gloucester, and at least equal to College Hall at Worcester.[10]

The Shire Hall at Worcester was built between 1834 and 1835 to a design by Charles Day, the County Architect, who chose to emulate the Greek Revival style favoured by Smirke and faced his building with a portico of six fluted Ionic columns. Worcester's secular concerts remained at the College Hall for almost half a century more, until a fine organ by Nicholson was installed in the Shire Hall. The change was made in 1884 in time for Dvořák's visit to Worcester; but surprisingly, with an ideal instrument available, no organ works were included in the secular concert programmes for that year.

The secular evening concerts, which had become such a popular feature of the eighteenth-century Music Meetings, continued regularly to be three in number until 1870. The balls which followed these concerts were gradually reduced to one only on the last night until, as part of the 'call to seriousness', they were dropped altogether in 1874(G).

> People whose judgement is not warped by excessive religious sentiment have often gravely shaken their heads at the Ball. Why? Is dancing sinful *per se*? ... But a chorus arises on all hands protesting that to dance in the evening, after hearing *Messiah* in the morning, is 'improper'. At what time is it proper then? Has anybody, armed with a gauge of propriety, investigated the subject, and ascertained exactly how many minutes after the 'Amen' chorus one may, without sin, stand up for a quadrille?[11]

The programme of the secular concerts contained a mixture of lightweight frivolities, glees, songs, assorted arias, overtures and instrumental showpieces; but gradually classic works of substance began to appear. Beethoven's Symphony No. 1 in C and the overtures *Prometheus* and *Egmont* were heard at Three Choirs in the composer's lifetime, and by 1853 all of his first eight symphonies had been performed. A limited selection of the symphonies of Haydn and Mozart were

[10] *MW* 1864, p. 569.
[11] *MW* 1874, p. 621.

played, and the overture to *The Magic Flute*, first heard in 1807(H), became a popular favourite, as did Cherubini's overture *Anacreon*. Of Schubert there was nothing. Vivaldi was all but forgotten.

Typical of these programmes before mid-century is that for the first secular concert in Gloucester in 1841:

Part I

Overture: Anacreon	Cherubini
Prize Ballad 1841 (Mr Hobbs)	Hobbs
Glee: 'Blow gentle gales', The Slave	Bishop
Air, Robert le Diable (Madame Dorus Gras)	Meyerbeer
Duetto: Il Fanatico per la Musica (Madame Viardot García and Signor Tamburini)	Fioravanti
Solo, violoncello (Mr Lindley)	Lindley
Ballad: 'I feel that thou art changed' (Miss Marshall)	Balfe
Duetto: 'Vanne se alberglie' (Mesdames Dorus Gras and Viardot García)	Mercadante
Song: 'The Sailor's Journal' (Mr H. Phillips)	Dibdin
Preghiera: Mose in Egitto	Rossini

Part II

Symphony No. 8[12]	Haydn
Ballad: 'I'll speak of thee' (Miss M. B. Hawes)	Hawes
Terzetto: 'Tremati, empi tremanti' (Miss Birch, Signori Brizzi and Tamburini)	Beethoven
Finale, La Cenerentola (Madame Viardot García)	Rossini
Aria: 'Cruda funesta smagnia' (Signor Tamburini)	Rossini
Ballad: 'Auld Robin Gray' (Miss Birch)	trad.
Duetto: Le Nozze di Darina (Madame Viardot Garciía and Signor Tamburini)	Mosca
Ballad: 'The three Ages of Love' (Mr J. Bennett)	E. J. Loder
Glee: 'The Chough and Crow' (Guy Mannering)	Bishop

London critics visiting the provinces found these programmes extremely tiresome. Even so eminent a musician as Robert Lindley (1777–1855), the leading cellist of his day, could become a target for their barbs when playing in such an indiscriminate setting:

> Mr Lindley, by courtesy 'the veteran', seems determined always to remind us how very long he has been the sole supreme, the great arch-violoncellist; for it is only to such archness that we can attribute his invariably choosing for his solos such antediluvian twaddle, as must have sounded old-fashioned and common-place to our mothers' grandmothers: of course he *delighted* his audience tonight.[13]

[12] Symphony No. 8 of the 'Salomon Symphonies' (i.e. No. 98 in B flat).
[13] *MW* 1841, p. 179.

But if the concert itself lacked interest, at least the unrestrained chattering of 'the elite, the wealth and the beauty of the three counties' could provide a source of innocent merriment – in this case at a concert in 1837:

> On Wednesday evening, the hall was exceedingly full, the attendants anticipating, if not a delightful concert, a *most* delightful dance; and this was evidently expressed upon numerous countenances during the former parts of the two last evenings' entertainment. Very shortly, therefore, after the commencement, endurance rather than enjoyment of the music began to be manifest. The Jupiter Symphony, excellently played, was scarcely noticed. Seeing at once how the game was likely to go, we amused ourselves with minuting down the remarks made around us upon the several pieces as they went off. First, on Hobbs' ballad, 'Oh, weep not mother'. – 'Ah, very pretty, but *very* long.' (Critique by a gentleman in jappaned pumps.) Rondo from La Cenerentola, 'Non piu mesta', by Mme. Albertazzi. – 'The sweetest thing she has sung. That's the length now I like for a song.' (Gentleman, in an uncorrugated cravat.) Glee, 'With sighs sweet rose', Calcott. – 'Sweet thing, if I could have heard Mr. Hunt. Sung *rather too slow*.' (The gentleman in pumps.) Lindley's violoncello concerto. – 'Very wonderful fiddling; but it was all so up and down – and *very long*.' (A flower-girl; at least a girl with flowers – in her hair.) 'Machin always chooses such long songs. That "Pirate crew" will never be over.' (Flower-girl aforesaid.) Ballad, Mrs. Knyvett, 'The auld wife', Griesbach. – 'Sweet thing; but too many verses. I applaud because it's over.' (A dancing gentleman.) Quartett from the Puritani, 'A te, o cara'. – 'Sweet thing indeed. Havn't [*sic*] they nearly done?' (Ditto.) 'Bonnie Prince Charlie', Miss Clara Novello – 'Dear – that's a sweet thing indeed. We must have that again. But O la! there are two pages more to come.' (The flower-girl.) Overture, Euryanthe. – 'Well, now that long thing's over, we have a chance.' Cavatina, Miss Woodyatt, 'Il braccio mio', Nicolini. – 'Charming voice! Belongs to Hereford. Sweet thing! Oh, she's not done yet. – There, now that's done.' Song, 'Invocation to Spring', Mr Phillips. – Oh Lord, are they going to have that again? It's quite ridiculous.' Ballad, Miss Hawes, 'The mermaid's cave', Horn. – 'Sweet thing! Oh, no! no!! no!!! we can-*not* have that again.' Grand Septuor (Beethoven), Blagrove, Moralt, Williams, Platt, Denman, Lindley, and Anfossi. – 'Very hot, ain't it? I wish those good people thought so. How they do go on! Look, how he is blowing with the horn. Why, we had a long overture before.' Glee, Mrs. Knyvett, Messrs. Hunt, Hobbs and Machin, 'Sweet thrush', Danby. – 'Dear, dear! a thing with four verses at this time o'night!' Duet, Mme. Albertazzi and Miss Clara Novello, 'Deh con te'. – 'I could almost give up dancing, to hear that girl's voice. Bravo, bravo! No, no! not again – go on.' Serenade, Mr. Bennett, 'Look, forth, my fairest', Balfe. – 'Six verses at *any* time are a bore – but NOW, twenty minutes after eleven!' Finale, Clemenza di Tito, 'Tu, e ver'. – 'Well! *at* last. Very fine! Bravo! bravo!! Now then for clearing away the benches. Sweet music, but too much of it. A devil of a bore; though I am partial to music. But dancing is more merry like.'[14]

---

[14] *MW* 1837, pp. 56–7 – part of a review of the Hereford Festival.

At which point Mr Adams and his celebrated Quadrille Band took their places on the platform.

The orchestral items with which each part of these concerts opened were frequently drowned out in the hubbub, augmented by the voices of the helpful but noisy Stewards, as members of the audience searched for their seats. Applause between the movements of a work was expected. The benches were uncomfortable; the lighting and ventilation poor; and the halls frequently packed to suffocation, with many people standing.

At Worcester in 1848 a crowd of 1,100 attended a concert in which Alboni, Castellan, Sims Reeves and Lablache were singing. So great was the crush that the doors of the College Hall had to be removed.[15] And in 1860 upwards of 300 people were turned away when not even standing room was available.

A further problem arose in the late 1850s due to the prevailing fashion for ladies to 'make broad the borders of their garments'. The College Hall at Worcester could normally hold about 900 people (600 in the body of the room and 300 in the gallery) but the wearing of crinoline dresses meant that over 100 seats at half a guinea each were lost at each concert: 'Perhaps when the present fashion is discarded (it cannot last for ever, that's one consolation), and ladies return to the straight and limp costume of their grandmammas … the "consummation devoutly to be wished" may be accomplished.'[16]

It is impossible to avoid the impression that until the latter part of the nineteenth century the secular concerts were as much, if not more, occasions for society display as for musical appreciation. Rarely was this so evident as at Worcester in 1857: the second evening concert was particularly well attended because it was known that the Duke of Cambridge would be present. He had not arrived by the time the concert started with a selection from Weber's *Der Freischütz*. Indeed, several numbers had already been performed and Madame Weiss, wife of the bass W. H. Weiss, was in the middle of singing Agatha's lovely Act III cavatina 'And though a cloud the sun obscure' when the Duke entered the hall. The music immediately stopped; the National Anthem was played, with Clara Novello and John Sims Reeves joining in as soloists; the audience applauded loudly; and, after all that, Mme Weiss was obliged to resume the abandoned aria from the beginning.

By mid-century these potpourris were becoming less popular, and it was George Townshend Smith at Hereford who laid the foundations for a more serious form of secular music-making. In 1861 he introduced an extra event on the fourth evening of the Festival: a Chamber Concert at the College Hall. His programme for the first of these included Mozart's Quartet in D minor, Mendelssohn's Quartet with Canzonet, op. 12, and the second movement of Beethoven's Septet; the soloists were Messrs H. Blagrove, Clementi, R. Blagrove, G. Collins, Blakestone, Williams (clarinet), Mann (horn) and Woetzig (bassoon). These pieces were interspersed with arias and duets by Buononcini, Haydn and Spohr, sung by Madame and Mr Weiss. This recital was so well received that at the next Hereford Festival, in 1864, Townshend Smith repeated the experiment and presented a programme which included Mozart's Quartet in G,

[15] *Annals* 1895, p. 160.

[16] *MW* 1860, p. 586.

Beethoven's Quartet in A, and a Quintet in D by George Onslow. The Hereford Chamber Concerts continued for many years, following the pattern of a series of Monday Popular Concerts which Arthur Chappell had successfully organised at the St James's Hall in London, but they were not taken up by Gloucester or Worcester.

The arrival of S. S. Wesley at Gloucester in time for the Festival of 1865 heralded a significant change in the content of the secular concert programmes. Mendelssohn's incidental music to *A Midsummer Night's Dream* had been popular at Three Choirs for thirty years, and *The First Walpurgis Night* for twenty: Townshend Smith had conducted the *Italian Symphony* in 1861. But Wesley, in his first Gloucester Festival programmes, included Mendelssohn's Piano Concerto No. 1 in G minor and Beethoven's *Fantasia*, op. 80 (the 'Choral Fantasy'), both with Arabella Goddard as soloist, thus beginning the trend away from the performance of unsatisfactory miscellanies and towards that of an increasing number of complete works from more or less classical masters, along with carefully selected shorter items.

As the century progressed, this same trend was to be seen in a gradual departure from the practice of devoting one day of the Festival to 'A Grand Selection of Sacred Music' in the cathedral. As in the evening concerts, these performances had comprised an overlong and unrelated mixture of overtures, airs and choruses, but extracted from popular sacred, rather than secular, pieces. Although the works of Handel had dominated these selections in the early years of the century (in 1816(H) for instance, of twenty-one items performed all but three were by Handel), it eventually became possible for a greater but hardly more satisfactory variety to be chanced.

At his last Music Meeting (1829(G)), William Mutlow went so far as to present the following seemingly interminable programme on the second morning:

Part 1

Opening Movement	Te Deum	Graun
Recit. and Air	'What, tho I trace'	Handel
Duett	'Qual Anelante'	Marcello
Quartett	'For this God'	Marcello and Knyvett
Recits. and Airs	'O Liberty'	
	'From mighty kings' ⎫	Handel
	'Shall I in Mamre's' ⎭	
Chorus	'For all these mercies'	
Recit. and Air	'With verdure clad' ⎫	
Recit.	'In splendour bright' ⎬	Haydn
Chorus	'The Heavens are telling' ⎭	

Part 2

First Grand Concerto		Handel
Offertorio	'The Hymn'	Dr Chard
Chorus	'Kyrie Eleison'	Rhigini

Air	'Agnus Dei'	Mozart
Chorus	'Rex Tremendae'	
Quartett	'Recordare'	} Winter
Chorus	'Lachrymosa'	
Air	'Gratias agimus'	Guglielmi
Recit. and Air	'The snares of death'	Stevenson
Recit.	'So will'd my father'	
Trio and Chorus	'Disdainful of Danger'	} Handel
Chorus	'If guiltless blood'	
Chorus	'Cum sancto Spiritu'	Mozart

Part 3

Luther's Hymn		
Air	'O magnify the Lord'	Handel
Scena	'The last man'	Callcott
Recit. and Air	'Ah! parlate'	Cimarosa
Chorus	'Glory to God'	Beethoven
Air	'O my God'	Ciampi
Quartetto	'Domine Jesu Christi'	Winter
Chorus	'The Lord shall reign'	Handel

Forty years later, in 1869(w), the Three Choirs audience on the second morning was well contented to hear Sullivan's *Prodigal Son*, extracts from Handel's *Judas Maccabaeus* and nothing more.

The Festival was of three days' duration until 1836, when Worcester added a fourth morning event (reverting to three days for the Festival of 1845 only). Gloucester followed this precedent in 1838 and Hereford in 1849. Typically, after 1847 *Elijah* would be performed on the first day (Tuesday), *Messiah* on the last, and Miscellaneous Sacred Concerts on the second and third days.

At Hereford in 1870, for a royal visit by Prince and Princess Christian, George Townshend Smith dropped the first evening secular concert altogether and replaced it with an oratorio performance in the recently gaslit cathedral. An even more important precedent set in 1870 was the performance of a symphony for the first time in the cathedral. (As late as 1870 some clergymen were doubtful about the propriety of allowing even a Beethoven symphony to be played in a cathedral.) Townshend Smith's success may well have been due to his canniness in obtaining approval to include Mendelssohn's *Reformation Symphony* in a programme which also contained the same composer's setting of Psalm 42 and part of *Christus*.

In the year following this innovation, Canon Tinling, preaching at the Opening Service of the Gloucester Festival, pleaded for 'more reverence in the Cathedral during the oratorio performances, and a higher religious tone and character to all that takes place within the sacred walls during Festival Week'.[17] He had good reason to rebuke his listeners: a not insignificant factor in the

---

[17] *Annals* 1895, p. 247.

hardening anti-Festival mood among many clergymen was the behaviour of Three Choirs audiences. It was not unusual for a large number of visitors to the cathedrals,

> feeling that they had come to a concert, and consequently disregarding the nature of the building in which it took place, complacently [to] lunch during the interval, and sometimes during the performance, even occasionally hanging their hats upon the recumbent figures on the tombs within their reach, and adopting a manner which seemed to show that they had come out for a holiday and were resolved to enjoy themselves.[18]

Many of those who did not remain in the cathedral for lunch would think little of stampeding out to nearby hostelries before the end of the morning performance.

Since the Music Meetings originated through the coming together of the three cathedral choirs to sing the daily Offices, it is perhaps surprising that details of the music sung at the services which marked the opening of each Festival in the nineteenth century are often only briefly referred to in the *Annals*; in the account of the Festival in some years no mention is made at all. It is, however, clear that the morning services followed the form of Matins: reference is made to the singing of the responses (for a long period to the setting by Tallis), while throughout the first half of the century Handel's Dettingen *Te Deum* and Utrecht *Jubilate* continued to hold pride of place. Also included were anthems – occasionally as many as three or four – by Boyce and Handel, and later by Knyvett, Kent, Attwood, Croft and other composers of their day.

Lysons, in a footnote to the *Annals* for 1812(w), complained about the interpolation of a song from Arnold's *The Redemption* (an adaptation of music by Handel) into the Dettingen *Te Deum*:

> The extremely bad taste in allowing the song 'Holy, Holy, Holy' to be thrust into a sublime composition, already perfect in itself, amounts to an act of positive desecration, and an insult to the Divine Majesty, when the fact is declared that the original words of this beautiful air in the opera of *Rodelinda*, are those of a love song, *Dove set, amato bene*?[19]

His objection was apparently not shared by others, the records showing that the same 'desecration' was repeated regularly until at least mid-century.[20]

It was not until mid-century that the music of J. S. Bach was heard at the services. Other so-called 'novelties' were heard later: the *Annals* for 1855(H) list no fewer than eight musical items at the Opening Service. Quite early in the century, though not regularly, an orchestral or organ overture preceded the service: for example, in 1823(G) Handel's overture to *Esther* was performed, and in 1825(H) his overture to *Saul*. Tradition was broken at Gloucester when, in 1874, 'the concluding act of the Festival was a grand Chorus Service in the nave ... on

---

[18] *MT* 1884, p. 584.

[19] *Annals* 1895, pp. 96–7n.

[20] See Watkins Shaw, *The Three Choirs Festival: The Official History of the Meetings of Gloucester, Hereford and Worcester, c. 1713–1953* (Baylis for Three Choirs Festival, 1954), p. 31.

Friday evening'.[21] At Gloucester in 1853 choral Matins sung by the cathedral choirs at 8 a.m. on the second and subsequent mornings of the Festival were introduced, presaging the Choral Evensong of the modern Festival. Not only did these services remove the 'scruples of many persons who were hostile to the musical performances in the Cathedral on the ground that they interfered with the legitimate object of the sacred edifice … that of divine worship', but they were also extremely well attended by the 'humbler classes', admittance being free.[22]

In 1876, for the first time, the Mayor of Hereford issued 'an earnest invitation … to his brethren at Gloucester and Worcester to come over (for the Opening Service), and thus enable the great desire of the civic bodies of each city for the continuance of the Festivals on the old lines'.[23] We read that this invitation 'was heartily responded to', and it is a practice which civil dignitaries, both of the three cities and of the counties, now regularly follow.

At Worcester in 1881 the Opening Service began at 3 p.m. on Sunday 3 September and took the form of Evensong instead of Matins.

The convenience of the hour, no doubt, helped to secure the attendance of an enormous crowd for all of whom indeed the great church was far too small. On going into the cathedral close, while the bells were still chiming, I found hundreds of people standing vainly before gates closed and guarded by policemen. 'Too late, too late, ye cannot enter now.' The refrain of Tennyson's mournful song may have occurred to some of the disappointed ones as they turned away. But a reference more distinctly scriptural possibly occupied the minds of others, who, having tickets for the reserved portion, found the way narrow and the gate straight. It was only too evident from the arrangements made that the cathedral authorities have little experience in dealing with crowds. They actually constructed at the doors for ticket holders a kind of funnel, through the narrow mouth of which applicants for admission had to filter one at a time. The result was unseemly crushing and crowding, so much that when the press was over the policemen congratulated one another on the close of a 'hot job'. Still worse were the regulations for the exit of the congregation. At one of the doors attempts were made to prevent persons from leaving, not only before the offertory but after it. In this instance a particularly zealous verger had more than he could do to carry out what I am bound to assume were his instructions. If he left his post for a moment the imprisoned people began to escape, seeing which he would push rudely through the throng with anything but solemn calm on his countenance, and interpose the barrier of his body and the authority of his gown. Under these circumstances a gentleman requested permission to retire, and being refused, flung the door open by main force. The verger grappled with him, and for a few moments a struggle of the liveliest description went on, ending in the discomfiture of the official, who, however, expressed

[21] *Annals* 1895, p. 256.

[22] Ibid., p. 174.

[23] Ibid., p. 267.

himself much consoled by reflecting that as the outer gates were locked his opponent could not get off the premises.[24]

Among the large crowds pouring into the ancient cities at Festival time were several visitors who had indeed come out for a holiday, and the expansion of the railway network by mid-century considerably increased their numbers. Of Gloucester in 1853 the *Musical World* reported that:

> We hear, upon the best authority, that there are at this moment only a few of the least desirable of the numbered tickets for the four morning performances left unsold. These places occupy about two-thirds of the whole area of the nave of the Cathedral, in which the morning performances of sacred music take place, and it is an unprecedented circumstance, that the majority of the holders of these tickets are strangers. Gloucester is peculiarly well placed for travellers, forming, as it does, an important centre of the western and south midland district, railways on both gauges meeting here. The Midland, Great Western, Gloucester and Dean Forest, and South Wales Railways meet here at one common station. At the last Gloucester Festival, in 1850, the South Wales line was not opened direct to Gloucester, a *hiatus* of twenty-seven miles having to be travelled by coach. There is, however, now a length considerably over one hundred miles of this line open – Gloucester to Carmarthen – and there can be little doubt that Taffy will avail himself of the opportunity of witnessing an English 'cwmrygeddion'. The South Wales Company, by way of encouraging the traffic, intend conveying passengers to and from Gloucester in one day for a single fare. The Midland Company also issue return tickets, available for the week; and the Great Western run special trains.[25]

In addition to local and visiting nobility, gentry and clergy who occupied the raised seats and nave, 'in the aisles were observed a strong muster of the humbler classes'.[26] And outside the cathedral on the last day, 'owing to the enormous press of individuals anxious to be present [at *Messiah*] … the police – whose regulations for preserving order and for avoiding collisions and mistakes, were admirably carried out – underwent no small difficulty in disposing of the equipages of the country visitors'.[27]

In 1843 Hereford Cathedral was in such a state of dilapidation that the Festival had to be held in All Saints' Church, but by 1846 the nave had been sufficiently restored for the cathedral to be used again. Something of the very special atmosphere of Victorian Hereford at Three Choirs can be gathered from *The Times* of 11 September 1846:

> The town of Hereford is now, perhaps, as full of gaiety and bustle as it is possible for it to be under any circumstances. The streets are

---

[24] *MW* 1881, pp. 575–6.

[25] *MW* 1853, pp. 589–90.

[26] Ibid., p. 591.

[27] Ibid., p. 609.

thronged – that is, thronged for Hereford, for a Hereford crowd and a London, or even a Birmingham crowd, are very different matters. Still there is little doubt that an average of two out of three of the comfortable population of 10,000 may be reckoned upon as interested, profitably or pleasurably, in the progress of the festival, which once in three years awakens the ancient city from its slumbers. And so, yesterday, a motley army of lookers-on covered the area on either side of Broad-Street, right up to the very mouth of the Cathedral, watching the more favoured children of fortune, as they entered the sacred edifice, to listen to the second morning's performance.

At the next Hereford Festival, in 1852, on the second morning came the news of the unexpected death of the Duke of Wellington:

> The solemn tolling of the Cathedral bell, which announced that England's most honoured son had quitted this world for ever, was not at first comprehended; but as soon as the cause was explained it became the theme of conversation and remark in every circle … at the Cathedral, before the oratorio commenced, the Dead March from Handel's *Saul* was performed in honour of the illustrious dead, the audience (the most crowded since the festival began) all standing. It was a most impressive and affecting scene. The simplicity of the music, which has so often commemorated the decease of great princes and greater soldiers; the measured blows of the drum, each, as it were, a warning to mortality; the significant expression upon every countenance, which told in unmistakable terms the deep regret of all, were not mere parts of an empty ceremony. There was nothing of show in the manifestation. It was a gratuitous and unanimous exhibition, in which the heart was prime mover, of sorrow for the loss of a great and good man, of sympathy and veneration for England's champion and the benefactor of the world.[28]

By 1855 the railway had come to Hereford by the extension of the Great Western, via Gloucester and Ross, and the completion of the Shrewsbury and Hereford Railways. As at Gloucester, the trains brought larger than ever crowds to the Festival and a marked increase in demand for accommodation in the city:

> The Herefordshire Militia, for some time quartered on the inhabitants of the town, has been ordered to Aldershot, and is expected to leave early on Wednesday morning. It was thought, I do not know why, that their presence might interfere with the conduct of the Festival. More likely the rooms occupied *gratis* by the men were in request.[29]

The pride and interest shown in the Festival at each of the three cities ensured that there would be an impressive display of street decorations during Three Choirs week. Although the smallest city, Hereford's effort was often the most spectacular. In 1882, for example, triumphal arches were erected in most of the important streets, one of them representing Cleopatra's Needle and one near

---

[28] *MW* 1852, p. 597.
[29] *MW* 1855, p. 542.

the Merton Hotel bearing the message 'Welcome to our city'. Venetian masts were erected around High Town and part of Commercial Street at intervals of 16 yards, and on each of these masts the name of a composer whose work was to be performed at the Festival.[30]

So, on to Worcester, and let us discover what the correspondent of the *Musical World* thought of that city in 1854:

> Worcester is not altogether the *beau ideal* of a cathedral city, nor is its church one of the very first class … Consistently with its clerical reputation, it is not so much put out of its way by these triennial festivals as some people would imagine. It gets up its excitements in a grave and sober way. Of course, on these occasions, there is an extraordinary influx of visitors, and, we believe, never more so than at the present festival. So, at least, goes our experience; for we can vouch that 'good accommodation for man and horse', during this week has been a thing not to be sought without patience under much denial, both in the city and neighbourhood. Yet with all this great extra population leavening the whole lump, as it were, and forcing the sober old city into a holiday mind, – with all the crowding about the streets, and gay dresses, and constant paradings to and from the Cathedral and College Hall, with a great deal of interpolated visiting and sight-seeing besides, there is no noisy and vulgar bustle. There is a brim-full but quiet happification about the whole scene that, to our taste, contrasts most favourably with the riot, heat, and turmoil emitted by those surging and crushing masses of humanity, which usually represent public beatitude in more populous places.[31]

This was the city which, in 1841, drew William Henry Elgar from his native Dover to earn a living as piano tuner, teacher and organist; the city where he met his wife, Ann, and where their first three children were born. In 1856 the Elgars moved to a rented cottage in the village of Broadheath, two miles west of the river, and there, on 2 June 1857, a fourth child, Edward, was born. By the time Edward was two years old the expansion of his father's business necessitated a reluctant move from Broadheath back to Worcester; back to the city where W. H. Elgar now supplied music to the cathedral and played the violin in the Three Choirs Festival orchestra, and where young Edward Elgar grew up to become the finest composer of English music since Henry Purcell.

[30] *Hereford Times*, 16 September 1882.
[31] *MW* 1854, p. 609.

Froissart

URING William Done's fifty-one years at Worcester he had worked with Gloucester colleagues John Amott, Samuel Sebastian Wesley, Charles Harford Lloyd and Charles Lee Williams; and with George Townshend Smith, Langdon Colborne and George Robertson Sinclair at Hereford.

Lloyd made his Three Choirs debut in the organ loft at the Hereford Festival of 1876. Selections from *Samson* and *The Creation* in the gaslit cathedral provided a special attraction at an evening concert: 'Lurid glares of gas fell upon the stately pillars, and pierced through gloom to the far-off roof, giving a weird-like appearance to nave and aisle.'[1]

A Gloucestershire man, born at Thornbury in 1849, Lloyd had graduated in Arts and Music at Magdalen Hall, Oxford. At his first Gloucester Festival, in 1877, it quickly became apparent that the young new cathedral organist was a musician of ability and distinction, and, moreover, one who seemed 'to possess the right stuff for a conductor, combining those essential attributes of firmness, quietude, and self-control, in the absence of which any hope of reaching eminence as a ruler in this particular sphere of art-demonstration must be altogether illusory.'[2] The *Musical Times* reserved to the end of a review of the week's events a notice of especial praise for Lloyd's conducting, praising 'not only his skill in conveying ... an accurate knowledge of the tempi of the several pieces, but his evident intimate acquaintance with the scores, and the intelligence he evinced in the endeavour to realise every point indicated by the composer.'[3]

Lloyd was an innovator. We have already noted his introduction at the Gloucester Festivals of Brahms's *Ein deutsches Requiem* in 1877 and of Beethoven's *Missa solemnis* in 1880, both drawing much-needed oxygen into the suffocating ultra-conservatism of nineteenth-century provincial taste. We have seen too that Parry's *Prometheus Unbound*, accepted by Lloyd for performance in the 1880 Festival, was later identified as the work which marked the birth of the renaissance of English music. But 1880 was to be Lloyd's second and last Festival as conductor. In 1882 he reluctantly resigned his post at Gloucester on appointment as Organist at Christ Church Cathedral, Oxford. Ten years later he succeeded Sir Joseph Barnby as Organist and Precentor of Eton College, and in 1914 he was appointed Organist at the Chapel Royal, London.

[1] *MW* 1876, p. 645.

[2] *MW* 1877, p. 600.

[3] Ibid., p. 480.

In his memoirs, Sir Herbert Brewer remembered Lloyd with affection:

He was the most unselfish and generous of men with an intensely keen sense of duty, and he consistently lived up to the very high ideals he had of life … His was an extremely highly strung, nervous temperament … I remember an occasion on which he was conducting in the nave of Gloucester Cathedral and his assistant at the organ failed to follow his beat. Throwing down his baton, Lloyd rushed up to the organ-loft and flung aside the assistant who came in audible contact with the floor, and played himself.[4]

Curiously, during his six years at Gloucester, Lloyd wrote no major work for the Festival. Then, having left, over a period of fifteen years he became a most prolific Three Choirs composer. His contributions were: *Hero and Leander*, 1884(w); *The Song of Balder*, 1885(H); *Andromeda*, 1886(G); *A Song of Judgement*, 1891(H); *Sir Ogie and Lady Elsie*, 1894(H); Concerto in F minor for organ and orchestra, 1895(G); *Hymn of Thanksgiving*, 1897(H); and an eight-part motet, *The Souls of the Righteous*, 1901(G) – in memory of Queen Victoria. It is curious, too, that although an organist all his life, as a cantata composer Lloyd was most drawn to secular subjects. He died at Slough on his seventieth birthday, 16 October 1919.

If Lloyd had been an excellent Festival conductor, the efforts of his contemporary at Hereford, Langdon Colborne, on behalf of Three Choirs from 1877 can perhaps at best be described as capable. Born at Hackney in 1835, Colborne was a pupil of George Cooper before being appointed Organist of St Michael's College, Tenbury, in 1860. The foundation stone of St Michael's was laid in 1854 and the college opened in 1856. The founder was the Rev. Sir Arthur Gore Ouseley, who, in 1855, was elected Professor of Music at Oxford and, in that same year, appointed Precentor of Hereford Cathedral. Colborne remained at St Michael's College for fourteen years before moving to Beverley Minster in 1874, Wigan Parish Church in 1875 and, briefly, Dorking Parish Church in 1877, the year of George Townshend Smith's death at Hereford.

At Colborne's first Festival as conductor, in 1879, the *Musical Times* reported that 'he endeavoured to earn, rather than to force, his position', and that 'if he did not venture any new readings of the standard works, he at least averted any catastrophe in ensuring the old ones'.[5] The *Musical World*, reviewing the performance of *Elijah*, noted that Colborne depended 'wisely on the occasional indications of Mr. Weist Hill, first violin in the orchestra, and a thoroughly experienced musician'.[6] Nor did Colborne, like Townshend Smith, attempt to fill the shoes of the Festival secretary in addition to those of the conductor; the Rev. Berkeley L. S. Stanhope took on those duties.

It is to Colborne's credit that he introduced the first and second parts of Bach's *Christmas Oratorio* to the Festival in 1879, and the same composer's *Magnificat* in 1882, but some of his choices were far less inspired: Dr G. M.

---

[4] Herbert Brewer, *Memories of Choirs and Cloisters* (Bodley Head, 1931).

[5] *MT* 1879, pp. 528 and 535.

[6] *MW* 1879, p. 578.

Garrett's *The Shunammite* and Molique's *Abraham* in 1882; Dr Joseph Smith's *Saint Kevin* – which tells how a young monk, tempted by the love of a maiden from whom he attempts to fly, eventually saves himself by hurling her, shrieking, into a lake – in 1885; and Colborne's own church cantata *Samuel* in 1888. The *Musical Times* suggested that Colborne's piece was 'on a par with a book written for children ... the music taxes nobody's powers of comprehension ... the work was manifestly out of place'.[7]

The Hereford Festival of 1888, Colborne's last, must have been a great disappointment to him. His *Samuel* failed to hit the mark, and his conducting of a selection from Handel's *Samson* was judged a double failure:

> The choice of pieces omitted some of the best numbers, and included a lot of recitative in the vain hope of sustaining the continuity and interest of the story, while in the performance all was confusion, even the Conductor seeming not to know, at times, what should come next. This state of things reached a climax when Dr. Colborne and the orchestra went on to the second part of an air which it was agreed with the singer should be omitted. The singer declined to follow, and a collapse ensued.[8]

The following day, Thursday, a fairly large audience assembled in the cathedral to hear Cherubini's Mass in D minor; Frederic Cowen's *Song of Thanksgiving*, written for the Centennial Exhibition at Melbourne and receiving its first performance in England; Hubert Parry's *Blest Pair of Sirens*; and Sir Frederick Ouseley's *Martyrdom of St Polycarp*. Cowen and Parry conducted their own works and scored significant successes. Colborne conducted the Mass in D minor and 'supported by the influence of the sacred place, Cherubini's strains subdued the audience till tears came unbidden to many eyes'.[9] But the Ouseley piece, a Degree exercise written thirty years previously, was a disappointment of which no mention is made in the *Annals*, even though the performance, in which Anna Williams, Hilda Wilson, Edward Lloyd and Charles Santley took part, was considered one of the best of the week: 'This is partly explained by the comparative easiness of the music; and it is clear that Dr. Colborne's natural desire to do the most possible for his old friend and patron met with sympathy on the part of the performers.'[10]

Colborne received the Lambeth doctorate in music in 1883.

Ouseley had been something of a prodigy, recognising at the age of five the key in which his father blew his nose, and at six playing a duet with Mendelssohn. He succeeded to his father's baronetcy in 1844. Ernest Walker, in his *History of Music in England*, summed up Ouseley's achievement as a composer:

> [he] always wrote with a lofty ideal; but inspiration, or anything approaching thereto, visited him rarely.
> His work is massive and sincere, but it is usually very dull; however,

[7] *MT* 1888, p. 603.
[8] Ibid., p. 604.
[9] Ibid.
[10] Ibid., p. 613.

he deserves a word or two of commendation not only for his excellent technical workmanship, sometimes of a brilliantly elaborate kind, but also for one or two emergences into a really vitalized atmosphere.

As the precentor of Hereford Cathedral, Ouseley seems to have taken little interest in the Three Choirs Festival. In 1858, a year in which Dean Dawes was said to have expressed his hostility to the 'abominable festival' by taking away the key to the choir, Ouseley absented himself from Hereford along with Archdeacon Freer and Lord Saye and Sele, one of the canons. It was rumoured that the Precentor was sulking at St Michael's College, Tenbury, because he did not want his anthem, *The Lord is the true God*, performed on Tuesday!

Thirty years later Ouseley agreed to preach at the Opening Service at Hereford. The congregation looked forward to the sermon being a 'vindication of sacred music in its widest sense. But Sir Frederick Ouseley said not a word regarding the art, limiting himself exclusively to the virtue of charity, and the opportunity then afforded for its particular exercise.'[11] In the event, the collections for the charity in 1888 were below average.

Sir Frederick Ouseley died on 6 April 1889 at the age of sixty-three. The following September, Langdon Colborne made his final Three Choirs appearance, playing the organ at the Gloucester Festival. A few days later, on 16 September 1889, he too died.

Gloucester 1883.   At the request of the Stewards 'rigid economy' was the text preached at this Festival, and the inevitable results of such preachment were speedily seen in the falling off in the sale of tickets.[12]

The period from 1873 to 1896, generally termed the Great Depression by economic historians, was a time in which agriculture in England was in sharp decline. A series of bad harvests and the challenge of imported wheat threatened the long-held supremacy of the landed gentry, the very men who in the Three Choirs counties had volunteered for stewardship of the Festival year after year, regularly underwriting deficits; now they found themselves compelled them to share their pre-eminence with financiers and industrialists. At Hereford the recession was felt more sharply than at Gloucester and Worcester because, then as now, the cathedral was smaller, resulting in a wider gap between ticket income and expenditure. Consequently, the Festival there depended upon some 300 Stewards contributing £5 each to a guarantee fund. In 1882 half of those Stewards refused to join; the Festival was a financial failure of such proportion as to excite comment in the national press: London audiences wanted new works and famous conductors; provincial audiences wanted only old favourites; the Festival needed to draw its audiences from both London and the provinces, *and* to attract a large privately funded subsidy through the stewardship scheme.

This was the dilemma facing Charles Lee Williams when he took over from Lloyd in Gloucester in 1882.

Williams was thirty-one years old when he arrived at Gloucester. He was born at Alton Barnes, Wiltshire, on 1 May 1851, and had been: a chorister at

[11] Ibid., p. 603.

[12] *Annals* 1895, p. 280.

New College, Oxford; a pupil of Dr G. B. Arnold, and Assistant Organist of Winchester Cathedral; Organist of Upton Church, Torquay, in 1870; music master of St Colomba's College, Rathfarnham, in 1872; and Organist of Llandaff Cathedral, where his uncle was dean, from 1876.

At a General Meeting of the Gloucester Stewards held on 15 March 1883, Williams faced thirty-seven gentlemen, among whom were several whose principal concern was to 'curtail the expenses and prevent the deficits which had occurred at the Festivals at Gloucester of 1877 and 1880'.[13] (The deficit in 1877 had been £136 15s. 5d., but in 1880 it had leapt to £470 0s. 7d., the highest amount for thirty-three years. Furthermore, in 1865, 1868 and 1871, the S. S. Wesley years, the Gloucester Festival had shown a worthwhile surplus.) The conductor presented his proposed list of principal singers and their anticipated fees; at the top of the list was Emma Albani. She would, said Williams, require a fee of at least 420 guineas. Opposition was immediate, and several around the table were fully prepared to dispense with the services of the star attraction altogether. Lloyd, still a committee member, was present to support Williams – perhaps a compromise could be reached by engaging Albani for fewer performances. The gathered wisdom was unable to make a decision on the number of principals to be engaged or the fees to be paid. A music committee would have to be formed. Could it, Williams asked, please sit immediately after the present meeting – time was running short?

The Music Committee met: Albani must be offered no more than 150 guineas for one oratorio and one concert; Edward Lloyd had asked for 150 guineas for five performances – he must be offered that amount for *six* performances; and reduced fees must be offered to Anna Williams and Hilda Wilson.

Not surprisingly, Frederick Gye would not allow Albani to appear on these terms. Undeterred, Williams pressed on with an ambitious plan to introduce more new works than ever before at the Gloucester Festival of 1883. The Stewards commissioned three short pieces from local men: one from Hubert Parry – *The Glories of our Blood and State* (a setting of James Shirley's poem *Death the Leveller*); one from C. H. Lloyd – *Allen a Dale*, to verses from Scott's *Rokeby*; and a choral setting of Byron's lines 'I wish to tune my quivering lyre', from Dr A. E. Dyer of Cheltenham College. Williams's teacher, Dr G. B. Arnold, the Organist of Winchester Cathedral, was invited to compose and to conduct a choral work. The result was *Sennacherib*, of which not even Williams could say more than that 'the composer's great knowledge of fugal writing and elaborate counterpoint was apparent throughout the cantata'.[14] The *Musical Times* judged it simply tedious. From more famous pens came the first performance of Sir John Stainer's *St Mary Magdalen*, thereafter known as his 'Gloucester Oratorio', and the second performance of Dr (later Sir) Charles Villiers Stanford's Symphony No. 2 (*Elegiac*), both conducted by their composers.

Richard Wagner died on 13 February 1883. Four weeks later Williams proposed to the Music Committee that the first Miscellaneous Evening Concert

---

[13] Gloucester Festival Minute Book, 1883. Gloucester Cathedral Archives and Library.

[14] *Annals* 1895, p. 281.

of the 1883 Festival should end with *Tannhäuser* (presumably the overture).[15] But no, the work actually played was Cherubini's overture to *Anacreon*. The Stewards were not yet ready for Wagner.

Nonetheless, Williams had achieved a great deal at his first Festival. London critics could not accuse him of neglecting new works; eminent composers had conducted their own pieces; and as a conductor himself, Williams was thought really rather good. If only the Stewards had allowed him to engage Albani, the Festival might have been a financial as well as an artistic success, instead of which the deficit amounted to £330 2s. 10d. – more than the saving in artists' fees.

While planning his next two Festivals, Williams determined to both raise standards and reduce costs – but not to compromise in the selection of soloists. He was acutely aware that lack of rehearsal time for both orchestra and chorus was the most effective brake on the artistic advancement of the Festival. The chorus, drawn from many towns, did not rehearse as a body until the day before the Festival, and the conductor was limited to only one orchestral rehearsal in London.

Williams tackled this second problem first; an entry in his notebook records:

London rehearsal Aug 28 & 29 [1889] at St. Andrew's Hall, Newman Street, at 9 for 9.30 a.m. Extra day put on in London at my urgent request. Quite impossible to do it with less – even with two days *more than half* the programme was performed *without any rehearsal at all*.[16]

He also noted his opinions on the orchestral players, marking down against each name, 'good', 'bad', 'too old', etc., concluding with, 'N. B. As vacancies occur in band, terms must be reduced – *especially* in *string*. There are any amount of excellent players ready and willing to attend the Festival. Good wind players are difficult to get and good terms must be offered.'[17]

The approximate numbers and costs of the chorus members for the 1886(G) Festival were as follows:[18]

Worcester	37	incl. Lay clerks & 4 boys	£166. 8. 0
Tewkesbury	9		£15. 1. 0
Cardiff	20		£57. 7. 0
Bradford	24		£109. 10. 0
Gloucester	68	plus Lay clerks and boys	£145. 19. 0
Bristol	20	incl. 6 Lay clerks	£94. 10. 0
Hereford	29	incl. 8 Lay clerks & 4 boys	£134. 8. 0
Cambridge	4	Lay clerks	£16. 0. 0
Oxford	8		£40. 0. 0
Single engagements	9		£38. 0. 0

[15] Gloucester Festival Minute Book, 1883. Gloucester Cathedral Archives and Library.

[16] Charles Lee Williams's notebook. Gloucestershire Archives.

[17] Ibid.

[18] Ibid.

At a meeting of the Music Committee in Gloucester on 13 March 1886, Thomas Gambier Parry said that he had been asked to suggest that the choruses should be selected from Gloucester, Hereford and Worcester.[19] Williams promised to consider the matter but no changes were made until 1892. It seems probable that it was Joseph Bennett who made this suggestion to Parry; he had joined the Music Committee in 1886 but was absent on 13 March. Bennett certainly raised the subject again immediately following the very successful 1889(G) Festival. 'The chorus', he said, 'relatively, was the most expensive in the kingdom, inasmuch as its 200 voices cost £800. There were means by which this expense could be lessened, and he should be prepared to lay before the committee a scheme which, without impairing its efficiency, would lessen the cost by £300. (Applause).'[20]

In 1892(G), the Festival Chorus was, for the first time, drawn entirely from the counties of Herefordshire, Worcestershire and Gloucestershire, the last including nearly 100 voices from Bristol. 'It was', the *Musical Times* said, 'a capital body of singers, fit for anything.'[21]

In the three Gloucester Festivals of 1886, 1889 and 1892, Williams continued to champion new music, including the first performances of Hubert Parry's *Judith* (1889) and *Job* (1892). Williams himself contributed two cantatas: *Last Night at Bethany* (1889) and *Gethsemane* (1892).

Meanwhile William Done, at the age of seventy-five, had decided that it was time to hand his baton to a younger man: he asked Williams to direct the Worcester Festival of 1890. On 1 January that year Done replied to a letter from Edward Elgar, who had asked if he would consider including a composition of his in the 1890(w) Festival:

> I shall be much pleased to receive the score of your new composition ... and I shall study it with much pleasure as the work of one whose talent I have always recognized and admired. It will be a pleasure to you to know that the proposal to introduce your orchestral piece at the Festival met with no opposition. I must not take the credit of it to myself, as it scarcely required a recommendation from me. I will take care to give you a good orchestra and fair opportunity of rehearsal.
>
> Will you kindly tell me whether any extra instruments will be required? I hope not as the orchestra is so small.[22]

Three days later Done wrote again:

> The score of your little work arrived safely. Many thanks to you for it. At the last Festival we had both Tuba and Contra Fag. but I do not intend to go to the expense of both this time. I myself much prefer the Contra

---

[19] Gloucester Festival Minute Book, 1886. Gloucester Cathedral Archives and Library.

[20] Gloucester Festival Minute Book, 1889. Gloucester Cathedral Archives and Library.

[21] *MT* 1892, p. 598.

[22] Letter from William Done to Edward Elgar (1 January 1890). Worcestershire Archive and Archaeology Service.

Fag. One of the two we must have, but as Mr. Williams will conduct throughout the Festival I must leave him to decide which and will let you known as soon as I hear from him.[23]

Elgar was thirty-two. In the previous year he had married his beloved Alice in London. On 24 June 1889 he was present at a St James's Hall concert conducted by Hans Richter in which the first performance of Parry's Symphony No. 4 in E minor, written at Richter's request, had been given. This splendid work, so shamefully neglected and so filled with just the sweep and brilliance which we now identify as 'Elgarian', must surely have had a seminal influence on a composer already mature in years but yet still feverishly seeking to establish his artistic reputation.

On 2 July 1890, Done wrote to Elgar once more:

Mr. Wheeler [the Worcester Festival secretary] has forwarded to me your note. I will take care to have your piece properly inserted in the programme.

The London rehearsals will take place at St. George's Hall on Wednesday and Thursday – September 3rd. and 4th. Our conductor has sent me a rehearsal programme, and I find that he has put you down for 3 o'clock on the first day – *Wednesday 3rd.* I hope to hear that that arrangement will suit you. You shall have a programme as soon as they are ready. I hope you are well.[24]

On 14 August the Elgars' only child, Carice, was born. Three and a half weeks later, on Wednesday 10 September, Edward Elgar's overture *Froissart* was heard for the first time, at the single evening secular concert of the 1890 Worcester Festival.[25] The occasion was vividly remembered by the twenty-one-year-old Assistant Organist at Hereford Cathedral, Ivor Atkins:

Never before had I heard such a wonderful combination of a first-rate Chorus and Orchestra. I was naturally specially interested in Elgar, knowing that he was to produce a new Overture whose very title attracted me, for I had just been reading Froissart's *Chronicles*. Sinclair pointed Elgar out to me. There he was, fiddling among the first violins, with his fine intellectual face, his heavy moustache, his nervous eyes and his beautiful hands.

The Wednesday evening came. I had no dress clothes with me, having come over from Hereford for the day, so crept up the steps leading to the back of the Orchestra and peeped from behind those on the platform. The new Overture was placed at the end of the first half of the programme.

The great moment came, and I watched Elgar's shy entry on to the platform. From that moment my eyes did not leave him, and I listened to the Overture, hearing it in the exciting way one hears music when among the players. I heard the surge of the strings, the chatter of the woodwind,

---

[23] Letter from William Done to Edward Elgar (4 January 1890). Worcestershire Archive and Archaeology Service.

[24] Letter from William Done to Edward Elgar (2 July 1890). Worcestershire Archive and Archaeology Service.

[25] A second evening concert in the cathedral was introduced in 1890.

the sudden bursts from the horns, the battle call of the trumpets, the awesome beat of the drums and the thrill of cymbal clashes. I was conscious of all these and of the hundred and one other sounds from an orchestra that stir one's blood and send one's heart into one's mouth.

But there was something else I was conscious of – I knew that Elgar was the man for me, I knew that I completely understood his music, and that my heart and soul went with it.[26]

Writing in the *Daily Telegraph*, Joseph Bennett said: 'Mr. Punch's memorable advice to persons about to marry [i.e. "Don't"] is that which true charity dictates in nine cases out of ten when young men propose to write overtures and symphonies. I regard Mr. Elgar as an exception. Let him go on. He will one day "arrive".' The *Musical Times* 'hoped, and, given opportunity, even expected' that Elgar would 'make his mark'.[27] And of Charles Lee Williams's direction of the Festival, 'no better man could have been found … enough cannot be said in acknowledging the unobtrusive efficiency which made the voyage of the Festival ship safe and pleasant … He is just such a conductor as these Festivals have long wanted.'[28]

[26] Wulstan Atkins, *The Elgar–Atkins Friendship* (David & Charles, 1985).

[27] *MT* 1890, p. 598.

[28] Ibid., pp. 596 and 599.

II

The Unreasonable Man

The reasonable man adapts himself to the world: the unreasonable one persists in trying to adapt the world to himself. Therefore all progress depends on the unreasonable man.

George Bernard Shaw (1903)

AT the time of Langdon Colborne's death in 1889, Charles Lee Williams had been in post at Gloucester for seven years, and William Done at Worcester for forty-five. Both men were, in their different ways, much liked and respected: Done, quietly persuasive and undemonstrative; Williams, clear in his purpose and firm but diplomatic. The new man appointed to Hereford was of a very different personality.

George Robertson Sinclair (1863–1917) was born at 3 Devonshire Villas, Sydenham Road, Croydon, on 28 October 1863. His ancestors were of Scottish descent but had for several generations been settled in Ireland, at Killiney, near Dublin. His father, Dr Robert Sharpe Sinclair, held the appointment of Director of Public Education in Bombay, and it was owing to the temporary residence of his mother in England that Sinclair happened to be born in Croydon. But he was extremely proud to call himself an Irishman, proclaiming his nationality during the Hereford Festival week by hoisting the Irish flag outside his house.

At the age of eight Sinclair entered the Royal Irish Academy of Music, where he studied under Sir Robert Stewart, who was an old friend of his father's and of Sir Frederick Gore Ouseley. Thus, in 1873, young Sinclair – aged ten – gained a choral scholarship at St Michael's College, Tenbury, where he was the only boy known to have been taught personally by Ouseley. His parents intended that he should take Holy Orders; but the death of his father when Sinclair was seventeen threw him upon his own resources. When Bishop (afterwards Archbishop) Benson, of Truro, asked Ouseley to recommend him an organist for the proposed Cornish cathedral, he at once nominated Sinclair.

In 1880, at the age of seventeen, Sinclair was appointed to Truro Cathedral as the first organist and choirmaster.[1] Even though still only twenty-six when he succeeded Langdon Colborne at Hereford, he already possessed an unusual degree of experience in addition to prodigious ability.

At the Worcester Festival of 1890 Sinclair shared the organ music with Done's assistant, Hugh Blair, and thus would have been present to hear the Three Choirs debut of the brilliant young Irish baritone Harry Plunket

---

[1] The building of Truro Cathedral, assisted financially by the Freemasons, began in 1880. The cathedral was completed and consecrated in 1887.

Greene; to hear the première of Elgar's overture *Froissart*; and at the same secular concert to hear Charles Lee Williams conduct, for the first time at a Three Choirs concert, a work by Wagner: the Prelude to Act III of *Lohengrin*.

The 'new music' of Wagner featured again in Sinclair's first Festival as conductor, at Hereford in 1891. He included the overture and Preislied (sung by Edward Lloyd) from *Die Meistersinger* in the single Shire Hall secular concert on Tuesday evening. The next morning in the cathedral he conducted a programme in honour of the centenary of the death of Mozart, beginning with that composer's Requiem and followed by Beethoven's Symphony No. 3 in E flat (*Eroica*); then came the first performance of a motet by Dr H. J. Edwards, *Praise to the Holiest* – a setting of words from John Henry Newman's poem *The Dream of Gerontius*; then, for the first time in an English cathedral, the prelude to Wagner's *Parsifal* – 'a fact which elicited some comment'.[2] The concert ended with Sullivan's *Te Deum* for the recovery of the Prince of Wales.[3]

The two principal works of the 1891(H) Festival were C. H. Lloyd's *Song of Judgement* and Hubert Parry's *De Profundis*, both performed under their composers' direction at the Thursday morning concert before a disappointingly small audience – only 921 tickets were sold. Of the Parry piece, a setting for soprano solo, orchestra and three choirs of four parts each, the *Musical Times* reported that 'shining through all, and giving it glory and splendour, are noble imaginings and exalted emotions … Men of varying tastes and judgement conceded to one another that in its way a great thing had been born into the world.'[4]

In addition to the musical achievements of the 1891 Hereford Festival, Sinclair was able to share in the satisfaction of a successful royal visit. On the first day of the Festival the Duke and Duchess of Teck and their children, Princess Mary (later the Duchess of York, then queen to King George V) and Prince Alexander, attended a performance of Mendelssohn's *St Paul* in which Emma Albani, Hilda Wilson, Edward Lloyd and Charles Santley were the soloists, and 'the conductor Mr G. R. Sinclair … showed much skill and tact'.[5]

But tact was the one quality which not everyone in Hereford would have attributed to Sinclair. In 1891 he had trodden on toes in order to get his own way with the Stewards. In spite of the poor audience for the première of Parry's *De Profundis*, the total attendance at the Festival was 8,978, an increase of 2,343 on the figure for 1888. Sinclair must have felt complete justification in his selection of music and was determined, like Charles Lee Williams at Gloucester, not only to meet the insatiable demand for stock oratorios (*Messiah* and *Elijah*), but also to support and encourage performances of new works. Unfortunately, his single-mindedness could all too easily be construed as obduracy, and his determination as petulance.

[2] *Annals* 1895, p. 300.

[3] In December 1891, the Prince of Wales caught typhoid, from which he recovered.

[4] *MT* 1891, p. 598.

[5] Ibid.

As preparations for the 1894(H) Festival got under way, an 'atmosphere' began to develop. The chairman of the Executive Committee was Mr J. H. Arkwright, and the Festival secretary the Rev. Prebendary G. G. Ashley (whose predecessor, the Hon. and Ven. Berkeley Stanhope, was now the Archdeacon of Hereford).

On 22 January 1894, Stanhope wrote to Arkwright:[6]

> You will probably receive a letter from Ashley tomorrow, on the subject of 'Sinclair'. He has been here this morning, & I feel there is not any probability of harmony between them. They cannot, and will not work together, which is essential …
>
> Ashley is bent on resigning – & who is to take up the work? For it needs a strong man to keep Sinclair in his proper place.
>
> If the breach cannot be permanently settled – better to have a fresh hand now, than later on when the work of Sec. is heavier.
>
> But perhaps with the aid of the Dean something may be done – Sinclair is a spoilt child.

Sure enough, Arkwright *did* receive a letter from Ashley the following day:

> The Hon: Sec: and the Conductor have each their own special business to transact, and it seems a pity that they cannot each do their own work in harmony & good temper without the one interfering with the work of the other. I am sure that no one would resent more keenly my interference with the Band and Chorus than Mr Sinclair, and I think courtesy and good sense demands, if nothing else, that he should show to the Hon: Sec: the consideration he would expect to be shown to himself.
>
> During the Festival of 1891 on many occasions Mr Sinclair interfered with the duties which devolved on me as Hon: Sec: and if the same line is to be adopted by him in reference to this festival it is obvious that we cannot work in harmony. I was in 1891 much annoyed by Mr Sinclair's interference but I had hoped no further unpleasantness would have occurred; I regret to find … that this is not the case.
>
> I feel much interest in the Festival work and I am ready and willing to do my best in the interests of this excellent charity but I see clearly that unless harmony exists between the Hon: Sec: and the Conductor that the Festival cannot be a success. Whilst I am quite willing to continue to act as Hon: Sec: I cannot do so except on the understanding that my duties are not interfered with. I shall be glad to hear your views before taking any decided action in the matter, or, if possible, the view that the Executive Com: hold on the subject.

Arkwright replied to Ashley on 26 January:

> I am extremely sorry that you have been again annoyed by Sinclair having reopened the question which I thought had been settled on the simplest grounds of common sense … unless Sinclair will shut up the Executive must be our referee. If you like I will write to him a very plain letter and

---

[6] All of the correspondence quoted in what follows is contained in the Arkwright Collection, Herefordshire Archive.

submit it to you and the Archdeacon, which ought to settle it. And I hope this would put all thoughts of your resignation out of possibility *or* we three might wait on the Dean in camera and plan an escape.

Ashley wrote back from a London address on 30 January:

I am very glad to find by your letter that you hold so strong an opinion on the matter in question. I prefer the second of your suggestions – for this reason – because Mr Dean has a real authority & power over Mr Sinclair beyond any that the Com: could assume. If the Dean spoke in earnest it would probably do more than anything else. I shall be at home after next Friday. If however you & the Archdeacon think the letter best, I will fall in with your views at once. Indeed I don't mind what course is adopted if only matters could be put on a footing of peace and harmony. I detest disagreement & quarrels; and it takes away all pleasure in doing my work, as I dread something unpleasant at every turn. I have no wish to resign unless it is forced upon me, but it is clear that if our respective duties cannot be carried out without constant friction the Festival must suffer.

Arkwright decided to write at once to the dean, who replied on 2 February:

I will see Sinclair & try & arrange matters. I fancy it would not be amiss if Berkeley Stanhope would call & talk the matter over with him – often there are faults on both sides.
      Then both Ashley and Sinclair respect & trust the Archdeacon.

The dean's arranging seems to have been successful. Ashley was persuaded to carry on. Sinclair pressed his purpose home, injecting new vigour into the Festival, raising the standard of music at Hereford Cathedral to new heights, gaining professional distinction, and attaining high office as a Freemason. When still only twenty-nine years old he received the Lambeth degree of DMus, an honour not accorded to William Done until the celebration of his Golden Jubilee at Worcester in 1894, the year before his death.

In 1899 Sinclair was appointed conductor of the Birmingham Festival Choral Society, and in that same year Elgar's *Enigma Variations* were performed for the first time. Among the 'friends pictured within' to whom Elgar dedicated his masterpiece, 'G. R. S.' (Variation XI) bursts energetically in between the intimate delicacy of 'Dorabella' and the meditative cello solo of 'B. G. N.' (Basil Nevinson). Elgar insisted that the variation had nothing to do with organs, cathedrals or, except remotely, G. R. S., but that the first few bars were suggested by the boisterous antics of Sinclair's bulldog, Dan. Even so, the music seems to match Dan's mercurial master remarkably well.

Away from the pressures of the cathedral and the Festival, Sinclair could be a kind and sociable man. He was a welcome guest at the home of the DuBuisson family from early in 1890. Margaret DuBuisson records in her diary the pleasure she found in Sinclair's visits when she was a young girl.[7] He frequently dined with them, as did a Miss Holland, and Sinclair entertained them himself and joined in other musical parties. Margaret DuBuisson shared his love for music

[7] I am grateful to Mr W. A. DuBuisson for this information.

and was fascinated by the skill with which he would improvise at the piano. He used to join in the games with the younger DuBuisson boys and was himself given dancing lessons by the family. In turn, he would play when a guest at parties and used to enjoy an evening pipe with his friends.

Sinclair's hobbies were cycling, yachting and photography. A bachelor, he shared his house with six cats and Dan, who followed closely in his master's footsteps, waiting patiently at the cathedral door whenever Sinclair went in. Dan was present at all Sinclair's lessons and at his rehearsals in the Shire Hall. A member of the Hereford Choral Society drew a caricature of Sinclair – 'the Metamorphosis of Dan' – which was passed quietly around during a rehearsal but was never intended to be seen by the conductor. As one London critic observed: 'Dan deserves to be made a Dogter of Music!'

Although by no means everyone in Hereford found Sinclair an unreasonable man, as the years passed by he became ever more set in his solitary ways. Percy Hull's wife, Molly, remembered the days when she had been Sinclair's pupil. She found him a fussy, typical bachelor. Dan had been succeeded by Ben, who snuffled, snorted and slobbered; the whole house smelt of a mixture of dog and general stuffiness – hardly an atmosphere in which a young girl could enjoy a music lesson.

> **Worcester 1893.** It was hoped that Worcester, at the 170th meeting of the Three Choirs, held there in 1893, would follow the excellent lead set by the conductor at the Gloucester meeting the year before, and dispense with other voices than those supplied by the three counties; but Worcester decided to walk in the old ways, and Mr Broughton's Leeds Choir of a hundred voices formed half the chorus.[8]

The continued dependence on a large and well-trained contingent of singers from Leeds was felt to be an increasing cause of shame to the Worcester Festival Choral Society, as was the humiliating fact that very few of their number were asked to take part in the Gloucester and Hereford Festivals. The debate, which had hitherto remained an internal matter within the Committee and Chorus, became public during 1893, when a visitor to the Festival wrote to *The Times*:

> THREE CHOIRS FESTIVAL
>
> Pray allow me to protest as publicly as possible against the further use of the above title at this festival. Out of a chorus of 200 voices (more or less) I observe the astounding statement that a large contingent – viz. nearly 100 voices – has been imported from Leeds. In these days of advanced musical knowledge, and with colleges and schools of music as plentiful as blackberries, do the authorities really mean to assert that in the combined counties of Worcester, Gloucester and Hereford 200 competent singers cannot be found to sing the very ordinary programme that the committee offer for performance this week? … Musical readers may recollect that at Gloucester last year the committee resolved, apart from the voices very properly contributed by Hereford and Worcester, to find their chorus exclusively within the bounds of the county. They made the experiment and

---

[8] *Annals* 1895, p. 306.

were not disappointed. The Gloucestershire singers, with a comparatively small number of allies from the sister shires, answered all requirements, and so was removed a long-standing provocation to criticism. I am told that some sort of agreement was come to among the organists of the three cathedrals with a view to make the festival dioceses sufficient unto themselves in the matter of chorus-singers, but this, if it ever existed, could not bind the committee, and the Worcester managers have here a hundred voices from Leeds … it may be of interest to state that Gloucestershire has just formally united its vocal resources for festival purposes. A meeting of representatives of choral societies within the county was held last week, under the presidency of Mr C. Lee Williams, with the result that festival performances may henceforth be organised anywhere within the shire in full assurance of a competent chorus … The example of its sister county is worth, at any rate, the serious consideration of Worcestershire.

The 1893(w) Festival was the first at which Hugh Blair took charge. The programme included only two new works: Parry's *Overture to an Unwritten Tragedy*, and a symphonic poem, *Gretchen im Dom*, by a Dresden organist called Fischer who had died in the previous December. (It was a flop – 'Enough of *Gretchen im Dom* and good-bye!' wrote the *Musical Times* critic.) The one bold choice of the Festival was Bach's Mass in B minor, which had been performed at Leeds in 1886 and 1892 and which, therefore, was dependent upon the northerners for its success. Blair's tempi were too slow but Sinclair 'did capital work at the organ'.[9]

Blair, born on 26 May 1864, was a Worcester man; a pupil of William Done and afterwards of George Macfarren and Dr G. M. Garrett. He became organ scholar at Christ's College, Cambridge, in 1883 and Assistant Organist of Worcester Cathedral in 1886, taking over from the elderly Done as acting organist in 1889 and succeeding to the full office on Done's death in August 1895.

It is perhaps understandable that Blair would choose the path of safety in his first Festival – but there is a hint in Charles Lee Williams's 1895 update of the *Annals* that the acting organist at Worcester might just have lacked a sufficient level of commitment. Writing of the 1893 repetition of Parry's *Job* and of Spohr's *Last Judgement*, both performed on the third day of the Festival, he says: 'band and chorus showed such perfect familiarity with the work as to reduce Mr Blair's labours and responsibility to a minimum.'[10]

This suspicion was confirmed by an anonymous letter published in the *Birmingham Daily Gazette* following the 1896 Festival:

Sir, it is all very well to lament over the small number of engagements sent to the Worcester choristers when the festivals are held at Hereford and Gloucester. No persons are more anxious for the entire chorus to be drawn from the three counties than the authorities in those two cities last named; but as one who may perhaps be allowed to speak on behalf of those authorities may I throw out a hint to our friends at Worcester? Some conductors do not consider that a few rehearsals of 40 minutes' duration

[9] *MT* 1893, p. 599.
[10] *Annals* 1895, pp. 307–8.

are sufficient to prepare the Worcester contingent for the Festivals held in Gloucester and Hereford, and until they are assured that the Worcester singers are well versed in the works to be produced, it is not surprising that the 'powers that be' at the two sister cities send so many engagements to a town where 60 rehearsals are not considered too much for a festival. We have had ample proof this week of what the three choirs are capable of, and it is a crying shame that such talent is not made the most of. – yours, &c.,

ONE FROM HEREFORD

The *Annals* tell a similar story, noting that 'An excellent programme had been arranged for the Festival [Blair's second], but owing to insufficient rehearsal the imposing array of executants went into action more or less unprepared.'[11] The *Musical Times* reported:

> Mr Blair, it is true, rehearsed his orchestra in London, where, also, some of the principals met him; but soloists, orchestra, and chorus were together in Worcester only one day and an evening – the last, it should be explained, being mainly devoted to the preparation of the music for the Opening Service.[12]

The 1896 Festival included the introduction to Three Choirs of the Requiem by Verdi, who was then in his eighty-third year; Schumann's *Rhenish Symphony* (No. 3); a cantata, *Blessed are they who watch*, by Blair himself; and the first performance of Elgar's *The Light of Life* (*Lux Christi*).

Hugh Blair and Edward Elgar were friends. Blair conducted the Worcester Festival Choral Society; Elgar had been the Leader of its orchestra. On 20 December 1891, Elgar wrote to his Yorkshire friend, Dr Charles Buck: 'Blair and I are pulling together & making things lively here.' And Elgar's diary contains many references to visits by Blair during 1892. Blair had provided much-needed encouragement to Elgar at a time when recognition of his talent seemed the remotest possibility. Now Blair was to be the first conductor to bring forward an Elgar choral work – and his preparations for the Festival were defective.

Fortunately, *The Light of Life* escaped the worst embarrassments of the lack of rehearsal. Elgar himself travelled up to Yorkshire to rehearse with the Leeds Choral Union and also directed the Festival première. All ran smoothly, and the soloists, Anna Williams, Jessie King, Edward Lloyd and Watkin Mills, were excellent.[13]

The *Musical Times* was unusually enthusiastic in its review of the new oratorio:

> Mr Elgar's *Light of Life* failed to secure a large audience on Tuesday evening. So much was expected. Does not the composer live near Worcester, and has he not yet to make a famous name? Facts of this kind were against him, but Mr Elgar, I hope, understands how 'to labour and to wait'. Time is on his side, and my trust is that, as years pass, he will make

[11] *Annals* 1931, p. 16.

[12] *MT* 1896, p. 666.

[13] Edward Lloyd described *The Light of Life* as 'one of the finest English works composed for some time' (*Worcester Daily Times*, 7 September 1896).

the best use of increasing experience in all that concerns the character and method of his art ... It is now clear that Mr Elgar has endowments sufficient for important results. He is no wayside musician whom we can afford to pass and forget, but one to be watched, encouraged, and, as he is still a young man, counselled. I think there is need for counsel, which, if tendered from a proper quarter in a fitting spirit, will not be spurned. Mr Elgar is not yet a master of oratorio, and the reason is partly to be discovered, perhaps, in the fact, indicated by his new work, that his sympathies are much more with the orchestra than with voices.[14]

Elgar's friendship with Blair continued, but in a letter to Charles Lee Williams written thirty-six years later he made it clear to whom he had felt equally indebted in 1896:

> Worcester, 1st September 1932
>
> I am deeply touched by your kind letter which brings back the happiest memories of your connection with the festivals: *you* made my first choral incursion into that somewhat *close* domain of the music meetings a pleasant experience. That was in 1896 & you have ever been the true friend you then proved yourself to me & to us all in the happy festival crowd.[15]

In 1897 Blair resigned his post at Worcester and became Organist of Holy Trinity, Marylebone. Charles Lee Williams, for some years troubled by a throat condition, also resigned in 1897, becoming an Examiner for the Associated Board of the Royal Academy of Music and Royal College of Music.

The year of Queen Victoria's Diamond Jubilee, 1897, brought new men to take charge of the Gloucester and Worcester Three Choirs – men whose abilities would match those of Sinclair at Hereford and who would lead the Festival strongly into the new century.

---

[14] *MT* 1896, p. 666.

[15] Letter contained in C. L. Williams's scrapbook. Gloucestershire Archives.

12

The Dream

AT Hereford in 1897 Sinclair broke with the tradition of an Opening Service and sermon on the Tuesday morning, and followed instead the example set by Worcester in 1881. An 'immense congregation' was present to hear the Festival Chorus, orchestra and some of the principal soloists take part in a special Opening Service on Sunday morning, 12 September. The music was magnificent. At Sinclair's request Elgar had composed a *Te Deum and Benedictus* especially for the occasion, pieces instantly recognised by the critics as masterpieces of their kind. Also performed were Schubert's Symphony No. 8 in B minor (*Unfinished*); 'How lovely is Thy dwelling-place' from Brahms's *German Requiem*; Elgar's *Imperial March*; and the 'Hallelujah' chorus from Beethoven's *Mount of Olives*. Here was a blazing fanfare to herald not only a celebration for the Diamond Jubilee of a queen, but also the beginning of a new era for Three Choirs.

For the first time at Hereford, the chorus was drawn entirely from the Three Choirs cities. Sinclair, with customary energy and commitment, arranged combined rehearsals for months in advance. Highlights of the Festival included a new *Magnificat* by Parry; the Good Friday music and the Finale to the first act of Wagner's *Parsifal*, with Lloyd Chandos and Harry Plunket Greene; the Symphony No. 6 in B minor (*Pathétique*) by Tchaikovsky; and Beethoven's *Missa solemnis* with Emma Albani, Hilda Wilson, Edward Lloyd and Watkin Mills – 'Rarely has that difficult music been attacked with greater spirit or more signal success.'[1]

Named in the programme for the first time in 1897 were the newly appointed Organists of Gloucester and Worcester: Herbert Brewer and Ivor Atkins. There, too, was Sinclair's eighteen-year-old Assistant Organist, Percy Hull, who had been present at Sinclair's house on 5 June 1897 when Elgar had taken over his manuscript of the *Te Deum and Benedictus*:

> I was privileged to hear Elgar play over his *Festival Te Deum and Benedictus* in Sinclair's house to see whether the work would be acceptable for the programme of the Festival at Hereford … He was as nervous as a kitten and heaved a huge sigh of relief when Sinclair said: 'It is *very very* modern, but I think it will do; you shall play it again after supper when Hull and I will give you our final verdict.' All this in Sinclair's stammering and somewhat patronising fashion.[2]

Within eight years the works of Elgar had established themselves as unassailable Festival favourites, equal in popularity to *Elijah* and *Messiah*.

[1] *MT* 1897, p. 678.

[2] 'Elgar at Hereford', *RAM Magazine* (1960), p. 6.

The pulse of the Festival now began to quicken. By perceptible degrees the Steward-dominated conservatism of the past gave way to a greater reliance upon the tastes of conductors with a broader vision allied to a keen sense of purpose.

Orchestral standards were rising too. The Queen's Hall had opened in London in 1893; two years later Henry Wood instituted his famous Promenade Concerts. Some seventy players from the Queen's Hall orchestra were engaged each year for Three Choirs under their Leader, Alfred Burnett (J. T. Carrodus died in 1895). In 1900, A. W. Paynes took Burnett's place; then, in 1904, the bulk of the players from the Queen's Hall orchestra left Henry Wood and formed the LSO – a case of good coming out of bad: Wood had insisted upon abolishing the practice of sending deputies to rehearsals and concerts. So began the long association of the LSO with Three Choirs.

When Herbert Brewer took over as Organist at Gloucester on 15 December 1896, he found the Stewards preparing once more to sharpen the knife of economy. The 1895(G) Festival had left them with a large deficit, and a special committee had been set up to consider and report on the best way to ensure future financial success:

> In their report they drew attention to the fees paid to the principal singers, which, they said, were increasing year by year and a stand would have to be made. They also found that the Friday evening Cathedral service was undoubtedly prejudicial to the funds of the Charity and recommended that the Festival should close with *Messiah*.[3]

They also recommended that only one new work should be given at the next Festival – 'novelties' always incurred a financial loss.

Brewer *was* able to economise on principal singers in 1898. Only Albani could have been considered an extravagance – but a necessary one. Brewer's other choices included Ella Russell, Hilda Wilson, Ben Davies, Hirwen Jones, Watkins Mills and David Bispham, the total cost for whom, including Albani, was little more than half of the fees paid to the four principal singers in 1895.

Cancellation of the Friday evening service was a more thorny problem. A general meeting of the Stewards was called on 30 June 1897 to discuss the proposal – but the Dean of Gloucester, Henry Spence, always took his holiday in June and July. A letter from him to the Festival secretary, P. Barrett Cooke, was read out at the meeting:

> I am very sorry the 30th June is fixed for the Standing Committee meeting to consider the Report. For several years past I have always been away for the last part of June and for July. I am still utterly opposed to giving up the 'free Service', and I hope nothing will be decided on that point until I can be present. Indeed, in my opinion, such a movement would be disastrous to the Festival.[4]

In spite of this, the committee unanimously resolved to retain the proposal that the Festival should close with the Friday evening oratorio, but the Stewards were

[3] Herbert Brewer, *Memories of Choirs and Cloisters* (Bodley Head, 1931).

[4] Gloucester Festival Minute Book, 1897. Gloucester Cathedral Archives and Library.

'willing to consider financially any suggestion from the Dean and Chapter as to the holding of the Sunday Service similar to the Opening Service at Hereford and Worcester'. Brewer tells us that this was his recommendation – and it averted the danger of reopening old wounds. The committee met again in October and were so enthusiastic about the success of the Opening Service at the recent Hereford Festival that the dean fell in with the wishes of the Stewards and agreed to preach the sermon at the first Sunday Opening Service held at the Gloucester Festival of 1898.

On the question of 'novelties', Brewer took a firm stand – and got his way: 'I pointed out that if musical interest was to be maintained and if the programmes contained no novelties, the Festivals would soon cease to attract and would pass away like other worn-out institutions.'[5]

The Stewards invited Sir Hubert Parry, Sir John Stainer, Charles Harford Lloyd, Charles Lee Williams, Rosalind Ellicott and Brewer himself to write new works. Such invitations customarily included a statement that the Stewards could offer no remuneration and that the works must be produced in print at the expense of the composer to the librarians of the Festival.[6] The financial worries of the Stewards concerning 'novelties' were nothing at all to do with commissioning fees, but rather with the loss of income due to poor attendance whenever new works were performed. In the view of the Stewards, merely to be invited to compose for Three Choirs was a privilege which might do much to establish the reputation of a composer and his work. Such terms could hardly be attractive to a penniless unknown or to an eminent and established composer.

Sir John Stainer declined his invitation. Parry accepted reluctantly: 'It has been almost impossible for me to write anything at all now, so constant are the claims upon every hour I have to dispose of. But undoubtedly I shall be proud to attempt something for the honour of my native County if I can possibly find time for it.'[7]

On 1 April 1898, Rosalind Ellicott wrote to Barrett Cooke regretting that she had no opportunity of composing a new orchestral work but offering her choral ballad, *Henry of Navarre*, written for Queen's College, Oxford, instead. Two weeks later, at a meeting of the Finance Committee, Brewer asked that an invitation be sent to Elgar to write a short orchestral work in place of Miss Ellicott's piece. He received a reply by return of post:

> Forli
> Malvern
> April 17, 1898

Dear Mr Brewer,

I have received a request from the Secretary to write a short orchestral thing for the Evening Concert. I am sorry I am too busy to do so.

---

[5] Brewer, *Memories*.

[6] See Gloucester Festival Minute Book, 1885, p. 92. Gloucester Cathedral Archives and Library.

[7] Gloucester Festival Minute Book, 1897. Gloucester Cathedral Archives and Library.

I *wish, wish, wish,* you would ask Coleridge-Taylor to do it. He still wants recognition and is far away the cleverest fellow amongst the young men. *Please* don't let your Committee throw away the chance of doing a good act!

Yours sincerely
Edward Elgar[8]

A month later Brewer received a letter from A. J. Jaeger, head of the publishing department at Novello & Co.:

London
May 12, 1898

Dear Mr Brewer,

My friend Mr Elgar told me a week ago that he has refused an offer to write an orchestral work for your Festival. I am glad to hear it for *his* sake for he has his hands full with *Caractacus* and the haste with which most of you good men have to compose their Festival works is on the whole the great bane of English music. Everybody seems to write under fearful pressure (especially Parry) and the consequences we all know, alas! Well, it is not my business, but I am awfully sorry it is so.

My object in writing is to draw your attention to a young friend of mine, S. Coleridge-Taylor, who is most wonderfully gifted and might write your Committee a *fine* work in a short time. He has a quite Schubertian facility of invention and his stuff is always original and fresh. He is the coming man, I'm quite sure! He is only 22 or 23 but there is nothing immature or inartistic about his music. It is worth a great deal to me – I mean I value it very highly, because it is so original and often *beautiful.* Here is a real melodist at last.

Why not try him and make the '98 Festival memorable by the introduction of young S. C-T. He scores very well, in fact he conceives everything orchestrally and never touches the P. F. when composing! I suppose you know that his father is a negro. Hence his wonderful *freshness.*

Why not give him a commission? He would rise to the occasion and do something good.

His symphony in A major is a most original work. We are doing a short Cantata of his, *Hiawatha's Wedding Feast*; delightful stuff! Won't that do for your Festival? You want a secular work don't you? I'll send you the M. S. score (P. F.) if you like (though at present in the printer's hands).

At any rate you keep your eye on the lad, and believe me, he is *the* man of the future in musical England.

Yours faithfully
A. J. Jaeger[9]

---

[8] Brewer, *Memories.*

[9] Ibid., p. 93. Jaeger's memory is perpetuated by Variation 9 ('Nimrod') in Elgar's *Enigma Variations.*

Brewer was obviously still not quite convinced about Coleridge-Taylor because on 21 April he suggested to the committee that Edward German be invited to write a new piece for the Festival. Nothing came of this, and it was not until 28 May 1898 that he recommended Coleridge-Taylor – leaving the young composer just three months to complete his work. The result, an Orchestral Ballade in A minor, caused a sensation at the 1898(G) Festival secular concert, and Coleridge-Taylor, who conducted his own piece, received a tremendous ovation. The programme also included Wagner's overture to *Die Meistersinger*, Rosalind Ellicott's *Henry of Navarre*, and Sullivan's *The Golden Legend*. The Gloucester Shire Hall was packed and 'the audience … expressed their appreciation … in a very forcible manner, despite the almost disabling heat'.[10]

Sir Hubert Parry's contribution to the 1898 Festival was his *A Song of Darkness and Light*, performed at the beginning of the Thursday morning concert, which also included Beethoven's Symphony No. 3 in E flat (*Eroica*); the Adagio and Finale from Stanford's Symphony No. 5 in D major (*L'Allegro ed il Pensieroso*), conducted by the composer; and Parts 1 and 2 of Bach's *Christmas Oratorio*.

The other 'novelties' were included in the Opening Service on Sunday 11 September. C. H. Lloyd had written a *Festival Overture*; C. Lee Williams a *Magnificat and Nunc Dimittis*; and Brewer a setting of Psalm 98. And for the first time at the Gloucester Festival a work by Elgar was performed: 'The Meditation' from *Lux Christi*.

But the most interesting item in Brewer's first Festival crept in almost by accident. He had intended that the Wednesday concert should include Brahms's *German Requiem* (Brahms died in 1897) and asked Barrett Cooke to hire copies from Novello & Co. However, the German publisher refused permission for the work to be performed from hired copies, and to purchase the music would have cost £20 – too much in the Stewards' view. An alternative suggestion, to perform Stanford's Requiem, was also considered, but for that Boosey's wanted a 16-guinea hire fee. Precious time was passing. Then a third possibility presented itself.

The first performance of Verdi's *Four Sacred Pieces* had been given at the Paris Grand Opera on 7 April 1898. Three weeks later Dean Spence proposed that this work should be included in the Festival programme. Barrett Cooke wrote to Verdi's publisher, Messrs Ricordi, but the hire fee which they quoted exceeded the cost of performing either the Brahms or the Stanford. He asked for a reduction, and on 16 May received a telegram from Messrs Ricordi:

> Price quoted exceptionally low considering importance of Works and right of first performance. However, relying on your securing thoroughly good performance will reduce to 15 guineas. Reply requested before Friday.[11]

Barrett Cooke accepted these terms. Three of the four Verdi pieces were hired for a guinea less than the cost of the Stanford Requiem, and received a 'thoroughly good' first performance in England under Brewer's baton on Wednesday 14 September 1898. The *Stabat Mater*, *Laudi alla Vergine* and *Te Deum* were given

---

[10] *MT* 1898, p. 667.

[11] Gloucester Festival Minute Book, 1898. Gloucester Cathedral Archives and Library.

in a manner with which the composer himself might well have been satisfied. The beauty of the quartet ... made a deep impression, while the two choral and orchestral pieces ... went to the hearts of all who listened. The effect was profound – as deep as the solemn stillness which reigned everywhere among the audience.[12]

Verdi wrote to Brewer – 'a letter full of gratitude' – and the following Christmas sent him a signed photograph. The pieces, which were Verdi's farewell to the earth, helped to launch Herbert Brewer's reputation as a Three Choirs conductor. His labours, reported the *Musical Times,* 'carried him to a recognised place among those who wield the baton as to the manner born'. And the 1898 Festival was a financial as well as an artistic success – the deficit was less than £50 instead of over £600 as in 1895.

In taking up his appointment at Gloucester, Alfred Herbert Brewer was returning home. He was born in Gloucester on 21 June 1865 and was a chorister in the cathedral from 1877 to 1880. Brewer began his musical studies, alongside G. R. Sinclair, under Charles Harford Lloyd. The two boys were so alike that they were often mistaken for each other – a confusion which persisted into their later lives.

Brewer obtained the first organ scholarship at the Royal College of Music (April 1883), where he studied under Sir Walter Parratt and other professors. His church organistships were St Catherine's and St Mary de Crypt, both in Gloucester (1881), St Giles, Oxford (1882), and St Michael's, Coventry (1886–92). He was organ scholar of Exeter College, Oxford, from 1883 to 1885 and then, briefly, Organist at Bristol Cathedral. From 1892 to 1897 he held the post of music-master at Tonbridge School. While there he had a curious experience:

> The organistship at Liverpool Town Hall became vacant through the resignation of W. T. Best. I applied and was chosen with two others to compete ... After hearing that I had been selected I dreamt most vividly that my friend, Lee Williams, was retiring from the organistship of Gloucester Cathedral, the post of all others which I wished to hold. The dream occurred on three successive nights and so unsettled me that I wrote to Liverpool to request that my name might be withdrawn from the list.[13]

A month later the organistship of Gloucester became vacant through the resignation of Charles Lee Williams due to ill health. Brewer obtained his FRCO in 1897 and took the degree of Bachelor of Music at Dublin University in the same year. In 1905 he received the Lambeth degree of DMus, and in 1926 he was knighted.

Brewer's contemporary at Worcester, Ivor Atkins, made a shaky start at his first Three Choirs Festival in 1899. The orchestra under its leader, Alfred Burnett, was praised for the excellence of its playing, but the chorus was badly criticised – and the blame was laid at the feet of the inexperienced Atkins for not being fully in touch with his singers. Lack of experience was also evident in some of the programme planning. At the Opening Service, for instance, Wagner's

[12] *MT* 1898, p. 667.

[13] Brewer, *Memories.*

Kaisermarsch was played during the offertory. Even the most ardent of Wagner's admirers might well have thought this piece of unrestrained jingoism, composed to celebrate the defeat of France and the founding of the German Empire in 1870 and 1871, somewhat out of place in an English cathedral on a Sunday afternoon.

The concert on Tuesday evening began with Charles Lee Williams's little piece *A Harvest Song*, during which the organ broke down. *Die Vätergruft* followed – an unaccompanied setting of Uhland's poem by Peter Cornelius for bass soloist and chorus. 'The solo was artistically interpreted by Mr Plunket Greene, who sang it in the original German, but the chorus appeared to be singing in an unknown tongue.'[14]

Coleridge-Taylor scored another Three Choirs success conducting the only 'novelty' of the Festival, his *Solemn Prelude*, at the beginning of the Wednesday morning concert. But the performance of Brahms's *German Requiem* which followed, conducted by Atkins, was a disappointment. After the interval Elgar conducted *The Light of Life*, in which the soloists were Esther Palliser, Marie Brema, Edward Lloyd and Andrew Black, and a very long programme ended with Dvořák's *Te Deum*.

Had Atkins's original intentions been realised, this concert would have included the first performance of a symphony by Elgar; something which Elgar had been keen to do when, in 1898, he had suggested to Atkins the idea of a symphony written round the subject of General Gordon. But by November 1898 Elgar was having second thoughts, which were passed on to his friend A. J. Jaeger: 'Then *unofficially*, poor old Worcester wants a symphony! ... Now as to Gordon: the thing possesses me, but I can't write it down yet: I *may* make it the Worcester work if that engagement holds.'[15]

The 'Gordon' symphony was never written. Elgar could not afford to spend many months working on a composition which brought no fee and, in any case, he had not reached the stage in his development where he was ready to write a symphony.

That evening, in the Worcester Public Hall, Elgar conducted the first performance of his *Enigma Variations* with the new coda written in response to a request from Jaeger that he should make more of the Finale. Jaeger had expressed his own faith in Elgar in the columns of the July edition of the *Musical Times*:

> Effortless originality – the only true originality – combined with thorough *savoir faire*, and, most important of all, beauty of theme, warmth, and feelings are his credentials, and they should open to him the hearts of all who have faith in the future of our English art and appreciate beautiful music wherever it is met.[16]

The next morning 'tip-toe expectation was rife' in the cathedral. For the first time in Three Choirs history an American composer was to conduct his work in the Festival. Atkins had invited Professor Horatio Parker of Yale University to

---

[14] *MT* 1899, p. 669.

[15] Document held by Worcestershire Archive and Archaeology Service.

[16] *MT* 1899, pp. 464–5.

conduct his oratorio *Hora novissima*, a setting of part of a twelfth-century Latin poem, *The Rhythm of Bernard de Morlaix on the Celestial Country*. Elgar was in the audience.

For some years Elgar had been considering *The Dream of Gerontius* as a possible subject for his music. At the heart of Newman's poem, Gerontius releases his hold on earthly life with that same cry: 'Novissima hora est.' Elgar was ready. There could be no doubt about the source of inspiration for his next major work.

Between Atkins's first Worcester Festival in 1899 and his second in 1902 the Boer War had begun and ended, Queen Victoria had died, and King Edward VII had ascended the throne. In those three years Atkins had gained in confidence and conducting ability sufficiently for him to follow the examples of Sinclair and Brewer in drawing his Festival Chorus only from the Three Choirs cities, and for the *Musical Times* to conclude that 'Mr Atkins has enormously improved since three years ago; he has got the grip of the thing well in hand now, and will develop assuredly into a really admirable conductor.'[17]

Ivor Algernon Atkins was born on 29 November 1869 in Cardiff, where his father, Frederick Pyke Atkins, was Organist of St John's Church. He received his earliest training in music from his father and took organ lessons from Charles Lee Williams, at that time Organist of Llandaff Cathedral. As a boy organist he officiated at two churches, Marstow and Pencoyd. In 1885, aged fifteen, he went to Truro as a pupil of, and assistant to, G. R. Sinclair, whom he followed to Hereford in 1890. Two years later Atkins took the degree of MusB at Oxford, and soon afterwards gained the FRCO. He became a DMus by examination at Oxford in 1920 and was knighted the following year.

Ivor Atkins and Edward Elgar were particularly close friends for over forty years, meeting almost every week until Elgar's death in 1934. The story of this friendship has been told in vivid and accurate detail by Atkins's son, the late E. Wulstan Atkins, in a book which gives greater insights into this relationship, and its bearing on Three Choirs, than is possible in the present history.[18]

T HE Festivals of 1900 and 1901 reflected the mood of the country: of patriotism born of the Boer War and of mourning following the death of Queen Victoria on 22 January 1901.

New works introduced at the Hereford Festival in 1900 included Horatio Parker's setting of Psalm 107 and Samuel Coleridge-Taylor's song cycle *The Soul's Expression*, for contralto and orchestra. The Tuesday morning concert was termed a 'Patriotic Performance', and included two 'novelties': Parry's *Thanksgiving Te Deum*, 'composed ... to commemorate the noble achievements of the British Forces in South Africa', and a setting by Stanford for chorus, orchestra and bugle *obbligato* of W. E. Henley's poem *Last Post*:

> The day's high work is over and done,
> And these no more will need the sun:
> Blow, you bugles of England, blow!

---

[17] *MT* 1902, p. 676.

[18] Wulstan Atkins, *The Elgar–Atkins Friendship* (David & Charles, 1985).

The Parry and Stanford pieces were both conducted by their composers, and in the same concert 'Dr Sinclair brought his forces through with flying colours' in performances of Brahms's Symphony No. 2 in D and the Verdi Requiem, in which the soloists were Emma Albani, Marie Brema, Edward Lloyd and Andrew Black. After the performance a telegram was despatched to the composer:[19]

Maestro Verdi   Busseto

Saluti affetuosi da tutti dopo una recita splendida del Requiem Festival di Hereford.

[signed] Albani-Gye, Brema, Lloyd, Sinclair, Elgar, Santley, Stanford

Determined to press ahead with innovations, Sinclair not only repeated the performances of Tchaikovsky's Symphony No. 6 in B minor (*Pathétique*) and the Good Friday music (Act III) and Finale (Act I) of Wagner's *Parsifal* which he had given in the cathedral in 1897, but also conducted a fine performance of Beethoven's Symphony No. 9 (*Choral*) with Albani singing in the work for the first time in her career. Even in a new century, Sinclair's audacity was seen as too much by some, including the critic of the *Musical Times*:

[The *Parsifal* extracts were] as much out of place – if not actually irreverent – in a Cathedral as Tchaikovsky's Symphony. Another attempted Cathedralisation was that of Beethoven's *Choral Symphony*, with a sacred (!) version of Schiller's words. Here again, while fully acknowledging Dr Sinclair's splendid qualities and the valuable services he has rendered to the cause of music in Hereford, I must part company with him on a question that has caused many misgivings in the minds of not a few thoughtful people in regard to the wisdom of admitting essentially non-sacred works into cathedrals.[20]

The year 1900 marked the farewell appearance at a Three Choirs Festival of Edward Lloyd. A Hereford lady presented him with a beautiful Jersey heifer named 'Symphony', and the Hereford Festival Choir gave a pair of silver candlesticks. In return, Lloyd wrote to members of the choir:

My dear Friends,

I much appreciate your kindness in presenting me with those handsome Candle Sticks & thank you most sincerely for the tangible proof of your regard & good will.

You may rest assured that I shall greatly value your gift & all the pleasant associations it will bring back to my memory.

It was at Gloucester under Dr S. S. Wesley that I made my first appearance at a Three Choirs Festival. That was in 1871 when Dr Sinclair was a nice little boy of four in pinafores. I have therefore been connected with these famous music meetings on & off – mostly on – for the long period of nearly thirty years, during which time I have endeavoured to pursue the even tenor of my ways.

[19] *MT* 1900, p. 661.
[20] *MT* 1900, p. 660.

I am very grateful for the kindness that has been shown to me during all those long years, & which has reached its culminating point in the presentation to me of this token of your regard.

I am forwarding each of you a signed photograph which I hope you will honour me by accepting.

With every good wish & sincere congratulations on your excellent singing at the recent Festival.

I am
Yours very truly
Edward Lloyd[21]

THE first, disastrous, performance of Elgar's *The Dream of Gerontius* was given under Richter's baton at the Birmingham Festival on 3 October 1900. Everything had conspired to ruin a work the worth of which Elgar knew only too well. The chorus master, Swinnerton Heap, who understood Elgar's music, died in May before the rehearsals began, and in the interval before G. R. Sinclair took his place the elderly W. C. Stockley took over. Stockley did not share Elgar's vision. The choir took a dislike to the music and failed to make an effort; Richter dragged the tempi. For Elgar the occasion was a nightmare. In spite of all, the critics hailed *The Dream of Gerontius* as a great work. An article by Otto Lessman for the *Allgemeine Musik Zeitung* was translated for the *Musical Times* of 1 January 1901:

> If I mistake not, the coming man has already arisen in the English musical world, an artist who has instinctively freed himself from the scholasticism which, till now, has held English art firmly bound in its fetters, an artist who has thrown open mind and heart to the great achievements which the mighty tone-masters of the century now departed have left us as a heritage for the one to come – Edward Elgar, the composer of *The Dream of Gerontius*.

No plans were made to include *The Dream of Gerontius* in the 1901(G) Festival, but Brewer invited Elgar to conduct the Prelude and 'Angel's Farewell' as part of the Opening Service, as well as his *Cockaigne* overture in the secular concert – part of a programme which included new works by Sir Frederick Bridge, W. H. Bell, Cowen and Hervey. But Elgar also played a vitally important part in ensuring the success of Herbert Brewer's own 'novelty' contribution to the 1901 Festival: his cantata *Emmaus*. Brewer, in his autobiography, recounted how this came about:[22]

> On receiving the invitation from the Stewards to write a work for the Festival I consulted my friend, Joseph Bennett, who, as is well known, had considerable experience and great gifts as a writer of libretti. His books are numerous and amongst them are to be found at least three Operas, some twelve Oratorios and half a dozen Cantatas. Who then could give better

[21] A. M. Broadley Collection. Gloucester City Library.
[22] Brewer, *Memories*.

advice or help in such a matter? The fact that he was a Gloucestershire man was another attraction to me. His reply to my appeal was that he would put on his thinking-cap and would do all he could to provide me with the necessary book.

I had not long to wait, for within a few days it arrived. It was on the subject of the Disciples journeying to Emmaus, and *Emmaus* was to be the title of the work.

With the words in my possession, I travelled to North Wales for a holiday, where I hoped to stay until the Cantata was finished.

The surroundings were so congenial and I became so interested in the subject that I finished the work within four weeks.

I took the first opportunity of going through it with Mr. Bennett before submitting it to a publisher, and as it satisfied his critical ear I lost no time in placing it in the hands of Messrs. Novello & Co.

Everything went smoothly until the programme was publicly announced in the early spring preceding the Festival. The final proofs had been passed and I was about to score the work when I received crushing news from the publishers. They had had a communication from another composer to the effect that he had noticed in the programme that my new work was a setting of Mr. Joseph Bennett's words entitled *Emmaus*. He went on to say that he had purchased these words from Mr. Bennett some years previously.

It transpired that Bennett, when searching through his manuscripts for a subject for my work, came across some loose sheets of paper on which was written a scene entitled *At Emmaus*, and forgetting all about the former transaction sent them to me as suitable material for a Cantata.

In reply to a letter of distress from me Bennett wrote that he had been in many a worse mess and all would come right! He would re-write the words.

This, however, entailed the re-writing of a great part of the music.

When this difficulty had been surmounted we were within a few weeks of the Festival – the chorus had their part to learn and not a note had been scored.

I was seriously thinking of withdrawing it from the programme when I received the following letter from Elgar:

Bettws-y-coed
N. Wales

June 14, 1901

My dear Brewer

Good! If I *can* I'll conduct *Cockaigne* for you but you would do it all right if I cannot come. I'll look out for you in town next week.

Jaeger – who has been in Malvern – but of course you know that – tells me by this post that you are somehow worried – (the exact *nuance* I don't quite understand – about getting your work ready) – he said something before we left home and I told him you must not be worried and that if necessary to make things smooth I would orchestrate some for you – that's all – I know it's a cheek to offer but if I can save you a little worry let me do so.

Yours ever

Edward Elgar

A more generous act could not be imagined. The proof copy of *Emmaus* was sent to him, and in a few days I received a letter which serves to prove the infinite trouble he took over the score:

Malvern

June 30, 1901

My dear Brewer,

I have scored Nos. 1, 4, 5, 6, 9 and 10. If that's not enough you must let me know. I send on my MS. I *hope* it will please you but I feel much at sea as to your wishes and I am sadly afraid you will not like my interpretation – the Tuttis may be all right.

No. 1 – see p. 7 of MS. (p. 2 in vocal score).

I *fattened* out the p.f. arrgt here – see strings especially last three bars, and on – you can easily sacrifice any of my orch: devices by a stroke of the pen.

I took the *bar before B* to be the actual 'chord of climax' and worked up to that: hence the brass alone and cumulative effect 3rd bar 3rd line.

See Andante Moderato p. 16 – I didn't know how much *force* you want and I have made you a fine burst, which will sound jolly but you may want to be more austere – It can easily be cut out.

p. 17, line 2, I gave this wholly (except final chords) for strings – I don't think it wants *colour* but you may have meant it for *wind* – but I give the soft wind a chance (contrasting) at letter R.

At O are these chords what you want? or do you want strings? at P I have to carry on the *flow* of the parts added a few notes for Vio: I – knock 'em out if you like.

2 bars before S. I've stuck *c* in first Vio: to avoid clashing with vocal part – also in the *rall.* near end – I have carried celli down to A.

The harp is effective but *ad lib.*

Thinking you will use the organ in other more likely places I've not put it in except a ped: or two in introduction.

I *have not* revised any of it I fear, as usual, there may be many errors but one of your pupils could look it thro': the first thing however is to know if it will *DO* at all for you.

Kind regards

Yours ever   Ed. Elgar

P. S. – I find I cannot send the parcel by post to-day: but will despatch it to-morrow. Send me a wire *in the a.m.* saying if you want me to continue any other numbers – *spell* the number (seven not 7) to avoid mistakes. If you are at liberty come over to see me, if necessary, and have lunch or something, let me hear if you are coming. I'm not let out on account of my chill.

I should be glad to see you. In haste.

A few days later he writes:

> Malvern
> July 7, 1901

My dear Brewer

I shall hope to despatch by an early post to-morrow the remainder of your score – it's all ready now but Sunday's a *dies non* with us as far as business posts are concerned.

I have taken great pleasure in trying to interpret your thoughts and feelings and only hope I have not grossly misrepresented them. Now: please *accept* my work on your score and never think I want any return whatever: keep a kind thought for a fellow sometime – that's all.

Please look very carefully thro' all the parts especially – once more – the transposing things.

I have enjoyed your themes immensely and they lend themselves to colour famously. I am especially pleased with No. 7 and (as far as I am concerned) with the first part of No. 11 – the end is good (as far as you're concerned) but I think you might have instrumented it better than I have.

I wish the work every success and if you have been saved any pin-pricks and have had a good rest I am happy in having done it!

Our kindest regards to your both.

> Yours always
> Edward Elgar

In the vocal score of *Emmaus* Elgar wrote – 'Began June 27, 1901. Ended July 7, 1901.' Brewer continues:

> What this unselfish act meant to me it is difficult to describe. It not only relieved me of an enormous amount of work at an anxious time, but the scoring of my work by the master hand has been an invaluable lesson to me and I feel that what measure of success *Emmaus* has attained is largely due to the effective orchestration. When one considers the number of big works Elgar then had on hand and the physical strain alone of the actual writing, one has some slight conception of the generosity of this most friendly act.
>
> And here I would record my gratitude to Lady Elgar for her untiring energy in preparing the score for her husband to work upon – work behind the scenes, unknown, unrecognised, yet how valuable!
>
> In spite of all these efforts to avoid the infringement of copyright the lawyers were not to be so appeased, and a week before the Festival we were warned that the performance of *Emmaus* would render us liable for heavy penalties.

This cheering (!) news greeted me on my arrival in London for the rehearsals of soloists and orchestra. Madame Albani, who was to be one of the soloists in the work, said that if imprisonment was to be the result, she would accompany me to prison!!

Legal interviews ensued and permission was given for the work to be performed on condition that it was afterwards withdrawn and the plates destroyed.

To such terms I naturally could not consent. The work must be given a chance to live or not be performed at all.

Eventually, through the good auspices of Messrs. Novello, the claim was withdrawn and the work allowed to be published and performed.[23]

Emmaus was given on Thursday evening, 12 September 1901, with Albani, Sobrino and Ben Davies, and was repeated in 1907(G). Brewer is said to have been so proud of the compliment which Elgar had paid him in orchestrating *Emmaus* that the manuscript score remained displayed in a place of honour in his music room thereafter. The original manuscript and orchestral parts of the work remained lost after Brewer's death, in spite of numerous attempts by scholars particularly interested in the Elgar scoring to find them. They were rediscovered quite by accident while researching this history, together with the original manuscript scores of Brewer's other works, wrapped in brown-paper parcels in the basement archive of the Gloucester City Library. The scores are now deposited in the Gloucestershire Archives.

B Y 1902, the engagement of choral singers from outside the Three Choirs counties having ended, the Festival settled into a regular annual pattern. The choral contingent from the Festival city of the year was normally the largest, but each was taught the music of the coming programme by its own conductor in the early part of the year, and the complete Festival Chorus met for combined rehearsal before the summer holiday. Rehearsals for the orchestra with solo voices were held in London in the week before the Festival. The orchestra came down on the Saturday in time for a hasty rehearsal with the chorus of the music for the 'Grand Opening Service' held in the cathedral on Sunday afternoon. Monday, from about 9.30 a.m. to 5.30 p.m., was given over to the general rehearsal in the cathedral; this was known to the chorus as 'Black Monday' – four days' music had to be hurried through in one day! *Elijah* was performed on Tuesday morning and *Messiah* on Friday morning. Other choral and orchestral works were given in the cathedral on Tuesday evening, Wednesday and Thursday morning and Thursday evening. Morning performances in the cathedral were interrupted by an interval of one hour for lunch and continued in the afternoon. On Wednesday evening there was a secular concert in one of the public halls and, at Hereford only, a chamber concert on Friday evening.

In spite of some opposition Sinclair, Brewer and Atkins were prepared to force the pace of change in Festival programming while retaining the

---

[23] For the complete correspondence between Elgar and Brewer on *Emmaus*, see Jerrold Northrop Moore, *Edward Elgar: Letters of a Lifetime* (OUP, 1990), pp. 97–100.

ever-popular *Elijah* and *Messiah*. These two pieces were, in any case, so familiar to the chorus and orchestra that little of the precious rehearsal time was thought to be needed each year to polish them up – a poor excuse but a practical one for falling in with public demand. In 1904 Brewer managed to increase the London orchestral rehearsals from two to three, but this was still inadequate to deal with the number of new and often difficult works.

Consider the pressures on Atkins during his two orchestral rehearsal days in London in 1902, the year of King Edward VII's coronation. His programme included Beethoven's fifth, Brahms's third and Tchaikovsky's sixth symphonies; the first performance at Three Choirs of a work by Richard Strauss – *Tod und Verklärung*; a Bach cantata, *The Lord is a sun and shield*; Percy Pitt's *Coronation March*; and Handel's coronation anthem *The king shall rejoice*. Then there was the music for the Opening Service. And time had to be found for composers who would be conducting new works at the Festival: Granville Bantock, *The Witch of Atlas*; Horatio Parker, Part III of *The Legend of St Christopher*; Walford Davies, *The Temple*; and Edward Elgar, directing *The Dream of Gerontius* personally for the first time – the highlight of a Festival which would also include his *Sursum corda*, composed in 1894 for a special cathedral service honouring a visit to Worcester by the Duke of York (the future King George V), *Cockaigne*, the national-anthem arrangement, and three of the *Sea Pictures*.

Just as he had recommended Coleridge-Taylor to Brewer, Elgar suggested to the Worcester Festival Committee that Henry Walford Davies (1869–1941) should be invited to write a new work for them. The result, *The Temple*, is an oratorio in two parts which tells two stories, one of David's desire to build 'an house unto the name of the Lord', and the other of Solomon's accomplishment of the task. In his biography of the composer, H. C. Colles described the problems and anguish which faced Walford Davies in bringing his work to performance at Worcester – an experience not unlike that of Elgar in Birmingham two years earlier:

> Walford had spent a good deal of time going to and fro to the sectional rehearsals earlier in the year, and in the process had made friends with the conductors, Atkins, Sinclair and Brewer, with officials and with the members of the choir. That was all to the good. They were all anxious to do their best for him, but none could disguise from themselves or him that he had unwarily piled up the obstacles to success.
>
> Mme Albani, the reigning star of the moment, was offered him as his soprano soloist. He took his score to her; she asked at once to see her 'Prayer', was disappointed to find it was only two pages long, found it 'beautiful but not her *tessitura*'. She was not keen to sing the narrative part which was all to be mixed up with choir. This was in May; later she was cajoled into compliance. But her instinct was right; it was not essentially her part. Walford succeeded in persuading the Committee to engage Gregory Hast for his tenor. They were a little doubtful of Hast's power to fill the Cathedral (either with people or with tone). But here Walford proved himself right. He got in Hast a tenor who understood him and his music intimately, and 'Solomon's Prayer' was the most impressive movement in the whole work. He would have liked to have had Forington

too; the baritone solo is clearly written for his voice. But this was not allowed. Lane Wilson was chosen; he took great pains with it and sang it very well.

The chorus had shown promise in their several rehearsals with the piano, but the clouds began to gather when Walford faced the orchestra in London. His orchestral experience, as either orchestrator or conductor, was still rudimentary, and he was naturally anxious. He talked too much. He tried to explain what the work was about when the hard-bitten orchestral players only wanted to know what they had to do, to do it, and pass on to the next feature of their long programme. There were mistakes in the parts, and time was wasted in correcting them. There were obvious miscalculations in the scoring and emendations had to be made at the last moment. These are the troubles which every young composer–conductor encounters at the outset, but Walford took them more hardly than most. From the rehearsals of *The Temple* he gained the reputation of being what an elderly critic called 'a worrying man', a reputation which it took him a long time to live down.

By the time that they all arrived at Worcester Walford certainly was worrying, and knew that he had cause. He realised too late that his music was very much more difficult than it ought to have been for such a purpose. The choir half knew their job, knew it in that way which allows all to go well in the practice-room and risks it going awry when the singers are placed on the tiers of a tall rostrum with a cumbersome orchestra between them and the soloists with whom they have to collaborate. Walford's ideal had been a chamber music *ensemble* on an immense scale. The anomaly was exposed in the result.

He begged for more rehearsal time, got it, but took more than he was given. His exigence did not increase his popularity with the overdriven choir. Ivor Atkins was patient, but when he tried to comfort Walford by suggesting that things were better than they seemed, Walford received his words merely as a confession of the low standard which it must be his mission to raise.

Atkins, however, was proved right. Walford had made no allowance for that innate capacity of Englishmen to pull themselves together in the face of the enemy. In our slipshod musical life it has become proverbial that a bad rehearsal means a good performance and *vice versa*. Never fully prepared, the semblance of preparedness which a lucky final rehearsal gives often leads to complacence in the subsequent performance, while a bad rehearsal puts everyone on their mettle to display their British phlegm. It is splendid, though it is not art.

On the day everyone played up (to use the sporting vernacular) extraordinarily well, and much of the work had its intended effect. Mme Albani led the narrative sections with a surprising amount of dramatic energy, and that scene of the consecration of the Temple which had first inspired Walford to the task was the most stirring moment in the narrative. The big choral numbers too did not fail of their effect. Any unprejudiced person could perceive that the choral writing was masterly and that there was strong lyrical feeling in the big solos, baritone and tenor. *The Temple* was in fact all good music, and some of it was quite evidently great music.[24]

The first Three Choirs performance of *The Dream of Gerontius* was hardly free from problems either. Ivor Atkins realised that there would be doctrinal difficulties; principally that the Invocations to the Blessed Virgin Mary and to the saints in the poem were contrary to the Thirty-nine Articles of the Anglican Church. Although, in informal discussions, both the Dean of Worcester, Dr R. W. Forrest, and Canon T. L. Claughton, chairman of the Festival Executive Committee, were anxious with Atkins for the performance to take place in the cathedral, written representation to the bishop had to be made.

Elgar understood the difficulties and agreed that if changes to the text of the poem were agreed he would approach his friend Father Richard Bellasis of the Birmingham Oratory, and, through him, Father William Neville, Cardinal Newman's executor and owner of the copyright.

By late April 1902 the Bishop of Worcester had given his approval to modifications to the text of *Gerontius* on the basis of omitting the Litany of the Saints, and of a substitution of 'Jesus', 'Lord' or 'Saviour' for 'Mary'; of 'souls' for 'souls in purgatory'; and, in the Angel's Farewell, of 'prayers' for 'Masses'. More than a month later Elgar had still not approached the Birmingham Oratory with the proposed changes, and the printing of Word Books for the Festival had become an imminent necessity. When on 16 May the Elgars had to leave for Germany to attend rehearsals of *Gerontius* at the Lower Rhine Festival, Atkins took the initiative, preparing two sets of drafts, the first embodying the word modifications approved by the bishop, and the second to a plan of his own of omissions only, which would be indicated by asterisks, which he rightly felt might be more acceptable and which he had already agreed with Elgar.

Father Neville gave his approval of the omissions; the bishop concurred, and printing of the Word Books went ahead. 'The libretto', said the *Musical Times*, 'had been purposely mutilated to suit Anglican tastes: but that was surely a deplorable blunder; at this rate how many works of art, when given in cathedrals, would "escape a whipping"? Surely this thing was too narrow and childish – as though the work were given from any sectarian standpoint!'[25]

But in spite of modification, the performance itself was deeply moving. William Green was to have taken the title role but was unable to attend the London rehearsal and so, at short notice, John Coates sang *Gerontius* for the first of what was to be very many times. Muriel Foster was memorable as the Angel, and Harry Plunket Greene took the part of the Priest and the Angel of the Agony. The chorus sang wonderfully well – only at the end did 'the tremendous strain of the work' begin to tell on them. Elgar, whose mother had died a few days earlier, conducted in mourning black. Granville Bantock wrote to his friend Ernest Newman on 11 September 1902:

> Never have I experienced such an impression before, as I did on hearing 'Gerontius' this morning in the Cathedral. If Elgar never writes another note of music, I will still say that he is a giant, & overtops us all. His

[24] H. C. Colles, *Walford Davies* (OUP, 1942), pp. 73–4.
[25] *MT* 1902, p. 676.

music moved me profoundly ... It is a great work, & the man who wrote
it, is a Master, and a Leader. We were all deeply affected, and gave way
to our feelings. While Elgar was conducting, the tears were running down
his cheeks. I want to hear nothing better. I have felt as if transfixed by a
spike from the crown of my head to my feet. Once on hearing *Parsifal*
at Bayreuth, when the dead swan is brought on, & today, at the words
'Novissima hora'.[26]

After the performance, Alice Elgar gave lunch to several friends. One of her
guests was Henry Walford Davies. Later, she wrote in her diary: '*Crowds* of
people came all the aftn. & to tea – & in the evening ... A most wonderful day
to have had in one's life. D. G.'[27]

---

[26] See Atkins, *The Elgar–Atkins Friendship*, pp. 80 and 89.
[27] See Jerrold Northrop Moore, *Edward Elgar: A Creative Life* (OUP, 1990), p. 375.2

13

Beyond these Voices

I N September 1900, Granville Bantock (1868–1946) was appointed Principal of the Birmingham and Midland Institute School of Music, and for the next thirty years was a regular visitor to Three Choirs. A number of his works received their first performances at the Festivals, many under Bantock's own direction. Some, such as *The Time Spirit*, a rhapsody for chorus and orchestra, performed at Gloucester in 1904, showed his gift for melodic charm and orchestral colour to pleasing effect; others missed the mark. Bantock's 'Fantastic Poem for Orchestra, in the form of a Prelude', *The Pierrot of the Minute* (1908(w) and 1924(H)) struck one young Festival-goer, Arthur Lloyd-Baker, as 'light but elaborately shapeless'.[1]

Bantock was well known for his oriental proclivities, of which a setting of Fitzgerald's translation of the *Rubaiyat of Omar Khayyam* is the most noted example. But such pieces found no place at Three Choirs. In 1909(H) he conducted his *Old English Suite*, an arrangement for small orchestra of sixteenth-century airs, which prompted the *Musical Times* to suggest that 'its example might be followed. Other suites as distinct from rhapsodies formed of old English airs, and particularly of folk songs, which have yet to be treated in this fashion, might be devised by British composers in search of new fields.'[2]

Ralph Vaughan Williams had already formed the Folk Song Society in 1904, writing in the *Morning Post* that 'whatever is done in the way of preserving traditional music must be done quickly; it must be remembered that the tunes, at all events, of true folk songs exist only by oral tradition, so that if they are not soon noted down and preserved they will be lost forever.'[3]

In his *Old English Suite*, Bantock 'lengthened lines and deepened shadows' in his adornment of airs by Orlando Gibbons, John Dowland, John Bull, Giles Farnaby and William Byrd, but 'all in the colours of the original'. The piece which followed in the programme was as refreshingly in the style of the twentieth century as Bantock's was rooted in that of the sixteenth: the first performance of the *Dance Rhapsody No. 1* by Frederick Delius, conducted by the composer in his single Three Choirs appearance.

Bantock's attempts at religious music were given a hearing at Three Choirs but none achieved a second Festival performance. Separate sections of his oratorio *Christus* were given over a period of eight years: an orchestral interlude entitled *The Wilderness* (1903(H)); *Christ in the Wilderness* (1907(G)) for soprano, baritone,

---

[1] Lt. Col. Arthur Barwick Lloyd-Baker of Hardwicke Court, Gloucestershire. (His diaries are deposited in the Gloucestershire Archives.)

[2] *MT* 1909, p. 665.

[3] *Morning Post*, 4 October 1904. See also Ursula Vaughan Williams, *R. V. W.: A Biography of Ralph Vaughan Williams* (OUP, 1964), pp. 69–70.

chorus and orchestra, with Agnes Nicholls (afterwards Lady Harty, CBE) and David Ffrangcon-Davies; and *Gethsemane* (1910(G)), a cantata for baritone, chorus, orchestra and organ in which Frederick Austin was the soloist. These were deeply serious pieces – sometimes dreary, sometimes thrilling, and even occasionally stirring, as in the soprano solo in *Christ in the Wilderness*, scored for harp, woodwind and tambourine – but overall they were failures. 'Mysticism' said Ernest Walker, was 'not part of his endowment.'[4] Perhaps if the whole of *Christus* could have been heard at a single sitting, the totality of Bantock's design and the appropriateness of his music would have made more of an impact. As it was, *Christus* remained a mysteriously hinted-at large work. It was, in any event, too late. The first performance of Elgar's two oratorios inspired by the story of the life of Christ had been given in Birmingham within the same few years: *The Apostles* in 1903 and *The Kingdom* in 1906. Knighted in 1904, Elgar had been appointed Peyton Professor of Music at Birmingham University the following year. He resigned in 1908 and Granville Bantock, who remained in Birmingham until 1933, took his place. Bantock was knighted in 1930.

Samuel Coleridge-Taylor (1875–1912) made his last Three Choirs appearance in 1903(H), conducting the première of *The Atonement* – a work which suffered badly from the libretto of Mrs Alice Parsons. The following day Arthur Lloyd-Baker was at Hereford to hear Sinclair conduct *The Dream of Gerontius*, with Muriel Foster, John Coates, Lane Wilson and Plunket Greene as soloists, and the first performance of Sir Hubert Parry's motet *Voces clamantium*. In his view '*The Dream* was very fine indeed. Sir Hubert's was more "popular" and easier to listen to.' The *Musical Times* expressed it rather more wordily: the Parry piece was 'an excellently written work, possessing a deeply true and intimate musical spirit, and constructed with a singular sense of fine equipoise'.[5]

The year 1904(G) was an important one for Three Choirs for many reasons: the first performance of Parry's *The Love that Casteth out Fear* and Brewer's *The Holy Innocents*; Elgar conducting *The Apostles* and his overture *In the South (Alassio)* for the first time at the Festival; and the unrehearsed and unpredictable appearance of a young Gloucester boy who was to grow up to become not only one of the half-dozen finest composers of song whom England has produced, but also a poet of rare individuality.

His appearance was unplanned. The principals in Part I of *Elijah* included Mesdames Sobrino, Hicks Beach and Foster. For Part II, after the luncheon interval, Albani was down to take over from Sobrino as first principal soprano, and Daisy Hicks Beach was not required. The part of the Prophet was taken by David Ffrangcon-Davies. Lloyd-Baker recorded his impressions: 'The best performance of *Elijah* that I've heard. Ffrangcon-Davies magnificent & looked the part: sang without book. Muriel Foster very good indeed. Sobrino rather painful. Albani better than 3 or 6 years ago, owing to visit to S. Africa: quite magnificent.' But when the soloists returned for Part II there was no second soprano with them. Brewer began nonetheless. Lloyd-Baker continues: 'For

[4] Ernest Walker, *A History of Music in England*, 2nd edn (OUP, 1924).
[5] *MT* 1903, p. 671.

"Lift thine eyes" Sobrino didn't turn up, owing to some misunderstanding. Daisy Beach was not to be found, & so the boy was hauled down to sing.'[6]

That 'boy' was the fourteen-year-old chorister who had accompanied Ffrangcon-Davies in Part I in the small part of the Youth in 'O Lord thou hast overthrown': Ivor Gurney. Writing to Marion Scott at the Royal College of Music years later, Gurney's mother recalled the excitement of the occasion:

> Ivor was top dog he sang with Madam Albani 3 Madams had to sing the trio lift thine eyes and the one when she was fetched down from the Bell Hotel said she didn't know it was time and so it had to be done and Dr Brewer said Ivor was to do it and Madam Albani would have him by her and he looked such a boy to her but they said he done it beautiful an unrehearsed piece and he was frightened at his success when he got home he hid in the kitchen everybody saying Ivor Gurney had been singing with Madam Albani.[7]

Sobrino, it seems, had taken lunch at the Bell Hotel and lingered too long over the decanter.

The audience for *Elijah* in 1904 was 2,324 – just 100 fewer than for *Messiah*: but by far the largest turnout of the week, 2,784, was for *The Apostles*. The popularity of Elgar's music had, for the first time, topped that of the old traditional favourites. And in 1905 his music occupied fully a quarter of the entire programme at Worcester: *The Dream of Gerontius*, *The Apostles* and the recently written *Introduction and Allegro* for strings (op. 47). *Gerontius* displaced *Elijah* from its traditional place at the beginning of the Festival, and before the performance Elgar was presented with the Freedom of the City of Worcester. Among the crowd of people lining the High Street from the Guildhall to the cathedral was a young violinist from the orchestra who had also appeared as a composer, conducting his own *Scenes from the Ballet* at the 1904(G) Festival – W. H. Reed:

> the procession making its way from the guildhall to the cathedral with the mayor, the high sheriff and all the aldermen in their civic robes and Elgar walking solemnly in their midst, clothed in a strange gown which puzzled most of the onlookers. Upon enquiry this turned out to be the Yale University gown and hood which Elgar hastened to wear on the very first occasion that a Doctor of Music's robes were needed at any of his public engagements.
>
> Remaining in the memory is another thing in connection with this procession and civic honour, and that is that Elgar turned as he passed a certain house in the High Street on his way to the cathedral and saluted an old gentleman whose face could just be seen looking out of an upper window. It was his father, who was watching the honour being paid to his son by the city of his birth. Being very old and feeble, he was unable to leave his room; but what must his feelings have been on looking out of

---

[6] Lloyd-Baker Diaries. Gloucestershire Archives.
[7] Ivor Gurney Archive. Gloucestershire Archives.

that window and seeing before his very eyes the fulfilment of his wildest dreams![8]

Back in the cathedral, 3,053 people heard Ivor Atkins conduct *The Dream of Gerontius*. After lunch the second part of the concert began with Atkins's own *Hymn of Faith*, in which Elgar had assisted with the orchestration. The concert ended with Brahms's Symphony No. 4 in E minor, which benefited immensely from not being interrupted by the custom of applauding between movements (as, indeed, did other symphonic works now being heard freely in the cathedrals).

A precedent was set in 1907(G) when the sixteen-year-old Mischa Elman, who had been engaged to play Beethoven's Violin Concerto in the Shire Hall secular concert, was invited to perform Beethoven's Romance in F as an 'extra' item in the cathedral on Thursday evening:

> The performance of the Romance in the crowded cathedral was a rare and memorable event in the long history of the Three Choirs Festival, and as from the organ loft I gazed at those magnificent Norman pillars in the nave, this thought crossed my mind: What would the earliest worshippers in Gloucester's stately nave have said to such a wonderful exhibition of a boy's skill on an instrument of music?[9]

In 1908(w), Elman returned to repeat his performance of the Beethoven Violin Concerto – but now that too was admitted to the cathedral. The same programme included a performance of *Everyman*, the cantata which secured Walford Davies's reputation following its première at the Leeds Festival of 1904 and which for a few years enjoyed great popularity. Sir Charles Villiers Stanford, whose *Stabat Mater* preceded Elman's playing of the Beethoven Concerto in the concert, considered that Walford Davies had reached a high level of creative achievement in *Everyman*, but the work fell out of vogue even before the start of World War I.

Throughout the early years of the twentieth century, the old argument about the suitability of cathedrals for Festival performances ground on, but with generally a little less venom than before. In his sermon at the Opening Service of the 1906 Festival at Hereford the Dean of Gloucester, who had been known to label Three Choirs critics as 'cranks', unearthed a precedent for church festivals which was as obscure as it was irresistible. He had discovered that a sacred mystery play by Roumanos had, as early as the fifth century, been given in the great cathedral of Hagia Sophia in Constantinople. Its title was *The Apostles*!

In 1907(G), Arthur Lloyd-Baker found himself sitting next to the Bishop of Gloucester, E. C. S. Gibson, during tea at the Palace. Gibson had been appointed in 1905 following the death of Bishop Ellicott:

> The Bishop said that he had not been able "to rise to the heights of the Apostles". He expressed no opinion as to the Festival, but it is generally understood that he approves of it so far: it is in a way on its trial, as the

---

[8] W. H. Reed, *Elgar* (Dent, 1946).

[9] *MT* 1907, p. 654.

Bishop's decision carries great influence even though he has no power to stop it.[10]

From the point of view of its contribution to art, this would have been no time to stop the Festival. Under Atkins, Brewer and Sinclair Three Choirs had taken on a new lease of life. By 1909(H) the *Musical Times* was able to report that:

> directed by earnestness and energy, the festivals have been gradually working up to a high pitch of excellence. The efforts of three organists may be said to have reached a definite stage on this occasion, for no better choral singing has ever been heard before at this festival. It reflects the condition of the day which finds choral singing in England in a higher state of efficiency than it has been for centuries. The possibility of securing notable results with the choir has been grasped, and to Dr Sinclair belongs the credit of being the first conductor to have charge of the best choir heard at these meetings.[11]

The Festival of 1910(G) opened with Sullivan's overture *In Memoriam*, in memory of King Edward VII. For the first time at Gloucester, Dean Spence-Jones permitted a complete performance of *The Dream of Gerontius* – but in the 'Protestantised' version. And at the same concert a new work was heard, the significance of which to British music was immediately apparent to a young student of music from Lydney in the Forest of Dean, Herbert Howells (1892–1983):

> In that year I had become an articled pupil of Dr (later Sir) Herbert Brewer. (In that classification I became a fellow musician with the unforgettable but tragic Gloucester-born composer-poet, Ivor Gurney). At the time I still feared Dr Brewer as much as I revered him. But round about April I was brave enough to ask him whether there was to be any 'new work' at September's Meeting. He seemed puzzled, slow to answer. He had, he admitted, heard of 'the strange composer' … who would be bringing a strange work, 'something to do with Tallis'. Lovely first week of September came. With it came the composer from Chelsea, a magnificent figure on the rostrum, a younger but more commanding version of the then Foreign Secretary, Sir Edward Grey. He was nearly thirty-nine. I gazed at him from the sixth row of the 'stalls' in the nave. (Beside me – in a crowded audience – an empty chair). I was seeing him for the first time. But what mattered was that it was Tuesday night, an Elgar night; a dedicated Elgar audience, all devotees of the by then 'accepted' masterpiece – *The Dream of Gerontius* … But there, conducting a strange work for strings, RVW himself, a comparative (or complete?) stranger; and his Fantasy would be holding up the *Dream*, maybe for ten minutes? In fact, for twice ten, as it happened.
>
> He left the rostrum, in the non-applauding silence of those days, thanks be! And he came to the empty chair next to mine, carrying a copy of *Gerontius*, and presently was sharing it with me, while Elgar

[10] Lloyd-Baker Diaries. Gloucestershire Archives.

[11] *MT* 1909, p. 664.

was conducting the first hearing I ever had of the *Dream*. For a music-bewildered youth of seventeen it was an overwhelming evening, so disturbing and moving that I even asked RVW for his autograph – and got it! I have it, still ... And I still have what I now know to be a supreme commentary by one great composer upon another – the *Fantasia on a Theme by Thomas Tallis.*[12]

In 1910(G) there was also another deeply significant first performance – but one given before a small and very private audience. W. H. (Billy) Reed had taken over in that year from Frye Parker (Burnett's successor in 1905) as Leader of the Festival orchestra. On the Saturday following the London rehearsals he called at Herbert Brewer's house. Sir Edward Elgar had finished his new Violin Concerto during the summer:

> At once I knew that something exciting was afoot, because Sir Edward had been twice to see if I had arrived.
>
> At all the Festivals of the Three Choirs it was customary for Sir Edward to take a house for the week and have a house-party of music-lovers. On this occasion he had taken one in College Green, a house normally used for the cookery school. It had a very large room containing a grand piano and several pictures. What these represented I never discovered, as they all had their faces turned to the wall. In many of the houses that Sir Edward had lent to him, or that he had taken for a short period (furnished), the pictures were either turned round the wrong way or covered over with some hanging material – even newspaper. No comment was ever made about the odd effect produced in the room. He just didn't want these family portraits, or whatever they were, staring at him; so he turned them round or covered them up.
>
> As soon as I heard I was wanted, I quickly found Sir Edward and learned that Frank Schuster had made a grand suggestion, which was: to invite a select number of people to come to that nice large room at the cookery school on the Sunday evening, when we – Sir Edward and I – could play them the Violin Concerto right through. I said it was an excellent idea, although I must confess I had some inward qualms. I knew every note of the concerto, and exactly how he liked it played: every nuance, every shade of expression; yet I felt a little overwhelmed at being asked to play the solo part at what would actually be the very first performance before an audience. It was one of those facts that you cannot annihilate by just calling it private.
>
> When the time arrived I went over to the house and found the guests assembled. Nearly all the prominent musicians engaged at the Festival were there: the three Festival conductors, Sinclair, Atkins and Brewer; the past organists of Gloucester Cathedral, Harford Lloyd and Lee Williams; some of the musical critics, and the house-party. The room was full; and

[12] Herbert Howells, 'Memories from the Twentieth Century', in Barry Still (ed.), *Two Hundred and Fifty Years of the Three Choirs Festival – A Commemoration in Words and Pictures* (Three Choirs Festival Association, 1977).

all the lights were turned out except for some device arranged by Frank Schuster for lighting the piano and the violin-stand.

Sir Edward took his seat at the piano, and after a tense whisper to me – 'You are not going to leave me all alone in the *tuttis*, are you?' – we began. My qualms vanished: I became so thrilled by the atmosphere created, by the evident appreciation of the listeners and the magnetic force that flowed from Sir Edward, that I threw my whole heart and soul into the performance, realising that the soloist is, after all, but the servant of the composer, and that he must strive to render, not merely the notes and brilliance of the passage-work, but the inmost thoughts and the most subtle shades of meaning expressed in the music. That evening is a never-to-be-forgotten memory to me; and I always, as I think of it, feel deeply grateful to him for giving me such an artistic experience.

The orchestration of the concerto was already finished (on August 5th). Fritz Kreisler arrived towards the end of the Gloucester Festival week and at once began to study the concerto for the first public performance, which took place at Queen's Hall in London on November 10th of that year. Such was the energy of Elgar at this period that, as soon as the concerto was finished he was writing another *Pomp and Circumstance* March and correcting proofs of the concerto and other things, besides lending a helping hand and giving the benefit of his advice to Ivor Atkins ... who was engaged upon a new edition of Bach's *St Matthew Passion*.[13]

Herbert Howells also heard something of Elgar and Kreisler working together:

On the Wednesday evening Dr Brewer gave me a telegram for Sir Edward Elgar, who, for that week, was renting a lovely house near the Cathedral. 'Take it across to Sir Edward,' he said. 'But give it to him yourself.' I took it ... waiting for the front door to open, I could hear the sounds of a violin and a piano. The door opened. I told the factotum I must give the telegram to Sir Edward myself. He asked me in, but with a polite warning. 'It might mean waiting. Sir Edward is upstairs with Mr Kreisler, practising.' He added, conspiratorially: 'I suggest you sit quietly at the top of the stairs, by the drawing-room door.' I did just that, for about forty minutes, entranced by hearing what I later knew was the slow movement of the Violin Concerto ... I carried out instructions.

Thursday, in the magical week, belonged to Kreisler in triplicate: sartorially, in public gesture and performance. And in historic misadventure. The initial white-tie array had to give way to a change into morning dress. As to gesture, the illustrious soloist bowed low and gracefully to the Cathedral audience, for the first time by any performer in Three Choirs history, and contrary to customary observance on holy ground. Finally, in performance, Bach's E major Concerto began as a matter of temperature-versus-stringed-instruments. In the very earliest phrase Mr Kreisler's E string snapped. Redemption was miraculously swift. The leader of the orchestra (beloved Billy Reed) handed his acclimatised fiddle to his great

[13] W. H. Reed, *Elgar as I Knew Him* (Gollancz, 1936; repr. OUP 1989), pp. 29–32.

friend. Fuss was avoided, continuity maintained. Mr K. smiled, enchanted and at ease … and there was no final bow. (And no applause, in that day, in any of the three Cathedrals. Silent thanksgiving is a lost art. But 1910 still clung to it in the Three Choirs).[14]

Brewer tells us that when Reed had put a new string on Kreisler's violin he handed it to Kreisler, who refused it and continued to use Reed's. 'The two instruments were twins – both being made by Joseph Guarnerius.'[15]

Parry was represented in 1910(G) by his motet *Beyond these voices there is peace*, which had been given its first performance under his baton at Worcester in 1908. The secular concert was given in the newly enlarged and decorated Shire Hall, the improvements to which, made possible by Parry's generosity, consisted mainly in the provision of an extensive balcony. During the evening Sir Hubert was the recipient of a grateful address from the Corporation of the city. In his reply Parry said that he looked to music as an antidote to socialism, hoping that people from the slums would be elevated by the power of the music. Brewer again:

> I had hoped that the gratitude of the city would take a more tangible form and that the Freedom of the City would have been conferred on Sir Hubert. I took steps to bring this about, but unfortunately Parry's political views were very pronounced … Party feeling, alas, runs very high in Gloucester as in most cathedral cities, and, as these views did not coincide with those of the party in power at the time, I was unable to achieve my project and secure this recognition of Parry's munificence.[16]

By 1911(w) the Festival had reached a new peak of confidence and artistic balance. The choir consisted of 63 sopranos and 24 boy choristers, 54 contraltos and 13 male altos, 56 tenors and 65 basses – 275 in all. The orchestra under its Leader, W. H. Reed, comprised 97 players selected mainly from the LSO and included 14 first violins, 12 second violins, 10 violas, 8 cellos, 9 double-basses, 8 flutes and a piccolo, 8 oboes (the extras being required for the *St Matthew Passion*), a cor anglais, 4 clarinets, 5 bassoons, 3 trumpets, 3 trombones and a tuba, percussion and 2 harps.

Wagner had by then, thanks to Sinclair's persistence, become an established name at the Festivals. Extracts from *Parsifal* were regularly included in the cathedral programmes, and other works at secular concerts. In 1911 the whole of Act III of *Parsifal* was given in Worcester Cathedral with John Coates, William Higley and Robert Radford.

Elgar's hard-won reputation was now established. His first symphony (1909(H)) and *The Kingdom* (1907(G)) had taken their places among the regular Festival favourites. And in 1911, the year of King George V's coronation, the second symphony, the unaccompanied six-part motet *Go, song of mine*, the *Coronation March*, and the Violin Concerto, with Fritz Kreisler as soloist, were added.

[14] Howells, 'Memories from the Twentieth Century'.
[15] Herbert Brewer, *Memories of Choirs and Cloisters* (Bodley Head, 1931).
[16] Ibid.

Another work only previously heard at the coronation was Parry's coronation *Te Deum*, and there were new compositions by Walford Davies (*Five Sayings of Jesus*, with the tenor Gervase Elwes) and Vaughan Williams (*Five Mystical Songs*, in which Campbell McInnes was the baritone soloist).

The *Five Mystical Songs*, conducted by the composer, preceded the Elgar Violin Concerto at the Thursday evening concert. Vaughan Williams, baton in hand, received something of a shock as his eyes ranged around the orchestra:

> I was thoroughly nervous. When I looked at the fiddles I thought I was going mad, for I saw what appeared to be Kreisler at a back desk. I got through somehow, and at the end I whispered to Reed, '*Am* I mad, or *did* I see Kreisler in the band?' 'Oh yes', he said, 'he broke a string and wanted to play it in before the Elgar Concerto and couldn't without being heard in the Cathedral.'

Years later, Vaughan Williams was telling this story to some players and one of them completed it. 'I was sitting next to Kreisler, one of our people had been taken ill, so he slipped in beside me: just before we started, he said, "Nudge me if there's anything difficult and I'll leave it out."'[17]

Kreisler also played the violin *obbligato* to the solo 'Have Mercy' in the performance of the Elgar–Atkins edition of Bach's *St Matthew Passion* given on the Thursday morning. His playing, reported the *Musical Times*, was 'one of those perfect things rarely heard'.[18]

Inspired by a visit to Rothenburg-on-Tauber in Germany, where he had heard a brass band playing from the top of the church tower, Atkins suggested to Elgar that an effective way to introduce their edition of the *St Matthew Passion* would be by playing before each part a Bach chorale from the top of the cathedral tower. He had it in mind that 'O Man, Bemoan thy Grievous Sin' and 'O Sacred Head, Surrounded' should be used, and Elgar agreed to orchestrate them for brass instruments. The playing of the chorales created a deep impression, and for many years they introduced the performances of the *St Matthew Passion* at Three Choirs.

Elgar was at the bottom of another enterprise, in the form of a handbill entitled 'Side Shows' which he circulated among his friends on the opening day. Wulstan Atkins explained its significance:

> The allusions were to well-known public figures, festival personalities and members of the Elgars' house-party. Most of them will be obvious, but perhaps a few need explanation.
>
> 'Burning of Heretics' refers indirectly to Granville Bantock, who was conducting his new work, *Overture to a Greek Tragedy* at the festival. Bantock was a co-founder of the STP Society, and signed himself the 'Arch Heretic' in their initiation ceremonies.
>
> 'Dr Elizabeth Pastoral' was Dr Herbert Brewer, the organist of Gloucester Cathedral, whose *Two Pastorals*, dealing with Elizabethan times, were being performed.

[17] Vaughan Williams, *R. V. W.: A Biography*, pp. 97–8.
[18] *MT* 1911, p. 666.

There had been a recent railway strike, with an orderly procession of banners and marching round 'Pitchcroft', a local open space by the river.

Canon J. M. Wilson, the cathedral librarian and a great authority on the architecture and history of the cathedral, had recently written an article about the probable origins of a stone coffin found during the cathedral restorations.

The local papers had reported the story of a fisherman who had caught a perch, which on being cleaned was found to have swallowed a gold ring.

St Kentigern, better known as St Mungo, lived about 518 to 603, and had ascribed to him a number of miracles, including the resuscitation of St Serf's favourite robin after it had been cooked in a pie, but alas, with no golden treasure.

A town house in Worcester had recently been bought for the Bishop, whose main residence was Hartlebury Castle, which was some miles outside the city.

'Bearpit in College Yard' – archaeological excavations were in progress outside the north side of the cathedral.

Worcester was gayer than ever before, with coronation decorations adding to the usual festival flags. The city and the county houses were full of guests, including royalty, and there was a festive mood over everything.[19]

The members of royalty present were the Princess Henry of Battenburg, Prince Leopold, and King Manoel of Portugal and his mother, Queen Amelia.

Another celebrated Festival prankster was the tenor John Coates, whose exploits were recounted in Sir Herbert Brewer's autobiography. One incident involving Coates and Billy Reed apparently fooled a large crowd of people outside Worcester Cathedral before a *Messiah* performance one Friday morning:

> They were both staying with me … and in the drawing-room of the house which I had taken for the week was a brass hearth-brush which looked uncommonly like a large telescope. Reed, on catching sight of it, exclaimed, 'What an excellent thing for a practical joke!' They immediately proceeded to action and took up their position in College yard and appeared to look through this imaginary telescope at the tower of the Cathedral. Very soon a huge crowd of people collected round them trying to discover what it was they were watching so intently … This continued for several minutes, the traffic meanwhile becoming very congested. Then Reed suggested to Coates that it was time for the crowd to see the business end of the hearth-brush. When they saw the bristles appear and spread out at the end of the brass tube and realised how they had been fooled there was a roar of laughter, the crowd rapidly dispersed and … proceeded on their way to the Cathedral.[20]

At Hereford in 1906 another tenor had been engaged to sing in *Elijah* and so John Coates had a day off:

[19] Wulstan Atkins, *The Elgar–Atkins Friendship* (David & Charles, 1985).

[20] Brewer, *Memories*.

But not being of an idle nature he occupied his time in other ways that morning. I had taken a house in the corner of the Close – Harley Court. There was a passage way in front of it leading from the Close to another part of town. To the surprise of Herefordians and visitors to the Festival they saw, on leaving the Cathedral for the luncheon interval, some notice-boards in front of my house which had not been there earlier in the day. One was placed on a privet hedge warning people 'Not to pluck the flowers'. On a few blades of grass and weeds was another, advising people to 'keep off the sward', and on a door leading to a rubbish heap near the house was the following notice – 'You are requested not to feed the wild Zigmollicans'.

It was highly amusing to watch these well-dressed people walk on tiptoe to the door and peer over cautiously, expecting to see some kind of wild beast in the pen; and then, on discovering only a heap of dead leaves, slink away, casting furtive glances around to see if their action had been observed.[21]

In the next edition of the *Musical Times*, the following comment appeared:

Much interest was aroused at Hereford by some specimens of that rare animal, the Zigmollican. They were kept in confinement by an eminent brewer residing near the Cathedral, and passers-by who managed to catch a glimpse of the elusive little creatures greatly admired their subtly-tinted coats. It was reported that they had been recently imported by Herr Johann von Ueberrock, the well-known zoological specialist!

By 1912 the days of innocent fun were fast coming to an end. Emma Albani, a Festival institution for thirty-four years, had made her final Three Choirs appearance, in *Messiah*, in 1911(w). In the two years of peace remaining, her place was taken by Ruth Vincent. 'It is not often' recorded the *Musical Times*, 'that we hear the *Messiah* solos sung so truly in tune.'[22]

Muriel Foster also retired after the 1912(H) Festival, in which she sang the solo cantata *O amantissime sponse Jesu* by Christian Ritter; the solo in Brahms's *Alto Rhapsody*; the *St Matthew Passion*; the first performance of Elgar's orchestrated version of (supposedly) Eastern European folk-songs, 'The Torch' and 'The River'; and, finally, *The Dream of Gerontius*, in a memorable performance at which her consummate artistry was joined with that of Gervase Elwes.

Walford Davies had been invited to compose a piece for the 1912 Festival, but was unable to complete his promised work. Elgar conducted the first concert performance of his orchestral arrangement of *The Crown of India* suite; Vaughan Williams presented his *Fantasia on Christmas Carols*, in which Campbell McInnes was once again his soloist; Billy Reed was present in his new capacity as Leader of the LSO; and Sir Hubert Parry made his last appearance at a Three Choirs Festival, conducting the first performance of his *Ode on the Nativity*, a work described by his biographer, Jeremy Dibble, as 'without doubt one of Parry's supreme choral achievements. No other of his choral works (with perhaps the

---

[21] Ibid.
[22] *MT* 1912, p. 666.

exception of *Blest Pair of Sirens*) displays such precision and formal tightness, and nowhere else does he show such a facility for thematic homogeneity.'[23]

So to 1913 – and Gloucester was to experience both a shock and an honour. The shock, remembered by the late Edith Sterry (née Deavin), who first sang in the chorus in that year, was the sight and sound of the soprano Aïno Ackté, who came from Finland to sing in the Verdi Requiem, the first performance of *Luonnotar*, op. 70, by Sibelius, and the closing scene from Richard Strauss's opera *Salome*. Not surprisingly the dean would not allow this last piece to be given in the cathedral, and so both the Sibelius première and the Strauss were included in the secular concert alongside such varied fare as Sullivan's overture *Macbeth*; the Hans Sachs monologue from Wagner's *Meistersinger*; Debussy's *Danse sacrée et danse profane*; Herbert Brewer's conventional ballad, *Sir Patrick Spens*; a scherzo caprice, *Will o' the Wisp*, by W. H. Reed; and Mozart's Piano Concerto No. 27 in B flat, K595, played by a most distinguished visitor.

Edith Sterry remembered how the chorus were hustled out of the Shire Hall when Aïno Ackté arrived to rehearse. Brewer described the same scene in his autobiography:

> At the rehearsal she [Ackté] caused much resentment by the way she insisted on the withdrawal of the audience, which consisted chiefly of the members of the chorus ... who were naturally anxious to hear the Finnish star. Her action was fully justified, for the music that she sang required so perfect an understanding between orchestra and singer that a detailed rehearsal was more than necessary. In fact parts of the score of *Luonnotar* were 'still in his head' a fortnight before the Festival, so the composer said. The orchestral parts were hastily copied out and full of errors.[24]

But Edith Sterry overcame Ackté's ban: she crept back in to the balcony and lay flat on the floor throughout the rehearsal![25] Brewer surmounted all the difficulties and in performance the piece made a great impression. He received a letter from Sibelius thanking him for an excellent performance and congratulating him on his success.

The Strauss was equally memorable. As Brewer recalled: 'Still more sensational was [Ackté's] singing of the closing scene from Strauss's *Salome*. Never in living memory had such singing in such music been heard at a Three Choirs Festival. It was electrifying and the audience was worked up to a wild state of enthusiasm.'[26]

The pianist in the Mozart concerto was none other than the French composer Camille Saint-Saëns (1835–1921), who had honoured the Festival with the première of his new oratorio, *The Promised Land*, which he was to conduct in the cathedral the next day. Since Saint-Saëns was the first living Continental composer to conduct at Three Choirs since Dvořák visited Worcester in 1884,

[23] Jeremy Dibble, *C. Hubert H. Parry: His Life and Music* (OUP, 1992), p. 454.

[24] Brewer, *Memories*.

[25] Recollections of Mrs Edith Sterry (private communication).

[26] Brewer, *Memories*.

it was perhaps appropriate that the secular concert should end with Dvořák's *Carnival Overture*.

The Promised Land failed to meet expectations, but nonetheless a glowing review appeared in the Paris *Figaro*:

> It is certain that in assigning the work to an English musical Festival, the French musician took means to ensure its production under the best conditions, and the most auspicious for an understanding of its true merits. Nowhere else, least of all in France, could he have discovered the magnificently sonorous choirs for which his finest and most significant pages were designed. Moreover, nowhere else would a presentation of the work so thoroughly in accord with its spirit have been realised.[27]

The Festival ended as usual with *Messiah*. The soloists were Ruth Vincent, Ada Crossley, John Coates and Robert Radford.

When Herbert Brewer laid down his baton on the afternoon of Friday 12 September 1913 the Three Choirs fell silent for seven years.

[27] *Le Figaro*, 15 September 1913.

14

An Essentially English Institution

As World War I drew to a close, speculation began about the future of the great national musical festivals. On 14 September 1918 a lengthy article appeared in the *Saturday Review*:

> Is the Musical Festival, triennial or otherwise, a thing of the past? For our part we think and hope not; but some people, who claim to speak with knowledge, are rather confident in their opinion that after the War there will be no regular resumption of these gatherings, which have naturally been suspended since the Autumn of 1914. And one thing is certain: if not held regularly they may as well not be held at all; for it is precisely because their occurrence hitherto has been as calculable as a solar eclipse or the landlord's demand for rent that they have been of real value in an artistic sense.

Going on to describe the provincial Festival as having been 'one of the prime glories of musical life in this country', the article stressed the key role which it had played in maintaining England's old supremacy in the department of choral singing, and ended with a plea for its future life: 'After all, at a Festival it is not the band, nor the soloists, nor the novelties, nor the conductor, but the choir that's 'the thing'. We could ill spare the institution that created the brilliant constellation to surround such a glorious central orb.'

Since the last Three Choirs Festival had been held in Gloucester in 1913, it was the turn of Worcester to lead off after the war – but the choral members in each of the three cities were all keen to accept the challenge. On the third Saturday in January 1919, Lord Coventry presided over a meeting of the Worcester Executive Committee. Four questions had been submitted to the Deans and Chapters and Festival Committees of Worcester, Hereford and Gloucester: (1) Should the Festivals be revived; (2) if so, what should their form and character be; (3) what should be the limit of expenditure incurred; and (4) where should the next Festival be held?

The Dean and Chapter of Worcester had passed a memorandum to the meeting in which, in answer to the first question, they said they did not think the Festivals should be revived in the form they had come to assume before the war, the cost involved amounting to considerably more than £3,000. In order to meet this expenditure the Dean and Chapter thought that:

> it became necessary to push the sale of tickets and advertise for patronage in a manner which they considered was not in accord with the character of the Cathedral, and which destroyed the idea that the Festivals were

religious in character and a noble illustration of God's gift of music employed for sacred objects.[1]

They were also worried that in the austere post-war climate it would be difficult to raise sufficient money for the Festival and, while they did not wish to see it abandoned altogether, suggested that it could be continued in a modified form:

> They suggested that the Festivals should be revived as a three-days' Festival, in which music would be rendered by the members of the Three Choirs, reinforced by local voices, orchestra, and one or two solo voices, and that at one meeting each day the main object should be the choral rendering of the highest degree of perfection of music – the finest examples of English Church music being selected.[2]

Lastly, the Dean and Chapter proposed that in any form in which the Festivals were revived the expenditure should not be allowed to exceed £1,000.

The Worcester Executive Committee postponed a decision on holding a Festival in 1919 until the Dean and Chapter had given a definite decision upon whether they would be willing to permit the Festivals to continue in traditional style or not.

Although the press had been excluded from the meeting, a report of it was supplied to them later. The danger was rising of a repetition of the filleted Festival of 1875. Then a letter from Sir Charles Villiers Stanford appeared in *The Times*:

> Sir,
>
> May I express an earnest hope that the Committee of the Three Choirs Festival should see their way to re-establishing that essential English institution on at least its former basis of efficiency and excellence? It is not wise to start again tentatively or hesitatingly. British music deserves and demands more than that; it has struggled successfully through four years of unexampled difficulty and is waiting for its reward. The Three Choirs Festival has the unique chance of taking the lead at a most important juncture; and I feel sure there will be forthcoming a surprising amount of outside support if it takes a large view and advances without flinching.

This brought a response, also in the columns of *The Times*, from the Rev. Arthur T. Bannister, Canon Residentiary and Precentor of Hereford:

> Sir,
>
> May I express my cordial agreement with Sir Charles Stanford's opinion that the Three Choirs Festival should be re-established *on its former basis*.
>
> I am sorry that the Worcester proposals should have been published before they had been thoroughly discussed by the Chapters and Stewards of Gloucester and Hereford. It may be that circumstances will prevent our making a start this year; but we in Hereford, both Dean and Chapter and

---

[1] *Gloucester Journal*, 1 February 1919.

[2] Ibid.

Stewards, are full of hope that in 1920, at any rate, the festival may be as efficient and excellent as of old.

The Times itself took up the question of the future of Three Choirs in the issue of 8 February 1919:

Musical festivals seem to be coming into the region of practical politics again ... [they] can hardly be regarded as local institutions, and their warmest friends are concerned to defend their existence on national rather than on local grounds. The question is not so much what part the triennial performance of oratorios and symphonies in the cathedral can play in the musical life of the place as whether the performances have a character of their own, some quality which musicians ... value for its own sake and fail to find elsewhere. Is [Three Choirs] to be maintained, widened, and improved (all admit the possibility of improvement), or is it to be allowed to lapse in the hope of building another tradition in its place? That is the decision which the authorities have to face at this moment after the compulsory standstill of the past four years. Two parties, the musical purist and the unmusical reactionary, join in favouring the latter decision. The former says honestly, Let the cathedrals study great Church music; the latter echoes him, but means, Let us cut down the expenses, because great Church music requires neither orchestra nor expensive soloists. What the purist forgets is that every cathedral in the land has maintained for centuries a permanent establishment solely for the cultivation of great Church music in its appropriate setting of the daily offices. If these establishments are not doing their duty (and many of them one knows are not), let him press his case against them with all vigour. A triennial or an annual festival could do little to supply their defect.

Looking at the financial side of the Three Choirs Festival, it appears that for many years a large deficit was borne annually by the stewards of the festivals, who were the wealthier residents of the neighbourhood, because they felt the music to be worth paying for; while many thousands of pounds taken in collections at the doors have been given to a deserving clerical, not musical, charity. We learn, however, that in recent years the festivals have paid their expenses. It seems clearly, then, a case on which musical people should have the decision. Do they still want this sort of music; is it vital to them, and if so, will they risk something to have it? The pause of four years may have given occasion for many a reflection, resulting in many a reform of detail and the casting off of some outworn conventions. So much the better, if the answer to the question is affirmative, that festivals have before them now a clearer course and a richer future.

In the face of indignation and opposition the Worcester Dean and Chapter decided to permit the Festival to go ahead as of old provided that 300 Stewards could be found. Ivor Atkins personally wrote 1,000 letters, an action which produced 90 percent of the guarantors needed to allow the Festival to be restarted, and the Bishop of Worcester set the seal of approval upon the proceedings by not only preaching at the Opening Service but singing as a tenor in the chorus too.

The long Three Choirs tradition resumed; in 1920 old friends met once more in Festival sunshine to celebrate the successful resuscitation of the ancient Meeting and to express sympathy for the very many who had sung and played for the last time at Gloucester in 1913. Apart from the victims of war, the intervening years had claimed the lives of Sir Hubert Parry, Charles Harford Lloyd and, at the early age of fifty-four, George Robertson Sinclair. For Elgar too, lodging alone, the Festival was a sad and mournful time. Lady Elgar had died on 7 April 1920.

Before the war the Festivals were numbered from the year 1724, when the charity collection was first made. Thus, the Festival of 1913 had been correctly described as the 190th Meeting of the Three Choirs for the benefit of the charity. However, Ivor Atkins decided to acknowledge the earlier beginnings of the Music Meetings. Settling somewhat arbitrarily upon 1715 as a starting point, and allowing for the suspension during the years 1914–19, he accorded the distinction of the 200th Meeting to the Worcester Festival of 1920. He also decided, wisely, that the time had come to dispense with the old system of engaging individual players for the orchestra, albeit that the majority of them had for some time past been members of the LSO. In spite of the higher overall contract cost, Atkins engaged the LSO as a complete ensemble.

Elijah was back on Tuesday – with Captain Herbert Heyner singing the role of the Prophet. On Wednesday morning Elgar conducted *The Dream of Gerontius*, with Kirkby Lunn superb as the Angel, John Coates in the title part, and Heyner singing the two baritone solos. For the afternoon there was 'a solemn music' in memory of Parry, Lloyd and Sinclair. It opened with Beethoven's *Three Equali* for four trombones, conducted in the Lady Chapel by Brewer:

> These solemn chords, played … at the eastern end of the building, and softening along the whole length until the instruments sounded much like the diapason notes of an organ, revealed the length of the building as nothing else had done, and made one realise anew the interdependence of music and architecture.[3]

Then followed Parry's motet *There is an old belief* from the *Songs of Farewell*, a setting of James Lockhart's lines wholly appropriate to the occasion:

> There is an old belief
> That on some solemn shore
> Beyond the sphere of grief
> Dear friends shall meet once more …

The rest of the concert comprised Parry's *Blest Pair of Sirens*, Walford Davies's *Fantasy* – founded on an episode in Dante's *Divina commedia*, scored for tenor solo, chorus and orchestra, and composed for the abandoned Festival of 1914 – and the Symphony in D minor by César Franck.

At the 1920 secular concert in the Public Hall, place was found for the music of no fewer than five West Country composers. Apart from songs by Brewer and Atkins, and Elgar's *Introduction and Allegro* for strings, there were *Four Worcestershire Sketches* by Julius Harrison, and Alexander Brent Smith's *Worcester*

[3] *MT* 1920, p. 667.

Rhapsody. This last, conducted by its elegant young composer, impressed both critics and public.

Alexander Brent Smith (1889–1950) was born in the village of Brookthorpe near Gloucester and was educated at the King's School in Worcester, was a cathedral chorister, studied music with Atkins and became his assistant organist. In 1912 he was appointed Director of Music at Lancing College in Sussex. While there he was an extremely popular master, not only engendering an interest and love of music in his charges but also organising 'Rag Concerts' for the last night of term. Among these were his 'Rag Operas': *Bacchus* in 1917, *Iphigenia* in 1921, *Circe and the Swine* in 1922, *Dido and Aeneas* in 1924, and a repeat of *Iphigenia* in 1926 in which sixteen-year-old Peter Pears made his stage debut. Pears also took part in Brent Smith's stagings of scenes from *HMS Pinafore* in 1927 and *The Mikado* in 1928.[4]

At Lancing, Brent Smith served under C. H. Blackistone, a headmaster whose popularity was as low as Brent Smith's was high.[5] Financial difficulties within the college led to staffing reductions, and 1934 saw the end of its much-admired Director of Music's work there. He returned to Brookthorpe, taught for some years at Pate's Grammar School in Cheltenham, and continued to serve Three Choirs as a member of the Music Committee of the Gloucester Festival. He was a regular contributor to several journals, including *Music & Letters* and the *Musical Times*, and composed a large body of works in most forms, a number of which were first performed at Three Choirs.

In addition to *Messiah*, the 1920 Festival included the Elgar–Atkins edition of the *St Matthew Passion*, Verdi's Requiem, and the first performance of Vaughan Williams's *Four Hymns* for tenor and string orchestra, written for and sung by Steuart Wilson, the youngest son of Canon J. M. Wilson of Worcester Cathedral, whose two elder sons were both killed in World War I. Steuart Wilson suffered injuries in the war, which affected one of his lungs and permanently damaged his health. Even so, his beautiful voice became one of the treasures of British music during the interwar years, and his interpretations of *Gerontius* and the Evangelist in Bach's *St John* and *St Matthew Passions* were greatly admired.

In 1920 all three of the singers whose voices were most closely associated with the name part in *Gerontius* during Elgar's lifetime appeared in the same Three Choirs Festival: John Coates, Gervase Elwes and Steuart Wilson. The styles of the two elder tenors were very different from each other but equally valid. Coates, whose career had begun as a baritone, brought the dramatic intensity and power to *Gerontius* which suited his voice so perfectly to the Wagnerian *Heldentenor* roles in which he also excelled. He was, said Gerald Moore, an aristocrat among singers. Elwes was noted for the spiritual commitment of his interpretations, especially, like Steuart Wilson after him, in *Gerontius* and the Bach *Passions*. Wulstan Atkins remembered him as a devout, almost saintly figure. But by 1920 Gervase Elwes was fifty-four years old and planning to retire from the profession on his return from an approaching tour in America.

Two other voices destined for stardom were heard at the Festival for the first time in 1920: the soprano Carrie Tubb and the superb bass Norman Allin,

---

[4] Memories of Mr B. W. T. Handford (private communication).

[5] Memories of Mr R. S. Thompson (private communication).

who dominated the British music scene for many years with his even, sonorous, flexible voice, and of whom Sir Henry Wood in his autobiography *My Life of Music* wrote:

> I have always thought it a pity that Allin is of such a retiring disposition, for, had he cared, he might have become one of the world's finest operatic basses. I believe his operatic roles numbered fifty. I imagine he loved the English countryside and his home too well, and who can blame him?

Charles Lee Williams, who had responded to Ivor Atkins's appeal for guarantors with a cheque for £10 ('put me amongst the *tenners* which you may think *base* of me'), wrote to Atkins on 14 September:

> My dear Atkins,
>
> I can only once again say that above all praise which rightly comes to you this week you will I know value the now well established fact that you have resuscitated & guided the Festival ship into harbour off your own bat most admirably.
>
> Please convey to your wife too my kindly greetings & say how much I appreciated being allowed to come in and out like a tame rabbit. It is just the spirit combined with tact & good humour that has carried you both through.
>
> In a quiet way I have propagated propaganda for you and your interests as much as I could, for I realised the big importance of a success *now* or never! – Thanks too dear boy for doing 'Williams in D'. 'Pon my life I didn't know I had a tune left in me. Lord! how they all played and sang it!
>
> *Don't write*: but get away right now & take a rod with you.
>
> Kindly greetings old Bean!
> Yours ever
> C. L. W.[6]

In November 1920, Ivor Atkins became a DMus by examination at Oxford, and his work in restarting the Festival after the war was recognised by the announcement of a knighthood in the New Year's Honours List of 1921.

Two weeks later the many friends and admirers of Gervase Elwes were stunned to learn that while travelling to an engagement at Harvard University he had been killed in a train accident.

---

[6] Letter in the possession of the late E. Wulstan Atkins.

15

The Elgar Festivals

THE interwar years were, above all, the years of the 'Elgar Festivals'. At a time when his music was out of fashion elsewhere in the country, Elgar was lionised at Three Choirs, and he in turn honoured the Festivals by regular appearances, usually conducting his own works. As the *Musical Times* put it in 1921, 'his world-wide fame finds its focus in the Three Choirs Festival, and if he owed something to them in his youth, he is now paying back the debt with interest'.[1] But worldwide fame and popularity are different things. Britain chose to neglect Elgar. Following a 1922 performance of *The Apostles* in a half-empty Queen's Hall, George Bernard Shaw, writing to the *Daily News*, apologised 'to posterity for living in a country where the capacity and tastes of schoolboys and sporting costermongers are the measure of metropolitan culture':

> *The Apostles* is one of the glories of British music ... It places Britain once more definitely in the first European rank, after two centuries of leather and prunella.
>
> It would be an exaggeration to say that I was the only person present, like Ludwig of Bavaria at Wagner's premieres. My wife was there. Other couples were visible at intervals. One of the couples consisted of the Princess Mary and Viscount Lascelles, who just saved the situation as far as the credit of the Crown is concerned, as it very deeply is. I distinctly saw six people in the stalls, probably with complimentary tickets.[2]

On the other hand, Three Choirs audiences for *Gerontius*, *The Apostles* and *The Kingdom* frequently exceeded in number those for *Elijah* and even *Messiah*. Nowhere else were Elgar's works performed with quite such dedication, and nowhere else so regularly under his own direction. At no other national festival or concert venue could performers and public alike mingle socially and meet so easily with leading composers – and the familiar figure of Elgar, often in company with his friend and champion Bernard Shaw, could hardly be missed, especially when he chose to wear full court dress with orders. His was a kindly presence too: he was once observed going into a store to buy sixpenny jewellery and then giving it to children he might pass on the way to the cathedral.[3] One of the choristers in 1925 later recalled: 'And here am I singing under the great Sir Edward himself – how majestic he looks on the rostrum – what a strangely nervous beat, and look at that delicate left hand resting on the score – now

---

[1] *MT* 1921, p. 692.

[2] *Daily News*, 9 June 1922.

[3] Herbert Howells, 85th birthday broadcast (BBC), October 1977.

he's placing it over his heart and his face beams on Billy Reed as a favourite orchestral theme approaches.'[4]

Elgar was, in each sense, at home at Three Choirs; and his Festival friends were real friends, as demonstrated not only in the *Enigma Variations* and the help he gave to Brewer with *Emmaus*, but also in the dedication of other works to Three Choirs conductors: the *Wand of Youth Suite No. 1* to Charles Lee Williams; *The Black Knight* to Hugh Blair; the *Pomp and Circumstance* marches nos. 3, 4 and 5 to Ivor Atkins, G. R. Sinclair and Percy Hull respectively; a setting of Lady Elgar's poem *A Christmas Greeting* to Sinclair and the Hereford Cathedral choristers; and to 'my friend, Percy Hull', a Serenade, a setting of a Russian text for unaccompanied choir.

Percy Clarke Hull (1878–1968) was the only ex-chorister of Hereford Cathedral, other than John Bull (1562–1628), to become its Organist. He became a chorister in 1889 and was afterwards a pupil of Sinclair and Assistant Organist from 1896. In recognition of his service to music he was awarded an honorary FRCO in 1920, the Lambeth degree of DMus in 1921 and, in 1947, a knighthood.

In 1914 Hull had been on holiday in Germany and, at the outbreak of war, was interned by the Germans. He spent the next four years at Ruhleben Prisoners of War Camp. Like Sinclair, Hull was a Freemason, and as such played an important part in bringing to the notice of the Grand Lodge the privations and sufferings of the Freemasons interned at Ruhleben, so that a large sum of money was raised for their assistance. He was appointed Deputy Assistant Grand Organist of England in recognition of his activities. On his release in November 1918, a sick man, he took over as Organist at Hereford, relieving Gordon Brown, an articled pupil of Sinclair who had deputised since February 1917. Although dogged by continuing illness Hull conducted his first Three Choirs Festival in 1921, achieving an unqualified success. 'His tempi', remarked the *Musical Times*, 'were on the side of vivacity, which afforded a contrast with those of his predecessor.'[5] Elgar assisted Hull, conducting *The Dream of Gerontius*, *The Apostles*, and the Cello Concerto, in which Beatrice Harrison, who had recorded the work in 1919, was the soloist. The chamber concert on Friday evening was all-British, including Ethel Smyth's Quartet in E minor and Elgar's Piano Quintet in A minor with Henry Ley, Organist of Christ Church, Oxford, joining W. H. Reed's quartet of players as pianist. The Festival also included pieces by Benjamin Dale, Edgar Bainton and Frederick Keel, all of whom had been Percy Hull's companions in captivity at Ruhleben. But the most strikingly original choral work of the week was the first Three Choirs performance of Gustav Holst's *The Hymn of Jesus*, conducted by the composer.

The Hymn of Jesus was heard for the first time, under Holst's baton, at a Philharmonic concert at the Queen's Hall in March 1920; it was an 'overwhelming success'. Holst 'knew that it was the best thing he had written, but this was the first time that his opinion and public opinion coincided'.[6] Although performed several times in the months following its première, it was at Hereford

[4] Melville Cook, 'Notes from my Three Choirs Diary', Hereford Festival programme book, 1988. Copy held in the Three Choirs Festival Office, Gloucester.

[5] *MT* 1921, p. 692.

[6] Imogen Holst, *Gustav Holst: A Biography* (OUP, 1938; repr. 1988).

in 1921 that the work was first heard under the most favourable and fitting conditions.

Before directing his first Festival in 1891, Sinclair had spent some time with J. T. Carrodus, gaining insights into the technique of conducting. After the 1921 Festival, Percy Hull acknowledged the great help of a similar sort which he too had received – from W. H. Reed. Under Hull, Hereford soon gained a reputation among members of the chorus as the most rigorously disciplined of the three Festivals, and the concentrated effort was well justified by remarkable results. Paying tribute to the choir in 1927(H) Harvey Grace wrote:

> It had much of the brilliance and vitality usually associated with the crack Northern bodies, together with the even greater virtue of beautiful tone for which we usually have to come farther south. And there can be no better tribute to these singers and their trainer than the fact of their being recruited on the 'let 'em all come' principle; for I am assured on the best authority that there is practically no voice trial. The singing would have been notable from a stringently chosen choir; from one that was simply collected it was astonishing.[7]

Herbert Sumsion also acknowledged Percy Hull's boundless energy:

> This took the form in music of a capacity for work, both on and off the platform, which has certainly not been exceeded by any other Festival Conductor within my knowledge … He was short in stature and by nature quick in all his movements – he always seemed in a hurry to get somewhere and to do something. As an administrator he took almost too much on his own shoulders, chiefly because he enjoyed being busy but also because he was so impatient to get a job done. It will be no surprise to learn that he was an early riser and could do with much less sleep than most people. His conversation was equally high powered, with most of the firing coming from his side. This developed into a manner which over the years became distinctly brusque. If you were unwise enough to greet him with 'Hello, Percy, how are you?' he would more than likely answer with 'What's that got to do with you?' – which could be disconcerting until one accepted that it was badinage and not meant to be taken literally. He was emphatic to a degree and things were either black or white – subtle tints of grey were not for him. This led to a certain rigidity in his personality and outlook, but he said what he meant and meant what he said and such an attitude can, and in his case did, pay handsome dividends.
>
> Particularly was this the case in his role as Conductor. Chorus, Soloists and Orchestra were never in any doubt as to what they had to do. Verbal instructions were clear, concise and unequivocal, and those given in writing were underlined, double underlined or even triple underlined and put in capital letters so that there could be no excuse for misunderstanding. The Orchestra liked his direct manner, the Soloists accepted their instructions (whether they agreed with him or not) and the Chorus, of course, loved being ordered about. It is almost superfluous to add that his beat was as

[7] *MT* 1927, p. 922.

clear as daylight, and under the conditions which inevitably prevailed at Festivals in his early days – chiefly lack of rehearsal time – such a beat was worth gold. Works such as Holst's *Hymn of Jesus*, with its complicated time patterns and unusual rhythms would have come to grief completely without that rock-firm and emphatic beat which steered everyone safely through what in those days were untravelled waters ... He had such an affection for Bach's B minor Mass that it became a 'must' at all Hereford Festivals. It also led to the one main criticism which was levelled against him – that he took some of it too fast. This applied almost entirely to the Choruses. In his desire to whip up his singers to give all they'd got he probably allowed excitement to get the better of him, and he took things faster than he realized.

... On the personal side friendship meant everything to him ... He was affectionately known to everyone as 'P. C.' – which in itself speaks volumes – and this is a distinction which he shared with only one other musician of his generation, namely V. W.[8]

In a flash of sharp wit hardly intended to offend his Gloucester and Worcester colleagues, Percy Hull once described Three Choirs as 'the three Ms', a reference to the magnificent headgear worn in the mayoral procession at Worcester and Herbert Brewer's keen business sense at Gloucester. 'The three Ms were', he said, 'at Worcester – Millinery; at Gloucester – Money; and at Hereford – Music!'[9]

B REWER'S close attention to box-office receipts was well rewarded at the Gloucester Festival of 1922. Attendances exceeded those of any previous Festival and the sum of £2,110 was made available to the charity. It is also much to Brewer's credit that he was prepared to include many new works in his programmes, even when they were alien to his own taste. This was certainly the case in 1922.

Once again, it was Elgar who suggested to the Festival Committee that they should invite three promising young men – Arthur Bliss, Eugene Goossens and Herbert Howells – to compose new pieces for the Festival. Charles Lee Williams, by then affectionately known as 'the Father of the Festival', had taken over as chairman of the Gloucester Executive Committee, which promptly agreed to commission new works from all three. The results were more than Lee Williams or Brewer had bargained for, especially in the work from Bliss: *A Colour Symphony*. Influenced by Stravinsky and *Les Six*, Bliss had painted a dazzling sound picture: superbly orchestrated, frequently dissonant, vigorous and forward-looking – but barely understood by many in the audience. Yet again, rehearsal time was woefully inadequate and, worst of all, just before the actual performance it was found that there was too little room on the platform to seat all the orchestra and the chorus. Even though the chorus were not required during the symphony, it was orchestral players who were ejected, leaving Bliss without several key instruments. None of this was mentioned by Brewer in his

[8] Herbert Sumsion, 'Percy Clarke Hull – A Tribute', Hereford Festival programme book, 1970. Copy held in the Three Choirs Festival Office, Gloucester.
[9] Memories of Watkins Shaw (private communication).

autobiography, but he does tell us that it was not until a fortnight before the Festival that the copies of Goossens's work, *Silence* (a choral setting of the poem by Walter de la Mare), were placed in the hands of the chorus, who agreed to a daily rehearsal to become acquainted with it. In his autobiography Goossens recalled the outcome:

> I went to Gloucester for the Festival and stayed at one of the oldest inns in England, the New Inn (fifteenth century). I had rehearsed *Silence* with the London Symphony Orchestra two days previously in London, and the fine choir had mastered its part quite satisfactorily at separate rehearsals under the late Dr. Brewer, organist of Gloucester Cathedral. All that remained, therefore, was to join the two forces at a final rehearsal. The chorus, unused to my chromatic idiom, was experiencing difficulty in arriving at the unison *pianissimo* B flat at the end of the piece anywhere near pitch. Brewer therefore installed a small harmonium at the back of the chorus to sound the crucial B flat as an aid to the chorus, and undertook to play it himself. He could as well have used the organ; as things transpired, it's a pity he didn't. The actual concert, with chorus and orchestra arranged picturesquely in the organ loft over the sanctuary, an impressive sight, began with a most inappropriate work for performance in a church – Scriabin's erotic *Poem of Ecstasy*. Awaiting my turn to conduct *Silence*, I sat with Elgar in the choir stalls, where, hidden from sight, we discussed the proceedings. 'To think that Gloucester Cathedral should ever echo to such music', sighed Elgar. 'It's a wonder the gargoyles don't fall off the tower. Heaven forgive Brewer!' The *Poem of Ecstasy* drew to a noisy, disorderly close, and the groined vaultings of the Cathedral turned the blare of trumpets into a shattering infamy. I started to leave for the choir-loft. 'Write a festival Mass, Eugene, and atone for this outrage.' 'All right, Sir Edward, but Mother Church won't approve of my modernisms.' 'Never mind. I'll be in Heaven by then; I'll make it all right for you! Don't forget, plenty of percussion in the *Sanctus*!
>
> One of the most impressive things about a Three Choirs Festival is the great silence of the audience at the Cathedral concerts. The Scriabine finished in shocked silence, and I faced a silent audience to start my own *Silence*. All went well until the final unison (and perfectly in tune) *pianissimo* B flat, when, just as Brewer started to play his helping note on the harmonium, a deep rattling boom shook the awe-inspiring silence of the church and persisted till the end of the piece. One of the low pedal bourdon pipes of the organ had ciphered, and broken the very silence which was the whole point of my work. Elgar, when I returned to the choir stalls, said he thought the piece atmospheric ('and the cipher was very effective'), but too short. 'All you youngsters are in far too great a hurry nowadays.' 'If that's what you think, just wait till you hear the next piece', I replied. This was the première of Arthur Bliss's *Colour Symphony*, which lasted forty minutes. Elgar had to admit there were exceptions, and immensely admired Bliss's vivid symphony. After the concert we ate an enormous roast-beef lunch at the New Inn, and with Arthur Bliss and Willie Reed, concert-master of the L.S.O. and close friend of Elgar, spent

the afternoon walking in open country along the banks of the Severn. Elgar not only outwalked us all, but completely out-matched us in matters of local history and topography. That evening, as proof of his energy, he conducted a Festival performance of his *Second Symphony*. An amazing, lovable man.[10]

The Gloucester audience failed to understand the new works:

the two compositions of Mr Arthur Bliss and Mr Eugene Goossens contained such terribly harsh progressions and positively ugly idioms of the ultra modern school, that opinions were freely expressed about the propriety of admitting such music into the programme for the Cathedral, where at any rate we may hope and expect to be edified by music suitable to the solemn and mysterious atmosphere of religious exaltation.

The *Colour Symphony* ... and ... *Silence* are obviously 'experiments' for secular concert halls only.[11]

On the other hand, Herbert Thompson, writing in the *Musical Times*, 'was not troubled by any sense of incongruity, for the music is not frivolous or distinctively secular in character. What I did feel was its intense vitality.'[12]

Bliss had to wait nearly forty years before his *Colour Symphony* was given a worthy performance at Three Choirs – again with the LSO and again under his own baton – at Hereford in 1955. Eugene Goossens's *Silence*, a work deserving of revival, never received a second chance. Herbert Howells's piece, *Sine nomine*, a 'fantasy' for wordless soprano and tenor soloists, wordless chorus, large orchestra and organ, received its second performance at the 1992 Gloucester Festival. In 1922 it was ridiculously placed – as a precursor to *Elijah*.

At luncheon immediately following *A Colour Symphony*, Howells, who always considered *Sine nomine* to be one of his best works, received a two-edged compliment from the trumpeter J. J. Solomon: 'Well, young man, after the Symphony this morning, even *Sine Nomine* seems tolerable.'[13]

The 1922 Festival was remembered locally less for the music performed than for the unveiling of a memorial tablet to Sir Hubert Parry during the afternoon of Wednesday 6 September, by Viscount Gladstone, a friend of Parry's from Eton days:

The ceremony was simple and appropriate. A procession was formed of musicians in their doctors' robes, who, with the Bishop and Dean, proceeded to where the tablet is placed on the west wall of the south aisle. Lord Gladstone, Sir Edward Elgar, Sir Charles Stanford, Sir Hugh Allen, Sir Henry Hadow, Professor Granville Bantock, and Dr Brewer took part in the procession. The tablet was formally presented to the Cathedral and unveiled. The Bishop read a couple of prayers, and then Lord Gladstone,

[10] Eugene Goossens, *Overture and Beginners* (Methuen, 1951), pp. 193–4.

[11] *Annals* 1931, p. 86.

[12] *MT* 1922, p. 706.

[13] Herbert Howells, 'Memories from the Twentieth Century', in Barry Still (ed.), *Two Hundred and Fifty Years of the Three Choirs Festival – A Commemoration in Words and Pictures* (Three Choirs Festival Association, 1977).

returning to the conductor's desk, spoke to the congregation of what Parry had been in the musical life of his time and of his character as a man.[14]

The ceremony ended with a moving performance of *Blest Bair of Sirens* – Sir Hugh Allen refusing to conduct until every choralist's copy was thrown to the ground.

The memorial tablet bears an inscription by the then Poet Laureate, Robert Bridges:

HUBERT PARRY
Musician
1848–1918

From boyhood's eager play called by the English Muse
Her fine scholar to be then her Masters' compeer
A spirit elect whom no unworthy Thought might wrong
Nor any Fear touch thee joyously o'er life's waves
Navigating thy Soul unto her holy Haven
Long these familiar Walls shall re-echo thy song
And this Stone remember thy bounteous gaiety
Thy honour and thy grace and the love of thy friends

It is surrounded by a decorative border into which are set the coats of arms of the thirteen institutions with which Parry was connected. Charles Lee Williams was as baffled by Bridges's words as he had been by *A Colour Symphony*, describing them as 'ten lines … from the Poet Laureate … which no one can understand or punctuate!'[15] And Robert Bridges excused himself from attending the ceremony, saying in a letter to Brewer: 'I am better away, because the tablet in the Cathedral is not what I wished it to be, and my disappointment and dissatisfaction, which I should not well disguise, would be out of place.'[16]

The 1922 Festival included one new Elgar work – the only one to receive a first performance at Gloucester – the transcription for orchestra of Bach's *Fantasia and Fugue* in C minor (BWV 537). In the previous year Elgar had said, 'Now that my poor wife has gone I can't be original, and so I depend on people like Johann Sebastian for a source of inspiration.'[17] At Worcester in 1923 there was the transcription of Handel's overture in D minor (from Chandos Anthem No. 2) and orchestrations of anthems by S. S. Wesley and Battishill. Among twenty-one British composers represented there were first performances of Alexander Brent Smith's *In Glorious Freedom* and, most importantly, a choral work by Arnold Bax, *To the Name above every Name*, a setting of a poem by the seventeenth-century writer Richard Crashaw. And an exciting young soprano made her Festival debut: Elsie Suddaby, 'who sang on five different occasions, and in all kinds of music, giving striking proof of her versatility and musical intelligence'.[18]

---

[14] *The Times*, 7 September 1922.

[15] C. Lee Williams's scrapbook. Gloucestershire Archives.

[16] Herbert Brewer, *Memories of Choirs and Cloisters* (Bodley Head, 1931).

[17] Goossens, *Overture and Beginners*, p. 298.

[18] *MT* 1923, p. 717.

63 Worcester Cathedral

64 Hereford, 1900: G. R. Sinclair conducting a rehearsal. C. V. Stanford is seated at right of rostrum (with hat on lap).

65 *(above left)* Percy Hull
66 *(above)* Emma Albani, 1902
67 *(above right)* Marie Brema

68 *(left)* Sir Charles Santley
69 *(right)* Edward Lloyd

70 Worcester, 1902: concert in the Public Hall

71 Worcester, 1902

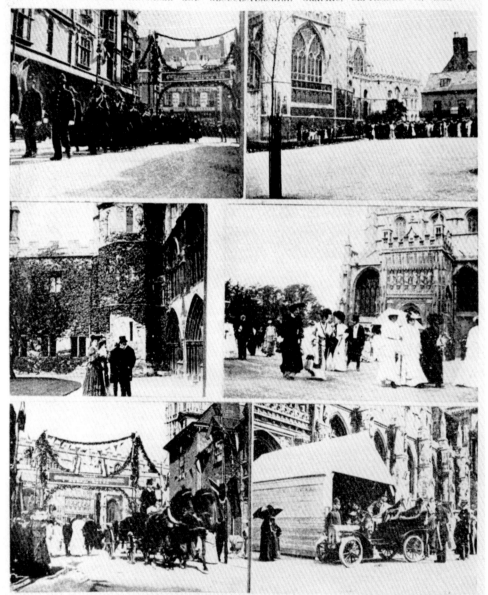

Photos by Miss Wheeler, Churcham, near Gloucester.

GLOUCESTER MUSICAL FESTIVAL.

Corporation Procession to Opening Service on Sunday Afternoon.

Very Rev. Dean Spence-Jones, Mrs. Spence-Jones, and Sir John Dorington in Deanery Gardens after the "Elijah."

Going to Opening Service.

Entering South Transept Door on Sunday.

Leaving after Morning Recital on Tuesday.

Mr. J. Dearman Birchall arrives on Motor-Car on Tuesday.

Printed and Published as a Gratis Supplement by the Cheltenham Newspaper Company.

72 Gloucester, 1904 (page from *Cheltenham and Gloucestershire Graphic*)

73 Gloucester, 1901: Herbert Brewer conducts a rehearsal in the cathedral. C. H. Lloyd is seated at the left of the rostrum.

74 Hereford, 1906: G. R. Sinclair conducts a rehearsal in the Shire Hall. His dog, Dan, is lying by his side on the rostrum, and Ivor Atkins is seated at the piano.

75 Hereford street decorations, 1906

76 Gloucester, 1907: Festival breakfast at the New Inn.   *Left to right: (front row)* – Lawrence, – F. Phillips, – Harman, – E. Rowley Lewis, R. H. Hillyard, J. Collins, – Fletcher, – Dickinson, – Lane and – Bubb; *(second row)* Precentor Fleming, G. R. Sinclair, Herbert Brewer, Sir Edward Elgar, Canon St John, Dean Spence-Jones, Archdeacon Hayward, C. H. Lloyd, Charles Lee Williams, Revd G. Ryley and the Revd A. Porter; *(third row)* – Dyson, George Smith, G. Banks, – Harden, – Proctor, Nigel Haines, P. Barrett-Cooke (Secretary of the Gloucester Festival), H. W. Young, G. Lewis, Howard Gray, W. Batey and – Tyrell; *(back row)* – Somerton, Percy Hull, – Carden, – Davis, Burton Barnes, Hatherley Bubb, H. N. Pitt, C. Rowles, Ivor Gurney, A. Castings and – Miller

GLOUCESTER MUSICAL FESTIVAL, SEPT. 8-13, 1907.

1. Mr. Ivor Atkins (on left) and Mr. P. Barrett Cooke (secretary to the stewards).
2. Group including Sir Hubert Parry (on left), Mrs. F. W. Waller, the City Member, and Miss Marie Brema (on right).
3. Mr. Lee Williams (on right), with Mr. Brewer, of Cardiff.
4. Mr. Ivor Atkins (on left), Sir Edward Elgar, Mr. W. H. Reed, and Mr. John Coates.
5. The Very Rev. Dean Spence-Jones.
6. Mr. Granville Bantock (on left), Dr. A. H. Brewer, and Dr. Harford Lloyd.
7. Mr. Gervase Elwes.

77 Gloucester, 1907 (page from *Cheltenham Chronicle and Gloucestershire Graphic*)

78 A Festival reception (probably 1907) given at Highnam Court by Sir Hubert Parry (seated at centre of front row, holding hat and cane)

79 Hereford, 1909: Sir Edward Elgar

80 Hereford, 1912

81 Gloucester, 1913: C. H. Lloyd, Herbert Brewer, Sir Edward Elgar and *(seated)* Camille Saint-Saëns

82 Sir Edward Elgar with Mr M. P. Price, MP, at Tibberton Court during the Gloucester Three Choirs Festival of 1913

83 Hereford, 1921: Percy Hull, Herbert Brewer and Sir Ivor Atkins

84 Gloucester, 1922: following the Dedication of the Parry Memorial. *Left to right: (standing)* Herbert Brewer, Sir Hugh Allen, Granville Bantock, Sir Henry Hadow; *(seated)* Sir Edward Elgar, Bishop Gibson, Lord Gladstone, Dean Gee and Sir Charles Villiers Stanford

85 Gloucester, 1922: Sir Edward Elgar and Herbert Brewer

86 Gloucester, 1922: Arthur Bliss, Herbert Brewer, W. H. Reed, Sir Edward Elgar and Eugene Goossens (the name of the lady is not known)

87 Worcester, 1923: Dorothy Silk, Agnes Nicholls and Elsie Suddaby

88 Harry Plunkett Greene

89 The Gramophone Company Ltd van parked outside Hereford Cathedral, 1927

90 Gustav Holst

THE THREE CHOIRS FESTIVAL AT GLOUCESTER CATHEDRAL.

Musical Celebrities of the Festival.

8.—Sir Ivor Atkins, the talented composer and organist of Worcester Cathedral, and Mr. Brent Smith.
9.—Miss Dorothy Silk, who sang the soprano parts in the " Elijah " performance.
10.—Mr. Herbert Heyner and Mr. Norman Allin, both of whom took principal parts.

11.—Mrs. Hathaway, Dr. Hathaway, and Dr. Lyon.
12.—Miss Margaret Balfour, the principal contralto in the " Elijah " and other performances.

13.—Mr. Horace Stevens, who has made a great name by his fine bass singing in many principal parts.

" Cheltenham Chronicle " Photos. Copies 1s. each, postage 2d. extra.

91 Gloucester, 1925 (page from *Cheltenham Chronicle and Gloucestershire Graphic*)

92 Hereford, 1930: Sir Ivor Atkins, Percy Hull, Herbert Sumsion and *(seated)* Sir Edward Elgar

94 Hereford, 1933: *Left to right: (standing)* Alexander Brent Smith, Sir George Dyson and Ralph Vaughan Williams; *(seated)* Herbert Sumsion, Percy Hull and Sir Ivor Atkins

96 Hereford, 1933: Percy Hull and Sir Edward Elgar

93 Gloucester, 1931: Dorothy Silk, Alice Sumsion, George Bernard Shaw and Herbert Sumsion

95 Hereford, 1933: George Bernard Shaw, Sir Edward Elgar and Herbert Sumsion

97 Hereford, 1933: Frank Titterton and his chauffeur

THREE CHOIRS FESTIVAL AT WORCESTER

The 215th meeting of the Three Choirs of Gloucester, Worcester and Hereford began on Sunday afternoon in Worcester Cathedral, and was attended by the Mayor and Corporation of that city.

1.—Mr. George Bernard Shaw, who attended the Festival.
2.—Canon Hereford (Capetown), Rev. G. V. Blois, with Miss Blois, from Hanbury Rectory.
3.—Mr. Francis Brett Young, the author, and his wife.

4.—The memorial window to the late Sir Edward Elgar, which was unveiled by Lord Cobham.
5.—Dr. Robertson and Dr. A. W. Davies (Dean of Worcester).

6.—A scene outside the Cathedral on Tuesday.
7.—Mr. A. K. Nicholson (designer of memorial window), Mr. John Stallard (Mayor of Worcester) and Dr. Perowne (Bishop of Worcester) and Lord Cobham.

98 Worcester, 1935 (page from *Cheltenham Chronicle and Gloucestershire Graphic*)

99 Gloucester, 1937: Zoltán Kodály rehearsing with Mary Jarred and Keith Falkner

100 Worcester 1938: Vera Wood, Ralph Vaughan Williams, Alice Sumsion and Herbert Sumsion

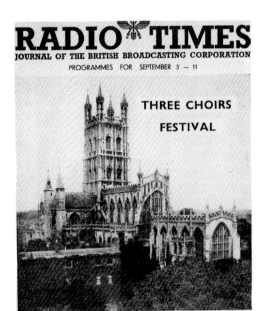

101 *Radio Times*, 5–11 September, 1937

102 Hereford, 1946: E. J. Moeran, Peers Coetmore, Herbert Sumsion, Jelly d'Aranyi, Alice Sumsion, Joy and Gerald Finzi

103 Gloucester, 1950: David Willcocks, Herbert Sumsion, Ralph Vaughan Williams, Gerald Finzi and Meredith Davies

104 Worcester, 1954. *(top left, clockwise)*: Ralph and Ursula Vaughan Williams; Herbert Howells; Gladys Ripley; Gordon Clinton; William Herbert; *(bottom left)* Norman Walker *(left)*, Wilfred Brown *(second right)* and Roderick Jones *(right)*; Edmund Rubbra *(left)* and Julius Harrison *(right)*

105 Hereford, 1958: Benjamin Britten and Peter Pears with the Ross High School Girls' Choir, following a rehearsal of *St Nicolas*

106 Hereford, 1958: Melville Cook conducting the Verdi *Requiem*

107 Worcester, 1960: *left to right:* Hugh McGuire (Leader of the LSO), Douglas Guest, Sir Arthur Bliss, Melville Cook and Herbert Sumsion

108 Hereford, 1964: Gerald English and John Shirley-Quirk rehearsing Britten's *Cantata Misericordium*

109 Gloucester, 1968: Festival soloists
(left to right):
(top) Rae Woodland, Barbara Robotham and Roger Stalman;
(centre) Norma Procter, John Mitchinson and Raimund Herincx;
(bottom) Elizabeth Harwood and Kenneth Bowen

110 Gloucester, 1968: garden party in the Cloister Garth

111 Worcester, 1969: composers *(left to right)* Luigi Dallapiccola, Jonathan Harvey, Elizabeth Maconchy and Peter Dickinson visiting Worcester Racecourse during the 1969 Festival

112 The Prime Minister, Rt. Hon. Edward Heath, and John Sanders – Gloucester Cathedral organ, 26 August, 1971

113 Gloucester, 1971: Sir Arthur Bliss and Mrs Eleanor Budge, Chairman of the Ladies Committee, with a presentation print of Gloucester Cathedral

114 Gloucester, 1974: *(left to right)*: Christopher Robinson, John Sanders and Richard Lloyd

115 Group of photographs: Gloucester, 1974: *(top)* John Sanders and the Gloucester Festival Chorus; *(centre)* Christopher Robinson and the Worcester Festival Chorus; *(above)* Richard Lloyd and the Hereford Festival Chorus

116 Her Majesty Queen Elizabeth the Queen Mother, John Sanders, Roy Massey and Donald Hunt – Malcolm Williamson's *Mass of Christ the King*, Westminster Cathedral, 3 November 1978

117 Worcester, 1978: Sir Charles Groves and Donald Hunt

118 Worcester, 1981: the three head choristers *(left to right)* John Padley, Hereford; Jonathan Garstang, Gloucester; and Rupert Harvey, Worcester

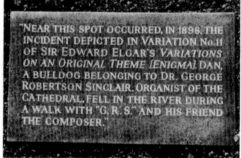

119 Hereford, 1991: Group of photographs: *(left, top to bottom)* Roy Massey acknowledging the Festival Chorus; Festival Chorus; Vernon Handley rehearses with Steven Isserlis and RLPO – Howard Blake's Diversions for Cello and Orchestra; *(top right)* Roy Massey, Wulstan Atkins and Winston, following the unveiling of the memorial to Dan and *Enigma* Variation XI

120 Gloucester, 1992: Chairman of the Gloucester Festival Fringe, Peter Wallace *(fourth from left)*, and the Mayor of Gloucester, Councillor Ben Richards *(eighth from left)*, receiving gifts from two representatives of Gloucester's Chinese Community. Also present *(left to right)*: Chairman of the Gloucester Festival, Dr H.J. Hoyland; Mrs Ann Richards; Mrs Anne Boden (Ladies Committee); Mrs Mandy Garstang (Ladies Committee); Councillor Tony Ayland; Mrs Margaret Macnair (Chairman of the Ladies Committee; Dr John Sanders (Festival Artistic Director); and Jonathan Boden (Fringe Co-ordinator)

121 Gloucester, 1998: Adrian Lucas and David Briggs

122 David Briggs at St Sulpice, Paris

123 Richard Hickox (1948–2008)

The great innovation of the 1923(w) Festival proved to be one of its most memorable features. Instead of ending with *Messiah* on Friday, an additional chamber concert, as at Hereford, was given on Friday evening in the College Hall by thirty-five players from the LSO. Symphonies by Haydn and Mozart, Wagner's *Siegfried Idyll*, the Scherzo from Mendelssohn's incidental music to *A Midsummer Night's Dream*, Debussy's *Danse sacrée et danse profane*, and songs by Megan Foster and Norman Allin made for a concert enjoyable from beginning to end. In 1925, Gloucester followed Worcester's lead, so that all three Festivals ended with a Friday evening secular concert.

After Sinclair introduced it in 1897, the 'Grail' scene from *Parsifal* was included in every Hereford Festival programme, except 1927, until 1930. Atkins included it at Worcester in 1923 with, as at Hereford, a small semi-chorus of choirboys hidden away in the central tower. Part of the tradition, and an object of pride, was the ability of the young singers to keep the pitch perfectly so that the entry of the orchestra which followed made a superb effect.

When, in 1926, Atkins decided to include the Prelude to *Parsifal* in his Festival programme, Dr Lacey, one of the Worcester Cathedral canons, wrote to the *Worcester Daily Times* protesting that Wagner was a 'sensualist'. Elgar replied angrily:

> The Canon quotes 'His emotions and spiritual experiences were those of the ordinary sensual man.' But 'Aren't we all?' If the Canon really believes that such emotions in early life debar a man from taking part in the services of the church in riper years he should at once resign his canonry and any other spiritual offices he is paid to hold.[19]

The Canon replied:

> Sir Edward Elgar misses the point. The writers whom I quoted were not criticising Wagner's life or character, but his art, in which they found sensuality of pietism matching the sensuality of his erotics. It was this that attracted my attention, for in my work as a priest I have had acquaintance with both kinds of sensuality, and I know what kind is the more dangerous.[20]

Canon Lacey seems to have missed the point made so well by Samuel Langford following the 1920(w) Festival, when comparing Walford Davies's *Fantasy* on Dante's *Divine Comedy* unfavourably with Elgar's *Gerontius*:

> Where ideas transcend, the power of the composer must transcend equally or the result is doubtful. Perhaps after all it is the strongly sensuous imagination, as in the example of Wagner, that can most safely attempt these heavenly flights, for there music is in little danger of losing its hold on our human feelings.[21]

---

[19] *Worcester Daily Times*, 18 March 1926.
[20] Ibid.
[21] *MT* 1920, p. 667.

Fᴏʀ the opening of the British Empire Exhibition at Wembley on St George's Day 1924, Elgar had composed the *Empire March* but, because the massed bands had been unable to rehearse the new piece separately, he was asked to conduct the old *Imperial March* instead, along with *Land of Hope and Glory*, Parry's *Jerusalem* and the National Anthem. The *Empire March* was played later in the year at the Exhibition Pageant and repeated at the 1924 Hereford Festival: 'a brilliant work, more distinguished in its very effective development than in its themes'.[22] Sir Charles Villiers Stanford, Sir Frederick Bridge and Sir Walter Parratt, the Master of the King's Music, all died in 1924. As a tribute to their memory, Beethoven's three *Equali* for four trombones preceded *Elijah*. It was the new Master of the King's Music, Sir Edward Elgar, whose works again dominated the Festival, but all was far from well when Elgar took up the baton to conduct *The Kingdom*. Sir Adrian Boult was present:

> It was at once apparent that the choir were perhaps resting too much on last year's laurels … Bad intonation was evident near the start, and I felt that Sir Edward was losing interest, as he began to drive the performance, getting faster and faster as if the one thing he wanted was to get out of the Cathedral and forget about music. We endured this for nearly an hour when we came to the wonderful scena 'The sun goeth down', which was written for that great soprano, Agnes Nicholls. She had, if I remember rightly, practically retired at that time, but returned at short notice to take over the part which she had made her own many years before. I shall never forget the intense concentration with which she began that gentle opening phrase, and the way the orchestra seemed instantly to spring to life and, immediately after, the disgruntled composer's interest quickened, and from that moment the performance returned to the extraordinary beauty of the year before.[23]

There were no problems in *Gerontius* – Astra Desmond, John Coates and Robert Radford joined a chorus determined to give of its best.

A short postscript to the 1924 Festival appeared in the *Musical Times*:

> No festival is without its anxieties, especially to the conductor, and even Dr. Hull's good humour must have been singularly tried at times by the requests launched at him from all quarters. The most embarrassing was, I imagine, a letter which reached him addressed to 'Dr John Bull, First Gresham Professor of Music, c/o Three Choirs Festival, Hereford Cathedral, Hereford.' It had also the superscription, 'Kindly forward', which Dr. Hull was unable to comply with, having unfortunately mislaid the address. The letter emanated from a press-cutting agency, which offered to supply Dr. Bull with references to himself and his compositions, and advised him that it had 'a large theatrical and musical department, under competent [*sic*] supervision.'[24]

---

[22] *MT* 1924, p. 908.

[23] Adrian Boult, 'Composer as Conductor', in H. A. Chambers (ed.), *Edward Elgar: Centenary Sketches* (Novello, 1957), pp. 9–10.

[24] *MT* 1924, p. 910.

To mark the tercentenary of the birth of Orlando Gibbons, Brewer decided to include an anthem by him in all but one of the 1925(G) Festival programmes. It was now Brewer's turn to receive letters, this time addressed to Orlando Gibbons, and again with a request that they should be forwarded![25]

Brewer had much else on his mind in 1925. Troubled for some time by the angina which forced him, when ascending to the organ loft, to climb slowly, one step at a time, and which prevented him from joining the choir at the top of the cathedral tower on Rogation Days, he was immersed in planning a Festival which was to include more new works than ever before.[26]

Sibelius had accepted an invitation to write a symphony for the Festival, but was unable to complete it in time or to visit Gloucester, so the *Variations on the St Antoni Chorale* by Brahms were substituted, along with Sibelius's *Finlandia*. Thirty-four British composers, twenty-five of them living, were represented in the programmes and services. Fifteen of them conducted their own works. There were ten 'novelties', the most important among which were Sir Walford Davies's choral suite *Men and Angels*; Basil Harwood's motet for chorus and orchestra, *Love Incarnate*; and two motets for unaccompanied chorus, *Glory and Honour and Laud* by Charles Wood (who, in 1924, had succeeded Stanford as Professor of Music at Cambridge and who died in 1926), and *The Evening Watch* by Gustav Holst. New orchestral works included Thomas Dunhill's *Three Short Pieces* for strings and organ, and *Paradise Rondel* by Herbert Howells. The poet F. W. Harvey, a fellow Gloucestershire man and a close friend of Brewer's former pupils Herbert Howells and Ivor Gurney, provided words for four old Irish airs under the collective title of *A Sprig of Shamrock*, which Brewer arranged for contralto or baritone voice with string quartet or piano accompaniment, and which were performed by Flora Woodman and four players from the LSO. Described by Charles Lee Williams as 'a tasty feast of double-Gloucester', this cycle – and pieces such as Brewer's most popular song, *The Fairy Pipers* – show the lightness of touch and delight in melody which, had his career taken a different direction, would have equipped Brewer for success as a composer of light opera.

One of the works chosen by Brewer for the 1925 Festival, Parry's *Job*, had been performed earlier in the year at the Royal College of Music. The Director of the college, Sir Hugh Allen, had selected a young bass-baritone, Keith Falkner, to sing the title role that Harry Plunket Greene had created at Gloucester in 1892. Dr Emily Daymond, who had been Parry's amanuensis, asked Plunket Greene to help Falkner. However, 'Help is hardly the word for it. He opened up a whole new world of declamation, colour and interpretation.'[27]

Though Falkner didn't know it, Sir Hugh had asked Brewer to come to the college to hear the performance. The next day Sir Hugh told Falkner that Dr Brewer had engaged him for the performance at the Gloucester Festival:

[25] Brewer, *Memories*.

[26] For these details of Brewer's infirmities I am grateful to Dr Arthur Pritchard (private communication).

[27] Memories of Sir Keith Falkner (private communication).

It was a great moment in my life … My father and mother were there and of course Dr Emily Daymond who gave me a conducted tour of Highnam. We stayed at 'The Dog' at Over, just outside Gloucester. The following day, in the bar, the landlord read out the critique in the Gloucester paper. In broad dialect he shouted, "Ee called thee a tenor. 'Ee don't know the difference 'tween a tenor an' a bass. 'Ee don't know the difference 'tween a sow 'na hog!'[28]

In his *Musical Times* review of the Festival, Herbert Thompson said that 'Special mention should be made of Mr Keith Falkner, a young baritone who essayed the exacting part of Job, and, in spite of his youthful personality and voice, sang it with remarkable intelligence.'[29]

Following World War I, one of Herbert Brewer's sons, Charles, had become a member of the BBC production staff; through his influence the first-ever radio transmissions from the Three Choirs Festival were made in 1925. Both of the secular concerts were broadcast, and during the interval of the first of these Sir Hugh Allen, unveiling a memorial to Sir Hubert Parry in the Shire Hall, said that 'for the first time a Three Choirs Concert was accessible in a way which Sir Hubert could not foresee, since thousands of people all over the British Isles and beyond were listening to it by wireless, via London'.[30] Frederick Delius, 329 miles away in Grez-sur-Loing, listening to a neighbour's wireless set, heard his *On Hearing the First Cuckoo in Spring* broadcast live from Gloucester; and loudspeakers were positioned in various parts of Gloucester itself, proving a great attraction to the crowds of people who gathered around them to listen to the concerts.

Other 'firsts' at the 1925(G) Festival included the performance of part of a Vaughan Williams symphony under the composer's baton: the last movement of the *Sea Symphony*, and the first appearance in the cathedral of Dame Ethel Smyth, who directed the *Kyrie* and *Gloria* from her Mass in D. She also won enthusiastic applause at the first secular concert with her overture *The Wreckers*.

Members of the chorus present at a rehearsal of Dame Ethel Smyth's Mass in D in the chapter house of Gloucester Cathedral were treated to an amusing sample of her eccentricity. The sun, shining through a window directly opposite to her with intense brilliance, dazzled Dame Ethel, who was unable to see the choir. 'Could one of the ladies please lend me a hat?' she asked. A hat was produced and Dame Ethel put it on, pulling the brim down over her eyes and, because her long hair was piled up into a bun, pulling the hat out of shape at the same time. Gradually, as she conducted, the hat was pulled further and further down, to hilarious effect. Then the wide belt which supported the skirt of her suit began to ride up. Brewer was sitting close by. 'Dr Brewer', called out Dame Ethel, continuing to conduct, 'could you please attend to my belt?' So there was Brewer, usually the epitome of dignity, embarrassedly tugging at Dame Ethel Smyth's waist while the choristers were hardly able to sing through their mirth.[31]

[28] Ibid.

[29] *MT* 1925, p. 924.

[30] *Annals* 1931, p. 92.

[31] Memories of Dr Melville Cook (private communication).

The 1925(G) Festival marked the climax of Brewer's career and new peaks in both attendance (19,973) and receipts. The number of Stewards was a record 434 and profits from all sources amounted to £3,700, which, because Brewer had been able to persuade the tax authorities to exempt Three Choirs from the payment of entertainments tax, was handed in its entirety to the charity.

Messiah drew the largest audience of the week: 3,410 tickets were sold. As Brewer conducted the 'Amen' chorus unrestrained tears rolled down his cheeks.[32] Perhaps he had been in pain, and certainly Lady Brewer recorded that

> after the 1925 Festival there were signs of failing health and walking became more and more of an effort. The Festival had undoubtedly been too great a strain, but his enthusiasm for work did not lessen and, in 1926, on the resignation of George Riseley from the conductorship of the Bristol Choral Society, he was invited to undertake and accepted the duties of that office.[33]

On New Year's Day, 1926, Brewer's name appeared in the Honours List, and on 5 February the king conferred the honour of knighthood upon him. Brewer was present at the 1927 Hereford Festival, taking his place in the organ loft for the historic recordings made during the week by The Gramophone Company.

Negotiations to record at the Three Choirs Festival had begun early in 1927. The Dean and Chapter had been somewhat doubtful about granting approval but, thanks to the intercession of Elgar and the enthusiasm of Percy Hull, finally agreed. The mobile recording van arrived in Hereford before the Opening Service on Sunday 4 September and took up its position at the west end of the cathedral. The first item to be recorded was the most important of all: a fanfare which Elgar had written especially for this Festival:

> At previous Three Choirs Festivals it had been the custom for the orchestra to play the National Anthem as the Mayor of the City and the Civic Party entered the Cathedral. During preparations for the 1927 Festival it had been pointed out that the National Anthem should properly be sounded at the appearance of the Sovereign's representative – in this case the Lord Lieutenant of the Shire, who made his entrance after the Civic Party. So Dr. Hull, as an old friend of Elgar's, had asked if he would compose a Fanfare to accompany the entry of the Civic Party. This Elgar had done, designing his music to lead up to the National Anthem. The performance at the Opening Service would therefore be an Elgar world premiere under the composer's direction.[34]

In spite of considerable difficulties of timing and balance, the recording engineers produced a total of twenty-five sides from the Festival performances. Many of these had to be destroyed, but among the items issued are memorable performances by Margaret Balfour, Tudor Davies and Horace Stevens, the

---

[32] Ibid.

[33] Brewer, *Memories.*

[34] Jerrold Northrop Moore, *Elgar on Record* (OUP, 1974), p. 72.

Festival Chorus, LSO, and Sir Herbert Brewer (organ), conducted by Elgar in excerpts from *Gerontius*.

Audience noise had been a particular problem in this essentially experimental recording project. One of the Gramophone Company men at Hereford was Bernard Wratten. In a letter to the editor of *The Gramophone* (2 October 1972) he recalled:

> One evening, after the day's music making was done, Dr. Hull invited us round to his house, where we found an impressive assortment of English composers, singers and musicians. Whilst we were there he told us that the wife of a local baronet, a lady with a considerable reputation for silliness, had been so taken with the hat of another member of the audience sitting just across the aisle during a rehearsal that she leant over to ask, under cover of combined choir and orchestra, where the hat had been bought. She had to raise her voice and at that moment the music stopped. She was clearly heard all over the Cathedral.
>
> The tale acquired its widely circulated form from our Public Relations Officer. It had nothing whatsoever to do with our recording but he felt there was a good news-story in it, and after decorating it he sent it out to the newspapers, most of which published it.[35]

In his book *Music on Record*, Fred Gaisberg, The Gramophone Company's pioneering chief recording engineer, recalled another intrusion by fashion: 'at the Three Choir performance of *Gerontius*, during a sudden silent pause after a *forte* climax, a lady's voice talking about "a lovely camisole for 11s 6d" was clearly exposed when the record was played back, and so ruined a fine set.'[36]

The Gramophone Company attempted to negotiate with the Dean and Chapter of Gloucester Cathedral to carry out recordings at the 1928 Festival but, in spite of pleading by Elgar, this was refused. The opportunity to establish a regular pattern of rare and valuable recordings was thus stopped.

Brewer's plans for the 1928(G) Festival were as ambitious as ever and intended to please all tastes, including hoped-for new works from Ravel, Honegger, Bantock, Holst and Ireland. He invited Zoltán Kodály to conduct his *Psalmus Hungaricus*; Dame Ethel Smyth, a complete performance of her Mass in D; Elgar, *The Dream of Gerontius* and *The Kingdom*; and Vaughan Williams, *The Lark Ascending*. Among the works which Brewer was to conduct himself was Verdi's Requiem, the work 'of all others [which] would have been his choice for his own requiem. He had been heard to say that if he was told to choose two works to hear before he died he would choose Verdi's Requiem and *The Dream of Gerontius*.'[37]

Sir Herbert Brewer suffered a heart attack and died at his house in Miller's Green, Gloucester, on 1 March 1928.

It is a strange coincidence that on the first Thursday in March, 1897, Herbert Brewer began his duties as organist in Gloucester Cathedral by

[35] Ibid., pp. 74–5.
[36] F. W. Gaisberg, *Music on Record* (R. Hale, 1948), p. 171.
[37] Brewer, *Memories*.

playing the organ at a Free Recital, and it was on the first Thursday in March, 1928, thirty-one years later, whilst a Concert of the Gloucestershire Orchestral Society was in progress, that he lay dying. Almost his last words were, 'I feel as if I were conducting the symphony.' Mozart's Symphony [No. 39] in E flat was then actually in progress.[38]

On 30 August 1928, the *Daily Mail* reported:

One of the chief events of the English musical year – the Three Choirs Festival at Gloucester next week – will be conducted by a virtually unknown musician, Mr Herbert W. Sumsion.

Sir Herbert Brewer's sudden death in the spring left vacant the conductorship of the festival and the organistship of the cathedral post which he had held for more than 30 years.

Names of many well known musicians, including a City organist who is of the first eminence as a conductor and choir-trainer, were canvassed; but the Gloucester Cathedral authorities did the unexpected thing in appointing a young man who has yet to win his spurs ...

He has a very heavy week before him ... Sir Herbert Brewer made a point of introducing into the Gloucester programme more unconventional music than is heard at Worcester and Hereford.

Thus the staid Three Choirs audience is on Thursday afternoon to have the shock of a performance of Arthur Honegger's *King David*. This is a particularly taxing work for a young conductor to take charge of at the last moment; but Honegger cannot come, and so it falls to Mr Sumsion.

Herbert Whitton Sumsion was born in Gloucester on 19 January 1899, became a probationer in the cathedral choir in 1908 and a chorister two years later. From 1914 to 1917 he was an articled pupil to Brewer, becoming an ARCO in 1915 at the age of seventeen and an FRCO (Turpin Prize) in the following year. In 1917 he was commissioned in the Queen's Westminster Rifles and saw active service in the Flanders trenches. On his return to Gloucester in 1919 he was appointed Assistant Organist at the cathedral.

An excellent piano accompanist, Sumsion played for Elgar's Festival Chorus rehearsals, becoming an ardent admirer of his music. He learnt exactly what Elgar wanted and how it was achieved. He never forgot how, after a rehearsal of *Gerontius*, the composer came across to the piano to shake his hand and nod his thanks – from Elgar such gestures of appreciation were rare.

In 1922, Sumsion became Organist at Christ Church, Lancaster Gate, in London and in addition, in 1924, accepted the post of Director of Music at Bishop's Stortford College and became an assistant instructor at Morley College. He also found time in 1924 to take lessons in conducting from Adrian Boult at the Royal College of Music. Boult was so impressed that he told Sumsion there was little that he could teach him which he didn't already know. At the RCM Sumsion met R. O. Morris, the Professor of Counterpoint and Composition, and when, in 1926, Morris was appointed to a similar post at the Curtis Institute of Music, Philadelphia, USA, he invited Sumsion to join him as his assistant.

---

[38] Ibid.

Sumsion sailed to America with R. O. Morris and his wife, Emmeline, whose sister Adeline was married to Ralph Vaughan Williams. On the voyage they were befriended by Professor W. B. McDaniel and his wife, returning home following a year of teaching Classics at the American Academy in Rome. Walton McDaniel was Professor of Classics at the University of Pennsylvania, Philadelphia, and it was on a visit to the McDaniels' home that Sumsion met their niece, Alice Garlichs. Herbert Sumsion and Alice were married in Philadelphia on 7 June 1927. One year later, on 10 June 1928, they embarked for England.[39]

Although appointed Organist at Coventry Cathedral, Sumsion was released in order to return to Gloucester as Brewer's successor. He was plunged immediately into preparations for the 1928(G) Festival while Alice, seven months pregnant, struggled to set up home at 7 Miller's Green. Fortunately, following Brewer's death, Samuel Underwood, Organist of Stroud Parish Church and a first-class choir trainer, stepped into the gap and trained the Festival Chorus until Sumsion's return.

Shortly before his death, Sir Herbert Brewer had said to the Dean of Gloucester (Dr Henry Gee), 'If anything happens to me, I want Herbert Sumsion to take over from me.'[40] His choice was now vindicated. There were uneven performances of course, but there were triumphs too. No little credit was due to the Gloucester Assistant Organist, Arthur Pritchard, whose playing was a notable feature of the Festival. And an old friend came to Sumsion's aid: Adrian Boult, by then the conductor of the CBSO, had driven down to Gloucester before breakfast one morning and helped Sumsion with his scores – a kind and selfless act.

The new works from Ravel, Honegger, Ireland and Holst had not materialised, and perhaps as well under the circumstances. Sumsion gave an assured performance of Honegger's *King David*, a work described by Harvey Grace as suggesting 'the unnecessary discomfort of a progress over broken bottles',[41] though after the performance he declared that 'the Ayes clearly had it'. Kodály conducted an excellent performance of his *Psalmus Hungaricus*, and Dame Ethel Smyth caused a stir conducting her Mass in D.

Required by the dean to cover her head while conducting in the cathedral, Dame Ethel wore her doctoral cap and gown – but quickly found the cap to be an irritating encumbrance which she discarded with a jerk of the head – and legend variously has it that it landed either on Billy Reed's desk or Dean Gee's lap![42]

At the Opening Service, Sullivan's overture *In Memoriam* was played in memory of Sir Herbert Brewer, and the Thursday evening programme was also made a special memorial performance by the inclusion of Lee Williams's unaccompanied anthem *Thou wilt keep him in perfect peace*, sung in the distance by

---

[39] Memories of Mrs Alice Sumsion (private communication).

[40] Memories of Dr Arthur Pritchard (private communication).

[41] *MT* 1928, p. 898.

[42] Memories of Mrs Edith Sterry and Miss Patience Gobey (private communication).

the cathedral choir. This was followed by a motet written by Brewer early in 1928 but never heard by him, *God Within*, and finally by Verdi's Requiem.

Vaughan Williams conducted *The Lark Ascending* and, of course, there was Elgar – conducting *The Dream of Gerontius*, *The Kingdom*, and the Cello Concerto with Beatrice Harrison as soloist.

Soon after the Sumsions' arrival in Gloucester, Elgar called on them at Miller's Green. Daisy, the parlourmaid and for many years a servant to Lady Brewer, opened the door to him. 'Oh! I know your face so well', she said, 'but I can't put a name to it.' Elgar was shown in to Alice's sitting room where he presented a large bouquet of roses to Herbert Sumsion's shy young bride.[43]

Among the soloists who appeared at the 1928(G) Festival were many established favourites: Dorothy Silk, Elsie Suddaby, Margaret Balfour, Muriel Brunskill, Astra Desmond, Steuart Wilson and Robert Radford, but there were even more newcomers who, in turn, would become famous names. The sopranos Dora Labbette and Joan Elwes had made their Three Choirs debuts in 1927(H) and returned in 1928. The tenors Parry Jones, Frank Titterton and Walter Widdop, and the baritones Roy Henderson, Stuart Robertson and Harold Williams appeared at the Festival for the first time. Horace Stevens, the outstanding 'Elijah' of his generation, repeated the part of the Prophet as well as singing in *Gerontius*, infusing dramatic intensity into his interpretations and, word perfect, singing without a score.

The ordeal faced by Sumsion in 1928 prompted Harvey Grace to question the accepted Three Choirs custom and to make a suggestion which presaged present practice:

> the way in which the three Cathedral organists have risen to the occasion has long been a matter of admiring comment. But need the ordeal be so severe? Is it necessary to limit their opportunities of conducting a professional orchestra to one week and a few odd rehearsals in three years? Surely the strain would be less, and the conducting better than it is, if the work were shared annually. Each Cathedral organist would then have the advantage of regular yearly experience of conducting under Festival conditions. Even that is little enough, seeing how much complex and unfamiliar music the programmes now contain. But it would be just three times better than the present arrangement, under which a conductor puts in a week of hectic struggle, and then says goodbye to first-class orchestral experience for three years.[44]

But the time for change was not yet and, under the circumstances, Sumsion had coped remarkably well, causing Elgar to make his famous remark: 'What at the beginning of the week was an *assumption* has now become a certainty.' And Charles Lee Williams sent Sumsion a dozen bottles of champagne.

Elgar had considered writing a new work for the 1929 Worcester Festival, a setting of two poems by Shelley, *The Demon* and *Adonaïs*, but this was vetoed by

---

[43] Memories of Mrs Alice Sumsion (private communication).

[44] *MT* 1928, p. 898.

the dean (Dr Moore Ede) on the grounds that *Adonaïs* 'is frankly pagan'.[45] Sir
Ivor Atkins tried hard to persuade Elgar to make the Festival 'memorable by a
great work', but was only able to interest him in orchestrating Purcell's motet
Jehovah, quam multi sunt hostes mei.[46] This was given, along with a Byrd five-part
motet, *Laetentur coeli*, before *Elijah* on the Thursday morning; Steuart Wilson
and Horace Stevens were the soloists. Elgar also conducted *Gerontius*, *The
Kingdom*, *Introduction and Allegro* for strings, and his Symphony No. 2.

The outstanding event of the 1929 Worcester Festival was the first
performance at Three Choirs of Bach's *St John Passion* in the edition prepared
by Sir Ivor Atkins. Canon Lacey of Worcester Cathedral, who three years earlier
had crossed swords with Elgar over the issue of Wagner's sensuality, assisted
Atkins by providing a new translation of the verses. The performance proved to
be one of the best of the week. The soloists were Dorothy Silk, Muriel Brunskill,
Steuart Wilson, Roy Henderson, Archibald Winter, and the bass-baritone Keith
Falkner, who had created such a great impression in 1925(G). From 1929 until the
outbreak of World War II, in which he served with the Royal Air Force, Falkner
sang regularly at Three Choirs. He succeeded Sir Ernest Bullock as Director of
the Royal College of Music in 1960 and was knighted in 1967.

Another singer who became a much-loved personality at the Festivals and
far beyond, Isobel Baillie, made her first Three Choirs appearance in 1929(W).
Her instantly recognisable voice, described by Richard Capell in *Grove*, had
'treble-like purity, "angelic" was sometimes applied to it; not so much personal
as brightly and serenely spiritual, made by her soaring and equable tones'. She
sang at every Three Choirs Festival from 1929(W) to 1955(H) with the exception of
1933. Isobel Baillie was made a DBE in 1978 and returned to Three Choirs in the
following year to give an autobiographical talk at the Hereford Festival.

It was in 1929(W) also that Myra Hess made the first of several appearances
at Three Choirs, playing Beethoven's Piano Concerto No. 4 in the cathedral. In
1941 she too received the DBE for her work in organising the National Gallery
wartime concerts.

New works presented in 1929 included Alexander Brent Smith's Choral
Concerto and Sir Walford Davies's *Christ in the Universe*, a setting of a mystical
poem by Alice Meynell, for soprano (Dorothy Silk), tenor (Steuart Wilson) and
orchestra, in which there is a prominent part for piano, on this occasion played
by the composer himself. There was also an *Idyll* for small orchestra and violin
obbligato, *At Valley Green*, by Herbert Sumsion – a piece which showed him to
have 'a feeling for gracious melody'.[47]

For Herbert and Alice Sumsion this was the first Three Choirs at which they
could enjoy to the full those house parties which were such a delightful feature
of the pre-war Festival. Along with Percy Hull's wife, Molly, Alice Sumsion
rented a house in College Green, Worcester, for a week. Among their guests
were several musicians, including Vaughan Williams, who was at the Festival
to conduct his *Sancta Civitas* and *The Wasps*. Billy Reed brought Elgar to join

[45] Wulstan Atkins, *The Elgar–Atkins Friendship* (David & Charles, 1985), pp. 408–9.
[46] Ibid., p. 410.
[47] *MT* 1929, p. 895.

in the fun – such as the rare sight of Vaughan Williams trying desperately to play ping-pong and not once succeeding in hitting the ball! This accompanied by roars of laughter. And more laughter as Elgar reminisced about his younger days: stories such as the one about him and his brother meeting in a Worcester street an acquaintance who was the worse for drink, taking him home and putting him to bed, only to discover later that it was in the wrong house![48]

Sir Keith Falkner recollects with particular pleasure how, apart from the music, the Festivals of the 1930s were great social affairs:

> tea parties, daily luncheons, with Receptions given by the Mayor, clergy and laity. Of this last category, two hostesses were famous: Mrs Holland-Martin (Worcester, Overbury Court) and Mrs Gwyn Holford (Gloucester, Hartpury House).
>
> The latter, a delightful eccentric with strong convictions regarding her Anglo-Catholic religion, was a stickler for social behaviour. A large hat always topped her tall and graceful figure at both breakfast and luncheon. One night, at dinner, a guest seated on her right poured his sherry into his soup announcing, 'I always have sherry in my soup!' The retort came: 'This will be the last time you dine in my house' (The cook had prepared a delicious consomme).
>
> With others Heddle Nash and I were at lunch. Halfway down the table I heard Heddle exclaim, 'It's alright! Gerontius is mine! Elgar has told me I'm the one!' Mrs Gwyn Holford, black hat a-tremble, said 'Mr Nash what did I hear you say?' 'Oh', replied Heddle 'Elgar has told me I'm Gerontius.' 'Mr Nash you don't have the slightest idea what Gerontius is about!'
>
> Deathly silence followed, everyone wondering what was to happen next. Heddle, of course, rose to the occasion saying: 'What's wrong with it? Can I come and talk with you about it?'
>
> Later when we sang the work together I found he was the best *bel canto* Gerontius I ever heard of his time, following in the steps of Gervase Elwes, John Coates and Steuart Wilson. And certainly in 1936 at Hereford – with Percy Hull – it was the finest *Gerontius* performance I ever took part in.
>
> The hospitality at Overbury Court with Mrs Holland-Martin for Worcester was equally luxurious and generous. One year the other guests included Sir Hugh Allen, Sir Walford Davies, Elsie Suddaby, Mary Jarred, Joyce Grenfell and Steuart Wilson:
>
> The gardens and lawns were spacious, while tennis and croquet provided relaxation from the Festival atmosphere. One evening, after dinner, Sir Hugh produced a copy of the 'notorious unintentionally comic' oratorio *Ruth* by George Tolhurst (1864). The evening became hilarious as we stood round the piano: Allen and Walford playing four hands, the rest of us singing the various parts. At moments we became quite hysterical, breaking many times for laughter and repeats. Joyce Grenfell pleased us enormously with her resonant voice and sense of fun.[49]

---

[48] Memories of Mrs Alice Sumsion (private communication).

[49] Memories of Sir Keith Falkner (private communication).

Another whose hospitality at Three Choirs was celebrated among regular Festival-goers was Charles Lee Williams. At every Gloucester Festival he and his son kept 'open house at College Green, and the happy family feeling that pervaded the Festival was due very largely to his hospitality, and not least to his constant care, shown in a hundred little ways, for the comfort and happiness of visitors'.[50] In 1929(w) Lee Williams conducted his *alla capella* setting of the Lord's Prayer at the Opening Service. Herbert Thompson, writing in the *Musical Times* commented that:

> He had grown old in the service of the Three Choirs, from the time of his appointment to Gloucester in 1882, and one of the pleasantest incidents of the Festival was when Sir Ivor Atkins announced, at the concluding concert, in the College Hall, that the Archbishop of Canterbury had declared his intention of conferring upon Mr Williams the degree of Doctor of Music. It is an honour long delayed, but most appropriate. He has been styled the Grandfather of the Three Choirs, and one trusts he may live long enough to be hailed as their Great-grandfather.[51]

When Lee Williams died on 29 August 1935, in his eighty-fifth year, the music critic of *The Times* wrote, 'The Three Choirs Festival was the passion of Lee Williams's life.'[52]

THE surprise of the 1930(H) Festival was less a matter of what was performed than of what was not. For the first time since 1847, excluding the 'mock' Festival of 1875(w), *Elijah* was dropped from the programme, and its inclusion was no longer an inevitability. *Elijah* was omitted in 1934 and 1936, and was performed only once or twice in each succeeding decade.

Instead of *Elijah*, the opening work of the 1930(H) Festival was *The Apostles*, a performance vividly remembered by Sir Keith Falkner, who appeared with Elgar, together with Elsie Suddaby, Astra Desmond, Heddle Nash, Roy Henderson and Norman Allin:

> Elgar took a piano rehearsal in the Close. All went normally until the Judas solo of his betrayal.
> Judas begins his marvellous song of anguish in which, to quote Elgar, 'a proud sinner is swayed by all sorts of feelings' while he sings to music that ranks among the most movingly intense that Elgar ever wrote.
>   Norman was half-way through, singing magnificently. Elgar burst into tears. Leaning on the piano he said 'I can't go on'. The rehearsal stopped. I had never seen him in such an emotional state. Whenever I hear this great aria now, I'm reminded of that occasion.[53]

---

[50] *MT* 1928, p. 901.

[51] *MT* 1929, p. 895. It is interesting to note that the use of the College Hall for a secular concert in 1929 was a revival – the hall had ceased to be a regular Three Choirs venue after 1878.

[52] *The Times*, 3 September 1935.

[53] Memories of Sir Keith Falkner (private communication).

At the actual performance Elgar, who was suffering from sciatica, 'had to be helped to the conductor's rostrum, where he *sat* to conduct through the performance and then was helped down again'.[54] At the Opening Service on the previous Sunday, Percy Hull had to conduct the *Introduction and Allegro* in Elgar's place. But as the week went on Elgar's condition gradually improved, and on Thursday evening he conducted a beautiful and memorable performance of *Gerontius* with Steuart Wilson singing the name part.

Only three new works were performed at Sumsion's second Gloucester Festival, in 1931. Holst had arrived for one of the chorus rehearsals soaked to the knees, having walked through mud and mire while following an ancient Roman trackway, and directed the rehearsal of his *Choral Fantasia* in a pair of Sumsion's trousers; there was a short orchestral work by R. O. Morris – the *Sinfonia in C major* – and an excellent performance under Sumsion's baton of Robin Milford's *A Prophet in the Land*, a 'Dramatic Oratorio' for soprano, tenor and baritone soloists and a large orchestra, including *ad lib* parts for treble recorder, harpsichord and organ.

George Bernard Shaw and his wife were accompanied at the Festival by T. E. Lawrence (Lawrence of Arabia, who by 1931 had joined the Royal Air Force under the name of Shaw, serving in the ranks until 1935, when he was killed in a motorcycling accident). On the Thursday, Alice gave lunch to a party of about twelve guests including the Shaws, R. O. Morris and his wife, and Dorothy Silk. Herbert Howells was also there: his song cycle *Green Ways*, with Isobel Baillie as soloist, had scored an outstanding success at the Wednesday evening concert. Sumsion had reverted to tradition and opened the Festival with *Elijah*. Howells remembered the conversation around the lunch table:

> Most of the company had heard *Elijah* on the Tuesday. So had G. B. S. And they had now gone to the luncheon just after hearing a famous and masterly Holst work [*The Hymn of Jesus*]. At table Shavian certitude galvanised proceedings. The voice of *The Perfect Wagnerite*, serenely infallible, was heard declaring both Mendelssohn's and Holst's weaknesses in their orchestration. In the constrained silence there was only one casualty. A glass of lemonade was knocked over. It was G. B. S.'s own.[55]

During the week Vaughan Williams conducted *The Lark Ascending* and *Job*, and Elgar *Gerontius*, the Violin Concerto (with Albert Sammons as soloist) and the *Nursery Suite*, composed in 1930 to celebrate the birth of Princess Margaret Rose to the Duke and Duchess of York.

Percy Hull's predilection for rapid tempi in his interpretation of Bach's Mass in B minor had earned for the Hereford Festival performances of that work the epithet 'the Hereford Stakes'. In 1931 it seemed as though Herbert Sumsion wished to take a leaf from Hull's book. He had conducted the Mass in B minor at a morning performance:

> In order to be over in time for the Mayor's luncheon he took it at a very fast speed. As it ended, I think at 12.55, Sir Hugh Allen was to be seen

[54] W. H. Reed, *Elgar as I Knew Him* (Gollancz, 1936; repr. OUP, 1989), p. 105.

[55] Howells, 'Memories from the Twentieth Century'.

walking furiously towards us – 'Disgraceful – all much too fast.' Steuart Wilson shouted, 'By the way, what *is* bogey for the B minor?'[56]

When the week was over Sumsion felt ill and somewhat depressed. Once more it was Adrian Boult who came to his aid, giving Sumsion an Hanovia ultra-violet lamp which he thought might be an effective pick-me-up – and it was![57]

W ILLIAM Walton first came into prominence in 1923, when his String Quartet was chosen for performance at the Salzburg Festival of the International Society for Contemporary Music. In the same year the first performance of *Façade*, at the Aeolian Hall, caused a scandal. In 1926 Walton's overture *Portsmouth Point* was performed at the Zurich Festival of the International Society, and the following year it was heard in London at one of the Proms. There followed the *Sinfonia concertante* for piano and orchestra, performed under Ansermet in 1928, and the Viola Concerto (with Hindemith as soloist) in 1929. Then, at the Leeds Festival of 1931, came the most excitingly original choral work of a generation – *Belshazzar's Feast*, conducted by Sargent. 'Every note hit its mark', said the *Musical Times*, 'and the composer had very definite notions of what those marks should be':

> Walton's first attempt to handle voices on a large scale showed an enormous increase on his already considerable grasp of saying something forceful and original without any kind of conscious striving to be like or unlike anyone else. His theme – expounded in a libretto by Mr. Osbert Sitwell, which balanced rapid dramatic narration with two big choruses of praise, one ironical to heathen gods of metal, wood and stone, and the other fanatical to the God of Israel – allowed him ample scope to depict with extreme vividness that barbaric mixture of monotheism and nationalism which lies just beneath the Bible narrative of the Captivity.

The shock of *Belshazzar's Feast* had, as Sir Adrian Boult put it, shattered the English musical world. Walton was invited to conduct at the 1932 Worcester Festival – but not *Belshazzar*, against which the Three Choirs cathedral doors remained bolted for a further twenty-five years.

Instead, Walton conducted his overture *Portsmouth Point* and, with Lionel Tertis as soloist, the Viola Concerto; Holst conducted the ballet music from his *Perfect Fool* as well as *The Hymn of Jesus*; and Vaughan Williams directed the first performance of his *Magnificat*, as well as his *Benedicite*. Sir Ivor Atkins presented a profoundly moving performance of Szymanowski's *Stabat Mater*. It seems the Festival was marred only by an unfortunate accident, when Muriel Brunskill broke down in the B minor Mass, having lost her place in the *Agnus Dei*. The bicentenary of the birth of Haydn was marked by Part I of *The Creation*, the *Te Deum* in C major, a string quartet, and a performance of the Symphony No. 93 – during which all the lights in the College Hall failed for quite a

---

[56] Memories of Sir Keith Falkner (private communication).
[57] Memories of Mrs Alice Sumsion (private communication).

long time but the LSO astonished everybody by continuing to play without interruption.

In 1930, Elgar had been persuaded to compose a piece to celebrate the twenty-fifth Brass Band Competition Festival, held every year at the Crystal Palace. The result was the *Severn Suite*. He later scored this work for orchestra and conducted the first public performance at the 1932 Worcester Festival, having recorded the new version with the LSO the previous April. G. B. Shaw was impressed: 'What a transfiguration! Nobody will ever believe that it began as a cornet corobbery. It's extraordinarily beautiful.'[58]

Elgar also conducted performances of his Symphony No. 1; *The Music Makers*, with Muriel Brunskill as soloist; 'For the Fallen', from *The Spirit of England*, with Isobel Baillie; and a superb *Gerontius* with Astra Desmond, Frank Titterton and Harold Williams. At the chamber concert Myra Hess and the Griller String Quartet played Elgar's Piano Quintet in A minor.

'Who will ever love these Festivals as you and I have?' wrote Elgar to Atkins during World War I.[59] In 1933 that love was as strong as ever:

> During these latter-day Festivals he is usually seated, but he's determined that the choir shall not fail him at the great outburst of 'Praise to the Holiest'. At rehearsal he is unimpressed – '*It wouldn't scare a mouse*'! On repetition, the choir responds with such vehemence that the Cathedral almost rocks![60]

Elgar and his daughter, Carice, rented a large house, 'The Priory', for the 1933 Hereford Festival. There was 'a convenient garden in front which was daily thronged with people coming to tea. They came in and out, and one hardly knew who they all were; but the Festival spirit prevailed – it was open door and hospitality throughout the week.'[61] Herbert and Alice Sumsion were among the throng. Elgar 'had the full score of *Elijah* by him and would show Bernard Shaw and others his pet points in it: things which appealed to him and of which he never tired'.[62] Sumsion joined Elgar and Shaw in this discussion, looking at the score over their shoulders – a moment captured by the camera of pianist Harriet Cohen (see Plate 95).

At the Opening Service, Elgar, wearing full court dress, conducted his March in B flat – a transposition from C of his Triumphal March from *Caractacus*, and the *Civic Fanfare*. Astra Desmond, Frank Titterton and Horace Stevens were the soloists in *Gerontius* under Elgar's baton on Tuesday evening; and in the Kemble Theatre on Wednesday evening he conducted the viola arrangement of his Cello Concerto with Lionel Tertis as soloist.

[58] Document dated 11 July 1932. Held by Worcestershire Archive and Archaeology Service.
[59] Atkins, *The Elgar–Atkins Friendship*, p. 447.
[60] Memories of Dr Melville Cook (private communication).
[61] Reed, *Elgar*, p. 106.
[62] Ibid.

Elgar mounted the Three Choirs rostrum for the last time at 11.30 a.m. on Thursday 7 September 1933. The work was:

> a better performance of *The Kingdom* than one had dared to hope. Miss Elsie Suddaby, Miss Astra Desmond, Mr Frank Titterton, and Mr Harold Williams formed a team of soloists second only to the first unforgettable interpreters of this masterpiece. And repeated hearings only confirm that this *is* a masterpiece, incomparably ahead of anything else which has been written this century ... The use Elgar makes of the harp alone would repay long study. But we do not prize and admire music because it is well-written. We prize it according to the degree of delight it gives us, and I am moved by *The Kingdom* as I am moved only by the greatest and noblest creations of musical art.[63]

Sir Edward Elgar died at his home, Marl Bank, Worcester, on Friday 23 February 1934. One week later, on Friday 2 March, a national memorial service was held in Worcester Cathedral. The players of the LSO and the soloists Elsie Suddaby, Astra Desmond and Harold Williams gave their services freely as a mark of their affection and respect for a great musician. Elgar's two dearest friends, Sir Ivor Atkins and Billy Reed, along with the Dean of Worcester, made all the necessary arrangements. The choir was made up of the Festival Chorus and members of the choirs of the three cathedrals.

The service opened with the Prelude to Part 2 of *The Apostles* and included the *Enigma* theme, Variation I (C. A. E.), Variation IX ('Nimrod'), and Variation XIII (***); from the *Dream of Gerontius*, the Prelude and final pages of Part I, the Angel's Song, and the Angel's Farewell; and, from *The Kingdom*, the Virgin's Meditation and the music from the Lord's Prayer to the end of the work.

Prayers and Lessons were read by the Archdeacon, the Dean, and the Bishop of Worcester, including the following words taken from a prayer read by the dean:

> We give Thee humble and hearty thanks that it pleased Thee to endow our fellow citizen EDWARD ELGAR with that singular mastery of music, and the will to use it in Thy service, whereby he being dead yet speaketh; now filling our minds with visions of the mystery and beauty of Nature; now by the concert of sweet and solemn sounds telling our hearts secrets of life and death that lie too deep for words; now soaring with Angels and Archangels and with all the company of Heaven in an ecstasy of praise; now holding us bowed with the broken and contrite heart before the throne of judgment.

> We thank Thee for the great place he holds in the glorious roll of England's Masters of Music.

> We thank Thee for the love and loyalty which ever bound this her son to the Faithful City.

---

[63] F. Bonavia, in *MT* 1933, p. 942.

16

Dona nobis pacem

THE year 1934 robbed English music not only of Sir Edward Elgar but also of Gustav Holst and Frederick Delius. Without Elgar or Holst there was a sense of grievous loss to the musical and social round of Three Choirs, and this was reinforced at the 1934(G) Festival by the additional absence of Vaughan Williams, who had cut his foot while bathing and was suffering from a poisoned abscess.

In 1933(H), Percy Hull, continuing a policy of gradual change, had decided to include *Elijah*, dropped in 1930(H), but to perform only an abridged version of *Messiah*. Sumsion, in 1934(G), omitted *Elijah* but followed Hull's lead by presenting only the abridged *Messiah*, thus making room on the Friday morning for W. H. Reed's *Symphony for Strings*, Haydn's *Te Deum*, and the Brahms Violin Concerto with Jelly d'Aranyi as soloist. In place of *Elijah* on Tuesday, *The Kingdom*, conducted by Sumsion, was given 'In Memoriam Edward Elgar', followed by Kodály's *Psalmus Hungaricus* and Vaughan Williams's *Pastoral Symphony*, conducted by Gordon Jacob in the composer's absence. Other contemporary pieces heard during the week included *Summer Music* and *St Patrick's Breastplate* by Arnold Bax; *Elegy* for strings and *Procession* by Herbert Howells; *Two Ballads* for baritone and orchestra by Howard Ferguson, in which Roy Henderson was the soloist; and Cyril B. Rootham's setting of Milton's *Ode on the Morning of Christ's Nativity*, with Isobel Baillie, Trefor Jones and Roy Henderson joining chorus, semi-chorus and orchestra under the composer's baton.

On Thursday evening, before a performance of *Gerontius*, G. D. Cunningham, the Organist of Birmingham Town Hall, played Handel's Organ Concerto in F major. When he had finished, 'an embarrassing gap appeared in the proceedings whilst waiting for the B.B.C. to relay the final part of the programme'. Herbert Sumsion summoned his Assistant Organist, Melville Cook, successor to Arthur Pritchard in 1932:

> 'Cook, what about playing an organ solo till they're ready to broadcast? Bach's D minor will fill the time nicely.' Me on to the organ bench in a jiffy, all stops drawn, now for it – diddle-de – and we're off, with the help of Sir Ivor Atkins to turn the pages. A great game of guessing after the concert – was it Cunningham? No, it was Cook, making his Festival debut without rehearsal![1]

Leaving Melville Cook's side, Sir Ivor Atkins made his way to the rostrum to conduct *Gerontius*, unrecognised by 'Crescendo', whose review in the *News*

---

[1] Melville Cook, 'Notes from my Three Choirs Diary', Hereford Festival programme book, 1988. Copy held in the Three Choirs Festival Office, Gloucester.

Chronicle commended 'Mr Sumsion, the orchestra, the chorus and the soloists, Mr Heddle Nash, Mr Harold Williams and Miss Astra Desmond, [who] have all sat under Elgar in the past and so know well his ways and wishes'. On the Tuesday evening Percy Hull had also taken a share in Sumsion's burden, conducting the Mozart Requiem. With Elgar gone, the conducting load was shared for the first time, each of the two visiting organists directing one work; a sensible precedent for future Festivals.

Shortly after Elgar's death, the Dean of Worcester and Sir Ivor Atkins launched a successful appeal for funds to erect a permanent memorial in the cathedral in the form of a stained-glass window. A design by Archibald Nicholson was chosen, drawing its inspiration from *The Dream of Gerontius*. The window, placed in the north aisle close to the spot where Elgar so often stood during performances at the Festivals, was unveiled by Viscount Cobham, the Lord Lieutenant, in a short ceremony at 11 a.m. on 3 September 1935, immediately before a Festival performance of *Gerontius*.

George Dyson (1883–1964) was a popular figure at the Festivals from 1933(H), in which year he conducted the first performance of his setting for tenor, chorus and orchestra of *St Paul's Voyage to Melita* with Trefor Jones as soloist. It was repeated in 1934(G), 1937(G) and 1952(H). The music of Dyson, owing nothing to Elgar and, unlike that of Vaughan Williams, barely influenced by folk song, casts back to the models of Stanford and Parry. A superb orchestrator, his work invariably drew contemporary critical praise. In addition to *St Paul's Voyage* two other compositions by Dyson for solo voices, chorus and orchestra received their first performances at Three Choirs: *Nebuchadnezzar* in 1935(W) and *Quo Vadis?* – Part I in 1946(H) and Parts I and II in 1949(H). Describing *Quo Vadis?* as 'a rare beauty ... perfect exposition in poetry and music of a deep spiritual longing for human harmony with the divine', the *Musical Times* of October 1946 concluded that 'Sir George Dyson showed ... a masterly command of his art, all the more admirable because at no point did he allow his superb craftsmanship to take on the appearance of conscious cleverness.'

In 1937, Dyson was appointed Director of the Royal College of Music in succession to Sir Hugh Allen. He was knighted in 1941, and conducted for the last time at Three Choirs in 1952(H), the year of his retirement from the RCM. The work was *St Paul's Voyage to Melita*, given a moving performance with Eric Greene as the tenor soloist. But its beauty was lost on two of the ladies in the audience, who were overheard on leaving the cathedral. 'Do you know where Melita is, dear?' one said. 'No', was the reply, 'but I was *so* grateful when he eventually got there!'[2]

THREE Choirs seems to have been affected little by the strikes and depression of the inter-war years. There was no shortage of applicants who, wishing to gain access to priority booking, were prepared to pay 5 guineas at Gloucester and Hereford, and 4 guineas at Worcester, for the privilege of stewardship. In the three years immediately preceding World War II the number of stewardships sold amounted to:

[2] Memories of Mr Rodney Bennett (private communication).

	Gentlemen	Ladies
1936(H)	117	123
1937(G)	205	187
1938(W)	237	286

For many years, separate conditions of stewardship were offered to ladies and gentlemen. When George Bernard Shaw first applied to become a Steward the Gloucester ticket secretary wrote to him 'to explain that he would not be able to sit with his wife as the Gentlemen Stewards were given seats in a separate reserved section'. Sumsion recalled that 'Shaw wrote back on a postcard, "Those whom God hath joined together, let no man put asunder."'[3]

It is interesting to compare the expenses of the Festival in these years with those of the nineteenth century. In 1886(G) Emma Albani had been able to demand 450 guineas; Edward Lloyd, 180 guineas; Anna Williams, 100 guineas; Janet Patey, 150 guineas; and Sir Charles Santley, 200 guineas. Even the lowest-paid principal, Watkin Mills, had received 50 guineas. Fifty years later, the payment of such astronomic sums would have been inconceivable: at Hereford, in 1936, Percy Hull was authorised to engage the artists chosen by the Music Committee – twelve singers and four solo instrumentalists – at fees not exceeding a total of £483. The lowest-paid principal singer received 10 guineas per performance, and even artists at the top of their profession, such as Astra Desmond and Heddle Nash, were offered only 18 guineas. The LSO was engaged by the Festival at a total cost of £1,121, exclusive of railway fares; each of the orchestral players received 12s. 6d. per performance, and 1 guinea was paid to the Leader.[4]

The Hereford Festival of 1936 was held under the patronage of King Edward VIII, whose abdication in December added crisis to uncertainty: Hitler had ordered his troops into the Rhineland in March, and the Spanish Civil War had begun in July. The composers who conducted their own works at the Festival were George Dyson – *Nebuchadnezzar* and the first performance of his *Prelude, Fantasy and Chaconne* for cello and orchestra, with Thelma Reiss as soloist; W. K. Stanton – an eight-part unaccompanied setting of Addison's *The Spacious Firmament*; and Vaughan Williams – his *Pastoral Symphony*, Part IV ('The Explorers') from *A Sea Symphony*, the Viola Suite and, composed for the Festival, two Hymn Preludes for small orchestra. At the Thursday morning concert an additional item was inserted into the programme: Roy Henderson sang 'Fare Well' from Stanford's *Songs of the Fleet* in tribute to Harry Plunket Greene, who had died three weeks previously.

Zoltán Kodály returned to Gloucester in 1937, making the second of four visits to the Festival. He conducted his *Dances of Galanta* and the Budávari *Te Deum*, written for the celebrations at Budapest in 1936 of the 250th anniversary

[3] Herbert Sumsion, 'Random Reminiscences', in Barry Still (ed.), *Two Hundred and Fifty Years of the Three Choirs Festival – A Commemoration in Words and Pictures* (Three Choirs Festival Association, 1977).

[4] Hereford Festival Minute Book, 1936–69. Hereford Cathedral Library and Archives.

of the city's liberation from the Turks – a wildly colourful piece which was much enjoyed by the chorus. Alas, their enthusiasm evaporated the next day.

Kodály had been described by 'Crescendo' in the *News Chronicle* as 'a little man, with thick flowing hair, and a keen face with bright eyes, and he seems rather shy, and probably is, for the surroundings must be very strange to him'. Certainly Kodály must have felt a great strangeness when conducting his unaccompanied motet, *Jesus and the Traders*, a work considered difficult in those days. At rehearsals the chorus had struggled to master Kodály's complex harmonies. They continued to feel insecure about the opening of the piece, and on the morning of the performance were very apprehensive. Melville Cook, the Assistant Organist, was aware of the problem, and had agreed to play a short organ improvisation immediately before *Jesus and the Traders*, giving the chorus a strong lead by ending on the same chord with which the Kodály work begins. Sadly, the chorus was caught unawares. That last, precious chord faded away unnoted as Kodály stepped on to the platform and raised his baton. A look of crumpled disappointment crossed his face as the chorus plunged into a ragged opening from which recovery was both slow and painful. At least one member of the chorus felt as if she was 'on a ship going down'. For another, the stress was altogether too great – she simply fainted away![5]

Characteristic of Kodály's music are a profound sincerity and the unmistakable influence of the music of his country's folk song. In 1906 he had written his university thesis on Hungarian folk song, afterwards collecting folk songs in collaboration with Bartók. He was, therefore, in some measure a Hungarian counterpart to Vaughan Williams, even though there is no similarity in their idioms.

Kodály met Vaughan Williams at Gloucester in 1937 and asked him 'searching questions about the reason and objects of the Festivals, and Ralph explained, with solemnity, that they became necessary after the Reformation, for in the days of celibate clergy there were neither widows nor orphans to support.'[6]

Vaughan Williams's own contributions to the 1937(G) Festival were the overture and songs from his opera *The Poisoned Kiss*, and the cantata for soprano and baritone soloists, chorus and orchestra, *Dona nobis pacem*, which had received its first performance at Huddersfield under Albert Coates on 2 October 1936. At Gloucester, and again at Worcester in 1938, the soloists were Elsie Suddaby and Roy Henderson. The text of *Dona nobis pacem*, formed of a fragment of the Latin mass, conflations from the authorised version of the Bible, an extract from a parliamentary speech by John Bright, and three poems by Walt Whitman, presents a clear message. Vaughan Williams, like Whitman, had seen war at first hand, saw its deathly hand reaching out once more, and sought to warn –

> I see a sad procession,
> And I hear the sound of coming full-keyed bugles;
> All the channels of the city streets they're flooding,
> As with voices and with tears.

[5] Memories of Mrs Diana Feilden (private communication).

[6] Ursula Vaughan Williams, 'Ralph Vaughan Williams at the Three Choirs Festival', in Still (ed.), *Two Hundred and Fifty Years of the Three Choirs Festival*.

The winter of 1937 brought the death of Ivor Gurney at the age of forty-seven – following fifteen years in an asylum, locked away from his beloved Gloucestershire in a Kent mental hospital and haunted by the horrors of World War I. Gurney's memory was honoured at the 1938(w) Festival in a performance, by Mary Worth, of 'Spring', one of his five exquisite *Elizabethan Songs*, as part of a group which included songs by Clifton Parker, Hubert Parry, and Gurney's friend and teacher from the Royal College of Music, Ralph Vaughan Williams. The accompanist was Edgar Day, who held the post of Assistant Organist at Worcester with distinction for half a century from 1912.

The orchestral concert at the 1938(w) Festival was given in the Gaumont Theatre, Worcester, by seventy members of the LSO, joined by other orchestral players. The Leader was W. H. Reed, and the soloist in a performance of Rachmaninov's Piano Concerto No. 2 in C minor was Benno Moiseiwitsch, who had become a British subject in the previous year.

By 1938, Thursday was generally known as the 'modern' day. The concert on the morning of 8 September began with Kodály's Budávari *Te Deum* and also included *The Blessed Damozel* by Debussy, the first performance of Lennox Berkeley's setting of Psalm 24, *Domini est terra*, conducted by the composer, and Vaughan Williams's *Dona nobis pacem*.

Three weeks later Neville Chamberlain flew back from meeting Hitler in Munich to tell cheering crowds that he had brought 'Peace for our time'.

Arrangements for the 1939 Festival at Hereford went ahead as usual. Tickets and programmes were printed, sold and distributed; soloists and orchestra engaged; and a full schedule of rehearsals completed. New works planned for performance included Sir George Dyson's *Quo Vadis?* Part I; the *Elegy in Memory of Edward Elgar* by Alexander Brent Smith; and *Dies natalis*, a cantata for high voice and strings by Gerald Finzi to words by the seventeenth-century Herefordshire poet Thomas Traherne.

The dates for the Festival were set at 3, 5, 6, 7 and 8 September. In August, Hitler signed an agreement with Russia, and war seemed inevitable. At midday on 28 August the Finance Committee of the Hereford Festival met, 'to decide whether or not to hold the Festival and, in the event of hostilities involving this country breaking out, what steps should be taken'.[7] Colonel Pateshall proposed that the Festival should immediately be abandoned, but his proposition did not find a seconder. Percy Hull had gone to London for rehearsals with the orchestra and principals on the previous day, not knowing until he got there whether or not the rehearsals would be held. He promised to telegraph the committee, but the telegram failed to arrive while they were in session.

The committee resolved that the secretary, R. A. Symonds, after consultation with the chairman, E. R. Dymond, should be authorised to cancel the Festival should hostilities break out before 30 August. On Thursday 31 August an announcement was broadcast that the government had decided to proceed with evacuation plans which, inevitably, involved restrictions on transport. Also, a ban was placed on the congregation of large assemblies for the time being. It was now impossible to carry on with the Festival. The next day German forces invaded

[7] Hereford Festival Minute Book, 1936–69. Hereford Cathedral Library and Archives.

Poland and, on Sunday 3 September, the date set for the Opening Service, Britain and France declared war on Germany.

One man remained undeterred. At the instigation of the Hereford Chapter and Three Choirs Festival Committee, the Archbishop of Canterbury had, on 1 May 1939, conferred the Lambeth degree of honorary Doctor of Music on W. H. Reed. Three Choirs Festival musicians, musical organisations and friends throughout the country subscribed towards his doctoral robes, and it was intended that they should be presented to him during the Festival. They were presented instead at a small ceremony at the Hereford deanery on the afternoon of Tuesday 5 September. Under the heading 'Little Festival', the *Hereford Times* reported that:

> Ever since 1902 Dr Reed has been coming to Three Choirs Festivals, and he related this week … that when Dr Hull telephoned him and said that the Festival was 'off', he recalled his long innings and asked himself, 'Am I stumped?' answering, 'No, I will not be put off.'
>
> He accordingly packed up his fiddle on Friday and came to Hereford, deciding that as this was Festival week he would play at it. 'I had always played at the Festival before', said Dr Reed, 'so I proceeded to the Cathedral on Sunday and played. So I think it is true to say I played at the Festival, though it may have been a small Festival lasting only five minutes.'

Billy Reed had played Mackenzie's *Benedictus* during morning service in the cathedral: '"I don't feel that my innings are at an end", he said. "I made one run on Sunday and my wicket is still up."'

Billy Reed never returned to Hereford; his wicket fell on 2 July 1942. But his long years of service to Three Choirs, and his friendship with Elgar, were marked by his burial in Worcester Cathedral, close to the Gerontius window.

17

Recovery

THE grim austerity of post-war Britain – shortages of food, petrol and paper, the continued requisitioning of city hotels, and greatly increased costs – could easily have deterred the Hereford Three Choirs Committee from embarking upon a resumption of the Festival in 1946. Percy Hull, the Hereford Cathedral Organist, was confident that all of the problems could be overcome, but there were pessimistic voices at a meeting of Stewards and supporters held on 27 October 1945. Once again the Festival was saved by the needs of the charity, whose fortunes at Hereford, according to Prebendary P. A. Lushington, were 'absolutely on the rocks'.[1] The Deans of Gloucester and Worcester made vigorous appeals for more faith, and further support came from Sir Ivor Atkins. But when the question was put to the meeting, several people refused to vote. The decision to hold a Festival in Hereford was carried by about twenty-five votes to six. A new secretary, Mr T. O. D. (Tom) Steel, was appointed and the dust blown from the programme planned for the abandoned Festival of 1939, which was used to form the basis of the revival. Detailed preparations went ahead and were well advanced when, just three months before the start of the Festival, came a major blow.

Percy Hull, who had been unwell since the beginning of 1946, now suffered a nervous breakdown. Hull's doctors were unable to predict how soon he would be well enough to resume his duties, and advised him that the organisers should be prepared for his complete absence from the Festival. At an emergency committee meeting held on 7 June 1946 it was resolved to ask Sir George Dyson to accept the position of deputy conductor for the Festival. The next day he travelled to Hereford and addressed the committee:

> He stressed very strongly that it was the very essence of the tradition of the Festival that the Conductor should be the local Cathedral Organist and he felt that if, for any reason, the local organist was not able to conduct this should be undertaken by the other two. He gratefully acknowledged the compliment implied by the invitation but did not feel that it would be wise to break with tradition, particularly as this Festival was a revival after the war. He was equally emphatic that an outside professional conductor should not be engaged and pointed out that all the preliminary work would have to be undertaken by the local Cathedral organists and their assistants and that it would, in his view, be very unjust to them to engage another conductor for the final performances. In any event he thought it

---

[1] Hereford Festival Minute Book, 1936–69. Hereford Cathedral Library and Archives.

very unlikely that an outside conductor would be able to spare sufficient time for rehearsals and would not get to know the chorus. He was himself ready and willing to do anything he could to help and, in particular, to do anything which had to be done in London.[2]

And so the devolution of the conductor's duties, which even before the war had begun to reduce the concentration of responsibility in the hands of the local organist, was carried still further as a result of Percy Hull's illness. Sir Ivor Atkins and Herbert Sumsion shared the work of preparing the 1946(H) Festival, greatly helped by the Hereford Assistant Organist, Colin Mann. Tom Steel and all concerned with the administration made Herculean efforts to ensure the smooth running of the Festival, even persuading the local MP to organise the derequisitioning of the Green Dragon and City Arms hotels. Although the incomes of those who formed the bulk of the Stewards had undoubtedly diminished since the previous Hereford Festival in 1936, fears of financial failure proved to be unfounded. Starved of live music throughout the war, greater numbers than ever applied for stewardships; indeed it was necessary to close the subscription list when, by June, it had reached 612.

The success of the Festival was, reported the *Hereford Times* on 4 January 1947, 'a tale of expectations surpassed and new records achieved', and £2,450 was raised for the destitute charity.

The LSO under its new Leader, George Stratton, was engaged in 1946. Among the principals were the sopranos Isobel Baillie, Mary Linde and Elsie Suddaby; contraltos Astra Desmond and Gladys Ripley; tenors Heddle Nash and Eric Greene; basses George Pizzey and Tom Williams; pianist Phyllis Sellick; violinist Jelly d'Aranyi; and Lionel Tertis, the most famous viola player of his time. Tertis had played at Three Choirs frequently from 1927, but had retired from the concert platform in 1936 only to re-emerge during the war; he died in 1975 in his ninety-ninth year.

Happily, by the time of the Festival Percy Hull had recovered sufficiently to conduct *Elijah* and *Gerontius*. Sir George Dyson took charge not only of his own *Quo Vadis?* and the Wife of Bath's song from his *The Canterbury Pilgrims* (with Isobel Baillie as soloist), but also of a fine performance of Vaughan Williams's *Pastoral Symphony*. The conducting load was further shared by other composers directing their own works: Alexander Brent Smith, *Elegy in Memory of Edward Elgar*; Edmund Rubbra, the orchestral suite *Improvisations on Virginal Pieces* (Giles Farnaby); E.J. Moeran, *Sinfonietta* in C; Gordon Jacob, the orchestral suite *William Byrd*; Samuel Barber, *Adagio for Strings*; and Gerald Finzi, *Dies natalis*. With this last, rapturously sung by Elsie Suddaby, it became clear that Three Choirs had returned with a work of lasting worth in its hand – 'inexpressibly rare and delightful and beautiful'.[3]

Although war had denied Three Choirs the first performance of *Dies natalis*, a return to peace ushered in a strong bond between Gerald Finzi (1901–1956) and the Festival. Finzi, his artist wife, Joy, and two sons, Christopher and Nigel, were

[2] Ibid.

[3] The quotation is from Thomas Traherne's *Centuries of Meditations* (First Century, sect. 31).

frequently to be seen among the familiar Festival faces, often in company with the magisterial figure of Vaughan Williams. When *Dies natalis* was repeated in 1947(G) the soloist was the tenor Eric Greene, who, as a relaxing preparation for the performance, joined the whole Finzi family in a game of rounders on the Gloucester King's School paddock[4] – a typical example of the offstage informality and fun that characterises Three Choirs.

During and immediately after the war the Rev. Walter Hussey of St Matthew's, Northampton, brought considerable distinction to his church through the commissioning of several works of art, including a number of festival anthems, the first of which, Britten's *Rejoice in the Lamb* (1943), was followed by pieces from Rubbra, Berkeley and, in September 1946 to mark the fifty-third anniversary of the consecration of the church, Gerald Finzi's *Lo, the full final sacrifice*. This exquisite setting of verses by Richard Crashaw (1612–1649) was conducted by Finzi at Three Choirs in both 1947(G) and 1948(W), establishing itself among the most distinguished pieces of 'sacred' music produced in England in the twentieth century.

Finzi had studied with Sir Edward Bairstow of York Minster and, as the late Christopher Palmer pointed out:

> doubtless what he absorbed there of the 'immemorial sound of voices' endowed him with a rare fluency and felicity in the handling of (voices). He … took pains in polishing and refining each of the comparatively small number of works he gave to the world. But they were vehicles for ideas and feelings rather than for beliefs. *Lo, the full final sacrifice*, *Dies Natalis*, *In Terra Pax* and *Intimations of Immortality* are all intensely 'religious' in this wider sense, even though they are the work of a confessed agnostic … The austerity of Finzi's harmonic language tempers and contains the ecstasy of the words; restraint controls the passion. His music is the diet of tranquillity, a glass of water drawn up from a deep cold well; the work, surely, of a man long subject to the authority and teaching of solitude.[5]

In 1920 Finzi had heard Elsie Suddaby, accompanied by Bairstow, practising a song by another who was no stranger to solitude: 'Sleep' from Ivor Gurney's *Five Elizabethan Songs*. He felt at once that it was one of the great songs, written with intense feeling; with hindsight, 'one can feel an incandescence in his songs that tells of something burning too brightly to last, such as you see in the filament of an electric bulb before it burns out'.[6] This led Finzi to discover Gurney, and for the rest of his life, with the assistance of Joy Finzi and his friend Howard Ferguson, he worked to save Gurney's poems and songs from absolute obscurity; and Finzi paid a further compliment to Gloucester's neglected son, orchestrating

---

[4] Gerald Finzi, 'The Composer's Use of Words', [three] Crees Lectures (1955), typescript held in the archive of the Royal College of Music, London. See also Stephen Banfield, *Gerald Finzi: An English Composer* (Faber & Faber, 1997), p. 393.

[5] Christopher Palmer, liner notes for recording of choral works by Bax and Finzi. Choir of King's College, Cambridge, directed by Stephen Cleobury (EMI EL 2704404 (1986)).

[6] Memories of the late Joy Finzi (private communication).

four of the *Five Elizabethan Songs*: 'Under the Greenwood Tree', 'Sleep', 'Spring', and 'Orpheus with his Lute'. It was fitting, therefore, that these four songs should be included in a programme played by the Jacques String Orchestra on the final night of the 1947 Gloucester Festival – and fitting too that they were sung by Elsie Suddaby.

THE year 1947 had begun well, with the announcement of Percy Hull's knighthood in the New Year's Honours List. In an effort to lift further the post-war gloom, the Festival Ball was revived for the first time since 1874 at Gloucester. Only one new work was heard at the Festival: Christopher le Fleming's *Five Psalms* for soprano solo (Elsie Suddaby), chorus and orchestra. Sir George Dyson conducted his overture *At the Tabard Inn* and *Quo Vadis?*; Edmund Rubbra, his Symphony No. 3; and Herbert Howells, his *Elegy* for strings, with Jean Stewart as soloist. The pianist Kathleen Long played the *Symphonic Variations* by César Franck and the *Ballade* for piano and orchestra by Fauré. Vaughan Williams conducted a broadcast performance of his Symphony No. 5 in D major which, under his baton, had been heard for the first time at a Promenade Concert in 1943, and the third movement of which, a *romanza*, has been linked with the *larghetto* of Elgar's Symphony No. 2 as one of the highest peaks of Romantic English music. The basses Norman Walker and Gordon Clinton were heard at Three Choirs for the first time, Clinton singing in *The Apostles*, Kodály's Budávari *Te Deum* and the *St Matthew Passion*. Walker also sang in the Bach as well as *Quo Vadis?* and *Messiah*. This year 900 stewardships were sold, compared with 400 in 1937. And it was in 1947, too, that the Archbishop of Canterbury conferred the Lambeth degree of DMus on Herbert Sumsion. A vintage Three Choirs year – but there was a single disappointment.

The name which was on everyone's lips was that of the sensational young contralto who had made her operatic debut in Britten's *Rape of Lucretia* at Glyndebourne in 1946: Kathleen Ferrier. Sumsion had tried to engage Ferrier for the 1947 Gloucester Festival, only to discover that she had been booked to appear during the same week at the very first Edinburgh Festival. The secretary of the Gloucester Committee, Anthony A. Scott, wrote to the Provost of Edinburgh as chairman of the Edinburgh Festival Committee, suggesting that even though no action might be possible for 1948, consideration should be given to the dates of the two festivals in future years.[7] Although his Lordship's reply expressed the hope that it would be possible to cooperate for a common purpose, the two festivals continued to coincide for many years.

Kathleen Ferrier did sing at Three Choirs in 1948, sharing the principal contralto parts with Mary Jarred. Ferrier's contributions included *Messiah* with Isobel Baillie, Heddle Nash and Norman Walker; *Gerontius* with Heddle Nash and Harold Williams; Debussy's *The Blessed Damozel* with Isobel Baillie; and the *St Matthew Passion*, in the Elgar–Atkins edition, with Elsie Suddaby, Bradbridge White and Gordon Clinton. Mary Jarred sang in *The Kingdom*, Szymanowski's *Stabat Mater* and Kodály's *Missa brevis*, orchestrated and, in part, rewritten for the Festival and conducted by Kodály himself.

[7] Gloucester Festival Minute Book, 1947. Gloucester Cathedral Archives and Library.

Kathleen Ferrier returned to sing in *Gerontius* with William Herbert and Hervey Alan at Hereford in 1952. Who, listening then to that glorious voice, could possibly have guessed that so shining a spirit would be extinguished in less than a year?

One significant and, until 1955, isolated break with a long tradition occurred in 1948. Because of Promenade Concert commitments the LSO was unable to play at Three Choirs, and the LPO was hired in its place.

This was Sir Ivor Atkins's last Festival as Director. He was entering his eightieth year, bore the brunt of the conducting, and was as indefatigable as ever. Sir Percy Hull, too, was coming to the end of a long career, and conducted for the last time as Director of the Hereford Festival in 1949. When both men retired in 1950 Sir Percy had been in post for almost thirty-two years and Sir Ivor for fifty-three, exceeding even the long record of William Done at Worcester. 'P. C.' returned to Three Choirs as a guest conductor in 1952(H), 1955(H) and 1957(W), when, at the age of seventy-nine, he took up the baton to direct the CBSO in a performance of the *Enigma Variations* – a final tribute to his old friend Edward Elgar.

Sir Ivor Atkins died on 26 November 1953. At his funeral in Worcester Cathedral the Very Rev. A. W. Davies, Dean Emeritus of Worcester, paid tribute to Sir Ivor as an honoured and familiar figure in the cathedral and the city, noting his strong sense of duty, devotion to truth, and attention to detail. 'He had sometimes been unbending in the presence of his fellow men, but in the presence of God he was a humble and devout Christian man.' Sir Ivor's ashes were interred below the Gerontius window, close to the resting place of W. H. Reed.

THE Gloucester Festival of 1950, remembered for the first performances of Gerald Finzi's *Intimations of Immortality* and Herbert Howells's *Hymnus Paradisi*, marked Herbert Sumsion's ascendancy from the junior member of the trio of conductors to 'the father figure, helping and advising two very much younger men'.[8] Both of these younger men, David Willcocks at Worcester and Meredith Davies at Hereford, had displayed brilliance as students, served with distinction in the war, established notable reputations and, with Sumsion, laid the foundations of the modern Three Choirs Festival before moving on to wider renown in national and international careers.

Sir David Willcocks (1922–2015) had been a chorister in Westminster Abbey, and afterwards organ scholar of King's College, Cambridge. After the war, in which he won the Military Cross while serving in the Duke of Cornwall's Light Infantry, he was successively Fellow of King's College and Organist of Salisbury Cathedral before his appointment to Worcester in 1950.

Meredith Davies (1922–2005) was only eight when he entered the Royal College of Music as a junior exhibitioner. In 1941 he went up to Oxford as organ scholar of Keble College, where his studies were interrupted by war service in the Royal Artillery. He gained the Limpus and Read Prizes for the FRCO, together with the Silver Medal of the Worshipful Company of Musicians, and held the

[8] Memories of Sir David Willcocks, Hereford Festival programme book, 1979. Copy held in the Three Choirs Festival Office, Gloucester.

post of Organist at St Alban's Cathedral for three years before his appointment to Hereford.

In association with David Willcocks and Meredith Davies, Herbert Sumsion embarked upon his happiest Three Choirs years. At the 1950(G) Festival, Willcocks conducted both of the two major Elgar works in the programme: the Cello Concerto, with Anthony Pini as soloist, and *Gerontius*, with Gladys Ripley, Heddle Nash and Norman Walker. Davies conducted the Fauré Requiem with Elsie Morrison and William Parsons, and the Symphony No. 5 by Sibelius. Both men took their place in the organ loft: Davies for morning and Willcocks for evening performances.

Another, even younger, man played the organ at the Sunday Service, the 5.00 p.m. Evensongs, and for the Fauré Requiem: this was the twenty-year-old Assistant Organist at Gloucester, Donald Hunt.

Herbert Sumsion conducted the first performance of *Intimations of Immortality*, a setting of Wordsworth's ode, dedicated to Adeline Vaughan Williams. The work was conceived and much of it written before 1939, when, interrupted by war, Finzi laid it aside, completing it only in 1950. The first tenor soloist was Eric Greene.

> One could not help thinking in this cathedral how Parry would have been pleased at this choice and setting of noble words. Finzi's melodic idiom has been nourished on English madrigals, folk-song, Bach, and Parry, but it is his own and his harmony has a modern richness not to be found in the tradition from which this noble cantata derives.[9]

Herbert Howells wrote *Hymnus Paradisi*, his masterpiece, to assuage a private grief. In 1935 he had taken his only son to cricket in Cheltenham. Only ten years old, Michael had said an extraordinary thing: 'I want to see Hammond score a century before I die.' Within a week the boy was dead, a victim of poliomyelitis.

Hit more by this death than by anything else, Howells was frozen mentally for three years. Then one day his daughter Ursula said, 'Why don't you write some music about Mick?'[10]

> The sudden loss of an only son, a loss essentially profound and, in its very nature, beyond argument, might naturally impel a composer, after a time, to seek release and consolation in language and terms most personal to him. Music may well have power beyond any other medium to offer that release and comfort. It did so in my case, and became a personal, private document.[11]

Howells kept the work 'under his pillow' for twelve years, showing it only to his wife and daughter, and to Herbert Sumsion, who suggested the title. In 1950, Ralph Vaughan Williams asked to see *Hymnus Paradisi* and insisted that Howells release it. The first performance, conducted by the composer, was given at the 1950(G) Festival, with soloists Isobel Baillie and William Herbert.

[9] *The Times*, 7 September 1950.

[10] Recorded memories of Herbert Howells, National Sound Archives (British Library).

[11] Christopher Palmer, *Herbert Howells: A Study* (Novello, 1978), ch. 6, pp. 46–7.

The Worcester Festival of 1951 was included as one of the principal musical attractions of the Festival of Britain – that great attempt to boost national morale and to celebrate the achievements of post-war recovery. From 3 May until 30 September huge crowds were drawn to the South Bank site in London, the permanent legacy of which is the Royal Festival Hall. Fears that Three Choirs might suffer as a consequence resulted in the first-ever Arts Council guarantee to the Festival against the possibility of loss – a grant of £750.

No new works were commissioned for the 1951 Worcester Festival (David Willcock's first), but *Intimations of Immortality* and *Hymnus Paradisi* were repeated, and Julius Harrison (1885–1963) was present in the county of his birth to conduct his *Worcestershire Suite* and to hear Willcocks direct his Mass in C, with Ena Mitchell, Grace Bodey, Richard Lewis and Harold Williams. Douglas Fox, who had lost his right arm in World War I, played Ravel's Piano Concerto for the Left Hand, and two singers made their final appearances at Three Choirs: Elsie Suddaby in Bach's Mass in B minor and Harold Williams in *Gerontius*. On the last evening, the Boyd Neel Orchestra gave a concert in the College Hall which, in addition to works by Handel and Bach, included Stravinsky's *Apollon Musagette*, Britten's *Les Illuminations* (with Richard Lewis) and the Prelude and Scherzo from Shostakovich's String Octet, op. 11.

K ING George VI died on 6 February 1952. In the minds of many, Britain was now about to enter into a new era of greatness matching that of the reign of the first Elizabeth, even though the Korean War continued to sap the nation's energy. In Hereford, Meredith Davies prepared for his first Festival as Director, intent on establishing confidence, trying to absorb all that he was being told about the true spirit and character of Three Choirs, but aware that the 'nascent festivals at Edinburgh and Aldeburgh were setting standards and winning musical prestige which could leave the Three Choirs looking like a very old-fashioned amateur junketing – as, indeed, some critics were beginning to suggest'.[12]

Davies knew that the key to any 'reform' lay in somehow rationalising the ludicrous rehearsal schedule. The chorus and orchestra still had only two opportunities to rehearse together: a full chorus rehearsal held in the cathedral on the afternoon of the Saturday preceding the Festival, and 'Black Monday'. However, as Davies recalls:

> Innovation in 1952 was modest, and more historical than radical: a harpsichord ousted the grand piano as a continuo instrument [in the *St Matthew Passion* and *Messiah*: Boris Ord was the player], Alfred Deller was a soloist [in Purcell's *My Beloved Spake* and Bach's *Erfreute Zeit im neuen Bunde*], and a Sunday evening organ recital was programmed [Harold Darke] – even then I thought it strange to assemble the Stewards on Saturday, with no official performance until the Tuesday morning.[13]

Davies wrote to Benjamin Britten asking for a new work for the Festival, but Britten was too busy to comply; he suggested a performance of his *St Nicolas*

---

[12] Memories of Meredith Davies (private communication).
[13] Ibid.

instead, but this was not given at Three Choirs until 1958(H), when Britten himself came to Hereford to conduct it. Only two new works were given in 1952: Donald Bridges was the soloist in the Concerto for oboe and string orchestra by George Stratton, the Leader of the LSO (Stratton died in 1954), and *Cantiones sacrae* by John Gardner, who had achieved great success with the performance of his Symphony No. 1 at the Cheltenham Festival of 1951. 'It was', wrote Martin Cooper in the *Musical Times*, 'these tit-bits which lured the London critics, like so many cats, to the feast at Hereford.' But of *Cantiones sacrae* he wrote that 'the choral writing provided the choir with considerable difficulties, some of which seemed gratuitous; but it is good that they should confront contemporary obstacles, and this work made an effective test-piece.'[14] The total combined rehearsal time available to choir and orchestra for this particular 'test-piece' had been forty minutes.

The schedule of full chorus and orchestra rehearsals on the afternoon of the Saturday and the 'Black Monday' preceding the 1953 Gloucester Festival gives a clear idea of the pressure facing all those involved. (Asterisks indicate music for the Opening Service on Sunday 6 September.)

Saturday 5 September

2.30	National Anthem*
	Three Hymns*
	Brewer in D*
	Handel, 'Let their celestial concerts'
3.00	Mendelssohn, Elijah
3.45	Bridge, A Prayer
4.00	Bach, St John Passion
4.00–4.15	Interval for orchestra
4.45	Walton, Te Deum*
5.15	Handel, 'Let the bright Seraphim'*
	Brahms, slow movement* from Symphony No. 4

Monday 7 September

10.00	Elgar, National Anthem
10.05	Handel, Israel in Egypt
	Vaughan Williams, Dona nobis
	Monteverdi, Magnificat
11.30–11.45	Interval for orchestra
12.00	Finzi, Intimations
12:45	Vaughan Williams, Job
1.00	Interval
2.00	Ireland, 'These things shall be'
2.30	Kodály, Psalmus Hungaricus
3.10	Elgar, Gerontius
3.50	Handel, Messiah
3.50–4.05	Interval for orchestra
4.05	Haydn, Coronation Mass
4.50	Brahms, Alto Rhapsody

[14] *MT* 1952, pp. 513–14.

THE coronation of Queen Elizabeth II had taken place on 3 June 1953, and so William Walton's *Coronation Te Deum* was a clear choice for inclusion in the Opening Service. The Wednesday evening concert in the cathedral began with Walton's stirring coronation march, *Orb and Sceptre*, and, although not programmed, the *Te Deum* was repeated. The only new work performed during the week was Anthony Scott's *Chorale Variations*. Richard Arnell made his single Three Choirs appearance conducting his *Sinfonia quasi variazioni*, op. 13; Herbert Howells conducted his *Elegy* for strings; and Vaughan Williams, *Job* and *Dona nobis pacem* with Joan Alexander and Bruce Boyce as soloists. Among the distinguished instrumentalists who performed during the Festival were Campoli (the Brahms Violin Concerto), Dennis Brain (Horn Concerto No. 2, K417, by Mozart), Gervase de Peyer (Finzi's Clarinet Concerto), and the Amadeus String Quartet. A startlingly successful and imaginative innovation was a performance of Monteverdi's *Magnificat* from the Vespers of 1610:

> Dr Sumsion had absorbed the style of the music unlike any other and still in these days of infinite regression into the past, virtually unknown. With the help of Dr Redlich's edition and half a dozen soloists he revealed for modern ears the strange mixture of what in 1610 was both old and new.[15]

The six soloists were Ena Mitchell, Joan Fullerton, Nancy Evans, Eric Greene, David Galliver, and Richard Stanton substituting for Thomas Hemsley, who was unable to appear.

After the 1951 and 1952 Festivals, David Willcocks and Meredith Davies had more time to think about the problems of inadequate rehearsal time. Davies remembered talking to Willcocks late into the night, and the rehearsal schedules for the Festivals of 1954(w) and 1955(H) reveal that modern practice, achieved in two strides, probably came out of that conversation.

At Worcester in 1954 full chorus rehearsals with orchestra were held on Saturday afternoon, Monday morning *and* Wednesday morning, thus releasing Monday afternoon and evening for performances: a Public Hall recital of songs and instrumental pieces in the afternoon, with Isobel Baillie, Thomas Matthews (violin), Eileen Ralf (piano), and Meredith Davies as accompanist; and a choral concert in the cathedral in the evening (Holst's *Hymn of Jesus* and the Verdi Requiem). New works during the week were Herbert Howells's *Missa Sabrinensis* and Vaughan Williams's Christmas cantata *Hodie (This Day)*, dedicated to Howells.

Sir David Willcocks remembered how Vaughan Williams, at the age of eighty-two was, by then,

> becoming very deaf, and somewhat infirm, so we had anxious moments at rehearsals. I shall never forget the difficulty that he experienced conducting the first movement of that work [*Hodie*] with its changing rhythmic patterns. At the final rehearsal there was a moment when things came apart, and in his endearing manner 'Uncle Ralph' shouted: 'I have told you 100 times – don't watch me!' The performance went without a hitch because singers and orchestra were determined to give of their best for this

[15] *The Times*, 12 September 1953.

great, beloved musician, who had inherited the mantle of Elgar as a father-figure of the Three Choirs Festival.[16]

Herbert Sumsion's memories of Vaughan Williams at Three Choirs reflected equal warmth:

> Never happier[17] than when sitting holding hands with a young damsel on either side of him, he was heard to remark: 'These Festivals would be marvellous, if it wasn't for the music!' ... If the conductor asked him in advance how he would like certain passages to be played, his advice was always the same: 'You play it as you would like it; and I will tell you if I don't like it.'

Vaughan Williams conducted not only *Hodie* in 1954 but also, on the previous day (Tuesday), his *Pastoral Symphony* (with Isobel Baillie). This followed a performance of *The Apostles* in which both Norma Procter and Wilfred Brown made the first of many Three Choirs appearances; the other soloists were Isobel Baillie, Gordon Clinton, Norman Walker and Roderick Jones. And on Thursday, John Carol Case began a twenty-year association with Three Choirs – singing the part of Christus in the *St Matthew Passion* alongside Joan Alexander, Grace Bodey, Eric Greene, Wilfred Brown and Norman Walker. It was during rehearsals for this that, astonished by one of Boris Ord's breathtaking keyboard runs on the harpsichord, Norman Walker produced a roar of laughter and, in a deep northern accent, said: 'Ee, Boris, there are too many beads on that curtain!'[18]

It was a week of many triumphs for David Willcocks, not least of which was his success in persuading the Dean and Chapter to give permission for the first time at Worcester for the audience to be seated facing the performers instead of each other across the centre aisle. Because the staging at Worcester (and Hereford) is erected at the west end of the cathedral there had formerly been strong opposition to any suggestion that the audience should turn their backs on the altar. Now at least some comfort was possible.

Meredith Davies again made ambitious plans for the 1955 Hereford Festival: Sir Thomas Beecham conducting Haydn's *The Creation*; Dietrich Fischer-Dieskau singing in Brahms's *Ein deutsches Requiem*; and Elisabeth Schwarzkopf, then at the height of her powers, as a principal soloist. These aspirations met with disappointment. Neither Beecham nor Fischer-Dieskau was able to accept, and Walter Legge, Elisabeth Schwarzkopf's husband and agent, replied to an offer of 500 guineas with an emphatic 'five hundred times *No!*'[19]

In spite of these setbacks, Davies was able to persuade the committee to accept a hugely innovative programme, the engagement of two orchestras instead of one, and a complete restructuring of the rehearsal schedule. All this in the face of financial difficulties which had left the 1952 Festival with a deficit of £217. Hugh Ottaway, writing in *Musical Opinion*, welcomed Davies's vision:

---

[16] Letter from Sir David Willcocks to the author, 27 June 1991.

[17] Memories of Herbert Sumsion (private communication).

[18] Memories of Meredith Davies (private communication).

[19] Memories of Rodney Bennett (private communication).

Worcester's innovations were retained and developed this year, though hardly, it seems, in any attempt to balance the account; for some radical changes, likely to alienate the older supporters, were made in the programme, and an expected deficit of £1,000 was announced at the outset. Such a policy is inevitably described as courageous or reckless, splendid or shameful, according to one's point of view. That changes *had* to be made in the type of programme, sooner rather than later, should not need special pleading: a tradition hangs with a dead weight when its emphasis is always on the past, or when it views the present with its own chosen type of blinkers. But in these western shires there is a good deal of blind conservatism, and such innocent steps as the omission of *Messiah* (for the first time since 1875!) and the inclusion of Stravinsky's *Symphony of Psalms* (composed in 1930 but not previously performed by the Three Choirs) are likely to lead to a palace revolution or, more appropriately, a storming of the organ-loft.

Those who had always stood in the way of *Belshazzar's Feast* found themselves quietly outflanked at Hereford by Humphrey Searle's *Night Music*, they also heard Racine Fricker's Prelude, Elegy and Finale (the first considerable orchestral work by a young Englishman to be included in the cathedral programme since Walton's Viola Concerto was given at Worcester in 1932), and the first performances in England of choral works by Francis Poulenc [*Stabat Mater*] with Jennifer Vyvyan as soloist, and Paul Huber [*The Prodigal Son*]. None of this is so very 'radical' by general musical standards, but it appears to have revived the capricious question as to what is suitable for cathedral performance. To judge by the chatter at a Festival luncheon, views on this are merely a reflection of personal taste; it is hard to find anything more objective, for wholly secular works, in the shape of classics from the orchestral repertory, have long been included in the Three Choirs programmes without objection. This is usually justified on the grounds that all great music is ennobling – but only, it seems, if it is long-established or its idiom accords with one's personal taste. Perhaps the only significant side to the question is that the passing of time seems to make it irrelevant: 'Time consecrates, and what is grey with age becomes religion.' However, the dissident voices were clearly in a minority and one found support for the programme in some unexpected quarters.[20]

The 1955 Festival represents a successful attempt by Meredith Davies to open up the week as never before and to place rehearsals nearer the related performances. The orchestra for the Opening Service and the Monday concerts was the CBSO. In addition to accompanying the choir in Stravinsky's *Symphony of Psalms* on Monday afternoon, they gave the *Concerto grosso* No. 1 in F by Handel, and a 'good, firm performance' of Beethoven's Symphony No. 3 (*Eroica*). For these two works they were under their own conductor, Rudolf Schwarz. The soloists in the Verdi Requiem on Monday evening were Amy Shuard, Constance Shacklock, Rowland Jones, and Owen Brannigan replacing Norman Walker, who was indisposed.

---

[20] *Musical Opinion*, November 1955, pp. 81 and 83.

The LSO took over on the second day for the rest of the week. The Wednesday programme included Lennox Berkeley's *Four Poems of St Teresa of Avila* (with Norma Procter) and the first performance of a choral suite by Geoffrey Bush, *In Praise of Mary* (with Isobel Baillie).

> Wednesday brought the fullest programme: a morning Chamber recital (Isobel Baillie and Julian Bream), three major orchestral works in the afternoon and, finally, a choral-orchestral concert which typified the Festival's 'new look'. The afternoon left a strong impression of Meredith Davies's grasp of the orchestra. Few cathedral organists would attempt *La Mer*, few indeed might be expected to bring it off convincingly, for it requires the utmost attention to detail and a complete mastery of orchestral values. Despite some sluggishness in the first movement, the performance was a triumph; it made a grand sound in the cathedral and was one of the highlights of the week.[21]

As the spacious grandeur of Debussy's seascape cascaded into the nave and eddied about the ancient pillars, Dr Sydney Watson, a long-time Steward of the Festival, turned to his neighbour and whispered: 'Ah, *la cathédrale engloutie!*'[22]

The Thursday evening concert ended with a brilliant performance of Sir Arthur Bliss's *Colour Symphony*, conducted by the composer, who, in 1953, had succeeded Arnold Bax as Master of the Queen's Music.

Ottaway's article in *Musical Opinion* summed up:

> Apart from one unfortunate venture [Huber's *The Prodigal Son*], the Festival may be reckoned an important success. All in all, the choral standard was very impressive, and a new interest was kindled in the tradition's future. Now that a more bracing climate has been introduced, steps should be taken to avoid a depression next year ... The Gloucester programme will be awaited with the keenest of interest.[23]

Both the LSO and the CBSO played again at the 1956(G) Festival, the latter in a concert in the Regal Cinema on the Wednesday afternoon, the Gloucester Shire Hall having been converted into an office block since the previous Festival! Rudolf Schwarz conducted the CBSO in a programme which opened with the overture to *Die Meistersinger*, a work which Sumsion had wanted to include in the 1950 cathedral programme but which had been vetoed by the Music Committee after Alexander Brent Smith had complained that 'the performance of such secular music was putting the Cathedral to a wrong use'.[24] The remainder of the CBSO concert comprised Dag Wirén's *Serenade* for strings; Bliss's *Meditations on a Theme by John Blow*; Beethoven's Piano Concerto No. 3, in which Phyllis Sellick was the soloist; and *La Valse* by Ravel.

---

[21] Ibid., p. 83.

[22] Memories of Meredith Davies (private communication).

[23] *Musical Opinion*, November 1955, p. 83.

[24] Gloucester Festival Minute Book, 1950. Gloucester Cathedral Archives and Library.

Ottaway's article of 1955 had suggested a number of works which came to mind as Three Choirs possibilities. Among these was Ernest Bloch's *Sacred Service*, an impulsively rhapsodic, intensely subjective setting of Jewish liturgy. This was given by Herbert Sumsion in 1956:

> The role of the Cantor, the leader of the exacting ritual, was effectively undertaken by Mr Hervey Alan … The lavish, vivid colours of Bloch's instrumentation, and the many Oriental inflections of his music, stood in the strongest possible contrast to the reticent rhapsody and peculiarly English atmosphere of Vaughan Williams's Romance for violin and orchestra, *The Lark Ascending*.[25]

Frederick Grinke was the soloist in *The Lark Ascending* and Vaughan Williams himself took up the baton to conduct. He was one month from his eighty-fourth birthday. As the great man took his place on the rostrum both audience and choir rose to their feet in tribute, and they stood again at the end. Ursula Vaughan Williams described that memorable Festival, the composer's last:

> The best week of all that summer was that of the Gloucester Festival. A large party stayed at the King's School House, just behind the cathedral; the whole Finzi family were there, the organist of Worcester, David Willcocks, and of Hereford, Meredith Davies, Howard Ferguson, and Harold Browne, the Treasurer of the South Western Arts Association. It was like an end of term week at a glorified educational school, Ralph said. We had a wonderful Sunday when the Finzi's drove us out to Chosen Hill[26] and Gerald described how he had been there as a young man on Christmas Eve at a party in the tiny house where the sexton lived and how they had all come out into the frosty midnight and heard bells ringing across Gloucestershire from beside the Severn to the hill villages of the Cotswolds. Gerald's Festival work, *In Terra Pax* [conducted by Finzi himself], was a setting of a poem by Robert Bridges about such an experience. For us it was still summer, with roses in the tangled churchyard grass where the sexton's children were playing; blackberries in the hedges and the gold September light over the country we all knew and loved. Another expedition we four made was to see Rutland and Kathleen Boughton. After much wandering we found their house [at Kilcot] and sat and talked through the morning.
> … One night we came out of the concert to find rainy clouds carrying shadows of the floodlit cathedral, four towers standing mighty and mysterious in the sky above the real tower.[27]

There is a sad postscript to this account of the visit to Chosen Hill. While there, the happy group again called at the tiny cottage in the churchyard. One of the sexton's children was suffering from chicken pox and Finzi, already weakened by leukaemia, contracted the virus. On returning home to Ashmansworth after the

---

[25] *Daily Telegraph,* 7 September 1956.

[26] Churchdown, close to Gloucester.

[27] Ursula Vaughan Williams, *R. V. W.: A Biography of Ralph Vaughan Williams* (OUP, 1964), p. 374.

Festival he became ill and the doctor sent him to hospital in Reading. He took a number of manuscripts with him but was unable to work and quickly became unconscious. Gerald Finzi died on 27 October 1956 at the age of fifty-five.

T HE 1956(G) Festival had included the first full orchestral version of Finzi's *In terra pax*, with Elsie Morrison and Bruce Boyce as soloists; Vaughan Williams's *Hodie* and Symphony No. 8, conducted by Meredith Davies, in addition to *The Lark Ascending* ('The choirs nearly fell out of their seats watching the timpani and percussion players in the last movement of *No 8*.');[28] and the first performance of Howard Ferguson's *Amore Langueo*, conducted by Herbert Sumsion and with Eric Greene singing the solo tenor part. *Amore Langueo* was dedicated to Gerald Finzi and his wife, Joy.

But there was *Gerontius*, and *Messiah* was back too. Hugh Ottaway was not impressed:

> When asked my opinion of the programme (*Musical Opinion*, August 1956), I had to let off steam – just one tentative puff. 'Any programme is third-rate', I said, 'if it insists on plugging *Messiah* and *Gerontius* to the total exclusion of the Mass in D and *Belshazzar's Feast*.' That did it! 'Plugging', it seems, is a rude word, Walton's work should never be mentioned, and perhaps the Beethoven has been socially smeared by Edinburgh's stooping to folly. At all events, I was strongly suspected of sapping and mining the cathedral fabric … What can you do with a supposedly responsible group of people – namely, the Stewards – who, when *Messiah* is miraculously dropped, as it was last year at Hereford, immediately demand its performance in full? I ask again, what can you do? I know what I should do, but we had better not go into that … So *Messiah* was given in full, 'by general request of the Stewards'. Respectability was thus restored and honour saved! And that brazen young man at Hereford is leaving anyway – stricken with remorse, no doubt, for his unpardonable sin … Now David Willcocks has done *Belshazzar's Feast* at Birmingham, and done it well. If he can persuade his committee to include the work next year at Worcester, I promise to march from Malvern and help defend his organ-loft; for some of those terrible Stewards would surely resort to fire and sword. And if he cannot? – well there will be other years. I shall not consign *Belshazzar's Feast* with Leamington Spa and the Baghdad Pact to the limbo of lost causes. On the contrary, I propose the formation of a Babylonian League – subject to a grant from O.U.P. – whose sole aim shall be that of securing a Cathedral performance of Walton's choral masterpiece. Once the ice has been broken, Belshazzar will probably do the hat-trick. That would indeed be occasion for feasting![29]

For almost thirty years Three Choirs had turned aside from a work which had become a standard part of the choral repertoire of leading choirs in the country. Mention of eunuchs and concubines in the text had resulted in *Belshazzar's Feast* being considered unsuitable for performance at the Festival. But the ice

---

[28] Ibid.

[29] *Musical Opinion*, November 1956, pp. 79 and 83.

was finally broken in 1957(w), when *Belshazzar* was at last accepted for cathedral performances: 'Without uncertainty it is possible to congratulate David Willcocks upon his performance of *Belshazzar's Feast* ... At last – in Worcester – it has been heard in a cathedral setting which vibrates sympathetically to the impact of its concentrated force and enhances the splendour of its scintillating clamour.'[30]

Hervey Alan, the soloist, distinguished himself also during the week in a repetition of Bloch's *Sacred Service*; *Elijah*; *Messiah*; the Mass in B minor; *A Tribute of Praise* by Anthony Lewis, Barber Professor of Music at the University of Birmingham; and the first performance of the Requiem by Julius Harrison, in which he was joined by Heather Harper, Marjorie Thomas and William Herbert. Heather Harper was also the soloist in the first performance of Anthony Milner's *The City of Desolation*; joined Hervey Alan in *A Tribute of Praise*; Marjorie Thomas in Debussy's *The Blessed Damozel*; Marjorie Thomas, Eric Greene and speakers Patricia Pilkington and Sir Steuart Wilson in Honegger's *King David*; and Pamela Bowden, Eric Greene and John Carol Case in Bach's *Magnificat*.

Denis Matthews played with the LSO under Willcocks in a performance of Mozart's Piano Concerto in A major, K488, and also gave a piano recital in the Public Hall which included works by Alan Rawsthorne and William Alwyn.

MEREDITH Davies and David Willcocks made immense contributions to Three Choirs, both in conducting and shaping policy. Both brought imagination and vitality to the Festival at a crucial time; and both left within the same year.

Davies moved to Oxford in 1956 as Organist and supernumerary Fellow of New College – but he already knew that his future lay in a different direction. He was encouraged by Sir Adrian Boult to become a full-time conductor, and the Hereford Dean and Chapter had the vision to release him for three months in 1954 and 1956 so that he could attend the Accademia di Santa Cecilia in Rome, where he studied conducting under Fernando Previtali. While at Oxford, Meredith Davies became associate conductor of the CBSO, returning to Three Choirs in that capacity each year from 1957 to 1960. He was also the conductor of the City of Birmingham Choir from 1957 to 1964. In 1959 he left New College for a career in conducting, appearing at Covent Garden and Sadler's Wells. Closely associated with the music of Benjamin Britten, Davies conducted, among much else, the first performance of *War Requiem* at the consecration of the new Coventry Cathedral in May 1962, when the soloists were Heather Harper, Peter Pears and Dietrich Fischer-Dieskau.

From 1964 to 1971 Meredith Davies conducted widely in the UK and abroad, while also holding the post of conductor of the Vancouver Symphony Orchestra. In 1971 he became conductor of the Royal Choral Society and joined the staff of the Royal Academy of Music, moving to Trinity College of Music as Principal from 1979 to 1988. He was appointed CBE in 1982. He died on 9 March 2005.

David Willcocks returned to Cambridge from Worcester in 1957 to take up the post of Organist and Director of the choir at King's College, remaining there

[30] A. T. Shaw, writing in the *Worcester Journal*, 6 September 1957.

for seventeen years, during which time the choir achieved international renown and Willcocks established a long and distinguished career at the heart of British choral music. He became conductor of the Bach Choir in 1960 and remained at Cambridge until his appointment as Director of the Royal College of Music in 1974, following the retirement of Sir Keith Falkner. He was appointed CBE in 1971 and was knighted in 1977. He died on 17 September 2015.

Following the resignations of Davies and Willcocks, Melville Cook was appointed Organist of Hereford Cathedral in 1956, and Douglas Guest of Worcester in 1957. Both men conducted at the 1957 Worcester Festival: Cook in *Elijah* and Guest the Symphony No. 6 of Edmund Rubbra.

Vaughan Williams was also expected to conduct in 1957 his *Five Variants of Dives and Lazarus*; but a day or two before the concert he had left a nursing home following an operation and was unable to be present. He did, however, send a message of good wishes, which was read out at the concert, given by the Three Cathedral Choirs.

Two weeks before the Hereford Festival of 1958, Ralph Vaughan Williams died quietly in his sleep.

18

Association

ALTHOUGH the committees of the Gloucester, Hereford and Worcester
Festivals had met together from time to time, usually to discuss financial
problems, no satisfactory arrangements had been made for regular meetings
and cooperation until 1946. On 14 March in that year, representatives from the
three cities met at the deanery in Hereford to discuss a proposition made by the
Dean of Gloucester, Dr H. Costley-White. There was, he said, a real need for a
central body to advise and assist, financially and otherwise, the diocese holding
the Festival.[1] That need became particularly apparent at Hereford in 1946 when
a decision had to be made on whether or not to revive the Festival. A new joint
advisory body was formed and continued to meet for the next ten years – and
financial problems continued to dominate the agenda.

Alarm bells began to ring following Hereford's small deficit in 1952. Then, in
1953, the LSO put the Festival on notice that its charges would be increased by
one fifth. Doubts were expressed about the ability of Worcester and Hereford
to continue to hold the Festival unless Gloucester was able to provide a subsidy.[2]
The Gloucester balance sheet showed a total surplus of £2,870 at the beginning of
1954 (collections for the charity amounted to £1,292 of this) but the total surplus
was down £730 on 1950. Worcester had been obliged to make alterations in the
programme of the 1954 Festival in the interests of economy, and Hereford was
anticipating a loss of as much as £1,000 in 1955.

Under these circumstances the Joint Standing Committee agreed that a
reserve fund was essential, and at Gloucester it was recommended that a quarter
of the 1953 Festival profits should be placed to a general reserve subject to the
other two Festivals agreeing to do the same in their turns.[3]

On 3 December 1953 a meeting was held in Worcester between representatives
of the Arts Council and the conductors and secretaries from the three cities.
The Arts Council of Great Britain, formed in 1940 as the Council for the
Encouragement of Music and Arts and whose charter was renewed under the
new title in 1946, was asked to throw Three Choirs a safety line. The Council
representative made it clear that the Council would be anxious to help the
Festival, 'but that this could only be done if some constitution linking the three
cities was adopted and that under such constitution no part of the proceeds from

---

[1] Hereford Festival Minute Book, 1936–69. Hereford Cathedral Library and
Archives.

[2] Gloucester Festival Minute Book, 1953. Gloucester Cathedral Archives and
Library.

[3] Ibid.

the concerts should be used for charitable purposes'.[4] Gloucester and Worcester rejected these conditions and it was left to Hereford to raise the matter again in 1955.

Meredith Davies, faced with rising orchestral fees, doubted that he could make appreciable economies without lowering musical standards. A partial solution was found in engaging the CBSO to play for the first part of the week in place of the more expensive LSO, thus setting a precedent for the next few years. Even so, an Arts Council grant was going to be necessary if ticket prices were to be held at a reasonable level and a large deficit avoided. A formal application seeking a guarantee of between £750 and £1,000 was submitted to the Arts Council – and the lower sum was approved 'with a view to keeping the Festival alive until a more permanent basis could be obtained'.[5]

In the autumn of 1955, Herbert Sumsion held discussions with the Music Director of the Arts Council on the possibility of regular assistance to the Festival. Once again the point was made that the Three Choirs Festival must be regarded as one undertaking, and any profits from concerts paid into a reserve fund, to which the Arts Council would contribute annually over a period of years until the fund was sufficiently in credit to obviate the necessity for support. The point was driven home by a warning that 'the Arts Council were prepared to support the Festival in this way now, but might not be so later on'.[6] The Joint Standing Committee reached a decision in time for the Festival year of 1956 to benefit from an Arts Council grant of £750, payable as soon as the new organisation, The Three Choirs Festival Association Ltd, became formally incorporated.

The assistant secretary of the Gloucester Festival, Mr Roland Pepper, a local solicitor, was asked to devise the necessary legal machinery – and incorporation was achieved on 18 March 1957. From this time the Charity for the Widows and Orphans of the Clergy would benefit only from collections and the proceeds of any events expressly organised for it, which in 1956 included the first Festival Garden Party organised by the Ladies Committee.

The association was fortunate in its first three years: in addition to an Arts Council annual grant there were special donations from ABC Television Ltd, the Gulbenkian Foundation, and the Trustees of the Gloucester Shire Hall Organ Fund, and both the Gloucester and Worcester Festivals made a profit. For the next triennium the Arts Council offered no grant but gave instead a cumulative guarantee spread over three years. Thanks to the Gloucester Festival again making a profit, this proved to be adequate. Thereafter the Arts Council never again offered a guarantee against loss other than on an annual basis.

Against this backcloth Melville Cook (1912–1993) rejoined the Three Choirs family after almost twenty years. A chorister of Gloucester Cathedral from 1923 to 1928, Cook became an articled pupil under Herbert Sumsion for three years from 1929 and Assistant Organist of Gloucester Cathedral from 1932 to 1937. He

---

[4] Hereford Festival Minute Book, 1936–69. Hereford Cathedral Library and Archives.

[5] Ibid.

[6] Gloucester Festival Minute Book, 1955. Gloucester Cathedral Archives and Library.

was also the Organist of All Saints' Church, Cheltenham, from 1935 to 1937. In 1938 he was appointed Organist of Leeds Parish Church, remaining there until December 1956, when he took over from Meredith Davies at Hereford. In 1940 Cook took the Durham degree of DMus after a period of study with Sir Edward Bairstow.

While working in Yorkshire, Melville Cook met Peter Pears, visiting Halifax to sing in *Messiah*. When, a little later, the English Opera Group visited Leeds, Pears introduced Benjamin Britten to Cook. This meeting led to an occasional correspondence and, when installed at Hereford, a determination on Cook's part to invite Britten to Three Choirs. Unaware that Meredith Davies had already tried unsuccessfully to tempt Britten to Three Choirs, Colin Mason, writing in *The Spectator* following the 1957(w) Festival, had suggested that 'the most important composer of religious music in England since Elgar and Vaughan Williams' had never yet been represented by the Three Choirs, and that this persistent ignoring of him seemed 'quite deliberate and rather suspect'. Of course, this was not strictly true: the *Variations on a Theme of Frank Bridge* had been given in 1948(w), *Les Illuminations* in 1951(w), and the *Seven Sonnets of Michelangelo* in 1953(G). But in 1958(H) Britten and Pears came to Three Choirs in person.

At long last, Mr Benjamin Britten has 'arrived' at the Three Choirs Festival. And about time too.

Tonight in Hereford Cathedral … Mr Britten conducted his *St Nicolas* cantata and his *Sinfonia da Requiem*. Tomorrow afternoon, in the Shire Hall, he is to give, with Miss Norma Procter and Mr Peter Pears, a recital which includes his *Abraham and Isaac* canticle.

I am not sure that *St Nicolas* … was the best choice for Mr Britten's West country 'arrival'. It suffers somewhat from the awkward naiveties of Mr Crozier's libretto and it does not suit a Cathedral quite so well as it suits, say, Aldeburgh Parish Church …

The iron-tongued *Sinfonia da Requiem* suited the Cathedral unexpectedly well. Not a detail, even in the macabre frenzy of the *Dies Irae*, was lost. If this performance, by the London Symphony Orchestra, was not the best the amazing and profoundly moving work has ever had, it sounded like it. Mr Britten has improved beyond measure as an orchestral conductor since he conducted the *Sinfonia* with a visiting orchestra at Birmingham Town Hall during the war years.

The concert had begun with Berlioz's *Te Deum*, which made it abundantly clear that in Dr Cook Hereford has again acquired an organist who is also an excellent conductor.[7]

In addition to Benjamin Britten, Cook also brought Peter Racine Fricker to Hereford to conduct his *Litany* for double string orchestra, and *The Light Invisible* by Kenneth Leighton and *Genesis* by Franz Reizenstein were given their first performances. From the past, *Messe des morts* by the seventeenth-century composer Jean Gilles and, from the present, Poulenc's *Stabat Mater* represented French ecclesiastical music. Peter Pears joined Jennifer Vyvyan, Ilse Wolf, John Whitworth, Nicholas Long, David Galliver, Richard Standen and Bruce Boyce

[7] *Birmingham Post*, 9 September 1958.

in a performance of Monteverdi's Vespers of 1610. The Sunday evening organ recital was given by the great Italian Organist of St Peter's, Rome, Fernando Germani, and popular tradition was followed in performances of the Verdi Requiem, *Messiah*, *The Kingdom*, and *Gerontius* with William Herbert singing the title role for the last time at Three Choirs.

Melville Cook took the lion's share of the conducting load upon himself, but Herbert Sumsion directed Finzi's *Fall of the Leaf* and Vaughan Williams's *Hundredth Psalm*, and Douglas Guest the Piano Concerto in C minor, K491, by Mozart (with Colin Horsley) and Poulenc's *Stabat Mater*. The CBSO orchestral concert, conducted by Meredith Davies, included Schubert's Symphony No. 3, the Brahms Violin Concerto (with Manoug Parikian), and Hindemith's suite for orchestra, *Nobilissima visione*.

Compared with such diversity, the programme of the 1959 Gloucester Festival contained little to surprise: an all-Vaughan Williams concert, *Missa solemnis*, *St Matthew Passion*, *Messiah*, *Gerontius*, and *Intimations of Immortality*. But there were new works: the first Three Choirs performance of the Requiem by Maurice Duruflé, with Helen Watts and Richard Standen; Adrian Crufts's *A Passiontide Carol*, again with Helen Watts; and the première of Howard Ferguson's *The Dream of the Rood* – a setting of an anonymous Anglo-Saxon poem translated for Ferguson by Dorothy de Navarro:

> Dr Ferguson, who never hesitates to speak out boldly, gives the story a powerful setting. It is impressive in its beauty and thrilling in its climaxes.
>
> The full and lovely voice of Heather Harper, who sang the solo part, gave us the first of these. There were others by the choir, though none the equal of the mighty annunciation, 'But the Lord arose by his great might to succour man' preceded by a vigorous and splendidly executed orchestral preface.
>
> [The *Dream of the Rood*] was the supreme moment of last night's music. It was intended that it should be and it was.[8]

Howard Ferguson dedicated *The Dream of the Rood* to Dame Myra Hess, and she acknowledged the honour by visiting Gloucester for the first performance, conducted by Herbert Sumsion. Two days earlier the Melos Ensemble gave a polished chamber recital in the cathedral (surely a contradiction in terms) of Schubert's Octet in F major, D803, and Howard Ferguson's boldly original Octet, op. 4 (1933), his largest chamber work.

By the early 1960s Howard Ferguson had come to a realisation that he had no more to say as a composer and made up his mind to stop writing, devoting himself instead to musicology. His bond with Three Choirs remained strong, Ferguson becoming a familiar and respected figure at the Festival.

Douglas Guest (1917–1996) was appointed Organist at Worcester Cathedral in 1957. Like David Willcocks, he came to Worcester from Salisbury Cathedral, and both were organ scholars at King's College, Cambridge. Guest was a student at the Royal College of Music from 1933 to 1935, and studied with Sir Ernest Bullock, among others. From 1935 to 1939 he was organ scholar at

---

[8] *Citizen*, 11 September 1959.

King's College under Boris Ord; David Willcocks succeeded him in 1939. From 1939 to 1945 Guest was on active service in the Royal Artillery. He commanded a battery in the D-Day assault force, on 6 June 1944, and was Mentioned in Despatches.

After the war, until 1950 he was Director of Music at Uppingham School. In that year he succeeded Willcocks at Salisbury and as conductor of the Salisbury Musical Society. From 1950 too he carried out frequent engagements as deputy conductor of the Bournemouth Symphony Orchestra. He also conducted other orchestras in London, including broadcast performances with the Philharmonia, as well as several provincial concerts with the LSO; he was chairman of the Governing Council of the National Youth Orchestra of Great Britain for thirty-four years.

Douglas Guest directed the Worcester Festivals of 1960 and 1963 before his appointment, in the latter year, as Organist of Westminster Abbey, a post which he held until 1987. He received the honour CVO in 1975.

Writing of the 1960(w) Festival in the *Musical Times*, Ernest Bradbury described Guest's work as 'invariably distinctive, energetic, and generally appealing'.[9] He might have added that Guest had also proved himself to be a very quick thinker.

After a week of rain, sunshine gilded the flag-bedecked streets of Worcester as the civic procession walked from the Guildhall to the cathedral for the Opening Service. Crowds of spectators watched as the Lord Mayors of Birmingham, Bristol and Coventry, ten mayors, a deputy mayor, local MPs and other civic representatives passed by. The procession reached the north door of the cathedral and waited ... and continued to wait for more than ten minutes.

Through a misunderstanding about the time of the service, the coach carrying members of the CBSO to Worcester had set out late. Realising that there had been an error, Douglas Guest rang the CBSO office in Birmingham, asking for a police escort. The police sent a patrol car to escort the coach – but the coach driver thought that the police were checking his speed and slowed down! Only when a police officer boarded the coach was the driver persuaded to put his foot down. The members of the orchestra arrived at the cathedral and scrambled into their places, the civic procession made its stately way into the nave followed by the Lord Lieutenant of Worcestershire, Admiral Sir William Tennant, in naval uniform, and his deputy lieutenants, then by the procession of the clergy.

The unfortunate start was soon forgotten in the combined splendours of church music and pageantry, and the congregation of 3,000 heard the Master of the Queen's Music, Sir Arthur Bliss, read the first lesson. (Bliss conducted his *Music for Strings* on the Thursday evening.)

Douglas Guest needed to think quickly too when, four months before the Festival, he learned that Anthony Milner would be unable to finish his new oratorio, *The Water and the Fire*, in time. To his great credit Guest chose not to substitute a well-tried warhorse but to give the first public performance in Britain of *In terra pax* by the Swiss composer Frank Martin. Described by Martin as an 'oratorio-brève', *In terra pax* was written in 1944 as a result of a commission from Radio Geneva to compose a choral work to mark the armistice

[9] *MT* 1960, p. 697.

of World War II; it was completed in 1945. In Worcester the soloists were Heather Harper, Jean Allister, David Galliver, John Carol Case and Hervey Alan.

> No one will deny that Douglas Guest had tackled his first 'official' Three Choirs with resolution and enterprise. Kodály's *Budávari Te Deum*, Petrassi's *Magnificat* and Janáček's *The Eternal Gospel* were relatively unfamiliar items in a programme that also included Verdi's *Quattro Pezzi Sacri*, Bruckner's E minor Mass and Berkeley's *Stabat Mater* ... and even the Bach Passion was changed this year, from the usual St Matthew to the St John.[10]

Kodály's Budávari *Te Deum* was given as the first item in the Monday evening programme and, unexpectedly, Kodály joined the audience to hear it. The soloists were Eileen Poulter, Marjorie Thomas, Wilfred Brown and Hervey Alan. During the performance, an alarmed Eileen Poulter noticed a smell of burning; the *Worcester Evening News* takes up the tale:

> Miss Poulter ... has an exceptionally keen sense of smell, and it seemed worse to her during an interval when she went to the artists' room below the stage.
> She mentioned it to Mr Wilfred Brown, tenor soloist, who diagnosed an electrical fault, and without further ado telephoned the Midlands Electricity Board. Their representative was promptly on the spot, a fuse box was found to be nearly red-hot, and a circuit seriously overloaded.
> The floodlighting on all but the North face of the Cathedral was turned off immediately, a circumstance which puzzled those who came out of the Cathedral later and found only one side illuminated.[11]

Benjamin Britten and Peter Pears returned to Hereford for the 1961 Festival, appearing with Barry Tuckwell in a Shire Hall recital which included Schumann's Adagio and Allegro for horn and piano and *Dichterliebe*, Britten's canticle *Still Falls the Rain*, and songs by Ireland and Bridge. On the Wednesday evening in the cathedral, Pears was a soloist, along with Jennifer Vyvyan, Helen Watts and Roger Stalman, in Mozart's Coronation Mass in C, K317, conducted by Herbert Sumsion; in Britten's *Nocturne*, op. 60, conducted by the composer; and in Fricker's *The Vision of Judgement*, with Jennifer Vyvyan, the Festival Chorus and the LSO conducted by Melville Cook.

John Mitchinson and Janet Baker both made their Three Choirs debuts in 1961: Mitchinson in *Messiah* and Baker in the first British performance of Paul Hindemith's *When Lilacs Last in the Door-Yard Bloom'd* (his 'requiem "for those we love"', setting words by Walt Whitman), a work described by Frank Howes in *The Times* as 'gray and interminable, for all its moments of redeeming lyrical beauty'.[12] Janet Baker also joined Ilse Wolf, Wilfred Brown and Donald Bell in *Three Latin Motets* by Bernard Naylor.

---

[10] Ibid.

[11] *Worcester Evening News*, article about Worcester Festival of 1960.

[12] *The Times*, 6 September 1961.

The year 1961 was a memorable one for Herbert Sumsion: he was awarded the CBE ('too little too late' wrote Sir Arthur Bliss in his letter of congratulation), became an Honorary Fellow of the Royal College of Music, and was elected an Honorary Associate of the Royal Academy of Music, all in that year – his thirty-third as Organist at Gloucester. 'I believe (and Hindemith, if I read *A Composer's World* aright would support me)', wrote Arthur Jacobs, 'that there is a moral worth in having performances conducted by men who belong to, and are loved by, the community which provides their audiences.'[13] Sumsion, known affectionately to all his friends as John, was just such a figure, and in retirement he retained the genuine warmth and respect born of long, dedicated service to music.

It is a measure of Sumsion's generous spirit that in 1962 he gave opportunities to two young musicians, one on the threshold of his career and the other rapidly establishing himself in the music-making life of Gloucester, to bring their compositions to a wider audience at Three Choirs. Both men chose to present a *Te Deum*.

John Sanders, Sumsion's Assistant Organist from 1958, conducted his *Te Deum* at the Opening Service:

> a splendid setting composed for the occasion. It owes – at any rate for purposes of description and categorization – something to Walton; it is sustained on a pervasive figure suggestive of bells and it is modern in its well-judged use of clanging dissonance; its scoring is clear and well adapted to a large church.[14]

During the organ recital which preceded the 1959(G) Opening Service, John Sanders had included a piece entitled *Whitsunday Procession* by Tony Hewitt-Jones. A Londoner, Hewitt-Jones went up to Christ Church, Oxford, but his studies were interrupted by war service in the Royal Navy. Returning to Oxford, where he was a pupil of Bernard Rose, he completed his musical studies and then took a teaching appointment in Gloucestershire. He was the first conductor of the Gloucestershire Youth Orchestra, formed in 1956; he studied with Herbert Sumsion, and was made an ARCO in 1957, when he was awarded the Limpus and Read prizes. Composing from 1951, Hewitt-Jones had completed a *Sinfonietta* for strings in 1959 and went on to write music in many forms, much of it for particular occasions. The Three Choirs Festival of 1962 was the first such occasion of major importance. Arthur Jacobs again:

> The last day brought Tony Hewitt-Jones's *Te Deum* for soloists [Norma Procter, Wilfred Brown and Hervey Alan], chorus and orchestra. The composer (born 1926) was unwise enough in the programme-note to allow his music to be wrapped in numerological mumbo-jumbo: we were told in all seriousness how the figure 3 (as in Three Choirs and in the Holy Trinity, to which the cathedral is dedicated) is symbolized in the musical forces used (violins 1, 2, 3; violas 1, 2, 3; triple woodwind, *etc.*) and even in the musical construction, with a canon in 27 parts (3^3)! For Mr Jones's sake one rejoiced that trumpets already have three valves. But three (if the composer

---

[13] *MT* 1962, p. 689.

[14] *The Times*, 4 September 1962.

will pardon the liberty) cheers for music with an arresting quality and a very individual approach.

A young composer might have set the traditional text with traditional church polyphony; or *à la* Britten; or with reverence to today's fashionable serialist models. Instead, Mr Hewitt-Jones has adopted a monumental, many-voiced, firmly diatonic style which one might almost call '20th-century Gabrieli'.[15]

The *Te Deum* was repeated at the 1968(G) and 1992(G) Festivals. Hewitt-Jones's association with Three Choirs extended over more than thirty years as composer, as music adviser to the county of Gloucestershire, and as a singer in the Festival Chorus whose solid bottom C was the pride of the second basses. He died in 1989.

Benjamin Britten and Peter Pears were unable to accept an invitation to appear at the 1962(G) Festival, but nonetheless the programme included Britten's *Nocturne*, sung by Gerald English, and the *Missa brevis* for boys' voices and organ. Sir Arthur Bliss conducted the first performance in an appropriate cathedral setting of his *Beatitudes*. (The première at the Coventry Festival was given in a theatre.) Honegger's *A Christmas Cantata* was conducted by Douglas Guest, with a capable baritone in James Walkley – a Gloucester Cathedral lay clerk. The London Mozart Players gave a concert under their conductor Harry Blech. The LSO played until Thursday, and the Bournemouth Symphony Orchestra appeared at Three Choirs for the first time on Friday afternoon, coincidentally marking three other 'firsts': Sir Adrian Boult as Festival conductor; Mahler's Symphony No. 4, with Elizabeth Harwood as the soprano soloist; and Tony Hewitt-Jones's *Te Deum*.

An even more surprising 'first' occurred on the Wednesday evening – a complete performance at Three Choirs of Vaughan Williams's *Sea Symphony*. The last movement had been given twice before, at Gloucester in 1925 and Hereford in 1936, but until 1962 the other sections had been banished from the cathedrals by Deans and Chapters set against the lack of orthodoxy in Whitman's texts.

> An unbeliever may rub his ears on hearing Vaughan Williams's *Sea Symphony* – with its prophecy of a poet whom Whitman pointedly calls 'the true son of God' – in a cathedral. Presumably (to alter a dictum ascribed to Rossini) what is too blasphemous to be said may be sung.[16]

Until 1962 books of words had been sold for each Festival concert in addition to an outline programme for the week. In that year, at Sumsion's suggestion, a single combined programme book was introduced – a precedent followed at all subsequent Festivals.

Herbert Sumsion, convalescing from illness, was unable to attend the 1963 Worcester Festival. His place was taken by John Sanders, conducting Carissimi's *Jephte*; David Willcocks, back to conduct the *Passacaglia, Chorale and Fugue* by Kenneth Leighton; and Christopher Robinson, Assistant Organist and Organist-Elect of Worcester Cathedral, in the traditional concert of the Three

---

[15] *MT* 1962, p. 691.

[16] Ibid., p. 689.

Cathedral Choirs. The CBSO and the RPO were both engaged, the latter for the first time at Three Choirs, and on the Saturday evening the National Youth Orchestra of Great Britain, conducted by Rudolf Schwarz, presented a sparkling programme, the principal work in which was Dvořák's Symphony No. 8 in G.

Sir Arthur Bliss was again present to conduct in 1963: Norma Procter, John Carol Case, the chorus and CBSO in the first performance of his cantata *Mary of Magdala*. The text, partly a reworking by Christopher Hassall of a seventeenth-century poem, deals with the mystery of the empty tomb in Gethsemane. Sadly, Hassall died soon after he finished the libretto and before hearing the completed work.

For Douglas Guest the abiding memory of the 1963 Festival, his last, is a sense of thrilling intoxication while conducting Benjamin Britten's *War Requiem*, only the third public performance anywhere. 'I never felt anything like it again', he told me. 'The Cathedral turned upside down.' Frank Howes expressed it perfectly:

> Britten's *War Requiem* was a bold undertaking for a choir and conductor with a week's festival to sustain, but Mr Guest's courage was amply justified and his own stature as a conductor made patent for all to admire. The geographical problem of placing the very large forces required was solved by putting the boys in one side aisle and the chamber orchestra in the other with the main stage between; the soloists also were at the sides with their backs to pillars, Miss Heather Harper to the left and Mr Gerald English and Mr John Shirley-Quirk to the right of the conductor.
>
> All three had entered into the spirit of the requiem – and what a spirit it is that reconciles into a single work of art the conflicting, distracted, and terrifying emotions of war as no other piece of music has ever done, but Mr English should perhaps have the recognition that he followed Mr Peter Pears in the part without at all resembling him.
>
> The chorus sang securely and Mr Guest controlled it all with a judgement that seemed hardly ever at fault even in so tricky a matter as balance. The result was that this masterpiece gripped with something like awe.[17]

B RITTEN'S *War Requiem* was again the centrepiece of the 1964 Hereford and 1965 Gloucester Festivals, conducted on both occasions by Melville Cook. In 1964 too the long-awaited oratorio by Anthony Milner, *The Water and the Fire*, at last received its first performance – performed by Heather Harper, Gerald English, John Shirley-Quirk, the chorus and the LSO, conducted by Melville Cook.

Anthony Milner (1925–2002), who was a Roman Catholic, based his dramatic oratorio on Man's emergence from the wastelands of life to a dream of perfect happiness. It was, according to Milner, inspired by pictures from the Bible. The composition contains a love duet, religious dance movements and a *Gloria* in which choirboys ring bells. The text includes passages from the Bible, the Liturgy and the Eucharist. *The Water and the Fire* was composed with the resonances of a

---

[17] *The Times*, 5 September 1963.

Gothic cathedral in mind, as was Bernard Naylor's *Stabat Mater*, the other work to receive its first performance at Hereford in 1964.

Written for a double chorus of women's voices and orchestra the *Stabat Mater*, dedicated to Melville Cook, was finished early in 1962. A note in the score reads: 'The work is designed for performance in a spacious building in which sounds last longer, or much longer, than their written notes indicate.'

Describing *The Water and the Fire* as 'the most powerful and evocative score' which Milner had yet composed, Felix Aprahamian, in a *Guardian* review, considered 'outstanding ... the depiction of the torrents of perdition in the first scene, of the waters of night in the second and the luminous beauty of the scene in which the Paschal Fire blazes'. Naylor, in his *Stabat Mater*, had 'succeeded in creating the kind of musical texture which floats through the spaces of Hereford Cathedral with magical effect ... Both works should be heard in London. But where?'

Melville Cook proved himself a true revolutionary by dropping *Messiah* from the programme – and this time it remained dropped for thirteen years. In addition to the Milner and Naylor premières, modern music included Stravinsky's *Symphony of Psalms* and Poulenc's *Gloria*, as well as the *War Requiem*. 'The ancient festival may not be *avant-garde*', declared John Waterhouse, 'but it is certainly no longer a museum.'[18] The old myth that Three Choirs was firmly cemented in an outmoded tradition seemed at last to be crumbling.

There might not have been any shortage of new works at Hereford but there was a very definite shortage of new voices in the Hereford contingent of the Festival Chorus, especially men. By 1964 Hereford could muster only five tenors, against ten from Gloucester and twenty-one from Worcester. Melville Cook placed an appeal for tenors and basses in the local newspapers, but numbers continued to fall. Hereford was only able to send three tenors and five basses, other than lay clerks, to Worcester in 1966. Overall balance seems not to have suffered from this deficit, and in reporting 1965(G) *The Times* praised the firm choral attack of the three choirs under Melville Cook in *The Hymn of Jesus*: 'Dr Cook brought dramatic understanding and an appropriate touch of flamboyance to his tempi and his timing, so as to recall something of the thrilling novelty which this music originally conveyed.'[19]

There was praise too for a performance of Anthony Milner's *Salutatio Angelica*, and especially for Janet Baker's interpretation of the contralto solos. But Herbert Sumsion was not spared the critical stripes of the London press. He was accused of providing an unyielding accompaniment in the Verdi *Te Deum* and the Sibelius Violin Concerto (with Yfrah Neaman), of a disappointing neutrality in Bach's Cantata No. 100 (with Janet Baker and Robert Tear), and of not demanding enough from his performers in Handel's early *Dixit Dominus*. On the other hand, there was warm praise for his realisations of *Gerontius* (Marjorie Thomas, Kenneth Bowen and Roger Stalman) and *Elijah* (Rae Woodland, Maureen Lehane, John Mitchinson and John Dethick). Sir Adrian Boult, who had arrived before breakfast to help Sumsion prepare for his first Festival in 1928, arrived on the final day of Sumsion's last Gloucester Festival – to conduct the

[18] *Birmingham Post*, 9 September 1964.
[19] *The Times*, 9 September 1965.

LSO in Vaughan Williams's *Norfolk Rhapsody* in E minor and Elgar's Symphony No. 1 in A flat. Between the two, Sir Arthur Bliss conducted his *Music for Strings*.

F ROM the beginning, cathedral concerts at Three Choirs had been received in reverent silence. This long and worthy tradition almost came to an end in 1965 – but not quite. The final work on the evening of Thursday 9 September was a vivid performance of *Belshazzar's Feast* under the baton of Christopher Robinson. The soloist was John Dethick. The chorus sang magnificently. In the highly charged moment following the final 'Alleluia!' a stifled cheer and ripple of applause broke the silence in the South Transept. The noise, which lasted only a moment, betokened that silent thanksgiving would not survive the end of the decade.

Melville Cook resigned his post at Hereford in 1966 and went to Canada to take up appointments as conductor of the Winnipeg Philharmonic Choir and as Organist of All Saints' Church, Winnipeg. After a year he moved to the Metropolitan United Church, Toronto, remaining there until his retirement and return to England in 1986; he died on 22 May 1993.

Herbert Sumsion conducted at Three Choirs for the last time in 1967(H): Haydn's *Nelson Mass* with Elizabeth Harwood, Janet Baker, Wilfred Brown, John Barrow, the Festival Chorus and the RPO. His thirty-nine years of service as Organist at Gloucester Cathedral came to an end on 28 September 1967. At a presentation ceremony in the King's School the Dean of Gloucester, the Very Rev. Seiriol Evans, paid tribute:

> He has the great and rare gift of being so completely in command as to inspire the utter confidence of all of us. You sometimes found this gift in the war among young commanders of destroyers and M.T.B.s [motor torpedo boats] – no side, no self-importance, no self-consciousness; as quiet as anything, yet able to be master of every situation.[20]

Herbert Sumsion to the letter.

---

[20] *Citizen*, 26 September 1967.

19

A New Epoch

Worcester 1966

When recalling impressions of the Opening Service, the one incident which looks biggest in retrospect is that Benjamin Britten's setting of the National Anthem was sung instead of the setting by Elgar, which has hitherto been heard at the opening of the festival for as long as most people can remember.

After hearing that modern setting of the familiar tune, which seemed – perhaps because of key affinity – to fall into place naturally and appropriately, as if it were born of the mood of trust and hope generated by Elgar's prelude to The Kingdom, a new epoch, I felt, had dawned upon the Three Choirs Festival: Christopher Robinson had made his mark![1]

CHRISTOPHER Robinson was born in 1936 at Peterborough and educated at St Michael's College, Tenbury, then at Rugby, and then Christ Church, Oxford. He was Assistant Organist at Christ Church from 1955 to 1958. During his last year at the university he was Assistant Organist at New College under Meredith Davies, and was then on the music staff at Oundle School for three years before taking the post of Assistant Organist at Worcester Cathedral in 1962. He succeeded Douglas Guest as Master of the Choristers and Organist in 1963, when he also became conductor of the City of Birmingham Choir in succession to Meredith Davies.

In 1966 Robinson brought to Three Choirs not only the impressive and grandiose *Grande Messe des morts* of Berlioz, but also, and long overdue, the music of Sir Michael Tippett in the year in which he was knighted: *A Child of our Time*, with Jennifer Vyvyan singing magnificently in the part of the Mother, and with Jean Allister, John Mitchinson and John Carol Case. At the Friday afternoon orchestral concert, Sir Adrian Boult conducted Tippett's Concerto for double string orchestra. There was also the first performance, commissioned by the National Federation of Music Societies, of *Changes* by Gordon Crosse. Described by the composer as 'A Nocturnal Cycle for Soprano, Baritone, Chorus and Orchestra', *Changes* is intended for large amateur choirs. The title refers to changes from day to night (symbolising life and death) and changes in bell-ringing, which provide many musical motifs of the work. Christopher Robinson conducted the Festival Chorus and the RPO (appearing at Three Choirs for the second time, in place of the LSO) in a spirited and assured performance, with excellent contributions in the important solo parts from Noelle Barker and John Noble.

---

[1] A. T. Shaw, *Hereford Evening News*, 6 September 1966.

254

Changes showed the strong influence on Gordon Crosse of Benjamin Britten, whose music was represented at the Festival by *St Nicolas*, conducted by David Willcocks (stepping in to replace Melville Cook) with Gerald English as the tenor soloist; and the *Cantata academica*, with Jennifer Vyvyan, Marjorie Thomas, John Mitchinson and Owen Brannigan under Robinson's own direction.

Sir Percy Hull was the principal visitor to the 1967 Hereford Festival: one month from his eighty-ninth birthday, accompanied by Lady Hull, carrying a walking stick which had belonged to Elgar, and which he used constantly. 'I am delighted', he said, 'to find the Festival still in a thriving condition and I do congratulate Hereford on acquiring its new young organist, Mr Richard Lloyd, a real find.'[2] Sir Percy Hull died at his home in Surrey on 31 August 1968.

Richard Hey Lloyd was born in Cheshire in 1933 and educated at Lichfield Cathedral School, at Rugby, and Jesus College, Cambridge, where he was Organ Scholar (1952–5). From 1957 to 1966 he was Assistant Organist at Salisbury Cathedral; he then moved to Hereford in succession to Melville Cook on 1 September 1966. He first appeared at Three Choirs conducting at the concert of the three cathedral choirs in the 1966 Worcester Festival, and in the following year directed his first Hereford Festival.

A long-time devotee of Three Choirs, Lloyd had been attending the Festival for nearly twenty years when he was appointed to Hereford. He was keenly aware that many in the Festival chorus had sung under the baton of Elgar and that there was, for instance, a 'Three Choirs way' of performing *Gerontius*. He was conscious, too, of the direct link to Elgar which had been maintained through Hull and Sumsion, and he had admired particularly the work which Meredith Davies had done in raising Festival conducting standards. From the outset, Lloyd set himself the task of building up the depleted Hereford chorus – and within a year all the deficiencies had been made good. The Hereford contingent of the Festival Chorus at the 1967(H) Festival with their chorus superintendent, Michael Morris, numbered ninety-three apart from choristers and lay clerks, and included fourteen tenors and eighteen basses.

Lloyd included several modern English works in his first Festival programme. Of these, Alun Hoddinott's *Dives and Lazarus*, commissioned for the 1965 Farnham Festival, was the most interesting. *The Annunciation* by Bernard Naylor, written in 1949 and broadcast in 1951, was given its first public performance at Hereford in 1967; in spite of fine solo work by Noelle Barker and Wilfred Brown it failed to please, and Norman Kay's *King Herod* fared little better.

On the other hand, Bruckner's Mass in F minor was given a stunning performance under Richard Lloyd on Thursday evening. On the last night Lloyd was blessed by that rare thing, a near-perfect group of soloists in *Gerontius*: Janet Baker, Ronald Dowd and Roger Stalman. But this memorable *Gerontius* was close to cancellation when, just before the performance, a hoaxer phoned to say that a bomb had been planted in the cathedral. Thanks to the action of the police (who merely said a parcel had been lost) a stampede was avoided.

In contrast, a metaphorical bombshell had burst on the previous day, following publication of an article by William Mann in *The Times*:

[2] *Hereford Evening News*, 7 September 1967.

It is difficult to be sure in what frame of mind one should approach the Three Choirs Festival. Is it a local jollification during which, for one week, the organists of the three cathedrals try their hands at the role of Toscanini and match their choir-master-organist talents (not necessarily those of a good conductor) against as wide a stretch of the choral and symphonic repertory as they fancy? Is it, as England's oldest musical festival ... to be regarded *ipso facto* as an event of natural cultural importance, to be judged by the standards of, say, Glyndebourne or Edinburgh? Or as a respectable shop window for all that is most worth while in choral and orchestral music of all countries and periods?

Or do we have to admit that an existence of 240 years inevitably induces some sort of senile decay and that, in its present form, the Three Choirs Festival needs to be replaced or retired for the musical health of the country?

In recent years, I have arrived at Three Choirs Festivals suspecting that the first or last of these attitudes must be the appropriate one, and either the choice of music or the setting, more rarely the quality of performance, has induced a more respectful frame of mind. First impressions this year, after two concerts today, are less favourable.[3]

William Mann went on to review the only two concerts which he had actually attended: one in which the Naylor and Kay works had been given; the other, a performance of the Verdi Requiem:

The fires did not blaze, the choir sang like mice, and the four soloists [Rae Woodland, Sibyl Michelow, Ronald Dowd and Roger Stalman] prophesied everlasting doom and searing physical agony as sedately as if they were rendering Victorian ballads about platonic love or the pleasures of life on the ocean. Musical drama was missing, and I am still waiting for a sign that this festival is as lively as it is old.[4]

Mann's attack generated considerable anger among Festival supporters, and it was rumoured that a petition condemning it had been organised from the Festival club. But there was no more unanimity among the critics in 1967 than at any other time, and there were those who praised Lloyd's Verdi Requiem as a performance of notable excellence. The more general attack upon the abilities of the organists to assume the role of conductors contained nothing new. It had been repeated innumerable times over the years and is still heard today. It is an argument which takes no account of the impossibility, clearly identified by Sir George Dyson in 1946, for an outside conductor to be able to spare sufficient time for rehearsals and to get to know the chorus, given the distance of Three Choirs from London and the number of works to be prepared for each Festival. Nor did it give a moment's consideration to the possibility that two factors, above all else, had for long contributed to the survival of the Festival: one, the needs of the charity; the other, the continuity guaranteed by the sure presence of the cathedral organists.

[3] *The Times*, 7 September 1967.
[4] Ibid.

Nonetheless, the advantages of relinquishing control of specific concerts to professional conductors are self-evident and, at the first Gloucester Festival under the direction of John Sanders, in 1968, the conducting load was shared by Hugo Rignold (the CBSO), Sir Adrian Boult (the RPO), and Raymond Leppard (the English Chamber Orchestra), in addition to Christopher Robinson and Richard Lloyd.

JOHN Sanders was born in Essex in 1933. He was educated at Felsted School, Essex, at the Royal College of Music, and at Gonville and Caius College, Cambridge, where he was Organ Scholar. After two years military service in the Royal Artillery he became Assistant Organist at Gloucester. In 1963 he was appointed Organist of Chester Cathedral, returning as Organist at Gloucester on the retirement of Dr Sumsion. In 1990 he received the Lambeth degree of DMus.

The year 1968 marked the centenary of the death of Rossini, whose *Stabat Mater* Sanders had chosen as the principal choral work for the Monday evening concert. And the Italian flavour continued on Tuesday afternoon with a performance of Verdi's *Four Sacred Pieces* conducted by Richard Lloyd in a concert which ended with the première of Christopher Steel's Mass in Five Movements, op. 18, conducted by John Sanders.

The Gloucester Festival of 1968 also managed to engage the most famous foreign singer to appear at Three Choirs for many years: the German soprano Rita Streich, celebrated for her singing of Mozart and Richard Strauss coloratura roles. However, two days before the Festival began John Sanders was told by the London agents, Ibbs and Tillett, that Rita Streich was ill and could not appear. They suggested that Richard Lewis, who was singing in Tel Aviv, might be engaged in her place. An urgent cable was sent to Tel Aviv. Lewis accepted and flew from Israel on Tuesday 27 August, sang in a broadcast recital from the Gloucester College of Education on the following Thursday morning, and left for the Edinburgh Festival the next day, where he sang the same programme: Purcell, Schubert, Beethoven, Vaughan Williams, Butterworth and Britten. In Gloucester the famous tenor was accompanied by Geoffrey Parsons.

Rita Streich had also been engaged to sing the *Four Last Songs* of Richard Strauss in the Tuesday evening concert, given by the CBSO under their principal conductor, Hugo Rignold. Her place was taken by Elizabeth Harwood, who, on the previous evening, sang in Christopher Steel's mass along with Kenneth Bowen, and on Wednesday evening in Beethoven's Symphony No. 9 (*Choral*), with Norma Procter, John Mitchinson and Raimund Herincx, the Festival Chorus and RPO conducted by John Sanders.

The fiftieth anniversary of Sir Hubert Parry's death fell in 1968. As a tribute to his memory Sir Adrian Boult gave his services to the Festival to conduct the *Symphonic Variations* for orchestra on Thursday evening. The last item in the same concert, Haydn's Mass in B flat (*Theresienmesse*), was conducted by Richard Lloyd and marked the last appearance at Three Choirs of the tenor Wilfred Brown.

Perfect diction, an unerring feeling for words, a faultless technique, and a golden personality: qualities which informed Wilfred Brown's superb artistry, and qualities which may still be experienced, not merely heard, in his gramophone recordings. Well-known as a radio broadcaster as well as a concert artist, Brown took exactly the same care over singing hymns on BBC religious programmes as he did when performing in great masterpieces. His recording of Gerald Finzi's *Dies natalis*, made in 1963 with the English Chamber Orchestra conducted by Christopher Finzi, is a never-to-be-bettered memorial to a great singer. Four years after making it, while on a cycling holiday with his wife on the Isle of Wight, Brown suddenly found that he couldn't pull on the brakes with one hand: this was the first ominous sign of a brain tumour. He died on 5 March 1971.

T HE National Youth Orchestra again visited Worcester in 1969 and – in response to youthful exuberance – the tradition of centuries was finally broken. On Sunday evening applause broke out spontaneously after the NYO and one of their young trumpeters had played the Trumpet Concerto in E flat by Hummel, conducted by Rudolf Schwarz – and sustained applause greeted each work for the rest of the concert. The audience were silent on Monday evening following Beethoven's *Missa solemnis*, but on Tuesday afternoon a single outburst of clapping was heard after Richard Lloyd had conducted Peter Maxwell Davies's *Five Carols* for boys' voices. More consistent applause was heard on Tuesday evening, though on Wednesday the audience was strangely silent following Rossini's effervescent *Petite Messe solennelle*. Both of Thursday's concerts were applauded – but then Sir Adrian Boult asked for no applause for Friday afternoon's concert by the RPO, much to the disappointment of the local press: 'The audience were getting used to the idea of clapping … and applause at a concert to be broadcast … would have ditched the outworn tradition once and for all.'[5] Not everyone agreed that applause in the cathedrals was a welcome precedent, and a lively correspondence was carried on in the Worcester and Hereford newspapers in 1969 and 1970. But the momentum of change was too great for effective protest; the silence had been broken for ever.

Four composers whose music was performed during the week were present at the 1969(w) Festival. Luigi Dallapiccola's *Due liriche di Anacreonte* and *Quadro liriche di Antonio Machade* were given in a Monday afternoon recital at Hartlebury Castle by the Vesuvius Ensemble of London; the soprano soloist in both works was Jane Manning. Dallapiccola was also present in the cathedral on Thursday afternoon to hear Christopher Robinson conduct the RPO and Festival Chorus in his *Canti di Prigionia*, a work described by John Waterhouse as 'among the most powerful gestures of "protest through music" ever made: the work may be regarded as the supreme musical symbol of all the anguish, suffering and frustrated idealism of the Italian people during the tragic last phase of the Fascist regime and the catastrophic events which followed.'[6]

Elizabeth Maconchy was in Worcester for the first performance by the three cathedral choirs and the Birmingham Brass Consort of her *And death shall have no dominion*; and a setting of Psalm 150 by William Mathias was heard for the first time in the Opening Service.

Heralded by A. T. Shaw in the *Worcester Evening News* as the first performance of a new work to make such a profound impression upon a vast

---

[5] *Hereford Times*, 30 August 1969.

[6] Worcester Festival programme book, 1969, p. 60. Copy held in the Three Choirs Festival Office, Gloucester.

audience in nearly fifty years, Jonathan Harvey's dramatic cantata *Ludus Amoris* was performed by Janet Price, Gerald English, Tony Church (speaker), the Festival Chorus and RPO conducted by Christopher Robinson on Tuesday evening. Importantly, it was the first work ever to be commissioned by Three Choirs with funds provided by the Arts Council. Free to applaud, the Festival audience gave *Ludus Amoris* a near-frenzied reception. The RPO manager even asked Christopher Robinson if he would bring the Festival Chorus to take part in a performance of the work at the Royal Festival Hall in the following June, and Kenneth Loveland, writing in *The Times*, praised: 'Not only the fact of Mr Harvey's work but the care and pride of presentation it received in Christopher Robinson's hands [which] suggested that the festival is rediscovering its relevance to the contemporary British musical scene.'[7]

The performance of *Ludus Amoris* went ahead at the Festival Hall on 16 June 1970 and was well received as the work of a composer equally aware of the conservative English choral tradition and of post-serial techniques, which Harvey had reconciled with remarkable success. Even so, it failed to take root and has not yet been repeated at Three Choirs.

Among distinguished visitors to the 1969 Worcester Festival was Edward Heath, then Leader of the Opposition, accompanied by Worcester MP Peter Walker. Within a year Mr Heath was the Prime Minister, and Peter Walker his Secretary of State for the Environment. The pattern of contemporary and new works woven together with the established, the familiar and the popular continued to provide the basis for Festival programme planning throughout the 1970s.

At Hereford in 1970 Richard Lloyd enveloped much new music in an Elgarian sandwich. The week began with *The Kingdom*, given by Sheila Armstrong, Norma Procter, Alexander Young, John Carol Case, the Festival Chorus, and the RPO conducted by Sir Adrian Boult. On Friday, Lloyd conducted *Gerontius* with Marjorie Thomas, Alexander Young, Roger Stalman, the chorus and CBSO. In between, among other things, there were Sir Lennox Berkeley's *Magnificat* and Benjamin Britten's *Spring Symphony*, both given for the first time at Three Choirs; *In the Beginning* by Aaron Copland; the first British performance of Psalm 150, op. 5, by the Argentinian composer Alberto Ginastera; and the premières of three British works: Christopher Brown's cantata *David*; Bryan Kelly's *Stabat Mater*, conducted by the composer; and *Notturni ed Alba* by John McCabe (1939-2015).

Notturni ed Alba, commissioned by the Festival, is a setting of four medieval Latin poems presenting different aspects of night, though in most cases approached from a subjective viewpoint. It was composed in response to a request made by Richard Lloyd while he and John McCabe were enjoying a pint of beer in Salisbury: 'What I want', Lloyd had said, 'is a *Dies Natalis* of the 70s.' *Notturni ed Alba* was the result. The first performance, given by the soprano Sheila Armstrong with the CBSO conducted by Louis Frémaux, remains in Richard Lloyd's memory as the single most important new work to be given at Hereford during his years there. It was repeated at the 1985 Festival.

A fourth new work promised for the 1970(H) Festival – a motet, *Out of the*

<hr />

[7] *The Times*, 28 August 1969.

deep have I called by Alun Hoddinott – had to be cancelled when the score failed to arrive in time. But the largest new work of the 1971 Gloucester Festival was also commissioned from Hoddinott: *The Tree of Life*, for soprano and tenor soloists, chorus, organ and orchestra. As Desmond Shawe-Taylor wrote in the *Sunday Times*:

> It was essentially a throw-back to our oratorio past, with little in the way of fresh impulse or idea to enliven the stale tradition; it even drew, amid loyal cathedral applause, a few hisses – the first I can recall in such surroundings, and surely among the first to complain of music as being not vanguard, but rearguard.[8]

The soloists in *The Tree of Life* were Margaret Price and Gerald English, with the Festival Chorus and RPO conducted by John Sanders.

Following a major rebuild which cost £35,000 and took a year to complete, the Gloucester Cathedral organ was rededicated at the Opening Service of the 1971 Festival. It was appropriate, therefore, that the programme should include the first performance of a substantial organ work: a specially commissioned concerto by Peter Dickinson. On Thursday evening the Prime Minister, Mr Edward Heath, and Mr and Mrs Peter Walker visited the Festival to hear a concert in which Richard Lloyd conducted the RPO and Festival Chorus in Haydn's *Harmoniemesse*, with Margaret Price, Alfreda Hodgson, William McAlpine and Benjamin Luxon; and Christopher Robinson conducted Samuel Barber's *Adagio for Strings* and Rachmaninov's *The Bells*, again with Price, McAlpine and Luxon.

At the end of the concert, and when the intrigued audience had finally been persuaded to leave, Mr Heath climbed to the organ loft and spent a few minutes playing the refurbished instrument – presumably a welcome break from the rigours of the Industrial Relations legislation then at the forefront of British politics.

Two soloists engaged for the 1971(G) Festival withdrew at short notice: the contralto Helen Watts was released from her contract in order to take up an offer to sing at the Salzburg Festival; and Robert Tear, who should have joined Alfreda Hodgson and Benjamin Luxon in *Gerontius* on the last night, fell ill. He was replaced by Gerald English.

The guests of honour at the Festival garden party on Monday were Sir Arthur and Lady Bliss. The chairman of the Festival, Mr Anthony Scott, presented Sir Arthur with a framed print of Gloucester Cathedral on behalf of the committee. Having admitted to being rather embarrassed, Sir Arthur thanked the committee not only for the gift, but also for his invitation to perform at Three Choirs in 1922. 'There is an atmosphere here unlike any other festival', he said. 'It is like being one member of a great big family.'[9]

I N a not very successful attempt to boost the numbers of young people attending the Festival, Wednesday 25 August 1971 was advertised as Youth Day. The idea was that for just £3 a student could purchase a 'package-deal' ticket to all the events for that day, winding up with a late-evening Folk Music Party (Steel

---

[8] *Sunday Times*, 29 August 1971.

[9] *Citizen*, 24 August 1971.

Eye Span, Pigsty Hill and The Song Wainers!) at nearby Highnam Court. This all-night pop concert was styled a 'Fringe Event' in the local press and, while not advertised or organised as a Festival Fringe, it seems to have been the first occasion upon which Three Choirs ventured into the sphere of modern light entertainment in an event outside the main programme.[10] A personality from the world of light entertainment ventured into the Festival, too: Eartha Kitt, in Gloucester to open a Samaritans Centre, caused heads to turn when she popped in to one of the mayor's Festival luncheons at the Guildhall, stopping long enough to chat with the Bishop of Gloucester, the Rt Rev. Basil Guy, and to sign autographs before leaving.

The centenary of the birth of Vaughan Williams was commemorated at Worcester in 1972 by a Sunday evening concert in which Sir Adrian Boult conducted the CBSO and soloists Jennifer Vyvyan and John Shirley-Quirk in the *Five Mystical Songs*, *Fantasia on a Theme by Thomas Tallis*, and *A Sea Symphony*. Ursula Vaughan Williams and Hugh Ottaway contributed essays on the composer to the programme book: 'The depths in Vaughan Williams's music are visionary and intuitive', wrote Ottaway, going on to praise his vitality, freshness and the force of his personality. 'Vaughan Williams will always appeal most keenly to listeners with an ear for the Englishness of English music; but those who only hear the Englishness, whether admirers or detractors, have failed to get to grips with the substance of his work.' During the week, Vaughan Williams's Mass in G minor and *Serenade to Music* were also given.

There was something akin to that peculiarly English institution, the Prom, at the Monday evening concert given by the RPO conducted by Meredith Davies and with the cellist Thomas Igloi. This was actually advertised as a 'Promenade Concert' and tickets for the promenade area in the side aisles were sold for a nominal 40p. The experiment was a partial success – but so many people wanted to sit that there was very little space for those who chose to stand. No matter, standing or sitting, the cathedral was filled to capacity. In his article in the programme book, Michael Kennedy described the four works given as 'Passionate Pilgrimages': Mendelssohn's overture *Fingal's Cave*, the *Walk to the Paradise Garden* by Delius, Walton's Cello Concerto, and a luminous and eloquent account of the Symphony No. 2 in E flat by Elgar. 'In the mastery and certainty of its orchestration', wrote Kennedy, 'in the emotional range of its expressive content, Elgar's Second Symphony remains one of the most searching musical experiences, incomparably described by its creator as "the passionate pilgrimage of the soul"'.

Two new works were given their first performances on Tuesday: in the afternoon recital by the three cathedral choirs, John Joubert's *Three Office Hymns of St Oswald* conducted by John Sanders; and in the evening, *Voyage* by John McCabe, with Jane Manning, Meriel Dickinson, Charles Brett, Brian Rayner Cook, the Festival Chorus and RPO conducted by Christopher Robinson. 'It was natural', wrote Kenneth Loveland in *The Times*, 'that the festival should return to McCabe after *Notturni ed Alba* (Hereford 1970), the best new work heard at the Three Choirs in recent years':

[10] *Citizen*, 19 August 1971.

This time a large-scale choral work has resulted. *Voyage* is about the legendary search of St Brendan for the promised land, a seven-year journey which makes him a kind of coracle-born flying Irishman.

Monica Smith's libretto reduces the story to manageable lengths, but retains the Celtic romanticism, twilight fancies and rather endearing belief in the unbelievable. There are quotations from the song of Taliesin, Marcus Aurelius and Shakespeare. McCabe translates all this into a similarly evocative score, generously endowed with glittering percussion sounds (maracas, marimbas, vibraphones) appropriately permeated with the touch of the visionary ... and generally matching the picturesque with the picturesque ... One hopes that he has a return ticket; there is much in *Voyage* that is exciting and deserving of an early repeat performance.[11]

Brian Rayner Cook, taking the part of St Brendan, was making the first of his many Three Choirs appearances. The work received a prolonged ovation punctuated by shouts of 'Bravo!' – the urgent spirit of applause had finally escaped completely from its dusty bottle. Even so, and surprisingly, *Voyage*, still awaits its second Three Choirs sailing.

Kenneth Loveland also pointed out that the choral writing in *Voyage*, richly varied with some moments of hysterical whispering and speech, was in the manner of Penderecki. Previously he had drawn attention to the position of Jonathan Harvey's *Ludus Amoris* in a continuing tradition extending from Bach through to Penderecki, in that the crowd is a strong vocal participant in the evolution of Harvey's narrative. The involvement of 'spoken whisperings rising to a hysterical crescendo and the fragmentary string writing and percussion textures' in *Ludus Amoris* seemed similarly reminiscent of Penderecki's *St Luke Passion*.

The first opportunity for Three Choirs audiences actually to hear the music of Krzysztof Penderecki came at the 1972(w) Festival: an excellent performance of the *Stabat Mater*, written in 1962. 'Had it been heard a few years earlier', wrote Loveland, the line of descent of more than one new work heard [at Three Choirs] might have been apparent ... In its immediacy and clarity the performance spoke volumes for the preparation with which Christopher Robinson had invested it.'[12]

To celebrate the seventieth birthday of Lennox Berkeley, Three Choirs commissioned from him a short orchestral work, *Voices of the Night*, which was played by the CBSO under the composer's direction at the Hereford Festival in 1973 at the start of an orchestral concert which also included the Schumann Cello Concerto in A minor (with Christopher Van Kampen) and Elgar's Symphony No. 1, both conducted by Andrew Davis.

Other new works in 1973(H) included the first Festival commission from Geoffrey Burgon, *The Fire of Heaven*, given by the three cathedral choirs conducted by Richard Lloyd; and *Let There be Light!* by Bryan Kelly, a setting of the first chapter of the Book of Genesis:

Such is the pace of technological progress that Mr Kelly manages to despatch the whole of creation in 25 minutes, as against Haydn's two hours.

[11] *The Times*, 31 August 1972.
[12] *The Times*, 2 September 1972.

That he is able to do this is due partly to the employment of a narrator [Gabriel Woolf] in addition to chorus, orchestra and soprano soloist [Jennifer Vyvyan] and partly to the lack of expansion of the musical ideas.[13]

Let There be Light! was accompanied by the RPO, again conducted by Richard Lloyd.

Two tenors for long associated with Three Choirs made their first appearances in 1973: Neil Jenkins and David Johnston.

Jennifer Vyvyan sang at Three Choirs for the last time on the evening of Thursday 23 August 1973, with Richard Lewis and the RPO, in the first performance in England of the *Te Deum* by Bizet, conducted by John Sanders, and also, appropriately, in *Hymnus Paradisi*, again with Richard Lewis and conducted by Richard Lloyd. Music was robbed of that lovely voice only seven months later, by Vyvian's untimely death at the age of forty-nine.

Richard Lloyd had begun the 1973 Festival with *Elijah*, not given in Three Choirs at Hereford since 1946; he ended the week with *The Apostles*. Wendy Eathorne and Marjorie Thomas sang in both works, joined by David Johnston with Raimund Herincx in *Elijah*, and Alexander Young, John Carol Case, David Thomas and Roger Stalman in *The Apostles*.

In 1974 Richard Lloyd was appointed Organist of Durham Cathedral, and in 1985 became deputy headmaster of Salisbury Cathedral School, remaining there until 1988, when ill health forced his retirement. In 1974, too, Christopher Robinson left Worcester to go to Windsor as Organist and Master of the Choristers of St George's Chapel, where he remained until 1991, when he was appointed Organist of St John's College, Cambridge. He conducted the Oxford Bach Choir from 1976 to 1997, and the City of Birmingham Choir from 1964 to 2002. In 1986 the queen bestowed upon him the honour of LVO and, in 1992, the CVO, and he received a CBE in the 2004 New Year's Honours List.

THROUGHOUT the 1960s and 1970s a notable feature of the Festival was the steadily increasing number and variety of events held in venues outside the cathedrals: song and chamber music recitals, exhibitions and displays, poetry readings, lectures and discussion groups – too numerous and diverse to describe in detail. This has remained the pattern for the modern Festival. Typically, in 1974(G) audience choices included a chamber concert at the Gloucestershire College of Education in which Ralph Holmes (violin) and Gillian Weir (harpsichord) performed works by Bach; another chamber concert, two days later, given by the Georgian String Quartet at Prinknash Abbey and devoted to Haydn's *The Seven Last Words of Our Saviour on the Cross*, op. 51; and an afternoon concert in Tewkesbury Abbey given by the Academy of the BBC conducted by Meredith Davies, which included, among works by Mozart, Elgar, Weber and Beethoven, the Symphonies for chamber orchestra, op. 11, by Gordon Crosse, written in 1964 for the Orchestra da Camera.

To celebrate the centenary of the birth of Gustav Holst in 1974 his daughter Imogen gave a lecture entitled 'Holst in Gloucestershire' in the Gloucestershire College of Education. Her father, she said, had been grateful to the Three Choirs

[13] *Daily Telegraph*, 21 August 1973.

for giving first performances of some of his works. Not all his visits to the Festival were happy occasions – sometimes standards had been disappointing – but there had also been some very good performances. An example was Holst's motet *Evening Watch*, first performed at Gloucester in 1925. There was, too, his great *Choral Fantasia*, composed at the request of Herbert Sumsion and hated by most people when first unveiled at Gloucester in 1931. This, *The Planets* and the *Hymn of Jesus* were given at the 1974(G) Festival. Of the *Choral Fantasia* Imogen Holst said: 'It is my father's best "thank you" to Gloucestershire for having given him his life. It is also the nearest he came to his own ideal of a tender austerity.'[14]

New works at the 1974 Gloucester Festival included two Festival commissions: Wilfred Josephs' overture, *The Four Horsemen of the Apocalypse*, op. 86, and *The Temple*, an unaccompanied triptych by Philip Cannon (1929–2016). There was also the first public performance of Christopher Steel's *Paradise Lost*.

Wilfred Josephs had predicted that *The Four Horsemen of the Apocalypse* might be his noisiest work, and so it proved: 'At the end there were decibel-battered eardrums and protesting echoes to prove the point.'[15] It was the first item in a concert given by the CBSO under Louis Frémaux which also included Saint-Saëns' Symphony No. 3 in C minor (with Ralph Downes at the organ) and Holst's *The Planets*.

'With *The Temple*', wrote Robert Henderson:

> Philip Cannon confirmed his reputation as one of the most accomplished of our choral composers. The text by the 17th-century poet George Herbert had the advantage of combining simplicity of language with precise, yet evocative imagery, making them particularly amenable to musical setting. And Cannon seized upon every inflection of this imagery with an admirable blend of discretion and imaginative tact.[16]

Although *The Temple* was well received by critics and public alike, it was the unwitting cause of John Sanders's closest brush with 'industrial action' by the Gloucester contingent of the Festival Chorus. Anxious to lighten the load on his singers, Sanders decided that the choral concert in the afternoon preceding the première of *The Temple*, a performance of the Monteverdi Vespers of 1610, would be given by a semi-chorus from Worcester and Hereford only. The evening concert, which included Bononcini's *Stabat Mater* and Holst's *Choral Fantasia* in addition to *The Temple*, was allotted to a semi-chorus from Gloucester only. Far from being delighted about his equitable distribution of the workload, angry voices were raised among the Gloucester contingent that they were being prevented from singing in the Monteverdi – and John Sanders was the unhappy recipient of a petition of protest against the imagined injustice!

The Guest of Honour at the 1974(G) Festival was Herbert Howells. Presenting him – at the Festival garden party – with a wine glass especially engraved by Mr Geoffrey Frith, John Sanders described Dr Howells as 'one of England's greatest living musicians, and one of the best loved. We thank him', he said, 'for all he has

[14] *Citizen*, 20 August 1974.

[15] *The Times*, 19 August 1974.

[16] *Daily Telegraph*, 24 August 1974.

done to enrich this Festival.' At a Gloucester Literary Luncheon Club meeting on the next day, Howells said that he was tempted to accuse Gloucester of showing insensibility to one of his greatest friends, Ivor Gurney:

> It would be most ungracious of me if I accused Gloucester of this, because I know the city has its deep interests, and has lived up to most of them throughout its long history.
>
> But some day this city and all its music lovers, and lovers of culture of any kind, have got to remember that remarkable man. I do hope – and I hope to see it before I die – that Gloucester really turns its face to Ivor Gurney.[17]

Happily, Herbert Howells lived just long enough to see a reawakening of interest in Ivor Gurney as both composer and major poet – an interest which has spread far beyond the city of Gloucester and which shows no sign of waning.

Iᴎ January 1975 Donald Hunt succeeded Christopher Robinson as Organist and Master of the Choristers at Worcester Cathedral. Born at Gloucester, Hunt was a cathedral chorister there and was educated at the King's School. Articled to Herbert Sumsion, he became Assistant Organist at the cathedral in 1947 at the age of seventeen, remaining there until 1954, when he went to Torquay as Organist at St John's Church. In 1957 he was appointed Director of Music at Leeds Parish Church – a post he held for seventeen years. In Yorkshire, Hunt was soon involved with the great West Riding choral tradition, becoming conductor of the Halifax Choral Society and the Leeds Philharmonic Society (following Sir Malcolm Sargent), and Associate Conductor and Chorus Master of the Leeds Festival. In 1971 he founded the Yorkshire Sinfonia Orchestra and in 1972 was appointed Leeds City Organist – the post having lapsed for over fifty years. In his years at Leeds he taught harmony and counterpoint at the Leeds College of Music and became well known as an adjudicator and recitalist. In May 1975 he received the degree of DMus, *honoris causa*, from the University of Leeds, for services to music in Leeds and Yorkshire. Three months later he directed his first Worcester Festival.

From the beginning, Donald Hunt imprinted his own authority upon the Festival, along with a determined blend of vigorous energy, ambitious dynamism, and stubbornness in the pursuit of self-imposed standards. From the beginning, too, his affinity with the music of Elgar, gained at one remove by Herbert Sumsion's side, was manifest in an instinctive feel for an authentic Elgarian style, and it was with the march composed by Elgar for the coronation of King George V that Hunt began the Opening Service of the 1975(w) Festival.

When the civic and ecclesiastical dignitaries had taken their places, the traditional act of worship began with the playing of the Meditation from Elgar's *The Light of Life*. 'It was', said A. T. Shaw, 'impossible to escape the feeling that the Order of the Service had been planned to take our minds off the "Pomp and Circumstance" inseparable from civic participation in the event, and to fix our thoughts upon love as a principle of life'.[18] The *Te Deum* of Verdi; selected

---

[17] *Citizen*, 21 August 1974.

[18] *Worcester Journal*, 28 August 1975.

readings from Coleridge, Hadow and Ruskin; and Vaughan Williams's *Serenade to Music* confirmed the mood.

Almost inevitably, it seemed, Hunt chose *The Dream of Gerontius* for his first concert of the Festival – a rapturous performance in which he conducted the Festival Chorus, the Worcester Cathedral Choir and the CBSO, with Alfreda Hodgson, David Galliver and Michael Rippon.

On the morning of the second day a brass band was heard for the first time in Worcester Cathedral: the Great Universal Stores Footwear Band under their conductor Stanley Boddington, and Ifor James (horn), gave a recital which included the first complete performance of McCabe's *Goddess Trilogy*. In the evening the cathedral was again crowded for Beethoven's *Missa solemnis* given by the RPO and the Festival Chorus conducted by Donald Hunt, with soloists Anne Conoley, Janet Hughes, John Mitchinson and Raimund Herincx.

On Tuesday afternoon in Perrins Hall at the Worcester Royal Grammar School, the Music Group of London and Ian Partridge (surely the natural successor to Wilfred Brown) gave a recital which included the première of *Severnside*, a song cycle in four seasons by Richard Benger for tenor voice and string quartet – settings of four poems by Mary Dawson, which were published for the first time in the programme book.

Settings for soprano, choir and orchestra by Richard Rodney Bennett of six poems by Kathleen Raine, under the title *Spells*, received their first performance on Thursday evening, sung by Jane Manning, to whom the work is dedicated. 'Unmistakably a major addition to the English choral repertory', wrote Martin Cooper. 'The choral and orchestral writing is precisely conceived to make a maximum impact and the RPO and Festival Chorus under Donald Hunt achieved an admirably disciplined and strongly characterised performance.'[19]

Richard Rodney Bennett's strong representation in the programme earned him the appellation Festival Composer 1975. His Piano Concerto, dedicated to Stephen Bishop-Kovacevich, was played by Malcolm Binns at the Wednesday evening orchestral concert given by the CBSO under Louis Frémaux, and this was followed by a late-night entertainment in the Swan Theatre featuring Richard Rodney Bennett and Marion Montgomery. The next afternoon, in his organ recital at Pershore Abbey, Christopher Robinson played Bennett's *Alba* (1973) in a programme which also included works by Messiaen (*L'Ascension*), and Frank Martin (*Passacaille*). Messiaen was again represented in the Friday morning recital given by the three cathedral choirs:

> Donald Hunt gave us a memorable performance of Messiaen's *Trois Petites Liturgies de la Présence Divine*. The choristers of the three cathedrals and the strings of the R.P.O. with piano played by Keith Swallow, Ondes Martenot operated by John Morton, and percussion, obtained effects of the utmost loveliness in a performance which is in my opinion the highlight of the festival.
>
> Over and again as the music revealed fresh aspects of the composer's sensibility and as the choristers astonished us by the brilliance of their

---

[19] *Daily Telegraph*, 30 August 1975.

singing I found myself wishing that a performance of such outstanding quality could have been recorded.[20]

Frank Martin's Requiem was written a year before his death in 1974 and received its first performance in this country under John Sanders at the 1975 Worcester Festival, in the presence of Madame Maria Martin, the composer's widow. The soloists with the RPO and Festival Chorus were Jane Manning, Jean Allister, Neil Jenkins and Michael Rippon. 'It is', wrote Martin Cooper, 'anything but a work of consolation and remains, from its uncomfortable opening almost to the end, full of the mediaeval fear of death and the final reckoning.'[21]

Earlier in this same concert, Neil Jenkins and Michael Rippon had sung in a good, strong performance of Vaughan Williams's *Sancta Civitas* under the baton of the new man at Hereford – Roy Massey.

BORN in Birmingham in 1934, Roy Massey was educated at Moseley Grammar School in that city, and received his musical education at the University of Birmingham and under David Willcocks at Worcester. While still a student he became accompanist and Organist to the City of Birmingham Choir, and worked closely with David Willcocks, Meredith Davies and Christopher Robinson. He was Organist of St Alban the Martyr, Bordesley, Birmingham, 1953–60, and of St Augustine's, Edgbaston, Birmingham, 1960–5. He then became Warden of the Royal School of Church Music at Addington Palace, Croydon, a post held concurrently with that of Organist of Croydon Parish Church. He returned to Birmingham as organist of the cathedral in 1968, and in 1974 took up his appointment at Hereford. In 1991 he received the Lambeth degree of DMus.

The 1976 Hereford Festival marked not only Roy Massey's Three Choirs debut as Director, but also the first Festival appearances of three outstanding soloists: Felicity Lott, Anthony Rolfe Johnson and Stephen Roberts, two of whom took part in Massey's first concert on Sunday evening – a confident reaching-back to Handel's epic oratorio of 1738, *Israel in Egypt*, receiving only its second Three Choirs performance since the beginning of the century. The soloists were Honor Sheppard, Felicity Lott, Margaret Cable, Neil Jenkins, David Thomas and Stephen Roberts, with Donald Hunt (organ), Roger Judd (harpsichord), the Festival Chorus and CBSO.

On Tuesday evening there was a concert entirely of French music. Donald Hunt conducted Poulenc's *Stabat Mater* (with Wendy Eathorne) and Saint-Saëns' symphonic poem *La Jeunesse d'Hercule*; Massey conducted the Requiem of Maurice Duruflé, with Wendy Eathorne, Alfreda Hodgson and Michael Rippon. The orchestra was the RPO. Among a number of Festival commissions and new works, by far the most important was the first performance, on Thursday evening, of the Requiem by Geoffrey Burgon, with Janet Price (a late substitute for Felicity Palmer), Kevin Smith and Anthony Rolfe Johnson, the Festival Chorus and RPO conducted by Roy Massey.

[20] A. T. Shaw, *Worcester Evening News*, 30 August 1975.
[21] *Daily Telegraph*, 28 August 1975.

At about the time of writing *The Fire of Heaven* for the 1973(H) Festival, in which he used the serenely mystical poetry of Thomas Traherne, Geoffrey Burgon (1941–2010) had discovered the poetry of the sixteenth-century Carmelite friar St John of the Cross. His first setting was a 1974 Cheltenham Festival commission, *Noche oscura*. With the Requiem of 1976 Burgon reached the culmination of his interest in St John of the Cross's poetry, combining it with the standard liturgical text of the Requiem to create his largest-scale work to date.

'It is not a mass in any sense', said Burgon, who expressed a horror of organised religion, 'but sets out to convey the concept of requiem by the dual idea of eternity "experienced" during life and after death.' As in several of Burgon's works, dreams played a part in the inspiration for the turbulent *Dies Irae*, which was omitted from his original conception.

In contrast to the Requiem of Frank Martin, full of tortured fear and lacking any trace of serenity, that of Geoffrey Burgon is entirely consolatory. 'The heart of the work', wrote Hugo Cole, 'lies in the serene and contemplative setting of the poems by St John of the Cross, in which the sense of timelessness and unity are matched by music that is often transparent, quiet, slow almost to the point of stasis.'[22]

> I entered in, I know not where,
> And I remained, though knowing naught,
> Transcending knowledge with my thought.

The 1976 Hereford Festival ended with *The Dream of Gerontius*:

> David Johnston brought to the name-part a sense of urgency and passion that was not dispersed or lost in the high-vaulted spaces of the great cathedral. Roy Massey took the music as freely and expansively as even Elgar himself could have wished.
>
> The Hereford semi-chorus sounded truly angelic. Clear, well-tuned, steady singing was needed, and was provided, and the Cathedral did the rest.[23]

---

[22] *Country Life*, 16 September 1976, p. 730.
[23] Ibid.

20

Jubilee

IT was a double celebration: the silver jubilee of Her Majesty the Queen and, dating Three Choirs from 1715, the commemoration of 250 years of music-making in Gloucester, Hereford and Worcester. In that same year Edinburgh was mounting only its thirty-first Festival and Cheltenham its thirty-third. The occasion was marked with six orchestras, more than thirty soloists, seven conductors, instrumental and choral groups, and a Festival extending over eight days from 20 to 28 August. There was a strong Commonwealth flavour with performers from Australia, New Zealand and Canada. Documentaries on Three Choirs were broadcast on radio and television. There were new works from Harrison Birtwistle, Peter Maxwell Davies, Rory Boyle, Ronald Tremain and Tony Hewitt-Jones, and the centrepiece – *Mass of Christ the King*, a large choral composition from Malcolm Williamson, Master of the Queen's Music – was dedicated to the queen for her jubilee. Certainly, the 1977 Gloucester Festival was an ambitious musical feast.

The programme had been planned to feature the music of composers who have had a major influence on the Festival during its long history: Bach's Mass in B minor; the Verdi Requiem; Kodály's *Jesus and the Traders*; Handel's *Messiah*; Holst's *The Hymn of Jesus*; Vaughan Williams's *Fantasia on a Theme by Thomas Tallis*; Beethoven's *Fantasia*, op. 80 (the 'Choral Fantasy'); Britten's *Cantata academica* and *Missa brevis*; Penderecki's *Stabat Mater*, and, of course, Elgar – the Cello Concerto, *Caractacus* and *Gerontius*. Herbert Howells was present to hear *Hymnus Paradisi* and had been commissioned to write a *Festival Fanfare* for the Opening Service, during which the first performance of Tony Hewitt-Jones's anthem *Let us now praise famous men* was also given. A wide sweep of musical history was embraced, from French medieval ballads, secular and sacred music of the English Renaissance and anthems by Victoria, Schütz and Gabrieli, to sounds with the freshness of new paint: Peter Maxwell Davies's *A Mirror of Whitening Light* and Harrison Birtwistle's *Silbury Air*, both played in a Contemporary Music Network concert by the London Sinfonietta.

An early disappointment had been the necessity to exclude from the programme the first performance of Richard Rodney Bennett's suite *The Christians*, based upon his music for the television series of the same name, due to Bennett's inability to complete the composition in time for the Festival. But there were early hints that there might also be problems with Malcolm Williamson's mass.

Australian-born Malcolm Williamson (1931–2003) had lived in England since 1953. A pupil of Sir Eugene Goossens at the Sydney Conservatorium, he studied piano there under Alexander Sverjensky, as well as French horn and violin. In London, struggling to make ends meet, he worked as a nightclub pianist, and

Organist at a Limehouse church. He studied composition with Erwin Stern and Elisabeth Lutyens, and Benjamin Britten helped him to get his first piano sonata published. Sir Adrian Boult introduced his music to Three Choirs in 1969(w): the overture *Santiago d'Espada*, composed in 1957 and dedicated to Boult.

In 1965, Williamson was one of four young composers commissioned to write an opera for Sadler's Wells and the result, his fifth opera, *The Violins of Saint-Jacques*, was produced with great success in 1966; but it was a success tinged with the pain of personal tragedy: the death some months earlier of a baby daughter.

Williamson's considerable output includes not only operas, symphonies, concertos, orchestral works, chamber music, piano and organ pieces but also, believing passionately as he did that music should be for everybody, church music in a pop-song style and mini-operas, which he called 'cassations', for performance by handicapped children. A remarkable man whose brilliance was framed by compassion, Williamson was master of six languages, had doctorates in medicine and psychology, and had held a university fellowship researching the problems of handicapped children.

Sir Arthur Bliss died in March 1975 and Williamson was appointed Master of the Queen's Music in his place. Pressures both personal and professional began to increase.

When the writer Paul Jennings visited him for a *Radio Times* interview before a BBC2 broadcast of *The Violins of Saint-Jacques* (6 November 1976), he found that Williamson had been up all night working on the *Mass of Christ the King*:

> Malcolm Williamson is a man utterly without the mask that most men (let alone creative artists) present to the world. His thoughts flash and subside, with sparks of allusion, tailings-off, recurrent grand central themes, darting side-flashes of wit, like a turning bird's wing in his own music, particularly in its Messiaen moods.

Williamson was a Roman Catholic, and his faith featured in the *Radio Times* interview:

> 'Messiaen said "Je suis musicien surtout catholique", and that's what I am: I became a Catholic when I was 20 – it was terrible, I can't imagine any other idea of life …'
>
> 'Come and look at this: I was struggling with it last night.' On the piano was the Kyrie of a Mass of Christ the King … 'The Feast of Christ the King was only created in modern times. I'm very interested in it: what we need is this gentle authority of God. See: the soprano calls out, higher each time, above the choir, *Kyrie Eleison*, have mercy on us. Come on, you're in a choir: let's have a go …'[1]

At the beginning of March 1977, a press conference was called at the offices of the Arts Council in Piccadilly to give details of the Gloucester Festival; Williamson had been invited to speak. He arrived late and, to the astonishment of the organisers and the relish of the press, launched into a bitter attack against the Arts Council, which had 'totally rejected' his application for a £5,000

---

[1] *Radio Times*, 31 October 1976.

commissioning fee for *Mass of Christ the King*. Major articles appeared in all the leading papers the next day.

> My feelings towards the Arts Council in regard to this are of total disgust because of their lack of support. I asked for £5,000 and got nothing … It is simply one more humiliation in a long list of humiliations I have suffered from the Arts Council over a great many years … A lot of the humiliation has been of the verbal kind, and it would certainly be denied by the people who luxuriate in this form of insult to composers. I think this is felt by many composers.

It was, he claimed, an unhappy fact that both the BBC and the Arts Council instituted 'reprisals' against people who spoke out against them:

> The lack of financial support for me to write this composition has impeded work on it very much. I hope somehow the difficulties will be solved and that it will be possible for the work to be presented. At the moment I have serious doubts about it … Given the concentration that goes into it, one is receiving less than a bus conductor gets pro rata.
>
> But what sustains me is the distinction of the occasion and the fact that one has the honour of having Her Majesty the Queen graciously accepting the dedication.

He had only been able to undertake the work because the Johnson Wax company had promised £2,000, to be paid after completion. The firm's ultimate contribution would be £3,500, including printing costs; and the RPO had lent him £1,000 to enable him to proceed.

> Mr Williamson said he had been speaking 'very much for the senior composers, many of whom had knighthoods and other distinctions, and had to behave like English gentlemen when applying for financial help.
>
> 'There is, of course, this vexed Anglo-Saxon habit of glossing over matters concerning money.'[2]

Here, of course, was all the stuff of a good gossip story: the Master of the Queen's Music denouncing the Arts Council and the BBC for their lack of artistic support for his work and insisting that both organisations had taken reprisals against composers who had displeased them – points pursued by the *Evening Standard* in the 'Londoner's Diary' column later in the day of the Arts Council press conference:

> 'I have certainly encountered this in the past', [Williamson] told me today. 'At the BBC there was the case of some lost tapes of mine. Afterwards when I complained, I was told my performance was below standard and my criticism was deplorable. In fact the work has never been broadcast.'
>
> 'People who I have spoken to today who have been on the receiving end of reprisals have pleaded with me not to be named. Nevertheless I cannot retract the statement. Composers, orchestral bodies, Festivals are conditioned to dumb acceptance of the Arts Council verdicts.'

[2] *Daily Telegraph*, 3 March 1977.

John Cruft, Music Director of the Arts Council, says: 'I am sorry Malcolm Williamson did not discuss with me the things troubling him rather than astonishing a gathering in this building who had come to hear about plans for the 250th Three Choirs Festival.'

Williamson again: 'Mr Cruft's assumption that I will starve and behave like a good little boy to protect the Arts Council's anonymity and at the same time write an enormous work is very unhelpful.'[3]

If Williamson had wished to make the maximum impact he could not have chosen a more telling time and place to make his protest. Under the title 'Just how much is a composer worth?', a lengthy article by Peta Levi appeared in the next edition of the *Sunday Times*. Triggered by Williamson's attack on the Arts Council, it contained an investigation into the hazards and rewards of composers, exposing the pitiful level of commission fees in this country. The article also revealed that in the following July, Williamson would be doing a tour in America – 'time he can ill afford since he has three years of composition to do in one'.[4] Inevitably, lack of funds forced him to accept too many commitments.

Malcolm Williamson was able to keep his bowl upright in 1977, subsidising himself by taking on the music for the film of Richard Adams's *Watership Down*. This on top of a twenty-minute jubilee mini-opera to be performed by thousands of schoolchildren in the queen's presence in the Liverpool streets on 21 June; an LPO commission for a symphony to be performed at a Royal Jubilee concert on 8 December; the *Mass of Christ the King* in Gloucester on 28 August; *and* the American tour in July.

By the end of July 1977 John Sanders knew that the mass would not be finished in time. There was no problem with the vocal score – prepared in three parts and separately colour-coded: red, white and blue – the last portion of which was received two weeks before the Festival. The orchestration was another matter.

One week before the Festival, John Sanders was in London for an orchestral rehearsal of the mass with the RPO; the parts had still not arrived and he was obliged to fill in with *Gerontius*. Halfway through the rehearsal a taxi pulled up and Simon Campion, Williamson's assistant, rushed in with orchestral parts for about two-thirds of the work. Back in Gloucester, more of the orchestral score continued to arrive piecemeal, by train, day by day.

Even more hair-raising, on the very day of the performance Malcolm Williamson himself arrived in Gloucester with additional missing parts and went into retreat in a feverish attempt to complete the orchestration. An eleventh-hour rehearsal was called, during which the drip feed of manuscript continued apace until, out of time, Sanders at last called a halt. The performance went ahead minus the *Gloria* and *Credo*; the responsorial psalm for solo tenor and orchestra, although fully scored, also had to be omitted, a casualty of Sanders's deadline. One other movement, the *Agnus Dei*, dedicated with the queen's permission to Benjamin Britten (who had died the previous December), was performed with

[3] *Evening Standard*, 3 March 1977.
[4] *Sunday Times*, 6 March 1977.

organ accompaniment. To compensate for the missing sections, Sanders revised the programme of the concert to include a repeat of Howells's *Festival Fanfare*, Elgar's arrangement of the National Anthem, and two anthems composed by Handel for the coronation of King George II in 1727: *Zadok the Priest* and *The King shall rejoice.*

In spite of such an inauspicious genesis, the incomplete *Mass of Christ the King* was received with considerable critical acclaim as a work containing some of the composer's most remarkable music. Ronald Crichton in the *Financial Times* was 'impatient to hear the whole work as soon as possible';[5] and in a thoughtful review for *The Times*, William Mann said that:

> It would be idle to assess *Mass of Christ the King* until it is performed complete. I can only assure those readers who spurn Williamson's simplistic music (its invention all the stronger because it has to be instantly performable) that the new Mass is an elaborate composition, grand and often surprising, for all that the choral music draws on ecclesiastical traditions, especially on plainsong. It makes a jubilant and variegated noise, approachable yet demanding concentration ... The solo vocal music, such as we heard of it, gave uplifting scope to April Cantelo's easy, pure high tones and Philip Langridge's fluent mellifluous tenor. Loris Synan ... displayed an impressive high mezzo register.[6]

The bass part was ably taken by Geoffrey Chard.

John Sanders, in spite of all the heart-stopping tensions of the previous weeks, had steered Williamson's work to success and shown it to be worthy of the effort. 'Sometimes it could be sensed', wrote William Mann, 'that balance was imperfect, the chorus slow to blaze, the orchestra battling bravely but tentatively, the conductor determined of spirit if he could not obtain at short notice real accuracy. It would be a pity if these forces were deprived of the glory of the work's first integral performance.'[7]

On the next evening Sanders, the Festival Chorus and RPO were on *terra firma* once more, and were granted their reward in a sublime performance of *Gerontius*: Maureen Guy a radiant, warm-voiced Angel; Ian Comboy a superbly dark-toned bass-baritone; and Robert Tear at the peak of his powers, and filling the cathedral with thrilling sound at 'Take me away' – magnificent.

On Saturday afternoon Donald Hunt conducted the three cathedral choirs and the Orchestra of St John's, Smith Square, in an exemplary performance of *Messiah*, with Felicity Lott, Paul Esswood, Anthony Rolfe Johnson and Stephen Roberts. And there was more glorious singing on Saturday evening: Dame Janet Baker and John Mitchinson, accompanied by the CBSO under Louis Frémaux, in Mahler's *Das Lied von der Erde*.

The extended Festival continued into Sunday 28 August: in the afternoon there was a concert by the Orchestra of St John's, Smith Square, conducted by John Lubbock at the Pittville Pump Room, Cheltenham. The final concert was

---

[5] *Financial Times*, 30 August 1977.

[6] *The Times*, 27 August 1977.

[7] Ibid.

given in the cathedral by the CBSO and the Festival Chorus. John Sanders conducted a repeat performance of Tony Hewitt-Jones's Festival anthem, and Beethoven's *Fantasia*, op. 80 (the 'Choral Fantasy'), in which Antony Peebles was the pianist. Donald Hunt took charge of performances of Britten's *Cantata academica* (with Felicity Lott, Jean Allister, Anthony Rolfe Johnson and Brian Rayner Cook) and the Poulenc Organ Concerto (with Roy Massey). And John Sanders brought the Festival to a close with Dvořák's *Te Deum*, first introduced to Three Choirs at Worcester in 1899. But before the vast audience dispersed, everyone joined in the singing of Vaughan Williams's setting of the Old Hundredth – a stirring climax to a memorable week.

After every Festival memories of performances and works jostle for favoured status in the mind. But some concerts are not simply remembered – they are impossible to forget, and one feels a sense of privilege at having been present. For this writer two memories of the 1977(G) Festival have this indelible quality. First, and in spite of the wholly inappropriate setting (the Gloucester Leisure Centre), Brian Rayner Cook's inspired singing in *Caractacus*. Second, a recital of English music at Prinknash Abbey: songs by Vaughan Williams, C. W. Orr, Ivor Gurney, and Herbert Howells – who sat in a monk's stall, head up, eyes closed in concentration and perhaps thanksgiving as Gloucestershire paid tribute to its own. Angela Malsbury played the Clarinet Sonata by Bax and Finzi's *Five Bagatelles* for clarinet and piano; and then, to end, the tenor soloist David Johnston was joined by his young son, Nicholas, and the pianist David Pettit in Benjamin Britten's canticle *Abraham and Isaac*. Here was perfect balance: music and place; innocence and experience.

D ONALD Hunt's obvious enthusiasm for French music was given full rein at the 1978 Worcester Festival: the overture *Le Carnaval romain* by Berlioz, Debussy's *Nocturnes*, and *Chant des captifs* by Jean Martinon were all heard on Monday evening in a RPO and Festival Chorus concert conducted by Hunt, with Meryl Drower, Neil Jenkins and Michael Rippon, ending with a sizzling performance of Walton's *Belshazzar's Feast* – linked to the Martinon piece by their common use of part of the same text: Psalm 136. Messiaen was represented on Tuesday by *Trois Petites Liturgies de la Présence Divine*, and on Wednesday by *L'Ascension*. Simon Preston's organ recital on Thursday was given over to Messiaen's *La Nativité du Seigneur*, and earlier in the afternoon, a century after its composition, the first complete British performance of the *Requiem Mass*, op. 54, by Saint-Saëns.

Compared with Malcolm Williamson's financial struggles in 1977, Saint-Saëns' fortunes 100 years earlier seem to have been provided for by a providential hand. Whit Sunday 1877 brought the death of the French Postmaster General, Saint-Saëns' friend Albert Libon. In his will, Libon left Saint-Saëns a legacy of 100,000 francs 'intended to take him away from the servitude of the organ at La Madeleine to allow him to devote himself entirely to composition'. In return Libon asked only that Saint-Saëns compose a Requiem to his memory, though a codicil, dictated only hours before his death, removed this condition which, he suggested, 'revealed a sentiment of vanity'. Even so, Saint-Saëns felt an obligation to complete the work, and in the spring of 1878 left Paris for Berne in search of quietness – again, a luxury apparently denied to Williamson. In his Swiss hotel room Saint-Saëns conceived, wrote and orchestrated the entire Requiem within eight days. The first performance was given at Saint-Sulpice, Paris, on 20 May 1878. Widor was the organist and Saint-Saëns conducted. In Worcester the soloists were Jane Manning, Margaret Cable, Kenneth Bowen and David Thomas, with the Worcester Festival Chorus and the BBC Northern Symphony Orchestra (now the BBC Philharmonic) under Donald Hunt. A beautifully written and orchestrated work, the Requiem deserves to be heard more often.

Earlier, Sir Lennox Berkeley's *Magnificat* and *Voices of the Night* were heard. Berkeley, who was designated 'The Festival Composer', celebrated his seventy-fifth year in 1978. In recognition of this, performances of several of his works were featured at the Festival, including the première of the motet *Judica me*, specially commissioned for the occasion.

Two guest conductors appeared at the Festival: Sir Charles Groves, who not only directed *Gerontius* on Sunday evening but also preached at the Opening Service earlier in the day, the first layman to do so; and the late Bryden Thomson, who conducted the BBC Northern Symphony Orchestra in music by Wagner, Messiaen and Elgar on Wednesday evening.

The concert on Tuesday evening, given by the three cathedral choirs and the BBC Northern Symphony Orchestra under Donald Hunt, began with Schubert's neglected Mass No. 3 in B flat, edited and published by Hunt in a new edition from the original manuscript in the British Museum. The programme also included Sir Lennox Berkeley's *Antiphon* for string orchestra, conducted by the composer from memory – he had forgotten to bring his spectacles – and the première of Anthony Payne's *Ascensiontide* and *Whitsuntide* cantatas, Festival commissions funded by the Arts Council. These two relatively brief pieces served to complete a process begun with the *Passiontide* cantata of 1974, whereby Payne had celebrated key festivals in the Christian year.

On Friday evening there was an all-Czech programme: Dvořák's setting of Psalm 149 and the *New World Symphony*, and Janáček's *Glagolitic Mass*, with Jane Manning, Maureen Guy, John Mitchinson and David Thomas, the CBSO, Worcester Cathedral Choir and Festival Chorus conducted by John Sanders.

Saturday was a day of startling contrast. In the afternoon, the British première of David Fanshawe's *African Sanctus*: the Worcester Chorus, cathedral choristers and the soprano Meryl Drower joined by an instrumental ensemble of piano, bass guitar, percussion and a pre-recorded tape of frogs, war drums, death laments, marriage songs and the Islamic call to prayer. The Festival ended on Saturday evening with Mahler's Symphony No. 8 in E flat, *Symphony of a Thousand*, performed for the first time at Three Choirs.

In a Thursday morning lecture at the Swan Theatre, David Fanshawe had explained how he had dreamt of hearing his work in an English cathedral as he had watched tribal natives lamenting the death of a fisherman in a small mud hut on Lake Victoria. For five years he had hitchhiked around Africa, collecting tapes of tribal music – a journey fraught with disasters, delays in jail and battles with wildlife. On one occasion he was recording a love song from a canoe when his paddle hit a hippopotamus on the head. The angry beast tossed him into the river along with his tape machine and twenty tapes, and he was chased to the river bank.

In the Sudan, Fanshawe heard of mountains that were thought to be like
Paradise. After many weeks on a camel, fruitlessly searching for music, he heard a
remarkable chanting on a mountain top, and on hearing the music had lain down
and wept. Four men were swaying from side to side on a prayer mat in a deep
trance, and Fanshawe managed to record them without their knowing that he
had been there.

Africa came to Worcester in 'a blaze of sound and colour', wrote A. T. Shaw.
'The order of the day for the chorus was informal, wear as garish as possible.'
Donald Hunt conducted in a red bush shirt. 'Such was the enthusiasm aroused
at the end of the work that applause continued until the conductor took the
unprecedented step of repeating the setting of The Lord's Prayer.'[8] And of the
Mahler:

> In its long history the Three Choirs Festival has produced a fine crop of
> memorable performances, but nothing quite so astonishing, so thrilling,
> and so ultimately satisfying as the performance of Gustav Mahler's eighth
> symphony given under the direction of Donald Hunt on Saturday night …
>
> The soloists in this gigantic work were: Elizabeth Harwood, Jane
> Manning, Meryl Drower, Anne Collins, Maureen Guy, John Mitchinson,
> Norman Welsby and John Tomlinson. The important organ part was
> played by Paul Trepte …
>
> The soul-shattering sound generated by this immense ensemble made
> it possible to understand what Mahler meant when he said: 'Imagine the
> whole universe beginning to sing and resound …'
>
> The last day of this the best festival of the century was a heady affair.
> The stupendous Mahler, the ebullient David Fanshawe throwing carnations
> to the chorus, and even an encore were things to remember and striking
> enough. But it was for Donald Hunt that the cheers went up. It was
> unquestionably his day.[9]

That was not the end of music-making for the Three Choirs in 1978. Malcolm
Williamson's *Mass of Christ the King* was performed for the first time in its
entirety on Friday 3 November 1978 in Westminster Cathedral. Sir Charles
Groves conducted the RPO and the Three Choirs, together with Goldsmiths
Choral Union, Elizabeth Connell, Philip Langridge and Brian Rayner Cook.
Queen Elizabeth the Queen Mother attended the performance, welcomed by
Cardinal Hume and Malcolm Williamson – an historic moment as a British
queen set foot in an English Roman Catholic cathedral for the first time in 400
years, and at the end she walked forward to thank Sir Charles and all who took
part. William Mann commented that:

> The music is characteristically eclectic in manner, its terms of reference
> ranging from plainsong to the neo-classic Stravinsky, via succulent
> Poulenc and austere Holstian harmony, with some piquant side-glances
> at Prokofiev's scoring. As a good Australian, Williamson selects at will,

[8] *Worcestershire Evening News*, 4 September, 1978.
[9] Ibid.

and then contrives that the finished product has his own personality to dominate the ingredients.[10]

John Sanders included Williamson's mass again in the 1986(G) Festival programme, thanks to generous funding from Central Independent Television plc. From early in the 1960s Three Choirs had become increasingly dependent upon commercial sponsorship. Without the support of Johnson Wax Ltd, *Mass of Christ the King* is unlikely to have been completed or the first London performance to have taken place. As the *Daily Telegraph*'s 'Mandrake' put it: 'Sponsorship of the arts by industry takes on a special glow with the news that Johnson Wax Ltd are subsidising the first full performance in Westminster Cathedral ... of Malcolm Williamson's *Mass of Christ the King* ... Long may it continue to shine.'

[10] *The Times*, 6 November 1978.

21

Theme with Variations

THE Monday evening concert at Hereford in 1979 began with a powerful performance of John Ireland's choral cantata *These things shall be*, and Ireland's song cycle *The Land of Lost Content* was the central work in a recital by Ian and Jennifer Partridge on Tuesday afternoon, both marking the centenary of the composer's birth. In *These things shall be* the soloist was Stephen Roberts, accompanied by the CBSO under Donald Hunt, taking over from John Sanders, who had been prevented by illness from appearing at the Festival.

Also on Monday evening, Roy Massey conducted the cantata *This Worlde's Joie* by William Mathias, with Janet Price, Kenneth Bowen, Stephen Roberts, Robert Green (organ), the choristers of the three cathedrals, the Festival Chorus and the CBSO. Contemporary British music was again well represented in the Tuesday morning recital by the three cathedral choirs: an *Easter Sequence* by Kenneth Leighton, *Two Carols* by Richard Rodney Bennett, and Geoffrey Burgon's *At the Round Earth's Imagin'd Corners*.

Donald Hunt beckoned the Festival to France on Monday evening, conducting Poulenc's last major work, *Sept Répons des ténèbres*. The soloist was Honor Sheppard, who also sang in the symphonic poem *King David* by the French-born Swiss composer Arthur Honegger, joining Margaret Cable and David Johnston, the Festival Chorus and CBSO under Roy Massey. The part of the Witch of Endor was taken by Elizabeth Evans, and the performance was further distinguished by the familiar voice of the popular broadcaster Richard Baker as the Narrator.

Of greater rarity was *Hymnus Amoris* by Carl Nielsen, given on Thursday evening by Julie Kennard, admirable in her first Three Choirs appearance, Brian Burrows, Stephen Roberts, David Thomas, the Festival Chorus and RPO conducted by Roy Massey. This was followed by the première of John Joubert's *Herefordshire Canticles*, a Festival commission repeated at Hereford in 1991 with the same soloists – Julie Kennard and Stephen Roberts, and again conducted by Massey.

A plea for peace and a condemnation of man's inhumanity to man are themes of Peter Maxwell Davies's opera *The Martyrdom of St Magnus*, commissioned by the BBC for the jubilee year of 1977 and included in the 1979 Hereford Festival – the first complete opera to be staged at Three Choirs. The production in the Nell Gwynne Theatre on Monday afternoon was given by The Fires of London conducted by John Latham-Koenig, with a cast which included Mary Thomas, Neil Mackie, Michael Rippon, Brian Rayner Cook and Ian Comboy. In the novel *Magnus* by George Mackay Brown, upon which the opera is based, Magnus is a Viking pacifist martyred in a (Nazi) concentration camp.

Although not the result of a deliberate design, choral works based on anti-war themes had been a feature of Roy Massey's Festival programmes, and four of these have left an especially profound and lasting impression upon him personally. Becomingly modest, Massey reflects that if, as he puts it, he 'had achieved nothing more at Three Choirs, then at least I have conducted those four works'. They are:

1985   Sir Michael Tippett, *A Child of our Time*, with Julie Kennard, Margaret Cable, Neil Jenkins, Michael George, the Festival Chorus and the CBSO

Michael Berkeley, *Or Shall We Die?*, with Wendy Eathorne, Stephen Roberts, the Festival Chorus and the RPO. This was only the second performance of the work, the première of which had been given at the Royal Festival Hall on 6 February 1983

1988   Benjamin Britten, *War Requiem*, with Julie Kennard, Maldwyn Davies, Michael George, choristers of the three cathedrals, the Festival Chorus and the CBSO

1991   Sir Arthur Bliss, *Morning Heroes*, with Brian Kay as the Narrator, the Festival Chorus and the RLPO

There had been near disaster in 1985. Janet Price, the soloist engaged for Berkeley's *Or Shall We Die?* developed tonsillitis. 'In less than a day, Wendy Eathorne studied and sang the immensely difficult soprano role with deservedly triumphant personal success', unforgettable as the desperate mother searching for her daughter among the rubble of a devastated Hiroshima:[1]

> All night I searched for my daughter.
> At dawn a neighbour told me
> she had seen her by the river,
> among the dead and dying ...

Although Roy Massey concedes that his programming might have been more conservative on the whole than that of his Gloucester and Worcester colleagues, it is surely clear that many rare, innovative or new things had been presented at his Hereford Festivals. For example, the first performance of William Mathias's *Veni Sancte Spiritus*, sung by the three cathedral choirs in 1985 – a Festival commission scored for four-part choir, organ, two trumpets and tuned percussion. 'This concise, immediately attractive piece', wrote Barrie Grayson in the *Birmingham Post*,

> a setting of the sequence for Whit Sunday, had all the hallmarks of the composer's style ... The words are a prayer requesting immortal light and Mathias with his singular imaginative skills, produced cathedral choir music that blowed and flashed with pictorial sound.
>
> It was an uplifting performance, directed convincingly by Roy Massey and sung with English cathedral choir panache ...

---

[1] *Birmingham Post*, 22 August 1985.

I have not forgotten the first time I heard Mathias's *This Worldes Joie* [it was repeated in 1985]. Now I am convinced the work has made a major contribution to the contemporary repertoire.[2]

In 1988 there was Paul Spicer's *The Darling of the World*, a setting of Robert Herrick's poem 'What Sweeter Music Can we Bring than a Carol'. Commissioned by the Birmingham Bach Society, it is dedicated to Richard Butt and was written as a companion piece to Britten's *St Nicolas*, being scored for tenor, choir, strings, piano, organ and light percussion. At Hereford the soloist in both works was Adrian Thompson. Roy Massey conducted *The Darling of the World*, and John Sanders *St Nicolas*, with the Girls' Choir of Hereford Cathedral School and the English String Orchestra.

Two notable birthdays occurred in 1988: the eightieth of Howard Ferguson and the eighty-ninth of Herbert Sumsion. Both were present at the Hereford Festival. On Tuesday evening John Sanders conducted a performance of Ferguson's *The Dream of the Rood*, with Wendy Eathorne, the Festival Chorus and the CBSO, and at the annual Finzi Trust Friends luncheon Andrew Burn gave a lecture on Ferguson's music. Sumsion's anthem *They that go down to the sea* was sung by the three cathedral choirs at Choral Evensong on Monday evening, when the canticles were to Paul Patterson's 'Norwich' service. And the Thursday evening concert ended with the first performance of Patterson's *Te Deum*. As Andrew Burn explained in his programme book note:

> With the *Te Deum*, Patterson has completed the last of three large-scale choral works which he likes to refer to as a 'Three Choirs Trilogy'. The *Mass of the Sea* was commissioned for Gloucester in 1983; such was its success that Roy Massey immediately requested a work for this year's festival [1988] and Patterson was also commissioned by the Huddersfield Choral Society to compose a work for their sesquicentenary in 1986 – the *Stabat Mater*. However, before Patterson had even put pen to paper, John Sanders decided to include this work in the 1986 Gloucester Festival, thus giving its second performance.

John Sanders, a serious, contemplative man whose professionalism inspired respect and loyalty, had been aware from his early days as Assistant Organist at Gloucester that the Festival was in danger of becoming a 'cosy club'. With the baton in his grasp he set about the task of widening its horizons, maintaining a staunch championship of English music but, at the same time, steadily introducing a more international flavour into his programming. Equally, his commitment to the improvement of choral standards became increasingly evident as the 1980s progressed.

In 1980(G) expected homage was paid to Elgar: *The Kingdom*, and the Cello Concerto with Amaryllis Fleming as soloist. There was music by Handel, Parry and Vaughan Williams; Tippett's String Quartet No. 1 (played by the Chilingirian String Quartet), and Walton's great Symphony No. 1 in B flat minor (the RPO conducted by Walter Weller); Richard Strauss's *Tod und Verklärung* in an otherwise all-Russian programme (the CBSO under Norman del Mar); the

---

[2] *Birmingham Post*, 20 August 1985.

Wagner *Wesendonck Lieder* (Sarah Walker); music of the thirteenth, fourteenth and fifteenth centuries and a concert of baroque choral and orchestral music.

Then, too, there was a repeat of David Fanshawe's *African Sanctus*; Janáček's *Glagolitic Mass* and, in honour of Sir Peter Pears's seventieth birthday, a moving account of Britten's *War Requiem* under Donald Hunt's direction, with Galina Vishnevskaya, Pears himself and Thomas Hemsley. There were the world premières of *Lord of Light* by Philip Cannon, Gerard Schurmann's *Piers Plowman*, commissioned by Netherlands Radio, *Buccinate Tuba* by Elis Pehkonen, together with the first English performances of Nicholas Maw's *Serenade*, Anthony Payne's *Footfalls Echo in the Memory*, and Peter Maxwell Davies's *Solstice of Light*.

Philip Cannon's *Lord of Light* is fittingly subtitled 'A Gloucester Requiem', since at the end the text passes into the medieval plainsong hymn *Christe Redemptor Omnium*, one of the Gloucester Chimes restored in 1979. It is set for soprano, tenor, baritone, boys' voices, chorus, orchestra (including organ) and, in its apotheosis, a recording of the Gloucester Chimes; the soloists in *Lord of Light* were Iris Dell'Acqua, Kenneth Bowen and Graham Titus.

Anthony Payne's *Footfalls Echo in the Memory* (deliciously misprinted in a *South Wales Argus* review as 'Footballs echo in the memory'!) takes its title from the first of T. S. Eliot's *Four Quartets*, 'Burnt Norton'. It is a short violin and piano piece in which the composer reworks some of the materials in his 1971 piano work *Paean*. *Footfalls Echo in the Memory* was given by Erich Gruenberg and John McCabe at a Friday morning recital in Prinknash Abbey. On Saturday afternoon in the Pittville Pump Room, Cheltenham, the Orchestra of St John's, Smith Square, under John Lubbock gave Nicholas Maw's revised *Serenade*. Deliberately lightweight and entertaining, there is, thought Andrew Clements writing in the *Financial Times*, 'the danger that the *Serenade* will fall between two audiences: not melodic enough for those who find contemporary music "difficult", while making too many concessions for Maw's admirers'.[3]

Peter Maxwell Davies's *Solstice of Light* was first performed at the 1979 St Magnus Festival, Orkney, and, as in *The Martyrdom of St Magnus*, the composer used a text by the Orcadian poet George Mackay Brown. The first English performance was given at Three Choirs in 1980 by Michael Power (tenor), the three cathedral choirs and the Organist Andrew Millington under the direction of Roy Massey during a Tuesday morning recital in Gloucester Cathedral. 'It was', wrote Kenneth Loveland, 'a model of how to achieve concentration and contrasts within a pattern of restrained but subtly varied textures ... it is wonderfully shaded, carefully shaped towards a growing climax.'[4]

The outstanding success of the 1980(G) Festival was the première of Gerard Schurmann's *Piers Plowman*. Born in Java of Dutch parents, Shurmann lived in England from childhood until 1981, when he settled in the United States. He studied composition with Alan Rawsthorne and piano with Kathleen Long, and his works include a Piano Concerto (commissioned by the late John Ogden); a Violin Concerto (premièred by Ruggiero Ricci); the orchestral song cycle *Chuenchi'i* on poems from the Chinese; the purely orchestral *Six Studies on Francis Bacon* and *Variants*; a work for unaccompanied chorus, *The Double Heart*,

[3] *Financial Times*, 30 August 1980.
[4] *South Wales Argus*, 29 August 1980.

on poems by Andrew Marvell; a wide variety of solo instrumental and chamber music; and incidental music for the theatre and for many feature films.

The text of *Piers Plowman* is based on incidents in William Langland's great fourteenth-century allegory, *The Vision of Piers the Plowman*, historically covering the latter part of the reign of Edward III and the succession of ten-year-old Richard II under the regency of the Duke of Lancaster, John of Gaunt. Langland, however, was more concerned with the prevailing moral issues than with political history, and it is the parallels between these and those of our own time which fired Schurmann's imagination.

The première of *Piers Plowman* was given during the Friday evening cathedral concert at the 1980(G) Festival by Felicity Lott, Sarah Walker, Anthony Rolfe Johnson, Norman Welsby, the Festival Chorus and RPO under the assured hand of John Sanders. A better performance is hard to imagine.

> In a direct modern tonal idiom, steeped in Britten, Walton and Gerhard, clean orchestration supported gloriously rich chorales, associated dramatic outbursts and soaring lyrical lines to which the four soloists ... generally responded sensitively. The Royal Philharmonic Orchestra ... excelled themselves.[5]

Piers Plowman was repeated at the 1989 Gloucester Festival, when the composer travelled from his home in California to be present.

> In its variety and balance, stretching from the comforting familiarity of Mozart and Schubert to the startling *avant-garde* freshness of Globokar, Ichiyanagi and Wiegold, the 1980(G) programme typifies John Sanders's continuing search to widen the horizons of the Festival.[6]

One work programmed in 1983(G) promised to be interesting but failed to live up to expectations. Handel's *Occasional Oratorio*, apparently not performed in full in England since 1763 and never sung at Three Choirs, was given in a new edition prepared by Merlin Channon. Douglas Drane wrote:

> Personally, after hearing the almost two hour abridged performance in Gloucester Cathedral, I would not regret it if that was my last occasion to hear it.
>
> It proved to be insipid and uninspiring. Unlike some of the other fine performances this week the [Gloucester] Festival Chorus could find no lustre to add and the principals: Wendy Eathorne, Angela Beale, Neil Jenkins and John Shirley-Quirk seemed unable to get it together.[7]

The *Occasional Oratorio* was accompanied by the Orchestra da Camera under John Sanders. The orchestra and its Leader, Kenneth Page, were popular visitors to Three Choirs for many years, and in 1983 the *Occasional Oratorio* was the last engagement of their silver jubilee celebrations. As Douglas Drane put it: 'Alas! It had to be this work to conclude them.'

The first performance of Paul Patterson's *Mass of the Sea* (*Missa Maris*), on the

[5] *Daily Telegraph*, 25 August 1980.

[6] In a morning concert at the Gloucester College of Education by Fresh Air Concerts: a programme of *avant-garde* music with an element of theatricality.

[7] *Citizen*, 26 August 1983.

other hand, scored a very considerable success at the 1983(G) Festival. Andrew Burn has explained that:

> the music of the Polish *avant-garde*, and in particular Penderecki, was a major formative influence on Paul Patterson, apparent in works like *Time-Piece* (1972) and *Kyrie* (1971), which established his reputation in the 1970s as a composer of a vivid, colourful imagination ... During the eighties he increasingly moved away from the textural configurations of his earlier works to a language that may be broadly summed up as a rapprochement between neo-classical sensibility and the 20th century English tradition of composers like Britten.[8]

Nigel Edwards, writing in the *Hereford Times*, expressed perfectly the enthusiasm felt by the great majority of those present at the première. Here was a new work for which further performances could hardly be in doubt:

> The 36-year-old composer ... was called to the platform again and again to the cheers of delighted music lovers both from the packed audience and from the 250-strong chorus which had just performed it.
>
> Lasting 40 minutes exactly, it proved to be one of the most striking, exciting and immediately likeable choral works to have been written for some years – a very fine piece indeed!
>
> ... The Kyrie is treated as a cry for help from the first chaos before creation when 'there was only sea and darkness was upon the face of the deep'.
>
> The Gloria becomes a rhythmic and vigorously structured dance of joy as the waters are divided and the glory of creation takes place. Christ the Saviour, walking upon the water, becomes the subject of an ethereal, loftily conceived Sanctus, while the Agnus Dei prepares us for that promised vision in the Book of Revelations of a time when there will be no more sea.
>
> Simple in concept, and yet a stroke of genius, it works extremely well. The Royal Philharmonic Orchestra and the Festival Chorus conducted by John Sanders responded magnificently. Only the soloists, Janet Price, Mary King, Kenneth Bowen and Christopher Keyte, failed to reach the highest demands of this work and were at times disappointing. But it must be added that their parts contained some of the most complex writing.[9]

In 1983 the city of Gloucester celebrated the 500th anniversary of the granting of the Charter of Incorporation by Richard III on 2 September 1483, elevating the town to the dignity of a borough. To commemorate this event the city commissioned the Gloucester-born composer Richard Shephard to write a celebratory piece, and the result, *Let us now praise famous men*, an extensive choral piece with organ and *obbligato* trumpet, was given its first performance by the St Cecilia Singers under Andrew Millington in their Friday morning cathedral recital. The trumpet was played by Crispian Steele-Perkins.

[8] Hereford Festival programme book, 1988, p. 156. Copy held in the Three Choirs Festival Office, Gloucester.

[9] *Hereford Times*, 26 August 1983.

Another distinguished son of Gloucester, the composer and writer Michael Hurd (1928–2006) (whose *Missa brevis* was performed at the 1968(G) Festival), presented the first of two talks on Ivor Gurney included in the 1983 programme of fringe events. Hurd, who was Gurney's biographer, spoke on 'Ivor Gurney – the Man and his Music'. Later in the week the poet Andrew Motion spoke on 'Ivor Gurney's Poetry' at the annual meeting of the Finzi Trust Friends, and John Shirley-Quirk included three songs by Gurney – *Severn Meadows*, *Black Stitchel* and *Sleep* – in his Friday afternoon song recital at Painswick Parish Church.

The first complete performance of Elis Pehkonen's Symphony for orchestra and soprano was given by April Cantelo and the Gloucestershire Youth Orchestra, conducted by Mark Foster, on the opening Saturday, and in an RPO orchestral concert conducted by Sir Charles Groves the next evening, John Scott (1956–2015) was the soloist in the première of the Concerto for organ, strings and percussion by Charles Camilleri.

Among the highlights of the 1983(G) Festival which linger in the memory is a luminous performance of Mahler's Symphony No. 10, given in the late Deryck Cooke's completed edition, by the CBSO under Simon Rattle. He had, wrote Helen Reid in the *Western Daily Press*:

> coaxed his string section into playing with a wonderful richness and the important woodwind and brass passages could not have been better played.
> The whole work rang with concentrated commitment and after the last movement, which is one of pure serene beauty, the audience paid the magical tribute of perfect silence before they applauded.[10]

Certainly the finest singing of the week was heard on the previous evening, Wednesday, when Jill Gomez was the soloist in the *Four Last Songs* by Richard Strauss, singing them 'with radiant purity, producing some notes of astonishing beauty'.[11] Perhaps the inspiration of this performance flowed into the Festival Chorus for the next work: Brahms's *Ein deutsches Requiem*, sung in German, with Jill Gomez and Brian Rayner Cook splendid in the solo parts.

No doubt the inclusion of Carl Orff's *Carmina Burana* in the last night programme was bound to excite comment – and it did. Monastic drunkenness, gambling and lust are not everyone's idea of appropriate topics for cathedral performance, no matter how exciting the music!

As we have seen, Malcolm Williamson's *Mass of Christ the King* finally achieved a complete performance at Three Choirs in 1986(G), when it was conducted by Donald Hunt. But the outstanding success of that Festival was yet another new work by Paul Patterson: his *Stabat Mater*, commissioned by the Huddersfield Choral Society for their 150th anniversary and first performed by them earlier in 1986. At Gloucester, John Sanders secured a fine performance. As Kenneth Loveland wrote:

> Mr Patterson writes music that strikes home. He has an imaginative fund of ideas, but is never out of reach of his audience, and always well within the physical capacity of the singers. In a phrase, he writes the sort of new

[10] *Western Daily Press*, 26 August 1983.
[11] *Western Daily Press*, 25 August 1983.

music which the choral tradition needs if it is to survive. It is very much of its time and looks forward, but it is all done with discipline and an eye to practicality.[12]

Hugely successful commercially, the first Three Choirs performance of Andrew Lloyd Webber's Requiem divided critical opinion far more sharply than did Patterson's *Stabat Mater*. Does it belong in a cathedral festival? 'For my money', wrote Kenneth Loveland after the convincing performance secured by John Sanders,

> it certainly does. The background of showbiz publicity and ballyhoo hardly prepares one for its high seriousness and more than competent writing.
>
> The elements of jazz and pop which are integrated are not out of place. Mr Lloyd Webber is writing in the idiom in which he best expresses himself, and it is never superficial music. He knows about originality of orchestral colour and detail, and like Mr Patterson, gives his choir something which is a challenge, but a practicable one.[13]

Barrie Grayson took an entirely opposite point of view:

> John Sanders, Miriam Bowen, Arthur Davies, Master Douglas Mason, Chorus and Orchestra [the RLPO] gave their all to a work which owes more to the popularity of the composer than in this instance, the quality of the music.
>
> This easily forgotten work with its borrowings and gimmicky pastiche sounds as though it was conceived bar by bar at the piano and passed on to a synthesizer expert for up-market sound colour.
>
> Unfortunately, there is little of uplifting spiritual quality in the music, and even less artistic cohesion.[14]

Of a quite different order was a concert given in Prinknash Abbey by the Amaryllis Consort: Jennifer Smith, Gillian Fisher, Charles Brett, Ian Partridge, Stephen Roberts and Michael George. Their programme was drawn from the court of Elizabeth I, a golden spring in the history of English music, and included pieces by Gibbons, Morley, Wilbye and Tomkins, among others, reaching a central climax with Byrd's settings of two funeral songs for Sir Philip Sydney: *Come to me, grief, for ever* and *O that most rare breast*.

The 1986(G) Festival ended with a revival after thirteen years of Mendelssohn's *Elijah*, in an abridged version and without an interval. The cuts, seen by some as judicious, were thought by others to be butchery of a masterpiece. Douglas Drane lamented:

> Two hours flat, no interval and some of the loveliest items cast aside – 'Cast thy burden', 'He that shall endure', the 'Holy, Holy, Holy' quartet and chorus. Poor old Elijah was not even allowed to 'go on his way in the strength of the Lord!' We realise that Liverpool is a long way away and

---

[12] *South Wales Argus*, 29 August 1986.
[13] Ibid.
[14] *Birmingham Post*, 25 August 1986.

the Band [the RLPO] wanted to get back to their hearth and home before midnight, but to do this is a travesty.[15]

Of the performance itself there were few grumbles: Brian Rayner Cook was dramatically authoritative in the title role; Helen Walker, Penelope Walker and Maldwyn Davies were all excellent; and the young treble, Andrew Wooldridge, sang with bright-toned confidence.

As always, one particular Festival memory is cemented into the mind – one lovely voice hovering above a spellbound cathedral audience: Sarah Walker, sublime in the song cycle *Les Nuits d'été* by Berlioz, and sensitively accompanied by the RPO under Sanders on Monday evening.

THE 1989 Gloucester Festival began on Friday 18 August: a day early to allow the children of the Downs School, Colwall, Malvern, to perform in the 'world première' of the concert version of a children's musical play – *Simpkin and the Tailor of Gloucester* by Douglas Young. This was repeated on Saturday afternoon. Originally expected to be of sufficient length to stand alone as a single-item entertainment mainly for children, it became clear at a very late stage that *Simpkin* would, after all, be quite a short piece. The headmaster of the Downs School (and conductor of *Simpkin*), Andrew Auster, was obliged to provide additional items to supplement the programme. Unfortunately, the result was a mismatch which reduced a kindly meant opportunity for children to contribute to the Festival into an embarrassing hybrid, unsuitable for either young or old.

'There are moments when the Three Choirs' planning can seem surprisingly amateur. It would be hard to imagine a more unwieldy programme than Saturday afternoon's concert in St Catharine's Church', wrote Simon Mundy in the *Independent*. He continued:

> *Simpkin and the Tailor of Gloucester* finally emerged in an abbreviated form. Why, one wonders, was that allowed to be so? Is it acceptable that Europe's oldest music festival should mount a bit of narration and a few pleasant choruses and call the result a world première? ... Douglas Young has written more interesting scores than this, even for youth forces, and a proper staging of the whole children's opera, without the hour of irrelevant music that had to be endured first, would have been a more worthwhile undertaking.[16]

Elizabeth Harwood generously agreed to assist in bridging the gap between *Simpkin* and an assortment of other, amateur, contributions. She sang Britten's *Cabaret Songs* and Strauss Lieder – tough fare for toddlers; and what a pity that this, her last recital at Three Choirs after so many years, should not have been set in a kinder acoustic.

1989(G) will be remembered for Parry, Pehkonen and pipistrelles.

---

[15] *Citizen*, 25 August 1986.

[16] *Independent*, 22 August 1989.

What Elgar is to Worcester Sir Hubert Parry is, or should be, to Gloucester, and a genuine attempt was made in 1989 to reverse a long neglect. Music by Parry was featured on seven days of the Festival:

Saturday   Symphony No. 5 in B minor – the Gloucestershire Youth Orchestra conducted by Mark Foster.

Sunday   The Great Service in D major setting of the evening canticles and the hymn *Laudate Dominum* at the Opening Service

Monday   *Symphonic Variations* – the RPO conducted by Roy Massey

Tuesday   Lecture by Michael Kennedy, 'Parry, Man of his Time'

Wednesday   Sonata for Cello and Piano in A major – Rachel Howgego (cello) and Stephen Lea (piano) in a fringe recital.

Part-songs ('Fair Daffodils', 'Music, when soft voices die', 'The sea hath many a thousand sands', 'Follow your saint', 'O love, they wrong you much', 'Better music ne'er was known') – the Renaissance Singers of Ontario conducted by Ray Daniels.[17]

Thursday   *Ode on the Nativity* – Festival Chorus and RLPO conducted by Donald Hunt

Friday   *Lady Radnor's Suite* – English String Orchestra conducted by William Boughton

Saturday   *Songs of Farewell* – the Rodolfus Youth Choir conducted by Ralph Allwood

On Thursday morning Parry's biographer, Dr Jeremy Dibble, gave an enthralling lecture on the composer – 'Hubert Parry: A Personal Sketch' – with musical illustrations by the Renaissance Singers of Ontario and most moving readings by Parry's descendant, Laura Ponsonby. The talk, given in the church at Highnam founded by Parry's father, Thomas Gambier Parry, was introduced by another descendant of the composer: the former Squire of Highnam, Tom Fenton.

The music of Elis Pehkonen was first heard at Three Choirs in 1980(G): *Buccinate Tuba*, scored for soprano solo, boys' voices, chorus, brass, timpani and organ, and ideally suited to the forces which John Sanders employed at the Opening Service throughout the 1980s: a brass ensemble, an effective and economical alternative to a full symphony orchestra. Pehkonen's Symphony was performed by the Gloucestershire Youth Orchestra under Mark Foster in 1983. His *Russian Requiem*, commissioned by the Birmingham Festival Choral Society, received its first performance in that city in November 1986, when it was described by the *Birmingham Post* critic, Barrie Grayson, as a 'momentous and

---

[17] This concert also included a wide range of renaissance and contemporary works; it ended with works by Elgar (*Go, song of mine*), Vaughan Williams (*Silence and Music*), and two songs by Gerald Finzi (*Clear and gentle stream* and *My spirit sang all day*). The Renaissance Singers of Ontario also presented a late-night Fringe concert of madrigals and Victorian songs.

memorable occasion … a profoundly moving experience'. The work was repeated on the Thursday afternoon of the 1989 Gloucester Festival.

Of Finnish extraction, Elis Pehkonen was born in Norfolk, studied at the Royal Academy of Music with Peter Racine Fricker, and at various times with Benjamin Britten, Richard Rodney Bennett and Anthony Payne.

Russian Requiem, directly influenced by documented events following the Russian Revolution of 1917, is dedicated to 'the stubborn child of Gorodietsky'. The work is a plea for the peace of reconciliation through the unifying love of Christ. Pehkonen does not set the entire *missa pro defunctis* (there is no *Sanctus*, *Libera me* or *In Paradisum*). Instead, he highlights selected passages with quotations from the Revelations of St John the Divine, Canto 3 of Dante's *Inferno*, Boris Pasternak's *Zhivago* poems 'Gethsemane' and 'Winter Night', as well as comments from the collected works of Lenin. The work is scored for soprano and contralto soloists (Christine Bunning and Susan Mason), chorus, oboe, cor anglais, two trumpets, timpani, percussion, organ and strings. The Gloucester performance was conducted by John Sanders.

> On paper [wrote Kenneth Loveland] the appearance of two requiems in one day looked heavy going. It did not turn out that way. Elis Pehkonen's *Russian Requiem* is the latest to blend liturgy and literature, including Dantë and Pasternak, and is a work of convincing statement, dramatic pulse and accessibility. The music, though often heavy with grief, suggests the glowing richness of the Russian Orthodox Church, and is at its best in the shimmering final quotations from *Winter Night* (an unexpected visitor in which Fauré seems to hover) where Sanders blended Pehkonen's gentle repetitions into a beautiful mosaic. Pehkonen's sincerity is a winning factor, and so, in a different way, is that of John Rutter, who conducted his *Requiem* later the same day. And he is a genial and pleasant hand at a tune. But one wonders whether the genial and the pleasant are really what one looks for in a requiem.[18]

And the pipistrelles? From the first note of the first concert an erratic squadron of tiny bats appeared from the cathedral tower to patrol the airspace above the audience. Kodály's Budávari *Te Deum* on Monday evening seemed to interest one musical *Fledermaus* in particular, who swooped down towards the conductor and caused Roy Massey to duck and weave. *Piers Plowman* followed – more bats 'scrambled', but were content to limit themselves to high-level reconnaissance. The *Birmingham Post* went so far as to interview Hilary Ward, a spokesman for the Nature Conservancy Trust, who said that the unusually high number of pipistrelles in the cathedral was probably due to the mild weather: most of the young had survived.

The Festival closed with a performance of Elgar's *Caractacus*, blessed with a perfect quartet of soloists: Julie Kennard, Robert Tear, Michael George and, in the title role, Brian Rayner Cook, with the Festival Chorus and RLPO under John Sanders. Brian Rayner Cook, who on Friday morning had woven magic spells of his own in a song recital with Clifford Benson at Painswick Parish

[18] *MT* 1989, p. 700.

Church, put the thoughts of many into words after *Caractacus*: 'That was John Sanders at his very best.'

Caractacus finished, the audience joined chorus and soloists in Parry's *Jerusalem* to the accompaniment of Elgar's 1922 orchestration. A fitting and proud ending to what was, above all, Parry's week.

Donald Hunt had drawn together two predominant themes in devising his programme for the 1981 Worcester Festival – looking north to Scandinavia and, yet again, south to France. But this time the French connection was further strengthened by invitations to internationally famous French performers and composers to make contributions to the Festival.

The Scandinavian theme, prompted by the fiftieth anniversary of the death of Carl Nielsen, was established not only by several of that most eminent of Danish composer's works, but also by the first British concert performance of the *Te Deum danicum* by his fellow-countryman Knud Jeppesen, whose two motets, *Herre! Hvor er mine fiender mange* and *Jeg slettede som tåge*, together with works by other Danish composers, were sung by the Copenhagen Boys Choir on Monday afternoon. The music of Finland was also featured: a magnificent performance of Sibelius's Symphony No. 2 by the RPO under Sir Charles Groves on Wednesday evening, and on Thursday *Finlandia* to open a concert given by the Festival Chorus and the BBC Northern Symphony Orchestra conducted by Donald Hunt, which included the first British performances of Aulis Sallinen's *Dies Irae* and, surprisingly, the *Missa solemnis* by Liszt.

The Sallinen piece is a setting of the poem *It was Christmas Day* by the Finnish poet Arvo Turtiainen: an apocalyptic vision of the world's nuclear destruction one Christmas Day. Sallinen hammers home the stark message of *Dies Irae* by stone-hard orchestration, percussive clamour and the austerity of an all-male choir. It is a journey from light to darkness, relieved only at the end by a single spark of hope born of a visit to the destroyed Earth by a space traveller, a representative of nobler and saner humanity elsewhere in the universe.

The inspiration for Edwin Roxburgh's *The Rock*, on the other hand, is the spiritual journey from darkness to light. Aware that his subject has inspired many of the world's greatest works of art, Roxburgh chose the Revelations of St John the Divine as the main text for *The Rock*, drawing also on a wide range of sources, from the Koran to T. S. Eliot.

In structure the work is woven around textual fragments from the medieval Worcester school: isolated manuscripts of fourteenth-century music recovered from book bindings and wrappers to bundles of accounts. *The Rock* was given at the Tuesday evening concert in 1981(w) with soloists Jane Manning, Mary King, Kenneth Bowen and John Noble, the Festival Chorus, cathedral choristers and the RPO under Donald Hunt. Critical opinion was sharply divided, not least on the matter of volume. For Nigel Edwards the work was a superb unfolding of the spiritual journey: 'we tasted the bitter depths of the dark and eventually rejoiced in the spiritual bliss of the heavenly realms with 'Alleluia Tympanum', quoted from the Worcester fragments with telling effect … the overall effect was magnificently convincing.'[19]

[19] *Worcester Evening News*, 26 August 1981.

Kenneth Loveland remained unconvinced by *The Rock* but found pleasure in the first performance of Herbert Sumsion's *In Exile: By the waters of Babylon*, heard in the cathedral on Tuesday morning:

> What can be said of Edwin Roxburgh's *The Rock* … the work's message is submerged in waves of indisciplined sound, and not all the advocacy of Donald Hunt, the chorus, the valiantly battling soloists, and the R.P.O. could bring it to the surface. Herbert Sumsion's *In Exile*, a setting for double choir of Psalm 137, was a happy event … a much loved figure at the festival, he had the maximum goodwill going for him, and a devoted account by the Donald Hunt Singers showed the new motet to be a skilled piece of professionalism … Of the new music, Jonathan Harvey's *Resurrection* made the strongest impression [given by the three cathedral choirs under Donald Hunt on the Friday morning]. Using mirror techniques, ascending chords for the resurrection text, descending ones for death, and allusive organ textures (Paul Trepte coped superbly) with muttered bass comments and treble insinuations, Harvey produced a sense of the inexorable by insistent repetitions.[20]

Friday 28 August 1981 was rather a special day for the Harvey family. Singing in Jonathan Harvey's commissioned work *Resurrection* were Worcester head chorister Rupert Harvey and his father, Dr Brian Harvey, the composer's brother and a voluntary cathedral bass lay clerk. Later in the day, father and son were singing Jonathan Harvey's anthem *I love the Lord* at Choral Evensong, and the organ voluntary that concluded the service, *Laus Deo*, was also by him.

Another Worcester Cathedral lay clerk to play a significant and versatile role at Three Choirs over many years was Trevor Owen. Apart from his valuable presence among the tenors of the three cathedral choirs and the Festival Chorus, Owen sang with the male-voice quintet Opus 5 (John Vickers, Trevor Owen, John Wilman, Roger Hemingway and Alan Fairs) at the 1977(G), 1979(H) and 1984(W) Festivals. At Worcester, as conductor of the Festival Junior Chorus, he directed several delightful performances of choral works and opera for young people, which included, in 1981, Purcell's *Dido and Aeneas* and Peter Maxwell Davies's *The Two Fiddlers* at the Worcester Technical College. And who should have been in the Junior Chorus and taking part in *Dido and Aeneas* but yet another member of the Harvey family: Rupert's young sister, Amanda! In 1991 Trevor Owen moved from Worcester to Chichester.

The 1981(W) Festival week had begun on Saturday evening with a recital of French organ music given by Jean Langlais (1907–1991), the celebrated Organist of the Basilique Sainte-Clotilde, Paris. In addition to works of his own, Langlais played pieces by Couperin and two of his predecessors at Sainte-Clotilde: César Franck and Charles Tournemire. At the Festival Eucharist on the following morning Langlais' mass, *Grant us Thy Peace*, commissioned by the Worcester Cathedral Choir Association for the Festival, was given its first performance, along with two motets by Pierre Villette: *O Sacrum Convivium* and *O Salutaris Hostia*.

---

[20] *MT* 1981, p. 690.

In 1976, Donald Hunt had approached Pierre Villette to write a new work for Three Choirs. The composer had already begun a mass to mark the sixth centenary of the foundation of Saint-Évode Choir School, Rouen Cathedral, and had completed the *Agnus Dei*. Originally commissioned to make a setting of the vernacular text with an accompaniment of two organs, Villette was now presented with the opportunity to complete the work on a larger scale. The terms of the original commission were amended, and Villette received a special grant for the composition from the French Minister of Culture. The first performance of Villette's *Messe en français* was given at the 1981(w) Wednesday afternoon concert by Wendy Eathorne, Margaret Cable, Alastair Thompson and David Wilson Johnson, the Worcester Festival Chorus and the BBC Northern Symphony Orchestra conducted by Donald Hunt, whose championship of the composer was entirely vindicated. The orchestral concert given by the RPO under Sir Charles Groves on Wednesday evening also began with a work by Villette – his beautiful *Trois Préludes pour cordes*, described by the composer as 'full of mystery and reverie'.

Jean-Claude Malgoire's interpretation of Handel's *Messiah* on the last Saturday afternoon was something of a disappointment. Conducting his chamber orchestra, La Grande Ecurie et la Chambre du Roy, the Worcester Cathedral choristers and lay clerks of the three cathedral choirs, Malgoire had the opportunity to break free from the nineteenth-century *Messiah* tradition. Instead, he attempted to produce a monumental idea of the work, unsupported by large-scale sound, leaving his audience in no man's land. Theresa Lister, Charles Brett, Alastair Thompson and Nicklaus Tüller gave wholly admirable accounts of their solos.

The 1981 Festival ended with a blazing performance of the *Grande Messe des morts* by Berlioz, played by the CBSO under Donald Hunt, and with the Festival Chorus rising magnificently to the challenge of the massive composition.

And a single, lasting memory of the Festival? The truly inspired singing of Rosalind Plowright and Alfreda Hodgson in Mahler's Symphony No. 2 (*Resurrection*) on Friday evening. Originally to have been conducted by Günther Herbig, and later advertised as under the direction of Bernhard Klee, finally it was Sir Charles Groves who took charge of the BBC Northern Symphony Orchestra and Festival Chorus, conveying superbly Mahler's dazzling vision of eternal certainty.

T HE centenary of Dvořák's visit to the Festival and the fiftieth anniversaries of the deaths of Delius, Holst and Elgar all fell in 1984. In that year, too, the Festival became an integral part of the Worcester Cathedral 900th anniversary celebrations.

Where better than Worcester to celebrate so important an Elgar anniversary? Certainly the BBC seized the opportunity, mounting an invitation-only television production with the Festival Chorus of *The Dream of Gerontius* on the opening Saturday evening, 18 August. Only the second occasion since 1977(G) that a part of the Festival had been televised, this well-intentioned tribute did not quite come off:

It would have been proper recognition of all he [Dr Hunt] has done to strengthen music at Worcester if he had been given the opening performance of *The Dream of Gerontius* [wrote Kenneth Loveland], but this had all the appearance of a starry package designed by the B.B.C. for its viewers rather than something intended by the festival for its own public. There was the tiring necessity of sitting through the ritual service dedication. To the stifling oppression of one of the hottest nights of the summer was added the almost unbearable heat and glare of television lights. In front of my seat a television camera repeatedly soared heavenwards as though trying to catch the soul of Gerontius in flight. It all worked against the atmosphere in which *The Dream* best conveys its message, and although Janet Baker, Stuart Burrows and Benjamin Luxon each did notable things, the chorus gave of their best, and Andrew Davis secured conscientious playing from the B.B.C. Welsh S.O. (the introduction to Part 2 was particularly beautiful), concentration was not possible.[21]

(Donald Hunt, having no part to play in these proceedings, changed into casual wear and took himself off to the Perdiswell Sports Centre to listen to Acker Bilk and his Paramount Jazz Band – only to be thrown out by the bouncer for failing to have a ticket!)

Rehearsals for this sweltering and mediocre *Gerontius* left no available time for the century-old traditional Opening Service. Hence the 'ritual service of dedication' which took its place: a thirty-minute service immediately preceding the first concert. In compensation, and taking an appropriate place on Sunday morning, a Festival Eucharist which incorporates the Festival Sermon was introduced. In 1984 this included the motets *A Spiritual Temple* by John C. Phillips and the first performance of *Most Glorious Lord of Life* by Donald Hunt, commissioned by the Worcester Cathedral Choir Association.

The television cameras remained in place for the 1984(w) Sunday evening concert – a programme of music taking America as its theme: Copland's *Fanfare for the Common Man* and *Appalachian Spring*; Bernstein's *Chichester Psalms*, with Worcester Cathedral chorister James Davis a clear and confident treble soloist; and two pieces composed by Delius on American visits, 'Sunset' and 'Daybreak' from the *Florida Suite*, and *Sea Drift*, in which Stephen Roberts was the baritone soloist with the Festival Chorus and the CBSO under Donald Hunt – altogether more enjoyable than the previous evening's *Gerontius*, in spite of equally torrid television lighting.

The American theme continued on Monday morning with a disappointing organ recital by Carlo Curley, who was struggling with an organ badly affected by heat changes in the cathedral over the previous days. And on Monday afternoon the American John T. Hamilton Chorale gave a recital of American choral music in All Saints Church, including pieces by Howard Hanson, Jerome Kern, Norman Luboff and Horatio Parker.

Almost inevitably, Dvořák's visit to Worcester in 1884 was linked coincidentally to the Festival's American theme. His String Quartet No. 12 in F,

21 *MT* 1984, p. 660.

op. 96 (*The American*) was included in a recital by the Delmé String Quartet at Hartlebury Castle on Tuesday afternoon, in addition to the Elgar String Quartet in E minor and *Meditation on an Old Czech Hymn: Saint Wenceslaus* by Dvořák's favourite pupil, Josef Suk.

On Monday evening Donald Hunt conducted the CBSO in a vigorous performance of Dvořák's Symphony No. 6 in D, one of the works conducted by the composer himself during his Worcester visit (the twenty-seven-year-old Elgar then among the first violins), and on Tuesday evening Dvořák's *Requiem Mass* was given an assured performance under John Sanders's direction, with Mimfred Sand, Fiona Kimm, Kenneth Bowen and John Noble, the Festival Chorus and the CBSO.

Three very different soundworlds were brought together on Friday evening in a concert given by the ladies voices of the Donald Hunt Singers and the BBC Philharmonic Orchestra conducted by Edward Downes: Elgar's *Froissart*; *Paris (The Song of a Great City)* by Delius; and Holst's masterpiece, *The Planets*. All three composers had been represented on Thursday morning in a programme of English choral music given in the cathedral by the Donald Hunt Singers and Osian Ellis (harp): *Unaccompanied Part-Songs*, op. 53, and *Go, song of mine* by Elgar; *On Craig Ddu* and *The Splendour Falls on Castle Walls* by Delius; and Holst's *Choral Hymns from the Rig Veda (Third Set)*, op. 26, No. 3. This fascinatingly varied programme also included William Mathias's *Three Improvisations* for harp, op. 10, Britten's Suite for harp, op. 83, and the first performance of Richard Rodney Bennett's *Sea Change*, an *a cappella* choral suite dedicated to Donald Hunt and commissioned by the Festival with funds provided by West Midlands Arts. The texts for *Sea Change* are taken from Shakespeare's *The Tempest*, from Andrew Marvell, and from Spenser's *Faerie Queene*.

> *Sea Change* was [wrote Hugo Cole] resourceful and imaginative, fairly lightweight music with a delightful setting of Marvell's *Remote Bermudas* (the prologue and epilogue most beautifully sung by an un-named tenor from the choir) [Trevor Owen].
>
> The evocation of sea monsters by means of *sprechgesang* was also effective, though Bennett's own individual voice was less apparent here, while in the setting of *Full Fathom Five*, the technical ingenuity of reflecting four upper voices with four lower voices muddied the harmonic waters without any great expressive gain.[22]

Monteverdi's Vespers of 1610 had been performed four times at Three Choirs between 1958 and 1979. In 1984 Donald Hunt programmed the work again – but this time for performance by the three cathedral choirs without augmentation by any element of the Festival Chorus. The performance, directed by Roger Norrington, was outstanding. Hugo Cole again:

> eight perfectly matched soloists, the three cathedral choirs and a familiar team of baroque specialists, the London Baroque Players, showed how few performers are needed to produce spectacular and brilliant effects

---

[22] *Guardian*, 24 August 1984.

in this kindly environment. In spite of Roger Norrington's fervour, the three choirs stuck to their normal serene and unimpassioned mode of singing; the contrast with the highly expressive singing of the soloists Gillian Fisher, Theresa Lister, Paul Esswood, Andrew Arthur, Martyn Hill, Joseph Cornwell, Michael George and Stephen Varcoe was in its way very effective.

Norrington's plain realization is consistent and unobtrusive. With performers of this calibre there is no danger in a high degree of exposure, and clarity of sounds brings us even closer to Monteverdi.[23]

In 1984 another important source of funding for new commissions became available to the Worcester Festival. Ken Pott's statue of Elgar, which gazes out at the cathedral from the southern end of High Street, had been unveiled by HRH The Prince of Wales on the composer's birthday, 2 June 1981. Such had been the response to the Elgar Statue Appeal that the project was realised with considerable funds to spare. Mindful of the spirit in which donations to the statue fund had been made, the Appeal Committee decided that surplus monies should be used to commission triennially a major work for the Worcester Festival. In 1987 the Elgar commission was Richard Rodney Bennett's Symphony No. 3, and in 1990 the song cycle *A Song for Birds* by Paul Spicer, but the first Elgar commission was Peter Racine Fricker's *Whispers at these Curtains*, op. 88, given by Stephen Roberts, the Festival Chorus and the BBC Philharmonic Orchestra conducted by Donald Hunt at the 1984(w) Thursday evening concert.

The text of *Whispers at these Curtains* is chosen from the devotions, sermons and prayers of John Donne. Fricker selected them from many different sources to illustrate three main lines of Donne's thinking: the obsession with bells and death, the voice of God and the whispers of the dead and of Christ's voice, and Donne's triumphant assumption of glory.

Whispers at these Curtains was followed by Elgar's Cello Concerto, with Robert Cohen an inspired soloist. His performance, wrote Kenneth Loveland,

> was remarkable as an example of the complete identification of player and music. With an accompaniment which spoke of instinctive rapport (B.B.C.P.O., Hunt) Cohen, filling the cathedral with a rich tone, explored eloquently the music's self-communing inner tragedy, and the despairing backward glance can rarely have been more poignant.[24]

The concert ended with the *Hymn of Jesus*, reminding us yet again of how very much was lost to English music by Holst's untimely death at only fifty-nine. As Donald Hunt pointed out in a programme note,

> much of Holst's musical language stems not only from the French-influenced fashions of his day, but also from his predilection for the music of Byrd, Palestrina and Bach. Indeed, it was following a performance of Bach's Mass in B minor in Worcester Cathedral that Holst said he found himself clutching the arm of his chair during the Sanctus. He felt he was

[23] Ibid.

[24] *MT* 1984, p. 660.

floating on air, and he feared lest he should find his head bumping against the groined roof![25]

The 1984(w) Festival had begun with *Gerontius*, and the spirit of Elgar was never far away. On Wednesday, Donald Hunt conducted Elgar's rare symphonic cantata *The Black Knight* and, even rarer, *Sursum corda* for strings, brass and organ. On Friday morning Michael Kennedy gave a fascinating talk on Elgar's oratorios in St George's Roman Catholic Church, where the composer had been organist in the 1880s. But the triumph of the week was reserved for Saturday, when Donald Hunt directed *The Apostles* in the afternoon and *The Kingdom* in the evening. The experience of hearing the two works in sequence invited reassessment, wrote Kenneth Loveland:

> The consistency of their creative urgency became more apparent; the motifs they share, and Elgar's transformation of them, were shown to have stronger relevance to changing situations; the almost operatic significance was heightened. The performances were devoted, with the choir providing eager response, tiring only a little at one point in *The Kingdom*, the R.L.P.O. immediately supportive of Dr Hunt's search for those subtleties of instrumental colour that are among the most interesting aspects of these works, and a totally committed team of soloists in Elizabeth Harwood, Alfreda Hodgson, Robert Tear and Michael Rippon plus, in *The Apostles*, Brian Rayner Cook a profoundly moving Jesus, and John Noble so powerfully involved as Judas. Dr Hunt's courage was completely justified, and late on the last night a packed cathedral audience rose to cheer him.[26]

As if to balance the American theme of the 1984(w) Festival, in 1987 Donald Hunt's musical compass swung to the east, pointing up distinctive Eastern European and Russian flavours: Szymanowski, Enescu, Borodin, Rachmaninov, Tchaikovsky and Penderecki.

The beautifully restored Countess of Huntingdon's Hall was used as a Three Choirs concert venue for the first time at the 1987(w) Festival, providing over 500 seats in a building of both local and national importance within a short walking distance of the cathedral. The hall, a converted chapel, was built in 1773 by Selina, Countess of Huntingdon, to accommodate early followers of the Huntingdon Connexion (related to Calvinistic Methodism), who were regarded – according to discriminatory legislation still active – as dissenters. The chapel was twice extended in the nineteenth century to house a growing congregation. The last service was held in 1976, and in 1977 the City of Worcester Building Preservation Trust was set up to save the fine Georgian chapel and to restore and adapt it as a concert hall, arts centre and music school to serve Worcester and the Severn region.

The inaugural concert in the Countess of Huntingdon's Hall was held on the afternoon of Sunday 23 August; it was an all-English programme, beginning

[25] Worcester Festival programme book, 1984, p. 152. Copy held in the Three Choirs Festival Office, Gloucester.
[26] *MT* 1984, pp. 659–60.

appropriately with William Boyce's *Worcester Overture* (Symphony No. 8 in D) played by the Worcester-based English String Orchestra, conducted for this special occasion by Sir David Willcocks.

Several other recitals were given in the hall during the week, three of them by the Medici String Quartet. On Monday afternoon their programme included Borodin's String Quartet No. 1 in A and Richard Rodney Bennett's *Lamento d'Arianna*; and on Friday afternoon three equally contrasted quartets – Beethoven's op. 130, Borodin's second, and Penderecki's first. On Wednesday morning the Medici Quartet were joined by Richard Pascoe, Barbara Leigh Hunt and the pianist John Bingham in a wholly delightful presentation of the life and music of Sir Edward Elgar written by Michael Kennedy: *Wood Magic*, an account, told as far as possible in Elgar's own words or in those of his friends and contemporaries, of how Elgar came to write the four masterpieces with which his composing life virtually closed in 1918–19: a violin sonata, string quartet, piano quintet, and the autumnal Cello Concerto.

On Thursday morning the Countess of Huntingdon's Hall was shown to be an ideal song-recital venue when John Shirley-Quirk, sensitively accompanied by Christopher Robinson, presented another all-English programme: Purcell, Vaughan Williams, Warlock, Gurney and Howells. Enveloped in all this was Donald Hunt's cycle *Strings in the Earth and Air*, settings of poems taken from the collection *Chamber Music* by James Joyce, and composed by Hunt as a wedding gift for his son Thomas and daughter-in-law Joanna.

The 1987 Elgar commission, Richard Rodney Bennett's Symphony No. 3, was performed for the first time at the Monday evening concert given by the BBC Philharmonic Orchestra conducted by Edward Downes (1924–2009), to whom it is dedicated.

Bennett (1936–2012) had intended to fulfil the commission with a short orchestral piece called *Tapestry* but subsequently extended the work to become his Symphony No. 3. In a programme note he explained that it

> was written in New York City and London between April and July 1987. My first two symphonies, commissioned respectively for the London Symphony and New York Philharmonic orchestras, were composed in the late 1960s and are primarily extrovert, display pieces in which I was exploiting the resources of the modern orchestra, creating show pieces for the virtuosity of the players.
>
> The new symphony, composed twenty years after the second, is a very different proposition. The orchestra is moderate … only nine wind players and modest percussion in addition to the usual strings, plus piano and harp.
>
> The music is mostly thoughtful and lyrical in nature, more or less monothematic, and has a strong feeling of tonality, particularly at the opening and closing of the score.

Among other major works performed in the cathedral during the 1987(w) Festival, Howard Blake's oratorio *Benedictus* and the *Te Deum* of Krzysztof Penderecki were, in their very different ways, memorable and important.

Howard Blake (b. 1938) grew up in Brighton and at eighteen won a scholarship to the Royal Academy of Music, studying piano and composition.

In the following decade or so he worked as a freelance session pianist, composer, conductor and orchestrator. In 1971 he went to live in a watermill in Sussex, where he began to forge a personal style of composition which is rhythmic, contrapuntal and, most importantly, melodic. *Benedictus*, started in 1978, was the 'culmination of this period of creativity and developed the idiom to the full, at the same time presenting in dramatic form Blake's other preoccupation of those years – a search for spiritual meaning'.[27] Orchestral works, choral works, songs, ballets, chamber and instrumental works have all followed, including the highly successful piece for narrator and orchestra, *The Snowman*, a perennial best-seller on disc and video.

Benedictus was inspired by the teachings of St Benedict as laid down in his book, *The Rule*, so called because 'it guides straight the life of those who obey'. Blake's work is a dramatic oratorio for tenor, speaker, large choir and orchestra; a solo viola is also employed to haunting effect in his absorbing score. At Worcester, the impressively operatic tenor soloist was Arthur Davies, with Jeffrey Fenwick (speaker), Christopher Balmer (viola), the Festival Chorus and RLPO in thrilling form under Donald Hunt.

Krzysztof Penderecki was born at Debrica, Poland in 1933. He studied composition with Malawski and Wiehowicz at the Krakow Music Academy, graduating in 1958. A year later, his *Threnody to the Victims of Hiroshima* won international acclaim for its intensely expressive use of new string sonorities, achieved through a thorough exploration of the instruments and playing techniques. The much larger *St Luke Passion* (1963–5), still unheard at Three Choirs, made an equally deep impression.

Penderecki's *Te Deum* received a gripping first Three Choirs performance on the Tuesday evening of the 1987(w) Festival, when it was conducted by the composer. As well as the *Te Deum* and the String Quartet No. 1, Penderecki's *Capriccio* for oboe and strings was also included in the Festival programme, performed at the Countess of Huntingdon's Hall on Saturday afternoon by Nicholas Daniel in an English String Orchestra concert conducted by William Boughton.

The Hungarian-born conductor Antal Dorati had been engaged to direct the Festival Chorus and RPO in Beethoven's cantata *Calm Sea and Prosperous Voyage* and the Symphony No. 9 in D (*Choral*) on Friday evening, with Alison Hargan, Alfreda Hodgson, Robert Tear and Gwynne Howell. Ill health prevented Dorati from appearing and his place was taken at short notice by the Swiss conductor Karl Anton Rickenbacher. Soloists and choir responded magnificently to Rickenbacher's clear, incisive command, but the orchestra maintained a strange and wayward detachment.

Alfreda Hodgson, Robert Tear and Gwynne Howell again joined the Festival Chorus and RPO on the last night of the 1987(w) Festival in a superb performance of *Gerontius* under the sure hand of Donald Hunt.

Between the lines of the Latin text of the central *Sanctus* section of his *Te Deum*, Penderecki interpolated lines from an old national hymn, its plea both ancient and modern, sung in Polish and translated as follows:

[27] Worcester Festival programme book, 1987, p. 19. Copy held in the Three Choirs Festival Office, Gloucester.

God of Poland, before all time, wrapped in great light, power and glory,
Before Thine altar we bear our petition:
Father, restore to us our rightful land.

As the 1980s came to an end the cries for freedom in Eastern Europe appeared to have been answered. Political change flowed at breathtaking speed behind the tearing down of the Berlin Wall in 1989, and by 1990 a new optimism had replaced the petrified gloom of more than four decades of Cold War. Certainly the mood of the Worcester Festival in that year seemed to reflect spontaneously a lighter-hearted internationalism: in the cathedral, Italian, Russian and English evenings; a French afternoon; Bach, Haydn, Beethoven and Mahler aplenty; Berg side-by-side with Elgar; and at outside events the music of Latin America and northern India, a brass band, jazz and much more – the whole a testimony to imaginative programming and planning.

One of the most keenly anticipated events of the Festival was the first UK performance of George Lloyd's Symphony No. 12, given on Friday evening by the BBC Philharmonic Orchestra under the composer's own direction – and how good it was to see a living British composer with a wide popular following on both sides of the Atlantic mounting the rostrum at Three Choirs to conduct a new, large-scale work.

George Lloyd (1913–1998) was born at St Ives, Cornwall. Illness precluded his attending school until the age of twelve, but after two years he left to pursue a full-time musical education, studying violin with Albert Sammons and composition with Harry Farjeon, then briefly attending Trinity College of Music in London. Lloyd began composing at the age of ten, and before World War II three symphonies and two operas, *Iernin* and *The Serf* (with libretti by his father), were performed – the former opera at Penzance in 1934 and the latter at Covent Garden in 1938. These early successes were brought to an end by the war. In 1942, while on an Arctic convoy in a cruiser, Lloyd was badly shell-shocked. After partially recovering his health, he was commissioned to write his third opera, *John Socman*, for the Festival of Britain in 1951. His health again deteriorated and he and his wife settled in Dorset, where they operated a market garden, growing carnations and mushrooms, and only composing intermittently.

By 1973 Lloyd had written six more symphonies and several concertos, and his health had recovered sufficiently for him to return to full-time composing. A broadcast of his Symphony No. 8 in 1977 marked a renewal of public interest in his music. Numerous performances with the BBC Philharmonic Orchestra followed, and in 1988 he was appointed Principal Guest Conductor with the Albany Symphony Orchestra of New York State, who commissioned his Symphony No. 11 and for whom he wrote No. 12.

George Lloyd's music aroused the considerable enthusiasm of those thirsting for lyrical beauty, melody and exuberance from a modern composer, and the disdain of others, who hear no more than skilful scoring in a nineteenth-century manner, derivative and banal to the point of being anodyne. 'But what music is not derivative in some sense and to some degree?' wrote David J. Brown in the *Musical Times*. 'Are some sources of derivation acceptable and some not? And was the same charge of banality not levelled at Mahler until fairly recently, before the discovery that it was really irony; *ergo* acceptable; *ergo* great?'[28]

In any event, the Worcester audience welcomed Lloyd's approachable clarity, even though the single-movement twelfth is far from his best symphony, the over-long *fugato* of its final section outstaying its welcome. 'No-one now living, though, can make an orchestra *sing* as he does, and our musical life has plenty of room for, and would be poorer without, his unique contribution.'[29]

The single 'world première' of the Festival was Mussorgsky's *Saint Nicholas Mass*, 'an unashamed hybrid', as Philip Lane, who realised and edited the work, described it in his programme note. Mussorgsky, of course, wrote no such mass. What Lane has done is to intersperse three choruses from *Salammbo* with the cantatas *Joshua* and *The Destruction of Sennacherib*, and substituted the Ordinary of the mass for the original texts – an ingenious if not entirely convincing device for making little-known music accessible. Donald Hunt conducted the RLPO and Festival Chorus, with Alison Pearce and Matthew Best the ideal soloists.

This Monday evening concert continued with the Tchaikovsky Piano Concerto in B flat minor, played on an inadequate piano by Boris Beresovsky, and ended with a thrilling account of Prokofiev's *Alexander Nevsky*:

> Roy Massey conducted both works, the latter being particularly distinguished by Linda Strachan's haunting obsequy for the dead of the Battle on the Ice (which itself made one fear premature collapse of Worcester Cathedral's structurally endangered central tower).
>
> The evening before was all-Italian, opened by Petrassi's half-hour *Magnificat*, arguably the most musically substantial and syntactically original of the Festival's unfamiliar big works, and one whose date of 1940 added further accusatory point. Though it was obviously a major challenge for the Festival Chorus, John Sanders's dedicated direction carried the day. Wisely, he allowed the R.L.P.O. (in splendid form for all five of their concerts) their head, and they duly relished Petrassi's pungently juxtaposed and often vividly exciting orchestral textures. Why is this composer, now 86, not heard far more often? One could ask the same about Respighi (leaving aside the Roman trilogy), but the ensuing not-ideally-paced performance of *Church Windows* under Donald Hunt will not, I fear, have made many converts.[30]

Wednesday evening brought the *St John Passion*, played on original instruments and at baroque pitch by the Hanover Band directed by Simon Preston, with the three cathedral choirs and a team of soloists of rare quality: Ian Partridge (Evangelist), Michael George (Christus), Luise Horrocks, Charles Brett, William Kendall and Peter Savidge.

Less satisfactory was the cathedral concert which on Saturday evening began the whole Festival. Again a first-rate team of soloists: Helen Field, Alison Pearce,

[28] *MT* 1990, p. 616.

[29] Ibid.

[30] Ibid.

Luise Horrocks, Sally Burgess, Linda Strachan, Neil Jenkins (stepping in for the indisposed Anthony Roden), Alan Opie and Stafford Dean; the RLPO in cracking form and, if not quite 'of a Thousand', a combined choir well capable of raising the roof – the Festival Chorus, choristers of Worcester Cathedral and the Worcester Junior Festival Chorus – in Mahler's vast Symphony No. 8 under Libor Pesek. But somehow the performance never added up to the sum of its parts, and an essential sense of unity between conductor and choir was noticeably lacking.

From such immensity it was refreshing to turn to the intimacy of the Countess of Huntingdon's Hall, where on Tuesday and Wednesday morning the Alberni String Quartet captured a magical mood. In both of their recitals the central work was a model of word-setting for singer and instrumental ensemble. On Tuesday, Samuel Barber's setting of Matthew Arnold's *Dover Beach* for baritone and string quartet, in which Thomas Hunt was the sensitive soloist. And on Wednesday the quartet was joined by Philip Dennis and Donald Hunt in Ivor Gurney's song cycle for tenor, string quartet and piano to poems by A. E. Housman, *Ludlow and Teme* – surely seven of the most beautiful of English songs.

Gurney was in the company of seven other composers, all with strong Three Choirs links, in an exquisite recital given by Ian and Jennifer Partridge at the Countess of Huntingdon's Hall on Friday morning: Stanford, Atkins, Brewer, Parry, Howells, Britten and Paul Spicer, whose song cycle *A Song for Birds* – settings of poems by Laurie Lee and medieval Latin poems translated into English by Fleur Adcock – was given its first performance.

Gerontius was again the climax to a dazzling week. The *Musical Times* reviewer noted that William Cochran's 'unequal assumption of the title role was fortunately compensated by Sally Burgess, substituting at the last minute for Alfreda Hodgson' (1940–1992), and went on to say that this:

> detracts in no way from the overwhelming emotional and spiritual impact of this of all works in this of all venues. [Alan Opie was powerfully impressive as the Priest and the Angel of the Agony.] The B.B.C.P.O., the Festival Chorus and Donald Hunt proved, as anticipated, worthy keepers of the Seal.

> The single finest performance, though, was of arguably the greatest work. On the Tuesday evening the Chorus and R.L.P.O., and (yet again), an exceptional solo team [Alison Pearce, Sally Burgess, Neil Jenkins and Matthew Best] were driven by Donald Hunt through an unfaltering (and uninterrupted) *Missa Solemnis* which, more than any other live performance I have heard, positively relished the stratospheric choral difficulties and constant challenges of balance in a superbly coherent projection of Beethoven's mighty and eternally unsettling vision. Malcolm Stewart's violin solo in the Benedictus touched perfection.[31]

---

[31] *MT* 1990, p. 617.

124 Gloucester Cathedral

125 Gloucester, 2007: Christopher Robinson and the Philharmonia Orchestra perform Vaughan Williams's *Serenade to Music*. Soloists, *left to right: (back row)* Andrew Staples, Nicholas Mulroy, Andrew Kennedy, Allan Clayton, Alex Ashworth, Allan Smith, James Birchall, Nicholas Perfect; *(front row)* Gillian Keith, Elizabeth Weisberg, Geraldine McGreevy, Nathalie Clifton-Griffith, Frances Bourne, Kate Symonds-Joy, Susanna Spicer, Jeanette Ager

126 Gloucester, 2007: Andrew Nethsingha with the Philharmonia Orchestra, Festival Chorus, Choristers of the Three Cathedrals at the end of the performance of Mahler's Symphony no. 8. Soloists *(left to right)*: Stephen Richardson, Alan Opie, Adrian Thompson, Gillian Keith, Catherine Wyn-Rogers, Sarah Connolly, Janice Watson, Judith Howarth

127 Worcester, 2008: Adrian Lucas with the Philharmonia Orchestra, Festival Chorus and the choristers from All Saints Worcester, Massachusetts, following the performance of *Carmina Burana*. Also on the platform are Geraint Bowen and Adrian Partington, as well as soloists Laurence Zazzo, Maureen Brathwaite and Christopher Purves

128 Hereford, 2009: Stephen Layton with the Music for Awhile Orchestra and the Three Cathedral Choirs following the performance of Handel's *Israel in Egypt*. Soloists *(left to right)*: Giles Underwood, Colin Campbell, Julia Doyle, Elin Manahan Thomas, Nathan Vale, Iestyn Davies

129 Gloucester, 2010: Jac van Steen with the Philharmonia Orchestra and Festival Chorus, following the performance of Mahler's Symphony No. 2. Soloists: Aylish Tynan and Susan Bickley

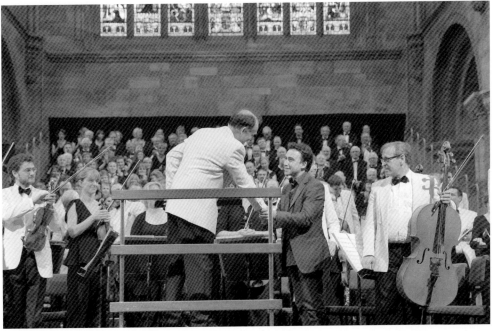

130 Hereford, 2012: Joseph Phibbs receives applause following the performance of his *Rivers to the Sea* by the Philharmonia Orchestra conducted by Adrian Partington

131 Hereford, 2009: Adrian Lucas

132 Hereford, 2012:
Martyn Brabbins and Peter Nardone

133 Hereford, 2015: Chairman's Reception.
Left to right: Adrian Lucas, Geraint Bowen, Peter Nardone, Roy Massey, Andrew Nethsingha

134 Hereford, 2015: Geraint Bowen

135 Gloucester, 2016: Adrian Partington

136 Gloucester, 2016:
Peter Nardone with Eleanor
Dennis and Sir Willard White

137 Gloucester, 2013: Vladimir Ashkenazy in rehearsal with Helena Juntunen and the Philharmonia Orchestra

138 Gloucester, 2013: the Festival Chorus

139 Gloucester, 2013: Edward Gardner conducts the Philharmonia Orchestra and Festival Chorus

140 Gloucester, 2013: Edward Gardner

141 Gloucester, 2013: Adrian Partington, the Philharmonia Orchestra, Festival Chorus and Njabulo Madlala following a performance of Walton's *Belshazzar's Feast*

142 The Three Cathedral Choirs singing a joint evensong in Worcester Cathedral, conducted by Geraint Bowen, June 2014

143 Worcester, 2014: Yeree Suh and Roderick Williams following the premiere of Torsten Rasch's *A Foreign Field*

144 Hereford, 2015: Opening Service

145 Hereford, 2015: Roderick Williams and Susie Allan, Holy Trinity Church

146 Massed Choirs in the Ballroom at Buckingham Palace, November 2015. Three Choirs Festival
Chorus, Three Cathedral Choirs and Three Choirs Festival Youth Choir, with Brass players from the
Royal Welsh College of Music and Drama. Geraint Bowen, Peter Nardone and Adrian Partington,
with organists Christopher Allsop, Peter Dyke and Jonathan Hope

147 HRH Prince Charles meets the choristers after the performance, Buckingham Palace, November 2015

148 HRH Prince Charles meets Dr Timothy Brain and Adrian Partington on the occasion of his visit to the Three Choirs Festival in 2016

149 HRH Prince Charles with Dr Timothy Brain following the performance of Mendelssohn's *Elijah*, which he attended at the 2016 Gloucester Festival

22

Houses of the Mind

THE 1991 Hereford Festival began on Sunday 18 August. Roy Massey, resplendent in the robes of his Lambeth doctorate, conducted the Festival Chorus and RLPO in a most impressive Opening Service, marred hardly at all by the lady who, during the prayer 'that through music we may raise man from the sorrows of this world to the joy of Your divine presence' called out loudly: 'and women!' A sign of the times?

The first cathedral concert of the 1991(H) Festival, given in memory of the late Bishop John Easthaugh, who had died in office in 1990, was a performance of the Beethoven *Missa solemnis*. 'There was much to admire', wrote David Hart in the *Birmingham Post*:

> the Festival Chorus was in fine collective voice, with tenors displaying a lively robustness and sopranos thrilling in the stratospheric upper reaches. And Julie Kennard, Catherine Wyn-Rogers, Neil Jenkins and John Noble made an extremely homogenous and tireless solo quartet. But this was largely negated by an orchestral accompaniment [RLPO] of often overwhelming proportions … The result was a performance light on subtlety, but full of grand gestures and a lot of noise.

On Monday a tremor of apprehension disturbed the festive atmosphere as news came through that in the USSR Mikhail Gorbachev had been toppled in a leadership coup. Were 'the sorrows of this world' again to overwhelm the nascent optimism in a new order? Against this background the performance of *Morning Heroes* on Monday evening was particularly piercing. The largest of the works by Sir Arthur Bliss included in the Festival to mark his centenary year, *Morning Heroes* was, for Roy Massey and many in his audience, an overwhelming emotional experience. Written by a composer who had seen the brutality of war at first hand through a soldier's eyes, its impact in performance is greater than can be anticipated from the printed score – especially so when the narration of 'Hector's Farewell to Andromache' (from *The Iliad*) and Wilfred Owen's 'Spring Offensive' are entrusted to a narrator of Brian Kay's ability. Here is Owen:

> Halted against the shade of the last hill,
> They fed, and, lying easy, were at ease,
> And, finding comfortable chests and knees
> Carelessly slept. But many there stood still
> To face the stark, blank sky beyond the ridge,
> Knowing their feet had come to the end of the world.

Earlier in the evening a small ceremony took place on the bank of the Wye opposite the cathedral – one of those slightly dotty and wholly delightful occasions which serve to make an English summer memorable. Organised by the city of Hereford's Environment Department, a suitably inscribed stone had been set in place to mark the approximate spot where G. R. Sinclair's bulldog Dan had so famously splashed into the river and the *Enigma Variations*. The site had been identified by Elgar's godson, Wulstan Atkins, and an unveiling ceremony was performed by Roy Massey, together with his dog, Winston, at 5 p.m. on 19 August. Winston dragged his master towards the small gathering and, once off the leash, pulled aside the artificial grass covering the plaque, paused while Dr Massey spoke a few well-chosen words, and then, like Dan before him, sped down the riverbank into the waters of the Wye!

THE bicentenary of the death of Mozart, an anniversary which at times in 1991 threatened almost to overwhelm national musical life, was not forgotten at Hereford. Kenneth Page conducted the Orchestra da Camera at Leominster Priory on Tuesday afternoon in lively performances of the Symphonies Nos. 40 and 41, and Stephen Coombs and Ian Munro played the Concerto in E flat, K365, for two pianos and orchestra. On the first afternoon in the cathedral, the same orchestra was conducted by Roy Massey in the *Sinfonia concertante* in E flat, K297b, for oboe, clarinet, bassoon, horn and orchestra; the youthful and brilliant soloists were Nicholas Daniel, Joy Farrell, Julie Andrews and Stephen Bell. The concert, which began with Denys Darlow's *Te Deum*, op. 12, ended with Mozart's Mass in C Minor, K427, a beautifully balanced performance, the Hereford Festival Chorus and soloists Jennifer Smith, Margaret Field, Andrew Tusa and George Banks Martin floating silver sound to the vault, and Roy Massey in seeming reverie at the end, leaving almost too late his acknowledgement of the orchestra and their Leader, Kenneth Page.

Wednesday and Thursday evenings contained the two high spots of the week:

> Vernon Handley brought from the Royal Liverpool P. O. playing of richness and character in Bliss's *Introduction and Allegro*. So he did in Gordon Jacob's arrangement of the Elgar Organ Sonata [Wednesday]. The chorus responded sympathetically to the many pleasantries of Howard Blake's *Song of St Francis*. It sounded grateful music to sing, something which could not be said of Joubert's *Herefordshire Canticles* [Thursday]. The chorus had a tough week, and it was no mean achievement that on the last day they should sing so jubilantly in the Poulenc *Gloria*, and so vigorously in the Berlioz *Te Deum*.[1]

By the last day, news bulletins had shown Boris Yeltsin defying the Moscow old guard from atop a tank and the restoration of the Soviet *status quo*. Worst fears again subsided – and full-throated singing affirmed our thankfulness.

> But ironically [wrote Kenneth Loveland] the best-remembered events had nothing to do with choralism. They were cellist Steven Isserlis's brilliant playing of Howard Blake's *Diversions* [Wednesday, with the RLPO

---

[1] *MT* 1991, p. 522.

and Handley], with its skilful commentary on traditional forms, Emma
Johnson's winning musicality in Stanford's Clarinet Concerto [Thursday,
with RPO and Sanders], and most of all, Vernon Handley's total authority
and control in a profoundly felt *Enigma Variations* [Wednesday].[2]

One Three Choirs tradition, the oldest of the Festival and more than once
the mainstay in preventing its abolition, had already been modified by 1991. The
Charity for the Benefit of Widows and Orphans of the Clergy in the three
dioceses had remained the largely unaltered *raison d'être* of the Festival from
1724 until 1986, but in that year important changes were made. As a result of
responsible funding by the Church and more adequate provision by the State,
Gloucester and Worcester had been finding it increasingly unnecessary to look
to the proceeds of Festival collections to assist their care of clergy widows and
orphans, though it was accepted that a similar position had yet to be reached
in Hereford Diocese. There remained a feeling that, in a Festival centred on
three great Christian churches, some charitable emphasis should abide, and,
while future policy was still under discussion, Gloucester broke with tradition
and divided the 1986 collection equally between the continuing needs of
Hereford Diocese for help with its clergy widows and orphans, and the Friends
of Cathedral Music, a charity concerned to safeguard the unique tradition of
cathedral and collegiate chapel music throughout the land.

In 1987, the Dean and Chapter of each of the three cathedrals agreed that
the purposes of the Festival collections should be widened to embrace the relief
and support of clergy families in special need, and that collections should be
taken only at the Opening Service (or after the first evening concert), at Choral
Evensong during the Festival week and after the last evening concert. And so, at
Hereford in 1991 collections were divided equally among the three dioceses and
allocated by them to such charitable work related to the needs of the families of
the clergy as they determined.[3]

ON the afternoon of Sunday 23 August – before the Opening Service
of the 1992(G) Festival – the people of Gloucester and Festival-goers
were surprised, and possibly deafened, by an unusual outdoor Fringe event:
a Unicorn Dance performed on College Green by children and adults of
the Gloucestershire Chinese community, with traditional (and very loud!)
instruments. Before the 1990s there had been too few children in the small
Gloucester Chinese community for a Unicorn Dance in the traditional manner
to have been possible, but by 1992 there were sufficient numbers to perform it
with gusto. The Unicorn Dance, believed to bring good luck to 'they who open
the eye', has a history that can be traced back 3,000 years.

After the dance, in a short but convivial demonstration of friendship, Peter
Wallace, Chairman of the Fringe, was joined by the Festival Chairman, Dr
Jim Hoyland; the Artistic Director, Dr John Sanders; members of the Fringe

[2] Ibid.
[3] See Rodney Bennett, 'The Three Choirs Festival Charity', Hereford Festival
programme book, 1991, p. 36. Copies of all the Festival programme books cited in
this chapter are held in the Three Choirs Festival Office, Gloucester.

Committee; the Mayor and Mayoress of Gloucester, Councillor and Mrs Ben Richards; Councillor Tony Ayland, and leaders of the Chinese community in a sociable exchange of gifts.

The main Festival in 1992 was centred upon a celebration marking the centenary of the birth of Herbert Howells (1892–1983). In his memory, a group of four stained-glass lights was unveiled in a side chapel within the Lady Chapel of the cathedral, among pre-existing memorial windows in memory of S. S. Wesley, C. H. Lloyd and Sir Herbert Brewer. The Howells windows were designed by Caroline Swash, fabricated at the Glantawe Studio, Swansea, and dedicated following Evensong on Tuesday 25 August:

> They incorporate musical illustrations from Howells's anthem *Like as the Hart*, his G major *Magnificat*, his motet *Take him, Earth, for Cherishing*, written in memory of President Kennedy, and a passage from perhaps his profoundest work, the *Hymnus Paradisi*. John Rutter donated a new anthem, *Hymn to the Creator of Light*, as a tribute to Howells's memory; it is a beautifully and originally crafted piece, whose textures are gradually overtaken by the haunting line of a German chorale. An opening lecture by Paul Spicer gave insight into the composer's life and achievement.[4]

Among the many works by Howells included in the 1992(G) Festival programme, both sacred and secular, his *Rhapsodic Quintet* for clarinet, two violins, viola and cello, op. 31 (1919), was played by the doyenne of English clarinettists, Thea King, with the Britten String Quartet.

By happy chance, the same team had recorded the piece for the Hyperion label in 1991 as part of a compact disc which was selected by Roderick Swanston as a 'record of the year' for the BBC's *Record Review* programme. 'It was', said Swanston, 'an example of twentieth-century clarinet music which I would have dismissed with contempt as a student.' But having listened to Howells's *Rhapsodic Quintet*, he was 'bowled over' by the piece, describing it as most sumptuous, and Howells as a vibrant and disgracefully neglected composer. Equal enthusiasm was expressed by the other members of the BBC review team. It was 'an elaborate stunner', said the not-easily-pleased Rodney Milnes; it contained 'a sense of regret at lost innocence'; there was in it 'the peace of ages'; and the ending contained 'one of the loveliest moments in music' – a timely discovery that there is more to Howells than Evensong.[5] Writing in 1977, Howells said:

> In my Gloucester-Worcester-Hereford wanderings during the past sixty years I have encountered half-truths (and sometimes their authors) often.
> One such experience lingers with me. A tightly-packed audience was slowly moving out of Hereford Cathedral after an evening performance. It suddenly heard – and was, doubtless, *meant* to hear – a man's pontifical voice, declaring that 'the trouble with these festivals is that they are so parochial' (A half-truth, innocuous – except for the ill-chosen moment. For the crowd round the 'loudspeaker' fellow had just been deeply moved,

---

[4] *Church Times*, 11 September 1992.

[5] *Record Review*, BBC Radio 3, Saturday 28 December 1991.

listening to beloved Kathleen Ferrier singing almost certainly for the last time at the Three Choirs Festival. And it was the 'Angel's Farewell'. The date: September, 1952.)

The parochial observation has a far-away historical truth. It implies, of course, a parish. That was no real concern for the near-cynic emerging with the rest of us from the Cathedral. But it might well be ours. And thinking constructively about the Parish could be a compelling and appropriate exercise for all devoted 'parishioners'.

As one of that company I have, for long years, tried to feel, define and express what is meant, to a potential musician, to have been nurtured in a countryside of companionable hills, two lovely but very diverse rivers, and three magical cathedrals: so that it has seemed that the Severn and the Wye could be flowing in one's veins, and that the three great churches of Worcester and Hereford and Gloucester had become the Houses of the Mind. Further: in one's youth, there might have been undisciplined music flaring in one's mind; but with it (providentially) the exciting certainty that for a whole week in early September there would be, in one or other of the three cities, the presence and spell of the reigning Festival giants – Hubert Parry, Edward Elgar, and the younger Ralph Vaughan Williams; and more than a glimpse of some other dedicated 'parishioners', their successors. All this. And a crowning certainty – that for *all* 'parishioners' (predestined leaders or not) *place* and *frame of mind* would be an unbroken unit.[6]

Two rarities by Howells were included in the 1992(G) Tuesday evening programme: *A Kent Yeoman's Wooing Song*, featuring Ann Mackay and Brian Rayner Cook, and *Sine nomine*, in which Ann Mackay was joined by the tenor Maldwyn Davies. In the first of these, the soloists, Festival Chorus and the RPO were directed by Donald Hunt, and in the second, by Roy Massey. The concert, recorded by the BBC, was broadcast on 31 December 1992.

A Kent Yeoman's Wooing Song, settings of two seventeenth-century poems, was composed in 1933. It is a complex work, far from easy for the chorus. A startling piece, especially so when heard in a cathedral setting, it had waited twenty years for its second performance (at the Proms under Sargent). The soprano sings of her determination to have a husband, and to 'have him out of hand!' The baritone boasts of his plow, his sow, his hog and his 'house and land in Kent', and demands that his maid should 'love me now':

> Or else he'll seek some otherwhere,
> For he cannot come every day to woo.

During the broadcast, Paul Spicer, introducing the work in discussion with the BBC's Chris Marshall, spoke of the high quality of Howells's score and the 'shock' of hearing such earthy music in the outer movements. By contrast, in the third of the work's four sections, 'a love-song brings us the Howells with whom we are familiar. The mood is lyrical and reflective, and the rich spread of

---

[6] Herbert Howells, 'Mementoes from the Twentieth Century', in Barry Still (ed.) *Two Hundred and Fifty Years of the Three Choirs Festival 1 – A Commemoration in Words and Pictures* (Three Choirs Festival Association, 1977).

choral-orchestral polyphony is like a sky with clouds floating in mist and sunset colours shifting and dissolving – the delectable mountains of *Hymnus Paradisi* are already in view.'[7]

Unfortunately, the *Kent Yeoman* proved to be the least successful performance in the 1992 programme. Writing of it later, Donald Hunt recalled that it was 'A strange choice – which found the choir in tentative form, unable to fathom the complexities of a work which felt like *Hymnus Paradisi* in a secular overcoat! I fear it was not a good performance and, to make matters worse, it was broadcast too.'[8] In spite of shortcomings, however, the *Kent Yeoman* was applauded enthusiastically. Moving on from an ardent yeoman to the radiance of Vaughan Williams's *Fantasia on a Theme by Thomas Tallis*, Donald Hunt directed a fine reading of an undoubted masterpiece.

Sine nomine, unknown to most of the audience, came as an unexpected and inspiring surprise. Following its first performance at the 1922(G) Festival the work, described by Howells as 'a spiritual meditation', lay mouldering on a shelf for seventy years. Scored for soprano, tenor, wordless chorus, large orchestra and organ, Howells clearly had in mind the acoustic of Gloucester Cathedral when composing it. In 1992, under the direction of Roy Massey, it proved to be a splendid piece: voices soaring into lofty spaces – exactly as Howells had imagined.

The *Financial Times* summarised the Festival week under the strap-line: 'Shared aims and age-old traditions':

> This year's director, John Sanders, produced perhaps the week's outstanding performance, a Bach B minor Mass, in which all aspects gelled: precise intonation, distinctive soloists led by Emma Kirkby [with Catherine Wyn-Rogers, Rogers Covey Crump and Stephen Roberts], period-instrument clarity from the Brandenburg Consort.
>
> The premières were mixed. Alongside a slightly dull brass piece from Hugh Wood [*Funeral Music*] and an unexpectedly-imaginative anthem from John Rutter [*Hymn to the Creator of Light*] came Philip Cannon's *A Ralegh Triptych*, settings of three poems penned in anticipation of execution. The angularity of Cannon's spare *a cappella* writing poses a challenge. That it came across well was due to the boys' alertness in tuning and attentive direction by Donald Hunt.
>
> ... Despite a valiant effort by the tenor, Maldwyn Davies, a tiring Royal Philharmonic Orchestra just took the edge off Finzi's sumptuous Wordsworth setting, *Intimations of Immortality* [conducted by Roy Massey], whose word-painting is as delicate as Britten's. A different problem is set in Janacek's inspirational *Glagolitic Mass* [conducted by Donald Hunt]. For all the flair in big climaxes, flat choral enunciation merged with a lethargic orchestral reading ... only John Mitchinson, the veteran tenor, found the required energy for its impassioned Gloria and Credo. The show was saved by Mark Lee, the young organ soloist, whose playing proved one of the distinctions of the week.

[7] Christopher Palmer, Gloucester Festival programme book, 1992, p. 87.

[8] Donald Hunt, *Festival Memories* (Osborne Heritage, 1996), p. 60.

... Of the visitors, Richard Hickox [in his Three Choirs debut] followed a scintillating Elgar *Alassio* with a Mahler Fourth Symphony of breath-taking indifference. But Michael Berkeley's ritualised, Messiaenic organ concerto (its inflections suggest a debt to Jehan Alain) easily prove its repertoire worth, with Thomas Trotter an articulate soloist. More striking was Meredith Davies conducting E. J. Moeran's cello concerto, eloquently played by Raphael Wallfisch, who has also recorded the work for Chandos. Davies's direction proved something of a revelation: he has been too long exiled from the podium.[9]

Meredith Davies had hinted that it would please him greatly should he ever be asked to return to the Festival, perhaps to conduct a single work. John Sanders readily agreed to extend an invitation, with the remarkable result that on Monday evening we saw the RPO players literally sitting up and taking notice under Davies's masterly direction.

The Moeran Cello Concerto was followed by Paul Patterson's *Mass of the Sea*, (commissioned for 1983(G)):

Paul Patterson's *Mass of the Sea* weaves a sequence of aquatic biblical texts into the fabric and music of the mass, with high, disembodied writing for soprano soloist [Ann Mackay], and vigorous, mocking choruses that recall Vaughan Williams's *Job*. When the anger subsides into the unexpectedly gentle Sanctus, underscored by the 'Ave Maris Stella' motif that sustains the whole work, it is a breathtakingly beautiful moment. *Mass of the Sea* provided one of the week's most authoritative performances. [Given by the Choristers of the Three Cathedrals, the Festival Chorus and the RPO conducted by John Sanders.]

If the wafting harmonies of Havergal Brian's setting of Psalm 23 somehow failed to illumine, plenty of zest was reserved for *Intimations of Immortality*, Finzi's resplendent large-scale setting of Wordsworth, directed by Roy Massey with the tenor, Maldwyn Davies, on good form, though occasionally swamped by the rich textures.[10]

An incident, minor yet deserving its small place in Three Choirs history, occurred during the Michael Berkeley Organ Concerto on Wednesday evening. At the beginning of the piece, two cornet players, required to enter the nave from the rear and to play while progressing slowly towards the platform, were unaware that one canine concert-goer, accompanying his young, partially sighted master, was lying patiently in the aisle. Concentrating on his instrument, one of the cornet players failed to see the labrador's outstretched paw – and trod on it, causing the hapless dog to stir visibly. But, giving no hint of suffering, he remained silent, and the concerto unspoiled. This attracted much attention in the local press and, in a short ceremony on the following evening, the brave labrador received acknowledgement from the Festival Committee: the Festival Administrator, Anthony Boden, presented him with a diploma 'Awarded for Pawbearance in the face of oncoming Cornet Players'!

[9] *Financial Times*, 5 September 1992, p. xiv.
[10] *Church Times*, 11 September 1992.

IN 1989, John Sanders revealed that over the years he had received a number of letters and telephone calls, especially from the USA, asking if he could advise on the whereabouts of the full score of Sir Herbert Brewer's cantata *Emmaus* in the orchestration by Elgar (see Chapter 12). Sadly, he had been obliged to tell enquirers that the score was lost. John asked me if, during researches into the Festival history, an eye could be kept open for it. And then, on the evening of 5 April 1990, serendipity came to our aid when, in Gloucester City Library with a small group of Ivor Gurney enthusiasts, we were deciding upon a list of items for an exhibition that would form part of a Gurney centenary celebration that was to be held in Gloucester in the following July. It was getting late, we had decided on most of the content of the exhibition and were about to call it a day. But then, in an afterthought, and knowing that as a youth Gurney had been a pupil of Herbert Brewer at Gloucester Cathedral, we decided that we should see if the library held anything by Brewer that might be worthy of notice. We looked in the card-index – and found a single card bearing just two words: 'Brewer scores'. Within minutes, we were in the strong-room, where, in a dark and dusty corner, we found a pile of large brown-paper parcels – untouched and unopened since they had been deposited there in 1928 by Sir Herbert's son, Charles Brewer. Presumably, librarians over time had thought that the parcels contained published scores, but not so: these were the leather-bound manuscript full scores of all Sir Herbert's choral works, including *Emmaus*. They have now been transferred to the Gloucestershire Archives, awaiting investigation by future researchers.

John Sanders directed the Festival Chorus and RLPO in the rediscovered *Emmaus* on the Friday evening of the 1992(G) Festival. (The printed vocal score had been published by Novello, and new orchestral parts were prepared by Nigel Taylor.) The soloists were the soprano Alison Hargan and tenor John Mitchinson.

In an article praising Brewer as 'one of the most gifted church musicians at the turn of the century', Roderic Dunnett wrote of *Emmaus*:

> The central chorus, 'O love most wonderful' is undeniably fine. The impassioned soprano arias look forward from Sullivan to Elgar's own *Sea Pictures*. The chord and canonic writing is well-judged throughout.
>
> Brewer skilfully framed *Emmaus* with two large-scale, orchestrally introduced choruses, whose sustained writing recalls his Gloucester predecessor S. S. Wesley and the English 17th-century tradition, as well as continental precedents. The opening has the sturdy feel of a chaconne. Elgar offered an alternative extended orchestral conclusion: in the event, Brewer preferred the more reflective, less elaborate version.
>
> Small as well as larger choral societies could easily attempt *Emmaus*, which is gratifying for chorus and soloists alike, and might make an alternative to Stainer's *Crucifixion* or yet another *Messiah*.[11]

Although unknown to most of us, in 1992 John Sanders was directing the Gloucester Festival in considerable discomfort, and for the last time. 'His conducting shoulder was becoming very painful and he was aware that if he wanted to make time for composing, he would have to give up the pressures

---

[11] *Church Times*, 12 February 1993.

and unremitting routine of the round of services, the enormous planning
and preparation for the world's oldest music festival and his teaching at the
[Cheltenham] Ladies' College' (where he was Director of Music).[12] He would
conduct at only three more Three Choirs Festivals – at Worcester in 1993 and
1996 – and he composed a new setting of the Evening Canticles to be sung
by the combined cathedral choirs at the 1997 Hereford Festival, where he also
conducted a performance of his own *Gloucestershire Visions*.

John Sanders, a man both admired and held in great affection by all who
knew him, died on 23 December 2003. For close to a century, the music of
Gloucester Cathedral had been directed by just three men: Sir Herbert Brewer,
Dr Herbert Sumsion and Dr John Sanders.

T HE music critic Roderic Dunnett, who has attended the Festival loyally
for over three decades, has written for many publications, including the
*Independent, New Statesman, Spectator, Classical Music, Early Music Today, BBC
Music Magazine, Church Times* and the *Financial Times*. At Worcester in 1993, a
time of financial strain and stress for all three Festivals, he wrote for both *Church
Times* and the *Financial Times*, and his comments on the 'business' of Three
Choirs, published in the latter, could have been made with equal validity in
regard to both Hereford and Gloucester:

> Programming to maintain diversity, ensure profitable sales and keep
> the Arts Council happy is a fine balance. The administration – much of
> it amateur and laid back, old style but efficient – annually falls to a local
> committee, led by the Festival Director, who is also the host cathedral
> organist. The conducting is shared with visiting professionals: this year the
> BBC Philharmonic brought with it the Bolshoi's Yuri Simonov, replacing
> the indisposed Sir Edward Downes, and BBC Scotland's Jerzy Maksymiuk.
> Some think there should be more guest conductors, but budget plays a role
> here.
>
> Full accounts date back to early performances of Handel's *Messiah*.
> One problem is that County Council and Arts Council support has fallen
> woefully behind in the last few years, while costs of orchestras, staging and
> closed-circuit TV have risen. Fire and safety checks have meant the loss
> of several hundred mainly cheaper seats, reducing Worcester's capacity to
> around 2,000.
>
> But the festival has its own resilience, as the Worcester treasurer, Peter
> Seward, explains. A tradition of stewardships guarantees the bulk of
> the central nave; sales are completed in March, providing a tidy sum for
> advance investment. Sponsorship from commerce and industry was
> initiated in 1976, at the same time as an organised 'Fringe' added diversity.
> A Royal Worcester [Porcelain] donation of £4,000 towards a performance
> of Britten's *War Requiem*, linked to Wilfred Owen's centenary and the
> 75th anniversary of the armistice, was matched under the Business
> Sponsorship for the Arts scheme administered by ABSA [Association for
> Business Sponsorship of the Arts]. The Great War has added meaning for

[12] Alan Charters, *John Sanders: Friend for Life* (Choir Press, 2009), p. 127.

Worcester: Geoffrey Studdart Kennedy, the pioneering forces' chaplain known as 'Woodbine Willie', was vicar of St Paul's Church.

Ticket sales account for well over half of the £370,000 budgeted expenditure, the bulk of which goes on orchestras and soloists. Sponsorship adds some £28,000, of which £10,000 is from county council sources. The dense programme book still makes a healthy profit. Most important, the administration takes up only 14 per cent of the whole. There are advantages in this quiet, in-house efficiency.[13]

Writing in his *Festival Memories*, Donald Hunt paid fitting tribute to the administrators with whom he had worked for two decades:

> One of the strengths of the Worcester Festival administration has been the longevity of service of the principal officers. Chairman and Treasurer have been in office in one capacity or another for nearly twenty-five years, and many of the committee have helped to guide us through a number of Festivals, creating a welcome continuity. David Wright, after two Festivals in which he created a newer dynamic and personal approach to the role of Secretary, gave way to Jean Armstrong, the first lady administrator in the Festival's history. As the Festival has expanded, so the role of the Secretary has become increasingly demanding, and Jean has gathered about her a team of helpers who give a professional standard of work, without destroying the unique family atmosphere which is perceived by those who visit us. But the greatest credit should go to Sam Driver White who, as Chairman, has guided Worcester through five Festivals with courage and distinction. Each of the three cities has its own special characteristics and, although the pattern of the concerts and programme content have changed considerably, the atmosphere of a Worcester Festival is thankfully still very much as I remember it as a youth.[14]

Undoubtedly, the gratitude expressed by Donald Hunt for the work of his supporting team would have been echoed equally by his colleagues at Hereford and Gloucester; and the cooperation between all three administrative teams, balancing serious hard work with a shared sense of camaraderie and sociable fun, was of incalculable value in smoothing efforts to deliver Festivals of high quality.

Elsewhere in his memoirs, Donald Hunt summarised his thoughts on the 1993(w) Festival:

> The Festival had followed a now well-established Worcester pattern: there was some international participation of conductors and artists, including the Gioia Della Musica from Prague, a generous helping of Elgar, and some special attention to the music of William Walton, aided by the effervescent personality of Susana, Lady Walton, who – with Richard Baker – narrated *Façade* at an entertaining concert at the Huntingdon Hall, now an essential venue in the Festival scene. I personally enjoyed two afternoon concerts, one with the strings of the BBC Philharmonic devoted to English Music [Parry, Finzi, Holst, and the first performance

[13] *Financial Times*, September 1993.
[14] Hunt, *Festival Memories*, pp. 58–9.

of the *Serenade* for strings by Robin Holloway], and the other a charming programme of Music for Spring, including a revival of Dame Ethel Smyth's *Canticle of Spring*, first heard at Worcester in 1926, and *Fynsk Foraar* by Nielsen, sung in Danish. This involved the Festival Junior Chorus, still going strong [and the tenor Ian Partridge, replacing Ian Thompson]. Earlier in the programme my valued colleague, Raymond Johnston [assistant organist], had conducted a delightful performance of Haydn's *Der Frühling* (Spring – 'The Seasons'), which we were surprised to find had never been sung at a Three Choirs, which only goes to show how many fine works have avoided the artistic scrutiny of a succession of conductors and committees. But perhaps the work that gave me the greatest personal satisfaction at the Festival was the thrilling performance of *Belshazzar's Feast*, the culmination of the opening broadcast concert. There was some marvellously incisive singing by the chorus, who even produced almost all of the famous *forte pianos*; and what an arresting start when the male voices proclaimed their potent message from memory. It really was exciting stuff!

That Festival was to herald the break-up of a long partnership for, shortly afterwards John Sanders announced his impending retirement. He had given long and distinguished service to the Festival, as well as providing it with much-needed stability, and it was typical of him that he should want to leave without fuss. In the event what was to be his last concert was in the opinion of many one of his finest, including Elgar's *The Spirit of England* [with soprano Julie Kennard] and, by a complete contrast of patriotic style and message, Walton's *Henry V* [with actor John Nettles]. The last-named did not meet with everyone's approval. I can accept that a work can be disliked, for whatever musical reason, but when the objections are wrapped up in pious clothing I find the argument much less convincing, especially when many of the objectors are the same as those who happily tolerate other very questionable works within the framework of a 'sacred' Festival. I have always been very sensitive to these matters and have tried to accommodate all tastes without offending people's feelings. Of course, mistakes have been made. I still feel guilty about the *Symphonie Fantastique* which I inherited in my first Festival programme. But clerical advice assured me that it was an expression of art which was acceptable. Mercifully, we are not in a situation now when such works as *Sea Symphony* would be rejected, or that Benjamin Britten might be excluded because he was thought to be agnostic (I once had a clergyman take me to task for having Britten's church music in the choir repertoire), but I exhort all Three Choirs' conductors to clear their programmes with clerical advisers, thereby avoiding some of these sensitive issues.[15]

Censorship of the music performed in churches and cathedrals is an issue of which, in the twenty-first century, the general public is barely aware, but one that, as we have seen, has prevented or delayed the performance at Three Choirs of a number of major works, Vaughan Williams's *A Sea Symphony* and Elgar's

[15] Ibid., pp. 57–8.

The Dream of Gerontius among them. Even Handel's *Messiah* had only gained admittance to Hereford Cathedral in 1759 because, with the Guildhall 'ruinous' and unusable, the Dean and Chapter were unwilling to lose the income from the Festival Charity (see Chapter 4). And Sir Ivor Atkins, deeming the text of Walton's *Belshazzar's Feast* to be unsuitable, excluded it from the 1932 Festival; it did not receive a Three Choirs performance until 1957.

Of course, a cathedral is not a concert hall, but, a decade before *Belshazzar's Feast*, Sir Herbert Brewer, with an ideal secular venue available to him, was able to surmount such obstacles. His innovative programming in 1922, for instance, included works such as Scriabin's *Poem of Ecstasy*, and the spine-chilling final scene from Richard Strauss's *Salome*, its libretto taken directly from Oscar Wilde's play of the same title. The Scriabin was performed in the cathedral (to the disgust of Elgar); the Strauss, in the Gloucestershire Shire Hall, which boasted a concert hall with orchestral platform, large auditorium and organ before its insensitive and apathetic conversion into an office block in the 1960s.

In 1880 the Shire Hall was the venue when Parry's choral/orchestral setting of Shelley's *Prometheus Unbound* received its première (see Chapter 9), an occasion of which Sir Henry Hadow was to write in 1898:

> There has arisen among us a composer who is capable of restoring our national music to its true place in the art of Europe. At the very nadir of our fortune, when we had entirely ceased to count among the musical nations of Europe, there appeared at the Gloucester Festival in 1880 a cantata entitled *Scenes from Shelley's 'Prometheus Unbound'* … No one seems to have had any idea that, on that evening in the Shire Hall, English music had, after many years, come again to its own, and that it had come with a masterpiece in its hand.[16]

Parry went on to more than fulfil Hadow's predictions (and to inspire Elgar), but, had there been no Shire Hall, it is doubtful that *Prometheus* would have been heard at all; it is certain that Parry's mould-breaking work would not have been permitted into the cathedral at that time, albeit that his sacred music was welcomed there. (Shelley, an unbeliever, had been expelled from university for sharing in the preparation of a pamphlet entitled *The Necessity of Atheism*.) Parry, although a man of deep spiritual sensitivity, like Vaughan Williams and Herbert Howells after him, was not an orthodox believer. There are church-music composers; and there are composers who write for the church – a very English dichotomy explained by Simon Heffer in relation to Howells: 'he shared with his hero Vaughan Williams an implicit understanding of the cultural importance of the Anglican rite, especially in musical terms, but without having to subscribe to the spiritual, religious or doctrinal aspects of it.'[17]

---

[16] See Charles L. Graves, *Hubert Parry*, vol. 2 (London, 1926), pp. 190–1.

[17] Simon Heffer, 'The Englishness of Herbert Howells', lecture given to the Herbert Howells Society in the Divinity Schools, St John's College, Cambridge, 17 October 2015. (Published by the Herbert Howells Society.)

AT the Sunday evening concert of the 1993 Worcester Festival, the European première of the American composer Dominic Argento's *Te Deum* was given by the Festival Chorus and BBC Philharmonic Orchestra conducted by Yuri Simonov (replacing Donald Hunt).

[It] is a highly gratifying work to sing, despite its vocally difficult leaps and shifting enharmonic changes, which demand particularly careful tuning from a chorus. In addition to the central text, the composer makes use of medieval lyrics, for example 'Ther is no rose of swich vertu', in a delightful female-voice setting with bassoon obbligato, to contrast what he terms an 'out-of-doors' quality with the often awesome feel he imparts to the words of the morning canticle itself.

But it is essential that those words be clearly heard; and it was here that this first performance fell down. The upper parts initially lacked confidence, and seemed confused by being left largely to their own devices by an unfamiliar conductor. The enunciation, which should be as crystalline as for, say, Benjamin Britten's *Hymn to St Cecilia* (Britten, Stravinsky and the Baroque aria being key influences for Argento), left much to be desired. In a work full of scherzo-like moments, many of the contrasts got lost.

The large chorus, to its credit, appeared more relaxed when heard alone or in section, where the fuzz of thicker chordings dissolved. Nowhere was this more evident than in the six-minute male semi-chorus section 'Farewell this world': it would have made a delightful ending. In the event, the long recapitulation, with the sole exception of the movingly sung final bars, seemed an unneeded elongation of an already satisfactory work.

... Simonov prefaced the Argento with a splendidly Elgarian, brassy display in Glazunov's overture *Carnaval* and a memorable peroration to Dvořák's B-minor Cello Concerto, with Robert Cohen the appealing young soloist.[18]

In 1976, Donald Hunt and the Worcester Cathedral Choir had recorded the beautiful *Hymne à la Vierge* by Pierre Villette; after hearing the recording broadcast on French radio, the composer contacted Dr Hunt. 'As a result a close friendship developed, and Worcester has had the privilege of being largely responsible for the works of Pierre Villette being widely appreciated in this country. It seemed natural to invite him to write a work for the Festival, and his *Messe en français* was premièred, and enthusiastically received' in 1981, along with other works by Villette, who attended the Festival.[19] Music by Villette was again featured at Worcester in 1990: his *Trois Préludes pour cordes*, included in a Friday afternoon concert, were, at Donald Hunt's invitation, directed by his Assistant Organist – marking the conducting debut at Three Choirs of Adrian Partington. The close link with Villette was again in evidence at Worcester in 1993: a concert of French music, programmed on Tuesday evening, opened with his *Tu es Petrus*. Originally written for an accompaniment of two organs, Donald Hunt had scored the work for organ and full orchestra for this Three Choirs performance: a rousing start to a striking evening of Gallic music.

---

[18] *Church Times*, 3 September 1993.
[19] Hunt, *Festival Memories*, p. 44.

THE opening concert of the 1994 Festival at Hereford, directed by Roy Massey, featured soprano Julie Kennard, tenor Adrian Thompson, the Festival Chorus, and the RLPO. At its heart was a performance of Howells's *Hymnus Paradisi*, which, 'while not the most polished imaginable, reached unerringly to the music's unsentimental heart. Its mood of shadowed radiance could not have come across more strongly.'[20] But for Roderic Dunnett the performance 'seemed fazed: choir and orchestra went their own amiable ways'.

> Things soon livened up. Kodály's *Budávari Te Deum* under Donald Hunt the next evening quickly reached for the jugular. Even where exposed, the choir were consistently lucid; the Magyar inflections of 'when thou lookest upon them' were memorable, as was the pairing of tenor and soprano that followed [Margaret Field and Neil Jenkins]. Some bizarre tuning at the end heralded a more awkwardly delivered Stravinsky *Symphony of Psalms*, with orchestra well on top but chorus visibly not. Carl Nielsen's early *Hymnus Amoris* lacks the controlled invention of his mature *Spring-time in Funen* ... but was nevertheless worth an airing. And there was poignancy [on Thursday evening] when Alan Ridout, whose contribution to church music has been so great like that of Kenneth Leighton, who was honoured at Thursday's evensong, emerged from a hospital bed to receive an ovation after the première of his festival commission, *Canticle of Joy*. The overriding aura here was one of charm. The work is like an extended scherzo, its launch sparkling like Bernstein, and other parts recalling Britten, Stravinsky or Lou Harrison. Much of Ridout's writing is as puckish as the material he used to provide for Canterbury's choristers. Texts included Vaughan, Eleanor Farjeon and Rupert Brooke.
>
> The soloists, Martyn Hill (tenor), and James Bowman (alto) – who presided like an amiable dowager – visibly enjoyed themselves. So did the orchestra. David Briggs, freshly arrived from Truro as organist of Gloucester Cathedral, prefaced it with an electrifying account of Beethoven's *Leonora III* Overture – as perfect a tale of love triumphant and light breaking out as you could ask for.[21]

Roy Massey's inclusion of *Lux aeterna* by William Mathias in the Tuesday evening programme paid especial tribute to one who was a Three Choirs composer through and through. Writing of Mathias, who died in 1992, Geraint Lewis recalled that

> Another of those tantalising might-have-beens of musical history was the full-scale new work he began to contemplate around 1991, following his first serious illness, for the 1994 Three Choirs. He so much enjoyed his last visit to Hereford in November 1990 to hear the Hereford Choral Society under Roy Massey performing *This Worldes Joie* that the new work took on a fairly tangible form in his mind – an intermingling of the *Veni Creator Spiritus* text with poems to do with the wide-ranging wonder of God's created Earth. He thought that a possible title might be *Earth Songs*,

[20] *Daily Telegraph*, 27 August 1994.
[21] *Church Times*, 9 September 1994.

though that would probably have changed! But I think he knew that he was actually living on borrowed time and when he wrote to Roy Massey he simply said, as if in premonition, that he hoped *Lux Aeterna* might return home in 1994 – and so it did.[22]

Indeed, *Lux aeterna* proved to be one of the most intense works of the week.

Wednesday evening brought the Bournemouth Symphony Orchestra in a thrilling all-English concert under the baton of Richard Hickox: *Froissart* by Elgar; Raphaël Wallfisch an ideal soloist in Gerald Finzi's powerful Cello Concerto; and a gripping performance of Walton's Symphony No. 1. In pleasing contrast, and equally rewarding, a recital of the seventeenth-century *Arie antiche* performed by the soprano Emma Kirkby and the lutenist Anthony Rooley at Dore Abbey on the following afternoon was both flawless and masterly. Beginning with the well-known *Lamento d'Arianna* from Monteverdi's lost opera of 1608, the recital concluded with John Weldon's virtually unknown but bewitching aria for Venus from *The Judgement of Paris* of 1701, the English opera that brought William Hine to prominence as a singer in London before his transfer to Gloucester Cathedral in 1707, a move of great importance in the genesis of Three Choirs. Anthony Rooley has written of the Weldon aria: 'Such invention, wholly enchanting – who could resist that final chromatic melisma? Purcell's death certainly did not leave England entirely without talent of great stature.'[23] In the programme book to the Festival, Rooley wrote of this concert that 'The journey [from Monteverdi to Weldon] explored the music of the first woman composer of real genius, Barbara Strozzi; the imagined lament of Mary Queen of Scots; an English answer to Ariadne's Lament, by Milton's favourite composer, Henry Lawes; and a fashionable reworking of the words of the ancient Greek poetess, Sappho, set by John Blow.'[24]

NINETEEN ninety-five was the first year in which arena-style seating was erected temporarily in a Three Choirs cathedral. At Gloucester, a steeply raked slope of seats was installed from mid-nave to the sill of the great west window; at ground level similar seats stretched eastward from the foot of the slope to the orchestral platform; and tiered chorus seating rose up from behind the orchestra to the choir screen.

THE Gloucester Festival of 1992 had, in part, been a celebration of the life and work of Herbert Howells. In 1995 the Festival turned to the music and verse of Howells's great friend, the dually gifted Gloucester-born poet and composer Ivor Gurney (1890–1937), in whose name a new Society was founded. Professor Kelsey Thornton gave a talk on Gurney's verse at a luncheon held in the Festival marquee on Tuesday to mark the inauguration of the Ivor Gurney Society, following which the mezzo-soprano Norah Sirbaugh and her accompanist Stephen Peet, who had flown from the USA for the occasion, were joined by the actor and broadcaster David Goodland in a packed St Mark's Church for an enthralling lecture recital: *Ivor Gurney and his Vision of Gloucestershire.*

[22] Geraint Lewis, Hereford Festival programme book, 1994, pp. 21–3.

[23] Anthony Rooley, sleeve note to United Classics CD.

[24] Anthony Rooley, Hereford Festival programme book, 1994, p. 137.

Writing in the 1995 programme book, the pianist Robin Hales cites a view that Gurney was a finer poet than composer:

> But he himself rated music the loftier inspiration, and there seems no doubt that his place among the best English songwriters is assured ... In his introduction to [Gurney's] songs, Howells sets out perceptively and eloquently the claims of Gurney to that prime position:
>
> 'It is my belief that not more than five or six (song composers) since Campion and Dowland have brought to their task a literary perception equal to his. It is a direct and experienced knowledge of poetry – the poet's 'creative' knowledge – that so often lends beauty and power to his approach. This it is that enables him so often to find the first engendering phrase of a song. It is this again which enables him to succeed just where most song composers signally fail – in that element of pace variation which is the birthright of speech and the despair of music-set-to-words. All union of music to words is based on compromise. It is the mark of genius that it does not stress that compromise. At his best Gurney nearly eliminates it. He has brought back to English song that identity of poet with composer which was a glorious commonplace in the time of his beloved Elizabethans.'[25]

It would have been difficult to avoid the Purcell Tercentenary in 1995. The music of arguably Britain's greatest composer, Henry Purcell (1659–1695), was to be heard across the land: the BBC broadcast every single piece that Purcell wrote, and at the Gloucester Festival his genius was richly celebrated. The Trumpet Sonata, played by the Fine Arts Brass Ensemble, was featured in the Opening Service. Choral Evensong on Monday evening included his Service in G minor and the anthem *O sing unto the Lord*. Tuesday afternoon brought His Majesty's Sagbutts and Cornetts, directed by Jeremy West, to join the three cathedral choirs conducted by David Briggs, Donald Hunt and Roy Massey in a programme that included Purcell's setting of 'Hear my prayer' (Psalm 102); one of only two choral pieces composed by Purcell to Latin texts, 'Jehovah, quam multi sunt hostes mei'; and the Funeral Music for Queen Mary. On Wednesday afternoon, in the cathedral, The King's Consort, directed by Robert King, presented a superb programme of Purcell's music for the theatre, the court and the Chapel Royal.

As Andrew Pinnock, Artistic Administrator of the Arts Council's Purcell Tercentenary Trust, put it:

> Cries of 'not more Purcell' were heard by the end of New Year's Day. TV jumped in with both feet and threatened to crush our Henry flat. The hype was, and remains, inevitable – it's the way we sell music these days: digging up bits of 'cultural heritage', parading them like Tutankhamen's treasures, burying them again when consumer interest fades.
>
> But Three Choirs has the Master in proportion. England's oldest music festival celebrates Purcell in the best possible taste. Purcell extravaganzas

---

[25] Robin Hales, programme note in the Gloucester Festival programme book, 1995, pp. 81 and 83.

come and go (1858, 1895, 1959 ... 1995 ...): Three Choirs has seen them all, and no doubt will see the next few too.

There's no need to 'revive' him here: Purcell has been regularly performed in all three cathedrals since the late 17th century. The man and his music fit into a longer, *living* church music tradition, which Three Choirs keeps alive (this is 'authenticity' in the deepest sense), and which it seeks to share with the wider public. The perfect antidote to Tercentenary fever![26]

David Briggs had taken over as Director of Music at Gloucester Cathedral in June 1994 and took up the baton at his first Gloucester Festival in the following year. But Three Choirs had for long been 'in the blood', as he put it.[27] He well remembered his mother talking about her coming to Three Choirs as a teenager in the mid-1950s and sitting behind Vaughan Williams in the audience; then later, in the 1970s, his father bringing him to Worcester to hear Jean Langlais play a recital on the recently rebuilt organ – and remembering all the wind noise. Little did he know that in 1985 he would be appointed Assistant Organist at Hereford, thus gaining the pleasure of being *répétiteur* for the Hereford Festivals of 1985 and 1988. He vividly recalled his first-ever Three Choirs concert, playing the organ part in *The Dream of Gerontius* at Hereford in 1985 – and of making 'an embarrassing initial blunder':

> For the first ten minutes of the rehearsal (illustrious soloists, chorus and CBSO) I was in the cathedral office desperately photocopying some descants for the choristers to sing at the Opening Service. Consequently, I missed the rehearsal of Elgar's very beautiful 'Prelude'. There is (as I now know) a 'general pause' in the middle of the Prelude, indicated in the score with the sign //. Even after three years of studying music at Cambridge, sadly I was unaware of the meaning of this sign, and, in the concert, plowed into this enormous silence with a huge organ chord. Dr Massey said afterwards 'Dear Boy, the man who never made a mistake never made anything.' Nevertheless, at that moment, I remember wishing I could disappear through a large trap-door at the Festival Organ![28]

These were years in which Briggs had gained valuable experience: playing the accompaniments to all the major Elgar scores, Walton's *Belshazzar's Feast*, Mathias's *Lux aeterna* and more, and it was amazing to him that there were still quite a few chorus members at that time who had sung under Elgar. He also enjoyed the camaraderie shared with his fellow assistant organists:

> The three then-Assistants used to meet up at least three times a year, at an event called 'The Three Bears'. Adrian Partington (Worcester) was 'daddy-bear', Mark Blatchly (Gloucester) was 'middle-bear' and I was 'baby-bear'. We used to talk mainly about our bosses! I vividly remember coming

---

[26] Andrew Pinnock, 'Henry Purcell: Tercentenary Fever', Gloucester Festival programme book, 1995, p. 25.

[27] David Briggs, email of reminiscences, sent to Anthony Boden, 10 December 2015.

[28] Ibid.

over to Gloucester for the Three Cathedral Choirs Evensongs and being completely blown away by Mark Blatchly's improvisations.[29]

Born in Birmingham in 1962, Briggs was a chorister in the cathedral there, going on to become an FRCO at seventeen and winning five prizes and the Silver Medal of the Worshipful Company of Musicians. As Organ Scholar of King's College, Cambridge, he had toured the Antipodes, Belgium, Holland and Germany with the choir, and had received a Countess of Munster Scholarship to study with Jean Langlais in Paris.

In 1989, following four years as Assistant Organist of Hereford Cathedral, Briggs was appointed Master of the Choristers and Organist at Truro Cathedral, becoming the youngest cathedral organist in the country. He was soon in great demand locally, nationally and internationally as an organ recitalist, recording artist, adjudicator, course director and tutor, particularly in improvisation. After five and a half years at Truro:

> In 1994 I had the immense privilege of being appointed Director of Music at Gloucester and conductor of the Gloucester Three Choirs. I particularly loved the idea of being associated with the famous Gloucester Organ, the cathedral choir and, of course, the Three Choirs. I was Festival Conductor in 1995, 1998 and 2001. I was greatly indebted to the wise and inspired council of Anthony Boden, the Festival Administrator. There were many quite radical changes made at that time, including the raked seating for the nave (which greatly improved sight lines for the audience, and made for a clearer acoustic ambience). I remember the stunningly powerful commission that year, a work called *My Heart Dances* by Francis Grier ... I had several intensive conducting lessons with the late, great Vernon Handley (always known as Tod) who lived about an hour away in Trellech. These were completely eye-opening. He was very big on complete clarity, not flapping, using the fingers (a lot), not opening my mouth like a fish, and memorizing the score. I remember the moment when he asked me to conduct the Prelude to *The Kingdom* in front of a mirror, and said 'would you like to try Sir Adrian's sticks?' [which were long]. Tod was a huge protégé of Boult. I think that having played the viola in the National Youth Orchestra of Great Britain for four years certainly helped, when it came to being on the podium.[30]

Those conducting lessons paid dividends. At the 1994 Hereford Festival, David Briggs had directed the Bournemouth Symphony Orchestra with distinction in fine performances of Beethoven's *Leonore* overture no. 3 and Mass in C; and in 1995 at Gloucester, on Monday evening, he would conduct the Philharmonia Orchestra in Stravinsky's *The Firebird* (1919 suite), Ravel's *Daphnis and Chloë* (suite no. 2) and, with the Festival Chorus, *Psaume: Du fond de l'abîme* by Lili Boulanger, all reflective of his studies in Paris and his close affinity with French music and musicians. This affinity was further underlined in 1995 by Briggs's invitation to Naji Hakim, Organist of Sainte-Trinité, Paris, to give a recital in

[29] Ibid.
[30] Ibid.

Gloucester Cathedral on the Friday afternoon of the Festival. And in the midst of this magnificent Gallic fare, Briggs also rose to the challenge of conducting the Festival commission – that work which he admired so greatly: the cantata *My Heart Dances* by Francis Grier.

E ARLY in the planning stage of the 1995 Gloucester Festival we were contacted by the Managing Director of the Philharmonia Orchestra, David Whelton, asking if we might consider including a Philharmonia performance of Mahler's Symphony No. 2 (*Resurrection*) in our programme. Gilbert Kaplan (1941–2016), a millionaire American publisher, had edited the original autograph score of the symphony, which he owned, and had made a considerable reputation as a conductor of the work.[31] He was coming to Europe to conduct the Philharmonia in a performance of the symphony at Salzburg and he would be in England at the time of Gloucester Three Choirs: the orchestra and conductor would cost the Festival nothing. Were we interested?

For some years, it had been customary at Gloucester to engage the Gloucestershire Youth Orchestra for the first Saturday evening, to divide the rest of the Festival week into two halves, and to engage two professional symphony orchestras – one for each half. Given that the Philharmonia is one of Britain's finest orchestras, that Gilbert Kaplan had already led twenty-five orchestras in this symphony to great acclaim, including with the Philharmonia, that the *Resurrection* is a mammoth work of about 85 minutes, and that for the Gloucester performance there were to be 115 musicians playing 126 instruments, the decision was not difficult to make. The Philharmonia was booked for three nights, starting with the Mahler on Sunday, followed by the Bournemouth Symphony Orchestra for the remaining four nights.

Leading soprano Rosa Mannion was engaged to sing in both the Mahler and, on Monday evening, Francis Grier's *My Heart Dances*, settings for soprano and baritone soloists, chorus and orchestra of texts by Rabindranath Tagore and Kabir. All seemed to be set fair until, at the eleventh hour, we received a doctor's letter: Rosa Mannion would be unable to sing.[32] Finding a substitute to replace an indisposed singer at short notice over a weekend might not be too difficult if the work in question is a repertoire piece – but when there are *two* works, both large-scale, one of them by Mahler and the other a première, the problem takes on a worrying aspect. But then, mercifully, as if in answer to prayer, Lynne Dawson answered the call to sing in the Mahler. She walked into the Festival office on Sunday morning – to our relief and thanks – soon to learn that a major anxiety remained. We explained about Rosa Mannion's illness and, without hesitation, Lynne asked to see the vocal score of the Grier commission. After only a few minutes consideration she agreed not only to sing in the Mahler (alongside Margaret McDonald) but also to sing, with baritone Graham Titus, in the first performance of *My Heart Dances* on the following evening.

---

[31] Gilbert Kaplan died on 1 January 2016, aged seventy-four.

[32] Rosa Mannion's singing career was cut short by illness in 1998.

Writing under the heading 'Mahler in the tropics', the *Church Times* reported on one of the hottest Festival weeks of the 1990s:

> One has to look to Edinburgh or abroad to find another festival as consistently enjoyable as Three Choirs, held this year in a sweltering Gloucester ... One landmark of the festival was the launch of the Ivor Gurney Society, dedicated to the life and works of the poet–musician, who began his all too short creative life as a Gloucester Cathedral chorister. Much of Gurney's output is ostensibly secular; but the quality of his response to all around him – akin to that of the Metaphysicals, Whitman and Hopkins, all of whom he emulated – came as close to the spirit of wonder as any piece heard during the festival.
>
> There were some fine ones: for example, the resurrection chorale by the German poet Friedrich Klopstock, as set by Mahler in the finale of his Second Symphony. To hear this pounded out by the full festival chorus and Philharmonia orchestra was a joy indeed. Yet was it only the scorching, dry acoustic that left one strangely unmoved by Gilbert Kaplan's interpretation?[33]

During the Mahler two or three of Gloucester cathedral's pipistrelle bats, awakened from slumber by heat, descended from the cathedral tower and presented a silent, aerial ballet high in the nave. Later in the evening a 'Bat Count' chart appeared on the wall of the Festival club; a nightly tally was logged, and by the end of the week it was clearly demonstrated that, in the bats' estimation at least, Mahler had been the favoured composer at the Festival by a wide margin – and I was not alone in being deeply moved by Gilbert Kaplan's interpretation.

In the same *Church Times* write-up we read:

> Tippett's Passion-inspired *A Child of Our Time* also felt suffocated. The choir rarely surmounted its chromatic sections, the glorious spirituals felt desultory, and the tenor John Graham-Hall, who can be so urgent and effective in opera, somehow lacked dramatic impact.
>
> The laurels went to Michael George in Vaughan Williams's *Five Mystical Songs*, from which Roy Massey's lavish beat produced none the less fine results; and to Donald Hunt's admirable orchestration of the *Introduction and Theme* by Herbert Sumsion, the former organist of Gloucester Cathedral who died last month.
>
> Shrewd, imaginative programme-planning encompassed one of the week's duds. Francis Grier's *My Heart Dances*, with its visionary text from Tagore, boded well. His *Sequence for the Ascension* is a rewarding work, full of delicate light and shade. Here, however, pruning would have helped both text and music. Mark Blatchly's *Gloucester Psalms* the next day had far more wit, variety and sensitivity to the needs of the chorus.
>
> One welcomed a chance to hear the setting of Psalm 130 ('Out of the deep') by Lili Boulanger, sister of the great teacher Nadia. *Du fond de l'abîme* rather loses its way amid over-cloudy textures; but the choir

---

[33] *Church Times*, 8 September 1995.

coped well, despite the problems French enunciation poses. Earlier, David Briggs ... gave an admirable, if drawn-out, account of Stravinsky's *Firebird* suite, and it was he, too, who wound up with Elgar's *The Kingdom*: if its unwieldy shape and some orchestral intransigence rather defeated him, the evening was made by Donald Maxwell's superb aria 'Ye men of Israel' (a marked contrast to his shambling recitatives), and some fine solo and duet work from all three other soloists [Judith Howarth, Catherine Wyn-Rogers and Peter Bronder].

But it was midweek which gave this year's Three Choirs its greatest lift: first, The King's Consort, with James Bowman and two splendid boy soloists from St Paul's Cathedral [Connor Burrowes and David Nickless] in an unforgettable afternoon of Purcell; and then, with the arrival of Richard Hickox, three memorable evening concerts: an Elgar *Apostles* out of this world [Judith Howarth, Catherine Wyn-Rogers (in place of the indisposed Jean Rigby), Neil Jenkins, Alan Opie, Paul Whelan and Robert Lloyd]; an entrancing performance by Tasmin Little of the rarely heard Delius Violin Concerto; and a clear vindication of the festival's risky decision to introduce *The Legend of King Arthur* by the mid-century American composer Elinor Remick Warren, greatly enhanced by two superb young soloists in Nathan Berg and Ivan Sharp. A Three Choirs coup.[34]

The Legend of King Arthur, welcomed wholeheartedly by Richard Hickox, was preceded by Walton's *Coronation Te Deum*, conducted by Roy Massey, and the tone poem *Death and Transfiguration* by Richard Strauss, conducted by David Briggs. The decision to introduce *King Arthur* to Three Choirs was thought 'risky' by some, a mistake by a few, and a *tour de force* by many, including Lewis Foreman, whose scholarly programme notes introduced many in the audience to the wholly unfamiliar name of Elinor Remick Warren (1900–1991).

While still at high school in California, Warren had been 'mesmerised' when she heard Alfred Lord Tennyson's great epic poem *Idylls of the King* read aloud by her English teacher. Already writing songs and choruses, she determined that one day she would set this magnificent text as a large-scale choral work. Two decades and many compositions later she felt ready to take on the challenge. Following the Los Angeles première of *The Legend of King Arthur* in 1940, with the Los Angeles Philharmonic Orchestra and Oratorio Society, conducted by the eminent British conductor Albert Coates, one music critic wrote that: 'so vital, complex, and at times so overwhelming a composition created a real sensation.'[35]

Warren was widely accepted in her time, and, even if briefly, her music was programmed by some of the leading musicians of the day. The main reason for her critical 'neglect' was surely her romantic idiom during the high

---

[34] Ibid.

[35] Quoted in CD liner notes: Elinor Remick Warren, *The Legend of King Arthur* (Cambria CD-1043), recorded in Krakow, Poland (November 1989): Thomas Hampson (baritone), Lawrence Vincent (tenor), Polish Radio and Television Symphony Orchestra and Chorus of Krakow; conductor: Szymon Kawalla; choral director: Bronislawa Wietrzny.

point of modernism, coupled with the comparative paucity of big works in her portfolio. Now that we can view a score such as *King Arthur* from the perspective of history, idiom matters far less than what she had to say, and the striking way she said it.

... Warren's young American contemporaries such as Copland and Carter, would not have identified with either the technique or the subject matter, but for example the parallel fifths when Bedivere goes to return the sword to the lake and the *pianissimo* descending chain of tritones as the arm draws Excalibur beneath the water, are effects of the twentieth rather than the nineteenth century. However, in many ways the score might be described as Wagnerian, and this certainly extends to the use of leitmotifs for the principal elements of the story, including King Arthur himself, Excalibur, the waters of the Lake and, later, the funeral barge.

... Remembering, in particular, her comparative inexperience, Warren exploits the colour of her romantic orchestra with remarkable flamboyance. Her choral writing, too, shows technical command and her music has real sweep and passion, with a fine ear for colour. The music is at once a traditional choral work, and a personal throw of genius, for there is nothing else quite like it, with its big romantic roles of Arthur and Bedivere. Yet its compact design focuses the music and maintains the narrative: its success owing much to the way the composer has structured her libretto, omitting irrelevances which would have caused it to ramble. This is surely a work crying out for performances by choral societies all over the UK – I do hope this first British performance will persuade many conductors of its rewards.

There is a curious footnote, a brief might-have-been. In 1952 the composer approached the Three Choirs with this very work. In reply to her exploratory letter of 3 March 1952, Herbert Sumsion wrote: 'The position with regard to settings of words for the Three Choirs Festival is that they have first to be submitted to the Dean and Chapter for their sanction. For the most part we keep to sacred words, i.e. words from the Prayer Book or Bible, and I doubt whether Tennyson's words would be considered suitable' ... Warren responded by sending the vocal score, but that was the last we, or she, heard of the matter, until today.[36]

A Festival commission, *Songs of the West – An Overture*, an ingenious and effective mix of folk-song arrangements by Paul Patterson, opened the Wednesday evening orchestral concert ahead of the Violin Concerto by Delius, played with total conviction by Tasmin Little and the Bournemouth Symphony Orchestra conducted by Richard Hickox.

Following the interval, Hickox and orchestra were joined by the soprano Patricia Rozario in a sublime performance of the *Sinfonia Antartica*, Vaughan Williams's masterly evocation of Scott's doomed expedition to the South Pole in 1912. The Prelude incorporates the title music of the film *Scott of the Antarctic*, composed by Vaughan Williams in 1947; two years later, he began to rework some of the themes from the film into this, his seventh symphony, prefixing a

---

[36] Lewis Foreman, programme notes, Gloucester Festival programme book, 1995, pp. 189–95.

verbal motto to each of the five movements. It is perhaps no coincidence that for the first of these, the Prelude (*andante maestoso*), Vaughan Williams chose the final stanza of Shelley's great poem *Prometheus Unbound* – the same masterpiece that had inspired Hubert Parry's cantata *Scenes from Prometheus Unbound*, composed for the 1880 Three Choirs Festival:

> To suffer woes which Hope thinks infinite;
> To forgive wrongs darker than death or night;
> To defy Power, which seems omnipotent ...
> Neither to change, nor falter, nor repent;
> This ... is to be
> Good, great and joyous, beautiful and free;
> This is alone Life, Joy, Empire, and Victory.

The Epilogue (*alla marcia, moderato ma non troppo*) opens with a reference to the Prelude, to heroic endeavour, transformed into a determined but not triumphal march – a march of heroism defeated. A snowstorm builds to a catastrophic blizzard; the solo soprano sings a wailing lament; voices mingle with the wind, dying away until unconquerable Nature reclaims the Antarctic for its own.

O N the Monday afternoon of the 1995 Festival, a recital from Three Choirs was broadcast for the first time by Classic FM. The Almira String Quartet, playing at Sir Hubert Parry's former Parish Church at Highnam, gave the first modern performance of Parry's String Quartet No. 3 in G major (1878), alongside works by Purcell and Vaughan Williams. For many years thought to be lost, the unpublished manuscript of this quartet was identified in 1992 by Philip Thomas and Stephen Banfield, who found it among the papers of Gerald Finzi; a performing edition was published by Michael Allis in 1995, and the quartet was repeated at the 1998 Gloucester Festival, when it was played by the Sorrel Quartet.

Also on Monday afternoon, at St Mark's Church, Gloucester, in a recital given by Brian Schiele (viola), Diana Nuttall (oboe) and Robin Hales (piano), the first performance of a Festival commission, a 'Soliloquy for Viola and Piano' by Ian Venables (b. 1955), was included amongst works by Max Bruch, Howard Ferguson, York Bowen, Gerard Schurmann, Malcolm Arnold and Robert Schumann. Over the following two decades Venables gained a considerable following, his work encompassing a number of genres. He has been especially admired for his many additions to the canon of English art song – and he has been hailed in the musical press as 'a song composer as fine as Finzi and Gurney'.[37] A characteristically stylish song by Venables, *Love's Voice*, setting a Venetian poem by the Victorian poet John Addinton Symonds, was included in a Tuesday morning recital given at St Mark's by the incomparable English lyric tenor Ian Partridge, accompanied by his sister Jennifer. Their programme also featured songs by Henry Purcell, Ivor Gurney, John Jeffreys, and the first performance of *The Julias and Simonettas* by Anthony Scott (1911–2000), a setting of a poem by Ursula Vaughan Williams. The composer Mary Chandler, in the penultimate year

---

[37] *BBC Music Magazine.*

of her life, was also present to hear the finest possible interpretation of her song cycle *The Time of Waiting*, settings of seven poems by Jennifer Andrews, who was also in the audience.

Venables was again represented in a lunchtime recital at St Mark's on Wednesday, in which the violinist Louise Vale and pianist Sally Bishop included his *Three Pieces* for violin and piano – pieces that clearly illustrate a diverse approach to composition and an ability to write striking and original melodic ideas.

On Friday morning at St Mark's, the Gloucester-born composer Christopher Boodle (b. 1952) was joined by clarinettist Gail Darby in a recital that ranged from Bach and Scarlatti to Poulenc and Stravinsky, and included two works by Boodle himself: a *Sonata* for clarinet and piano, written in 1992 and described by the composer as being in a twentieth-century idiom according to eighteenth-century principles; and *Six Little Piano Pieces*, each miniature embodying a different aspect of twentieth century composition and adopting a linear rather than a chordal approach to piano writing.

Also on Friday morning, the Medici String Quartet shone at Cheltenham's Pittville Pump Room in a recital that included Ravel's String Quartet in F, Beethoven's op. 59 no. 3 (*Rasumovsky*) and, with the composer present, Philip Cannon's String Quartet of 1964. Cannon achieved international recognition with this work a year later when he submitted it for the Eighth International Composer's Competition in Paris. Competing against forty-eight other entrants, he had been awarded not only the *Grand Prix* (the first British composer to achieve this), but also the *Prix de la critique*, an unprecedented double honour. Following their success with it at Three Choirs, the Medicis went on to record the Cannon String Quartet for the Olympia CD label.[38]

In a candle-lit late-night concert in the Lady Chapel of the cathedral on Tuesday, the *a cappella* group Opus Anglicanum (countertenor, two tenors, baritone, bass and reader) presented *All Creation Rejoices over Thee, Mary*, a programme in which readings depicting aspects of the natural creation were placed among settings of texts in praise of Mary the Mother of God. One member of the group – a former boy chorister at New College, Oxford; choral scholar at King's College, Cambridge; and a qualified doctor – the tenor James Gilchrist, may not yet have been aware that he was standing on the threshold of a very busy and successful international career.

THE opening concert of the 1996 Worcester Festival, given on the first Saturday evening of the week, contained two works: Beethoven's Symphony No. 5 and a work long thought to have been destroyed by its composer: the *Messe solennelle* by Berlioz. It was not until 1992, 165 years after its second performance, that Frans Moors, an Antwerp schoolteacher, reported his discovery of the Berlioz manuscript among the music stored in an old oak chest in the organ gallery at the church of St Charles Borromaeus, Antwerp. John Eliot Gardiner

[38] Olympia CD (OCD 623). As well as the String Quartet, the disc also includes Cannon's Clarinet Quintet and String Sextet, in which the Medici String Quartet were joined by David Campbell (clarinet), Jane Atkins (viola) and Melissa Phelps (cello).

conducted the first modern performance at the church of St Petri in Bremen on 3 October 1993, and the first London hearing, in Westminster Cathedral, nine days later. To Donald Hunt's great credit, the second UK performance was given in November 1994 by the Worcester Festival Choral Society.

On 1 September 1996, Dr Donald Hunt OBE retired from his appointments as Organist and Master of the Choristers of Worcester Cathedral and Principal Conductor of the Worcester Three Choirs Festival, positions he had held with great distinction for two decades. It was entirely fitting, therefore, that he should also direct the Festival Chorus, the RLPO and soloists Susan Black (soprano), Peter Bamber (tenor), and Alan Fairs (bass) in the first Three Choirs Festival performance of Berlioz's long-lost *Messe solennelle*.

H ECTOR Berlioz was twenty years old and a reluctant medical student when, in 1823, M. Masson, the conductor of the church of Saint-Roch in Paris, asked him to write a mass to celebrate the Feast of Holy Innocents (28 December).

> We were to have a hundred picked musicians in the orchestra, and a still larger choir, with a month for practice. The copies were to be made *gratis* by the Saint Roch choir-children, etc, etc. I set to work heart and soul ... As soon as it was finished I gave my manuscript to M. Masson, who handed it over to his young pupils to copy and study. He swore by all his gods that the performance should be grand and perfect. We only wanted a good conductor, as neither he nor I was accustomed to direct such a large body of performers. [Henri] Valentino was at that time the leader at the Opéra ... and promised to help us, although he evidently felt no confidence in the material I had at my disposal. On the day of our full rehearsal, our *great choral and instrumental forces* resolved themselves into a choir of twenty singers (consisting of fifteen tenors and five basses), twelve children, nine violins, a viola, an oboe, a horn, and a bassoon. Imagine my shame and despair at having to introduce Valentino, the celebrated conductor of one of the first orchestras in the world, to such a phalanx of musicians! ... 'Never fear', persisted Masson, 'they will all be here at the performance tomorrow. Let us begin.' Valentino took up his baton with a resigned air, tapped his desk, and began; but he was obliged to stop almost immediately, because of the endless mistakes in the parts; flats and sharps were missing from the key-signatures; a pause of ten bars was left out in one place, and thirty bars omitted in another. It is a miserable hash; I suffer the torments of the damned; and at last am forced to resign my long-treasured hope of hearing one of my works performed by a large orchestra.[39]

But at least the 'miserable hash' caused an unavoidable delay, giving Berlioz the opportunity to rewrite much of the work. He was loaned 1,200 francs by a wealthy aristocrat, Augustin de Pons, who was only too happy to finance the performance, telling Berlioz: 'We will engage the chorus and orchestra from the

[39] *Memoirs of Hector Berlioz*, ed. Ernest Newman (Tudor Publishing / Knopf, 1932), pp. 28–9.

Opéra, Valentino must be satisfied, we must be satisfied, and by heaven it shall succeed!'[40] And succeed it did. The first performance of Berlioz's *Messe solennelle* was given at Saint-Roch on 10 July 1825, with Henri Valentino conducting; Berlioz himself played the tamtam; the press was unanimously favourable; and after the performance François Lesueur, Berlioz's composition master, greeted his pupil with the memorable words: 'Come let me embrace you! By Jove, you're not going to be a doctor or an apothecary; you're going to be a great composer. You have genius – I say it because it's true.'

THE 1996 Festival celebrated the fourth centenary of the appointment in 1596 of Thomas Tomkins (1572–1656), who served Worcester Cathedral as Organist and Master of the Choristers for fifty years. Tomkins, a major figure of the Golden Age of British music, was arguably the greatest of all Welsh-born composers. Living through one of the most revolutionary periods in British history, his professional life was spent in the service of the Crown and the Church at both the Chapel Royal and Worcester Cathedral. He survived the Civil War, the suppression of the English Church, the closure of the Chapel Royal, the destruction of his organ at Worcester, the devastation of Worcester itself, and the bombardment of his house in the shadow of the cathedral. Even so, Tomkins was still able to find the strength and inspiration to continue composing secular music of fine quality.

Much of Tomkins's output has survived, including his collection of music for the Anglican rite, *Musica Deo sacra*, published posthumously in 1668. His work embraced both sacred and secular vocal music, pieces for keyboard and for viol consort, thereby proving him to be one of the most versatile figures of English Renaissance music.[41]

Examples of Tomkins's instrumental music were heard at the Huntingdon Hall on Monday morning in a recital given by the English Consort of Viols; these included his *Fantasia* for three viols, *In nomine* for three viols, and the *Pavan and Almain* for four viols. Evensong in the cathedral on Monday, sung by the three cathedral choirs, was devoted entirely to Tomkins, including his glorious Third Service and the anthem *O praise the Lord*.

ON Sunday afternoon, the Alberni String Quartet was joined by tenor John Mark Ainsley and pianist Susan Tomes in a memorable recital at the Huntingdon Hall. The 100th anniversary of the writing of *A Shropshire Lad* by the Worcestershire-born poet A. E. Housman was marked by Vaughan Williams's song cycle *On Wenlock Edge*, performed between Mozart's String Quartet in B flat, K458 (*The Hunt*), and Elgar's Piano Quintet, op. 84. The Alberni Quartet returned to the Huntingdon Hall on Wednesday morning. Opening their second recital with Ravel's shimmering String Quartet in F, dedicated to Fauré, they continued with an all-too-rare performance of a work by Edmund Rubbra: his String Quartet No. 1 in F minor, op. 35.

[40] Ibid.
[41] See Anthony Boden, *Thomas Tomkins: The Last Elizabethan* (Ashgate, 2005).

Rubbra's polyphonic and lyrical style is ideally suited to the quartet medium. It is also one in which, along with his church music, his engagement with the Tudor and Jacobean inheritance is most clearly perceived. His art is also in a direct line from his teacher, Holst, and his friend and mentor, Vaughan Williams. The first quartet, in fact, bears the dedication 'To R.V.W. whose persistent interest in the original material of this work has led to the present revisions and additions'.[42]

Continuing the Housman link on Monday morning – and repeated in the afternoon – a celebration of his life and work in words and music, *To Look at Things in Bloom*, was presented at Hartlebury Castle by Claire Nielson and Paul Greenwood of the Royal Shakespeare Company, Tim Jones (baritone), and the then Assistant Organist at Worcester, Adrian Partington (piano).

On Monday evening, in the cathedral, the RLPO, conducted in turn by Roy Massey and David Briggs, was joined by soprano Alison Pearce, baritone Robert Hayward, pianist Kathryn Stott and the Festival Chorus in a refreshingly varied programme including, before the interval, Schoenberg's transcription of the Prelude and Fugue in E flat (BWV 552) by Bach, and Henryk Górecki's *Beatus Vir*, written for Karol Wojtyła, Cardinal of Kraków (later Pope John Paul II). The second half of the concert was devoted to two French masterpieces: Kathryn Stott was the impressive soloist in Ravel's Concerto for piano and orchestra in G major, and the concert ended with Poulenc's exhilarating *Gloria*.

Kathryn Stott returned on Tuesday morning to give a bravura performance at the Huntingdon Hall, playing works by Liszt, Chopin, Fauré, Chabrier, Ravel and Poulenc. Equally 'at home' as a remarkable exponent of Tango and other Latin dance music as in a wide range of European repertoire, her work has been recognised by the French Government, from whom she received the award of *Chevalier dans l'Ordre des arts et lettres*, and she has made many recordings, including rarities such as Herbert Howells's Ravel-inspired Piano Concerto No. 2.[43]

While attending a London conference in 1985, Donald Hunt met Barry Smith, Director of Music at St George's Cathedral, Cape Town; their meeting would lead to an invitation for Hunt to visit South Africa in 1985. He returned regularly for the next two decades, building a rapport with the Cape Town Symphony Orchestra and Philharmonia Choir and, thanks to these connections, was able to extend an invitation to the St George's Singers and Barry Smith to take part in the 1996 Three Choirs Festival. They proved a very welcome addition, and were praised by the late Felix Aprahamian in his *Church Times* review of the Festival:

> The visiting St George's Singers from Cape Town and their conductor Barry Smith gave evidence of his, and their, sterling qualities [on the final Saturday morning] in a variety of choral pieces that included Schütz,

[42] Adrian Yardley, programme notes, Worcester Festival programme book, 1996, p. 124.

[43] Hyperion CDA66610, Howells Piano Concerto No. 2 in C minor, etc., Kathryn Stott (piano), Royal Liverpool Philharmonic Orchestra; conductor: Vernon Handley.

Brahms and Mendelssohn. South African works by Stephen Carletti, Hubert du Plessis and Peter Klatzow used traditional material, without achieving the simple beauty of John Joubert's 'There is no Rose'.[44]

The St George's Singers, the three cathedral choirs, Worcester Junior Festival Chorus and the Bournemouth Sinfonietta were directed by Joshua Rifkin on Tuesday evening in a rare performance of Bach's *St Matthew Passion* based on the première, in 1911, of the Elgar–Atkins edition. The soloists on this occasion included Robert Johnston (Evangelist), Laurence Albert (Christus), Deborah York (soprano), Catherine King (contralto), John Mark Ainsley (tenor) and Thomas Hunt (bass).

The American conductor, keyboard player and musicologist Joshua Rifkin, famed for his theory that most of Bach's choral works were originally sung with only one singer per choral line, came to prominence in the UK in 1994 when he and his Bach Ensemble performed the *St Matthew Passion* at the BBC Promenade Concerts, but he is also well known for his ragtime revival in the 1970s, including his recordings of works by Scott Joplin.

As part of a programme of English and French music in the cathedral on Wednesday afternoon, Richard Studt conducted the Bournemouth Sinfonietta, with trumpeter Mark Calder as soloist, in the first performance in England of the *Concertino* for trumpet and strings by Pierre Villette. Edwin Roxburgh (b. 1937) conducted two of his compositions at the Festival, one with the Bournemouth Sinfonietta at the Wednesday afternoon concert, when he directed four soloists – oboe, horn, violin and cello – in a performance of his *Sinfonia concertante*. In the evening, Gervaise de Peyer was the distinguished soloist in the première of Roxburgh's Clarinet Concerto with the BBC Philharmonic Orchestra under the composer's own direction. Felix Aprahamian reviewed the Wednesday to Saturday concerts:

> The discreet sprinkle of novelties brought a Clarinet Concerto by Edward Roxburgh on Wednesday. To its echoed melodic motifs and more angular episodes, under the composer's direction, Gervase de Peyer's honeyed tone lent its usual distinction. Before it, Butterworth's *Shropshire Lad* Rhapsody seemed to belong more truly to the surroundings, as did the curtain raiser, Elgar's version of Bach's Fantasia and Fugue in C minor. So did the First Symphony, in Dr Hunt's masterly account. It was totally Elgarian in his scrupulous regard for every indicated nuance and the BBC Philharmonic Orchestra's magnificent playing.
>
> On Thursday, Walt Whitman, whose name was linked to an untypical though early Gustav Holst overture, provided text and inspiration for two masterpieces: Delius's *Sea Drift*, and Vaughan Williams's *Sea Symphony*. Here, again, Dr Hunt, the orchestra and Festival Chorus, with Paul Whelan [winner of the Lieder prize at the 1993 Cardiff 'Singer of the World' competition] and Judith Howarth, communicated the essential spirit of both scores.
>
> Friday morning [with Thomas Holme (speaker), Gervase de Peyer (clarinet), the Donald Hunt Singers, the St George's Singers, Cape Town,

[44] *Church Times*, 30 August 1996.

and the Bournemouth Sinfonietta conducted by Donald Hunt and Barry Smith] the indefatigable conductor [Dr Hunt] regulated the consolatory strains of Vaughan Williams's *Oxford Elegy* as skilfully as he accompanied Gervase de Peyer in Gerald Finzi's ever-melodious Clarinet Concerto. Dr Hunt's own plainsong-inspired *Hymnus Paschali* was worthy of the best native traditions of the Festival. [On Friday evening with Judith Howarth, Sally Burgess, Evelyn Glennie, the Festival Chorus and BBC Philharmonic.] Exciting, if less appropriate, despite its dependence on another plainsong tune and text, was *Veni, veni, Emmanuel*, a concerto for percussion and orchestra by James Macmillan. Under Martyn Brabbins, it gave Evelyn Glennie's display of prodigious virtuosity ample scope, but only the composer's own description of his work alerted the viewing listener to its religious significance.[45]

In addition to *Veni, veni, Emmanuel*, the Friday evening concert included the Stokowski orchestration of Bach's Toccata and Fugue in D minor; the ballet *El Amor Brujo* (Love the Magician) by Manuel de Falla; and Richard Rodney Bennett's *Spells*, a setting of poems by Kathleen Raine, which received its first performance at the 1975 Worcester Three Choirs Festival.

Also impinging on the memory was 'For all the saints', sung by the three cathedral choirs at Evensong on Friday; and Parry's 'Jerusalem', ending the Festival on Saturday night, and coming after Elgar's *The Dream of Gerontius*, which could hardly ever be less than profoundly moving in Worcester Cathedral, its ideal setting. Sally Burgess, Arthur Davies and Laurence Albert, vocally versatile soloists, helped Dr Hunt in making it an unforgettable *Dream*.[46]

And so Dr Donald Hunt OBE came to the end of his long and dedicated service to both Worcester Cathedral and the Three Choirs Festival: a fine conductor who, should he have chosen to do so, could have made a permanent transition from organ loft to rostrum. In his own words:

I gave up a promising career in Yorkshire to work in Three Choirs Country because I felt the draw of its 'special' atmosphere. Elgar had something to do with it, but so did the cathedral. The three cathedrals make the Festival; it would be nothing without them. Conversely it must be said that for two hundred and sixty-nine years the Festivals have enhanced the life of the cathedrals. The benefits that accrue to the cathedral and its community from this triennial outburst of artistic and religious activity are incalculable. Worcester let down the show in 1875 with a sanctimonious proclamation which was really a cover-up for the fact that they were bowing to the wishes of the Earl of Dudley, because they coveted his pelf. It is to be hoped that present and future generations of cathedral administrators will not see the Festival as a means of 'making financial hay while the music plays', disregarding the benefits that the Festival unquestionably brings

[45] Ibid.
[46] Ibid.

to the cathedral, and indeed the city and community which it should be privileged to serve.[47]

Donald's interpretations of the works of Elgar have been widely acknowledged as among the very best. Typical of such plaudits, the late Michael Kennedy CBE (1926–2014), writing in 1997 on the subject of Three Choirs standards, expressed the view that

> Indeed, when I have attended, I have been impressed by the excellence of the performances, the obvious care in preparation and the skill of the conductors, who no longer seem as if they are in some alien environment and are longing to rush back to the anonymity of the organ-loft. Invidiously to name only one, the genuine Elgar tradition has been nobly upheld by Donald Hunt.[48]

This, of course, is not to say that Donald is a single-composer specialist. Happily, he is an accredited BBC conductor and he has made several recordings, including an excellent Three Choirs performance of Howells's *Hymnus Paradisi* from the 1977 Gloucester Festival, with soprano April Cantelo, tenor David Johnston, the Three Choirs Festival Chorus and the RPO.[49]

The then chairman of the Worcester Festival and chairman of the Three Choirs Festival Association, Sam Driver White (ob. 2017), wrote a fitting tribute to Dr Hunt, published in the 1996 Festival programme book:

> For over twenty years I have worked with Donald on the Elgar Foundation, and have learned to appreciate his very great knowledge and understanding of Elgar's music. Donald has ensured that Elgar has always featured strongly at the Worcester Festival and those of us who have been present at his many performances of the great Elgar oratorios will never forget the quality of those performances, his conducting ability, his chorus control and the depth of true understanding that he has brought to the interpretation of Elgar's music.
> ... Donald has striven for better and better performances from chorus and orchestras and although a very talented conductor himself has brought in a specialist guest conductor where he felt that the performance required this. He also introduced to the festival the concept that Baroque music, where appropriate, should be performed on early instruments and by smaller choral forces ... [He] has also introduced many early twentieth-century and contemporary pieces previously unknown to the festival.
> He has stamped his considerable and lasting influence on this great and long-lived festival ... Donald goes forward to undertake the artistic direction of the new Elgar Centre that is being developed at Lower Broadheath adjoining Elgar's Birthplace, and he will continue his

[47] Hunt, *Festival Memories*.
[48] Michael Kennedy, 'Musings on the Three Choirs', Hereford Festival programme book, 1997, p. 21.
[49] BBC Radio Classics [licensed to Carlton Classics] No. 15656 91982. Recorded 23 August 1977; released 1997.

conducting career unabated. He will lecture, he will teach and, hopefully, he will compose.[50]

Donald Hunt was soon to fulfil Sam Driver White's predictions: he appeared as both conductor and composer at the 1997 Hereford Festival:

> In a week's programme of mixed success, Donald Hunt, now director of the Elgar School of Music in Worcester, returned to the Festival to preside over one of his own choral works, *A Song of Celebration*, which was most touching in a shy soprano solo from the choir (amid some uneasy chorus tunings), and for the baritone Thomas Hunt's warmly appealing approach to the newly-added movement, 'Our Good Shepherd Lives'.[51]

It was also at the 1997 Hereford Festival that Donald Hunt's successor at Worcester, Adrian Lucas, made his Three Choirs debut. Before taking up the organ studentship at St John's College, Cambridge, in 1980 Lucas had held an organ scholarship at Salisbury Cathedral. While at Cambridge he was awarded the John Stewart of Rannoch Scholarship in Sacred Music and toured with the choir in Australia, Scandinavia and across Europe. He was appointed Assistant Organist at Norwich Cathedral in 1983 and then, in 1990, as Organist and Master of the Choristers at Portsmouth Cathedral. During this time he directed the music for the consecration of the completed cathedral (formerly St Thomas's Church) in 1991 and, in 1994, that for the Drumhead Service of Commemoration of the fiftieth anniversary of the D-Day landings. Other television appearances with the choir included work for American Cable TV, Meridian, and special programmes for *Songs of Praise* and *Highway*. By the time of his move to Worcester he had given recitals at such prestigious venues as the Royal Festival Hall and Birmingham Town Hall and, in 1994, played for the annual British Legion Service of Remembrance at the Royal Albert Hall. He also toured frequently as a recitalist in the USA and Canada.

Adrian Lucas, who studied conducting under Colin Metters at the Royal Academy of Music, became Organist and Master of the Choristers at Worcester Cathedral and conductor of the Worcester Festival Choral Society in 1996. In the following year he was invited by Roy Massey to conduct two works, both by Brahms, at the Monday evening choral and orchestral concert of the Hereford Three Choirs Festival. Lucas opened the concert with the Bournemouth Symphony Orchestra in a stirring performance of the *Academic Festival Overture*, op. 80, described by Brahms as 'a very jolly potpourri of student songs à la Suppé':

> Adrian Lucas, the new music director at Worcester, caused a cheerful stir on his Three Choirs debut, by eliciting a memorably stylish performance of Brahms's *Academic Festival Overture*. Brahms's bombastic *Triumphlied* [with baritone Brian Rayner Cook] was, by contrast, embarrassingly unmemorable.[52]

[50] Sam Driver White, Worcester Festival programme book, 1996, p. 6.
[51] *Church Times*, 12 September, 1997.
[52] Ibid.

Triumphlied, op. 55, for massed voices in an eight-part choir, was composed during the Franco–Prussian War of 1870. The war prompted Brahms to 'develop a violent fit of patriotism and [he] even considered joining the Prussian forces'.[53] Lucas was unlucky to find himself facing *Triumphlied*, a rarely performed tub-thumping work, at his first Three Choirs rehearsal – and it brought the chorus very close to open rebellion. Yet again, still-unresolved rehearsal problems continued to bedevil rehearsal schedules:

> I made it a personal goal, through my years at the Festival, to improve the cohesion of arrangements for chorus rehearsals. In my early days, it was common to turn up to a massed rehearsal with no knowledge of which works were to be scheduled, quite apart from any information about details of breathing, phrasing, pronunciation or other essentials. My first festival (1997) gave me the opportunity to conduct Brahms's *Academic Festival* Overture and the almost completely unknown *Triumphlied*. This latter piece was not only unknown to audiences, but also to members of the chorus as the copies, rather poorly produced vocal scores, arrived late and surfaced only briefly before the Festival itself. My allotted 30 minutes of full chorus rehearsal was soon up and I was about to leave the stage when the chorus started stamping their feet and shouting 'we want Brahms ... we want Brahms'. So, with little negotiation, I returned and managed another 20 minutes before the rehearsal ended! I don't think the performance was much better, but I had learned a crucial lesson about the way things worked. Shortly afterwards, we developed a detailed schedule, accompanied by rehearsal notes and a growing use of technology to spread this information. Of course, we were still at the mercy of the individuals taking the local rehearsals to cover all the music in equal measure, but things were moving in the right direction.[54]

Adrian was soon to prove his worth as both a fine conductor and choir trainer.

O N Monday evening John Sanders returned to conduct Three Choirs for a final time in a performance of his *Gloucestershire Visions*, an evocative work of great beauty comprising settings of the Gloucestershire poets Roland Pepper, Ivor Gurney, Eva Dobell and Leonard Clark, and ending with 'A Hymn of Thanksgiving', using the words of the ancient canticle *Te Deum laudamus*.

> John Sanders, Herbert Sumsion's recently retired successor at Gloucester, was also honoured. His Responses and his Good Friday Reproaches are well known. His new *Hereford Service*, sadly rendered a travesty by external noise, made for a highly personal Thursday evensong.
>   Sanders's work for chorus and tenor solo [Adrian Thompson], *Gloucestershire Visions*, provides evidence of eclecticism, but also, in quieter passages, of a fine ear for orchestration. The opening and close of the initial and second movements (the latter derived from a mesmerising clarinet-led

---

[53] Peter Latham, *Brahms*, Master Musician Series (Dent, 1948), p. 55.

[54] Adrian Lucas, 'Three Choirs Festival Jottings for Anthony Boden', 20 January 2016 [personal communication].

movement in his chamber cycle *In Praise of Gloucestershire*) were as intoxicating as anything by, say, E. J. Moeran; later movements proved chorally more viscous and orchestrally more overbearing than they had at the work's better-balanced Gloucester première.[55]

The Monday evening concert ended with a particularly significant British choral work deserving of more frequent revival, *Cantiones sacrae* by John Gardner (1917–2011). This work was first heard at Hereford in 1952, and in 1997(H) was sensitively conducted by Roy Massey, with the soprano Ann Mackay as the superlative soloist. A prolific composer of some 250 works, including three symphonies and six operas, Gardner is assured his place in our national consciousness, even if he should be remembered only for his wholly delightful modern English carol *Tomorrow shall be my Dancing Day*: 'whole-hearted dance, at once pagan, erotic, and symbolically Christian – the spirit of Christmas past and present.'[56]

On the previous evening, Sunday, Richard Hickox achieved a *tour de force*, setting the scene with one of Elgar's most brilliant and picturesque works, the concert overture *Cockaigne*, and following it with a memorable performance of Beethoven's monumental Symphony No. 9 in D minor (*Choral*), with soloists Cara O'Sullivan, Jean Rigby, Nigel Robson and Matthew Best, the Festival Chorus and the Bournemouth Symphony Orchestra.

Tuesday morning brought the sheer delight of *I Fagiolini* to the cathedral. (*I Fagiolini* translates as 'Little Beans'.) Founded by Robert Hollingworth, a former chorister at Hereford Cathedral, this supremely versatile group gave its first concert in 1986 while its members were students at Oxford, and soon earnt a reputation as one of Europe's most challenging vocal ensembles. At 1997(H) their programme ranged widely over the classics of renaissance and twentieth-century vocal repertoire, including, before the interval, plainchant, Tallis, Victoria, Palestrina and Lassus; after it, Poulenc, Tippett and Britten.

Just as James Gilchrist had been in company with Opus Anglicanum at the Gloucester Festival in 1995, an outstanding baritone, Roderick Williams, an early member of *I Fagiolini*, was making his first Three Choirs appearance at Hereford in 1997.

D AVID Briggs opened the 1997(H) Tuesday evening choral and orchestral concert with Arthur Bliss's powerful suite *Things to Come*, the first great score for a British film. Alexander Korda's 1934 screen adaptation of H. G. Wells's *The Shape of Things to Come*, a terrifying prophecy of total, near-annihilating war, was matched perfectly by Bliss's blistering score. 'As Bliss wrote in his autobiography, *As I Remember*, Wells viewed his novel as a parable, wanting it to be "an educative lesson to mankind, to emphasise the horror and uselessness of war, the inevitable destruction of civilised life, the rise of gangster dictatorship and oppression".'[57]

---

[55] *Church Times*, 12 September 1997.

[56] Nicolas Robertson, liner notes to *20th-Century Christmas Collection* – The Sixteen, dir. Harry Christophers (Collins Classics: CD12702 (1990)).

[57] Andrew Burn, Hereford Festival programme book, 1997, p. 93.

Following the Bliss, David Briggs went on to conduct the première of the orchestral version of John Joubert's *Rochester Triptych*, the three texts of which reflect contrasting but complementary views of life, all by the seventeenth-century poet John Wilmot, 2nd Earl of Rochester, the 350th anniversary of whose birth fell in 1997. A return to Brahms brought contralto Penelope Walker to sing the *Alto Rhapsody*, and the concert concluded with soprano Alison Pearce joining the chorus, boys' choir and orchestra under Roy Massey in Paul Patterson's *Te Deum*, op. 65:

> Oddly, the works by Hunt, Sanders, and John Gardner all end in a kind of cop-out, a canticle setting that sits uneasily with what precedes it. Paul Patterson's full-blooded *Te Deum*, however, is a carefully mapped-out orchestral setting of marked variety and invention. Roy Massey elicited a tremendous performance, with vigorous, bongo-led prestos, tidy horn and clarinet soli to offset the glorious soprano of Alison Pearce, and an enchanting, precisely intoned *a cappella* movement for chorus.
>
> Indeed, this was Roy Massey's week. To his restrained flamboyance and sensitive conducting we owed, too, both the première of a new secular cantata, *Below the Surface Stream*, by Judith Bingham, and a well-poised, exemplary performance of John Gardner's *Cantiones sacrae*.
>
> Given deft work from the Festival Chorus and Bournemouth Symphony Orchestra strings alike, this psalm-based Hereford commission, first heard under Meredith Davies in 1952, proved well worth its revival. Gardner says *multum in parvo*: eerie nocturne and dark, contrabassoon-led textures are interspersed with exciting dance movements as pithy as Britten's *Gloriana* interludes, and pared-down neo-Baroque scoring such as not even Stravinsky dreamed up.[58]

On Wednesday afternoon, the three cathedral choirs joined Catherine Bott, Susanne Rydén, Rogers Covey-Crump, Charles Daniels, William Kendall, Michael George, Simon Birchall and the period-instrument Brandenburg Consort under the direction of Roy Goodman in a timeless masterpiece: the Vespers of 1610 by Claudio Monteverdi. 'I hope you can sit back', wrote Goodman in the programme book, 'and picture yourself in beautiful Mantua, Rome or Venice almost 400 years ago.' We were not disappointed.

> For many who attended this summer's Three Choirs Festival at Hereford, the abiding memory will be the opening concert – Beethoven's Ninth Symphony, in an exciting performance under Richard Hickox – and perhaps, too, the young baritone Paul Whelan, a strong Elijah in the final evening's anniversary tribute to Mendelssohn.
>
> Some will cherish memories of the midweek's Monteverdi Vespers, which aligned the reduced forces and lucid textures of the three cathedral choirs with the period-instrument Brandenburg Consort; or memories of visiting vocal groups such as the Rodolfus Choir and I Fagiolini.
>
> While the young cellist Natalie Klein entranced audiences with Haydn [the NYO under Roger Norrington at Wyastone Leys], the week's high

---

[58] *Church Times*, 12 September 1997.

point was Robert Cohen's beautifully poetic and involved reading of Walton's Cello Concerto – as intoxicating under Hickox's direction as the ensuing Elgar Second Symphony was noisy and depressing.[59]

Mendelssohn died in Leipzig on 4 November 1847, a little more than fourteen months after the première of his *Elijah* in Birmingham on 26 August 1846. He was only thirty-eight. The first of many Three Choirs performances of *Elijah* was given in Gloucester, also in 1847, and 150 years later this perennial favourite was selected by Roy Massey, directing the Festival Chorus and Bournemouth Symphony Orchestra, as the work with which to close the 1997 Festival at Hereford. The soloists on that occasion were soprano Patricia Rozario, mezzo Catherine Wyn-Rogers, tenor Mark Tucker, and the title role was ably sung by Paul Whelan, a young bass-baritone of fine quality, his tall, bearded figure epitomising a youthful Old Testament prophet: a worthy upholder of a very long Festival tradition.

[59] Ibid.

23

'A Gold-Plated Orchestra'

MICHAEL Kennedy's essay 'Musings on the Three Choirs' has already been mentioned. Published in the programme book of the 1997 Festival at Hereford, it embraced Kennedy's reflections on Three Choirs past and present and, as the twentieth century drew ever closer towards the twenty-first, posed a few timely and pertinent questions about repertoire. Kennedy also looked back to Elgar's involvement with the Festival, considered the steady decline in the great man's reputation in London during the composer's lifetime, but pointed out that, in spite of this, 'in his own West Country [Elgar] was sovereign in his kingdom'. Kennedy then moved on to write of that other undisputed 'giant personality', Ralph Vaughan Williams, whose Three Choirs association lasted unbroken (except for two world wars) from 1911 to 1957: 'Where Elgar was autocratic', wrote Kennedy, 'Vaughan Williams was democratic.' Kennedy himself had been in Worcester in 1954:

> when, at the age of 82 and now a stooping oak-like figure, [RVW] conducted the first performance of his Christmas cantata *Hodie*. 'Far too difficult', he told me afterwards, but no-one else has quite captured its essence as he did. Gerald Finzi was there that day, another much-missed figure, whose *Dies natalis* belongs to the walls of the three cathedrals as potently as any of Elgar's works, and 'John' (Herbert) Sumsion, whose recent death [in 1995] severed the last significant musical link with Elgar. At that period Sumsion, David Willcocks and Melville Cook were a triumvirate easily the equal of their predecessors and successors. They laid the foundations of the modern festivals while preserving the hallowed traditions.
>
> William Walton was never a Three Choirs composer, although his Viola Concerto, first performed in 1929, was included in the Worcester programme in 1932 and was hated by Elgar. For some extraordinary reason, *Belshazzar's Feast* was not admitted into the cathedrals until 1957, 26 years after its sensational Leeds première. There had been a plan to include it in the 1932 Festival – this is why the Viola Concerto was chosen instead – but Atkins banned it because he considered the libretto was unsuitable for cathedral performance, whereupon a letter appeared in the press asking why it was more unsuitable than the Demons' Chorus in *Gerontius* or, for that matter, Wagner excerpts and an extract from *Salome* [Strauss]. Walton was asked to write something for the 250th anniversary [of the Festival] in 1977, but declined. Has Delius's

Mass of Life ever been performed at Three Choirs? I ought to know, but don't.[1]

The answer to that last question was 'No', and it is an uncanny coincidence that Kennedy should have asked it in 1997: in the previous year I had approached the Dean of Gloucester to discuss the possibility of including the Delius *Mass of Life* in the programme for the 1998 Festival. It seemed wrong that one of the towering peaks of English choral and orchestral music, a work of epic grandeur, should never have been heard at Three Choirs. But the dean's response was unequivocal: the text used by Delius is by Nietzsche and, as such, is inimical to Christian doctrine. Such a position implies that Delius deliberately set out to use *A Mass of Life* as a vehicle to disseminate Nietzsche's philosophy, but *can* the relation between a work of art and a philosophical treatise ever be so simple? Philip Heseltine (Peter Warlock), writing on the relation between music and text, makes the point that *A Mass of Life* is 'not an attempt to set philosophy to music, as it has been foolishly described':

> It is Nietzsche, the poet – an incomparably greater man than Nietzsche, the philosopher – who has been drawn upon for the text; one might almost say Nietzsche, the musician, for when his creative imagination soars highest his very words 'aspire towards the condition of music', seeking to express a wider significance than words alone can ever convey. Nietzsche, the philosopher, is often at variance with himself as well as with the world, but Nietzsche the poet-musician, is at one with the great mystics of all ages.[2]

Delius's amanuensis, Eric Fenby, who was a committed Christian, tells us that:

> Two years (1904–5) were spent in the composition of a paean to the Will, *A Mass of Life*, the grandest of Delius's choral works. The title suggests a unique non-conformity. The text which [the conductor Fritz Cassirer] helped him to select from Nietzsche's *Thus Spake Zarathustra* is biblical in style; poetry, metaphor and irony blending in a revelation of Nietzsche's gospel of the Eternal Recurrence ... Delius produced his masterpiece by concentrating on the poetic fragments he felt were most apt to the full expression of his musical symbols rather than by attempting deliberately to disseminate philosophical ideas.[3]

A Mass of Life is not a conventional mass setting; rather, it is a glorious outpouring in praise of Life itself. Delius was not the only great composer to turn to the poetry of Nietzsche: both Gustav Mahler and Richard Strauss were inspired by his verse to compose masterpieces, one of which, Mahler's Symphony No. 3, was to receive a stunning first-ever Three Choirs performance at Worcester Cathedral in 1999 (the Nietzsche setting is in the fourth movement).

[1] Michael Kennedy, 'Musings on the Three Choirs', essay in the Worcester Festival programme book, 1997. Copies of all the Festival programme books cited in this chapter are held in the Three Choirs Festival Office, Gloucester.

[2] Philip Heseltine, *Frederick Delius* (Bodley Head, 1923), pp. 105–6.

[3] Eric Fenby, *Delius*, The Great Composers Series (Faber and Faber, 1971), p. 57.

When, two years in advance, plans for the 1998 Gloucester programme were being drawn up, *A Mass of Life* had to be excluded. However, in 1997, a change of dean and a change of attitude made it possible for this great work to be scheduled for 2001; Richard Hickox was duly engaged to conduct it. It was hoped that the Festival audience would at last discover that a performance of *A Mass of Life* presents a life-affirming and numinous experience. In the meantime, considerable effort was made to ensure that the 1998 programme at Gloucester would be both ambitious and eclectic:

> Shudder, Salzburg: eat your heart out, Edinburgh. In a hot, high August, forget the Salzgammmergut, yea, a pox on Princes Street. The place to be is glorious English Severnside. They say the Three Choirs Festival is old hat. What piffle. I have just attended nine days of the most extraordinary, daringly planned and exciting music I have encountered at any British festival in years.
>
> Nicholas Bury, the Dean of Gloucester, fired the starting gun. 'Why not go over the top?' he urged. Well, this year's Three Choirs organisers got the message. What could be more OTT than *Parsifal* [on Friday evening] – the whole, long drawn-out first act – with a solo cast of thousands? Matthew Best's Gurnemanz, magnificent; Mark Beesley's Titurel, unnerving, a kind of male Erda; and Alan Opie's Amfortas, outstanding. The Philharmonia, true heroes of the week, delivered for Richard Hickox, making his first assault on the Grail a dream of a performance. The audience's hushed silence could have been cut with a knife.
>
> And all this only the night after David Briggs – a Francophile to put it mildly – had delivered a Berlioz *Damnation of Faust* [on Thursday evening] to knock you off your seats. Opie terrific as Mephisto, and the baritone Roderick Williams adding a bouncy Brander to his exquisite solo recitals and appearances elsewhere. Bach's B minor Mass the evening before was an equal joy – thanks chiefly to Nicki Kennedy and Robin Blaze: no need to jet in Andreas Scholl – we already have our own.
>
> Briggs is still new to the game; his conducting is immensely promising (witness a cracking *Carnaval romain* and thrilling *La Mer*), but too self-conscious; he has yet to learn to nurse a large chorus. But it was undeniably his week; as if to prove it, fine recitalist that he is, he prefaced Friday's *Parsifal* by delivering the entire Mahler Fifth Symphony in his own new transcription for organ, and truly magnificent in the brilliant colourings of the Gloucester organ.
>
> Howard Ferguson was the oldie of the festival: he may be 90, but he looks and sounds 30, and his lovely full choral setting of the mediæval *The Dream of the Rood* [on Monday] sounds as gorgeous and lovely as ever. (Why doesn't everybody do it, for gawd's sake?) Michael Hurd, 70 in December and a Gloucestershire lad heart and soul, was the not-quite-so-oldie. His *Concerto da Camera* for oboe is a small gem; *Shore Leave*, his cycle of settings of Charles Causley ('See the noon her yellow landau draws against the fainting sky': so who's been pilfering *The Merchant of Venice*?). Christian Wilson trysted with Mahler; Christopher Boodle delivered a spicy new trumpet sonata; but highlight among the youngsters

was Ian Venables' riveting, moody *Piano Quintet*, which lends a new late 20th-century dimension to the English pastoral. If anyone deserves a clutch of West Midlands Arts commissions, this promising young Worcester composer does.

And I almost forgot to mention Parry. True to form Gloucester gave us the lot – chamber, choral, keyboard, his Joachim-like *Overture to an Unwritten Tragedy*, the recently rediscovered, expansive Piano Concerto, plus a clutch of new books and reissues.[4]

Following Gloucester custom, the first Saturday evening concert featured the Gloucestershire Youth Orchestra, and it is to their credit and the credit of their conductor, Charles Peebles, that they were able to rise admirably to the challenging programme asked of them. Even the opening work was, at that time, a rarity: the Bridal March from *The Birds* by Hubert Parry, composed in 1883 as part of the incidental music for a Cambridge University production of Aristophanes's satirical comedy of that title. The march (which in the original contained a chorus) came to prominence again in 1947, when an organ arrangement of it by Walter Alcock was used at Westminster Abbey during the royal wedding of HRH Princess Elizabeth and Philip, Duke of Edinburgh. Parry's biographer, Jeremy Dibble, provided a programme note for the 1998 performance at Gloucester:

> Parry's broad tune, cast in C major and set low in the tessitura of the violins, provides an example of that 'nobilmente' Englishness which we more readily associate with Elgar – and yet this music predates the *Pomp and Circumstance* marches by seventeen years. The ebullient coda, full of bold appoggiaturas and sequences, also seems to foreshadow the confident *Schwung* of Elgar's music and surely confirms the irrefutable stylistic and influential link between the two men.[5]

This opening concert continued with more rarities: the Cello Concerto by Delius – Raphael Wallfisch the masterly soloist; Grieg's *Norwegian Bridal Procession*, in the orchestration by Delius; and, perhaps asking too much of the young players, the Symphony No. 5 in D (*L'Allegro ed il Pensieroso*) by Stanford.

Wallfisch returned on Sunday morning to give an enthralling solo recital – Bach's Cello Suite No. 3 and the Sonata for unaccompanied cello by Kenneth Leighton (1929–1988). The venue, Gloucester's newly refurbished St Mary de Lode Church, is an ideal recital room for both Three Choirs and the Gloucester Music Society. Later in the day, coaches delivered a good-sized audience to Blaisdon Hall, a Victorian mansion set high over the Severn Vale in the west of Gloucestershire, a lovely setting for the Sorrel Quartet recital in which Parry's early String Quartet in G (played by the Almira Quartet at the 1995 Festival) was performed in company with Frank Bridge's *Three Idylls* and the Quartet in B flat major, op. 67, by Brahms. At the same time, back at St Mary de Lode, American mezzo-soprano Nora Sirbaugh, previously heard singing Gurney in

[4] *Independent*, 24 August 1998.
[5] Jeremy Dibble, programme note, Gloucester Festival programme book, 1998, p. 37.

1995(G), returned to Gloucester, this time to introduce a recital with pianist Roger Buckley. Their programme comprised songs by Delius, Balfour Gardiner, Frederic Austin and Roger Quilter, as well as settings of poems by the Gloucester-born poet W. E. Henley in the rarely heard song cycle *Love Blows as the Wind Blows* by George Butterworth.

FOLLOWING the success of the Philharmonia's participation in the 1995(G) Festival, it was decided for 1998(G) to discontinue the practice in Gloucester of dividing the Festival week into two halves, each with a different orchestra, and to engage the Philharmonia for the whole week. This proved to be a great success, not only in eliminating the difficulties of a mid-week, nocturnal changeover but also in engendering a greater sense of commitment on the part of the players, who were now able to settle into their task knowing that they were not to be uprooted after only three days in the west. The change also made economic sense for both the Philharmonia and the Festival and, given the consistently high standards of rehearsal and performance, David Briggs was soon to be heard heaping praise upon the Philharmonia as 'a gold-plated orchestra'! His recollections of preparing to rehearse with them in London are revealing:

> I remember sitting in the Novotel [hotel], Lambeth the night before rehearsing the Philharmonia for twenty-seven hours over the following three days, with a huge mound of full scores, and thinking 'oh my goodness, why am I putting myself through this?' It was a very daunting feeling indeed, leading up to standing on the rostrum for the first time, in front of an orchestra who had literally tens of thousands of hours of combined experience. I was grateful that I'd spent over 100 hours learning the scores, inside out. When it came to it, the sense of osmosis was palpable, and I think that no other experience has ever influenced me more, as a musician. It felt as if the players were actually 'inside' my head, and all that I had to do was imagine the sound, and it would happen. It has certainly influenced my playing as a Concert Organist, in a very real sense, particularly in terms of colour, rhythm and organic control of rubato.[6]

The fruits of our Philharmonia decision were already apparent at the Sunday evening choral and orchestral concert, in which David Briggs and Adrian Lucas shared the conducting honours. Beginning with Parry's *Blest Pair of Sirens*, the masterpiece hailed by Elgar as 'one of the noblest works of man', Briggs moved on to scale the heights of Delius's rapturous settings of poems by Ernest Dowson, *Songs of Sunset*, characterised by the Delius expert Lionel Carley as 'a requiem for lost love, a prolonged and profound reflection on the transience of life and the transience of human emotions'.

> They are not long, the weeping and the laughter,
> Love and desire and hate;
> I think they have no portion in us after
> We pass the gate.
> They are not long, the days of wine and roses;

---

[6] David Briggs, email to Anthony Boden, 10 December 2015.

Out of a misty dream our path emerges for a while,
Then closes within a dream.

As Martin Lee-Browne and Paul Guinery observe:

The instrumentation [of *Songs of Sunset*] is typically lavish for this period in Delius's career, and includes a family trio of oboe, cor anglais and bass oboe, whilst three bassoons are reinforced by a sarrusophone (the double bassoon being the practical substitute for that nowadays). On the other hand, the choral writing is less ambitious than in *A Mass of Life* and only rarely do the voices divide.[7]

The soloists in this performance were the Swedish mezzo-soprano Katarina Karneus, who in 1995 had won the Cardiff Singer of the World Competition, and the distinguished English baritone Peter Savidge, who, after the interval, returned to the platform as an excellent soloist in a spine-tingling performance of Walton's *Belshazzar's Feast* under the baton of Adrian Lucas.

The revelatory Three Choirs debut of the baritone Roderick Williams and his regular accompanist, Susie Allan, was made at St Mary de Lode Church in Gloucester on the morning of Monday 17 August 1998. Opening their recital with Schubert Lieder – settings of words by Goethe and Rückert – they continued with songs in Russian by Tchaikovsky, Rachmaninov and Shostakovich, and then returned to Rückert (the same poems chosen by Mahler for his *Rückertlieder* settings with orchestra) in *Five German Songs* by the Gloucester-based composer, pianist and organist Christian Wilson (1920–2014); these were followed by a group of English songs by Ireland, Gurney and Britten, and the recital ended with a setting of a poem by Roger McGough composed by Roderick Williams himself: 'I asked my lady'. (In 2005, Roderick Williams and Susie Allan recorded a number of songs by Ivor Gurney, Herbert Howells, John Sanders, Christian Wilson, and Ian Venables, including a number of première recordings.)[8]

A trumpet and piano recital at St Mary de Lode on Monday afternoon featured Gavin Wells (trumpet) and Christopher Boodle (piano). In addition to works by Handel, Ernst (arr. Bach), and Domenico Scarlatti, this included the first performance of Boodle's Trumpet Sonata, the Sonata for trumpet and piano by Halsey Stevens (1908–1989), and *Quatre Variations sur un thème de Domenico Scarlatti* by Marcel Bitsch (1921–2011).

An orchestral concert at Cheltenham Town Hall on Monday afternoon featured the Gloucestershire Symphony Orchestra conducted by Mark Finch, the first half of which was given over to two works by Hubert Parry: one, the *Overture to an Unwritten Tragedy*, thought (correctly) by Herbert Thompson, critic of the *Yorkshire Post*, to be 'suited admirably as a prelude to Shakespeare's *Othello*'; the other, the colourful, exuberant Piano Concerto in F sharp major (1880), with Anthony Goldstone (1944–2017) an ideal soloist. One member of the Cheltenham audience, delighted by the Parry Concerto, was overheard to say, 'Ah well, Parry was obviously influenced by the César Franck *Symphonic*

---

[7] Martin Lee-Browne and Paul Guinery, *Delius and his Music* (Boydell, 2014), p. 229.

[8] SOMM Recordings, 'Severn & Somme' (SOMMCD 057).

Variations' – an understandable comment given the comparably inventive élan of both works – except for the fact that the Parry Concerto actually pre-dated the Franck *Variations* by a full five years. 'This revival of what could be described as the first major Romantic British piano concerto', wrote Jeremy Dibble, 'has been long overdue.'[9]

The Monday evening concert ended with the first performance of a Festival commission, David Briggs's *Te Deum*, described in his words as a work 'permeated by the Gregorian chant setting of the text: strongly influenced by my own love of French orchestral and organ music, particularly Debussy, Ravel, Lili Boulanger, Messiaen, Duruflé and Cochereau'.[10] An undisguised Francophile, Briggs was no less committed on Monday evening when transferring from Berlioz and Debussy to tackle, in the presence of the composer, Howard Ferguson's moving and under-rated *Dream of the Rood*. On Tuesday evening, Briggs directed a fine performance of the Bach Mass in B minor; and then on Friday, in his own splendid organ transcription of Mahler's Symphony No. 5, revelled in post-Wagnerian romanticism.

As well as attending *The Dream of the Rood*, Howard Ferguson (1908–1999) was again present at St Matthew's Church, Cheltenham, on Wednesday afternoon, as was Michael Hurd (1928–2006), to hear Nora Sirbaugh, Ian Partridge and Roderick Williams as soloists with the Cheltenham Chamber Orchestra, conducted by Denise Ham, in a concert of British music that began with Parry's *English Suite*. Roderick Williams was the outstanding soloist in *Shore Leave*, a cycle of five songs for baritone and strings by Michael Hurd to words from Charles Causley's 1960 collection *Union Street*. Ian Partridge, whose recordings of Gerald Finzi's *Farewell to Arms*, op. 9, and *Two Milton Sonnets*, op. 12, can surely never be bettered, sang both works at this concert, which also included Finzi's Romance in E flat for strings, op. 11, and his orchestrations of Parry's 'When I survey the wondrous Cross' (no. 2 of the *Three Chorale Fantasias*), as well as the four of Ivor Gurney's *Five Elizabethan Songs* that were orchestrated by Finzi, beautifully sung by Nora Sirbaugh.

The orchestral concert on Wednesday evening presented a rare opportunity to hear the Philharmonia conducted by Richard Hickox in Parry's Symphony No. 4 in E minor, a stunning work, enriched by the brilliance and heroic sweep, the rhythmic hesitation, and the elegiac sound picture which we have come to recognise as 'Elgarian'. (Elgar, still an unknown at the age of thirty-four, was in the St James's Hall audience at the première of Parry's fourth symphony, conducted by its dedicatee, Hans Richter.) In Hickox's hands, the Three Choirs performance was a thrilling one, preceded by superb interpretations of Brahms's *Tragic Overture*, and Elgar's Violin Concerto with Tasmin Little an impeccable soloist.

Even before the orchestral concert had come to an end, a long queue was forming outside the cathedral. A late-night performance of Rachmaninov's Vespers, op. 17, had attracted a capacity audience – perhaps unsurprising as it was to be sung by the Corydon Singers directed by Matthew Best, whose recording of the Vespers is considered one of the finest interpretations of this sublime

[9] Dibble, programme note, Gloucester Festival programme book, 1998, p. 72.

[10] David Briggs, programme note, Gloucester Festival programme book, 1998, p. 78.

piece. Since leaving Cambridge, where he was a Choral Scholar at King's College, Matthew Best had pursued a dual career as conductor and bass singer, and it was in this latter capacity that he returned to the Festival two nights later to be heard as Gurnemanz, the shrewd old knight of the Holy Grail, in the first act of Wagner's *Parsifal*.

A DIVERSE and lengthy recital of British music given by pianist Margaret Fingerhut at St Mary de Lode Church on Thursday morning opened with Parry's *Theme and Nineteen Variations* in D minor; continued with the first performance of a piece commissioned by Margaret Fingerhut herself, Paul Spicer's *Pilgrimages* (after a poem of the same name by R. S. Thomas); the Piano Sonata No. 3 (1926) by Arnold Bax; *Six Fantasy Waltzes* by William Alwyn; and concluded with *Four Romantic Pieces*, op. 95, by Kenneth Leighton.

In the afternoon cathedral concert, the three cathedral choirs, directed by David Briggs, Roy Massey and Adrian Lucas, presented a richly varied programme including works by Delius (*To be Sung of a Summer Night on the Water*), Parry (*Songs of Farewell*), Patrick Gowers (*Viri galilaei*), Henryk Górecki (*Totus Tuus*), Arvo Pärt (*The Beatitudes*), and two pieces by Kenneth Leighton (*Paean* and *Let all the world in every corner sing*). David Briggs also conducted a work of his own, *The Music Mountain*, which, scored for two organs, chorus, treble and tenor, was commissioned in 1991 by the Three Spires Singers of Truro to mark their tenth anniversary.

Also on Thursday afternoon, at St Mary de Lode Church, three members of the Emerald Chamber Players – Roger Huckle (violin), Rachel Howgego (cello), and John Bishop (piano) – played familiar trios by Haydn and Mendelssohn and, between them, gave a brilliant performance of the virtually unknown but very fine Piano Trio in E minor (1877) by Hubert Parry.

Thursday ended with the first-ever Three Choirs performance of Berlioz's 'Dramatic Legend in Four Parts', *La Damnation de Faust*, which was first performed at the Opéra Comique in Paris, in concert form, in 1846. Two parts of the work were produced in London at Drury Lane in 1848 under Berlioz's direction, again in concert form, and the first complete concert performance in England was given at the Manchester Free Trade Hall in 1880. It proved very difficult to stage as an opera until, adapted by Raoul Gunsbourg, the first operatic performance was produced at Monte Carlo in 1893.

The inclusion in a Three Choirs programme of *The Damnation of Faust*, an exciting and challenging masterwork, was potentially controversial. However, the performance was a sell-out, the cast was of the first rank, and Gloucester Cathedral – with much-improved seating and platform arrangements – proved a near-ideal setting for a large-scale concert performance. In his *Guardian* review of 'Faust's journey to the Other Place', Barry Millington wrote that:

> In Berlioz's vision of damnation and redemption, the chorus adopt the personae of demons, soldiers, students, gnomes, sylphs and prying neighbours. The genteel ladies of the combined Festival Chorus adopted a hilariously coarse tone for the peasants by the wayside Cross; this was well-drilled choral singing in the best Three Choirs tradition.

Richard Edgar-Wilson had to do battle with a similarly taxing solo tenor part, rising to top C sharp, but he generally met the demands of this tough lyric role in style. Alan Opie's Mephistopheles was ideally minatory; Marguerite herself was sung by Ann Murray not with naïve wonder but with full-toned passion. Roderick Williams supplied an admirable Brander.

Under David Briggs's confident direction, the Philharmonia conjured everything from pastoral tranquillity to a hair-raising ride to the abyss.[11]

Cheltenham's nineteenth-century Pittville Pump Room was the venue for Friday morning's recital by The Chilingirian Quartet; their programme included string quartets by Delius and Grieg, and, with pianist Nigel Clayton, the three-movement Piano Quintet, op. 27, by Ian Venables, written in 1995 and commissioned from Kendall Wadley for performance at the 1996 Malvern Festival by the Duke Quartet and pianist Scott Mitchell. In the words of Graham Lloyd:

> Virgil Thompson wrote of Samuel Barber that he created 'Romantic music, predominantly emotional, embodying sophisticated workmanship and complete care … his melodic line sings and the harmony supports it.' This sentiment can equally be applied to Ian Venables, whose music, like Barber's, inhabits a deep sound world, dominated by individually crafted melodies and a rich and often sensuous harmonic palette.[12]

Venables's reputation was destined to continue on its deservedly upward trajectory: in 2016, in an edition of *Musical Opinion* that featured his portrait on the front cover, he was acclaimed as 'Britain's greatest living composer of art song'.[13] And more of Venables's music was included at Gloucester in 1998: on Friday afternoon his *Fantasy* was featured at St Mary de Lode in an oboe, viola and piano recital given by Diana Nuttall, Brian Schiele and Robin Hales that also included, *inter alia*, the delightful *Concerto da camera* by Michael Hurd in the version for oboe and piano.

DAVID Briggs made a most persuasive case for organ transcriptions on Friday afternoon. His dazzling organ recital in the cathedral included E. H. Lemare's transcription of the *Carnival Overture* by Antonín Dvořák and two transcriptions of Briggs's own: a Symphonic Scherzo *L'Apprenti sorcier* by Paul Dukas and an impressive arrangement of Gustav Mahler's mighty Symphony No. 5, a recording of which was released at the recital and awarded a five-star rating by the *BBC Music Magazine*: 'Briggs's arrangement … is splendid in every way, full of imaginative touches, thoroughly organistic, and performed here with an unerring sense of style and architectural proportion.' *Gramophone* magazine's review was equally complimentary: 'Briggs does it better than anyone else

---

[11] *Guardian*, review of 1998(G) performance of Berlioz, *The Damnation of Faust*.

[12] Graham J. Lloyd, liner note to SOMM Recording: Ian Venables, Piano Quintet, op. 27, etc. (SOMMCD 0101).

[13] *Musical Opinion*, no. 1506, Jan–Mar 2016, p. 9.

could; his performance is truly virtuosic, and Priory's recording of the stunning Gloucester organ is first-rate.'[14]

In his Three Choirs reminiscences, David has written of his Mahler transcription:

> Since the age of 14, I have been in love with the symphonies of Gustav Mahler. I'll never forget Mahler 8 in the 1986 Gloucester Festival, conducted by my distinguished and much loved predecessor, John Sanders. For me this was a completely life-changing experience. In the 1998 Festival I gave the first performance of my organ transcription of the Fifth Symphony. It was in the middle of an epic heatwave and I remember that most of the Philharmonia came to the concert. James Clarke (the incredibly supportive leader of the orchestra) said afterwards 'that was great, David: but I don't think we're out of a job just yet!'[15]

THE decision to present the whole of Act I of Wagner's *Parsifal* for the Friday evening choral and orchestral concert was a gamble. Extracts from *Parsifal* had been included at Three Choirs in the past, but a whole Act had not been attempted since 1911(w), when Act III was given. Born of an idea suggested by the then chairman of the Gloucester Festival Committee, Martin Lee-Browne, it was necessary to consider not only the cost and scale of such a production, including a cast of eleven singers and a large orchestra, but also the possibility that some of our Stewards and other regular attenders might dislike the inclusion of a Wagnerian music drama at Three Choirs. However, these fears were offset by a total confidence in our ability to present a successful concert performance under the direction of Richard Hickox – especially given the skill of the 'gold-plated' Philharmonia, our selected soloists, and, above all, the ability of the Festival Chorus.

Parsifal requires an atmosphere and singers suited to its solemn story, and both requirements could be met at Gloucester. As one writer expressed it in 1920, we 'should enter the auditorium as if passing through the doors of a cathedral, out of the glare and noise of the busy world. It is argued that to take one's luxurious seat in an opera house, pleasantly flushed with good cheer, is to assist at this work in a spirit at variance with its sacred import.'[16]

In the event, and as feared, a number of regular Festival-goers stayed away. However, the shortfall was much reduced by the attendance of a goodly number of Wagner enthusiasts. One of these, a member of the Wagner Society, sought me out to say that he had attended performances of *Parsifal* around the world over many years, including at Bayreuth, but that he had never heard a finer performance of Act I than this. The cast was as follows:

Kundry: Pamela Helen Stephen, mezzo-soprano
Parsifal: Adrian Thompson, tenor

[14] Priory Records Ltd: Gustav Mahler, Symphony No. 5 in C sharp minor, transcribed and played by David Briggs on the Organ of Gloucester Cathedral, 1998 (PRCD 649).

[15] Briggs, email to Boden, 10 December 2015.

[16] *Opera at Home* (The Gramophone Company Ltd, 1920), p. 266.

Amfortas: Alan Opie, baritone
Gurnemanz: Matthew Best, bass
First Knight: Ivan Sharpe, tenor
Second Knight: Roderick Williams, baritone
First Esquire: Nicki Kennedy, soprano
Second Esquire: Benedikte Moes, soprano
Third Esquire: Ian Yemm, tenor
Fourth Esquire: Henry Moss, tenor

Reviews were favourable, including from Barry Millington in the *Guardian*:

Neither Wagner's *Parsifal* nor Berlioz's *Damnation of Faust* was intended for a performance space quite like Gloucester Cathedral, but both lived triumphantly up to expectations as highlights of the 1998 Three Choirs Festival. *Parsifal* may have been intended for the mystically darkened auditorium of the Bayreuth Festspielhaus, though the looming vastness of Siena Cathedral also left its mark on the Grail scenes.

The no less breathtaking architecture of Gloucester may have encouraged Richard Hickox in the breadth and amplitude of his approach to Act I. Hickox's roots are in the Anglican cathedral tradition, but it is heartening to witness the command with which he tackles new territory like *Parsifal*. This was a deeply spiritual reading, patiently unfolding the long paragraphs with their shimmering coloration, piling on the agonies and the ecstasies of this anguished score, and responding to the climactic peaks with genuine empathy.

So intense was the spirituality, however, that the drama suffered. Whatever the overall pace, the action must never stand still, as it did here from time to time. The very protracted prelude also seemed to stretch the ensemble of the Philharmonia, which otherwise played superbly. Several of the soloists were charting new and exciting territory too. Matthew Best, for all his youth, has the gravity, wisdom and weight of tone for a magnificent Gurnemanz, all he lacks at the moment are the diction and animation of line so memorably demonstrated recently by John Tomlinson. The latter qualities were evident in Adrian Thompson's Parsifal – a lieder singer's intelligence allied to ample tone. I had thought that Pamela Helen Stephen might be too refined a mezzo for Kundry, but she found a highly convincing dusky tone colour for the wild woman.

The massed ranks of chorus suggested more an Elgarian Last Supper than a Wagnerian, but it was a glorious sound, as it had been the previous evening for Faust's journey to the Other Place.[17]

On the following morning, Saturday, our thoughts returned from the Knights of the Holy Grail and their stronghold high in the Pyrenees, to a choice between two recitals in the familiar surroundings of Gloucestershire. At St Mary de Lode, tenor Richard Edgar-Wilson and pianist Eugene Asti gave a recital of English song (Hubert Parry, Ivor Gurney and George Butterworth) and German Lieder (Robert Schumann's *Liederkreis*, op. 39, settings of poems by Eichendorff).

[17] *Guardian*, review of 1998(G).

In total contrast, at Prinknash Abbey, set in the wooded hills overlooking Gloucester, the Hungarian cimbalom player Viktória Herencsár and organist Malcolm Rudland presented a recital of works for each of their instruments, both separately and in combination. Organ solos included the Prelude and Fugue in A major (BWV 536) by Bach, and *Sportive Fauns* by the Hungarian-born organist–composer Dezsö Antalffy-Zsiross (1885–1945); Viktória Herencsàr played two cimbalom solos, by Liszt and Géza Allega, and joined Malcolm Rudland, who was born and bred in England but is half-Hungarian, to perform arrangements of works by Handel and Albinoni, *Secessionist Glass Windows* by Zoltán Györe (b. 1947), and the first performance of the Gregorian sketches *Vázlatok gregorián dallamokera* for organ and cimbalom by István Koloss (b. 1932). This composition, which uses four plainsong melodies, unfolds in four movements; helpfully and enjoyably, before the performance Dom Charles Watson of Prinknash taught the audience to sing the plainsong melodies from which the sketches were derived: *Veni creator Spiritus*, *Adore te devote*, *Ubi caritas* and *O filii et filae*.

After lunch, at Highnam Parish Church, the Chalumeau Wind Quintet was joined by Christopher Boodle (organ) in a programme that included works by Arrieu, Debussy, Ibert, Hindemith, Parry, and Gershwin – the latter in celebration of the centenary of his birth in 1898. Gershwin's music was also centre stage in a Swing Band concert performed at St Nicholas Church in the city by the Gloucestershire Youth Jazz Orchestra directed by Tony Sheppard.

The 1998 Festival ended on Saturday evening with a choral and orchestral concert in the cathedral which had, as its centrepiece, *The Soul's Ransom* by Sir Hubert Parry.

> Between 1898 and 1908 Parry embarked on a cycle of ethical oratorios. In these works he hoped to express the kernel of his artistic and philosophical beliefs strongly influenced by the moral values of Ruskin, the Utilitarian Rationalism of John Stuart Mill and the Social Darwinism of Herbert Spencer. This began with his cantata *A Song of Darkness and Light*, written for Gloucester in 1898, and concluded with *Beyond These Voices There Is Peace* [written] for Worcester (1908). Of all these works it was perhaps *The Vision of Life* (written for the Cardiff Festival in 1907), based on his own poem, that captured the essence of his humanitarian principles. But arguably most successful of all these reflective essays was *The Soul's Ransom: A Psalm for the Poor*, written for Hereford in 1906.[18]

Composed for soprano, bass, chorus and orchestra, *The Soul's Ransom* was performed by Anne Dawson, Mark Beesley, the Festival Chorus and the Philharmonia Orchestra under the direction of Roy Massey. The performance drew plaudits from the *Church Times*:

> On the last night came Roy Massey's inspired conducting of Parry's 45-minute 'ethical cantata', or 'Sinfonia Sacra', which Parry subtitled 'A Psalm for the Poor'. Dr Massey is a true professional when it comes to

[18] Dibble, programme note, Gloucester Festival programme book, 1998, p. 211.

this kind of stuff. Nursed and nurtured by him, the massive Three Choirs chorus served up its best offering of the week.[19]

The concert began and ended with masterpieces of ceremonial music: Handel's *Zadok the Priest* and Parry's *I was glad*. Following *The Soul's Ransom*, David Briggs took over from Roy Massey to direct a deeply moving performance of Elgar's *The Music Makers*, with Catherine Wyn-Rogers an inspiring mezzo-soprano soloist in a work that is itself a reflection on the theme of 'inspiration' – entirely fitting given that Parry's music was an inspiration to Elgar. The Festival as a whole was summed up enthusiastically in the *Independent* as a 'mind-boggling enterprise … framed by *Blest Pair of Sirens* and *I was Glad*. A humdinger of a week.'

A DRIAN Lucas, already very familiar to Three Choirs audiences, came fully into his own as Musical Director at Worcester in 1999, exactly 100 years after the debut of Sir Ivor Atkins. His goal to improve rehearsal arrangements and chorus cohesion has already been mentioned above, and he, like David Briggs, documented some recollections of his years with the Festival:

Orchestras

In my early years at the Festival, it was the practice to share the orchestral work between two main orchestras, certainly at Worcester. The Royal Liverpool Philharmonic Orchestra and Bournemouth Symphony Orchestra were engaged in 1999 partly, I gather, to alleviate issues of summer vacation and hours. At the point of changeover, where not only players but also music stands were moving swiftly in and out of the building, there was a noticeable tension in the air, and usually some comments flying about which pieces each ensemble were playing and which they might have liked to perform. Latterly, the Festival made a conscious decision to settle on one orchestra across the full week and across all three locations. This arrangement with the Philharmonia has now been operating solidly, I believe, since 2003 and was formalised in 2011, allowing much better opportunities for forward planning, as well as some leverage with a broader range of international conductors and soloists. The Philharmonia was always inspirational to work with, showing support and great musical insight across a great breadth of music genres and styles.

Cathedral Choirs and Chapters

The Festival started with the Cathedral Choirs and I felt a strong leaning towards bringing them back to the centre of the event. For many years, whilst an essential ingredient, they had become somewhat shadowed by the orchestral concerts with the Festival Chorus. Over the course of my 15 years with the Festival, I instigated a number of special showcase events to shine some light in their general direction. The opening night [Saturday] in 1999 saw the Cathedral Choirs with the Stan Tracey orchestra performing a Duke Ellington centenary concert with music from his *Sacred Concerts*, inevitably to the distaste of many of the older attendees, but hugely enjoyed by those present. The final item, *David Danced*, saw the assembled

---

[19] *Church Times*, 18 September 1998.

boy choristers dancing down the cathedral nave, following the spectacular hoofer, Will Gaines. Later that week, the choristers assembled to perform *Cassocks Away* in the Chapter House, where the main item was the musical *Nero* by Paul Drayton – a rare opportunity to hear the boys performing secular music. Latterly, there were regular late-night slots by the lay clerks of the three cathedral choirs, but it was a great achievement that in 2005 the BBC started to broadcast Choral Evensong regularly from the Festival.

Returning choristers and supervision

With the rise in levels of supervision for choristers, as well as the expectations of the choristers themselves, new ways were sought to find suitable staffing with local knowledge and plenty of energy. Where better to look than amongst former choristers? Over the years, it was with great pleasure that a number of former choristers returned from all three cathedrals to assist with these duties, allowing a degree of reunion previously difficult to achieve. Much of this was overseen by Clive Marriott, at the time Deputy Head of St Paul's Cathedral School and latterly Head of Salisbury Cathedral School. Clive brought a great deal of friendship and professionalism to the job and managed to strike the balance perfectly between hard work and good fun.[20]

ADRIAN Lucas's influence was apparent from the outset of the 1999 Worcester Festival. The Opening Service on Saturday afternoon, 21 August, ended with his own arrangement of the National Anthem; the Eucharist on Sunday morning included his *Sacerdotes Domini*, along with Howard Blake's *Festival Mass* and *Tu es Petrus* by Pierre Villette; and, on Saturday evening, he widened the Three Choirs experience with an adventurous departure from the norm: a jazz concert featuring soprano Tina May, baritone Niall Hoskin, tap dancer Will Gaines, actors Kevin Whately and Madelaine Newton (who are husband and wife), the three cathedral choirs, and the Stan Tracey Orchestra. The pieces performed were *Genesis*, a suite in seven parts by Stan Tracey, and Duke Ellington's *Heaven in Ordinarie* (see Adrian's comments above, on 'Cathedral Choirs and Chapters').

On Sunday afternoon, at Perrins Hall, Royal Grammar School, the Kingsdown Duo – Roger Huckle (violin) and John Bishop (piano) – gave a recital of English music including the very rarely heard Sonata in D major by Rutland Boughton, a work in which the movements are prefaced by quotations from Nietzsche's *Also Spake Zarathustra*. They also played Granville Bantock's Sonata No. 1 in G for violin and piano, and the *Three Pieces* for violin and piano, op. 11, by Ian Venables.

The cathedral concert on Sunday evening comprised two works: the sublime *Four Last Songs* by Richard Strauss and the large-scale *Te Deum* that Berlioz called the brother to his Requiem. The soloists were Judith Howarth, an effortless soprano in the Strauss, and Lynton Atkinson, a refulgent tenor in the Berlioz. They sang with the Festival Chorus, the cathedral choristers, the Festival

---

[20] Adrian Lucas, 'Three Choirs Festival Jottings for Anthony Boden' (personal communication).

Youth Chorus, the RLPO, and Adrian Lucas, who directed his vast forces with spirit and panache. It was a performance that he remembers well:

> The opening night [Sunday] of my first 'home' Festival involved Strauss's *Four Last Songs* and the mighty *Te Deum* of Hector Berlioz. In those days, we were still at the mercy of the ageing Bradford electronic organ in the nave, whose sound was rather uninspiring and lacking quality. However, the pipe organ in the quire was still playable, despite its various idiosyncrasies, and Berlioz was quite used to the problems of organs being remote from orchestral forces. The decision was made to use the pipe organ for this performance, though with a strongly worded warning in the programme book ['Members of the audience seated near the pipe organ should be aware that BOTH ORGANS WILL BE USED AT MAXIMUM VOLUME AT CERTAIN TIMES in an attempt to fulfil Berlioz' written instructions!']. For those seated towards the East end of the cathedral, the effect was quite astonishing: from here the sound of the orchestra was relatively remote, while the pipe organ was extremely close and potent in its volume. I am told that the second chord of the piece (organ alone after the initial orchestral *forte*) caused many in the audience to jump out of their seats![21]

The next morning, Monday, brought contrasts in both scale and repertoire in a concert featuring the Canadian choir 'Anna Magdalena' at the Countess of Huntingdon's Hall. Named after the manuscript notebook of music presented by J. S. Bach to his second wife, Anna Magdalena, in 1725, the choir – a group of thirty-six young lady members of the Vancouver Bach Choir – was formed in 1996. Directed by Bruce Pullan and accompanied by pianist Joyce Maguire, they presented a delightfully varied programme of works ranging through Bach, Purcell and Mozart; Schubert, Stanford and Britten; the *Missa brevis* (1995) by the Canadian composer Stephen Hatfield, and the first performance of a John Clare setting, *Song's Eternity*, for children's chorus (four-part) and piano by Mark Edgley Smith (1955–2008). Anna Magdalena also sang at the Tuesday evening concert in the cathedral.

Historic Pershore Abbey, a beautiful building with a perfect acoustic, was the venue for the afternoon concert given by the Fine Arts Brass Ensemble (two trumpets, a horn, a trombone and a tuba). Their programme included: an arrangement by trombonist Simon Hogg of the Prelude from Marc-Antoine Charpentier's *Te Deum*; the Violin Concerto in A minor (BWV 1041) by Bach (arr. Toreilles/Barre); *Music for His Majestie's Sackbuts and Cornets* by Matthew Locke; *Helensburgh Derive* (1992) by Gordon McPherson; an arrangement of a *canzona* by Giovanni Gabrieli; Elgar's *Chanson de matin*; Philip Flood's *Movement and Repose, in memoriam* Paul Clarke, former promotions manager of the Arts Council, a piece first performed at the 1992 Cheltenham Festival; and, finally, four songs by George Gershwin.

[21] Ibid.

THE artists in the Monday evening concert in the cathedral were Emma Silversides (soprano), the Festival Chorus and the RLPO, directed by Donald Hunt and David Briggs.

The first item, conducted by Dr Hunt, was something of a rarity: the *Benedicite* of 1929 by Vaughan Williams. Michael Kennedy wrote that the work

> combines lusty choral jubilation with a gentler hymn for soprano in pastoral style, and rather harsh, unrelenting orchestration – the piano is used as a percussive instrument – with 'a cappella' choral passages ... The work is essentially for wholehearted admirers of the composer, who relish its vigorous style ... and it is grand to sing ... Aaron Copland was present [at the première in 1931] and wrote afterwards of the work's 'bourgeois grandeur' and 'inherent banality' ... 'His [RVW's] is the music of a gentleman farmer, noble in inspiration but dull.' Mr Copland was young then, and he had the grace to eat his words in the light of later works.[22]

No such reservations could be applied to the next item on the programme, a performance marking the centenary of one of the glories of English music and an undoubted masterpiece: Elgar's *Enigma Variations*. The conductor was Donald Hunt, whose excellent book, *Elgar and the Three Choirs Festival*, was published in timely fashion to coincide with 1999(w) Festival week.

IN the course of a lengthy and penetrating programme note, the newly appointed editor of the Worcester programme book, David Harrison, reopened the long-argued question of the 'Enigma':

> [It] is one that has concentrated the minds of musicians the world over. Elgar had indicated that over the main theme there ran another, but steadfastly refused to give any hint of what it might be. 'Old Lang Syne won't do', was the terse reply to an early suggestion and seems to be about the nearest he got to giving any kind of clue. The solution to one of the most famous puzzles in music remains as elusive as the Loch Ness Monster. Whatever the answer, Elgar was devoted to his 'japes', and it would have pleased him enormously to think that he had set the world a brain-teaser that would run and run.

Soon after the 1999(w) Festival, while working on a biography of Thomas Tomkins, I met and befriended Professor Denis Stevens (1922–2004), musicologist, conductor, champion of Claudio Monteverdi, and a Tomkins expert. He too had set his mind to a reassessment of Elgar's 'Enigma'. Three years before his death, Stevens set down his conclusions in writing, and for me his theory remains the most persuasive of many:

> Here ... we are faced with a theme that does not occur at the beginning of a melody. It is heard in the middle. It has to combine with harmonies in the major and minor and go with both. A clue as to the source was given by Elgar in the notes he fed to the writer of the Crystal Palace concert programme when the piece was first performed in 1899: 'The principal

---

[22] Michael Kennedy, *The Works of Ralph Vaughan Williams* (OUP, 1964), pp. 225–6.

theme never appears.' Elgar loved a play on words. Did he not rather mean, 'The principal theme, NEVER, appears'?

What then is NEVER? It was an interpolation by Arne into his famous song: 'Rule Britannia, Britannia rule the waves, for Britons NEVER, NEVER, NEVER shall be slaves.' The phrase is set to the notes B G C♯ A D♯; in the minor, B-flat, G C♯ A D♯. This tiny phrase appears in all the variations as well as in the theme.[23]

Denis Stevens's theory also provides an answer to the question asked of Elgar by Dora Penny, 'Dorabella' of Variation X, on a visit to the Elgars at Craeg Lea in 1899. She had asked 'what *was* the tune that "goes and is not played"?' But Elgar told her that she must find it out for herself, saying 'I thought you, of all people, would guess it.'

Could it be that young 'Dorabella' had gained admission to 'the friends pictured within' because her surname, Penny, was linked in Elgar's mind to the (pre-decimal) penny coin, the reverse of which featured a seated image of Britannia with spear and shield?

THE last item in the concert, Poulenc's powerful *Stabat Mater*, scored for large choir and full symphony orchestra, was conducted by David Briggs. Poulenc wrote no music for the Church before August 1936 but, having heard that a close friend – the young composer and music critic Pierre-Octave Ferroud – had been killed in a car accident, he made a pilgrimage to the remote shrine of the Black Madonna of Rocamadour in the south of France. This journey proved to be a turning point in Poulenc's life, prompting him to compose *Litanies à la Vierge Noire*, a short but sublime piece based on the prayers of pilgrims, and suffused with a deep sense of loss. It was to be heard in a concert given by the three cathedral choirs on Tuesday afternoon. Before it, at 11.00 a.m. in the Countess of Huntingdon's Hall, the superb Florestan Trio (Anthony Marwood, violin; Richard Lester, cello; and Susan Tomes, piano) had performed the Piano Trio in B flat major by Schubert and the Trio *élégiaque* in D minor by Rachmaninov.

Christopher Robinson, the then Organist and Director of Music at St John's College, Cambridge, who had directed music at Worcester Cathedral and at Three Choirs from 1963 until 1975, returned to Worcester on Tuesday afternoon to conduct the three cathedral choirs, the English String Orchestra, and soloists Sally Bruce-Payne (mezzo-soprano) and Roderick Williams (baritone) in Poulenc's aforementioned *Litanies à la Vierge Noire*, scored for a choir of women's voices and orchestra. It was a disappointing performance. The choristers of the three cathedrals, who took the place of the ladies, missed their first entry and, to Christopher Robinson's evident consternation, all too clearly struggled thereafter. Fortunately, this ill-starred ten minutes was followed by polished performances of Schönberg's haunting *Verklärte Nacht* and the Requiem by Maurice Duruflé.

On Tuesday evening Mark Elder (who was knighted in 2008), conducted the Philharmonia Orchestra, the Festival Chorus, the Festival Youth Chorus, the cathedral choristers and the Canadian group Anna Magdalena in a stunning

[23] Denis Stevens, *Fragmenta autobiographica* (Schola Antiqua Press, 2001), p. 24.

performance of Mahler's vast Symphony No. 3, with Catherine Wyn-Rogers a warmly sensitive mezzo-soprano soloist. This was a momentous and unforgettable occasion, marking the Three Choirs debuts of both the symphony and the conductor.

One of the longest symphonies ever written, Mahler's Symphony No. 3 is also scored for one of the largest orchestras. Mahler gave descriptive titles to the movements. There were originally intended to be seven, but the last, 'What the child tells me', based on Mahler's *Wunderhorn* song *Das himmlische Leben*, was later transferred to the fourth symphony as the Finale. The final programme for the third symphony is therefore:

I   Pan awakes – summer marches in.

II   What the flowers in the meadow tell me.

III What the beasts in the wood tell me.

IV   What Man tells me.

V   What the angels tell me.

VI   What love tells me.

'Mahler had contemplated calling the symphony *Pan*, or even *The Joyful Science*, after Nietzsche's book *Die fröliche Wissenschaft* ... These titles are pointers, no more: the symphony is an exultant celebration of life, physical and spiritual, sensuous and animal.'[24] Given a great performance such as this was, it is a celebration which vindicates the maxim that all great music is a force for good.

THE next morning, Wednesday, the Brodsky Quartet, in their memorable recital at the Countess of Huntingdon's Hall, gave a performance of works by Stravinsky, Britten and Elgar. At the same time in Tewkesbury Abbey, Adrian Lucas, playing the historic 'Milton' Organ, gave a recital that included Ian Venables's Rhapsody for Organ, op. 25, Elgar's Sonata in G major, op. 28, *Three Miniatures* by Herbert Sumsion, and the *Toccata in memoriam Brian Runnett* by Patrick Gowers (1936–2014).

The English Symphony Orchestra conducted by William Boughton presented a programme of English music in the cathedral on Wednesday afternoon, including Benjamin Britten's suite on English folk tunes *A time there was* ...; *The Walk to the Paradise Garden* by Delius; Vaughan Williams's Symphony No. 5; and, with pianist David Owen Norris, *Fragments of Elgar* by Robert Walker (b. 1946). This last was a realisation of the sketches, drafts and a recording of half an hour of music improvised at the piano by Elgar. These ideas for a piano concerto had been begun by Elgar in 1913, but, though he continued sketching it in his final years, he left no hint of how the separate elements could fit together, and never completed the work. Robert Walker's realisation had been commissioned by Gavin Henderson for the Dartington International Summer School, and his score was first performed in the Great Hall, Dartington, on 17 August 1997, by David Owen Norris and the Dartington Festival Orchestra conducted by Graeme Jenkins.

---

[24] Michael Kennedy, *Mahler*, The Master Musicians Series (J. M. Dent, 1974), p. 125.

Following its Three Choirs outing at Worcester, *Fragments of Elgar* was performed in Canada and the Netherlands, all the time being revised and polished. In his programme essay for the Worcester performance, Walker had written of the *Fragments*: 'This should be stressed with all force: this is NOT Elgar's Piano Concerto and should never be referred to as such.'[25] Seven years later, when Walker's work was concluded and his score recorded by David Owen Norris and the BBC Concert Orchestra conducted by David Lloyd-Jones, the CD was released under the title: *Sir Edward Elgar: The Sketches, Drafts and Recordings of his Piano Concerto, realised for performance by Robert Walker.*[26]

INTERNATIONALLY recognised as a conductor of the highest stature, Leonard Slatkin took up the position of Principal Guest Conductor of the Philharmonia Orchestra at the beginning of the 1997/8 season. In this role, he came to Worcester on Wednesday 25 August 1999 to direct a performance of Elgar's *The Kingdom*, a work that he had recorded for RCA Victor in 1988. At Worcester his soloists were Jennifer Bates, Sally Burgess, John Mark Ainsley and Peter Savidge; his choir, the Festival Chorus. A knowledgeable audience, steeped in Elgarian tradition, filed into a packed cathedral – and their expectations were entirely fulfilled.

Charles Owen, a pianist of rapidly rising reputation, was the dazzling young soloist at a recital in the Countess of Huntingdon's Hall on Thursday morning, in a programme featuring pieces by Schubert, Chopin, Poulenc and Debussy. A busy and popular performer, Charles Owen is now (2016) Professor of Piano at the Guildhall School of Music and Drama in London.

Two contrasting concerts were scheduled for Thursday afternoon: at Great Witley Church the five musicians of Florilegium (flute/recorder, oboe, violin, cello and harpsichord) performed music of the eighteenth century, including pieces by Telemann, Fischer, Vivaldi, J. C. Bach, J. S. Bach and Vivaldi; while at the Countess of Huntingdon's Hall, Brian Davis (harp) and Daniel Phillips (organ) explored a wide range of pieces from both the classical and romantic periods.

The evening concert in the cathedral included the Festival Commission: *A Song for the End on the World* by Francis Pott. It was conceived many years previously as a Requiem alternating poetic texts with those of the mass, but, as the composer explained in his programme notes:

> Much changed in the making. *A Song on the End of the World* now takes from liturgical sources only the *Agnus Dei* and *Recordare, Jesu Pie*. Our pre-Millennial media, however, present us daily with inextricably linked

---

[25] Robert Walker, Worcester Festival programme book, 1999, pp. 156–9.

[26] Dutton Digital Epoch, *Sir Edward Elgar: The Sketches, Drafts and Recordings of his Piano Concerto, realised for performance by Robert Walker*, played by David Owen Norris (piano) and the BBC Concert Orchestra conducted by David Lloyd-Jones (CDLX 7148). The CD also includes (with the BBC Singers) Elgar's *Spanish Serenade*, op. 23, 'The Immortal Legions' (from *Pageant of Empire*) and *So Many True Princesses* (orch. Anthony Payne); other works by Elgar orchestrated by Haydn Wood and Henry Geehl; and the *Elegy in Memory of Edward Elgar* by Anthony Collins.

images of communal mourning and the incitement to ethnic vengeance (drowning the pleas for peace of those who have not so suffered). Inasmuch as *A Song on the End of the World* both embodies these and presumes by its choice of texts to articulate a renewed protest against the horrors of our age, it remains a Requiem of sorts.[27]

That choice of texts is extensive and includes quotations from George Mackay Brown, William Blake, Czesław Miłosz, Georg Heym (translated by Patrick Bridgewater), Isaac Rosenberg, Thomas Merton, Randall Jarrell, Mervyn Peake, Thomas Traherne, Dylan Thomas and Charles Causley, as well as from Psalms 22, 130 and 139.

The Francis Pott world première performance was preceded by Szymanowski's *Stabat Mater* and the Concerto for two pianos by Poulenc. The singers were Judith Howarth (soprano), Sarah Fryer (mezzo-soprano) and William Clements (bass); the piano duo partners in the Poulenc Concerto were Nicola and Alexandra Bibby; the Festival Chorus and Philharmonia Orchestra were conducted by Roy Massey in the Szymanowski, and by Adrian Lucas in the works by Poulenc and Pott. Barry Millington, who attended for the *Guardian*, penned an enthusiastic review:

> The penultimate concert featured an enterprising commission from the composer Francis Pott, prefaced by an unobvious pairing of works by Poulenc and Szymanowski. When in sacred mode, both the Frenchman and the Pole are liable to ravish the ear with textures of shameless sensuality, though on this occasion the Poulenc was his Concerto for Two Pianos, a jovial, effervescent piece that makes no pretence of sacred aspirations. Nicola and Alexandra Bibby caught the mood of droll wit, complete with Mozartian pastiche, and Lucas and the Philharmonia accompanied ably.
>
> Szymanowski's *Stabat Mater*, for all its heartwarming sonorities, sets the far from frivolous medieval sequence of texts depicting the grief of the Virgin Mary. There is a powerful expressive punch to be packed here, as Roy Massey and the Festival Chorus with soloists Judith Howarth, Sarah Fryer and William Clements, demonstrated. However, even Szymanowski's grandiose gestures were outstripped in the Pott commission, entitled *A Song on the End of the World*. This juxtaposes verse by poets as diverse as Blake, Dylan Thomas, Mervyn Peake and Georg Heym with Psalms and other liturgical quotations, but musically there are throwbacks to both the English pastoralist tradition and even the choruses, angelic and demonic, of Elgar's *Gerontius*. The idiom is contemporary and original, and Pott's response to the graphic imagery of his selected verse – sustained over an hour in seven movements – is impressive and profoundly affecting.
>
> The splendid Festival Chorus was given some thrilling music in the fourth section (Heym) and the sixth (Peake), the wind and brass unleashing apocalyptic counterblasts. Pott's new work is unfashionably ambitious. The Festival's faith in him was amply rewarded.[28]

[27] Francis Pott, programme note, Worcester Festival programme book, 1999, p. 198.

[28] *Guardian*, review of 1999(w).

And so we came to the last day of the 1999(w) Festival, starting with a superb chamber recital given at the Countess of Huntingdon's Hall by the renowned Brodsky Quintet. Both halves of their programme contained a *Quartettsatz* in C minor by Schubert (D703 before the interval, D103 after it), and a String Quintet by Mozart (K514 before the interval, K515 after it). In the afternoon the focus transferred to Hartlebury Castle, where the Gentlemen of St John's, a vocal ensemble comprising the alto, tenor and bass choral scholars, and the organ scholars of the choir of St John's College, Cambridge, impressed and entertained with a programme that ranged from *The Lamentations of Jeremiah* by Tallis to works by Delius, Vaughan Williams, Poulenc and Finzi.

The last night was given over to a thrilling, unashamedly operatic and perennially favourite work: the *Messa da Requiem* by Giuseppe Verdi. Only a handful of choral/orchestral works can guarantee a packed cathedral – and the Verdi Requiem is most certainly one of them. In 1999 the soloists were Sarah Leonard, Catherine Wyn-Rogers, William Kendall and Matthew Best, and the splendid Festival Chorus and Philharmonia Orchestra were directed with spirited finesse by Adrian Lucas.

24

A New Millennium

As the Festival passed over its third new-century boundary, it was becoming clear to some within the organisation that the model that had served it so well for so long was perhaps beginning to creak. For how long could the Festival remain as tripartite as it was, with its three local committees operating almost entirely autonomously under the delegated authority from the legal entity – the Three Choirs Festival Association? Granted, the Artistic Directors met from time to time, over a slap-up lunch in the Feathers in Ledbury, and the Association fulfilled its legal oversight functions in signing off both Festival programmes and budgets, but the music world was changing. Costs, both artistic and logistical, were rising, and the Festival was beginning to ask itself where the money was going to come from in the future, and indeed how best to manage itself. As annual budgets ticked past half a million pounds, with a little over half of that coming in as ticket revenue, key to the Festival's future was not only sponsorship, but also the prudent management of Festival resources.

The Festival Society held the organisation's reserves, which were not insubstantial, but which were very unevenly distributed, mainly down to substantial legacies given for the benefit of one or other city. Understandably, of course, local volunteer treasurers, who were taking on the direct management of very large sums, were defensive about 'their' money, and local committees tended to work in their own way, towards their own festival. This is not to say that the cities were hostile to each other, simply that their focus was continually on their own year, in their own milieu, with their own people. This is what had worked for many years, and arguably what made Three Choirs the entity that it was, with the clear individuality of each city and cathedral, and a particular identity recognised by audience and volunteer alike. However, there was a growing feeling that there could be potential benefits from more integration.

The audience base was becoming more diverse – undoubtedly a good thing – but at the price of a continuing decline in stewardship numbers. Fewer and fewer people were coming to the Festival for the week, and this slowly began to have a profound impact on audience expectation regarding the concert experience. The focus on driving up artistic standards was clear, as was the recognition that with artists and orchestras of higher standing also comes higher cost. However, the new tendency for concert-goers to come to Festival events for just one or two days brought with it additional challenges, involving issues as wide-ranging as audience comfort in the venues, standards and availability of catering, and even the provision of toilet facilities. In broadening its reach, the Festival began to put itself in comparison with the purpose-built concert spaces in, for example, Birmingham and Cardiff (both within two hours' drive of any of the three cities), as well as the recognised halls in Cheltenham and Malvern. The days were passing in which Three Choirs audiences would 'grin and bear it', or see such compromises as 'part of the charm'; their passing was hastened by the financial imperative to increase ticket prices, particularly for the prized nave seats, as higher costs inevitably upped the expectations of the non-seasoned Festival goer. The drive to raise artistic standards had knock-on effects here, too: Artistic Directors secured more rehearsal time, both before and during Festival week, the latter limiting the time available for performance in the cathedral spaces.

It was in this context that, in early 2001, the Festival's first abortive attempt at some form of centralisation took place: an effort to appoint a central administrator. The three local administrators were interviewed, but the panel could not agree on any one of them taking up a central role, or indeed how it should be paid for, and the proposal was shelved. This did not stop some inside the organisation making the argument, particularly as the average term of an administrator decreased, that the continual 'reinvention of the wheel' year on year, both between Festivals in one city and across the three cities, was not a process that could continue indefinitely.

T HE first Festival of the new millennium was to be Roy Massey's last home Festival as Organist of Hereford Cathedral before he retired from the post at Easter the following year, following a tenure of twenty-six years, and nine Hereford Festivals as Artistic Director. What could be a more 'Three Choirs' finale than a centenary-marking performance of *Gerontius*, with Catherine Wyn-Rogers, Adrian Thompson and James Rutherford?

> There was a great sense of occasion in the packed Hereford Cathedral. Festival Choruses are smaller these days but that didn't take anything away from the passion of the singing of those opening Kyries.
>
> Perhaps as we are getting used to smaller Messiah choirs, even Elgar works will have smaller choral resources? This Festival chorus were soon giving us all the feelings for the poor dying Gerontius, and in this the Bournemouth Symphony Orchestra were well attuned in their accompaniment. They had given a splendid Prelude ...
>
> It was in every sense a Three Choirs Festival Performance. The audience willed it to succeed and succeed it did. The great sounds created by the semi-chorus and then the tutti dynamics of all resources will ever move us ... they did last week.[1]

Choruses were indeed getting smaller, partly due to health and safety restrictions on the number of people on the platforms, but also for artistic reasons. Over the following years, particularly with the arrival of new Artistic Directors at both Hereford and Gloucester, the raising of chorus standards was a key focal point for development.

In many ways, the 2000(H) programme typifies Massey's years in charge at Hereford, and his skilful art in satisfying the public's taste for the known while also encouraging and facilitating performances of the unknown. Nowhere was this more visible than in Monday evening's cathedral programme, which combined the richness and beauty of Vaughan Williams's *Serenade to Music* and

[1] *Hereford Times*, 31 August 2000.

the emotional drive of Elgar's Cello Concerto (with Raphael Wallfisch as soloist) with a new work for soloists, chorus and orchestra by Francis Grier – *Around the Curve of the World*. This cantata celebrates the 150th anniversary of the journeys to New Zealand of the so-called Canterbury Pilgrims, led by John and Robert Godley, and their correspondence forms part of Sue Mayo's libretto.

> Woven into the work's psalms and canticles are the universal themes of emigration, pilgrimage, diaspora, exile and new homelands. … The journey is treated on many levels. There is the reality of the daring and gruelling sea voyage. This is the dimension of religious quest and pilgrimage, which becomes another central level of interpreting the voyage and which has prompted the librettist to start each narrative section with a well-known biblical text.
>
> In addition to a purely religious interpretation – and intermingling with it – there is a psychological perspective to the Journey: one might say that all the struggles and conflicts, which the travellers contend, symbolise their inner emotional journey.[2]

An ambitious, hour-long piece, subtitled 'A musical parable for the new millennium', *Around the Curve of the World* draws musically on both free-rhythmed psalmic material and a more dramatic, almost Britten-esque language. However, attractive though parts of the piece undoubtedly are, and though it was assisted by some fine solo singing from the tenor Daniel Norman in particular, there were reservations expressed about the exclusively Western, rather colonial, tone of the libretto; others were unconvinced by the music itself, including Douglas Drane, writing in the *Hereford Times*: 'The libretto deserved better music than this score. Much too long, with Grier's persistent use of "harmonised" plainsong. It was tedium ad nauscam.'[3]

Thursday's evening concert was another case of Massey's programming flair, here combining the verve and drive of twentieth-century American music – Bernstein's ebullient *Chichester Psalms* alongside Copland's ballet suite *Appalachian Spring* – with Stravinsky's *Firebird* suite and a newly commissioned work by Judith Bingham: *Otherworld*. This last piece was jointly commissioned by the Three Choirs Festival (with funding from West Midlands Arts) and the Minnesota-based Plymouth Music Series, one of the foremost choral organisations in America. As Bingham herself wrote in her accompanying programme note:

> In writing a piece for the start of the third millennium, I wanted not only to try and embrace as large a range as I could of literature in the choice of texts, but also look beyond the planet for the subject. I was kick-started by two things: firstly, pictures from the Hubble telescope, and secondly a little booklet on how the ancient Egyptians believed that the souls of the Pharaohs went on testing star journeys after death, ending up, hopefully,

---

[2] Composer's programme note, Hereford Festival programme book, 2000, p. 78. Copies of all the Festival programme books cited in this chapter are held in the Three Choirs Festival Office, Gloucester.

[3] *Hereford Times*, 24 August 2000.

as stars themselves. This gave me the starting point for a piece about star journeys, both real and symbolic, and the mystery and immensity proved a wonderful symbol for the elusiveness of truth and God.[4]

True to her word, the texts are varied, from an ancient Egyptian religious poem (which is strikingly similar to the Christian Creed), through twelfth-century Sufi mysticism and the Emperor Hadrian to the American poet Jerome Rothernberg's translation of a Passamaquoddy Indian ritual. This diversity is mirrored in the musical material, incorporating off-stage chorus, tubular bells and a wind machine, held together by the continual return of a ritualistic timpani part, and concluding in dance-like mystic positivity. Paul Conway reviewed the concert for the *Independent*:

> Otherworld is a substantial work (lasting about 35 minutes), and instantly communicative. Roy Massey, conducting the Festival Chorus and the Bournemouth Symphony Orchestra, gave the piece a solid first performance, while leaving room for future readings to draw out the myriad magical elements in the score with even greater empathy.[5]

Adrian Lucas shared the podium with Roy Massey for this concert, taking charge of an 'exuberant' reading of Bernstein, a 'tuneful' *Appalachian Spring*, and a 'vibrant' *Firebird*, with both Festival Chorus and Bournemouth Symphony Orchestra on fine form.[6] Lucas indeed recalls the Stravinsky as one of the highlights of his Festival career.[7]

The other significant première of the week came in Wednesday evening's cathedral concert with the Bournemouth Symphony Orchestra under the baton of Paul Daniel. Kenneth Leighton's Concerto for oboe and strings (1953) was written shortly after the composer's spell studying in Rome under Goffredo Petrassi. It conspicuously shows the hallmarks of that period, perhaps to the dismay of his mentor, Gerald Finzi, who expressed reservations about the piece, and avoided programming it. However, unlike many other 'rediscovered' works, this piece was not lost, or forgotten, but simply filed away by the composer as 'a piece rooted in a very specific time and stage in his life'.[8] Formally, it is a traditional piece, but one that avoids the overt virtuosity of many concertos, while giving the player license to explore the expressive and technical potential of the instrument.

> The soloist's opening rhapsodic theme establishes the prevailing mood of the concerto (a mercurial juxtaposition of the lyrically contemplative and the intensely passionate) while the central lento molto is the emotional core of the work: soloist Virginia Shaw expertly charted the music's brooding inner landscape. A brief but enjoyably skittish finale brings this eloquent work to a satisfying close. The Bournemouth strings, under Paul

---

[4] 2000(H) programme book, p. 185.

[5] *Independent*, 27 August 2000.

[6] *Hereford Times*, 31 August 2000.

[7] 'Festival Reflections' – a short note to the authors by Adrian Lucas.

[8] Stephen Jackson, 2000(H) programme book, p. 158.

Daniel provided a sympathetic accompaniment for Virginia Shaw, whose musicianship shone through in this belated but welcome addition to the genre.[9]

Having opened with a lively account of Sir Arthur Bliss's *Introduction and Allegro*, this fine orchestral evening concluded with a first Three Choirs performance of Anthony Payne's realisation of Elgar's Symphony No. 3, to a packed house. The story of the sketches is well known – the few pages of full score, and various snatches of ideas that the veteran composer jotted down in the final year of his life, but knew he would not be able to complete. After various abortive attempts, notably by senior figures at the BBC, the Elgar family finally decided to commission Anthony Payne to make an authorised version. Payne later wrote:

> It was during this process that I became more consciously aware of the overall sweep of the symphony. It was different in its sheer breadth of emotion from any of his other symphonic works: there was the raw vigour and magic lyricism of the opening movement, the use of a lighter manner in the second which went far beyond his established symphonic practice, and the searing intensity of the Adagio, tragic in its import, while the finale revealed a world of chivalric action and drama.[10]

The 'enthusiastic welcome' expressed by the audience on the symphony's *pianissimo* tam-tam conclusion was not only testament to Paul Daniel's 'flawless performance', but also recognition that 'Payne had communed, as it were, with our favourite composer and what we heard was very good.'[11]

Less successful, perhaps, though not for the expected reasons, was Wednesday afternoon's *St John Passion*, with the three cathedral choirs and Roy Goodman's period-instrument Brandenburg Consort. An excellent roster of soloists, including a characteristically forthright Evangelist in Rogers Covey Crump, a carefully measured Stephen Varcoe as Christ, and fine singing from Emma Kirkby, Robin Blaze, Michael George and William Kendall, should have made this a definitive tribute, marking 250 years since the death of J. S. Bach. However, confusion reigned in the audience as the alternative order of words was used, which differed significantly from the order printed in the Festival programme book, while the correct order was not distributed to many until the interval. Though in one sense one can simply sit back and allow the great music to speak, the narrative drive in *St John Passion* is so strong that missing the story rather risks missing the point.

No such troubles dogged Roy Massey's opening night *Creation*, which was 'magnificent in every way', with 'first class accompaniment by the Orchestra of St John's, Smith Square' and a Festival Chorus 'as good as you can get';[12] the performance also included memorable singing from Ruth Holton, James Oxley and Robert Rice. John Lubbock's orchestra excelled themselves here, and in their

[9] Paul Conway, *Independent*, 27 August 2000.
[10] Notes to NMC recording D053.
[11] *Hereford Times*, 31 August 2000.
[12] *Hereford Times*, 24 August 2000.

two other engagements: the Opening Service and an orchestral programme the following day at Wyastone Concert Hall. This latter concert consisted mainly of staples of the English repertoire – Vaughan Williams's *Fantasia on a Theme by Thomas Tallis*, and Elgar's *Serenade* and *Introduction and Allegro* – alongside a new work by Jeremy Lubbock (*Dialogue for Viola and Strings*, featuring Jane Atkins), and Laurence Ashmore's arrangement of Finzi's evergreen *Five Bagatelles*.

A hugely varied daytime recital programme took Festival-goers through experiences as diverse as music from the French court of the Sun King, Louis XIV, through the humour and wit of modern writing for Brass Quintet, via Emma Kirkby's lute-song recital, French impressionism with Cécile Ousset at the piano, and the drama of Olivier Latry's Widor on the cathedral organ. Particular mention perhaps should be made of Thursday morning's cathedral concert given by the Joyful Company of Singers, under their founder and director, Peter Broadbent. Few choirs can bring off entirely *a cappella* performances on this scale, not least when they include Bach motets alongside contemporary music, as well as a fine account of Copland's Genesis setting *In the Beginning*.[13]

AFTER the European grandeur of the 1998 Gloucester Festival, with its inclusion of Berlioz and Wagner, the 2001(G) programme was always going to take a different path. Gloucester chairman, Martin Lee-Browne, put it thus in his foreword to the 2001 programme book: 'The first year of the new Millennium seems to be an appropriate occasion for celebrating the wealth of music that has been written in the British Isles since Tudor times.'[14] The Festival included works by no fewer than twenty-five British composers, beginning with William Byrd and ending with the millennial piece *Creation* by David Briggs, and a new commission for the three cathedral choirs from former Artistic Director John Sanders: *Urbs Beata*. It was also to be David Briggs's last Festival as Artistic Director, as he took the decision in the period following the Festival to pursue his freelance career as a concert organist and composer.

After the success of engaging one orchestra for the whole week in 1998, the Philharmonia returned to Gloucester and, breaking with established tradition, it was they who opened the first night, with an orchestral programme conducted by Richard Hickox. The concert was an interesting combination of the extremely popular (Vaughan Williams's *Fantasia on a Theme by Thomas Tallis*, and Elgar's Symphony No. 2) with the first public performance of *Whispers of Heavenly Death* by Vaughan Williams, and a rare outing for Granville Bantock.

> Any pretence at objectivity about RVW's immortal *Tallis Fantasia* in the setting and acoustic it was written for would be futile – Hickox's measured pace was just right, and the effect was sublime and indescribably moving. Immediately afterwards, we were treated to the remarkable experience of a Vaughan Williams world première – after 93 years languishing in an attic,

---

[13] The contemporary music at this concert included recent works by Judith Bingham – *The Drowned Lovers*, a reworking of Stanford's famous *Bluebird* – and Anthony Payne – *Break, Break, Break* – commissioned by the Spitalfields and Cheltenham Festivals in 1996.

[14] Foreword to Gloucester Festival programme book, 2001, p. 4.

his setting of Walt Whitman's 'Whispers of Heavenly Death' was sung by mezzo Pamela Helen Stephen. And most extraordinary it was too.

Then, at last, an airing for Granville Bantock's 'Sappho' of 1906. Once very much a force to be reckoned with, Bantock's work has been virtually eclipsed in recent years. Judging from this prelude and selection of songs this is unfair. These settings of sultry lyrics by the poetess of Lesbos would have had the founders of Three Choirs spinning in their graves. Pamela Stephen gave a committed and vocally svelte performance of this lusciously scored music.[15]

Michael Kennedy, writing in the *Sunday Telegraph*, while 'fascinated' to hear a new insight into the evolution of Vaughan Williams's developing style (the song manuscript is dated January 1908 – presumably shortly before he began his studies with Ravel), was less convinced by the Bantock songs, describing them as 'opulently scored but fatally deficient in variety of mood and tempo'.[16] More telling generally, however, and an observation which will doubtless resonate with generations of Festival goers, was this:

> the impact of all the works I heard was intensified by the cathedral's acoustics. To hear the *Tallis Fantasia* in the building for which it was written and to undergo the ecstasies and agonies of Elgar's Second Symphony amid these pillars and arches is an experience unique to the Three Choirs and something no other British festival can rival.[17]

A large proportion of Sunday's programming was devoted to the music of Frederick Delius, beginning with two sets of songs performed in a recital at St Mary de Lode Church by the mezzo-soprano Helen Withers and pianist Roger Buckley. The four settings of poems by the French symbolist poet Paul Verlaine (1844–1896) were composed in two pairs, almost fifteen years apart (1895 and 1910–11), during the extended period in which the composer lived in Grez-sur-Loing, near Fontainebleau. They are, as Lionel Carley puts it, 'markedly different in style from other groups of songs by Delius ... French in spirit, yet truly Delian'.[18] Music by Howells, Rebecca Clarke and John Ireland was also on the menu, along with the first performance of three songs by Christian Wilson, setting poems by Ursula Vaughan Williams. Helen Withers was on sparkling form according to Michael Kennedy:

> in voice and looks, this impressive singer seems to have been born to sing Debussy's Mélisande, a judgement I formed after her exquisite performance of Delius's five Verlaine settings. ... Her tone is strong and pure, her diction good and she gives full weight to the meaning of the texts.[19]

---

[15] Laurence Hughes, *Independent*, 24 August 2001.

[16] *Sunday Telegraph*, 26 August 2001.

[17] Ibid.

[18] Gloucester Festival programme book, 2001, p. 63.

[19] *Sunday Telegraph*, 26 August 2001.

The evening concert was given over to the first Three Choirs performance of Delius's *A Mass of Life*, conducted by Richard Hickox, with Susan Gritton, Catherine Wyn-Rogers, Adrian Thompson and Alan Opie joining the Festival Chorus. (See pp. 336–8 in Chapter 23 for comment on why it took almost 100 years for the piece to be programmed.) In his programme note, Stephen Lloyd makes a fascinating comparison between it and that great Three Choirs work, Elgar's *Dream of Gerontius*.

> While these two works are poles apart in matters of faith, just as the two composers were dissimilar in temperament and outlook, there are nevertheless some interesting parallels to be drawn. The texts of both works have caused problems for their acceptance in hallowed surroundings. Too overtly Catholic references in *The Dream of Gerontius* seemed likely to delay the work's initial acceptance at the 1902 Three Choirs Festival until certain passages had been reworded, while as recently as 1996 some objection was voiced (by a very small minority) against a London performance of *A Mass of Life* in St Paul's Cathedral, the Archdeacon finding it necessary to assure the audience beforehand that the work's 'affirmation of life' was not irreligious. (Walton's *Belshazzar's Feast* – to be heard on Thursday – had for similar reasons to wait until 1957 for a Three Choirs performance.) The newcomer can be easily misled by the title of Delius's work. It is, of course, no religious mass at all. Perhaps we should instead interpret it as a *celebration* of life. *The Dream of Gerontius*, on the other hand, in its divisions can be seen in some ways to follow the pattern of the Mass.[20]

Paul Conway reviewed the concert for the *Independent*:

> The grand scale and visionary power of Delius's 'A Mass of Life' from 1904 belies the composer's reputation as a miniaturist. Horn calls, forest murmurings and an *echt*-Teutonic text based on *Also Sprach Zarathustra* suggest echoes of Wagner's *Ring Cycle*. Richard Hickox's firm belief in this headstrong hymn to nature galvanised this year's Three Choirs Festival performance. Adopting a brisk pace, he caught its essential drama and concentrated on the work's potent mixture of iron strength and melting beauty …
>   The main glory of this reading was the Philharmonia's playing. Atmospheric antiphonal horn calls at the start of the second half seemed to summon each other from the Urwald, while the woodwinds floated some ravishing solos. Hickox's unerring understanding of the massive work's complex architecture resulted in a climax of breathtaking inexorability. A stunned silence followed by vigorous applause set the seal on a life-affirming experience.[21]

Following such an event was always going to be difficult. Two concerts shared the burden: at Tewkesbury Abbey there was a performance of Purcell's *Dido and Aeneas* by the Gloucester-based St Cecilia Singers, and in the cathedral there was another evening performance steeped in the British musical renaissance of the

[20] Gloucester Festival programme book, 2001, p. 71.
[21] *Independent*, 24 August 2001.

first half of the twentieth century, but with a new addition by one of the home team. Michael Kennedy again:

> At Monday's Philharmonia concert, the Gloucester director of music, David Briggs, conducted his own *Creation* for soprano, chorus and orchestra, first performed last year (not at the Three Choirs), wide in scope and unembarrassedly eclectic. In the same programme, perhaps unfortunately were VW's *Five Mystical Songs* (Garry Magee the vibrant baritone soloist), Walton's Viola Concerto, expertly played by Paul Silverthorne on a golden toned 1620 Amati, and Holst's *Hymn of Jesus*, incandescently sung by the chorus.[22]

The BBC returned to the Festival for the first time since 1992 to record two chamber concerts, the first of which took place in St Mary de Lode on the Tuesday morning, where the Sorrell Quartet were joined by clarinettist David Campbell for Britten's Quartet No. 3 (op. 94), *Three Idylls* by Frank Bridge, and Sir Arthur Bliss's mournful Clarinet Quintet. Friday afternoon's recital of Byrd and Gibbons by the counter-tenor Robin Blaze and the viol consort Fretwork was the second concert recorded for later broadcast, perhaps indicating that the relationship between the BBC and the Festival was beginning to be rebuilt.

The feast of British masterpieces continued in the evening concert, the focus of which was two significant and very personal works relating to loss: Howells's *Hymnus Paradisi* and Finzi's Wordsworth setting *Intimations of Immortality*. Both were premièred, though not together, at the 1950 Gloucester Festival, and have been performed at Three Choirs several times since. Howells selected texts from Psalms 23 and 121, along with sections from the Burial Service in the Book of Common Prayer, which encapsulate, in the composer's own words, the 'transient griefs and indestructible hopes of mankind'. Some felt that the Wordsworth poem was entirely unsuitable for a music setting, being too meditative an introspection, but Finzi's love of poetry and his instinctive and profound understanding of language shape both the macro-structure of the piece, and its colour and detail. In both works, the chorus under Roy Massey's experienced baton took centre stage, contemplative when required in Howells and thrillingly declamatory when required in Finzi.[23] Perhaps something of the humanity of this flowering of music in Britain is illuminated by the closing words of Wordsworth's ode:

> The Clouds that gather round the setting sun
> Do take a sober colouring from an eye
> That hath kept watch o'er man's mortality;
> Another race hath been, and other palms are won.
> Thanks to the human heart by which we live,
> Thanks to its tenderness, its joys and fears,
> To me the meanest flower that blows can give
> Thoughts that do often lie too deep for tears.

[22] *Sunday Telegraph*, 26 August 2001.
[23] *Independent*, 24 August 2001.

In a clever twist of programme planning, Wednesday's focus shifted to an 'Honorary Englishman', to use Martin Lee-Brown's phrase – Handel. Indeed, no composer has been more performed at Three Choirs Festivals than he. The London Handel Festival Orchestra, joined by violinist Adrian Butterfield, flautists Rachel Brown and Daniel Pailthorpe, and sopranos Rachel Nicholls and Camilla Darlow, provided welcome contrast in the form of Handel's Grand Concerto in D major (op. 6, no. 5), the cantata *Diana Cacciatrice* (Diana the Huntress), and a selection from the opera *Giove in Argo* (Jupiter in Argos). A *Messiah* at Three Choirs is now a comparative rarity, so its place in this programme, conducted by David Briggs with the impressive cast of Nicki Kennedy, Robin Blaze, James Gilchrist and Michael George, makes it all the more significant. It was very clearly a formative work for this Festival, and its influence can be felt across time and music. This particular performance was memorable for a different reason, however, as over the course of the first half it became clear to many that Michael George was not simply 'a bit off colour', but that his voice was rapidly disappearing. Recognising that he could not deliver the second half, he withdrew, leaving a gaping hole in the solo line-up and a major problem for the Festival. Up stepped William Armiger, Festival secretary and long time cathedral lay clerk, to take the bass arias for the second half, an effort that was greeted with 'thunderous applause from the 2,000-strong audience'.[24]

Following this opportunity to taste a different wine, the audience were invited again to drink deeply from the cup of British music over the final three days – Walton's *Belshazzar's Feast*, Elgar's *The Apostles* and *Sea Pictures*, Vaughan Williams's *A Sea Symphony*, as well as music from the lesser known Frederic Austin, and Arnold Bax's *The Garden of Fand*. And drink they did, until they were satisfied, or perhaps even drunk. All was not quite so well, however, in the chorus. While they had coped admirably with the volume of new music during Festival week and produced some wonderful moments, it is notable that much of the critical praise for the Festival as a whole made no mention of the chorus contribution. Other contemporary reports suggest that the objective quality of the chorus was not where the Festival subjectively thought it to be. A certain complacency seems to have developed over this period relating to choral standards, which was soon to be challenged head-on, most notably by David Briggs's successor at Gloucester.

T HE 2002 Three Choirs Festival in Worcester marked a significant point in what one might call the 'changing of the guard'. A few short years earlier, in 1993, three figures held the august positions of Artistic Directors, with a combined total of sixty-four years in the jobs. With Geraint Bowen succeeding Roy Massey at the beginning of the academic year 2001–2, and Andrew Nethsingha arriving in Gloucester at Easter 2002, the conducting roster now had a very different feel, with Adrian Lucas as the 'old hand' after just five years in post. His first major innovation was to encourage single-conductor concerts, as opposed to the traditional practice of sharing the podium, particularly among the 'home team'.

---

[24] Richard Savill, *Daily Telegraph*, 24 August 2001.

Hereford Cathedral had appointed a known quantity in the person of Geraint Bowen, who had been Assistant Organist at Hereford from 1989 to 1994 under Roy Massey (replacing David Briggs when he moved to Truro Cathedral), and had seen two home Festivals in that time. A chorister at Hampstead Parish Church under Martindale Sidwell, he went up to Jesus College, Cambridge, as Organ Scholar in 1982. He was appointed Assistant Organist at St Patrick's Cathedral, Dublin, the year after he graduated, and he took a BMus at Trinity College, Dublin, during his time there. Taking over the reins at St David's Cathedral in Pembrokeshire in 1995 brought with it the artistic directorship of the St David's Cathedral Festival, a ten-day event in May and June centred around the cathedral space. Bowen's introduction to much Three Choirs repertoire was through his father, Kenneth Bowen, a highly regarded tenor who performed many times at the Festival as a soloist, and to whose concerts Bowen had frequently gone in his formative musical years.[25] A fine pedigree, then, to step into the shoes of his long-time predecessor in Hereford, along with useful and relevant experience.

Geraint Bowen seems to have drawn the shorter straw in terms of his Festival debut, taking charge of a concert which no one would term as 'repertoire', save perhaps for the choral parts of Walton's great anthem *The Twelve*. Setting a poem by W. H. Auden, written specifically for the piece, it is a challenging work for any choir, not least in its effervescent fugal conclusion, very much in the manner of the final pages of *Belshazzar's Feast*. Piano concertos are also notoriously difficult to bring off in cathedral acoustics, and it is only really in Worcester that they work at all. So the prospect of a first Festival performance of Stanford's second concerto, with its echoes of Rachmaninov's masterpiece (his second concerto is in the same key and was championed by Stanford from the podium), must have been somewhat daunting. Bowen, however, rose well to the challenge, steering the Philharmonia and Charles Owen 'capably' through this little-known score, programmed to mark the composer's 150th anniversary (his Symphony No. 3 also appeared later in the week).[26]

The second half comprised Constant Lambert's jazz-influenced *The Rio Grande*, scored for piano, chorus and orchestra, and 'Four Dance Episodes' from *Rodeo* by Aaron Copland. Lambert's early work (the piece was written when he was just twenty-two years old) established his reputation both in England and the USA after its first broadcast performance in February 1928, and it was performed some 200 times over the following decade. As Michael Barlow put it in his programme note, 'It is an extremely original piece, and one of the relatively few successful attempts in making use of jazz in concert music.'[27] The chorus clearly enjoyed the syncopation and jazz rhythms of Lambert's extrovert score, and Bowen came across very well, too.

Copland's ballet *Rodeo* was composed some fifteen years later, and first performed by the Ballet Russe de Monte Carlo in New York in October 1942, with the 'Four Dance Episodes' heard in a New York Philharmonic concert in

---

[25] Interestingly, however, the young Geraint only came once to Three Choirs, at the age of fifteen, in 1978.

[26] *Church Times*, 13 September 2002.

[27] Worcester Festival programme book, 2002, p. 70.

June 1943. It is a clear tribute to Copland's skill that only five minutes of music from the ballet are omitted in the *Episodes*, which last less than 20 minutes in their entirety. The Philharmonia were characteristically incisive here, and were unflustered even when their conductor's glasses fell to the ground during the last movement. In all, it was a hugely promising debut for the new man at Hereford, whose first home Festival would, of course, come around next.

Andrew Nethsingha, newly arrived at Gloucester, was entrusted with much more familiar repertoire, in the form of Handel coronation anthems, a solo Bach cantata (*Ich habe genug*), and Haydn's ever popular *Nelson Mass*, with a 'dream team' of soloists including Emma Kirkby, Robin Blaze and Michael George, accompanied by the Philharmonia Orchestra. He made an impressive debut, playing to the largest house of the week, at nearly 2,000 people.

Of Sri Lankan heritage, Nethsingha was steeped in what makes Three Choirs Festival what it is. He spent his early years in Tenbury, where his father, Lucian Nethsingha, was Organist at St Michael's College, and also played the organ at numerous Three Choirs Festivals for his great friend Christopher Robinson. A pupil of Howells, Lucian Nethsingha went on to take up the post of Organist at Exeter Cathedral, where Andrew was later a chorister. Winning a place at the Royal College of Music, Andrew won seven performance prizes before being appointed Organ Scholar at St George's Chapel, Windsor, under Christopher Robinson in 1986. He went up to Cambridge the following year, to the organ scholarship at St John's College under Dr George Guest. Four years as Assistant Organist at Wells Cathedral followed, before he was appointed to the top job at Truro Cathedral, becoming the youngest cathedral organist in the country. His reputation as a choir trainer grew as he began to make musical waves in the south west, and the lure of a Three Choirs cathedral position was to prove irresistible when David Briggs announced his plan to move on from Gloucester.

As a whole the 2002 programme suffered in comparison with the previous two years, where an overarching theme ran through the week. In 2002 there was less cohesion, though two particular threads did run throughout: a focus on the music of William Walton in his centenary year (with performances of twelve of his works), and links to the Royal Jubilee celebrations.

Lucas himself took the podium for Walton's Symphony No. 1 on Monday evening; the Philharmonia did justice to the complexity and drive of the piece, in a performance that was 'forcefully delivered'.[28] On Wednesday the guest conductor Tugan Sokhiev made his Festival debut with the *Spitfire Prelude and Fugue*, also with the Philharmonia, before Lucas took the reins again on the last night of the Festival, tackling both *Orb and Sceptre* and Walton's great *Coronation Te Deum* written for the 1953 service in Westminster Abbey, this time joined by the Bournemouth Symphony Orchestra and the Festival Chorus.

The other anniversary celebration to fall in 2002 was the centenary of the birth of Maurice Duruflé. An organist of considerable note, he found composition extremely difficult, feeling the need continually to revise his works before allowing them to be heard publicly. His entire published output consists of just fourteen works, only four of which are secular. His *Trois Danses* were included in Wednesday evening's concert, conducted by Tugan Sokhiev, and

[28] Geoff Brown, *The Times*, 23 August 2002.

paired with Rachmaninov's brooding Symphony No. 2. Unlike the introverted mood of much of Duruflé's sacred output, this piece is 'gregarious and outgoing', though it shows the hallmarks still of the composer's craft, and his 'self-critical and self-conscious' nature.[29] Sokhiev conducted admirably – the young Russian conductor was undoubtedly one to watch.

A notable Festival returnee, Sir David Willcocks (1919–2015), took charge of the three cathedral choirs for a concert on Wednesday morning, just over half a century after his appointment to the organist position at Worcester Cathedral. He was joined by Ruth Holton, Julie Cooper, John Bowley (an ex-Worcester chorister) and Peter Savidge, along with the Bournemouth Symphony Orchestra, for a finely crafted programme of Mozart – a rare performance of the *Salve Regina* (K276) and a 'touching' account of the Mass in C minor (K427).[30]

The Festival programme included two substantial pieces of new music, in the form of a commission from Andrew Gant, and the first public performance of Lionel Sainsbury's Violin Concerto, completed in 1989. The latter, championed by the soloist for the concert, Lorraine McAslan, failed to convince Hilary Finch in *The Times*: 'At 35 minutes long, its three movements form a garrulous, confident, late-Romantic showpiece, teeming with bravado and bravura, somewhat over-orchestrated, and behaving as though the past 100 years of musical history had never existed.'[31]

The Gant commission, *The Vision of Piers Plowman*, was perhaps more successful, and took on board Adrian Lucas's request for some element of jazz to be included. The composer also speaks in his programme note of a desire to 'reflect the unique nature of the Three Choirs Festival, its participants, its venues, its roots in the local community and landscape, respecting and renewing its great tradition of new choral works'.[32] The text would clearly be key for the piece, and Gant himself explains the background to his choice of Langland's poem:[33]

> I wanted a text that plugged directly into the local nature of the Festival and its musicians, and this poem opens with the dreamer wandering on the Malvern Hills and meeting a 'Field full of folk', the butchers, bakers, lawyers, doctors, priests and professional people of Malvern and its environs: the chorus play the parts themselves. I wanted a text which would let the audience and the performers do things that they are not normally allowed to do in an oratorio: laugh, tap their feet, have fun: this poem is very funny, very moving, very profound and very rude, all done in roistering alliterative couplets. ... this poem takes a uniquely English view of the central Christian story, personalising it to the experience of ordinary English people and presenting it in a vivid, dramatic and highly unusual way.[34]

[29] Gareth Price, Worcester Festival programme book, 2002, p. 112.

[30] *Church Times*, 13 September 2002.

[31] *The Times*, 29 August 2002.

[32] Worcester Festival programme book, 2002, p. 87.

[33] This was the second time that a Three Choirs commission used this text, as Gerard Schurmann had chosen it for his 1980 work, repeated in 1989.

[34] Worcester Festival programme book, 2002, p. 87.

Geoff Brown reviewed the concert for *The Times*:

> Gant's conception of jazz turned out to be safe, old, white: a few
> syncopated rhythms here, the faint twang of an American spiritual there,
> plus a distant memory of blues in the night …
>
> All very decorous; and all slotted into an ingenious 50-minute stylistic
> melange, often inventively orchestrated.
>
> Trouble is, the text Gant uses – a rowdy and moving poem by the local
> 14th-century cleric William Langland – deserves something stronger than
> music that glides by the ear. Langland presents a quasi-allegorical vision of
> earthly frenzy and heavenly peace in language often raw, always alliterative,
> sometimes rude: if you want to know what medieval life smelt like,
> read this.
>
> It's a tough bird to set to music, and bolder melodic and rhythmic
> material would have let the work fly further.[35]

Paul Daniel's account of Mahler's Symphony No. 2 on Thursday evening was
rather better reviewed, with praise for the chorus's singing, though less for their
command of German. Judith Howarth was on spine-chilling form, particularly
in the second movement, where her soprano 'and those apocalyptic trumpets at
the opposite end of the nave from the orchestra, made us glimpse heaven itself at
the moment of Resurrection'.[36] Plaudits too for Daniel here, who 'decided to play
Mahler's Second Symphony wiry and highly strung. Rhythms were taut enough
to snap; tension surged through every sustained note; and Daniel knew when to
move things on, and when to allow Mahler's sweet pastoral interludes to fan out
into the vaulting.'[37]

Just as memorable for some was the sight of three dragon boats racing up the
river past the cathedral, the three deans of the three cathedrals in their prows,
drums beating the rhythm of the strongmen paddlers. For the record, the race
was won by Gloucester.

ALL eyes turned to Hereford for the 2003 Festival, the first non-Massey
programme there for thirty years, and the first major test of Geraint
Bowen's stewardship. His idea for the programme was to focus on marking
several significant anniversaries: 200 years since the birth of Hector Berlioz,
fifty years since the deaths of Arnold Bax and Sergei Prokofiev, and anniversary
performances of works first performed at Three Choirs in 1803 and 1903.

After the traditional Hereford pattern of a Sunday morning Eucharist (with
a newly commissioned but rather non-descript mass setting by Geraint Lewis)
and an orchestral Festival Service, the opening major concert of the week paired
Mozart's Coronation Mass in C, K317, with William Mathias's extended cantata
This Worlde's Joie. The choristers of Hereford Cathedral joined the Festival Chorus
for an opening rendition of Parry's *I was glad*, before Ruth Holton, William

---

[35] *The Times*, 23 August 2002.

[36] Hilary Finch, *The Times*, 29 August 2002.

[37] Ibid.

Towers, James Oxley and Jeremy Huw Williams took centre stage, alongside Geraint Bowen and the Bournemouth Symphony Orchestra.

The Mathias work was first given at Three Choirs in Hereford in 1979 (and repeated in 1985), and is scored for soprano, tenor and baritone solo, children's choir and orchestra. In the composer's own words:

> The four sections carry no separate titles in the score, but are designed to reflect both the seasons of the year and the span of human life: I Spring (Youth); II Summer (Maturity); III Autumn (Decline); IV Winter (Death), leading to a transfigured Spring and re-birth.[38]

Rian Evans reviewed the concert for the *Guardian*:

> Bowen was occasionally a little heavy-handed with his forces – the Bournemouth Symphony Orchestra in strong form – but it was his underlining of the work's natural vigour and colour that made this performance so vibrant.
>
> Jeremy Huw Williams was easily the best of the three soloists, delivering the line, 'Of this worlde's joie, how it cometh to nought', most potently. Yet that dynamic force was dissipated abruptly when baritone and chorus then spoke rather than sung the poem's despairing climactic stanza. Not even the glorious conviction of the final chorus heralding a joyous new spring could quite make up for that.[39]

Roy Massey was not absent from the Festival for long, returning to give an organ recital at Tewkesbury Abbey the following morning, before a fine concert of British orchestral music at Wyastone Leys given by William Boughton and the English Symphony Orchestra, with the pianist Mark Bebbington. The programme included not only Finzi's *Eclogue* for piano and strings, but also a rare performance of Constant Lambert's Piano Concerto No. 1, as edited and orchestrated by Edward Shipley and Giles Easterbrook.

The first of two nights focused on the music of Hector Berlioz saw the Festival Chorus joined by the Bournemouth Symphony Orchestra and conductor Stephen Cleobury to perform *L'Enfance du Christ*. Cleobury is known for his 1990 recording of this work with King's College, Cambridge, and the RPO; his knowledge and understanding of the narrative and musical arc of the score shone through, and his rapport with the orchestra was extraordinary. The chorus struggled, but there was some fine solo singing, especially from Stephen Varcoe, Michael George and Brindley Sherratt, though John Mark Ainsley was disappointing. And, although it is a substantial piece, it was performed here without an interval – there was simply a five-minute pause between parts one and two – an approach which worked well. Unbeknownst to either audience or conductor, Stephen Cleobury's wife went into premature labour that evening, and their daughter was born late that night, appearing at the end of the week as possibly the youngest-ever Festival attendee, at the age of three days.

Andrew Nethsingha was entrusted with the other substantial Berlioz work, *Les Nuits d'été*, in a programme that also included Lennox Berkeley's orchestral

---

[38] Note to EMI recording, 1975.

[39] *Guardian*, 19 August 2003.

work *Voices of the Night* (commissioned by the 1973 Three Choirs Festival in Hereford), and a rare outing for Beethoven's dramatic oratorio *Christus am Ölberge* (Christ on the Mount of Olives). Sarah Connolly was on radiant form in the Berlioz songs, and the trio of Ailish Tynan, James Gilchrist and Robert Rice did justice to a piece that is often regarded as not quite living up to the general standard of Beethoven's œuvre.

No one doubts the calibre of Elgar's Symphony No. 1, of course, and both Tasmin Little and Vernon Handley were sparkling in Wednesday evening's orchestral programme. Perhaps the finest interpreter of Bax's music, one could choose none better than Handley to conduct what was only the second Three Choirs performance of Bax's programmatic *Tintagel*. This was followed by a revelatory reading of Finzi's neglected Violin Concerto, which Little had recorded for the first time a couple of years earlier.

The three cathedral choirs were joined this year by the period orchestra Florilegium, in an attractive programme of Bach and Handel. Handel's *Gloria in Excelsis Deo*, unknown until its discovery at the Royal Academy of Music in 2001, was an interesting novelty, and there was fine solo singing from Ruth Holton and Jonathan Arnold in particular, alongside a superb contribution from the boys and men of the cathedral choirs. All was not so smooth behind the scenes, however, as Florilegium's artistic director, Ashley Solomon, was involved in a car accident while travelling to Hereford on the morning of the concert; as a result, both he and the orchestral parts arrived very late.

A typically varied daytime programme provided much to enjoy across this Festival, including a fine concert of early polyphony from The Cardinall's Musick, recitals by David Owen Norris and Lada Valešová (piano), Nathan Vale (tenor) and John Scott (organ), Rubbra from the Dante Quartet, and a fascinating programme of early South American music by the Birmingham-based chamber choir Ex Cathedra. New music was not absent either, as the Okeanos ensemble presented an entirely contemporary programme containing no fewer than four world premières, from Judith Bingham, John Joubert, Priaulx Rainer and Howard Skempton.

The most significant commission at 2003(H) was from the Hereford-based composer Anthony Powers: his setting of poems by John Donne (1572–1631) for soprano and baritone solo, chorus and orchestra, entitled *Air and Angels*. The other works in the concert were Elgar's *Froissart*, Sir Hubert Parry's *Voces Clamantium* (commissioned for the Hereford Festival in 1903), and Prokofiev's *Scenes from Romeo and Juliet*. Adrian Lucas and Geraint Bowen shared the podium (Bowen taking charge for the Powers commission), alongside soprano Carys Lane and baritone Matthew Brook.

Air and Angels is Powers's attempt to explain and elucidate the characteristically opaque language of Donne's love poetry, intending also to transcend the physical aspect of the music, with it becoming, in some form, an angel itself. Rian Evans reviewed the concert for the *Guardian*:

> Powers's *Air and Angels* is a striking setting of love poems by John Donne, conceived in seven sections that merge imperceptibly into a continuous arching sequence. The overall quality of the work is indeed darker than the title would suggest, with the vast instrumental forces … underlining the

sense of deep tumult. Its alchemy was at its strongest when textures were at their most translucent. ...

It says much for this committed performance of *Air and Angels*, under the direction of Geraint Bowen, that the scenes from Romeo and Juliet by Prokofiev seemed oddly superfluous, however passionate. But that hardly constitutes a complaint.[40]

The final concert of the week was a slightly tired, but nonetheless bombastic, Verdi Requiem, in which a massed RPO and Festival Chorus (including at least one Artistic Director) were joined by Judith Howarth, Catherine Wyn-Rogers, Adrian Thompson and Michael George, conducted by Geraint Bowen.

I N the later years of David Briggs's tenure as Gloucester's Artistic Director, he had become rather less directly involved in the process of programming for the Festival. One might say that his activity culminated in the 2001 'Celebration of British Music'. Partly for this reason, the gestation of the 2004 programme was rather more difficult. Even before his arrival in Gloucester in May 2002, Andrew Nethsingha had begun to work in earnest on his 2004 programme. This was a wise move, given the Three Choirs tradition of launching one year's programme at the previous year's Festival. However, it soon became clear that the then chairman of the Gloucester Festival and his administrator had been thinking in similar fashion, and by the autumn of that year it emerged that there were two programmes in planning: one compiled by the Artistic Director, and one by his colleagues. What followed was an extremely difficult period for the new Gloucester man, as those involved negotiated their precise remits and areas of artistic responsibility. Among the issues was significant disagreement regarding the required 'Britishness' of what was being planned, where the chairman felt that Gloucester's unique selling point, in relation to the Festivals in the other two cities, was its focus on British music. Moreover, even within the British music programming, Nethsingha felt there was an east–west divide between the so-called Three Choirs composers (Elgar, Finzi, Vaughan Williams, and so on) on the one side, and, on the other, those grouped around Benjamin Britten, who were curiously 'out of fashion' and under-represented. Other very significant names in British music, such as Michael Tippett and Oliver Knussen, also fell into this camp, their music considered as being outside 'traditional Three Choirs territory'.[41] Eventually, however, the critic Christopher Thomas praised Nethsingha's 2004 approach, commenting that 'a notable but balanced accent on British music remains'.[42]

These fundamental disagreements, along with deteriorating health, led the chairman to step down. He was replaced by a previous Gloucester treasurer who had been outside the organisation for some years before this period, but who was to be a very significant figure in future: Bernard Day.

---

[40] *Guardian*, 26 August 2003.

[41] Interview with Andrew Nethsingha, 25 January 2016.

[42] Christopher Thomas, 'Seen and Heard Festival Review', online at http://www. musicweb-international.com/SandH/2004/May-Aug04/3c88.htm [accessed 29 September 2016].

Clearly, this programming dispute highlights some of the organisational issues that were beginning to affect the running of the Festival, having been bubbling under the surface for some years. Questions began to be asked in earnest about longer-term strategy, both artistic and in terms of the business, and it became essential to consider how such questions might be addressed in the existing tripartite structure. The chairmanship had also recently changed in Worcester, with the long-serving Sam Driver White stepping down after the 2002 Festival to be replaced by a former BBC employee and artist agent, Paul Vaughan. How should this historic Festival modernise, and compete with other major annual events, particularly in terms of factors like its relations with the BBC? Could the Festival carry on being run in the same way, and could it continue to rely on amateur supporters to run its affairs?[43] Many such individuals had served the Festival extremely well, bringing their skills and experience to the fore to deliver extraordinary concerts and events over many years; but as complexity and cost rose, would suitable people still volunteer to take on such significant responsibility? And, as charitable supporters (in particular local authorities, the Charity Commission and the Arts Council) tightened their requirements, and significant local businesses were bought by larger national concerns, the financial stewardship of the organisation was coming under closer scrutiny, and gaining the required monetary backing was proving more and more difficult. Indeed, in his introduction to the 2004 programme book Bernard Day spoke of the artistic and logistical costs of putting the Festival on, signalling not only the need for financial support into the future, but also some of the challenges the Festival was to face over the coming years.

Andrew Nethsingha's first home Festival programme did indeed have a very different feel from the 2001 Gloucester week. The familiar was certainly present, in the form of Haydn's *The Creation* and Elgar's *The Kingdom* and *The Music Makers*, bookended by Germanic masterpieces in the form of Brahms's *A German Requiem* and Beethoven's mighty Symphony No. 9. Partnered with the Brahms on the opening night was the first public performance of *Five Songs from the Norwegian* by Frederick Delius, sung well by the soprano Alwyn Mellor though perhaps lacking some clarity of diction. The concert also included the first of several performances of works by former Artistic Director John Sanders, who had died the previous year, and to whose memory the Festival as a whole was dedicated: his *Festival Te Deum*.

True to Nethsingha's words regarding neglected composers, Sunday evening's orchestral concert opened with *Choral* by Oliver Knussen, an early orchestral work written when the composer was only eighteen years of age. Essentially a decoration of a single and immensely slow sequence of four chords, its sound world resonated around the glorious acoustic of the cathedral just as Nethsingha had hoped it would. A first Festival performance of Delius's Violin Concerto followed, with Tasmin Little the fresh and persuasive soloist; with the assistance of Richard Hickox on the podium, she allowed the music 'to breathe in the way that it needs'.[44] The orchestra took centre stage after the interval for a rare

---

[43] 'Amateur' is used in its traditional sense here – a person who engages an activity for pleasure rather than for financial benefit or professional reasons.

[44] Thomas, 'Seen and Heard Festival Review'.

performance of the original version of Vaughan Williams's *A London Symphony*, as recorded three years earlier by Hickox himself to some acclaim:

> It is true to say that the original is somewhat sprawling in comparison to the version we have come to know but the quality of the music the composer removed is immediately evident and shone through in this performance. The slow movement was imbued with a feeling of twilit mystery and sadness for a London that is lost, the scherzo wonderfully fluent and bustling with life.[45]

Contemporary British music was never far from sight here, with the Festival's first official 'composer-in-residence', John McCabe, involved in a plethora of concerts over the week. These ranged from a choral setting of words by James Clarence Mangan and performed by Bath Camerata, to the orchestral *The Golden Valley* (2000) in Saturday's Gloucestershire Symphony Orchestra concert, via McCabe's own piano recital on Wednesday morning. Most significant, however, was the Festival's innovative commission this year, a set of variations on Vaughan Williams's great hymn tune, *Down Ampney*, in which five different composers each contributed a section.[46] Led off by McCabe, variations by Robert Saxton, James Francis Brown, David Matthews and Judith Bingham follow, producing an interestingly varied whole. As one reviewer put it: 'With a little adjustment, the variations (published by Maecenas Music) might earn a foothold in the repertoire; but the unbalance needs addressing, and a peroration restoring Vaughan Williams' lovely disguised tune would have been welcome.'[47]

Some did criticise Nethsingha's decision to commission a purely orchestral work as opposed to a choral one, but his focus at this point was on standards in the chorus, and in further rationalising and improving the way that the chorus was recruited, operated and rehearsed. Changes to the use of lay clerks, and the beginnings of standardisation in audition procedures, were beginning to have an impact on the outright quality of the singing, though exclusions, particularly of singers who had been part of the Festival for many years, are never easy.

Friday's evening concert, which contained the *Down Ampney* variations, was notable for another reason, too: the Festival debut of Martyn Brabbins on the podium, a relationship which was to become even more significant for the Festival after the untimely death of Richard Hickox in 2008. Alongside a rare outing for Howells's *King's Herald* (in its orchestral version) and a fine performance of Elgar's Cello Concerto with the returning Raphael Wallfisch, Brabbins also conducted the Philharmonia and Festival Chorus in a characterful reading of Elgar's nostalgic, autobiographical cantata *The Music Makers*, with the soloist Catherine Wyn-Rogers. This concert was dedicated to the memory of Wulstan Atkins, a giant of the English music scene and stalwart of Three Choirs.

---

[45] Ibid.

[46] The inspiration for this came from the *Variations on an Elizabethan Theme*, written in 1952 to celebrate the forthcoming coronation in 1953, by Lennox Berkeley, Benjamin Britten, Arthur Oldham, Humphrey Searle, Michael Tippett and William Walton.

[47] *Church Times*, 3 September 2004.

He attended eighty-two consecutive Festivals up to 2002, before his death in May 2003 severed one of the last direct links to Edward Elgar.

Another favourite at Three Choirs, Emma Johnson, graced the stage in the cathedral on Monday evening to play Mozart's evergreen Clarinet Concerto with Adrian Lucas and the Philharmonia, in a programme that included two much less-known works – the Concerto for double string orchestra by Sir Michael Tippett, and, marking his 150th anniversary, Janáček's mighty *Glagolitic Mass*. The immense effort put in by the Artistic Directors in drilling the chorus for this work paid off, and their singing stood well alongside excellent solo work by Adrian Thompson and Matthew Best in particular, and some stunning playing on the Gloucester Cathedral organ from the Assistant Organist, Robert Houssart.

The organ was in significant use again on Thursday evening, though this time in the immensely experienced hands of David Briggs, for a rip-roaring account of Saint-Saëns' *Organ Symphony*, brought to life in electrifying style by another Three Choirs 'old hand', Christopher Robinson. The first half of this concert was perhaps the most daring of the entire week, opening as it did with Charles Ives's *The Unanswered Question* (marking fifty years since the composer's death), before Andrew Nethsingha and the Philharmonia Orchestra were joined by that most other-worldly of electronic instruments, the ondes martenot, and the choristers of the three cathedrals for a performance of *Trois Petites Liturgies de la Présence Divine* by Olivier Messiaen. A hugely ambitious piece to attempt in this context, it was perhaps a stretch too far for the choristers, whose difficulties were exacerbated when the amplification failed to function as intended. But even so, the performance elicited warm applause from the audience, who had clearly been challenged.

Other highlights of the week included scintillating and moving singing from Carolyn Sampson, James Gilchrist's *Liederkreis*, Olivier Latry putting the cathedral organ through its paces, as well as early music from Robin Blaze and Fretwork, and a sumptuous *Missa Pappae Marcelli* from the three cathedral choirs, interspersed with movements from Couperin's *Messe pour les paroisses*. David Briggs's improvisation accompanying the 1925 silent film *The Phantom of the Opera* starring Lon Chaney junior was doubly impressive, not just for his playing but also for the fact that the film feed to his monitor in the organ loft failed, leaving his only option to watch the film backwards on the projection screen, through the organ console tracery.

Roderick Williams was fast becoming both a fixture and a favourite with the audience, and he did not disappoint in 2004. He delighted Festival-goers with a magnificently varied and powerful performance as Peter in Elgar's *The Kingdom*, and a highly praised song recital with Iain Burnside that included songs by Peter Warlock, Charles Dyson and Ian Venables, John Sanders's cycle *The Beacon*, and Finzi's *Before and After Summer*.

The Festival Chorus raised themselves in impressive fashion to tackle a mammoth sing on the final night, combining Poulenc's effervescent *Gloria* with the majestic outpouring of joy that completes Beethoven's last symphony, easily outclassing the soloists in a fine performance of a work that John Sanders, in his time at Gloucester, had undoubtedly made his own. What better tribute to a hugely significant figure in the recent history of this Festival?

THE arrival of the new chairman into the Worcester committee was very much a case of 'a new broom sweeps clean'. Unencumbered by, and at times resolutely dismissive of, how the Festival had been run in the past, Paul Vaughan brought in a raft of sweeping changes. For some, these changes were wholly to be welcomed:

> infinite congratulations to the Worcester committee for coming up with such a welcome transformation of what used to be a fusty, dutiful old fixture. Elgar, who criticised the moribund attitudes of this ancient institution a century ago, would have been delighted to see this injection of life and gaiety into the proceedings.
>
> And artistically the week-long programme has blossomed, with a pleasing range of appropriate offerings and a standard of execution of the highest professional order. Sorry you missed the 20th century, Three Choirs, but welcome to the 21st.[48]

However, all was not well under the surface. There was uproar in the chorus after it was revealed that the Sunday night concert including Rachmaninov's *The Bells* would not be performed by them, but by Adrian Lucas's City of Birmingham Choir. Stewards and volunteers who were informed that they would no longer be required, voted with their feet. And, most significantly, the joint treasurers resigned several months before the Festival opened, passing senior members of the Association a 'real' budget (figures different from those presented at the formal meetings) that predicted a loss of between £80,000 and £180,000.[49] This left the directors of the Association with a hugely difficult decision. Should they pull the Festival, in accordance with the removal of delegated authority allowed by the Articles of Association, with all that such a momentous decision would entail? Should they parachute in an alternative team to take over the running of the enterprise, and if so what could they do at such a late stage, and who would be prepared to take it on? Or, should they let the Festival run, knowing the considerable financial and reputational risk they were taking in doing so? Faced with this choice, the directors (who are, of course, also trustees of the charity) felt that the least damaging option was to allow the Festival to go ahead, making every effort behind the scenes to mitigate the situation. It was a calculated risk, and one that the directors only felt able to take because there were safety-net funds in the Festival Society that were restricted for the use of the Worcester Festival, and which could be drawn upon if the treasurers' assessment proved correct.

Once again, organisational issues were dogging this great institution. Inter-city competitiveness had become negative, and the atmosphere at Association level somewhat poisonous between representatives of the three committees. Meetings were not actually hostile – they were often perfectly cordial – but they avoided direct discussion of the problematic issues (assuming the relevant people actually attended), as senior figures tried to work behind the scenes to avoid overt disagreement and strife, and allow the Festival's public face to continue to shine.

[48] Christopher Morley, *Birmingham Post*, 9 August 2005.

[49] The projected expenditure for the Festival at this time was around £650,000.

And shine it did, in many ways, in Worcester in 2005. The weather, too, was fine and warm all week, and England's cricket fans were basking in the glow of a famous Ashes victory. Perhaps the most significant innovation at the Festival itself was the 'Club on the Green', which erected a large marquee on the grassed area enclosed between the cathedral cloisters and the King's School. High-quality real ale and a significant step up in the catering on offer made this the heart of the social side of the Festival. It proved an excellent addition, and one that Gloucester and Hereford would try to replicate in their cities, too, though neither has such a well-suited physical space for it as Worcester. Unbeknownst to Festival goers, however, the contractual arrangements with the external catering providers were disastrous; as a result, instead of making a five-figure contribution towards the Festival (as it had done in the past), the extremely popular offer on the green made a substantial five-figure loss.

Musically, there were some particularly high spots in the course of the week, most notably on Wednesday. For the first time, the BBC broadcast Evensong live from the Festival, and this broadcast has continued (though not always live) since that point: a significant move in the relationship between the Festival and Radio 3. Wednesday's evening concert, with the CBSO (in residence for the week) conducted by Martyn Brabbins, saw the first Festival performance of Gershwin's concert version of his opera *Porgy and Bess*. Gweneth-Ann Jeffers and Keel Watson in particular were superb soloists, joined by the Festival Chorus, who sang with commitment for a conductor who clearly inspires them. Linked to *Porgy and Bess* by their common 'spiritual' material, the second half of the concert was a very fine performance of Tippett's *A Child of our Time*, which proved an extremely successful bedfellow to Gershwin's jazz-inspired opera. For many, this was the highlight of the week, despite the delay to the beginning of the second half, on account of the conductor's having been inadvertently locked in his dressing room.

American music had featured in the opening concert, too, with Bernstein's effervescent overture from *Candide*, paired with only the second Three Choirs outing for Finzi's 'Ceremonial Ode' *For St Cecilia*, which is dedicated to Finzi's close friend Howard Ferguson. Edmund Blunden's text was as clearly articulated as you would hope by James Gilchrist, well supported by the Festival Chorus. Mendelssohn's *Lobgesang* made up the second half, with Rachel Nicholls and Gillian Webster joining Adrian Lucas and the CBSO for a fine opening concert.

Sunday evening's cathedral concert was an all-Russian affair, with the first performance of Rachmaninov's *The Bells* at the Festival since 1987(w), alongside the cantata by Prokofiev based on his film score for Sergei Eisenstein's 1938 film *Alexander Nevsky*, and Shostakovich's *Festive Overture*. This is the sort of programming that shows the best of Three Choirs, in its ability to showcase repertoire that others cannot and, joined by the CBSO, Adrian Lucas made a convincing case for this music to be performed much more often.

> Sunday's all-Russian concert dispensed with the home-team Festival Chorus, bringing instead the City of Birmingham Choir for its Three Choirs debut.
>
> This is Festival director Adrian Lucas' 'other' choir, and they have already performed Rachmaninov's The Bells at Symphony Hall. It sounded better

in this less searching, more generous acoustic, great washes of colourful sound bathing our ears, though the vastness of the space did not suit all the soloists.

Singing with great confidence in Russian, the choir brought a fine tone, shapely and nuanced, and with lively articulation, as they did for Prokofiev's *Alexander Nevsky*. Mezzo-soprano Frances McCafferty sounded eerily Russian in her solo, rich with plaintive lament, and the CBSO (resident orchestra after a long absence) gave Lucas a wonderfully alert and dramatic account of this admittedly derivative score.[50]

To take three days to get to any significant work by the Worcester's favourite son could be seen as unfitting for a Festival so steeped in his music, but come it did, in the form of Elgar's *The Light of Life*. This relatively early work was premièred under the composer himself at the Worcester Festival in 1896, and had, surprisingly, only been performed at Worcester since then.

Writing for the *Guardian*, Rian Evans observed that:

the exemplary baritone of James Rutherford carried both the authority and compassion to achieve the devotional focus that Elgar intended; the fine Festival chorus made the final Light of the World a paean of praise worthy of The Dream of Gerontius.

While the debt to Wagner is audible in The Light of Life – Elgar had visited Bayreuth prior to its composition – it was a Brahmsian dignity that characterised Bowen's approach, with the lyricism of the instrumental introductions and postludes carefully shaped and the City of Birmingham Symphony Orchestra warmly responsive.

Andrew Kennedy, who sang the role of the blind man with an affecting clarity of delivery, was also the eloquent soloist in Britten's Serenade for tenor, horn and strings which opened the concert.[51]

Elgar's music was also a focus on Thursday in the cathedral, though here represented by several smaller-scale pieces, and programmed alongside Adrian Lucas's own *Creation Canticles*. The great novelty here was the second-ever performance of Elgar's *The Holly and the Ivy*, unheard since its première in January 1899, and rediscovered by chance in 1970. Ruth Holton was superb in Lucas's work, brought to life in a convincing reading by Andrew Nethsingha and the CBSO, with perhaps some of the best singing of the week from the Festival Chorus. The evening was rounded off by a spellbinding late-night Rachmaninov Vespers, delivered in characteristic style by Nigel Short and his chamber choir, Tenebrae.

It was perhaps a mistake, however, to programme the Armonico Consort's well-reviewed and interesting staging of Purcell's *The Fairy Queen* against the main cathedral events on the last three nights of the Festival. The Purcell was well attended, and seems to have hit audience numbers in the cathedral concerts, perhaps because there was not much early music on offer during the

---

[50] Morley, *Birmingham Post*, 9 August 2005.

[51] *Guardian*, 11 August 2005.

rest of the week: Ex Cathedra gave an excellent programme of Tudor music on the Tuesday evening, but the performance suffered both from the cavernous space of the cathedral and from its late start time (9 p.m.). Other than this, the only pre-Elgar work in the main programme was Saturday's Mendelssohn. Unsurprisingly, those seeking a fix of earlier music sought out the Armonico Consort's Purcell rather than what was on offer in the cathedral.

Unfortunately for the Festival, audience numbers were down over much of the week, and in no concert was this more apparent than the cathedral programme on Tuesday afternoon performed by the three cathedral choirs and CBSO Wind Ensemble under David Hill. Doubtless, the Bruckner Mass in E minor is a beautiful work, but it needed a larger choir to do it justice, and the choristers seemed ill-prepared both in Bruckner and in Kenneth Leighton's *Easter Sequence*, though David Hill drew some fine singing from them nonetheless.

Classic chamber music programmes were scattered through the week, including The Cardinall's Musick marking the 400th anniversary of the Gunpowder Plot, Mark Bebbington playing Ravel, Prokofiev and Liszt, and concerts by the Wihan String Quartet, the Elgar Chorale, and the Festival debut for the *a cappella* gospel group Black Voices. David Owen Norris, joined by Amanda Pitt and Joanne Thomas, gave a fascinating insight into the music of Dyson and Quilter, and two late-night concerts were recorded by BBC Radio 3 for their 'Jazz Line-Up' programme.

The final major concert of the week (it was not the last, as Sir David Willcocks returned to the Festival on the Saturday to direct a 'Bring and Sing' performance of *Messiah*) was Britten's *War Requiem*. Adrian Lucas, the Festival Chorus and the CBSO were joined by the Russian soprano Elena Prokina, Worcester-born tenor John Mark Ainsley, and baritone James Rutherford in marking the sixtieth anniversary of the end of World War II. It was a highly charged evening, its atmosphere built by the cathedral bells tolling before the concert began, and although this was not a definitive account of Britten's masterwork, it was a telling one, enhanced by the cathedral space itself.

Christopher Morley, writing in the *Birmingham Post*, called this week 'the most successful Three Choirs Festival I can remember in 35 years'.[52] Yet, despite the wonderful weather, hugely successful innovations in terms of the non-musical provision, and some fine performances over the week, the prediction of the treasurers proved correct. Insufficient money was raised, resulting in an overall loss in excess of £130,000. This left the organisation with much soul-searching to do. The chairman and his committee resigned, and the deficit was covered by those Worcester-only funds.[53] However, significant damage had been done to the organisation's finances and reputation, particularly among its financial supporters. Pressure was soon brought to bear from the Arts Council (among others), who doubted that the Festival's organisational structure was fit for purpose, and was similarly sceptical of its governance and oversight procedures. Perhaps another chairman could have handled the situation

[52] *Birmingham Post*, 18 August 2005.

[53] It should be observed that had such a loss occurred in a Hereford or Gloucester year, no such parachute funds were available, and the result could well have been the end of Three Choirs Festival.

differently – introduced the same positive innovations without setting noses out of joint, managed partnerships and contractual relations in a way that was more beneficial to the Festival. Whatever mistakes were made, it is clear that the events of 2005 forced the Festival to make vital changes to its structures and processes over the following years, changes which transformed the organisation into the professional arts body that it is today. Such crises, while painful at the time, in hindsight can be seen to have been beneficial.

AFTER the financial difficulties of 2005(w), Hereford rose manfully to the challenge of righting the ship in 2006. A solid Three Choirs programme was put together by Geraint Bowen, his second as Artistic Director, but not one without innovation. Granted, the stalwarts were treated to their Elgar (*The Kingdom* on the opening night, marking the centenary of its first performance), a sell-out Three Cathedral Choirs Mozart Requiem, and a final night *Belshazzar*, but in between there was a first performance at Three Choirs for Schumann's *Das Paradies und die Peri*, a revival of Kodály's boisterous Budávari *Te Deum* (last performed in Gloucester in 1989) and a new commission from the Scottish composer James MacMillan.

It was perhaps this last work, *Sun Dogs*, jointly commissioned with the Indiana University Contemporary Vocal Ensemble and receiving its UK première at Hereford, that had the largest impact. This is a piece inspired directly by a richly metaphorical and highly colourful poem by Michael Symmons Roberts. The title refers to the astronomical phenomenon in which, under certain conditions, the sun appears to have two mini-suns at its feet, like guard dogs, though it seems that for both composer and poet it was the symbolism and iconography of the idea that particularly appealed. The astronomical crosses into the animal, posing the question of what these dogs would be like if they were real. As James MacMillan himself put it: 'One of the very first poems I had ever seen by [Michael Symmons Roberts] was this fabulously elusive and allegorical poem from the early 1990s called 'Sun Dogs'. I knew as soon as I saw it that one day I would set it.'[54] It is a text about deliverance and redemption, in which the encounters depicted are seemingly mundane, and are therefore dismissed rather than being recognised as meetings with grace. The outsiders (whether dogs or beggars), though seemingly powerless at the beginning, become powerful through their acts of compassion.

A very difficult work for *a cappella* choir, the hard work put in by the Festival Chorus came good in a fine account under the direction of the composer himself. They coped valiantly with the demands of singing in free rhythm, chanting and whistling, and made a good fist of communicating the vivid text, lifting themselves 'to a whole new level in one bound'.[55] Perhaps the most successful Three Choirs commission for some years, the concert also attracted BBC Radio 3, who returned to record an evening concert for the first time since 1996.

This new work was paired with some varied but core Three Choirs fare conducted by Andrew Nethsingha, who shared the podium duties with James MacMillan. A rousing account of Finzi's *God is Gone Up* in its full orchestral

[54] Interview with James MacMillan on Radio 3, before the broadcast of the concert.

[55] *Church Times*, 1 September 2006.

version was followed by a very convincing performance of Vaughan Williams's *Five Variants on Dives and Lazarus*, the lustrous Philharmonia strings filling the cathedral acoustic in characteristic English pastoral style. After the interval, James Gilchrist was on sparkling form in a typically intense and expressive *Dies natalis*, originally written for the 1939 Hereford Festival (which was cancelled because of the outbreak of war). This setting of words from *Centuries of Meditation* by the Hereford-born poet Thomas Traherne draws inspiration from landscape and art as well as text, and the subtlety and expressive power of Finzi's musical language was finely wrought here by musicians who visibly feel and live this music. Perhaps the best concert of the week was concluded by a 'beautifully sensitive' reading of Vaughan Williams's *Five Mystical Songs*, with Matthew Brook as soloist.[56]

However, the difficulty of the MacMillan work had meant that *Sun Dogs* dominated rehearsals, resulting in a rather lacklustre *Belshazzar* the following night. While Neal Davies shone, the Festival Chorus struggled to match his energy, coming across as slightly wayward in Walton's fizzing score. In the first half, Geraint Bowen's measured approach to Shostakovich (*Tahiti Trot*) and his careful phrasing and particular attention to the woodwind in Ravel's *Ma mère l'oye* produced a pleasing account of both works, with the Philharmonia's characteristic warmth shining through.

Given the composer's minimal choral output, the centenary of Shostakovich's birth was not perhaps an anniversary one would expect to be significantly marked by Three Choirs. However, the great Russian's music was to be heard throughout the week across six different events. Orchestrally, his Chamber Symphony was performed in an interestingly varied concert at Wyastone Leys by the Stratford-based Orchestra of the Swan, alongside works by Finzi and Bliss, and the world première of Julian Philips's *Masque for Caliban*, 'an inventive and poignant new work for baritone and orchestra'.[57] Shostakovich's solo vocal work appeared in a recital given by James Oxley, Roderick Williams and Caroline Dowdle, and his *Passacaglia* as an Evensong voluntary on Friday night, played by Peter Dyke. However, most significant here was a superb reading of the Cello Concerto by Steven Isserlis in Wednesday evening's orchestral concert, conducted by Richard Hickox with the Philharmonia Orchestra. Its pairing with Janáček's folk-infused suite from *The Cunning Little Vixen* provided an interesting first-half foil, before a sure-footed performance of Vaughan Williams's Symphony No. 5.

The supporting programme was typical of both Three Choirs in general and Geraint Bowen's input in particular, spanning the large (the first appearance at the Festival of the National Youth Orchestra of Wales, playing Mahler) and the small (the Brodsky quartet), the early (viol consort Phantasm) and the more recent (James Oxley and Roderick Williams singing Sibelius and Korngold).

Monday's evening concert was a Festival highlight for many, primarily for its first half: Kodály's rumbustious Budávari *Te Deum*, where the chorus were superb under the baton of Adrian Lucas, followed by perhaps the discovery of the week, John McCabe's *Notturni ed Alba*, commissioned by the Herefordshire

[56] Ibid.
[57] Ibid.

Arts Association for the 1970 Hereford Festival. To use the words of Michael Kennedy, this is 'the most exotically and seductively beautiful music McCabe has written'.[58] The audience was captivated by Carys Lane's luminous tone and utter command of the material of these 'riveting nocturnes'.[59] Her stamina was also amazing, as she sang both works in the first half, as well as the Schubert Mass in A flat that followed the interval, alongside Catherine King, Andrew Kennedy (returning after his debut at Worcester in 2005) and Robert Rice.

The inclusion of Schumann's 'oratorio ... for cheerful people' in the 2006 Festival programme was perhaps the most significant talking point in the run-up to the Festival.[60] Unknown by most, audience and performers alike, the piece had never been given at Three Choirs before, though it enjoyed a period of popularity after its first performance in Leipzig in 1843. Since its Hereford performance, it has appeared more regularly on European stages, and has been championed in more recent years by the conducting luminaries Sir Simon Rattle, Nikolaus Harnoncourt and Sir John Eliot Gardiner in the concert hall as well as on disc. The piece takes its libretto from the German translation of Thomas Moore's *Lalla Rookh: An Oriental Romance* (1817), which seems to have both enchanted and captured Schumann's musical imagination. It also seems that Schumann saw something of a 'gap in the market' for a piece that took advantage of the general popularity of the biblical oratorio, but taking a non-religious tale, and one steeped in the middle-eastern exoticism that was so 'in vogue' at the time. As Schumann wrote: 'I am involved in a major project – the greatest that I have ever undertaken – it is not an opera – I nearly think of it as a new genre for the concert hall.'

Carefully structured across three parts, but avoiding the conventional set-piece numbers, the narrative tells the tale of a Peri (according to Persian mythology, the impure child of a fallen angel and human female) who tries to re-enter paradise by bringing gifts to redeem her sin. Her first two efforts – the last drop of blood of a hero slain in the pursuit of liberty, and the final sigh of a maiden who sacrifices her life for love – are deemed worthy, but insufficient. The pearly gates only open to admit her on her presentation of a tear from a sinner who repents at the sight of a child at prayer. Moralistic and sentimental, perhaps, but Schumann's score ripples with original touches, and with flashes of both his symphonic writing and his Lieder, skilfully lit here by Richard Hickox's assured direction. Despite a few odd moments, Joan Rodgers made a convincing Peri, and James Gilchrist's characteristic grasp of text ensured his narration was never lost. Other performances manage to combine certain solo parts more effectively than was managed here – Alan Ewing in particular seemed under-used – but audience, chorus and orchestra alike were all taken by the piece in some form, and it seems certain that it will reappear on Festival programmes in the future.

One other work that clearly falls into this category is Mozart's Requiem, this year performed by the three cathedral choirs and the Cheltenham-based period instrument ensemble The Corelli Orchestra, conducted by Geraint Bowen

---

[58] Hereford Festival programme book, 2006, p. 108.

[59] *Church Times*, 1 September 2006.

[60] This is the composer's own description of the work.

himself. A feisty *Nozze di Figaro* overture, directed by Warwick Cole, followed by a fine Symphony No. 40 provided a fully Mozartian first-half prelude to the main course. The audience that filled the cathedral were doubtless not aware of the efforts at authenticity, which centred around pitch – the period instruments here were tuned to A = 430 Hz, as opposed to the normal A = 440 Hz of modern concert pitch. Those few in the building with perfect pitch were bemused, but the packed house welcomed the performance with great acclaim, particularly for the virtuosic and thoroughly convincing work of the cathedral choirs.

It was, perhaps, an evolutionary Festival rather than a revolutionary one, but certainly this was a week in which the audiences were strong and support consistent. A steadying year, and one upon which the Festival could build.

THE Gloucester Festival programme in 2007 was always going to have a distinct Elgarian focus, given the significant celebration of 150 years since the composer's birth. Needless to say, this would involve a *Gerontius*, conducted by Andrew Nethsingha. More significantly, this would be the first time the piece had appeared on a Festival programme since 2002, the longest period without a performance since it was first given (complete) in 1902.[61] Much anticipated, then, and with a trio of soloists to whet the appetite of any Three Choirs audience – the much-loved Sarah Connolly's first Festival appearance as the Angel, the return of the ever-popular Roderick Williams, and the well-known and much-respected face of James Gilchrist in his first 'title role' performance. However, as John Quinn reported for MusicWeb:

> I had hoped for great things but this is not a Gerontius that will live in my memory and, though it was warmly received by the audience, I don't think it will go down in the annals of the Three Choirs as one of the best performances that this masterpiece has received at Festivals over the years.[62]

Despite a triumph in the same work just a few weeks earlier in Cheltenham, Gilchrist was not on top form vocally, particularly in the more heroic passages, and some criticised Andrew Nethsingha's over-ambitious tempi. Sarah Connolly, however, was stunning, singing with 'dignity and sincerity in her voice' and with a tone that 'was consistently rich and full'.[63] Roderick Williams was similarly impressive, and while the chorus perhaps did not reach the heights of certain other concerts over the course of the week, 'the choral singing was excellent overall'.[64]

Other major Elgar works in the programme included the Symphony No. 1, given alongside Rossini's overture *The Silken Ladder* and the Tippett Triple Concerto (its first performance at Three Choirs). This Sunday orchestral concert – an event fast becoming a feature in Gloucester programmes – was a triumph, with excellent playing from the trio of soloists from the orchestra in the Tippett,

---

[61] Not including the two interruptions for war.

[62] John Quinn, 'Seen and Heard Concert Review: Three Choirs Festival (3)', online at http://www.musicweb-international.com/SandH/2007/Jul-Dec07/three_choirs3.htm [accessed 29 September 2016].

[63] Ibid.

[64] Ibid.

and a rip-roaring Elgar inspiringly led by Martyn Brabbins.[65] There was an electric atmosphere immediately following the concert, with musicians coming off the stage clearly energised in a new way by the performance of a very familiar work.

Adrian Lucas's grasp of this repertoire was clear, too, in a memorable account of Elgar's war elegy *The Spirit of England*, paired with Holst's contemporaneous *The Planets*, making an intriguing contrast with the Britten *War Requiem* which opened Festival week. There was a magical conclusion to the Holst, as the ladies' chorus moved away down the east cloister walk, their siren-like, ethereal sound becoming ever more distant and seeming to melt into the silence of the spheres. John Quinn reviewed the concert for 'Seen and Heard International'. Of the Elgar, he wrote: 'This was a splendid and very faithful account of an underrated masterpiece. Coming just a few days after War Requiem it was very good to hear a contrasting but no less effective and eloquent musical testimony to the wastage of war.' And of the Holst: 'This was a very fine account of Holst's orchestral masterpiece and the performers deserved the ovation that they received from the audience.'[66]

Andrew Nethsingha had shown similar charge in the opening concert of the week, in an emotionally charged *War Requiem*. Joined by the Philharmonia Orchestra, Festival Chorus, the choristers of Gloucester Cathedral, Judith Howarth, Stephen Roberts and the incomparable James Gilchrist, this was a memorable performance, and an 'auspicious' opening to the week. John Quinn again:

> Andrew Nethsingha was in sole charge and he exerted an impressive control, clearly having the full measure of the piece. His was a very convincing interpretation of the score. ... The Festival Chorus sang their demanding parts with great assurance and fine tone. ... The outstanding solo performance was given by James Gilchrist. As in so many Britten works a key challenge for the tenor soloist is to banish the listener's memories of Peter Pears. So compelling was Gilchrist's performance that this was never an issue. He sang with a wonderfully plangent tone yet there was ample steel in the voice also.[67]

The return of Christopher Robinson after some years was a welcome feature of the Monday evening performance, featuring a fine reading of Howells's *Hymnus Paradisi*, and a revelatory *Serenade to Music*, performed by '16 first-rate young soloists taking up the parts originally assigned to Isobel Baillie, Heddle Nash, and Eva Turner ... The Vaughan Williams was out of this world.'[68] No

---

[65] The soloists in the Tippet were James Clark (violin), Vicci Wardman (viola) and David Cohen (cello).

[66] John Quinn, 'Seen and Heard Concert Review: Three Choirs Festival (5)', online at http://www.musicweb-international.com/SandH/2007/Jul-Dec07/three_choirs5.htm [accessed 29 September 2016].

[67] John Quinn, 'Seen and Heard Concert Review: Three Choirs Festival (1)', online at http://www.musicweb-international.com/SandH/2007/Jul-Dec07/britten0408.htm [accessed 29 September 2016].

[68] *Church Times*, 31 August 2007.

less impressive was the choral singing in Howells's complex score, with a chorus who were 'quite superb' showing 'total commitment' to their maestro.[69] Clearly, Nethsingha's focus on the chorus, assisted of course by his colleagues in the other two cities, was paying dividends, raising standards as well as attracting a wider age range to audition.

This concert also included the first significant piece from the Festival's composer-in-residence, Robin Holloway: the UK première of his orchestration of Debussy's 1915 Great War elegy for two pianos *En blanc et noir*. It was a 'splendidly lucid' realisation, 'over which the German hymn *Ein feste Burg* glowers like some vast howitzer',[70] but one in which even that was 'swept away, like poisonous fumes'[71] by the new order. Other works in this mid-week showcase of Holloway's music included the *Serenade* in D flat (performed by the Okeanos Ensemble), and his reworking of Bach's *Goldberg Variations*, titled *Gilded Goldbergs*, and delivered in stunning style by the Micallef-Inanga Piano Duo.

Other new music of note included: a stunning collection of *Robert Graves Songs* by Hugh Wood, in a recital by the inimitable young tenor Andrew Kennedy; first and second performances respectively for chamber works by Howard Skempton and Nicola LeFanu; and fascinating modern pieces for solo guitar by Lionel Sainsbury and Nigel Westlake, expertly rendered by Craig Ogden. The music of Elizabeth Maconchy was featured, too, in her centenary year, along with works by the local composer Graham Whettam, who sadly died shortly after the Festival.

Early music was perhaps more visible, both in some stunning small recitals and on a larger scale on the main platform. Most notable perhaps was Catherine Bott's concert with the gut-fiddle players Pavlo Beznosiuk and Mark Levy – for one critic, it was 'the early music highlight of the week'.[72] The sure hand of Geraint Bowen was also to be felt, not least in the novelty of a short arrangement by Bach of Kuhnau's *Der Gerechte kommt um*, confidently performed by the cathedral choirs and Corelli Orchestra, prior to their Vivaldi *Gloria*. No less scintillating was Gillian Keith in Bach's Cantata No. 51, *Jauchzet Gott*, in which she and Crispian Steele-Perkins (period trumpet) played off each other in astonishing style.[73]

The Birmingham-based chamber choir Ex Cathedra returned to the Festival for an exquisite Monteverdi Vespers, played to a packed house on the Thursday evening, taking a main evening concert spot for the first time. As John Quinn observed:

> The placing of this performance right in the middle of a week that has contained many large scale, rich textured choral and orchestral works was

[69] John Quinn, 'Seen and Heard Concert Review: Three Choirs Festival (1)', online at http://www.musicweb-international.com/SandH/2007/Jul-Dec07/britten0408.htm [accessed 29 September 2016].

[70] *Church Times*, 31 August 2007.

[71] Paul Drayton, Gloucester Festival programme book, 2007.

[72] *Early Music Today*, October/November 2007.

[73] Steele-Perkins and Bowen were also together on the platform later in the week for the Haydn Trumpet Concerto.

very shrewd. It provided an excellent contrast with the music of Britten, Elgar *et al.* and thereby refreshed the ears of the audience in a most effective way. ... This superb account of Monteverdi's Vespers is one that I will not quickly forget.[74]

Perhaps the largest challenge of the 2007 Festival actually took place in the week preceding it: torrential rain and the river Severn bursting its banks resulted in much of Gloucester and the surrounding countryside being submerged. The main electricity substation was saved by sterling military efforts, though the flooding resulted in contamination of the normal water supplies, and bowsers on every street corner.[75] It was also thanks to the commitment and understanding of the Gloucestershire police (whose then Chief Constable, Timothy Brain, took over the chairmanship of the Gloucester Festival in 2012) that the staging and seating was escorted through closed and flooded roads to enable the Festival to go ahead. Bottled water, temporary toilets and extensive restrictions on catering notwithstanding (on the opening night, there was not a restaurant open in the city), it was important for the city that the Festival go ahead, and the drinking-water supplies were restored by Tuesday of Festival week. US news networks did not assist, however, showing a flooded Tewkesbury – the Abbey an island – with the caption 'Gloucester flooded', which resulted in inundation of the Festival's phone lines. (The planned Tewkesbury concerts were hastily moved to Cheltenham.) The watery theme was taken up in competitive style by the cathedral clergy, who, in their introductions to each concert, sought ever more inventive and aquatically themed puns to ensure that the music was not interrupted by mobile phones. As John Quinn judged: 'His colleagues tried their best to match him but didn't quite succeed and I declare the Dean to be the winner of this friendly little "contest" – by a short head.'[76]

One much-anticipated feature of the Festival's programme was the first-ever Festival performance of an Arnold Bax symphony, which was due to be given in an afternoon orchestral concert alongside Vaughan Williams's *Lark Ascending* and Elgar's *Enigma Variations*. The venerable conductor Vernon Handley,

[74] John Quinn, 'Seen and Heard Concert Review: Three Choirs Festival (4)', online at http://www.musicweb-international.com/SandH/2007/Jul-Dec07/three_choirs4.htm [accessed 29 September 2016].

[75] As the dean of the cathedral, Nicholas Bury, quipped in characteristic style in his address at the Opening Service: 'A new word has entered our daily language in Gloucester these past weeks – "Bowser". What did you think when you first heard it? The council and the water board and the army are responding to the crisis in Gloucestershire over the water shortage by bringing in bowsers, I heard on the news. I imagined a kind of special hound trained by the City Council with a barrel of clean drinking water around its neck. Instead it was a rather mundane tank on wheels – named oddly enough after the Australian who invented the petrol pump – Sylvanus Bowser, who died in 1933. Nevertheless thank God for them.'

[76] John Quinn, 'Seen and Heard Concert Review: Three Choirs Festival (5)', online at http://www.musicweb-international.com/SandH/2007/Jul-Dec07/three_choirs5.htm [accessed 29 September 2016].

whose recording of the complete Bax symphonies with the BBC Philharmonic (Chandos, 2003) is generally regarded as without equal, was engaged to conduct.

However, by summer 2007 his health was failing. He arrived in the cathedral on the morning of the concert in a wheelchair, and was assisted up on to the platform with a stool wedged on to the relatively small podium. By the rehearsal break it was clear that all was not well, and Handley's collapse on leaving the stage necessitated the calling of the Festival doctor. Cancellation of the afternoon's performance (which was nearly sold out) seemed imminent. Emergency decisions were taken by the Festival Secretary, Chairman and representatives of the orchestra resulted in a delayed second part of the rehearsal. The principal percussionist, David Corkhill, took the podium for *The Lark Ascending*, so giving the Festival's Artistic Director time to fetch his *Enigma Variations* score, and re-rehearse it. The concert was saved, but there was to be no Bax. Unfamiliar to the orchestra and with no conductor and no rehearsal time, it was the only choice available. Meanwhile, a quick trip to the Gloucester music library revealed a set of parts for Elgar's *Introduction and Allegro*, which there was barely time to run through before the end of the rehearsal. The programme was augmented by the Mozart C minor Wind Serenade, the parts hastily faxed over from Oxford, and arriving on the platform minutes before the performance was due to begin. A very attractive concert was mounted, to an appreciative audience, though it was not the programme advertised, and it should be noted that there has still not been a Bax symphony performed at a Three Choirs Festival.

Andrew Nethsingha did fulfil one dream, however, conducting massed Festival forces in a 'rip-roaring reading'[77] of Mahler's Symphony No. 8. This was Nethsingha's last concert as Artistic Director before moving to Cambridge to take the reins of the choir at his *alma mater*, St John's College. The fine cast of soloists (Stephen Richardson stepping in at the eleventh hour for an indisposed Graeme Broadbent) all added to the occasion, with notable mentions for Gillian Keith, whose 'voice soared sweetly from on high as the "Mater Gloriosa"' and Adrian Thompson, who 'radiantly invoked the Eternal Feminine'.[78] While this was far from a definitive account of a great masterpiece, particularly in its pacing in the early stages, the atmosphere created over the course of the second half in particular was priceless, and fully deserving of the standing ovation from the full house that greeted the epic conclusion. For Nethsingha, perhaps, it was as Goethe's *Faust* has it in the symphony's final chorus:

Alles Vergängliche	(All that is ephemeral
Ist nur ein Gleichnis;	is but a symbol;
Das Unzulängliche,	the incomplete
Hier wird's Ereignis;	is here fulfilled;
Das Unbeschreibliche,	the indescribable,
Hier ist's getan ...	is here accomplished ...)

---

[77] *Church Times*, 31 August 2007.

[78] Jim Pritchard, 'Seen and Heard Concert Review: Three Choirs Festival (6)', online at http://www.musicweb-international.com/SandH/2007/Jul-Dec07/three_choirs6.htm [accessed 29 September 2016].

25

Reorganisation

THE organisational issues that had dogged Three Choirs over the previous decade, and which came to a head in 2005, resulted in increasing pressure, both from inside and out, to find a model on which the Festival could move forwards. Over the course of the 2006–7 cycle, much work had been going on behind the scenes to assess possible solutions, all of which became focused on recruiting some sort of central manager to work across the three cities. A job description was drawn up, and advertisements placed in the music and arts press, as well as the national papers. These attracted a varied field of applicants. The whole process was directly supported by the Arts Council, which, despite lauding many aspects of the 2005 Worcester Festival, was perhaps the loudest voice calling for organisational change. In particular, the Council gave a significant grant to assist the Festival with the appointee's first year's salary. The successful candidate would be the first full-time employee the Festival had ever taken on. The purpose of the role was advertised thus: 'To establish and operate a central professional management system within the organisation leading to high quality delivery of Festivals.' It also included a very clear responsibility regarding longer-term strategy and direction, and organisational development.

This was the Festival making a statement of intent about where it both needed and wanted to go in the future, and marked a recognition that the time had come for a professional core to assist local committees, and to provide key consistency and services to the local teams in the three cities. It was a huge shift. To use the words of Bernard Day, chairman of the Three Choirs Festival Association, in the published press release: 'the new structure enables this historic festival to meet the challenges and opportunities of the 21st century. It will go from strength to strength.'

The unanimous decision of the two interview panels (administrative and artistic) was to offer the job to Dr Paul Hedley, who took up the post from the beginning of February 2008.[1] Clearly, given the timescales required for festival planning, his direct impact on the Worcester Festival that summer was limited (the programme having already been announced the previous summer), but this appointment marked a significant change in how the Festival was managed, and in the direction of the organisation as a whole.

Of more direct significance for Worcester was the new chairman, Sir Michael Perry, a businessman of significant repute who had previously been chairman of Unilever and chairman of the Shakespeare's Globe Trust, and had retired to the

---

[1] Dr Hedley had held the post of Local Administrator for the very successful 2007 Festival in Gloucester, and at that time was also a lay clerk in Gloucester Cathedral choir.

Worcester area. His reconstituted committee combined some 'old hands' with new blood, and brought substantial business experience with it, particularly in financial terms, along with a drive and focus that Worcester greatly needed.

Adrian Lucas's 2008 programme was built around a desire to place the cathedral choirs closer to the centre than they had been in previous years. The primary vehicle for this was the return of Bach's great *Christmas Oratorio*, where the massed boys and men of the three cathedrals were joined by the Academy of Ancient Music, with Edward Higginbottom, the renowned early music specialist from New College, Oxford, on the podium. Unusually, this performance included all six parts of the oratorio; the concert began at 6 p.m., with a Glyndebourne-esque 'dinner interval'.[2] The cathedral bell-ringers took a major part too, though ringing throughout the interval rather than before the concert, as had been the case in 2005. The combination of fine preparatory work, a top-notch ensemble and a highly skilled conductor used to getting the best from boy choristers resulted in a very fine performance:

> In musical and textual terms, this brilliant *Christmas Oratorio* was like sitting at the feet of Gamaliel. The young tenor Andrew Tortise ... excelled ... while the three choirs, lifted to a whole new level or *étage*, sang as if they were the Maîtrise of Versailles itself.[3]

More controversial, perhaps, were the changes to Choral Evensong, long a staple of the Festival programme. Instead of the usual pattern of joint 'massed' Evensongs, each cathedral choir was asked to sing one service on its own, in addition to two joint Evensongs, one of which was recorded for BBC broadcast. This was an interesting innovation, partly driven by a desire to make more joint rehearsal time available, and one that would be watched closely over the ensuing years. On the final Saturday, Worcester Cathedral choir were joined by their counterparts from All Saints, Worcester, Massachusetts, who also performed in Friday's evening concert – an attention-grabbing performance of *Carmina Burana* under Adrian Lucas's assured baton.

Worcester's girl choristers, a front row launched only two years earlier, played their part, too, in both the Festival Eucharist (Vaughan Williams's Mass in G minor), and Wednesday's evening concert, which also marked the arrival of the new man at Gloucester – Adrian Partington. Known to many in Three Choirs circles, not least due to his time as Assistant Organist under Donald Hunt at Worcester (1981–91), Partington did not follow the traditional cathedral organist route to his new post. He had been a chorister at Worcester (1966–71), and still recalls the 'high watermark' of Three Choirs Festivals in 1969: Christopher Robinson's programme, which famously included the second British performance of Janáček's *Glagolitic Mass*, a major commission from Jonathan Harvey (*Ludus Amoris*, see Chapter 19), and Beethoven's *Missa solemnis*.[4] In those days, home choristers would have typically sung as part of the main chorus, and those

---

[2] In true Festival style, there was an option to have a full turkey dinner in the Cathedral School in between the two halves.

[3] *Church Times*, 29 August 2008. The other soloists for this performance were Lorna Anderson, Sarah Connolly and Michael George.

[4] Interview with Adrian Partington, 16 May 2016.

experiences as a boy clearly left a huge impression on the ten-year-old Partington. He went from Worcester to the Royal College of Music, and became Organ Scholar at St George's Chapel, Windsor, before going up to King's College, Cambridge, as Organ Scholar in 1978. Following his time as Assistant Organist at Worcester, he spent three years as Head of Music in a small independent school, before taking on the formation of the new CBSO Youth Choir, assisting Simon Halsey. This appointment and other work with the CBSO chorus, alongside various keyboard-playing engagements with the orchestra, allowed him to give up teaching and concentrate on his freelance work. This was shortly afterwards joined by a position at the Royal Welsh College of Music and Drama, and the beginning of his long (and ongoing) association with the BBC National Chorus of Wales.

Partington's first concert as away Artistic Director was an interesting mixture of non-standard repertoire, opening with Elgar's *Froissart* overture, followed by the much less performed Stokowski orchestration of Mussorgsky's *Pictures at an Exhibition*. This latter piece in particular, Partington recalls, was a very good introduction for him to the Philharmonia. The piece was not already in their repertoire, which made it much easier for the two parties to find and begin to build a musical relationship.[5] The second half of the concert, with a nod to the Christmas theme initiated by the *Christmas Oratorio*, was Britten's *St Nicolas*, in which the chorus and Worcester choristers were joined by James Gilchrist. Perhaps the most significant element to come out of this performance, at least for Partington, related to a matter of chorus preparation. Much had been done over the previous years to improve the rehearsal process for the chorus, both in matters of recruitment and the use of the cathedral lay clerks, but the standard model was based on the school term – rehearsals stopped at the end of the summer term, restarting two nights before the Festival began. In this case, the upshot was that the work done at the massed rehearsal almost a month previously had been largely forgotten. As a direct result of this experience, Partington resolved that at least in his home Festival, he would endeavour to do away with this rehearsal break. His experience with the CBSO chorus and the BBC National Chorus of Wales was clearly going to inform his approach to the Festival Chorus, too.

The other new arrival at 2008(w) was the brand new Tickell organ, installed over previous months at triforium level above the quire. Many festival-goers were anxious to both see and hear this all-new instrument, which would be used for the Festival Evensongs, and put through its paces in an inaugural recital by the renowned British organist Dame Gillian Weir in the latter part of the week. Despite some rehearsal issues, primarily caused by the difficulty of finding practice slots in a building that was in constant use during Festival week, this was an exhibition of very fine playing, and one which showcased the extremely varied colours and great impact of the new organ. The omission of the programmed Bach Preludes did affect the balance of the recital, but Weir's playing of Messiaen (*L'Ascension: Four Symphonic Meditations* and *Les Anges*) in particular was no less than one would expect from such a luminary of the organ world. An auspicious inauguration.

[5] Ibid.

Just as varied was the daytime programme, with certain conspicuous highlights over the course of the week: dazzlingly virtuosic recorder playing by Piers Adams and Red Priest, a sold-out Tewkesbury Abbey performance from the King's Singers (covering music from Byrd to Geoffrey Poole, alongside their typical close harmony), fine piano recitals by Bobby Chen and Mark Bebbington, and, for the first time at Three Choirs, Shakespeare's Globe Touring Company performing *The Winter's Tale* in College Hall. The 2005 Festival's 'Club on the Green' was again in evidence, though this time catered by a combination of the Friends and the school, and was a popular social hub across the week, no doubt assisted by the quality real ale organised by the Worcester Cathedral Guild of Bellringers.

Three significant anniversaries were marked in Adrian Lucas's programme. Perhaps most significantly for Three Choirs, fifty years had passed since the death of Vaughan Williams in 1958. There were performances of no fewer than sixteen of his works, from the largest scale – *A Sea Symphony* (Martyn Brabbins, Festival Chorus and the Philharmonia, alongside Britten's *Four Sea Interludes* from *Peter Grimes*), to the choral (*Lord, thou hast been our refuge* in the Opening Service, and a whole concert by the Elgar Chorale), as well as organ and song repertoire. Two centenaries were marked too – one either side of the Channel – as Adrian Lucas continued the Worcester tradition begun by his predecessor, Donald Hunt, of showcasing French music. The hundredth anniversary of the birth of the great French organist and composer Olivier Messiaen was marked in a variety of concerts: orchestral (*Les Offrandes oubliés* the opener for Martyn Brabbins's Philharmonia programme), organ (several recitals over the week), and chamber (a hugely powerful performance of the *Quatuor pour la fin du temps* in a late-night concert in College Hall with soloists of the Philharmonia Orchestra and Matthew Schellhorn).

The other centenary was that of the birth of Howard Ferguson – less significant perhaps, perhaps, but worthy of attention nonetheless. His dazzling fanfare-based *Overture for an Occasion* proved a fine opening item in Friday's evening concert, alongside a revival of his *Amore Langueo*, premièred in Gloucester in 1956, and only performed once at the Festival since. Among Ferguson's small published œuvre (only nineteen works), the two large-scale pieces for chorus and orchestra arguably sit at the pinnacle, with *Amore Langueo* the earlier of the two. In reviewing Richard Hickox's recording of the piece on EMI for *Gramophone* magazine, Michael Oliver writes:

> Its language is reassuring: recognizably within the mainstream of the English choral tradition, at times post-Walton as well as post-Elgar, but in two respects it stands at a tangent from that tradition and avoids being merely 'traditional'. ... It achieves its directness through economy of means: the choral textures are often beautiful (there is an especially fine unaccompanied chorus of contemplation towards the end) but there is no wallowing in lush harmonies, no indulgence or 'fatness', and the structure of the piece is closely controlled.[6]

---

[6] Michael Oliver, review of EMI catalogue number el749627-4, *Gramophone*, February 1988.

'Closely controlled' would be a fine description of Lucas's performance, too, ably assisted by the flawless diction and the communicative skills of tenor James Gilchrist, and some assured singing from the Festival Chorus.

The other significant work in this concert was this year's Festival première, *A British Symphony* by Andrew Gant. This is a piece not without controversy, however, as its first performance had been pulled at the last minute the year before by the conductor Barry Wordsworth. He declared to the audience in a short speech at the beginning of the concert in Brighton that he 'did not believe in the work' – an event which made headlines in the national press. No such problems troubled the Three Choirs performance. *A British Symphony* is about cultural identity, and aims to 'explore the diversity of the nations of the United Kingdom while at the same time celebrating their unity and the critical elements which make them one'.[7] Its musical material is substantially drawn from British folk songs, with an ever-present link to the sea surrounding these isles. David Hart reviewed the concert for the *Birmingham Post*, under the byline 'Polite generosity afforded to premiere of A British Symphony':

> Gant's 'folk-song' symphony is no compendium piece. The various tunes are often little more than melodic fragments, surrounded by a bewildering assortment of alarums and excursions.
>
> In his programme note Gant refers to unity, diversity and a 'psychological narrative', but it's a bitty, quirky journey in which the various musical elements are glimpsed through the distorting mirror of a funfair.
>
> Despite its serious intent and intriguing sound-canvas (Gant has an undoubted ear for strange orchestral textures and colourful percussion) this is at best an allusive and elliptic work; at worst it's a worrying, nihilistic view of nationhood that many will find disturbing.[8]

Perhaps the most innovative concert of the week, however, was that presented on the second Saturday, with the inimitable John Wilson at the helm of an effervescent Philharmonia Orchestra in a programme of classic British film music:

> he conducted like one inspired, and his introductions, in which he wore his vast learning lightly, were killingly amusing. The music was Vaughan Williams, Walton, and Eric Coates, all doing their belated bit for the war; some non-militaristic Malcolm Arnold and delicious Richard Rodney Bennett; together with glimpses of the Carry On films (Eric Rogers) and Harry Potter (John Williams).[9]

This concert was given in partnership with the Worcester Festival – a separate, locally run and extremely diverse event that ran in parallel that year. Though much of the main Festival audience chose not to attend, effective cross-promotion between the two festivals ensured a good house: one that

[7] Andrew Gant, Worcester Festival programme book, 2008. Copies of all the Festival programme books cited in this chapter are held in the Three Choirs Festival Office, Gloucester.

[8] *Birmingham Post*, 6 August 2008.

[9] *Church Times*, 29 August 2008.

was significantly different in character, and demonstrably more local. Clearly, this was a laudable and reasonably successful effort to draw in a new audience. Such outreach is a continual challenge for any festival, but it was increasingly becoming a requirement for any endeavour hoping to receive financial support from bodies such as the Arts Council and local authorities, particularly as their budgets are squeezed ever tighter.

THE 2009 Hereford Festival was planned against a very uncertain backdrop. Granted, the new central administration was having an effect, and in the middle of 2009 the Association also appointed a part-time Development Manager to oversee and assist with fund-raising across the three cities. However, the clouds of the 2008 international financial crisis were dark, and with turmoil in the United States spreading to the European stock markets and financial infrastructure, no one was quite sure whether there would be a knock-on effect in terms of the consumption of culture. When the programme was planned, UK interest rates stood at 5 percent; by the time tickets went on sale at Easter, they stood at 0.5 percent, with the government having pumped billions of pounds into the banking sector.

However, the Festival need not have worried on that score. Despite having had to take some difficult decisions to control artistic and logistical costs, ticket sales were strong, outperforming any previous Hereford Festival, and outstripping predictions by over 15 percent. Clearly the audience was attracted by Geraint Bowen's programme, with its carefully crafted blend of youth and experience, of new and old, of known and unknown. The thread holding it all together was a seasonal one – an idea that has inspired generations of composers, and which grew out of the desire to perform Haydn's *Die Jahreszeiten* (The Seasons), to mark 200 years since the composer's death. As Bowen puts it in his introduction to the Festival programme book:

> First performed in 1801 when Haydn was at the height of his fame, the work has always been rather overshadowed by his other oratorio, *The Creation*. Along with his six great masses, however, *Die Jahreszeiten* is full of wonderful music by a man who, while in his late 60s when he wrote it, was still clearly full of zest for life, and I hope that in the bicentenary of the composer's death this unjustly-neglected work will once again enjoy the same popularity which it has always enjoyed in Germany and Austria.[10]

Happily, the audience was both substantial and appreciative, while the critics lauded both the piece's inclusion and the performance itself. Rian Evans wrote in the *Guardian*:

> Even in this, the bicentenary of his death, performances of Haydn's oratorio Die Jahreszeiten are rare, so all credit to the Three Choirs festival and artistic director Geraint Bowen for daring to stage it. ... The festival chorus acquitted itself admirably, but it was conductor Bowen's willingness to bring out the irrepressibly exuberant aspects of the score that made this account so vivid. The dramatic summer storm, the glorious hunting

---

[10] Geraint Bowen, Hereford Festival programme book, 2009, p. 9.

horns of autumn, and the peasants' hiccuping, rollicking merry-making are every bit as realistic as Beethoven's Pastoral Symphony, usually seen as the beginnings of Romanticism. The suggestion here was that good old Haydn did it first.[11]

While the *Church Times* offered this:

Haydn's *The Seasons*, with the unmatched solo trio of Gillian Keith, James Gilchrist and Roderick Williams, proved itself far more than a quaint pastoral ... This was a magnificent performance, in which the ability of the Philharmonia – led by James Clark and beautifully nursed by Geraint Bowen – to match Haydn's fine texturing with delicate, almost period-instrument touches was crucial to making this God-fearing and moral work the spiritual centrepiece of the festival.[12]

The seasonal theme radiated out from this core, touching virtually all aspects of the Festival programme. Sunday afternoon, for example, saw another sold-out concert, this time at Wyastone Concert Hall, where the baroque violinist Rachel Podger was joined by her own handpicked team of period players (Brecon Baroque) for a scintillating Vivaldi *The Four Seasons*. (Podger was to be heard in the cathedral too, late on Thursday night with some spellbinding solo Bach.) Wednesday afternoon saw the return of the young tenor James Oxley performing Schubert's *Winterreise* at Holy Trinity Church, alongside evocations of the natural world at different points of the year in Libor Nováček's piano recital of Janáček (from *Na zarostlém Chodníčku* (On an Overgrown Path)) and Liszt (*Années de pèlerinage: Suisse*).

Perhaps more obvious were the overtly seasonal items in the evening programme, launched in stunning style by Tugan Sokhiev's primal reading of Stravinsky's *Rite of Spring*, prefaced by a wonderfully touching Mendelssohn Violin Concerto with Jennifer Pike the fine-toned and hugely impressive soloist. For many, this was a defining concert of the week, as the 'Russian firebrand' revelled in the primal energy of Stravinsky's masterpiece in an acoustic that could barely contain it, having already treated his audience to Mendelssohn's lyricism and Beethoven's poetry (the *Egmont Overture* opened the concert).[13]

The following night in the cathedral had a completely different tone, with Adrian Lucas joined on the stage by Emma Johnson, this time returning to the Festival to play Finzi's wonderfully characterful Clarinet Concerto, and the Festival Chorus opening with a rousing account of Haydn's *Te Deum* in C. The second half picked up the seasonal thread in the form of Britten's sunlit *Spring Symphony*, not a work that comes up particularly often, anywhere.

Britten's *Spring Symphony*, another seasonal work fiendishly difficult to pull off with clarity as well as dynamism, achieved both under Adrian Lucas's assured direction and first-rate pacing. He and the orchestra caught both the Tippett-like flair, a sort of musical equivalent of Gerard Manley

---

[11] *Guardian*, 18 August 2009.

[12] *Church Times*, 4 September 2009.

[13] *Church Times*, 4 September 2009.

Hopkins's spring rhythms, found in much of this early Britten work, and its subtle anticipations of the *War Requiem*.

From the superbly modulated opening movement, the massed choir rose to the challenge.[14]

The music of John McCabe (1939–2015) was featured this year, marking his seventieth birthday. Performances included a UK première, a newly commissioned orchestration of an existing work, and a completely new piece, too. The new piece, a setting of the medieval carol *Woefully Arrayed*, was given on Tuesday afternoon by the conductorless vocal ensemble Stile Antico, who were then beginning to make waves in the early-music world. Commissioned by the Festival, this was the first contemporary piece they had performed. The idea for the commission sprang from a conversation over lunch, where, having just heard of Stile Antico's proposed 'Passion and Resurrection' programme, which included a setting of the same text by William Cornysh (1465–1523), McCabe mentioned in passing that he had always wanted to set the carol himself. So successful was the piece that Stile Antico has performed it many times in several different countries, and it is typically offered as an option to promoters in Passiontide programmes – a fantastic foil to the Renaissance polyphony for which the group is known.

The new orchestration was programmed in the evening concert conducted by Adrian Partington. It is a full version of the 2004 *Songs of the Garden*, originally conceived for soloists, chorus, brass quintet and organ, and taking as its inspiration an eighteenth-century Japanese book of pictures of insects, birds, plants and animals by Kitigawa Utamaro, interspersed with short verses by his contemporary Tsutaya Jūzaburō. The texts selected by McCabe were varied, though virtually all English, and range in time from *c.* 1500 to the era of Thomas Hardy, and which in combination convey a rough calendar from spring to autumn. In the composer's own words:

> Another element in the concept of the work, and one which explains the more general texts, is that I wanted at least to indicate that it is worth exploring the relationship of man to nature and through it, to God – in many minds the three are inextricably intermingled.[15]

Joined by Carys Lane, Jeanette Ager, Simon Wall and Giles Underwood, Partington, the Festival Chorus and the Philharmonia gave a convincing account of both the piece and this newly orchestrated version. An interesting contrast, too, was provided by the concert opener, a bright and breezy rendition of Poulenc's extrovert and lively *Gloria*. A fine concert was rendered extraordinary, however, by a ravishing account of Strauss's *Four Last Songs* from the soprano Sally Matthews. Increasingly in demand both on the concert platform and on the opera stage, Matthews gave a hugely memorable and communicative performance that showed her to be a maturing singer utterly in command of her extremely colourful instrument, and blessed with a striking musical instinct that shone through bright and clear:

[14] *Church Times*, 4 September 2009.

[15] John McCabe, Hereford Festival programme book, 2009, p. 210.

It was Strauss's *Four Last Songs* under Adrian Partington ... which confirmed the Three Choirs' ability – as often, but especially with the Philharmonia in residence – to match or excel London, and, indeed, Continental standards.[16]

This was a wonderful and unexpected way to round off a truly varied and interesting seasonal thread of programming, and a concert well worthy of the presence of the BBC, who recorded it for broadcast in the following September.

McCabe's *Les Martinets noirs* was given its first UK performance by David Curtis and the Orchestra of the Swan, who had made their impressive Festival debut in Hereford in 2006. Inspired by the 'vertiginous athleticism' of the swift (the 'martinets noirs' of the title), it is a small-scale concerto for two violins, or more accurately violin duo given that they never play separately, here ably performed by David Le Page and Catherine Leech.[17] A joyful and energetic work, it provided a fascinating counterpart to a first half of Handel and Finzi, before the concert concluded with a rare outing for Vaughan Williams's *Concerto grosso*, only performed once before at Three Choirs. Composed in 1950 for the Rural Schools Music Association, this piece is unique in that the orchestra is split into three sections based on skill: Concertino (advanced), Tutti (intermediate) and Ad lib (novice), the latter part entirely played on open strings. Earlier in the day, players from the orchestra had been in workshop with local young string players, who had the opportunity to join the professionals on the cathedral platform for the concert. This was a good performance (notable in part for the eagle-eyed by the appearance of John McCabe at the back of the second violins), and indicative of the fine work that this Festival in particular had done in including young performers. The choristers of the three cathedral choirs acquitted themselves very well under the steely direction of Stephen Layton in Handel's dramatic oratorio *Israel in Egypt*, the Rodolfus Choir gave a very convincing performance of Bach's Mass in B minor in Tewkesbury Abbey, and the National Youth Orchestra of Wales 'excelled in Mahler'.[18] Youth was very much in evidence across the week.

Most notable of all, though, was the first performance of *The Prophecy of Joel*, written by the sixteen-year-old Patrick Dunachie, in the first Choral Evensong of the week, and some extremely fine solo singing on the last night:[19]

> After his previous weekend's *Dream of Gerontius*, Geraint Bowen delivered the *pièce de résistance* with a bicentenary performance of Mendelssohn's *Elijah* that produced at least three wonders: the stupendous uplift and command of the Three Choirs Festival Chorus; the bass-baritone Matthew Brook, electrifying as the beleaguered prophet; and the Hereford chorister

[16] *Church Times*, 4 September 2009.
[17] McCabe, Hereford Festival programme book, 2009, p. 229.
[18] *Church Times*, 4 September 2009.
[19] Patrick went from Hereford to King's College, Cambridge, and in 2016 replaced David Hurley as the first countertenor in the King's Singers.

Rory Turnbull, musically astute and utterly note-perfect as Elijah's keen-eyed youthful sidekick.[20]

ANTICIPATION was running high in the Festival audience for Adrian Partington's first programme as a home Artistic Director, due in part to the impression he had made in his two 'away' Festivals, alongside his reputation in Birmingham and Cardiff. He had excellent material from which to draw for his 2010 programme, too, most notably an anniversary that no Artistic Director could pass up – the centenary of the first performance of Vaughan Williams's *Fantasia on a Theme by Thomas Tallis*, which was, of course, premièred in 1910 in Gloucester Cathedral. Not only would this be the perfect opportunity to programme the piece, but, given its popularity at the time (it had been in the top three in the Classic FM Hall of Fame for the previous three years), it was sure to attract a new audience too. It was partnered with Elgar's masterly Violin Concerto, which, although premièred later in 1910 in London, had been played through in two private performances during the Festival at Gloucester that year. Holst's *St Paul's Suite* completed the programme.

This was to be no ordinary centenary-marking concert, however. The French violinist Philippe Graffin (who had recently recorded the Elgar concerto to great critical acclaim) performed the original version, and that great classical iconoclast Sir Roger Norrington was engaged to conduct.[21] Norrington was known for his impassioned advocacy of historically informed performance practice, and most particularly for his interest in orchestral vibrato – or rather the lack of it.[22] It seems clear from both historical sources, and indeed gramophone recordings, that the general use of vibrato in orchestral playing did not become widespread until the late 1920s and 1930s, and that in 1910 only a few soloists were starting to employ the technique away from particular expression, or occasional decoration.[23] Norrington's argument is that permanent orchestral vibrato was unknown in England at the time these pieces were premièred, and that for a historically informed performance, the orchestra should therefore play with 'pure tone'. He puts it thus in his programme note entitled 'The Sound of 1910?' (note the question mark):

> In this concert, I am hoping you will hear the old traditional sound of each piece. … The wonderful Philharmonia Orchestra … make the most beautiful sound when I ask them to play with pure tone. …
>
> So is this older way worth reviving? Some people think the idea is foolish antiquarianism. For myself, and for a growing number of younger conductors, it is a passion. If a composer like Elgar or VW (or Brahms

[20] *Church Times*, 4 September 2009.

[21] Graffin recorded the concerto with the RLPO conducted by Vernon Handley, on Avie Records. At 2010(G) he also gave a children's concert the following morning, including Ridout's *Ferdinand the Bull*, and his own creation, *The Hidden Fairy*.

[22] Norrington's general fame had risen significantly as a result of his chairing of the judging panel on the BBC's reality television show *Maestro* two years previously.

[23] Notably, in this context, the shift was perhaps begun by Fritz Kreisler, to whom the Elgar concerto is dedicated.

or Wagner) expected a particular sound, then I feel a duty and also a fascination to hear what it was like. And once I hear it I am in thrall.[24]

John Quinn reviewed the concert for *Seen and Heard International*:

So the audience at this concert were faced with something of a musical experiment. All well and good, perhaps; we all need to be challenged from time to time. Unfortunately, the experiments in sound were coupled with very unsatisfactory interpretation from the podium.

There were interesting aspects in the performance of Vaughan Williams's great masterpiece. To my surprise I felt that the 'pure tone' worked quite well when Tallis's tune was heard for the first time. Norrington also ensured that the three separate string choirs were properly differentiated. The solo quartet played as well as the prohibition of vibrato would allow but it was in their solo lines that I particularly missed the warming effect of vibrato. On the debit side, however, Norrington's pacing of the music was unsatisfactory. The basic pulse was just too brisk and the music was never really allowed to breathe or expand naturally.[25]

Of the Elgar, Quinn wrote:

In the Elgar concerto I found that the lack of orchestral vibrato was not as much of an issue as had been the case in the first half. Perhaps my ears had become attuned. I rather think, however, that it was more the case that the scoring of the Elgar work is richer and fuller, whereas the sparer scoring of the Vaughan Williams and the Holst had accentuated the bareness of the sound. ... Graffin threw off the demanding virtuoso passages with great skill and he gave a fine account of the long and highly original cadenza. So there was a good deal to admire overall in this performance of the concerto.[26]

Whether one agrees with this assessment of the performance, or subscribes to the alternative opinion heard in certain quarters of the cathedral describing it as 'a revelation', the matter undoubtedly split the audience down the middle; the issue was still a hot topic of conversation by the end of Festival week, four days after the concert itself.

The Festival had begun in true Three Choirs style, with brass fanfares by Elgar, Bliss and Paul Patterson to accompany the processions of dignitaries arriving for the Opening Service, before a fine performance of *The Kingdom* which acted as the focal point for the Festival's first day.

Slice through *The Kingdom* at any point and you'll be in the thick of first-rate, sometimes inspired music, brilliantly written for the voice, marvellously orchestrated. Adrian Partington, directing Saturday's performance, made the most of these qualities, sending glorious orchestral

---

[24] Gloucester Festival programme book, 2010, pp. 112–13.

[25] John Quinn, 'Seen and Heard Concert Review: Three Choirs Festival 2010 (4)', online at http://www.musicweb-international.com/SandH/2010/Jul-Dec10/three_choirs1008.htm [accessed 30 September 2016].

[26] Ibid.

sonorities echoing round the huge Norman columns of this greatest of West Country cathedrals. The Philharmonia Orchestra was on top form, the Festival Chorus immaculately prepared, singing with focus and precision, in music that makes steep demands on their control and coordination.[27]

More Elgar works were dotted throughout the week, in organ recitals and Evensongs, alongside two more substantial pieces: the overture *Cockaigne* opened the final night programme, while Sarah Connolly was 'gloriously even and warm-toned' in *Sea Pictures* on Friday evening, under the baton of Adrian Lucas.[28] This latter programme paired the Elgar with Finzi's *Intimations of Immortality*, alongside a previously unheard orchestration by Philip Lancaster of Ivor Gurney's 1925 setting of Edward Thomas – *The Trumpet*.[29] It is a piece undoubtedly worth its place in the canon. So, too, is the other work by Gurney which was premièred at this Festival – *A Gloucestershire Rhapsody*, first performed nearly a century after its completion, in Martyn Brabbins's orchestral programme at Cheltenham Town Hall. 'An attractive and assured work', the piece is a paean to the local landscape, its history (ancient and Roman), its fertility, its being, and has since been recorded by the BBC Scottish Symphony Orchestra.[30] It is to the Festival's great credit that it continues to support such works, and to champion them far and wide, not least when they are so deeply rooted in the Three Choirs' own territory.

The new music was not all by Gurney. There was also a major new commission from the Birmingham-based composer John Joubert – *An English Requiem*.[31] Modelled on Brahms's *Ein deutches Requiem*, it sets passages of Scripture (in the New Revised Standard Version) to form a 'succession of meditations on the subject of death'.[32] The listener is led from the realisation of the inevitability of passing to an embracing of it, through prayer (beautifully and passionately sung by Neal Davies), hope (ardently portrayed by Carolyn Sampson) and faith.[33] Richard Morrison was there for *The Times*:

> Stylistically, … this is a very English requiem. … one could easily imagine Elgar, VW, Howells, Britten and Walton nodding their heads

[27] Stephen Walsh, review for the*arts*desk.com, 8 August 2010, online at http://www.theartsdesk.com/classical-music/kingdom-three-choirs-festival [accessed 30 September 2016].

[28] Andrew Clements, *Guardian*, 16 August 2010.

[29] The manuscript of the piece is written for choir with short score piano accompaniment, but one that is so dense and impractical as to leave one in little doubt that it was intended for orchestra.

[30] *Church Times*, 27 August 2010.

[31] Alongside a smaller commission – a *Jubilate* premièred at the Opening Service.

[32] John Joubert, Gloucester Festival programme book, 2010, p. 92.

[33] The six movements of the piece have illustrative titles to provide, in the composer's own words, 'guidance as to their content and meaning as they proceed from the earliest premonition of death towards a realisation of its ultimate inevitability – and beyond'. Those titles are: 1. Intimations; 2. Prayer; 3. Judgement; 4. Hope; 5. Faith; 6. Solace.

in approval (and perhaps, recognition) as Joubert's majestic climaxes, astringent harmonies and poignant melodies echoed round the Gothic arches. ... Under Adrian Partington's assured direction – and, happily, with the composer present – the Three Choirs Festival Chorus and the Philharmonia Orchestra gave a thoroughly prepared and committed performance of the piece. I hope that it, too, has an afterlife.[34]

Pairing this new piece with two Teutonic giants proved successful: a fine account of Brahms's *Academic Festival Overture*, here performed with the rarely used choral parts, and a well-judged Beethoven Symphony No. 5, provided a useful and illustrative musical foil for Joubert's journey towards solace.

Such a journey was also evident in Sunday night's performance of Mahler's Symphony No. 2, where the Philharmonia were joined by Ailish Tynan and Susan Bickley, under the utterly inspiring leadership of the Dutch conductor Jac van Steen, who was making his Festival debut. For many, this was a highlight of the week – a chance to experience music-making of the highest quality by artists at the top of their game, and to witness the absolute mastery of both craft and score displayed on the podium. Able, unlike many, to work the acoustic to his advantage, van Steen cleverly used the spatial possibilities of the cathedral nave, positioning offstage players in the north transept (to his left and behind the stage), and having the final trumpet calls ring out above the chorus (who sang from memory) from the organ loft. For John Quinn, it was the moment that the week was set alight: 'The audience in Gloucester cathedral witnessed a masterly demonstration of conducting which motivated all the performers to give of their considerable best and deliver a performance that will long be remembered by all those lucky enough to be present.'[35]

Memorable too, and for all the right reasons, was the debut concert of the newly formed Three Choirs Festival Youth Choir, in a programme of Bach and Handel with the Corelli Orchestra at Tewkesbury Abbey. This new initiative, led by Adrian Partington and informed by his experience of setting up the CBSO Youth Choir in Birmingham, was a significant one, aiming to provide a route for promising young singers to high-level music-making, with the intention, too, of feeding the Festival Chorus. This group of nearly sixty teenagers and young adults 'delighted and thrilled with the brilliance of its singing', reflecting very positively on the depth of talent in the local area, and also boding very well for the future of choral singing, and of Three Choirs itself.[36]

Not content with developing choral singing, this year also saw the advent of a new project aimed at conservatoire students wanting to go into professional music-making: a masterclass series. Simon Carrington led the first of these for young choral conductors, which was also filmed by the Masterclass Media Foundation as a teaching aid. This is an exciting initiative, combining a series of masterclasses with showcase performance opportunities, and constituting

---

[34] *The Times*, 11 August 2010.

[35] John Quinn, 'Seen and Heard Concert Review: Three Choirs Festival 2010 (2)', online at http://www.musicweb-international.com/SandH/2010/Jul-Dec10/three_choirs0808.htm [accessed 30 September 2016].

[36] *Church Times*, 27 August 2010.

further evidence, if it were needed, that Three Choirs is a Festival looking to the future.

After the enormous success of Ex Cathedra's Monteverdi Vespers in 2007, 2010(G) went a stage further into early opera, with Jonathan Miller's beautifully stylised production of Monteverdi's *Orfeo*, performed by Philip Pickett and his New London Consort. Perhaps the first time that a fully staged opera has been performed in the cathedral at a Three Choirs Festival, it presented significant logistical challenges, particularly in lighting and rehearsal requirements, necessitating a 'Cheltenham day' for the rest of the concerts taking place on that Thursday. It was an extraordinary experience against such a wonderful sacred backdrop, and one in which Pickett's intimate understanding of the layers of Monteverdi's score and the careful pacing of the drama paid great dividends, regardless of whether the audience could follow the libretto in the gathering gloom.

Two days earlier, the festival-goer had had a foretaste of this sound world when the three cathedral choirs, eschewing a major work, presented a programme of Venetian polychoral music. The choirs were joined by the early-music specialist Harry Bicket and His Majestys Sagbutts and Cornetts, to perform pieces including Gabrieli's *Exultet iam angelica a 14* and his *Magnificat a 33*. There are few opportunities to hear such repertoire, and fewer still to do so in an acoustic to rival that of St Mark's, Venice, where much of this music was first given. While the programme as a whole perhaps didn't quite hang together, 'both the full choir and the many solos emerging from the choir captured convincingly the energy and special idiom of this music of the early Italian baroque'.[37]

The final night's programme, in fine Three Choirs style, combined the joyful shouts of Parry's *I was glad* with the pastoral, folk-song-tinged *The Banks of Green Willow* by George Butterworth. Before the interval there was a rare performance of a rather neglected work by Parry, his *Ode on the Nativity*, sung here in sensitive and unaffected style by the soprano Amanda Roocroft. The high point, however, was a revelatory reading of Holst's *Hymn of Jesus*, in which the chorus in particular were on stellar form, Adrian Partington giving just the right amount of space to allow the acoustic to work its magic, without affecting the necessary direction of the work. As Ivan Hewitt wrote in the *Telegraph*:

> it was in Holst's Hymn of Jesus that the concert really took wing. The tremendous implacable tread of the orchestral basses, the boy trebles floating from the gallery above, and the tenors calling mysteriously somewhere out of sight – all this was powerfully moving, and left any purely local feelings far behind.[38]

This last comment seems particularly apt, and not just in the context of Holst's visionary score. The first major fruits of the Festival's efforts to transcend the local were being revealed in the form of an official residency partnership with the Philharmonia Orchestra, which was announced late in Festival week.

[37] *Church Times*, 27 August 2010.
[38] *Telegraph*, 16 August 2010.

To begin in 2012 and run for an initial three years, this agreement placed that relationship in the context of the other residency partnerships that the orchestra maintained, in Basingstoke, Bedford, and Leicester, and opened up significant new opportunities for both partners. To quote the press release:

> The Three Choirs Festival and the Philharmonia Orchestra have cemented their long-established relationship with the announcement of a three year partnership, which will see them working together to realise the Festival's artistic vision and ambitions as well as to develop a comprehensive new programme of education and audience development activity.

Here is a very clear case of mutual interest, and one with huge potential. Such a move would simply not have been possible without the organisational changes that had taken place over the previous years, driven by the chairman of the Association, Bernard Day. Recognition was growing, particularly in the media, and artistic ambition was running high. Administrative and organisational improvements were becoming more and more visible, too, a case in point being the successful implementation of a new ticketing system for the 2010 Festival – a significant step forward, particularly in relation to online sales.

G IVEN that this was to be Adrian Lucas's last Festival as Artistic Director, one can forgive him a certain amount of contemplation of the past in putting together his 2011 programme for Worcester. However, perhaps the most striking and original element of this contemplation was the desire to mark the tenth anniversary of one of the most significant world events of modern times – the terrorist attacks on the United States of 11 September 2001. A new anthem was commissioned from the American composer Jackson Hill, *Still in Remembrance*, which was broadcast by the BBC in Wednesday's Choral Evensong. In the evening concert slot on Sunday, Lucas's cleverly crafted approach placed that most recognised of requiems – Mozart's – alongside two works, one American and one European, much associated with times of tragedy: the *Adagio for Strings* by Samuel Barber, and Mahler's famous *Adagietto*, from the fifth symphony. These two works flanked the direct response to the events of 9/11 by the American composer John Adams, *On the Transmigration of Souls*, first performed in 2002.[39] Written for orchestra, chorus, children's choir and pre-recorded tape, the piece is intended as what Adams calls a 'memory space' – a place for individual contemplation, whether of the specific historical event that is its focus, or beyond it. Perhaps the most striking visual image referred to by Adams himself, which acted as some sort of 'way in' to the piece, was a short section of amateur video taken minutes after the first plane struck, and showing a shower of millions of pieces of paper cascading out of the windows of the burning building. This image, and the myriad implications it contains, he aimed to capture in the music. The chorus parts set words from signs posted around the site, Ground Zero, by families of the missing, which interweave with pre-recorded city-scape sounds, and the reading of the names of those killed that day. It is a hugely affecting and effective work, and the logistical challenges

---

[39] In that original première concert by the New York Philharmonic, the piece was paired with Stravinsky's *Symphony of Psalms* and Beethoven's Symphony No. 9.

both for the live performers and of integrating of the tape track were admirably surmounted in the resonant acoustic of the cathedral nave. John Quinn was there:

> I thought Mr Partington controlled his large forces superbly and it seemed to me that the composer's intentions were very accurately conveyed – the resonant acoustics of the cathedral didn't obscure too much detail but lent a suitable aura to the sound. I found it very moving. At the end, after the piece had faded into a long silence, applause seemed almost an impertinence but it was justified out of respect for the performers, for the piece and, let's not forget, for those who were caught up in that terrible day.[40]

Some fine solo singing, particularly from Julia Doyle and Simon Wall, and some tight chorus work in the reading of Mozart after the interval seemed all the more poignant in the context of what had gone before. John Quinn again: 'Overall this was a strong and affirmative account of Mozart's masterpiece and it was a fitting and often stirring conclusion to a dignified and thoughtful commemoration of 9/11.'[41] Adrian Lucas noted, too, that many of the choristers involved in the performance were not even born when these events took place, which is both a sobering reminder and also a positive sign of renewal – something evident too in the extremely diverse audience which filled the cathedral for this concert.

Adams's vision of transmigration, while not something that Elgar would have recognised, does have common ground with the journey taken by the dying Gerontius, whose passage the Festival audience had had opportunity to experience the previous night, under the baton of Adrian Lucas. While Sarah Connolly's radiant Angel, and Alan Opie's commanding Priest/Angel were familiar to many, John Graham-Hall's title role was not. Known for his opera rather than his work on the concert platform, and performing much of the work from memory, Graham-Hall undoubtedly drew significantly on that stage experience in a uniquely characterised performance, though some found the more lyrical passages in Part II suited his approach better than the higher, more forceful material in Part I. Lucas's Festival Chorus performed well, though perhaps not quite reaching the heights of the previous year's vintage in Gloucester, and Lucas himself showed his vision of the piece, drawing fine playing from the Philharmonia Orchestra.

More notable Elgar was to come, first in a masterly organ transcription of the Symphony No. 2 by David Briggs, using the main Tickell instrument to great effect, and secondly in a rare performance of *Caractacus* with Sir Andrew Davis at the helm. As many have noted, it is in his orchestral writing that Elgar is most often at his best. Striking colour and imaginative detail abound in this oratorio, too, despite its neglect, and it is not hard to see prefigured what was to

[40] John Quinn, 'Seen and Heard Concert Review: Three Choirs Festival 2011 (2)', online at http://seenandheard-international.com/2011/08/three-choirs-festival-2011-2-a-dignified-and-moving-commemoration-of-911 [accessed 4 October 2016].

[41] Ibid.

come from Elgar's pen in the subsequent years (*Enigma* the following year and *Gerontius* the year after that), even if it is not quite fully formed, and not assisted by the libretto.

> Elgar's *forte* is the orchestral extension of text, so performance stands or falls on orchestra and conductor. Andrew Davis and the Philharmonia were superlative, technically brighter and sharper than the London Symphony Chorus were for Richard Hickox on their recording almost 20 years ago. Davis delineates the underlying themes so precisely that the music seems to come alive, whispering meaning much as the trees the Druids worshipped whispered meaning to them. Tight dynamics built drama into what might otherwise be fairly stolid Victorian melodrama.[42]

There was truly committed singing from a good team of soloists too, notably Judith Howarth and Brindley Sherratt (replacing an indisposed Matthew Best), and led by an incomparable performance as Caractacus himself by the baritone Peter Savidge. A further vote of confidence came from the BBC, who recorded the concert for future broadcast – clear evidence that that relationship was growing again, alongside the now customary live broadcast of Choral Evensong.

The other visiting conductor for 2011(w) was entrusted with marking the centenary of the death of Gustav Mahler with his monumental Symphony No. 3. A new name to many, if not most, Susanna Mälkki came highly recommended by the orchestra, and won Festival hearts in very short order. A product of Finland's highly regarded Sibelius Academy, she has made a name for herself particularly in contemporary music, but her versatility is widely recognised, and she showed both a deep connection with Mahler's music and a gestural language well adapted to developing close ties and understanding with her musicians. Joined by the ladies of the Festival Chorus, the choristers of the three cathedrals and Catherine Wyn-Rogers, the Philharmonia and the audience were drawn, rapt, under Mälkki's spell – but really this was Mahler's spell, as however impressive the conductor was, it seemed that it was the music speaking through her, rather than her interpretation riding atop the orchestral waves. John Quinn recounts the spellbinding conclusion:

> Mahler's Third Symphony has a loud, majestic ending, which at the Proms, for example, habitually results in an immediate eruption of cheering and clapping. Not here. Instead, as the last great chord died away in Worcester Cathedral there was ... silence! For several seconds there was no applause or even movement from the capacity audience.[43]

This was not the only Mahler in the programme either. The soprano Jane Irwin joined the National Youth Orchestra of Scotland, who were making their Festival debut at Worcester, in his *Lieder eines fahrenden Gesellen*. Masterfully led by their conductor, Christoph Mueller, this was a hugely impressive

[42] Anne Ozorio, *Opera Today*, 27 August 2011.

[43] John Quinn, 'Seen and Heard Concert Review: Three Choirs Festival 2011 (4)', online at http://seenandheard-international.com/2011/08/three-choirs-festival-2011-4-a-memorable-mahler-performance-from-the-philharmonia-and-susanna-malkki/ [accessed 30 September 2016].

display by a group of talented and committed young players, who not only gave a thoroughly professional Ravel (his *Rapsodie espagnole*) and convincing Mahler, but also converted members of the audience to the music of their countryman James MacMillan; they played his Symphony No. 3 – the first time a major MacMillan orchestral work has been performed at Three Choirs Festival.

Not to be outdone, the Festival's very own Youth Choir, formed in 2010 at Gloucester, were given a significant raise of status that evening, in the form of a cathedral concert with the Philharmonia Orchestra. It was a bold and courageous decision by Adrian Lucas to entrust such a programme to the fledgling ensemble, not least with Beethoven's Mass in C on the bill. Adrian Partington took the reins again, and despite ending up in hospital later that night with gallstones, he led a well-crafted and youthful reading, after a first half of Beethoven's overture *Coriolan* and the Violin Concerto by Max Bruch, with soloist Tai Murray. The concert was well received: 'The Three Choirs Youth Choir [produced] a performance of professional standards, not least in the prolonged Credo, where the girls' singing at the 'Crucifixus' was out of this world.'[44]

Picking up the trend initiated in 2010, youth was becoming an increasingly important feature of the Festival programme. The pattern of recitals by young organists selected by the Royal College of Organists was repeated. The Festival also saw a well-supported and ably presented concert by the choir of Royal Holloway, the return of the Eton Choral Course, and the second year of the new masterclass series – this year focusing on brass, and led by senior members of the Philharmonia brass section. As in 2010, the 'winning' group was offered a concert slot at the Hereford Festival in 2012. Tom Hammond-Davies, who was selected from the 2010 cohort of young choral conductors, took charge of Oxford-based Musica Beata in a programme of secular *a cappella* fare, including a fascinating polyphonic commission from Nicholas Brown.

Following the three cathedral choirs' experiment with Venetian polychoral music at Gloucester, their programme for 2011(w) returned to more familiar ground with Charpentier's *Te Deum* in D and Handel's great *Dixit Dominus*. The singers also had the great opportunity of working again with some of the top period-instrument players in the country, in the form of the Academy of Ancient Music. Adrian Lucas conducted a lively and virtuosic concert, which also included Bach's second orchestral suite and Vivaldi's Double Trumpet Concerto in C, with soloists Alison Balsom and Crispian Steele-Perkins vying for supremacy at the front of the platform. This was one of the first times that Alison Balsom had played natural trumpet in concert, something for which she has become much better known in more recent years. Balsom and David Goode (organ) also gave an excellent recital the following morning, including works by Alain, Bach, Naji Hakim and Petr Eben; Balsom's ringing tone and understated virtuosity were complemented by the versatile instrument at St Martin's Church, and by Goode's sensitive playing.

Petr Eben's music was in evidence on Tuesday evening in the cathedral too, though as a supporting element in a fascinating programme of music inspired

---

[44] *Church Times*, 2 September 2011.

or influenced by the Orthodox tradition, and presented by Harry Christophers and The Sixteen: Stravinsky, Rachmaninov and Arvo Pärt, happy bedfellows with John Tavener and James MacMillan. However, although the audience was clearly transported by some beautiful singing, the cathedral's electronic nave organ intervened in such a realistic manner as to develop a cipher mid-concert; fortunately, it was swiftly remedied by the Assistant Organist, who was in the building at the time.

At the previous Worcester Festival (2008), the second Saturday had seen a departure from the norm, and a successful effort to engage a different sort of audience, in the form of a concert of film music.[45] Worcester reprised the idea in 2011, with a twist, presenting an Opera Gala evening, expertly compèred by Sir Thomas Allen, and dedicated to the memory of the great English tenor and long-time Festival artist Heddle Nash. The chorus was also involved, taking advantage of the opportunity to sing some different repertoire, including Verdi, Wagner and Borodin, and making a good fist of it, under Adrian Lucas's direction. But it was Sir Thomas Allen who held the limelight, joined by two young female singers, successfully managing to bridge the gap into this lighter fare.

Geraint Bowen had been in charge the previous evening, in a 'haunting and emotionally searing' account of Brahms's *Ein deutches Requiem*, in which the chorus produced perhaps their best singing of the week.[46] Their sound was 'fresh and accurate', resulting in a performance of 'utmost distinction'.[47] This was complemented by high-quality solo singing from Elizabeth Watts and William Dazeley, the latter having given an excellent and varied recital the day before in Huntingdon Hall.[48] In a typically Three Choirs twist of programming, the first half was given over to a rare performance of Vaughan Williams's *An Oxford Elegy*, including perhaps a Festival first – the part of the narrator was expertly taken by the Dean.

This work hinges on the quality of the narration, and here the Dean of Worcester, the Very Revd Peter Atkinson, showed skill and acumen worthy

---

[45] Hereford and Gloucester had also begun to engage with larger events at the edges of the Festival, both aimed at different audiences, and intended to involve the local population. Hereford in 2003 saw the first 'Gathering Wave' performance, a joint project with a local group which grew over subsequent Festivals (including a significant commission from Ken Burton in 2006), graduating to a spot on the main cathedral stage on the night after the final main Festival concert. Gloucester had similarly utilised the cathedral platform on the second Sunday for *The Song of the Earth* in 2007, and Scott Stroman's *Jazz Psalms* in 2010. More significant coverage of these projects is beyond the scope of the present work, but their importance in the local communities, and indeed in the Festival's 'outreach', should not be underestimated.

[46] *Church Times*, 2 September 2011.

[47] John Quinn, 'Seen and Heard Concert Review: Three Choirs Festival 2011 (8)', online at http://seenandheard-international.com/2011/08/three-choirs-festival-2011-8-a-wonderful-account-of-brahmss-requiem-in-worcester/ [accessed 30 September 2016].

[48] His programme included Finzi and Barber, alongside songs by Somervell, Richard Pierson, and Kit and the Widow.

of a seasoned actor. His beautiful, apt, and lulling delivery, and Bowen's delicate shaping, married with the Philharmonia's sensitive solo touches and a wordless chorus to produce a memorable, nicely understated, finessed performance of this work.[49]

For much of its history the Festival had taken place in September; then, for a time, it was held in late August. Since 2004, however, it had been scheduled slightly earlier in the month, thereby avoiding the late-August bank holiday. But 2012 brought with it a significant decision, as on the recent pattern its dates would have placed it at the same time as the London Olympics. Despite some research indicating that the core Festival audience chose to attend based upon the programme rather than the dates, the decision was taken to move the Festival two weeks ahead of its normal pattern – as early in the summer holiday as it could realistically be, given the time needed for logistics and setting up. It would then run right up to the day of the Opening Ceremony. An additional potential benefit of doing this would be to assist Adrian Partington's agenda for preparing the chorus, making it much easier for them to rehearse through to the beginning of Festival week, rather than have a break before it. It did, however, raise significant challenges in ensuring that all was ready in the cathedral, despite the extreme demand nationally for temporary toilet blocks, seating, and, indeed, cameramen.[50]

Geraint Bowen also faced an interesting programming conundrum – whether to stick to a traditional Festival programme or to try to link to the national event in a characteristically 'Three Choirs' way (avoiding the obvious Olympic-themed ideas). His solution was a neat one – to view the Olympics as a sort of 'secular pilgrimage', and to draw in themes of travel and of the island host nation surrounded by sea, to provide a relevant but unforced narrative string through the week. The centrepiece of this idea was to be a performance of a major work by a composer who had a strong relationship with the Festival, but is little known except for a few liturgical works: Sir George Dyson. *The Canterbury Pilgrims* (1930) established Dyson as a major figure in British music in the inter-war years, and three commissions from Three Choirs Festival followed: *St Paul's Voyage to Melita* (1933), *Nebuchadnezzar* (1935) and *Quo Vadis?* (1939, though not completed until some years later). It is therefore astonishing that the 1930 work had never been heard at Three Choirs.

Lewis Foreman, in his programme note, quotes the composer's own description of the piece as 'Portraits chosen from the Prologue to Chaucer's *Canterbury Tales* and set to music for chorus, orchestra and three soloists'.[51] The importance of the chorus in Dyson's vision is clear, and the piece is defined by its 'dramatic and effective choral writing', alongside the composer's gift for colourful orchestration.[52] The 'tableaux' of characters that we see are lucidly defined as

---

[49] *Church Times*, 2 September 2011.

[50] The standard of TV coverage on the screens inside the cathedral had been consistently high, but the BBC was calling in every available cameraman to cover the massive number of Olympic events.

[51] Hereford Festival programme book, 2012, pp. 182–3.

[52] Ibid., p. 183.

they are presented, from the chivalric Knight to the personable Squire, from the gold-loving Physic to the dutiful Parson, Dyson's music providing a series of vivid pictures, though not necessarily prescriptive ones. As Andrew King observed:

> the Three Choirs Festival is the perfect forum for such a work when one considers that the characters depicted, rich and poor alike, are assembled all by their faith in God to make their humble pilgrimage to Canterbury to pray, and the audience of the festival journey hence to Hereford, Gloucester and Worcester cathedrals annually, called by their love of music and begin every concert with a prayer.[53]

Who better to oversee this performance, too, than Martyn Brabbins, who has shown a great affinity with this repertoire over the years, and is a firm favourite with audience and chorus alike? In the words of John Quinn: 'Brabbins was ... adept at bringing out the more subtle and poetic aspects of the score – of which there are many. Under his energetic and committed leadership this came across as a convinced and convincing performance.'[54] There was fine singing, too, from a trio of soloists – Susan Gritton, Alan Oke and Simon Bailey – who managed the switches of character and style admirably in their diverse portrayals. They were surpassed perhaps only by the chorus, who 'tackled Dyson's score with great enthusiasm and assurance'.[55] The concert was recorded by BBC Radio 3, for broadcast in September.

The Festival Chorus had been in fine fettle earlier in the week, marking the queen's Diamond Jubilee with a rare performance of *O Lord our Governour* by Healey Willan (commissioned for the Queen's coronation) in the Opening Service, and a lively account of Haydn's *The Creation* with Geraint Bowen and the Philharmonia. The performance of Vaughan Williams's *A Sea Symphony* on the Monday evening found them on 'magnificent form', with 'fine attention to detail, indicating a very well-prepared chorus'.[56] Perhaps the changes to the rehearsal process in the run-up to Festival week were having an impact. Also evident over the opening days was the direct advantage of the relationship between orchestra and Festival that had been developing over some years, and which had now been formalised with the beginning of the Philharmonia's official residency. For John Quinn the effect was clear: '[The Philharmonia is] a splendid

[53] Andrew H. King, 'Dyson's *Canterbury Pilgrims* at the Three Choirs Festival in Hereford', *Bachtrack*, 28 July 2012. Online at https://bachtrack.com/review-three-choirs-2012-dyson-canterbury-pilgrims-philharmonia-brabbins [accessed 30 September 2016].

[54] John Quinn, 'A Splendid Three Choirs Pilgrimage to Canterbury', *Seen and Heard International*, 28 July 2010. Online at http://seenandheard-international.com/2012/07/a-splendid-three-choirs-pilgrimage-to-canterbury/ [accessed 30 September 2016].

[55] Ibid.

[56] John Quinn, 'The Three Choirs Festival Takes to The High Seas', *Seen and Heard International*, 25 July 2016. Online at http://seenandheard-international.com/2012/07/the-three-choirs-festival-takes-to-the-high-seas/ [accessed 30 September 2016].

orchestra in any case but the benefits of a close alliance between orchestra and festival over the last few years are readily apparent.'[57]

The early fruits of this partnership were noticeable in both repertoire and personnel, with the inclusion of a new work by Joseph Phibbs, commissioned by the Philharmonia and Anvil Arts, and first performed earlier in the year under Esa Pekka Salonen.[58] A complex score, and one that had clearly benefitted from revision after its first performances, it is a series of musical 'snapshots' each of which draws 'on a specific harmonic and orchestral palette to evoke a particular sound world', where 'the presence of the sea acts as a constant driving force behind the work as a whole'.[59] The *Church Times* was complimentary: 'a magnificently contrasted, vividly orchestrated journey ... and a real sense of tight structure which confirms Phibbs as one of the rising – arguably risen – stars on the composing scene'.[60] Alongside Mendelssohn's *Calm Sea and Prosperous Voyage*, this new piece acted as a fascinating foil to Vaughan Williams's *A Sea Symphony*, and was impressively rendered under Adrian Partington's leadership.

The maritime theme was picked up in Sunday's orchestral concert by a new face on the podium, again a direct result of the collaboration with the orchestra. The Venezuelan conductor Diego Matheuz is a product of 'El Sistema', and one of the most promising talents emerging from South America.[61] He treated a full cathedral to a finely judged account of Debussy's masterpiece *La Mer*. This was paired with Stravinsky's *Firebird Suite*, the Delius Cello Concerto (marking 150 years since the composer's birth) with Julian Lloyd Webber as soloist, and, in a sideways nod to the following week's events in London, Ravel's famous *Boléro*.[62]

Such a significant Delius anniversary could not be marked at Three Choirs without a major choral work, which came on Thursday evening in the form of *Sea Drift*. With Ireland's *London Overture* and Elgar's *The Music Makers* sharing the billing, expectations would have been high in any case, and doubly so as this was the debut concert for the new Artistic Director at Worcester, Peter Nardone. Born in Elderslie in Renfrewshire, and educated in Paisley (he was a chorister at Paisley Abbey), he studied at the Royal Scottish Academy of Music and Drama, before moving to London to study singing at the Royal Academy of Music in 1986. An accomplished countertenor and organist, he held positions at Croydon Parish Church while pursuing his singing career with top chamber groups in London, including the Monteverdi Choir, the Tallis Scholars and the King's Consort, before being appointed Director of Music at Chelmsford Cathedral in

---

[57] Ibid.

[58] The piece was commissioned to celebrate the eighteenth anniversary of the Anvil Arts Centre is Basingstoke, where the Philharmonia was also resident.

[59] Joseph Phibbs, Hereford Festival programme book, 2012, p. 116.

[60] *Church Times*, 3 August 2012.

[61] 'El Sistema' is the famous Venezuelan model of music education, which prioritises ensemble participation and has changed the lives of so many children in that country, particularly those from disadvantaged backgrounds. Its products also include Gustavo Dudamel and the Simón Bolívar Youth Orchestra.

[62] So famously the music that provided the backdrop for Torvill and Dean's triumph at the 1984 Winter Olympics.

2000, where he also ran the Chelmsford Cathedral Festival. His first experiences of Three Choirs were trips to Festival concerts as a teenager, which introduced him to the rich seam of larger-scale choral repertoire, as well as the fundamental nature of the Festival and its locality.

Nardone's debut certainly impressed Andrew King, who described his Ireland as 'beautifully paced' and 'stirring', while in Elgar he 'coaxed from chorus and orchestra a dynamic range that might have been the envy of any professional or amateur chorus'.[63] John Quinn was effusive of the Delius too, describing Nardone as 'alive to the poetry' of Delius's score.[64] James Rutherford was an impressive soloist in the Delius, and Sarah Connolly radiant in the Elgar.

Early music always plays a significant part in Geraint Bowen's Festival programmes, and 2012 saw a focus on the music of Johann Sebastian Bach. Rachel Podger's crack period group Brecon Baroque, who had such a success in 2009, returned to Wyastone Concert Hall with three of the six Brandenburg Concertos (numbers 2, 4 and 5), along with the Triple Concerto in A minor, for flute, violin and harpsichord. The viol consort Fretwork played their arrangement of the incomparable *Goldberg Variations*, hampered somewhat by one of the players being taken ill in the intense heat inside St Francis Xavier.[65] The three cathedral choirs, however, provided the main focus to this strand of the programme, with a dramatic and carefully structured account of the great *St John Passion*, conducted by Geraint Bowen, with the period-instrument Music for Awhile Orchestra. Tackling any such work with boy choristers is a substantial undertaking, but the young voices rose admirably to the challenge, well supported by the men of the back rows. Special mention should go to a 'superb Evangelist', James Oxley, who stepped in on the day of the concert for an indisposed John Mark Ainsley.[66] This was singing of the highest order, often with little reliance on the copy, and demonstrating a complete focus on communicating Bach's extraordinary music and fulfilling the Evangelist's responsibility for the narrative drive of the work. Iestyn Davies was the pick of a very fine group of other soloists.

The Three Choirs Festival Youth Choir had distinguished themselves as one of the first music-based projects to be awarded an 'Inspire Mark' from the

[63] Andrew H. King, 'Three Choirs Festival: Ireland, Delius and Elgar with Nardone and the Philharmonia', *Bachtrack*, 7 August 2012. Online at https://bachtrack.com/review-three-choirs-festival-2012-philharmonia-elder-ireland-delius-elgar [accessed 30 September 2016].

[64] John Quinn, 'More Superb Singing at Three Choirs Festival', *Seen and Heard International*, 29 July 2012. Online at http://seenandheard-international.com/2012/07/more-superb-singing-at-three-choirs-festival/ [accessed 30 September 2016].

[65] After a wet beginning to July, Festival week was the hottest of the year by some margin, and the heat took its toll on a significant number of Festival-goers, too. Many ambulances were called, but fortunately there were no long-lasting effects.

[66] John Quinn, 'A Deeply Satisfying and Moving St. John Passion at Three Choirs Festival', *Seen and Heard International*, 26 July 2010. Online at http://seenandheard-international.com/2012/07/a-deeply-satisfying-and-moving-st-john-passion-at-three-choirs-festival/ [accessed 30 September 2016].

2012 Cultural Olympiad. Now, after the previous year's triumph at an evening concert with the Philharmonia, they were presented with a new challenge – a commission from Bulgarian-born Dobrinka Tabakova: *Centuries of Meditations*. Inspired by Tom Denny's (2009) stained glass windows in Hereford Cathedral's Audley Chapel, which explore aspects of the philosophy of the local seventeenth-century poet and mystic Thomas Traherne, the four movements set Traherne's poetry. Tabakova's music is immediately approachable and attractive, the piece being seen by many as the perfect vehicle for the youthful sound of this hugely promising Festival innovation. David Hill returned to the Festival to conduct, having last appeared in 2005(w). The Youth Choir benefitted from some excellent supportive playing from the Orchestra of the Swan, who gave a pleasing performance of Debussy's *Danse sacrée et danse profane*, and complemented the vitality and freshness of the young voices in a serene Fauré Requiem, with soloists Katie Trethewey and Marcus Farnsworth.

New music was present elsewhere, not least in the liturgical context, with a world première by Francis Pott, sung at Evensong by Hereford Cathedral Voluntary Choir, and a Festival commission from Richard Rodney Bennett for the Festival Eucharist – *One Equal Music*.[67] There was also a new piano sonata by David Briggs for Mark Bebbington, and the English première of Judith Bingham's *Celticity*, included in a varied programme of Gershwin, Ravel and Beethoven by the National Youth Orchestra of Wales. Bingham was joined by Dobrinka Tabakova and Joseph Phibbs for a fascinating discussion on the state of modern classical music, chaired by the renowned music journalist Stephen Johnson.

Contemporary repertoire also featured in a Festival first – a solo saxophone recital on the main cathedral stage in a late-night slot. Gerard McChrystal produced a spellbinding display of virtuosity, extended technique and use of technology (both tape and loop station were in evidence, producing multi-phonic music from a monophonic instrument). But the wizardry was all in the service of the music, whether that were Bach and Telemann, Barry Cockroft, or the world première by Joe Cutler – *Loopable Music*. There was a first appearance at Festival too from the lyricist and performer Kit Hesketh-Harvey – a late-night cabaret performance that left little to the imagination, but brought the house down in the Shire Hall.

For the closing event, timed to finish before the highly anticipated Opening Ceremony of the London Olympics, Geraint Bowen and the Philharmonia Orchestra were joined by the Festival Chorus and Welsh tenor Wynne Evans. What better beginning than an epic account of Tchaikovsky's *1812 Overture* – complete with masonry-shaking cannon effects – and with the majesty and scale of Berlioz's great *Te Deum* to conclude the programme? And in between, to mark the centenary of his death, Samuel Taylor-Coleridge's *Petite Suite de concert*: a refreshing sorbet between the main courses.

[67] The commission was supported by the Frank Clarke-Whitfield Trust.

THE 2013 Gloucester Festival marked the second year of the residency partnership with the Philharmonia Orchestra, and it was here that the real potential of this agreement began to become apparent. The series of recitals by young prize-winners of the Royal College of Organists was expanded into a 'Young Artists Series' incorporating recipients of the Philharmonia's own Martin Musical Scholarship.[68] Particularly striking here was an extraordinary accordion recital by the Lithuanian player Martynas Levickis. This educational strand, which was one of the stated aims of the partnership, also saw the orchestra's renowned digital department bringing their 'Universe of Sound' pods to Gloucester Quays shopping centre for six weeks over the summer. These experiential immersive devices, first seen at the Science Museum in London in 2012 and given the 2013 Royal Philharmonic Society Award for Audiences and Engagement, offer a virtual opportunity to explore an orchestra from the inside, and to 'conduct' parts of Holst's *The Planets* with virtual coaching from Esa Pekka Salonen. (The pods use cutting-edge digital technology to track hand movements, and allow a realistic virtual experience.)

Notable too was the presence of Philharmonia players on the platform for the first performance of John O'Hara's new community opera, *The Bargee's Wife*, part of what had been termed 'Three Choirs Plus' over recent years. A major project involving the Festival's sister dementia charity, Mindsong, and singers old and young from around the area, the piece tells the story of a child who died after falling into a frozen canal lock in 1938 – a real event etched into the memory of numerous care-home residents, whose words and memories were brilliantly woven together by the librettist Karen Hayes.[69] Roderic Dunnett reviewed the production for the website *Behind the Arras*:

> The whole work is a kind of Requiem for Solomon Pavy, with shades of the similar ditties in John Tavener's landmark 1960s work *Celtic Requiem*. (If one had to cite or compare another modern work, it would be Steve Reich's mesmerising *Different Trains*, with its groped-after echoes of the Holocaust.) …
>
> It is this kind of intensity which makes *The Bargee's Wife* one of the best children's operas I have never [*sic*] seen staged. Two vocal soloists soared through the air, evoking past and future, but the main soloists were the shimmering Philharmonia Orchestra members, plus harp and keyboards, evincing a marvellous cycle of sounds in O'Hara's quite wonderful, often syncopated, vibrant score.[70]

Projects such as this are the real stuff of meaningful education work in the arts. It is to be hoped that the Festival can find a way to continue along this path

[68] A fund designed to enable exceptionally talented students to bridge the difficult gap between full-time study and professional status.

[69] Mindsong is a project that takes music therapy to dementia sufferers in residential care. After being successfully piloted in 2007, it spread out from Gloucester and was formed as a charity in its own right in 2012.

[70] Roderic Dunnett, 'The Midland's Golden Oldie: Three Choirs Festival 2013', *A View from Behind the Arras*. Online at http://www.behindthearras.com/Reviewspr/ReviewsPRjulyDec13/three_choirs_08-13.html [accessed 30 September 2016].

(and similar ones being explored in Worcester and Hereford), engaging in a substantive way with local communities while not losing sight of or diminishing the core identity of the Festival.

In the main programme, the most obvious effect of this deepening partnership between orchestra and Festival was the presence of the Philharmonia's Conductor Laureate, Vladimir Ashkenazy, who opened the Festival with a gala concert featuring music by Elgar, Sibelius and Rachmaninov. Increasingly admired for his interpretations of Elgar's music, the Russian maestro did not disappoint here, 'clearly relishing the score's broader phrases, without neglecting the textural contrasts and many fine timbral details – and without slipping into sentimentality'.[71]

The Sibelius, a rare performance of the tone poem for soprano and orchestra *Luonnotar*, was programmed to mark the centenary of its first performance just down the road in the Shire Hall, at the 1913 Gloucester Festival. A fiendishly difficult piece for the singer, on account of its extreme range and its Finnish text (taken from the mythological epic *Kalevala*), the stunning soloist on this occasion was the Finnish soprano Helena Juntunen. She 'brought such wonderment ... I might not have minded hearing nothing else all week', and her singing 'made one come out of Gloucester Cathedral at the interval walking on air, like Gurney and Howells when they first heard Vaughan Williams's *Tallis Fantasia*'.[72] Ashkenazy's grasp of the score was evident too, capturing the other-worldly soundscape and oscillating tonality in the generous cathedral acoustic to magical effect, and drawing 'cool, watery images from the Philharmonia Orchestra, on subtle and imaginative form'.[73]

The second half was given over to a Russian masterwork – Rachmaninov's *The Bells*, also written in 1913, which sets words by Edgar Allen Poe. Helena Juntunen was joined by tenor Paul Nilon, baritone Nathan Berg and the Festival Chorus for a glorious conclusion to the opening night's concert: 'the combined forces of Philharmonia and Festival Chorus were magnificent, with Ashkenazy seeming to conduct from inside the sound itself to produce a performance of elemental power.'[74]

The other celebrity conductor gracing the podium with the Festival Chorus was Edward Gardner, returning to the cathedral where he was a chorister to perform a bicentenary programme of Wagner and Verdi (both of whom were born in 1813). Increasingly in demand in the opera house and on the concert stage, Gardner's star was very much in the ascendant: in 2013 he held the post of Music Director at English National Opera, following a spell with Glyndebourne Touring Opera, and had received both Royal Philharmonic Society and Olivier awards.[75] The programme entrusted to Gardner eschewed the obvious Requiem

[71] Steph Power, writing for *Wales Arts Review*, 7 August 2013. Online at http://www.walesartsreview.org/three-choirs-festival-ashkenazy-philharmonia-orchestra-elgar-sibelius-rachmaninoff/ [accessed 30 September 2016)].

[72] *Church Times*, 30 August 2013.

[73] John Allison, *Telegraph*, 2 August 2013.

[74] Power, *Wales Arts Review* (online).

[75] Gardner has since taken over as Chief Conductor of the Bergen Philharmonic Orchestra.

in favour of Verdi's lesser known, and much less performed, *Four Sacred Pieces*.[76] These were paired with Wagner's overture to *Tannhäuser*, followed by his *Tristan and Isolde*-inspired and Schopenhauer-influenced *Wesendonck Lieder*, performed here in the customary Felix Mottl orchestration.

To the dismay of many ticket holders, Festival favourite Sarah Connolly was indisposed, but it took just a few phrases of the first of Wagner's songs to banish that disappointment as the warm richness of Emma Bell's voice filled the cathedral space. A 'vocal revelation' following a 'stunning'[77] overture, this was singing which was 'expressive without any trace of unwanted histrionics'.[78] The Verdi pieces are difficult to bring off in concert, not least because of the demands of the two *a cappella* movements, but the Festival Chorus, and most notably the semi-chorus within it, made an excellent job of capturing Verdi's musical language, clearly assisted by the 'surefooted and dynamic' leadership from the podium, and 'consistently fine playing' from the orchestra.[79] The significant period of silence after the final orchestral chords was a fitting response from a rapt audience, as was the warm applause for one of Gloucester's own which followed.

Edward Gardner had, of course, been a chorister under Dr John Sanders, who had died in 2003, and whose liturgical music in particular was much in evidence over the course of the week. The notable exception, however, was his secular song cycle *The Beacon*, performed in a recital due to be given by Andrew Kennedy, who was replaced at short notice by Robert Murray. Murray gamely took on much of Kennedy's planned programme, including both the Sanders work and a commission from John O'Hara. (The planned Britten, *Les Illuminations*, was replaced by *Winter Words*.) Again, Partington's programme avoided the obvious in this centenary year by programming no large-scale Britten works at all, but concentrating on his art song and smaller-scale choral output. The locally based St Cecilia Singers gave an entirely Britten programme with astute narration and commentary from Stephen Johnson, and Roderick Williams's recital included the dark-hued *Songs and Proverbs of William Blake*. This latter event was memorable, but not entirely for the right reasons – as ever, Williams's singing was impeccable, and his programming innovative, including new songs by the German composer Torsten Rasch, but the concert was marred by 'noises off' in the newly refurbished Blackfriars Priory.[80]

[76] The first performance of these pieces in England had been at the 1898(G) Festival, when three of the four were given – the *Ave Maria* was omitted.

[77] *Church Times*, 30 August 2013.

[78] John Quinn, 'Local Boy Makes Very Good in Gloucester', *Seen and Heard International*, 1 August 2013. Online at http://seenandheard-international.com/2013/08/local-boy-makes-very-good-in-gloucester/ [accessed 30 September 2016].

[79] Ibid.

[80] The Rasch was a foretaste of things to come, as Rasch had been commissioned to write a major new work to be premièred at Worcester the following year, marking the centenary of the beginning of World War I.

Contemporary music was much in evidence elsewhere too, not least in the inclusion of Brett Dean's *Komarov's Fall* as a fascinating foil to a masterly performance of Holst's *The Planets*, and in the featuring on Tuesday and Wednesday of the music of the Estonian composer Arvo Pärt. A conductor much associated with Pärt's music, Stephen Layton, and his choir, Polyphony, took to the stage for an evening performance with the Philharmonia. Opening with Pärt's tribute to the Englishman he never met – *Cantus in memoriam Benjamin Britten* – there followed a fine performance of the *Berliner Messe*, its first outing at Three Choirs. Later that night, Pärt's rarely performed *Stabat Mater* made use of the cathedral's fine acoustic; bassoonist Jarek Augustyniak played *Spiegel im Spiegel* in recital the following morning; and Pärt's *Magnificat* was included in the BBC Evensong broadcast. A fitting tribute to a composer of great significance in contemporary music, and whose compositions had never featured at Three Choirs before.

Lovers of period instruments were not denied their fill of suitable Festival fare either, as there were two significant events. Geraint Bowen took the reins for a Beethoven Symphony No. 9, with the Festival Chorus and Florilegium (prefaced by Mozart's *Sinfonia concertante* in E flat), and John Butt brought his own splendid team of players from the Dunedin Consort for a (now) rare festival performance of *Messiah*, in the original Dublin version as reconstructed by Butt himself. The three cathedral choirs were on excellent form, and joined by a fine team of soloists, who collectively made a good case for Butt's scholarly edition, despite rumblings from some in the audience who missed their favourite numbers from Prout or Watkins Shaw. The concert was recorded for future broadcast by Radio 3.

The BBC also recorded the conspicuous novelty of this year's programme: a complete performance of *The Song of Hiawatha* by Samuel Coleridge-Taylor. Rarely done at all, and almost never with all three parts, its programming here was a direct result of increased cooperation and collaboration between the three Festival committees, facilitated by the now irreplaceable central organisational structure (whose leadership had passed to Dominic Jewel early in the year). Initially proposed for 2012, marking the centenary of the composer's death, it was deemed too risky to include *Hiawatha* as well as Dyson's *The Canterbury Pilgrims*, and the piece was taken up by Adrian Partington instead – absolutely not something that would have occurred a few short years before, when relationships between the cities were stretched almost to breaking point. Based on Henry Wadsworth Longfellow's narrative poem of the same name, and written in three distinct sections over three years, the piece is perhaps best remembered for the infamous and immensely popular costumed performances by the Royal Choral Society under Sir Malcolm Sargent in the inter-war years, which drew capacity audiences in the Royal Albert Hall.[81]

Peter Nardone oversaw this performance with soprano Hye-Youn Lee, tenor Robin Tritschler and bass Benedict Nelson, though of course it was the Festival Chorus who took centre stage. As Andrew King remarked:

[81] It is interesting to note in the context of the 2013 Festival, that Longfellow's poem consciously imitates the Finnish epic *Kalevala*, from which Sibelius drew his *Luonnotar*.

The chorus, for whom the music is almost relentless, gave a stunning performance ... In particular the brief unaccompanied sections such as 'Thus the gentle Chibiabos' revealed a choral sensitivity that might be the envy of any professional or amateur choir. In telling the story, the chorus held the audience's attention completely, spurred on by Coleridge-Taylor's wonderfully vivid characterisations.[82]

John Quinn was also impressed by Peter Nardone's contribution in what was only his second major Three Choirs Concert: 'This seemed to me to be anything but a dutiful performance of a neglected score. He conducted with belief and inspired his performers.'[83]

Undoubtedly *Hiawatha* was a worthwhile inclusion, but it seems unlikely to be repeated any time soon. Not so the pieces programmed for Adrian Partington's other two concerts in the week, which featured choral masterpieces by Walton and Elgar. This was a memorable *Belshazzar's Feast*, not just for some sterling work from the chorus, but also for some 'expressive and characterful' singing from South African-born Njabulo Madlala, and for Partington's clear and decisive lead from the podium.[84] The other works on the bill were an orchestrated organ piece by Vaughan Williams, *Prelude and Fugue* in C minor from 1930 (premièred at Hereford that year), and Elgar's Shakespearean symphonic poem *Falstaff*, written for the 1913 Leeds Festival.

Most memorable of all, however, was the final night's *Gerontius*. Elgarians among the Festival faithful were doubtless eager to hear Adrian Partington's reading of Elgar's great score, having had Adrian Lucas's in 2011, and Geraint Bowen's in 2009, and having followed Partington's very convincing interpretations of other major Elgar works since his arrival. They were not disappointed. In characteristic style, the Artistic Director had chosen to preface Elgar with the piece that arguably shaped and informed it – Wagner's Prelude to Act I of *Parsifal*. For John Quinn 'the choice was as apposite as it was perceptive', with refined tone and an admirable sense of space providing a musical context into which this *Gerontius* might fall.[85]

> But it was what followed that took the breath away. A chorus director with awesome conducting experience (above all with the BBC National Chorus

[82] Andrew H. King, 'Samuel Coleridge-Taylor's *The Song of Hiawatha* at the Three Choirs Festival, Gloucester', *Bachtrack*, 6 August 2013. Online at https://bachtrack.com/review-three-choirs-2013-gloucester-coleridge-taylor-hiawatha [accessed 30 September 2016].

[83] John Quinn, 'A Heart-Warming Evening in the Gloucester Wigwam', *Seen and Heard International*, 3 August 2013. Online at http://seenandheard-international.com/2013/08/a-heart-warming-evening-in-the-gloucester-wigwam/ [accessed 30 September 2016].

[84] Dunnett, 'The Midland's Golden Oldie' (online).

[85] John Quinn, 'An Excellent, Moving Gerontius at the Three Choirs Festival', *Seen and Heard International*, 4 August 2013. Online at http://seenandheard-international.com/2013/08/an-excellent-moving-gerontius-at-the-three-choirs-festival/ [accessed 30 September 2016].

and Orchestra of Wales) … Partington found ingredients in *Gerontius* one had simply never spotted before. Not so much his pacings as the quality of his inner ear, sensing tension and signalling it before it even arose, reading the undercurrents of the work, holding back where others might surge, keeping a lid on things.[86]

Toby Spence, recently returned from serious illness, showed what a fine singer he had become in a role that he will surely sing many times in the future. His combination of intensity and introspection, and his clear grasp of both narrative and musical line make him ideally suited to the dying man despite his youthful appearance, leading Roderic Dunnett to dub him 'the most exquisite young Gerontius'.[87] The Festival Chorus, too, despite a week of intense performance, showed huge range: freshness and light as well as steel and, indeed, sheer volume when required. The revelation, however, was in the 'outstanding' contribution of the Estonian mezzo Kai Rüütel.[88] For Dunnett, she was 'the most affecting Angel I have ever heard, Janet Baker included'.[89] That is high praise from a man who has heard many performances of this work in his time, and not just at Three Choirs.

Gerontius, then, was an undoubted high point to conclude a fine Festival, and one signalling the ambition and upward trajectory of artistic delivery. Good performances were clearly no longer good enough, and the combination of the Philharmonia residency and the organisation's administrative development were having their impact. As Adrian Partington remarked in his Foreword to the programme book, 'the music of Elgar is still, and probably will remain, the essence of the festival'.[90] But what is essence without a means to deliver it, or a context in which it can both be enjoyed in and of itself, and seen in relation to the other?

I T would have been difficult for any Artistic Director running a Festival in 2014 to avoid some sort of recognition of the most significant centenary of recent times – the marking of the beginning of World War I – but Peter Nardone's challenge was a more particular one: ensuring that the programming was authentic both to him as Artistic Director and to the history of the Festival, while not allowing retrospection and horror to overwhelm what is, after all, a celebratory festival. His intentions were summed up in his 'Welcome' remarks in the Festival programme book: 'Like a seam of precious metal, the spirit of optimism, hope and joy runs through the 2014 Three Choirs Festival.'[91] Perhaps the first three nights' concerts exemplify this sense of a journey that begins with recognition of what man can do to man (Britten's *War Requiem*), and then passes through contemplation and faith (Dvořák's *Stabat Mater*) towards reconciliation and light in Mahler's Symphony No. 2 (*Resurrection*). These concepts of light, of

---

[86] Dunnett, 'The Midland's Golden Oldie' (online).

[87] *Church Times*, 30 August 2013.

[88] Quinn, 'An Excellent, Moving Gerontius' (online).

[89] *Church Times*, 30 August 2013.

[90] Gloucester Festival programme book, 2013, p. 4.

[91] Worcester Festival programme book, 2014, p. 4.

what comes after, of what is left behind are also central to Torsten Rasch's new work, *A Foreign Field*, jointly commissioned by the Three Choirs Festival and the Städtische Theater Chemnitz.

As with any substantial commission, this project had a very long gestation, the kernel of the idea, in terms of Festival involvement at least, going back to the autumn of 2011.[92] A composer was eventually selected, through which process the idea began to emerge of a joint commission, and, indeed, a cross-border one. There was clear interest in the idea of an English choral festival commissioning a 1914 piece from a German composer, but the advent of the Chemnitz partnership brought with it another dimension: a link to World War II in the form of the fiftieth anniversary (the following year) of the destruction of Chemnitz by allied bombing in 1945. In addition, if it could be logistically managed, there were possibilities of singers from both places taking part in both performances.

Work was already well under way before Peter Nardone was appointed to the position at Worcester, and it is to his credit that he not only took the project on in his first home Festival, but also spearheaded the trip to Germany in March 2015 for the Chemnitz performances, accompanied by a group of choristers and members of the Festival Chorus. For the world première at Worcester an external conductor was engaged in the person of the Swiss contemporary music specialist Baldur Brönnimann. He appeared along with soprano Yeree Suh and baritone Roderick Williams, joined too by singers from the Kantorei der Kreuzkirche, in Chemnitz.

A Foreign Field is, in Rasch's own words, emphatically not a war requiem, or mass for the dead, or even an oratorio. Rather, he uses the structure of Anglican Evensong – though utilising large-scale forces – to construct a work that draws on liturgical texts (notably the psalms) and poetry by Edward Thomas, Rupert Brooke and Ivor Gurney in English, and Rainer Maria Rilke and Georg Trakl in German. The musical centrepiece is an *a cappella* setting of Psalm 91, the so-called Soldier's Psalm, which was carried by many soldiers in the trenches on both sides of the conflict. At the real heart of the work, however, is a scene depicting the last night that Edward Thomas and his wife, Helen, spent together before he went off to war, never to return:

> On the one hand, it depicts the sentiments of the one who has to go away and is going to lose his life, but on the other hand also that of the woman who stays behind and has to go on living with that feeling of being left behind, and that he will never come back.[93]

The piece undoubtedly contains elements of the horror of war, but it is this very human loss that transcends the battlefield, and indeed the two sides, which stands out. That loss, however, is counterbalanced by the Latin psalms that speak of the hope of salvation, and the redemptive 'lux perpetua' with which the piece ends.

---

[92] The idea should properly be attributed to Anwen Walker, who was involved in the project from the outset, and without whose drive, tenacity, and, indeed, knowledge of the Dymock Poets, it would most likely not have succeeded.

[93] Interview with Torsten Rasch as part of the World Waw I Centenary Art Commissions project (14–18 November).

Programmed alongside *A Foreign Field* were Elgar's *Spirit of England*, setting Binyon's jingoistic 1914 poem 'For the Fallen', and Vaughan Williams's transcendent *The Lark Ascending*, with its cliff-top backstory of naval manœuvres. The soloist for the Elgar was the tenor Peter Hoare, with violinist Matthew Trusler taking centre stage for the Vaughan Williams.

Although very difficult for the chorus in particular, not least given the constraints on rehearsal and preparation time (parts of the piece were, in fact, rewritten to make them more performable by an amateur group), the critics' response to *A Foreign Field* was very positive:

> One of the finest, most worthwhile premieres I have heard in many years.
> (Christopher Morley)[94]

> The musical score was as many-layered as the text. Washes of glittery metal percussion, creating an otherworldly atmosphere, sat cheek-by-jowl with a densely expressive texture that often harked back to Berg, or even Wagner.
> (Ivan Hewitt)[95]

> The work is full of chromatic harmonies slithering downwards like a world subsiding into chaos, and orchestral interludes that fiercely evoke the screaming shells and ear-shattering artillery as well as (in a magnificently moving, Berg-like ending) the heroism and sacrifice of the millions who died ... the best movement is also the simplest: a superbly crafted, unaccompanied choral setting of Psalm 91.   (Richard Morrison)[96]

> You sense that honesty and integrity, dignity and beauty in Rasch's music, and you sense, too, the man in the kind of poetry he is drawn to ... A Foreign Field will (I feel), and certainly should, be done in the next four commemorative years by choruses across the land, and in Germany, too.
> (Roderic Dunnett)[97]

Roderick Williams came in for high praise too, as did the Festival Chorus and choristers, not least for their performance of the unaccompanied setting of Psalm 91, and their suitably full throated rendition (despite some balance problems) of the Elgar. *The Times* dubbed it 'a superbly assured first performance', and it was recorded by Radio 3 for broadcast in September.[98]

This programming thread of, as Thursday's concert title termed it, 'Reflections of 1914', was ably set off by Roderick Williams on the first afternoon, who performed an exemplary recital, both in planning and execution, exploring 'The Great War in English Song'. Butterworth, Finzi and Gurney were all represented, alongside lesser-known songs by Martin Shaw, Elaine Hugh-Jones and Ian Venables. Despite the heat, both singer and pianist (Gary Matthewman) made their mark. The opening cathedral concert, with Peter Nardone on the podium to tackle Britten's great *War Requiem*, was also a

[94] *Birmingham Post*, 4 August 2014.
[95] *Telegraph*, 1 August 2014.
[96] *The Times*, 4 August 2014.
[97] *Church Times*, 22 August 2014.
[98] *The Times*, 4 August 2014.

success. Unfortunately, Susan Gritton was indisposed, but the key soprano part was thrillingly taken by Katherine Broderick, who was 'shattering' when required, but showed her versatility by producing a beautifully gentle tone when the texture allowed.[99] David Wilson-Johnson impressed too, and in the famous duet 'Strange Meeting' the 'subtle interaction' between him and James Oxley produced a memorable effect.[100] Fine singing from the chorus set a positive tone for the week, as did the firm hand of Peter Nardone (perhaps too firm, if truth be told, in certain places), marshalling his massed forces to good effect.

The Festival Youth Choir took this thread further still, with a fine *a cappella* performance on the cathedral stage on Monday morning. The programme included Vaughan Williams's Mass in G minor, and the 2010 piece *Shadows of Sleep* by Joseph Phibbs. This latter work weaves war poetry with Hilaire Belloc's 'The Night', resulting in a series of dreams 'each of which casts its own particular shadow, before fading away to reveal a new, contrasting image'.[101] It was convincingly given by these young voices under the direction of Adrian Partington. On Thursday evening there was a complete contrast in tone and experience, with a programme of Russian music from Nigel Short's exemplary chamber choir, Tenebrae.

New music was to be heard later in the week, too, played by the young instrumentalists of the National Youth Orchestra of Scotland. With the virtuoso celebrity trumpeter Håkan Hardenberger, they gave a fine account of Sally Beamish's new Trumpet Concerto, alongside thoroughly committed performances of Walton and Strauss under their conductor Michael Francis. The days when such orchestral works were considered 'out of reach' of such youth ensembles are well and truly passed.

Lovers of the earlier side of the repertoire were not excluded, as the three cathedral choirs, joined by the Academy of Ancient Music, tackled another masterwork in the form of Bach's immense Mass in B minor. A difficult piece for any choir, the boys in particular scaled the heights of Bach's genius with aplomb, supported by some very stylish and assured playing from the orchestra, and ably directed by Nardone himself. By chance, after the 2014 programme was published, Peter Nardone discovered that the programme for the 1914 festival, which was cancelled shortly after the outbreak of war, had also included the Bach Mass in B minor, and, indeed, Parry's *Blest Pair of Sirens*, both of which he had chosen to include himself 100 years later.

A more celebratory programming thread came in the form of the 450th anniversary of the birth of Shakespeare, serendipitously falling in a year when the Festival is closest to the birthplace of England's most famous poet and playwright. Shakespeare's Globe Touring Company returned to Worcester with their acclaimed production of *Much Ado About Nothing*, taking over the

---

[99] *Church Times*, 22 August 2014.

[100] John Quinn, 'The Three Choirs Festival Commemorates the Great War with War Requiem', *Seen and Heard International*, 26 July 2014. Online at http://seenandheard-international.com/2014/07/the-three-choirs-festival-commemorates-the-great-war-with-war-requiem/ [accessed 30 September 2016].

[101] Joseph Phibbs, Worcester Festival programme book, 2014, p. 62.

space of College Hall to form a wonderfully historic 'in the round' performance space. Soprano Julia Doyle, sensitively accompanied on the harpsichord by Steven Devine, gave an attractive recital of Shakespeare settings by Purcell and Arne in Huntingdon Hall, and the King's Singers included George Shearing's *Songs and Sonnets from Shakespeare* in their typically varied afternoon cathedral programme. Of more substance, perhaps, was the performance of Walton's *Henry V* in the evening programme on Wednesday, where the Philharmonia Orchestra was joined by the ever-popular John Wilson, returning to Worcester after his film music concert in 2008, and the actor Samuel West. This programme was completed by Strauss's great tone poem *Don Juan*, marking 150 years since the composer's birth, and an 'eloquent' reading of Korngold's Violin Concerto with soloist Andrew Haveron.[102]

The Dvořák *Stabat Mater* is not a piece that is performed a great deal, and had not been given at Three Choirs since 1956 in Gloucester. An attractive work, though lengthy, Geraint Bowen made a good case for its more frequent performance, particularly in his well-judged tempi and his grasp of its overall architecture, and the Festival Chorus clearly relished the opportunity to get to grips with a new score. A different challenge lay in Adrian Partington's turn on the rostrum later in the week: Elgar's *The Apostles*, following his memorable renderings of Elgar in 2010(G) and 2013(G). Here again, Partington showed himself to be steeped in this music, with an intuitive grasp of the Elgarian idiom, and a balance of sweep and space that allowed the detail of orchestration and colour to be revealed without harming the narrative arc. The male soloists stole the show here, particularly Brindley Sherratt singing the part of the misguided Judas, and the 'calm and dignified' Marcus Farnsworth, a youthful and wholly believable Jesus.[103]

Two other soloists shone in Monday night's Mahler Symphony No. 2 – the 'refined and graceful' singing of Jennifer Johnston, and the 'spine tingling' control of Katherine Broderick, though it was the guest conductor, the Slovakian Juraj Valčuha, who really stole the limelight with a masterful touch.[104] This is repertoire with which he clearly has a close affinity, and his ability to adapt to, and indeed utilise, the spatial and acoustic possibilities of the vast cathedral space was exemplary. The addition of the main cathedral organ, sounding from behind the main body of the audience in the final pages, was a masterstroke, whoever's idea it was.

Worcester's emphasis on local audience engagement was carried through this year, following forays into film and opera in the last two festivals, to a last night with distinct overtones of another great British music Festival:

[102] *Church Times*, 22 August 2014.

[103] John Quinn, 'A Triumphant and Moving Account of *The Apostles* at the Three Choirs', *Seen and Heard International*, 2 August 2014. Online at http://seenandheard-international.com/2014/08/a-triumphant-and-moving-account-of-the-apostles-at-the-three-choirs/ [accessed 30 September 2016].

[104] Holly Harrison, 'An Exultant Mahler "Resurrection" Symphony in Worcester Cathedral', *Bachtrack*, 29 July 2014. Online at https://bachtrack.com/review-three-choirs-philharmonia-worcester-july-2014 [accessed 30 September 2016].

Nardone suffered mutterings and gentle flak for programming 'Best of British: Festival Finale', a sort of Last Night of the Proms with the Philharmonia Orchestra for the concluding Saturday night … But an on-form Nardone went on to deliver a scintillating programme with real flair and a great deal of excellence. Sarah Connolly sang Elgar's Sea Pictures with ten times the wisdom and insight she brought last time she did it here. And what wondrous Parry![105]

The audience that filled the cathedral nave certainly felt it a fitting end to the Festival, and the Philharmonia's playing was exemplary. Again it could be seen that the residency partnership was having an appreciable effect on the standard of music-making, in the cathedral concerts in particular, and not just through the presence of first-rank international conductors. The Festival Chorus raised their game too, producing consistently fine singing throughout the week, even with the additional challenges of a newly commissioned work.

ACCORDING to the dating scheme set out by Sir Ivor Atkins, although the 2015 Hereford Festival would be the 288th Festival, it would also mark the tercentenary of the date used for the first 'Music Meeting' (1715). Any organisation that reaches such a milestone can be forgiven for wanting to celebrate it, and Three Choirs Festival was no exception. Of course, 2015 also saw the anniversaries of three other great events in British history: 800 years since Magna Carta, 600 years since Agincourt, and 200 years since Waterloo.[106] This meant that the programme could draw on swathes of history and music covering the entire lifespan of the Festival, and look to its future too: an exciting, though hugely daunting, task for Geraint Bowen and his team.

It was also an opportunity to significantly raise the profile of the Festival nationally and internationally, on the back of the marking of that date. As Dominic Jewel (former Chief Executive) put it: 'The reason for celebrating the tercentenary was not because we were pleased to get to 300 years, but to say "look at what we can do with it". That was the driving force for persuading people to sit up and notice us.'[107] And notice they did, with a considerable number of reviews and features in the press, and even a significant article in the *New York Times* (the first time a full review of the Festival had been published that side of the Atlantic). BBC Radio 3 featured the Festival in the daily 'Composer of the Week' slot, and the celebration was not forgotten by the Festival's royal patron, the Prince of Wales (see Chapter 26).

The fact that such a celebration was mounted also highlights another significant change in the way the Festival is run, and one which had been

---

[105] *Church Times*, 22 August 2014. The programme included Handel's *Zadok the Priest*, Vaughan Williams's *Five Variants on 'Dives and Lazarus'*, Delius's *The Walk to the Paradise Garden*, alongside shorter pieces by Elgar and Parry, Finzi's *A Severn Rhapsody*, and Parry's *Blest Pair of Sirens* and Elgar's *Pomp and Circumstance March* no. 1.

[106] Each of these significant historical events was explored in lectures across the course of the week.

[107] Interview with Dominic Jewel, 16 May 2016.

evident in 2014 as well: planning now begins much further in advance. A few years before, it would not have been unusual for a local committee to convene for the first time eighteen months before 'their' festival, in order to begin to plan the programme (to be published that same year). In the modern climate, particularly in terms of relationships with the top orchestras, and especially with commissioning new works from significant composers, even a three-year planning period has become rather short, certainly in terms of realising the Festival's growing musical ambition. Clearly, such timeframes necessitate longer-term strategy across years and across committees, something that was not really possible before the advent of the professional administrative core. As Geraint Bowen put it, 'it is testament to how necessary the central administration has become that everyone now sees a return to how it was before as unthinkable.'[108]

The opening day of the Festival was to be one that looked back, but also looked forward. The Opening Service featured, alongside the Festival Chorus and Hereford Cathedral choir, the period instruments of the Corelli Orchestra performing works by Purcell and Handel that would have been well known to performers and audiences alike across the first century of the Festival's history. The evening concert was given over to the piece which has become synonymous with Three Choirs, and which some doubtless said it would have been sacrilegious to leave out – *The Dream of Gerontius*. Unfortunately, the advertised tenor, Peter Auty, was indisposed. He was replaced at short notice by Paul Nilon, who gave an 'admirably pained and passionate' performance in a 'galvanising reading that showcased the Festival Chorus.'[109] There was also 'committed and beautifully nuanced' singing from Sarah Connolly as the Angel.[110]

It was left to Festival-regular and favourite baritone Roderick Williams to look forwards, though in his meticulously crafted way. His recital 'Song of the Hero' carried on the 'Great War' thread that ran through much of the 2014 programme, though here with more focus on the home front – on those left behind. This included a rare male-voice rendition of Elgar's *Sea Pictures*, the *Four Last Songs* by Vaughan Williams, works by Tim Torry and Herbert Howells, and a newly commissioned cycle by Rhian Samuel – *A Swift Radiant Morning*. She sets words by one of the lesser-known soldier poets, Charles Hamilton Sorley, who was killed in action on the Western Front in October 1915 at the age of just twenty. 'A work of striking originality', this is a fine addition to the contemporary canon of World War I settings, faultlessly and movingly captured by Williams and his pianist, Susie Allan.[111]

This was not the only new music during the week, though given the scale of the previous year's commission it was no surprise that there was no substantial contemporary choral work in the evening cathedral programme. Instead, a new set of evening canticles commissioned by the Festival from the former King's

[108] Interview with Geraint Bowen, 13 September 2016.

[109] *Church Times*, 21 August 2015.

[110] John Quinn, 'The Three Choirs Festival's *Gerontius* Tradition Upheld in a Worthy Manner', *Seen and Heard International*, 26 July 2015. Online at http://seenandheard-international.com/2015/07/the-three-choirs-festivals-gerontius-tradition-upheld-in-a-worthy-manner/ [accessed 30 September 2016].

[111] *Church Times*, 21 August 2015.

Singer Bob Chilcott was broadcast in Wednesday's Evensong, sung by the three cathedral choirs, and *Stargazer* by Alec Roth was given its première by the vocal ensemble Voces8. The winning piece in the tercentenary composition competition – George Arthur's setting for double choir of *Prayer of Thomas Ken* – was premièred by the Hereford Cathedral Voluntary Choir.[112] The Festival also featured Pete Churchill's *Echoes – A Polish Tale*, given in the Gathering Wave Concert,[113] and John Scott gave the first performance of *O Gott, du frommer Gott* by Anthony Powers. It was to be one of the last performances that he gave, as shortly after returning to New York following his European concert tour he was taken ill and died of a suspected heart attack on 12 August. A formidable and admired musician, he had performed several times at Three Choirs, and his legacy to cathedral music will be long remembered.

The 2015 Hereford Festival also saw the third new commission in three Festivals from the German composer Torsten Rasch, this time in the form of six settings of words by the Welsh poet Alun Lewis (1915–1944), written for Sarah Connolly and performed with Joseph Middelton on the last afternoon of the week.[114] This concert cleverly mirrored Roderick Williams's recital which opened the week, acting as a salutary reminder of the continuing legacy of war, and indeed that great human cost can yet give rise to extraordinary inspiration and artistic endeavour. No backslapping jamboree here to celebrate a significant birthday or milestone.[115] Rather, 'Song of the Widow' allowed Purcell to speak 'of the penitential and consoling possibilities which song can afford the soul', before the real focus and perspective was offered by the combined forces of poet and composer.[116] Sarah Connolly was on stunning form, communicative as ever with fabulous support from her pianist, Joseph Middleton; the changes to the advertised programme were entirely justified, as moods shifted and light and shade played among the pillars and stained glass of Holy Trinity Church. Of the commission:

> Rasch is one of those composers who has absorbed deeply the music of the Second Viennese School, and by his gifts evolved a musical format both approachable and entrancing. Thus the second song, 'Black dog barking at the moon', may recall Schoenberg's *Pierrot Lunaire* (1912) or *Das Buch der hangenden Garten* (1908–9), and yet emerges wholly fresh and original.
>
> Rasch can evoke the dark and cavernous ... the witty and yet atmospheric and sympathetic ... His evocative piano accompaniments,

[112] The competition was judged by the composer Paul Mealor, and Jonathan Wikeley, Choral Editor at Music Sales Ltd, who would publish the piece.

[113] As in previous years, this community event was held on the main cathedral platform on the Sunday at the end of Festival week.

[114] Alun Lewis was born in one world war, killed in another.

[115] The programme had evolved somewhat between printing and performance, so in fact ran as follows: Purcell, *Three Divine Hymns*; numbers 1, 2 and 6 from Timothy Watts, *Equal Mistress*; Gurney, *Sleep*; Gurney, *Three Cabaret Songs*; Rasch, *A Welsh Night*; Howells, *Gavotte*; Gurney, *Thou didst delight my eyes*; Novello, *Glamorous Night*; and Wood, *Roses of Picardy*.

[116] Gwilym Bowen, Hereford Festival programme book, 2015, p. 243.

mostly independent of the voice, often conjure a mood in counterpoint and contrast to the singer …

This was a richly engaging cycle, which urgently invites a repeat hearing.[117]

The other element in the programme that continued this World War I Centenary strand was a rare performance of *Morning Heroes* by Sir Arthur Bliss – his great elegy for the fallen (which included his beloved brother), setting texts both classical (Homer) and contemporary (Walt Whitman, Wilfred Owen). Partnered by an urgent reading of Sibelius's fifth symphony (written in 1915, though revised in 1916 and 1919), a very different product of World War I, Sir Andrew Davis made a good case for Bliss's troubled work to be performed more often.

> *Morning Heroes* is music of immense dignity and beauty; Bliss's instincts are lyrical, and it's full of quiet expressive string lines and woodwind solos of the sort that thoughtless people call 'English pastoral' – though there was very little comfort to be had here. Davis, who conducted the work in London earlier this year, opened up the grain of the texture, bringing out the clash of unquiet harmonies, and letting the inner and lower orchestral voices – violas, cellos, a hollow-sounding bass clarinet – throw long shadows over the music.[118]

Malcolm Sinclair replaced the advertised Samuel West as narrator to great effect, and despite the sheer quantity of text given to the chorus, they acquitted themselves extremely well. There was also exemplary orchestral playing from the Philharmonia.

High standards of musicianship were also very much in evidence in perhaps the standout concert of the week – the first Three Choirs performance of Messiaen's great song of love, his immense *Turangalîla-symphonie*. 'Superlatively conducted by the magisterial Jac van Steen', this was prefaced by the Prelude and Liebestod from Wagner's *Tristan und Isolde*.[119] This concert was further evidence of the deepening and fruitful relationship between the Festival and the orchestra, and indicative of its ambition and confidence, as well as showing clearly how far the Festival has come since the days of the 'secular concerts' and the sanitisation of Cardinal Newman's poem for Anglican ears. The opportunity to hear this masterpiece of the orchestral repertoire in a cathedral acoustic with one of the top orchestras in the world was electrifying.

> Pianist Steven Osborne played the fiendish solo piano writing with the same dazzling command he was to bring to a superbly intimate recital of late Beethoven and Schubert sonatas two days later. The Philharmonia

[117] *Church Times*, 21 August 2015.

[118] Richard Bratby, 'Philharmonia, Davis, Three Choirs Festival', the*arts*desk.com, 29 July 2015. Online at http://www.theartsdesk.com/classical-music/philharmonia-davis-three-choirs-festival [accessed 30 September 2016].

[119] Roderic Dunnett, 'The 300th Anniversary of the Three Choirs Festival', *bachtrack*, 7 August 2015. Online at https://bachtrack.com/review-gerontius-three-choirs-300-anniversary-hereford-july-2015 [accessed 30 September 2016].

Orchestra, brilliantly directed by Jac van Steen, romped through the dizzying score, the blowsy brass particularly splendid. Sitting amid all the clamour and rampant ardour of this colossal 10-movement work, Messiaen has one moment of blissful calm, a visit to the Jardin du sommeil d'amour, when that electronic curiosity, the ondes martenot, which up to then has been whopping with decidedly frisky joy, sings an ethereal song of love against a background of birdsong, trilled sweetly from the piano. It's an exquisite moment and one beautifully realised in this ecstatic performance.[120]

Just as notable, however, but for very different reasons, was Geraint Bowen's *St Matthew Passion* in the middle of the week, with the three cathedral choirs, and the Festival debut of the Orchestra of the Age of Enlightenment. There was exquisite playing from this premier period band, and Bowen showed a great ability to drive the dramatic narrative of Bach's masterpiece, while also allowing the moments of reflection and the crucifixion scene to breathe where they needed to. The boys in particular excelled, particularly in their command of the original German text, but the real laurels went to a fine team of soloists: James Oxley, Matthew Brook, Elizabeth Watts, William Towers, Anthony Gregory and Roderick Williams. As Stephen Pritchard noted: 'few could have been prepared for the dramatic intensity of Evangelist James Oxley's performance. For three hours he lived the role, singing without a copy, freighting each utterance, first with urgency and then resigned solemnity as his narrative slid towards the inevitability of Golgatha.'[121] Matthew Brook was peerless, too, in the part of Christus, in an intense and beautifully projected portrayal of Bach's 'man of sorrows' – an altogether more human figure than the 'hero' of the *St John Passion*. Praising Geraint Bowen, the *Church Times* reviewer wrote: 'This elevating performance, and the deep feeling it engendered in all, was a personal triumph.'[122]

Youth was conspicuously on show in 2015(H) with the return of the Young Artist thread from previous years, alongside a recital by the singers selected at the previous year's competitive masterclass in Worcester, Emily Garland and Dominic Sedgwick. The Festival Youth Choir performed Bob Chilcott's Requiem, alongside Bernstein's effervescent *Chichester Psalms* under the baton of Peter Nardone. Freshness of voice combining with 'poise and precision', and some fine solo singing from Ruairi Bowen and Patrick Dunachie in particular, produced a fine impression.[123] Outclassing them all, however, was the National Youth Orchestra of Wales, in a stunning programme of real rarities: Dukas's last major published work, *La Péri* (marking the 150th anniversary of the composer's birth), Florent Schmitt's 1907 ballet score *La Tragédie de Salomé*, and, to conclude, a memorable reading of Stravinsky's *Rite of Spring*, conducted impeccably by Paul Daniel.

[120] Stephen Pritchard, *Guardian*, 2 August 2015.

[121] Ibid.

[122] *Church Times*, 21 August 2015.

[123] Stephen Pritchard, *Guardian*, 2 August 2015.

Unusual repertoire was the order of the day on Thursday evening too, when Peter Nardone took to the podium for two works that had previously only been performed in Hereford years: William Mathias's *Lux aeterna*, commissioned by Roy Massey for the 1982 Festival, and *Hymnus Amoris* by the Danish composer Carl Nielsen, celebrating the 150th anniversary of his birth, and only given once before at Three Choirs (in 1979). Mathias's work was written in memory of his mother, with the concept of 'light' being foremost in the composer's mind. The Festival Chorus, with soloists Sarah Fox, Jennifer Johnston and Claudia Huckle, conjured 'shimmering washes of sound' in a performance that undoubtedly justified the revival.[124]

There was also a welcome revival for a masterwork of the choral repertoire that, unbelievably, had not been given at Three Choirs for almost a quarter of a century – Beethoven's fearsome *Missa solemnis* (the last Festival performance had been in 1991(H)). The piece is regarded by many as one of Beethoven's supreme achievements, and as an 'Everest of the choral repertoire', and this concert found Adrian Partington and the Festival Chorus equal to the task.[125] The composer makes huge demands on soloists and chorus alike, and despite Marcus Farnsworth's late withdrawal, the solo team did him proud, eclipsed only by the contribution of the Chorus:[126] 'This was a performance by the choir that was as memorable as it was tireless. … after all that had gone before they were just as committed and secure in the closing pages of the Agnus Dei as they had been in the opening Kyrie.'[127] Special mention should be made of the orchestra, particularly the Leader, Zsolt-Tihamér Visontay, for a radiant solo alongside the quartet in the 'Benedictus', where the strings produced an almost viol-like quality of tone.[128] Partington, too, was 'magnificent at all key points', showing not only his grasp of Beethoven's thematic development but also his skill with, and ability to inspire and lift, large choirs.[129]

And so it was left to the Artistic Director to close the main evening concert programme with a committed account of Verdi's great Requiem, with soloists Katherine Broderick, Catherine Wyn-Rogers, Gwyn Hughes Jones and Alastair Miles. Unsurprisingly, the most telling interventions here were from the Philharmonia brass, thrilling in the cathedral acoustic but with such fullness of tone, the operatic drama of the piece melting away with the final chords of the 'Libera me'.

Who can tell what the next 100 (or even 300) years have in store for this historic event, which has outlived all expectations, overcome the vagaries of society, politics and economics, and has shown itself in rude artistic health in

---

[124] Andrew Clements, *Guardian*, 31 July 2015.

[125] John Quinn, 'Beethoven Storms the Heavens in Hereford', *Seen and Heard International*, 31 July 2015. Online at http://seenandheard-international.com/2015/07/beethoven-storms-the-heavens-in-hereford/ [accessed 30 September 2016].

[126] The soloists were Eleanor Dennis, Jennifer Johnston, Mark le Brocq, and the late change, Edward Grint.

[127] Quinn, 'Beethoven Storms the Heavens' (online).

[128] Dunnett, 'The 300th Anniversary' (online).

[129] *Church Times*, 21 August 2015.

recent years. It is no small task for Artistic Directors and management in the future to realise the ambitions begun all those years ago in the cathedrals and music clubs of these three provincial cities, and to lead them through whatever the future may hold.

26

An Invitation to the Palace

IT was on an afternoon in early June 2015, while working on final preparations for the Hereford Festival, that the Three Choirs management were invited to attend a meeting at the London residence of the Festival's president, the Prince of Wales. Despite knowing very little about what would be discussed, there was no doubt that the invitation would augur something quite significant.

The Chief Executive and his assistant found themselves, some days later, in a beautiful room in Clarence House with a surprising number of others, including representatives from the Prince's staff and senior members of the firm that runs events at Buckingham Palace. In short, it transpired that Prince Charles was offering to recognise the tercentenary of the Festival by hosting a performance in the ballroom at Buckingham Palace. In terms of the numbers of performers, this would be perhaps the largest concert ever held in that space. Organising the event was to prove hugely challenging, and required much dedicated work; but the result was extremely successful from all angles.

Organising a concert in any such significant space is never straightforward, but the challenge of doing so with a massed choir of 300, an invited audience in excess of 400 (all of whom had to be vetted), and a little-used historic organ was immense. Very early in the planning the decision was taken to involve all of the Festival's 'in house' choirs – massed chorus, cathedral choirs and Youth Choir – who would each perform alone and together in a programme intended to capture the nature of the Festival, past and present. Logistically, it was no small feat to transplant such a large number of performers to London, particularly given the Prince's wish to spend time with each group of performers following the concert. Little rehearsal time was available – a constraint which impacted significantly upon the assistant organists, who were required to adapt extremely quickly to a difficult instrument. The Palace organ pre-dates such modern niceties as registrations, and so three organists were required at any one time: one organist playing, one selecting stops to his left, and one selecting stops to his right. Preparation time on the day was limited to a few minutes per item – barely time to play through the pieces, let alone rehearse meaningfully. Put all of this alongside the need for Royal Footmen to escort anyone moving between different rooms in the Palace, and the stringent regulations on mobile phones, and it soon becomes apparent why the organisation needed precision and detail to almost military standards.

The evening came, and guests began arriving at the gates of the Palace – not just Festival-goers from the three cities, but supporters from around the country, and a sizeable group of the Festival's American friends. Filling the ballroom that November evening was a hugely diverse cross-section of those involved or associated with Three Choirs, from long-time members of Friends committees to previous Artistic Directors, from Stewards to sponsors. All were gathering to mark this auspicious occasion in the splendour of the Royal household. The huge age-range among the performers should be marked here too, from the youngest chorister to the 'elder statesmen' of the Festival Chorus, with decades of experience on the Festival platform.

Following a short speech from Dr Timothy Brain, the chairman of the Three Choirs Festival Association, the programme opened with perhaps the finest rendition of the National Anthem heard anywhere, down at least in part to the musical experience of the audience as well as the chorus. The massed choirs then broke into Handel's joyous *Zadok the Priest*, a piece almost as old as the Festival itself, and performed many times at Three Choirs over the years, as well as at every coronation since 1727. Accompanied by brass players from the Royal Welsh College of Music and Drama (an organisation of which Prince Charles is also patron), the effect was breathtaking: a stunning sound, ably supported by the playing of Peter Dyke, and conducted by Geraint Bowen. Focus then shifted to the cathedral choirs, performing Parry's 'My soul, there is a country' from his *Songs of Farewell* (1915), conducted by Peter Nardone. Then followed youthful beauty conjured by the girl choristers of Worcester Cathedral and the Festival Youth Choir in Rutter's ever-popular *The Lord Bless you and Keep you*.

No such tour of Three Choirs repertoire would be complete without music from its most famous son, Edward Elgar, and what better source than the end of Part I of *The Dream of Gerontius*? The massed choirs were joined by one of the most popular Three Choirs Festival soloists in recent years: Roderick Williams. While it is always difficult to take short sections from a larger work, Williams's commitment and the belief of the chorus, with Jonathan Hope's sensitive work in the organ loft and the guiding hand of Adrian Partington, resulted in a finely atmospheric performance that succeeded in creating a sacred space into which the soul of the dying Gerontius could 'Go forth' with confidence.

From Elgar to Purcell's *Hear my Prayer* – a jump back in time to the music of the Festival's early days, and no less harmonically arresting than it must have been on its first performance well over 300 years before. Adrian Partington then returned the baton to his Hereford colleague for another Three Choirs staple: two movements from Vaughan Williams's *Five Mystical Songs*, skilfully rendered by the cathedral choristers and Festival Chorus, and heroically accompanied by Peter Dyke. With Roderick Williams in attendance, some felt that it was a shame not to use him in the Vaughan Williams too, but tight time constraints on the overall programme length precluded that possibility. So tight were the constraints, indeed, that there were contingency plans in place to shorten the programme mid-flow were things not to have run to time.

An excerpt from the most recent large-scale Festival commission followed, in Torsten Rasch's setting of verses from Psalm 91, taken from his piece *A Foreign Field* which was premièred at the 2014 Festival. It was a deftly wrought and sensitively handled performance by the three cathedral choirs, conducted by Peter Nardone, who had travelled with the Festival singers to Chemnitz in 2015 to take part in the German première of the piece. This was, of course, a significant inclusion, underscoring the fact that the Festival is still commissioning and performing contemporary music, as it has across its entire history.

The programme closed with two of the most familiar pieces in the choral canon. Parry's *I was glad* was composed for the coronation of Edward VII in 1902, and has been performed at every coronation since, its grandeur a worthy match to the palace ballroom in which we were seated, and lifted here by the brass players from the Royal Welsh College and by Adrian Partington's declamatory reading. And what better way to close such an event than with a rousing 'Hallelujah Chorus' from Handel's *Messiah*, a piece performed perhaps more than any other over the course of the Festival's 300 years, programmed as it was first in 1757, and given in all but two Festivals between then and 1963.

This was truly an event worthy to mark such a significant anniversary of what is thought to be the oldest non-competitive music festival in existence. That claim is testament not only to Three Choirs' longevity, but also to how it has developed and reinvented itself over the course of its long history. The event was not without effect, either, as the 2016 Festival in Gloucester was honoured with two separate royal visits: by the Duke and Duchess of Gloucester, and by Prince Charles himself.

This concert was a shining example of what can be achieved through unity and collaboration – of the heights that can be reached when the Festival communities pull together to produce something extraordinary, regardless of city affiliation, age or experience. It is this commitment to the endeavour, alongside a tangible and heartfelt respect for the music, which is at the very heart of the Festival as it embarks upon its fourth century.

APPENDIX

Three Choirs Festival Timeline

EIGHTEENTH CENTURY

1709 Early evidence of 'friendship and fraternity' was shown in 1709 when Henry Hall, the Organist of Hereford Cathedral, and his counterpart at Gloucester, William Hine, collaborated in the composition of a morning service, 'Hall and Hine in E flat', possibly for a joint celebration at Worcester in 1710. The *Te Deum* is by Hall, the *Jubilate* by Hine.

1715(G) The year from which the Music Meetings are counted. It is believed that the annual gatherings were fully established by 1715, albeit that the earliest actually recorded Meeting was held in 1719(w). Wars have interrupted the continuity of the Festival twice, from 1914 to 1920, and from 1939 to 1945. Until the late 1750s only music for services was permitted in the cathedrals, where the *Te Deum and Jubilate* in D of Purcell, for example, was sung regularly for almost forty years from the inception of the Meetings. Other concerts, including oratorio performances, were held in various secular venues. Even *Messiah* was not at first admitted within the cathedrals.

1724(G) Thomas Bisse successfully proposed that the Music Meetings should be held for a charitable purpose, i.e. for the benefit of the orphans (later 'the widows and orphans') of the poorer clergy of the three dioceses. This remained the principle *raison d'être* for the Festival Charity until 1986.

1731(W) William Hayes, a pupil of William Hine at Gloucester and an ardent Handelian, was Organist at Worcester until 1734 but did not conduct at the Meetings during those years. Handel became the dominant composer in the programmes, which from 1733 featured 'the most eminent performers from the metropolis'. Hayes went on to become Professor of Music at Oxford and to build a national reputation as composer, conductor, singer and organist, appearing at Three Choirs many times in the 1750s and 1760s.

1737 William Boyce took over as conductor of the Music Meetings, serving for many years. His anthems were performed regularly at Meetings during the eighteenth century and, in the secular concerts, both his *Solomon* and *The Shepherd's Lottery* were featured.

1745(G) Maurice Greene, accompanied by several Gentlemen of the Chapel Royal, Westminster Abbey and St Paul's, performed Greene's dramatic pastoral *Love's Revenge* at the Music Meeting.

1755(W) Stewards now two of the gentry.

1757(G) First *Messiah* performance at a Music Meeting, but not in the cathedral. Hayes conducted at Gloucester in 1757, 1760 and 1763.

1759(H) *Messiah* was admitted to performance in the cathedral for the first time. Richard Clack, Organist of Hereford from 1754 to 1779, was in charge of the Meeting and was the first of the cathedral organists to be recorded as conductor. Thereafter, *Messiah* was performed in whole or in part every year until 1963 (and from time to time since then).

1772(G) First appearance of ladies to assist the boys in the choruses. 'Miss Radcliffe and others of the celebrated female chorus singers from the North of England' were engaged.

1781(G) William Cramer leads the orchestra for the first time.

1784(G) Second morning given to oratorio type of music.

1786(H) The west end of Hereford Cathedral collapsed. Music Meeting held in St Peter's Church.

1788(W) King George III attended a performance of *Messiah*.

1798(H) Stewards six in number.

NINETEENTH CENTURY

1800(W) First Three Choirs performance of *The Creation* by Haydn. François Cramer succeeded his father as Leader, and continued to appear at the Meetings until his retirement at the age of seventy-six.

1817(G) Concerts moved from Booth Hall to Shire Hall.

1819(H) Concerts moved from Music Room to Shire Hall.

1830(W) Princess Victoria attends the Music Meeting. Maria Malibran, making her second Three Choirs appearance, is hailed as the great star of the occasion.

1832(H) Samuel Sebastian Wesley appointed Organist at Hereford, appearing at a Meeting for the first time, as a pianist, at Worcester in 1833. He remained at Hereford until 1835.

1834(H) Performances transferred from the choir to the nave.

1836(W) Fourth morning added.

1838(G) The first Music Meeting to be designated a 'Three Choirs Festival'. Queen Victoria was crowned in the previous year.

1847(G) Mendelssohn's *Elijah* performed in the year following its first performance in Birmingham. Thereafter, it featured at every Festival until 1929, and many times thereafter.

1853(G) Liturgical services by combined cathedral choirs.

1864(H) Chamber concert introduced.

1865(G) S. S. Wesley appointed Organist at Gloucester.

1871(G) S. S. Wesley conducts the first Three Choirs performance of Bach's *St Matthew Passion*.

1875(W) The 'Mock' Festival.

1878(W) Elgar first played in the Festival orchestra.

1879(H) Arthur Sullivan conducted his *Light of the World*.

1880(G) Hubert Parry conducted the première of his *Scenes from Shelley's 'Prometheus Unbound'*, a work hailed by Sir Henry Hadow as the birth of modern English music.

1881(W) First Sunday Opening Service.

1883(G) John Stainer conducted the first performance of his *St Mary Magdalen*, which was repeated at Hereford in 1891. Charles Villiers Stanford conducted his Symphony No. 2 in D minor (*Elegiac*).

1884(W) Antonín Dvořák conducted performances of his *Stabat Mater* and Symphony No. 6 in D, op. 60 (formerly No. 1).

1889(G) Sullivan conducted his *In Memoriam* and *Prodigal Son*; Parry conducted *Judith*.

1890(W) Second evening performance added. Parry conducted his *Ode on St Cecilia's Day*. Elgar conducted the first performance of his overture *Froissart*.

1891(H) George Robertson Sinclair's first Festival as Artistic Director at Hereford. Première of Parry's *De Profundis* under the composer's direction.

1892(G) Chorus for first time drawn only from local singers. Parry conducted *Job*, which was repeated under his baton in 1893(w), 1894(H), 1901(G) and 1909(H).

1893(W) First Three Choirs Festival performance of the Bach Mass in B minor.

1895(G) Frederic Cowen conducted the première of his *The Transfiguration*.

1896(W) Elgar conducted the première of his *The Light of Life* (*Lux Christi*).

1898(G) Herbert Brewer's first Festival as Artistic Director at Gloucester. The first appearance of Samuel Coleridge-Taylor at Three Choirs, where he conducted the première of his *Ballade* in A minor. Parry conducted the first performance of his *A Song of Darkness and Light*. The first performances in England of the *Stabat Mater*, *Laudi alla Vergine* and *Te Deum* from *Quattro pezzi sacri* by Giuseppe Verdi.

1899(W) Ivor Atkins's first Festival as Artistic Director at Worcester. Coleridge-Taylor conducted the first performance of his *Solemn Prelude* for orchestra. The American composer Horatio Parker conducted the first British performance of his *Hora novissima*, and Elgar conducted the first Three Choirs performance of his *Enigma Variations*.

TWENTIETH CENTURY

1900(H) Horatio Parker returned to conduct the première of his *A Wanderer's Psalm*. Elgar conducted *Caractacus* (Scene III).

1901(G) First performance of Herbert Brewer's *Emmaus*, orchestrated by Elgar, who also conducted his *Cockaigne* overture in an orchestral concert, and the Prelude and Angel's Farewell from *The Dream of Gerontius* as part of the Opening Service.

1902(W) First Three Choirs complete performance of *Gerontius*, conducted by Elgar, who regularly directed his own works at the Festival for the next thirty years. Other composers conducting premières of their works included Walford Davies (*The Temple*) and Granville Bantock (*The Witch of Atlas*).

1903(H) First performances of *The Wilderness* by Bantock and *The Atonement* by Coleridge-Taylor. Parry directed his own *Voces clamantium*.

1904(G) First Three Choirs performances of *The Apostles* and the overture *In the South*, both conducted by Elgar. The première of Parry's *The Love that Casteth Out Fear*, under the composer's direction.

1907(G) First Three Choirs performance of *The Kingdom*, conducted by Elgar.

1908(W) First performance of Parry's *Beyond these voices there is peace*, conducted by the composer.

1909(H) Frederick Delius conducted the first performance of his *Dance Rhapsody No. 1*.

1910(G) Ralph Vaughan Williams directed the première of his *Fantasia on a Theme by Thomas Tallis*. Thereafter he conducted his own works regularly at the Festival.

1911(W) Fritz Kreisler was the soloist in the first Three Choirs performance of the Elgar Violin Concerto, under the composer's direction. Vaughan Williams conducted the first performance of his *Five Mystical Songs*.

1912(H) Premières of two works conducted by their composers: *Ode on the Nativity of Christ* by Parry, and the *Fantasia on Christmas Carols* by Vaughan Williams.

1913(G) Camille Saint-Saëns conducted the première of his oratorio *The Promised Land*, and was the soloist in a performance of the Piano Concerto No. 27 in B flat, K595, by Mozart. The soprano Aïno Ackté travelled from Finland to sing in the Verdi Requiem, the first performance of *Luonnotar*, op. 70, by Sibelius, and the hair-raising closing scene from Richard Strauss's opera *Salome*.

1914 Outbreak of World War I stops the Festival.

1920(W) Resumption of the Festival following World War I. Elgar conducted his setting of Binyon's *For the Fallen*, and Vaughan Williams the first performance of his *Four Hymns* for tenor and strings. Bach's *St Matthew Passion* was performed using two organs for the first time in Worcester, and with chorales played from the tower by brass instruments.

1921(H) Percy Hull's first Festival as Artistic Director at Hereford. Elgar conducted the first Three Choirs Festival performance of his Cello Concerto, in which Beatrice Harrison was the soloist. Gustav Holst conducted his *Hymn of Jesus.*

1922(G) First performances of Elgar's orchestral transcription of the *Fantasia and Fugue* in C minor by Bach (BWV 537); *A Colour Symphony* by Arthur Bliss; Eugene Goossens's setting of a poem by Walter de la Mare, *Silence*; and *Sine nomine* by Herbert Howells.

1923(W) First performance of *To the Name above every Name* by Arnold Bax.

1925(G) Dame Ethel Smyth conducted performances of the overture to *The Wreckers* and of the *Kyrie* and *Gloria* from her Mass in D. *The Evening Watch* by Gustav Holst received its first performance. This was the first year in which a Three Choirs Festival concert was broadcast by the BBC.

1928(G) Herbert Sumsion's first Festival as Artistic Director at Gloucester. Zoltán Kodály conducted his *Psalmus Hungaricus* in the first of three visits (1928, 1937 and 1948) to Three Choirs. The Festival programme also included *King David* by Honegger, and the first performance of *The Burden of Babylon* by Bantock, which was conducted by the composer. Dame Ethel Smyth returned to conduct a complete performance of her Mass in D.

1929(W) First performance at Three Choirs of Bach's *St John Passion.*

1931(G) Holst conducted the première of his *Choral Fantasia* and a performance of the *Hymn of Jesus.* Vaughan Williams conducted the first Three Choirs Festival performance of *Job.* Robin Milford's *A Prophet in the Land* received its first performance, and Herbert Howells conducted the première of his song cycle *In Green Ways.*

1932(W) William Walton conducted his *Portsmouth Point Overture* and Viola Concerto, and Vaughan Williams the first performance of his *Magnificat.*

1933(H) The last Festival in which Elgar took part, conducting *Gerontius*, *The Kingdom*, and the Concerto in E minor, arr. for Viola. George Dyson conducted the première of his *St Paul's Voyage to Melita.*

1935(W) The first performances of *The Morning Watch* by Arnold Bax, and of Dyson's *Nebuchadnezzar*, which was conducted by the composer.

1936(H) Vaughan Williams conducted the first performance of his *Two Hymn Preludes* for orchestra.

1937(G) Kodály conducted both his Budávari *Te Deum* and *Jesus and the Traders.*

1938(W) Dyson conducted his Symphony in G; Vaughan Williams, his *Dona nobis pacem*; and Lennox Berkeley, the première of his *Domini est terra.* The programme included the first Three Choirs performance of Debussy's *The Blessed Damozel.*

1939 Outbreak of World War II stops the Festival.

1946(H) Resumption of the Festival following World War II. First Festival performance of *Dies natalis* by Gerald Finzi. E. J. Moeran conducted his *Sinfonietta* in C, and Dyson the first performance of his *Quo Vadis?* (Part I).

1947(G) Vaughan Williams conducted his Symphony No. 5. Finzi conducted his *Lo, the full final sacrifice*, and Edmund Rubbra his Symphony No. 3.

1948(W) Kodály conducted his *Missa brevis* (partly rewritten for this performance). Rubbra conducted his setting of *The Morning Watch*.

1949(H) Last appearances of Hull and Atkins as conductors. Vaughan Williams conducted his Symphony No. 3 (*Pastoral*); Finzi, the première of his Clarinet Concerto; and Dyson, *Quo Vadis?* (Parts I & II).

1950(G) Howells conducted the première of *Hymnus Paradisi*, and Vaughan Williams his Symphony No. 6 and the première of his *Fantasia on the 'Old 104th'*. Finzi's *Ode on the Intimations of Immortality* received its first performance, conducted by Sumsion.

1951(W) David Willcocks's first Festival as Artistic Director at Worcester. Finzi conducted his introduction and aria *Farewell to Arms*, and Julius Harrison his *Worcestershire Suite*. Douglas Fox was the soloist in Ravel's Piano Concerto for Left Hand. Stravinsky's *Apollon Musagette*, Britten's *Les Illuminations*, and the *Prelude and Scherzo* for string octet, op. 11, by Shostakovich were featured in a chamber concert.

1952(H) Meredith Davies's first Festival as Artistic Director at Hereford. First performance of *Cantiones sacrae* by John Gardner. *Aubade héroique* by Constant Lambert was performed.

1953(G) Richard Arnell conducted his *Sinfonia*, op. 13. *These things shall be* by John Ireland received its first Three Choirs performance.

1954(W) First performances of *Missa Sabrinensis* by Howells and *Hodie* by Vaughan Williams, both conducted by their composers.

1955(H) First performances in Britain of the *Stabat Mater* by Francis Poulenc and of *The Prodigal Son* by Paul Huber. Humphrey Searle's *Night Music*, and the *Prelude, Elegy and Finale* by Peter Racine Fricker were also featured. Sir Arthur Bliss conducted his *Colour Symphony*, and a choral suite, *In Praise of Mary*, by Geoffrey Bush, received its first performance.

1956(G) Vaughan Williams's last appearance at Three Choirs, conducting *The Lark Ascending*. First full orchestral version of Finzi's *In terra pax*. First performance of *Amore Langueo* by Howard Ferguson.

1957(W) First (long overdue!) Three Choirs performance of Walton's *Belshazzar's Feast*. First performances of the Requiem by Julius Harrison and *The City of Desolation* by Anthony Milner.

1958(H) Melville Cook's first Festival as Artistic Director at Hereford. Benjamin Britten conducted his *St Nicolas*, with Peter Pears as soloist, and the *Sinfonia da Requiem*; he also gave, with Norma Procter and Peter Pears, a recital which included his *Isaac and Abraham* canticle. Fricker conducted his *Litany* for double string orchestra. Kenneth Leighton's *The Light Invisible* and Franz Reizenstein's *Genesis* received their first performances.

1959(G) Première of *The Dream of the Rood* by Howard Ferguson.

1960(W) Douglas Guest's first Festival as Artistic Director at Worcester. Bliss conducted his *Music for Strings*. First performance in Britain of *In terra pax* by Frank Martin. Kodály was in the audience to hear a performance of his Budávari *Te Deum*. Goffredo Petrassi's *Magnificat* and *The Eternal Gospel* by Leoš Janáček were featured.

1961(H) Britten and Pears returned to Hereford to appear in a chamber recital. Britten also conducted his *Nocturne*, op. 60. Fricker's *The Vision of Judgement* was given, as was the first British performance of Paul Hindemith's *When Lilacs Last in the Door-Yard Bloom'd* (his 'requiem "for those we love"').

1962(G) First performances of *The Beatitudes* by Bliss, under the direction of the composer; the *Te Deum* by John Sanders; the *Te Deum* by Tony Hewitt-Jones; and, surprisingly, the first complete Three Choirs performance of *A Sea Symphony* by Vaughan Williams.

1963(W) Britten's *War Requiem* given its third performance anywhere, conducted by Douglas Guest.

1964(H) First performances of *The Water and the Fire* by Anthony Milner and the *Stabat Mater* by Bernard Naylor. Also included were the *War Requiem*, Stravinsky's *Symphony of Psalms* and Poulenc's *Gloria*.

1965(G) Anthony Milner's *Salutatio Angelica* was featured, with Janet Baker as soloist.

1966(W) Christopher Robinson's first Festival as Artistic Director at Worcester. First Three Choirs performance of Michael Tippett's *A Child of Our Time*. Sir Adrian Boult conducted Tippett's Concerto for double string orchestra. First performance of *Changes* by Gordon Crosse.

1967(H) Richard Lloyd's first Festival as Artistic Director at Hereford. Performances of Alun Hoddinott's *Dives and Lazarus* and Bernard Naylor's *The Annunciation* were featured.

1968(G) John Sanders's first Festival as Artistic Director at Gloucester. Boult conducted the *Symphonic Variations* for orchestra by Parry.

1969(W) The première of Jonathan Harvey's *Ludus Amoris* and the first Three Choirs performance of Janáček's *Glagolitic Mass* were given. Elizabeth Maconchy was present for the first performance of her *And Death Shall Have No Dominion*. Luigi Dallapiccola was also in the audience for performances of his *Due liriche di Anacreonte*; *Quadro liriche di Antonio Machade*; and *Canti di Prigionia*. Peter Maxwell Davies's *Five Carols* for boys' voices was also featured. A setting of Psalm 150 by William Mathias was heard for the first time at the Opening Service.

1970(H) First performance of John McCabe's *Notturni ed Alba*, conducted by Louis Frémaux.

1971(G) First performances of *The Tree of Life* by Alun Hoddinott and the Organ Concerto by Peter Dickinson.

1972(W) First performances of John Joubert's *Three Office Hymns of St Oswald*, and *Voyage* by John McCabe. First Three Choirs performance of the *Stabat Mater* by Krzysztof Penderecki.

1973(H) A short orchestral work, *Voices of the Night*, by Lennox Berkeley, was performed under the composer's direction. Other new works included *The Fire of Heaven* by Geoffrey Burgon and *Let there be Light* by Bryan Kelly.

1974(G) First performances of two commissions: Wilfred Josephs' overture *The Four Horsemen of the Apocalypse* and Philip Cannon's unaccompanied triptych *The Temple*; and the first public performance was given of Christopher Steel's *Paradise Lost*.

1975(W) Donald Hunt's first Festival as Artistic Director at Worcester. First performances of *Spells* by Richard Rodney Bennett and *Sequentia V* by David Ellis. First performance in Britain of the Requiem by Frank Martin, at which the composer's widow was present. Hunt conducted, *inter alia*, a memorable performance of Messiaen's *Trois Petites Liturgies de la Présence Divine*.

1976(H) Roy Massey's first Festival as Artistic Director at Hereford. First performance of the Requiem by Geoffrey Burgon.

1977(G) The 250th Three Choirs Festival. New works by Harrison Birtwistle, Peter Maxwell Davies, Rory Boyle, Ronald Tremain and Tony Hewitt-Jones; and the centrepiece – the *Mass of Christ the King* by Malcolm Williamson.

1978(W) The first complete British performance of the *Requiem Mass*, op. 54, by Saint-Saëns. Sir Lennox Berkeley conducted his *Antiphon* for string orchestra, and his motet *Judica me*, and Anthony Payne's cantatas *Ascensiontide* and *Whitsuntide* received their first performances. The British premières of Jean Martinon's *Chant des captifs* and the *African Sanctus* by David Fanshawe were heard, and the Festival ended with the first Three Choirs performance of Mahler's Symphony No. 8 in E flat (*Symphony of a Thousand*).

1979(H) The première of John Joubert's *Herefordshire Canticles*. Peter Maxwell Davies's *The Martyrdom of St Magnus* was the first complete opera to be staged at Three Choirs. The first Three Choirs performance of *Hymnus Amoris* by Carl Nielsen.

1980(G) World premières of *Lord of Light* by Philip Cannon, Gerard Schurmann's *Piers Plowman*, Elis Pehkonen's *Buccinate Tuba*, and the first English performances of Nicholas Maw's *Serenade*, Anthony Payne's *Footfalls Echo in the Memory*, and Peter Maxwell Davies's *Solstice of Light*.

1981(W) First British performances of Aulis Sallinen's *Dies Irae*, Knud Jeppesen's *Te Deum danicum*, the *Trois Préludes* by Pierre Villette and, surprisingly, the *Missa solemnis* by Liszt. First performances of Herbert Sumsion's *In Exile: By the Waters of Babylon*, Jonathan Harvey's *Resurrection*, Paul Trepte's *God's Grandeur* and Pierre Villette's *Messe en français*.

1982(H) First performances of the *Hymn to St Thomas* by Geoffrey Burgon and *Lux aeterna* by William Mathias.

1983(G) First performance of *Mass of the Sea* by Paul Patterson. Simon Rattle conducted a luminous performance of Mahler's Symphony No. 10, given in the late Deryck Cooke's completed edition.

1984(W) First performances of William Mathias's *Let us now praise famous men*, Richard Rodney Bennett's *Sea Change* and Peter Racine Fricker's *Whispers at these Curtains*. BBC television cameras were present for a performance of *The Dream of Gerontius*, conducted by Andrew Davis, in which the soloists were Janet Baker, Stuart Burrows and Benjamin Luxon, and for a concert of music by Copland and Bernstein.

1985(H) Michael Berkeley's *Or Shall We Die?* And the first performance of *Veni Sancte Spiritus* by William Mathias.

1986(G) The first Three Choirs performances of Andrew Lloyd Webber's Requiem and Paul Patterson's *Stabat Mater*. Revival, after thirteen years, of *Elijah*.

1987(W) The first performance of Richard Rodney Bennett's Symphony No. 3, conducted by its dedicatee, Edward Downes. The *Te Deum* of Krzysztof Penderecki was conducted by the composer, whose *Capriccio* for oboe and strings, and String Quartet No. 1 were also included in the Festival programme. Howard Blake's oratorio *Benedictus* was also performed.

1988(H) *The Darling of the World* by Paul Spicer and the first performance of the *Te Deum* by Paul Patterson.

1989(G) Music by Parry was featured on seven days of the Festival, including the *Ode on the Nativity*, the Symphony No. 5 in B minor, and the *Symphonic Variations*. The *Russian Requiem* by Elis Pehkonen received its first Three Choirs performance.

1990(W) The first UK performances of Leonard Bernstein's *Missa brevis*, Ned Rorem's *Te Deum* and George Lloyd's Symphony No. 12, the latter conducted by the composer. The première of Mussorgsky's *Saint Nicholas Mass* – 'an unashamed hybrid', as Philip Lane, who realised and edited the work, described it in his programme note.

1991(H) Brian Kay was the narrator in a performance of *Morning Heroes*, the largest of the works by Sir Arthur Bliss, which was included in the Festival to mark his centenary year.

1992(G) *Sine nomine* and the *Kent Yeoman's Wooing Song* were among the works included in the programme to mark the centenary year of Herbert Howells. The newly discovered manuscript score of Herbert Brewer's *Emmaus*, orchestrated by Elgar, enabled the work to be heard at the Festival for the first time since 1907. Parts for this performance were prepared by Nigel Taylor.

1993(W) The European première of the *Te Deum* by Dominick Argento, and the first performance of Robin Holloway's *Serenade* for strings. The British première of *Tu es Petrus* by Pierre Villette.

1994(H) The first performance of Alan Ridout's *Canticle of Joy.*

1995(G) David Briggs's first Festival as Artistic Director at Gloucester. First UK performance of *The Legend of King Arthur* by Elinor Remick Warren, conducted by Richard Hickox. Premières of *My Heart Dances* by Francis Grier, and Paul Patterson's overture *Songs of the West.*

1996(W) Donald Hunt's *Hymnus Paschalis* and the première of Edwin Roxburgh's Concerto for clarinet. First Three Choirs performance of *Veni, veni, Emmanuel* by James MacMillan, and the British première of the Trumpet Concerto by Pierre Villette.

1997(H) Donald Hunt's *A Song of Celebration* and the first performance of Judith Bingham's *Below the Surface Stream.*

1998(G) The Festival celebrated the 150th Anniversary of Sir Hubert Parry's birth; the programme included several of his works, including his Symphony No. 4 and *The Soul's Ransom*; the first performance of the *Te Deum* by David Briggs; first Three Choirs performances of *The Damnation of Faust* by Berlioz and the first act of *Parsifal* by Wagner.

1999(W) Adrian Lucas's first Festival as Artistic Director at Worcester. The *Stabat Mater* by Karol Szymanowski and the première of Francis Pott's *A Song on the End of the World.*

TWENTY-FIRST CENTURY

2000(H) Francis Grier's *Around the Curve of the World*, the first performances of Judith Weir's *Otherworld* and Kenneth Leighton's Concerto for oboe and strings.

2001(G) The Festival was billed as 'A Celebration of British Music' and included the first public performance of *Whispers of Heavenly Death* by Vaughan Williams and the first Three Choirs performance of *A Mass of Life* by Delius.

2002(W) The first performance of *The Vision of Piers Plowman* by Andrew Gant.

2003(H) Geraint Bowen's first Festival as Artistic Director at Hereford. The first performance of *Air and Angels* by Anthony Powers.

2004(G) Andrew Nethsingha's first Festival as Artistic Director at Gloucester. Five composers were each invited to contribute a variation on *Down Ampney* as an orchestral tribute to Ralph Vaughan Williams. The five composers were John McCabe, James Francis Brown, Judith Bingham, David Matthews and Robert Saxton. The new work, *Orchestral Variations on Down Ampney*, was conducted by Martyn Brabbins.

2005(W) Adrian Lucas's *Creation Canticles* performed. The first performance of *Songs of Truth and Glory* by Howard Blake.

2006(H) The UK première of *Sun Dogs* by James MacMillan, conducted by the composer. The first Three Choirs performance of Schumann's *Das Paradies und die Peri.*

2007(G) The UK première of Robin Holloway's orchestration of Debussy's *En blanc et noir*, originally for two pianos. Unfortunately, a scheduled performance of the Symphony No. 1 by Arnold Bax had to be abandoned following the collapse of the conductor, the late Vernon Handley, during a rehearsal.

2008 Paul Hedley appointed as the Festival's central manager, and its first full-time employee.

2008(W) The first performance of *A British Symphony* by Andrew Gant, and an innovation: an orchestral concert of classic British film music.

2009(H) First UK performance by David Briggs of his composition entitled *Three Preludes & Fugues: Hommage à Marcel Dupré*. World première of the newly commissioned orchestral version of John McCabe's *Songs of the Garden*. UK première of John McCabe *Les Martinets noirs*.

2010(G) Adrian Partington's first Festival as Artistic Director of Gloucester. World première of two Festival commissions from John Joubert: *Jubilate* (at the Opening Service), and *An English Requiem* (conducted by Adrian Partington). The first Festival masterclass was held, as part of a new initiative for aspiring professionals from UK music colleges; it was a choral masterclass with Simon Carrington, filmed by the Masterclass Media Foundation. Centenary performance of Vaughan Williams's *Fantasia on a Theme by Thomas Tallis*, written for the Gloucester Festival in 1910, conducted by Sir Roger Norrington without vibrato! First performance of Ivor Gurney's *A Gloucestershire Rhapsody*, written in 1921 but never performed; it was edited for this première by Philip Lancaster and Ian Venables. Debut performance of the newly formed Three Choirs Festival Youth Choir.

2011(W) World première of Festival commission by Cheryl Frances-Hoad: *Songs and Dances*, written for the cellist Jamie Walton. First use by the Festival of 'surround sound' for the performance of John Adams's *On the Transmigration of Souls*. World première of Festival commission by David Briggs: an organ transcription of Elgar's Symphony No. 2, performed by David himself to commemorate the centenary of its composition. World première of Festival commission by Jackson Hill: *Still in Remembrance*. World première of Festival commission by Ian King: *A Worcestershire Song Cycle*, with words by Chris Jaeger. World première of Festival commission by Nicholas Brown: *On the Operations of the Sun*.

2012(H) The start of a formal three-year residency for the Philharmonia Orchestra. World première of Festival commission by Dobrinka Tabakova: *Centuries of Mediation*. World première of the Piano Sonata by David Briggs; *All Across this Jumbl'd Earth*, by Bernard Hughes; *One Equal Music*, by Richard Rodney Bennett; and *The Love of God is in Eternity*, by Francis Pott. English première of Judith Bingham's *Celticity*. First performance at the Festival of Dyson's *The Canterbury Pilgrims*. Dame Felicity Lott appointed as President of the Three Choirs Festival Society.

2013(G) Centenary performance of Sibelius's *Luonnotar* (the first performance was given in Gloucester in 1913). World première of *Venite* by James d'Angelo,

Fanfare by John Hardy, and *The Bargee's Wife* and a song cycle by John O'Hara. First appearance at the Festival of conductors Vladimir Ashkenazy and Edward Gardner.

2014(W) Peter Nardone's first Festival as Artistic Director of Worcester. World première of Festival commission by Torsten Rasch: *A Foreign Field*, commissioned jointly with Chemnitz Opera to commemorate events in the two world wars.

2015(H) Celebration of the Festival's 300th anniversary marked by performances of masterpieces of the repertoire from the three centuries. including Beethoven's *Missa solemnis*, the Verdi Requiem, Elgar's *The Dream of Gerontius*, and Bernstein's *Chichester Psalms*. Period instruments played at the Opening Service, which included music by Purcell and Handel that would have been familiar to early concert-goers. Seven premières: Three Choirs Service (Mag & Nunc) by Bob Chilcott; two song cycles – *A Swift Radiant Morning* by Rhian Samuel, for Roderick Williams (baritone) and Susie Allen (piano), and *A Welsh Night* by Torsten Rasch, for Sarah Connolly (mezzo-soprano) and Joseph Middleton (piano); *Prayer of Thomas Ken* by George Arthur, an introit for Hereford Cathedral Voluntary Choir chosen through an anniversary competition; Alec Roth's *Stargazer* for Voces8; *O Gott du frommer Gott*, by Anthony Powers, for Organist John Scott, who gave his last recital in England at the Festival; Pete Churchill's *Echoes: A Song of Poland*, for The Gathering Wave community choir project. Sir Andrew Davis conducted a rarity by Arthur Bliss, *Morning Heroes*, and the Philharmonia performed Messiaen's *Turangalîla-Symphonie* to great acclaim, probably the first time the work had been heard in any Three Choirs city.

The Three Choirs Festival Foundation was launched with a reception at the House of Lords in January 2015, and the anniversary year concluded with a performance in the State Ballroom of Buckingham Palace on 24 November, in the presence of HRH The Prince of Wales, President of the Three Choirs Festival. The massed Three Choirs Festival Chorus, Youth Choir and the three cathedral choirs were conducted by Geraint Bowen, Peter Nardone and Adrian Partington, and the organ was played by Christopher Allsop, Peter Dyke and Jonathan Hope. Roderick Williams was the baritone soloist, and brass players from the Royal Welsh College of Music and Drama also took part.

Select Bibliography

ARCHIVES

Gloucester Cathedral Archives and Library
Gloucestershire Archives
Hereford Cathedral Library and Archives
Herefordshire Archive
Worcester Cathedral Library and Archive
Worcestershire Archive and Archaeology Service

EARLIER PUBLICATIONS DEVOTED
TO THE THREE CHOIRS FESTIVAL

Boden, Anthony, *Three Choirs: A History of the Festival* (Alan Sutton, 1992)

Hunt, Donald, *Festival Memories* (Osborne, 1996)

Lee Williams, C., H. Godwin Chance, and T. Hannam-Clark, *Annals of the Three Choirs of Gloucester, Hereford and Worcester: Continuation of History of Progress from 1895 to 1930* (Gloucester, 1931)

Lysons, Rev. Daniel, *History of the Origin and Progress of the Meeting of the Three Choirs of Gloucester, Worcester and Hereford and the Charity connected with it* (Gloucester, 1812)

    Carried on to 1864 by John Amott (Gloucester, 1864)

    Carried on to 1894 by C. Lee Williams and H. Godwin Chance (Gloucester, 1895)

Shaw, Watkins, *The Three Choirs Festival: The Official History of the Meetings of Gloucester, Hereford and Worcester, c. 1713–1953* (Baylis for Three Choirs Festival, 1954)

Still, Barry (ed.), *Two Hundred and Fifty Years of the Three Choirs Festival – A Commemoration in Words and Pictures* (Three Choirs Festival Association, 1977)

Young, Barbara, *In our Dreaming and Singing: The Story of the Three Choirs Festival Chorus* (Logaston Press, 2000)

FURTHER READING

Arnold, Samuel, *Cathedral Music*, 4 vols (published by subscription, London, 1790) [a supplement to William Boyce, *Cathedral Music*, 3 vols (London, 1760–73)]

Atkins, E. Wulstan, *The Elgar–Atkins Friendship* (David & Charles, 1985)

—— *1890–1990: The Centenary of the Birth of a Friendship: Edward Elgar and Ivor Atkins and their Influence on the Three Choirs Festival* (Trinity Press, 1990)

Aylmer, Gerald, and John Tiller (eds), *Hereford Cathedral: A History* (Hambledon Press, 2000)

Banfield, Stephen, *Gerald Finzi: An English Composer* (Faber & Faber, 1997)

Barlow, Michael, *Whom the Gods Love: The Life and Music of George Butterworth* (Toccata Press, 1997)

Barrett, Philip, *The College of Vicars Choral at Hereford Cathedral* (Hereford Cathedral, 1980)

Bennett, Joseph, *Forty Years of Music, 1865–1905* (Methuen, 1908)

Best, G. F. A., *Temporal Pillars* (CUP, 1964)

Bliss, Arthur, *As I Remember*, rev. edn (Thames Publishing, 1989)

Boden, Anthony, *The Parrys of the Golden Vale* (Thames Publishing, 1998)

—— *et al.*, *Thomas Tomkins: The Last Elizabethan* (Ashgate, 2005)

Bortin, Virginia, *Elinor Remick Warren: Her Life and her Music* (Scarecrow Press, USA, 1987)

Brewer, Herbert, *Memories of Choirs and Cloisters* (Bodley Head, 1931)

Bridcut, John, *Essential Britten* (Faber & Faber, 2010)

Butcher, Vernon, *The Organs and Music of Worcester Cathedral* (Worcester Cathedral, 1981)

Carley, Lionel, *Delius: A Life in Letters*, 2 vols (Scolar, 1988)

Charters, Alan, *John Sanders: Friend for Life* (Choir Press, 2009)

Colles, H. C., *Walford Davies* (OUP, 1942)

Cook, Andrea Theodore, *A History of the English Turf* (H. Virtue & Co., 1905)

Cox, Nicholas, *Bridging the Gap: A History of the Corporation of the Sons of the Clergy over Three Hundred Years, 1655–1978* (OUP, 1978)

Dean, Winton, *Handel's Dramatic Oratorios and Masques* (OUP, 1959)

Dibble, Jeremy, *C. Hubert H. Parry: His Life and Music* (OUP, 1992)

—— *Charles Villiers Stanford: Man and Musician* (OUP, 2002)

—— *John Stainer: A Life in Music* (Boydell, 2007)

Fenby, Eric, *Delius*, The Great Composers (Faber & Faber, 1971)

Ferguson, Howard, and Michael Hurd (eds), *The Letters of Gerald Finzi & Howard Ferguson* (Boydell, 2001)

Foreman, Lewis, *Bax: A Composer and his Times* (Boydell, 2007)

—— (ed.), *The John Ireland Companion* (Boydell, 2011)

Frith, Brian, *The Organs and Organists of Gloucester Cathedral* (Gloucester Cathedral, 1972)

Gaisberg, F. W., *Music on Record* (R. Hale, 1947)

Gee, Very Revd Henry, *Gloucester Cathedral: Its Organs and Organists* (Chiswick Press, 1921)

Goossens, Eugene, *Overture and Beginners* (Methuen, 1921)

Graves, Charles L., *Hubert Parry* (Macmillan, 1926)

Green, Bertram, *Bishops and Deans of Worcester*, rev. edn (Worcester Cathedral, 1979)

Hawkins, Sir John, *A General History of the Science and Practice of Music*, 5 vols (1776; repr. Novello, Ewer & Co., 1853 and 1875)

Heighway, Caroline, *Gloucester: A History and Guide* (Alan Sutton, 1985)

Heseltine, Philip, *Frederick Delius* (Bodley Head, 1923)

Holst, Imogen, *Gustav Holst: A Biography* (OUP, 1938; repr. 1988)

Horton, Peter, *Samuel Sebastian Wesley: A Life* (OUP, 2004)

Hunt, Donald, *Samuel Sebastian Wesley* (Seren Books, 1990)

—— *Festival Memories* (Osborne, 1996)

—— *Elgar and the Three Choirs Festival* (Osborne, 1999)

Jacobs, Arthur, *Arthur Sullivan: A Victorian Musician* (OUP, 1984)

Kennedy, Michael, *The Works of Ralph Vaughan Williams* (OUP, 1964)

—— *Mahler*, The Master Musicians, 2nd edn (J. M. Dent, 1990)

Lee-Browne, Martin, and Paul Guinery, *Delius and his Music* (Boydell, 2014)

McVeagh, Diana, *Gerald Finzi: His Life and Music* (Boydell, 2005)

—— *Elgar the Music Maker* (Boydell, 2007)

Moore, Jerrold Northrop, *Edward Elgar: A Creative Life* (OUP, 1990)

Myers, R. M., *Handel's Messiah: A Touchstone of Taste* (Macmillan, 1948)

Palmer, Christopher, *Herbert Howells: A Study* (Novello, 1978)

—— *Herbert Howells: A Centenary Celebration* (Thames Publishing, 1992)

Phillips, Henry, *Musical and Personal Recollections during Half a Century* (Skeet, 1864)

Plumb, J. H., *The Commercialisation of Leisure in Eighteenth-Century England* (University of Reading, 1973)

Reed, W. H., *Elgar as I Knew Him* (Gollancz, 1936; repr. OUP 1989)

—— *Elgar* (Dent, 1946)

Rosenfeld, Sybil, *Strolling Players and Drama in the Provinces* (CUP, 1939)

Shaw, Watkins, *The Organists and Organs of Hereford Cathedral* (Hereford Cathedral, 1988) [updated edn of John E. West, *Cathedral Organists Past and Present* (London, 1899)]

Spicer, Paul, *Herbert Howells* (Seren Books, 1998)

—— *Sir George Dyson: His Life and Music* (Boydell, 2014)

Walker, Ernest, *A History of Music in England*, 2nd edn (OUP, 1924)

Welander, David, *The History, Art and Architecture of Gloucester Cathedral* (Alan Sutton, 1991)

West, John E., *Cathedral Organists Past and Present* (London, 1899) [the updated edn is Watkins Shaw, *The Succession of Organists of the Chapel Royal and the Cathedrals of England and Wales from c. 1538* (OUP, 1991)]

Whyte, J. C., *History of the British Turf*, 2 vols (Henry Colburn, 1840)

Vaughan Williams, Ursula, *R.V.W.: A Biography of Ralph Vaughan Williams* (OUP, 1964)

Index

Locators for illustrations include group number (G1, G2, or G3), followed by plate number in parentheses; so, G1(10) refers to plate ten in the first group of illustrations. Page numbers followed by 'n' refer to footnotes.